What they're saying about *Head First*

Amazon named Head First Java
a Top Ten Editor's Choice for
Computer Books of 2003
(first edition)

Software Development Magazine named
Head First Java a finalist for the 14th Annual
Jolt Cola/Product Excellence Awards

"Kathy and Bert's 'Head First Java' transforms the printed page into the closest thing to a GUI you've
ever seen. In a wry, hip manner, the authors make learning Java an engaging 'what're they gonna do
next?' experience."

> **— Warren Keuffel, Software Development Magazine**

"...the only way to decide the worth of a tutorial is to decide how well it teaches. Head First Java excels at
teaching. OK, I thought it was silly... then I realized that I was thoroughly learning the topics as I went
through the book."

"The style of Head First Java made learning, well, easier."

> **— slashdot (honestpuck's review)**

"Beyond the engaging style that drags you forward from know-nothing into exalted Java warrior status,
Head First Java covers a huge amount of practical matters that other texts leave as the dreaded "exercise
for the reader..." It's clever, wry, hip and practical—there aren't a lot of textbooks that can make that claim
and live up to it while also teaching you about object serialization and network launch protocols. "

> **— Dr. Dan Russell, Director of User Sciences and Experience Research**
> **IBM Almaden Research Center (and teaches Artificial Intelligence at Stanford University)**

"It's fast, irreverent, fun, and engaging. Be careful—you might actually learn something!"

> **— Ken Arnold, former Senior Engineer at Sun Microsystems**
> **Co-author (with James Gosling, creator of Java), "The Java Programming Language"**

"Java technology is everywhere—If you develop software and haven't learned Java, it's definitely
time to dive in—Head First."

> **— Scott McNealy, Sun Microsystems Chairman, President and CEO**

"Head First Java is like Monty Python meets the gang of four... the text is broken up so well by puzzles
and stories, quizzes and examples, that you cover ground like no computer book before."

> **— Douglas Rowe, Columbia Java Users Group**

Praise for *Head First* Java

"Read Head First Java and you will once again experience fun in learning...For people who like to learn new programming languages, and do not come from a computer science or programming background, this book is a gem... This is one book that makes learning a complex computer language fun. I hope that there are more authors who are willing to break out of the same old mold of 'traditional' writing styles. Learning computer languages should be fun, not onerous."

> — **Judith Taylor, Southeast Ohio Macromedia User Group**

"If you want to *learn* Java, look no further: welcome to the first GUI-based technical book! This perfectly-executed, ground-breaking format delivers benefits other Java texts simply can't... Prepare yourself for a truly remarkable ride through Java land."

> — **Neil R. Bauman, Captain & CEO, Geek Cruises (www.GeekCruises.com)**

"If you're relatively new to programming and you are interested in Java, here's your book...Covering everything from objects to creating graphical user interfaces (GUI), exception (error) handling to networking (sockets) and multithreading, even packaging up your pile of classes into one installation file, this book is quite complete...If you like the style...I'm certain you'll love the book and, like me, hope that the Head First series will expand to many other subjects!"

> — **LinuxQuestions.org**

"I was ADDICTED to the book's short stories, annotated code, mock interviews, and brain exercises."

> — **Michael Yuan, author, Enterprise J2ME**

" 'Head First Java'... gives new meaning to their marketing phrase `There's an O Reilly for that.` I picked this up because several others I respect had described it in terms like 'revolutionary' and a described a radically different approach to the textbook. They were (are) right... In typical O'Reilly fashion, they've taken a scientific and well considered approach. The result is funny, irreverent, topical, interactive, and brilliant...Reading this book is like sitting in the speakers lounge at a view conference, learning from – and laughing with – peers... If you want to UNDERSTAND Java, go buy this book."

> — **Andrew Pollack, www.thenorth.com**

"If anyone in the world is familiar with the concept of 'Head First,' it would be me. This book is so good, I'd marry it on TV!"

> — **Rick Rockwell, Comedian**
> **The original FOX Television "Who Wants to Marry a Millionaire" groom**

"This stuff is so fricking good it makes me wanna WEEP! I'm stunned."

> — **Floyd Jones, Senior Technical Writer/Poolboy, BEA**

"A few days ago I received my copy of Head First Java by Kathy Sierra and Bert Bates. I'm only part way through the book, but what's amazed me is that even in my sleep-deprived state that first evening, I found myself thinking, 'OK, just one more page, then I'll go to bed.' "

> — **Joe Litton**

Praise for other *Head First* books co-authored by Kathy and Bert

 Amazon named Head First Servlets
a Top Ten Editor's Choice for
Computer Books of 2004
(first edition)

 Software Development Magazine named
Head First Servlets and Head First Design
Patterns finalists for the 15th Annual
Product Excellence Awards

"I feel like a thousand pounds of books have just been lifted off of my head."

> **— Ward Cunningham, inventor of the Wiki
> and founder of the Hillside Group**

"I laughed, I cried, it moved me."

> **— Dan Steinberg, Editor-in-Chief, java.net**

"My first reaction was to roll on the floor laughing. After I picked myself up, I realized that not only is the book technically accurate, it is the easiest to understand introduction to design patterns that I have seen."

> **— Dr. Timothy A. Budd, Associate Professor of Computer Science at Oregon State University
> author of more than a dozen books including *C++ for Java Programmers***

"Just the right tone for the geeked-out, casual-cool guru coder in all of us. The right reference for practical development strategies—gets my brain going without having to slog through a bunch of tired stale professor-speak."

> **— Travis Kalanick, Founder of Scour and Red Swoosh
> Member of the MIT TR100**

"FINALLY - a Java book written the way I would'a wrote it if I were me.
Seriously though - this book absolutely blows away every other software book I've ever read...
A good book is very difficult to write... you have to take a lot of time to make things unfold in a natural, "reader oriented" sequence. It's a lot of work. Most authors clearly aren't up to the challenge. Congratulations to the Head First EJB team for a first class job!

> **— Wally Flint**

"I could not have imagined a person smiling while studying an IT book! Using Head First EJB materials, I got a great score (91%) and set a world record as the youngest SCBCD, 14 years."

> **— Afsah Shafquat (world's youngest SCBCD)**

"This Head First Servlets book is as good as the Head First EJB book, which made me laugh AND gave me 97% on the exam!"

> **— Jef Cumps, J2EE consultant, Cronos**

Other Java books from O'Reilly

Head First Design Patterns
Head First Servlets
Head First EJB™

Ant: The Definitive Guide™
Better, Faster, Lighter Java™
Enterprise JavaBeans™
Hibernate: A Developer's Notebook
Java™ 1.5 Tiger: A Developer's Notebook
Java™ Cookbook
Java™ in a Nutshell
Java™ Network Programming
Java™ Servlet & JSP Cookbook
Java™ Swing
JavaServer Faces™
JavaServer Pages™
Programming Jakarta Struts
Tomcat: the Definitive Guide

Be watching for more books in the Head First series

Head First Java™
Second Edition

Wouldn't it be dreamy if there was a Java book that was more stimulating than waiting in line at the DMV to renew your driver's license? It's probably just a fantasy...

Kathy Sierra
Bert Bates

O'REILLY®

Beijing • Cambridge • Köln • Paris • Sebastopol • Taipei • Tokyo

Head First Java™

Second Edition

by Kathy Sierra and Bert Bates

Printed in the United States of America.

Published by O'Reilly Media, Inc., 1005 Gravenstein Highway North, Sebastopol, CA 95472.

O'Reilly Media books may be purchased for educational, business, or sales promotional use. Online editions are also available for most titles (safari.oreilly.com). For more information, contact our corporate/institutional sales department: (800) 998-9938 or corporate@oreilly.com.

Editor: Mike Loukides

Cover Designer: Edie Freedman

Interior Designers: Kathy Sierra and Bert Bates

Printing History:

May 2003: First Edition.

February 2005: Second Edition.

(You might want to pick up a copy of *both* editions... for your kids. Think eBay™)

In other words, if you use anything in *Head First Java*™ to, say, run a nuclear power plant or air traffic control system, you're on your own.

ISBN: 0596009208

[M]

To our brains, for always being there

(despite shaky evidence)

Creators of the Head First series

Kathy Sierra

Bert Bates

Kathy has been interested in learning theory since her days as a game designer (she wrote games for Virgin, MGM, and Amblin'). She developed much of the Head First format while teaching New Media Authoring for UCLA Extension's Entertainment Studies program. More recently, she's been a master trainer for Sun Microsystems, teaching Sun's Java instructors how to teach the latest Java technologies, and a lead developer of several of Sun's Java programmer and developer certification exams. Together with Bert Bates, she has been actively using the concepts in Head First Java to teach hundreds of trainers, developers and even non-programmers. She is also the founder of one of the largest Java community websites in the world, javaranch.com, and the Creating Passionate Users blog.

Along with this book, Kathy co-authored Head First Servlets, Head First EJB, and Head First Design Patterns.

In her spare time she enjoys her new Icelandic horse, skiing, running, and the speed of light.

kathy@wickedlysmart.com

Bert is a software developer and architect, but a decade-long stint in artificial intelligence drove his interest in learning theory and technology-based training. He's been teaching programming to clients ever since. Recently, he's been a member of the development team for several of Sun's Java Certification exams.

He spent the first decade of his software career travelling the world to help broadcast clients like Radio New Zealand, the Weather Channel, and the Arts & Entertainment Network (A & E). One of his all-time favorite projects was building a full rail system simulation for Union Pacific Railroad.

Bert is a hopelessly addicted Go player, and has been working on a Go program for way too long. He's a fair guitar player, now trying his hand at banjo, and likes to spend time skiing, running, and trying to train (or learn from) his Icelandic horse Andi.

Bert co-authored the same books as Kathy, and is hard at work on the next batch of books (check the blog for updates).

You can sometimes catch him on the IGS Go server (under the login *jackStraw*).

terrapin@wickedlysmart.com

Although Kathy and Bert try to answer as much email as they can, the volume of mail and their travel schedule makes that difficult. The best (quickest) way to get technical help with the book is at the *very* active Java beginners forum at javaranch.com.

Table of Contents (summary)

Table of Contents (the full version)

Intro

Your brain on Java. Here *you* are trying to *learn* something, while here your *brain* is doing you a favor by making sure the learning doesn't *stick*. Your brain's thinking, "Better leave room for more important things, like which wild animals to avoid and whether naked snowboarding is a bad idea." So how *do* you trick your brain into thinking that your life depends on knowing Java?

1 Breaking the Surface

Java takes you to new places. From its humble release to the public as the (wimpy) version 1.02, Java seduced programmers with its friendly syntax, object-oriented features, memory management, and best of all—the promise of portability. We'll take a quick dip and write some code, compile it, and run it. We're talking syntax, loops, branching, and what makes Java so cool. Dive in.

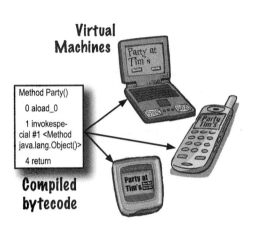

Virtual Machines

Method Party()
0 aload_0
1 invokespe-
cial #1 <Method
java.lang.Object()>
4 return

Compiled bytecode

2 A Trip to Objectville

I was told there would be objects. In Chapter 1, we put all of our code in the main() method. That's not exactly object-oriented. So now we've got to leave that procedural world behind and start making some objects of our own. We'll look at what makes object-oriented (OO) development in Java so much fun. We'll look at the difference between a class and an object. We'll look at how objects can improve your life.

DOG

size
breed
name

bark()

one class

many objects

3 Know Your Variables

Variables come in two flavors: primitive and reference.
There's gotta be more to life than integers, Strings, and arrays. What if you have a PetOwner object with a Dog instance variable? Or a Car with an Engine? In this chapter we'll unwrap the mysteries of Java types and look at what you can *declare* as a variable, what you can *put* in a variable, and what you can *do* with a variable. And we'll finally see what life is truly like on the garbage-collectible heap.

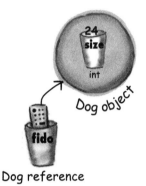

Dog reference

4 How Objects Behave

State affects behavior, behavior affects state. We know that objects have **state** and **behavior**, represented by **instance variables** and **methods**. Now we'll look at how state and behavior are *related*. An object's behavior uses an object's unique state. In other words, ***methods use instance variable values***. Like, "if dog weight is less than 14 pounds, make yippy sound, else..." ***Let's go change some state!***

pass-by-value means pass-by-copy

copy of x

00000111 → 00000111

X — int

Z — int

```
foo.go(x);   void go(int z) { }
```

Extra-Strength Methods

5

Let's put some muscle in our methods. You dabbled with variables, played with a few objects, and wrote a little code. But you need more tools. Like **operators**. And **loops**. Might be useful to **generate random numbers**. And **turn a String into an int**, yeah, that would be cool. And why don't we learn it all by *building* something real, to see what it's like to write (and test) a program from scratch. **Maybe a game**, like Sink a Dot Com (similar to Battleship).

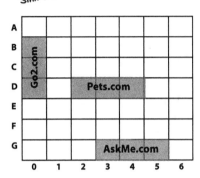

We're gonna build the Sink a Dot Com game

Using the Java Library

6

Java ships with hundreds of pre-built classes. You don't have to reinvent the wheel if you know how to find what you need from the Java library, commonly known as the **Java API**. *You've got better things to do.* If you're going to write code, you might as well write *only* the parts that are custom for your application. The core Java library is a giant pile of classes just waiting for you to use like building blocks.

"Good to know there's an ArrayList in the java.util package. But by myself, how would I have figured that out?"

- Julia, 31, hand model

7 Better Living in Objectville

Plan your programs with the future in mind. What if you could write code that someone *else* could extend, **easily**? What if you could write code that was flexible, for those pesky last-minute spec changes? When you get on the Polymorphism Plan, you'll learn the 5 steps to better class design, the 3 tricks to polymorphism, the 8 ways to make flexible code, and if you act now—a bonus lesson on the 4 tips for exploiting inheritance.

Make it Stick

Roses are red, violets are blue.
Square IS-A **Shape**, the reverse isn't true.

Roses are red, violets are dear.
Beer IS-A **Drink**, but not all **drinks** are **beer**.

OK, your turn. Make one that shows the one-way-ness of the IS-A relationship. And remember, if X **extends** Y, X **IS-A** Y must make sense.

8 Serious Polymorphism

Inheritance is just the beginning. To exploit polymorphism, we need interfaces. We need to go beyond simple inheritance to flexibility you can get only by designing and coding to interfaces. What's an interface? A 100% abstract class. What's an abstract class? A class that can't be instantiated. What's that good for? Read the chapter...

```
Object o = al.get(id);
Dog d = (Dog) o;
d.bark();
```

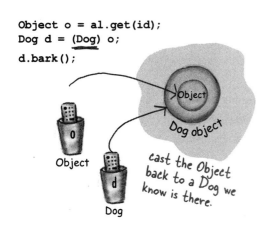

cast the Object back to a Dog we know is there.

9 Life and Death of an Object

Objects are born and objects die. You're in charge. You decide when and how to *construct* them. You decide when to *abandon* them. The **Garbage Collector (gc)** reclaims the memory. We'll look at how objects are created, where they live, and how to keep or abandon them efficiently. That means we'll talk about the heap, the stack, scope, constructors, super constructors, null references, and gc eligibility.

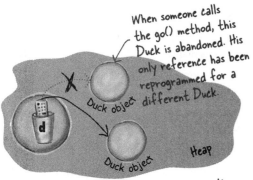

When someone calls the go() method, this Duck is abandoned. His only reference has been reprogrammed for a different Duck.

'd' is assigned a new Duck object, leaving the original (first) Duck object abandoned. That first Duck is toast.

10 Numbers Matter

Do the Math. The Java API has methods for absolute value, rounding, min/max, etc. But what about formatting? You might want numbers to print exactly two decimal points, or with commas in all the right places. And you might want to print and manipulate dates, too. And what about parsing a String into a number? Or turning a number into a String? We'll start by learning what it means for a variable or method to be *static*.

Static variables are shared by all instances of a class.

static variable: iceCream

kid instance one   kid instance two

instance variables: one per **instance**

static variables: one per **class**

11 Risky Behavior

Stuff happens. The file isn't there. The server is down. No matter how good a programmer you are, you can't control *everything*. When you write a risky method, you need code to handle the bad things that might happen. But how do you *know* when a method is risky? Where do you put the code to *handle* the **exceptional** situation? In *this* chapter, we're going to build a MIDI Music Player, that uses the risky JavaSound API, so we better find out.

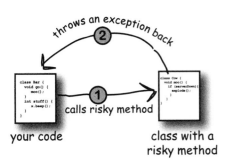

throws an exception back

calls risky method

your code

class with a risky method

12 A Very Graphic Story

Face it, you need to make GUIs. Even if you believe that for the rest of your life you'll write only server-side code, sooner or later you'll need to write tools, and you'll want a graphical interface. We'll spend two chapters on GUIs, and learn more language features including **Event Handling** and **Inner Classes**. We'll put a button on the screen, we'll paint on the screen, we'll display a jpeg image, and we'll even do some animation.

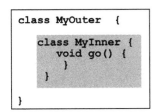

```
class MyOuter  {

    class MyInner {
        void go() {
        }
    }

}
```

The outer and inner objects are now intimately linked.

inner

outer

These two objects on the heap have a special bond. The inner can use the outer's variables (and vice-versa).

13 Work on your Swing

Swing is easy. Unless you actually *care* where everything goes. Swing code *looks* easy, but then compile it, run it, look at it and think, "hey, *that's* not supposed to go *there*." The thing that makes it *easy* to *code* is the thing that makes it *hard* to *control*—the **Layout Manager**. But with a little work, you can get layout managers to submit to your will. In this chapter, we'll work on our Swing and learn more about widgets.

Components in the east and west get their preferred width.

Things in the north and south get their preferred height.

North

West Center East

The center gets whatever's left

South

14 Saving Objects

Objects can be flattened and inflated. Objects have state and behavior. Behavior lives in the class, but *state* lives within each individual *object*. If your program needs to save state, *you can do it the hard way*, interrogating each object, painstakingly writing the value of each instance variable. Or, **you can do it the easy OO way**—you simply freeze-dry the object (serialize it) and reconstitute (deserialize) it to get it back.

serialized

Any questions?

deserialized

15 Make a Connection

Connect with the outside world.

It's easy. All the low-level networking details are taken care of by classes in the java.net library. One of Java's best features is that sending and receiving data over a network is really just I/O with a slightly different connection stream at the end of the chain. In this chapter we'll make client sockets. We'll make server sockets. We'll make clients and servers. Before the chapter's done, you'll have a fully-functional, multithreaded chat client. Did we just say *multithreaded*?

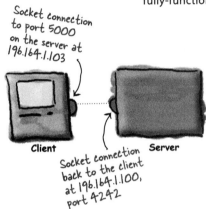

Socket connection to port 5000 on the server at 196.164.1.103

Client

Socket connection back to the client at 196.164.1.100, port 4242

Server

16 Data Structures

Sorting is a snap in Java. You have all the tools for collecting and manipulating your data without having to write your own sort algorithms The Java Collections Framework has a data structure that should work for virtually anything you'll ever need to do. Want to keep a list that you can easily keep adding to? Want to find something by name? Want to create a list that automatically takes out all the duplicates? Sort your co-workers by the number of times they've stabbed you in the back?

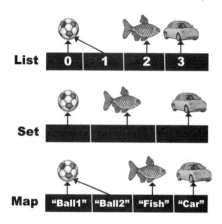

17 Release Your Code

It's time to let go. You wrote your code. You tested your code. You refined your code. You told everyone you know that if you never saw a line of code again, that'd be fine. But in the end, you've created a work of art. The thing actually runs! But now what? In these final two chapters, we'll explore how to organize, package, and deploy your Java code. We'll look at local, semi-local, and remote deployment options including executable jars, Java Web Start, RMI, and Servlets. Relax. Some of the coolest things in Java are easier than you think.

18 Distributed Computing

Being remote doesn't have to be a bad thing. Sure, things *are* easier when all the parts of your application are in one place, in one heap, with one JVM to rule them all. But that's not always possible. Or desirable. What if your application handles powerful computations? What if your app needs data from a secure database? In this chapter, we'll learn to use Java's amazingly simple Remote Method Invocation (RMI). We'll also take a quick peek at Servlets, Enterprise Java Beans (EJB) , and Jini.

 Client

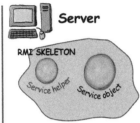 Server

A Appendix A

The final Code Kitchen project. All the code for the full client-server chat beat box. Your chance to be a rock star.

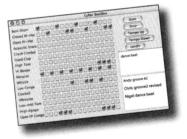

B Appendix B

The Top Ten Things that didn't make it into the book. We can't send you out into the world just yet. We have a few more things for you, but this *is* the end of the book. And this time we really mean it.

i Index

Intro

In this section, we answer the burning question: "So, why DID they put that in a Java programming book?"

Who is this book for?

If you can answer "yes" to *all* of these:

(1) **Have you done some programming?**

(2) **Do you want to learn Java?**

(3) **Do you prefer stimulating dinner party conversation to dry, dull, technical lectures?**

this book is for you.

> **This is NOT a reference book. Head First Java is a book designed for *learning*, not an encyclopedia of Java facts.**

Who should probably back away from this book?

If you can answer "yes" to any *one* of these:

(1) **Is your programming background limited to HTML only, with no scripting language experience?**
(If you've done anything with looping, or if/then logic, you'll do fine with this book, but HTML tagging alone might not be enough.)

(2) **Are you a kick-butt C++ programmer looking for a *reference* book?**

(3) **Are you afraid to try something different? Would you rather have a root canal than mix stripes with plaid? Do you believe than a technical book can't be serious if there's a picture of a duck in the memory management section?**

this book is *not* for you.

[note from marketing: who took out the part about how this book is for anyone with a valid credit card? And what about that "Give the Gift of Java" holiday promotion we discussed... —Fred]

We know what you're thinking.

"How can *this* be a serious Java programming book?"

"What's with all the graphics?"

"Can I actually *learn* it this way?"

"Do I smell pizza?"

And we know what your *brain* is thinking.

Your brain craves novelty. It's always searching, scanning, *waiting* for something unusual. It was built that way, and it helps you stay alive.

Today, you're less likely to be a tiger snack. But your brain's still looking. You just never know.

So what does your brain do with all the routine, ordinary, normal things you encounter? Everything it *can* to stop them from interfering with the brain's *real* job—recording things that *matter*. It doesn't bother saving the boring things; they never make it past the "this is obviously not important" filter.

How does your brain *know* what's important? Suppose you're out for a day hike and a tiger jumps in front of you, what happens inside your head?

Neurons fire. Emotions crank up. *Chemicals surge.*

And that's how your brain knows...

This must be important! Don't forget it!

But imagine you're at home, or in a library. It's a safe, warm, tiger-free zone. You're studying. Getting ready for an exam. Or trying to learn some tough technical topic your boss thinks will take a week, ten days at the most.

Just one problem. Your brain's trying to do you a big favor. It's trying to make sure that this *obviously* non-important content doesn't clutter up scarce resources. Resources that are better spent storing the really *big* things. Like tigers. Like the danger of fire. Like how you should never again snowboard in shorts.

And there's no simple way to tell your brain, "Hey brain, thank you very much, but no matter how dull this book is, and how little I'm registering on the emotional richter scale right now, I really *do* want you to keep this stuff around."

Your brain thinks
THIS is important.

Great. Only 637 more dull, dry, boring pages.

Your brain thinks
THIS isn't worth saving.

We think of a "Head First Java" reader as a learner.

So what does it take to *learn* something? First, you have to *get* it, then make sure you don't *forget* it. It's not about pushing facts into your head. Based on the latest research in cognitive science, neurobiology, and educational psychology, *learning* takes a lot more than text on a page. We know what turns your brain on.

Some of the Head First learning principles:

Make it visual. Images are far more memorable than words alone, and make learning much more effective (Up to 89% improvement in recall and transfer studies). It also makes things more understandable. **Put the words within or near the graphics** they relate to, rather than on the bottom or on another page, and learners will be up to *twice* as likely to solve problems related to the content.

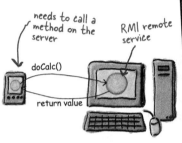

needs to call a method on the server

RMI remote service

doCalc()

return value

Use a conversational and personalized style. In recent studies, students performed up to 40% better on post-learning tests if the content spoke directly to the reader, using a first-person, conversational style rather than taking a formal tone. Tell stories instead of lecturing. Use casual language. Don't take yourself too seriously. Which would *you* pay more attention to: a stimulating dinner party companion, or a lecture?

> It really sucks to be an abstract method. You don't have a body.

Get the learner to think more deeply. In other words, unless you actively flex your neurons, nothing much happens in your head. A reader has to be motivated, engaged, curious, and inspired to solve problems, draw conclusions, and generate new knowledge. And for that, you need challenges, exercises, and thought-provoking questions, and activities that involve both sides of the brain, and multiple senses.

`abstract void roam();`

No method body! End it with a semicolon.

> Does it make sense to say Tub IS-A Bathroom? Bathroom IS-A Tub? Or is it a HAS-A relationship?

Get—and keep—the reader's attention. We've all had the "I really want to learn this but I can't stay awake past page one" experience. Your brain pays attention to things that are out of the ordinary, interesting, strange, eye-catching, unexpected. Learning a new, tough, technical topic doesn't have to be boring. Your brain will learn much more quickly if it's not.

Touch their emotions. We now know that your ability to remember something is largely dependent on its emotional content. You remember what you care about. You remember when you feel something. No we're not talking heart-wrenching stories about a boy and his dog. We're talking emotions like surprise, curiosity, fun, "what the...?", and the feeling of "I Rule!" that comes when you solve a puzzle, learn something everybody else thinks is hard, or realize you know something that "I'm more technical than thou" Bob from engineering *doesn't*.

Metacognition: thinking about thinking.

If you really want to learn, and you want to learn more quickly and more deeply, pay attention to how you pay attention. Think about how you think. Learn how you learn.

Most of us did not take courses on metacognition or learning theory when we were growing up. We were *expected* to learn, but rarely *taught* to learn.

I wonder how I can trick my brain into remembering this stuff...

But we assume that if you're holding this book, you want to learn Java. And you probably don't want to spend a lot of time.

To get the most from this book, or *any* book or learning experience, take responsibility for your brain. Your brain on *that* content.

The trick is to get your brain to see the new material you're learning as Really Important. Crucial to your well-being. As important as a tiger. Otherwise, you're in for a constant battle, with your brain doing its best to keep the new content from sticking.

So just how *DO* you get your brain to treat Java like it was a hungry tiger?

There's the slow, tedious way, or the faster, more effective way. The slow way is about sheer repetition. You obviously know that you *are* able to learn and remember even the dullest of topics, if you keep pounding on the same thing. With enough repetition, your brain says, "This doesn't *feel* important to him, but he keeps looking at the same thing *over* and *over* and *over*, so I suppose it must be."

The faster way is to do **anything that increases brain activity,** especially different *types* of brain activity. The things on the previous page are a big part of the solution, and they're all things that have been proven to help your brain work in your favor. For example, studies show that putting words *within* the pictures they describe (as opposed to somewhere else in the page, like a caption or in the body text) causes your brain to try to makes sense of how the words and picture relate, and this causes more neurons to fire. More neurons firing = more chances for your brain to *get* that this is something worth paying attention to, and possibly recording.

A conversational style helps because people tend to pay more attention when they perceive that they're in a conversation, since they're expected to follow along and hold up their end. The amazing thing is, your brain doesn't necessarily *care* that the "conversation" is between you and a book! On the other hand, if the writing style is formal and dry, your brain perceives it the same way you experience being lectured to while sitting in a roomful of passive attendees. No need to stay awake.

But pictures and conversational style are just the beginning.

Here's what WE did:

We used *pictures*, because your brain is tuned for visuals, not text. As far as your brain's concerned, a picture really *is* worth 1024 words. And when text and pictures work together, we embedded the text *in* the pictures because your brain works more effectively when the text is *within* the thing the text refers to, as opposed to in a caption or buried in the text somewhere.

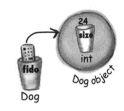

Dog

Dog object

We used *repetition*, saying the same thing in different ways and with different media types, and *multiple senses*, to increase the chance that the content gets coded coded into more than one area of your brain.

BE the compiler

We used concepts and pictures in *unexpected* ways because your brain is tuned for novelty, and we used pictures and ideas with at least *some emotional content*, because your brain is tuned to pay attention to the biochemistry of emotions. That which causes you to *feel* something is more likely to be remembered, even if that feeling is nothing more than a little *humor*, *surprise*, or *interest.*

This is PuzzleVille

We used a personalized, *conversational style*, because your brain is tuned to pay more attention when it believes you're in a conversation than if it thinks you're passively listening to a presentation. Your brain does this even when you're *reading*.

We included more than 50 *exercises* , because your brain is tuned to learn and remember more when you *do* things than when you *read* about things. And we made the exercises challenging-yet-do-able, because that's what most *people* prefer.

BULLET POINTS

We used *multiple learning styles*, because *you* might prefer step-by-step procedures, while someone else wants to understand the big picture first, while someone else just wants to see a code example. But regardless of your own learning preference, *everyone* benefits from seeing the same content represented in multiple ways.

Java Exposed

We include content for *both sides of your brain*, because the more of your brain you engage, the more likely you are to learn and remember, and the longer you can stay focused. Since working one side of the brain often means giving the other side a chance to rest, you can be more productive at learning for a longer period of time.

And we included *stories* and exercises that present *more than one point of view*, because your brain is tuned to learn more deeply when it's forced to make evaluations and judgements.

Brain Barbell

We included *challenges*, with exercises, and by asking *questions* that don't always have a straight answer, because your brain is tuned to learn and remember when it has to *work* at something (just as you can't get your *body* in shape by watching people at the gym). But we did our best to make sure that when you're working hard, it's on the *right* things. That *you're not spending one extra dendrite* processing a hard-to-understand example, or parsing difficult, jargon-laden, or extremely terse text.

We used an *80/20* approach. We assume that if you're going for a PhD in Java, this won't be your only book. So we don't talk about *everything*. Just the stuff you'll actually *use*.

Here's what YOU can do to bend your brain into submission.

So, we did our part. The rest is up to you. These tips are a starting point; Listen to your brain and figure out what works for you and what doesn't. Try new things.

cut this out and stick it on your refridgerator.

- -

(1) Slow down. The more you understand, the less you have to memorize.

Don't just *read*. Stop and think. When the book asks you a question, don't just skip to the answer. Imagine that someone really *is* asking the question. The more deeply you force your brain to think, the better chance you have of learning and remembering.

(2) Do the exercises. Write your own notes.

We put them in, but if we did them for you, that would be like having someone else do your workouts for you. And don't just *look* at the exercises. **Use a pencil.** There's plenty of evidence that physical activity *while* learning can increase the learning.

(3) Read the "There are No Dumb Questions"

That means all of them. They're not optional side-bars—they're part of the core content! Sometimes the questions are more useful than the answers.

(4) Don't do all your reading in one place.

Stand-up, stretch, move around, change chairs, change rooms. It'll help your brain *feel* something, and keeps your learning from being too connected to a particular place.

(5) Make this the last thing you read before bed. Or at least the last *challenging* thing.

Part of the learning (especially the transfer to long-term memory) happens *after* you put the book down. Your brain needs time on its own, to do more processing. If you put in something new during that processing-time, some of what you just learned will be lost.

(6) Drink water. Lots of it.

Your brain works best in a nice bath of fluid. Dehydration (which can happen before you ever feel thirsty) decreases cognitive function.

(7) Talk about it. Out loud.

Speaking activates a different part of the brain. If you're trying to understand something, or increase your chance of remembering it later, say it out loud. Better still, try to explain it out loud to someone else. You'll learn more quickly, and you might uncover ideas you hadn't known were there when you were reading about it.

(8) Listen to your brain.

Pay attention to whether your brain is getting overloaded. If you find yourself starting to skim the surface or forget what you just read, it's time for a break. Once you go past a certain point, you won't learn faster by trying to shove more in, and you might even hurt the process.

(9) Feel something!

Your brain needs to know that this *matters*. Get involved with the stories. Make up your own captions for the photos. Groaning over a bad joke is *still* better than feeling nothing at all.

(10) Type and run the code.

Type and run the code examples. Then you can experiment with changing and improving the code (or breaking it, which is sometimes the best way to figure out what's really happening). For long examples or Ready-bake code, you can download the source files from headfirstjava.com

What you need for this book:

You do *not* need any other development tool, such as an Integrated Development Environment (IDE). We strongly recommend that you *not* use anything but a basic text editor until you complete this book (and *especially* not until after chapter 16). An IDE can protect you from some of the details that really matter, so you're much better off learning from the command-line and then, once you really understand what's happening, move to a tool that automates some of the process.

SETTING UP JAVA

- If you don't already have a **1.5** or greater **Java 2 Standard Edition SDK** (Software Development Kit), you need it. If you're on Linux, Windows, or Solaris, you can get it for free from java.sun.com (Sun's website for Java developers). It usually takes no more than two clicks from the main page to get to the J2SE downloads page. Get the latest *non-beta* version posted. The SDK includes everything you need to compile and run Java.
  If you're running Mac OS X 10.4, the Java SDK is already installed. It's part of OS X, and you don't have to do *anything* else. If you're on an earlier version of OS X, you have an earlier version of Java that will work for 95% of the code in this book.
  Note: This book is based on Java 1.5, but for stunningly unclear marketing reasons, shortly before release, Sun renamed it Java 5, while still keeping "1.5" as the version number for the developer's kit. So, if you see Java 1.5 or Java 5 or Java 5.0, or "Tiger" (version 5's original code-name), *they all mean the same thing.* There was never a Java 3.0 or 4.0—it jumped from version 1.4 to 5.0, but you will still find places where it's called 1.5 instead of 5. Don't ask. (Oh, and just to make it more entertaining, Java 5 and the Mac OS X 10.4 were both given the same code-name of "Tiger", and since OS X 10.4 is the version of the Mac OS you need to run Java 5, you'll hear people talk about "Tiger on Tiger". It just means Java 5 on OS X 10.4).

- The SDK does *not* include the **API documentation,** and you need that! Go back to java.sun.com and get the J2SE API documentation. You can also access the API docs online, without downloading them, but that's a pain. Trust us, it's worth the download.

- You need a **text editor**. Virtually any text editor will do (vi, emacs, pico), including the GUI ones that come with most operating systems. Notepad, Wordpad, TextEdit, etc. all work, as long as you make sure they don't append a ".txt" on to the end of your source code.

- Once you've downloaded and unpacked/unzipped/whatever (depends on which version and for which OS), you need to add an entry to your **PATH** environment variable that points to the /bin directory inside the main Java directory. For example, if the J2SDK puts a directory on your drive called "j2sdk1.5.0", look inside that directory and you'll find the "bin" directory where the Java binaries (the tools) live. Tha bin directory is the one you need a PATH to, so that when you type:

```
% javac
```

at the command-line, your terminal will know how to find the *javac* compiler.
  Note: if you have trouble with you installation, we recommend you go to javaranch.com, and join the Java-Beginning forum! Actually, you should do that whether you have trouble or not.

Note: much of the code from this book is available at wickedlysmart.com

Last-minute things you need to know:

This is a learning experience, not a reference book. We deliberately stripped out everything that might get in the way of *learning* whatever it is we're working on at that point in the book. And the first time through, you need to begin at the beginning, because the book makes assumptions about what you've already seen and learned.

We use simple UML-*like* diagrams.

If we'd used *pure* UML, you'd be seeing something that *looks* like Java, but with syntax that's just plain *wrong*. So we use a simplified version of UML that doesn't conflict with Java syntax. If you don't already know UML, you won't have to worry about learning Java *and* UML at the same time.

We don't worry about organizing and packaging your own code until the end of the book.

In this book, you can get on with the business of learning Java, without stressing over some of the organizational or administrative details of developing Java programs. You *will*, in the real world, need to know—and use—these details, so we cover them in depth. But we save them for the end of the book (chapter 17). Relax while you ease into Java, gently.

The end-of-chapter exercises are mandatory; puzzles are optional. Answers for both are at the end of each chapter.

One thing you need to know about the puzzles—*they're puzzles*. As in logic puzzles, brain teasers, crossword puzzles, etc. The *exercises* are here to help you practice what you've learned, and you should do them all. The puzzles are a different story, and some of them are quite challenging in a *puzzle* way. These puzzles are meant for *puzzlers*, and you probably already know if you are one. If you're not sure, we suggest you give some of them a try, but whatever happens, don't be discouraged if you *can't* solve a puzzle or if you simply can't be bothered to take the time to work them out.

The 'Sharpen Your Pencil' exercises don't have answers.

Not printed in the book, anyway. For some of them, there *is* no right answer, and for the others, part of the learning experience for the Sharpen activities is for *you* to decide if and when your answers are right. (Some of our *suggested* answers are available on wickedlysmart.com)

The code examples are as lean as possible

It's frustrating to wade through 200 lines of code looking for the two lines you need to understand. Most examples in this book are shown within the smallest possible context, so that the part you're trying to learn is clear and simple. So don't expect the code to be robust, or even complete. That's *your* assignment for after you finish the book. The book examples are written specifically for *learning*, and aren't always fully-functional.

We use a simpler, modified faux-UML

Dog
size
bark() eat() chaseCat()

You should do ALL of the "Sharpen your pencil" activities

Sharpen your pencil

Activities marked with the Exercise (running shoe) logo are mandatory! Don't skip them if you're serious about learning Java.

Exercise

If you see the Puzzle logo, the activity is optional, and if you don't like twisty logic or cross-word puzzles, you won't like these either.

Technical Editors

"Credit goes to all, but mistakes are the sole reponsibility of the author...". Does anyone really believe that? See the two people on this page? If you find technical problems, it's probably *their* fault. :)

Valentin Crettaz

Jessica's MINI

Jessica Sant

Valentin's tie

Jess works at Hewlett-Packard on the Self-Healing Services Team. She has a Bachelor's in Computer Engineering from Villanova University, has her SCPJ 1.4 and SCWCD certifications, and is literally months away from receiving her Masters in Software Engineering at Drexel University (whew!)

When she's not working, studying or motoring in her MINI Cooper S, Jess can be found fighting her cat for yarn as she completes her latest knitting or crochet project (anybody want a hat?) She is originally from Salt Lake City, Utah (no, she's not Mormon... yes, you were too going to ask) and is currently living near Philadelphia with her husband, Mendra, and two cats: Chai and Sake.

You can catch her moderating technical forums at javaranch.com.

Valentin Valentin Crettaz has a Masters degree in Information and Computer Science from the Swiss Federal Institute of Technology in Lausanne (EPFL). He has worked as a software engineer with SRI International (Menlo Park, CA) and as a principal engineer in the Software Engineering Laboratory of EPFL.

Valentin is the co-founder and CTO of Condris Technologies, a company specializing in the development of software architecture solutions.

His research and development interests include aspect-oriented technologies, design and architectural patterns, web services, and software architecture. Besides taking care of his wife, gardening, reading, and doing some sport, Valentin moderates the SCBCD and SCDJWS forums at Javaranch.com. He holds the SCJP, SCJD, SCBCD, SCWCD, and SCDJWS certifications. He has also had the opportunity to serve as a co-author for Whizlabs SCBCD Exam Simulator.

(We're still in shock from seeing him in a *tie*.)

Other people to ~~blame~~ credit:

At O'Reilly:

Our biggest thanks to **Mike Loukides** at O'Reilly, for taking a chance on this, and helping to shape the Head First concept into a book (and *series*). As this second edition goes to print there are now five Head First books, and he's been with us all the way. To **Tim O'Reilly**, for his willingness to launch into something *completely* new and different. Thanks to the clever **Kyle Hart** for figuring out how Head First fits into the world, and for launching the series. Finally, to **Edie Freedman** for designing the Head First "emphasize the *head*" cover.

Our intrepid beta testers and reviewer team:

Our top honors and thanks go to the director of our javaranch tech review team, **Johannes de Jong.** This is your fifth time around with us on a Head First book, and we're thrilled you're still speaking to us. **Jeff Cumps** is on his third book with us now and relentless about finding areas where we needed to be more clear or correct.

Corey McGlone, you rock. And we think you give the clearest explanations on javaranch. You'll probably notice we stole one or two of them. **Jason Menard** saved our technical butts on more than a few details, and **Thomas Paul**, as always, gave us expert feedback and found the subtle Java issues the rest of us missed. **Jane Griscti** has her Java chops (and knows a thing or two about *writing*) and it was great to have her helping on the new edition along with long-time javarancher **Barry Gaunt**.

Marilyn de Queiroz gave us excellent help on *both* editions of the book. **Chris Jones**, **John Nyquist**, **James Cubeta**, **Terri Cubeta**, and **Ira Becker** gave us a ton of help on the first edition.

Special thanks to a few of the Head Firsters who've been helping us from the beginning: **Angelo Celeste**, **Mikalai Zaikin**, and **Thomas Duff** (twduff.com). And thanks to our terrific agent, David Rogelberg of StudioB (but seriously, what about the *movie* rights?)

Some of our Java expert reviewers...

Corey McGlone

Jef Cumps

Johannes de Jong

Jason Menard

Thomas Paul

Marilym de Queiroz

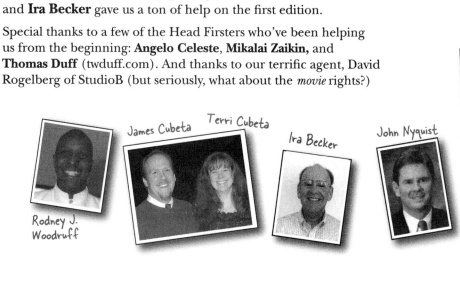

James Cubeta   Terri Cubeta

Ira Becker

John Nyquist

Chris Jones

Rodney J. Woodruff

Just when you thought there wouldn't be any more acknowledgements*.

More Java technical experts who helped out on the first edition (in pseudo-random order):

Emiko Hori, Michael Taupitz, Mike Gallihugh, Manish Hatwalne, James Chegwidden, Shweta Mathur, Mohamed Mazahim, John Paverd, Joseph Bih, Skulrat Patanavanich, Sunil Palicha, Suddhasatwa Ghosh, Ramki Srinivasan, Alfred Raouf, Angelo Celeste, Mikalai Zaikin, John Zoetebier, Jim Pleger, Barry Gaunt, and Mark Dielen.

The first edition puzzle team:

Dirk Schreckmann, Mary "JavaCross Champion" Leners, Rodney J. Woodruff, Gavin Bong, and Jason Menard. Javaranch is lucky to have you all helping out.

Other co-conspirators to thank:

Paul Wheaton, the javaranch Trail Boss for supporting thousands of Java learners.
Solveig Haugland, mistress of J2EE and author of "Dating Design Patterns".
Authors **Dori Smith** and **Tom Negrino (backupbrain.com)**, for helping us navigate the tech book world.
Our Head First partners in crime, **Eric Freeman and Beth Freeman** (authors of Head First Design Patterns), for giving us the Bawls™ to finish this on time.
Sherry Dorris, for the things that really matter.

Brave Early Adopters of the Head First series:

Joe Litton, Ross P. Goldberg, Dominic Da Silva, honestpuck, Danny Bromberg, Stephen Lepp, Elton Hughes, Eric Christensen, Vulinh Nguyen, Mark Rau, Abdulhaf, Nathan Oliphant, Michael Bradly, Alex Darrow, Michael Fischer, Sarah Nottingham, Tim Allen, Bob Thomas, and Mike Bibby (the first).

*The large number of acknowledgements is because we're testing the theory that everyone mentioned in a book acknowledgement will buy at least one copy, probably more, what with relatives and everything. If you'd like to be in the acknowledgement of our *next* book, and you have a large family, write to us.

Breaking the Surface

Come on, the water's great! We'll dive right in and write some code, then compile and run it. We're talking syntax, looping and branching, and a look at what makes Java so cool. You'll be coding in no time.

Java takes you to new places. From its humble release to the public as the (wimpy) version 1.02, Java seduced programmers with its friendly syntax, object-oriented features, memory management, and best of all—the promise of portability. The lure of **write-once/run-anywhere** is just too strong. A devoted following exploded, as programmers fought against bugs, limitations, and, oh yeah, the fact that it was dog slow. But that was ages ago. If you're just starting in Java, **you're lucky**. Some of us had to walk five miles in the snow, uphill both ways (barefoot), to get even the most trivial applet to work. But *you*, why, *you* get to ride the **sleeker, faster, much more powerful** Java of today.

The Way Java Works

The goal is to write one application (in this example, an interactive party invitation) and have it work on whatever device your friends have.

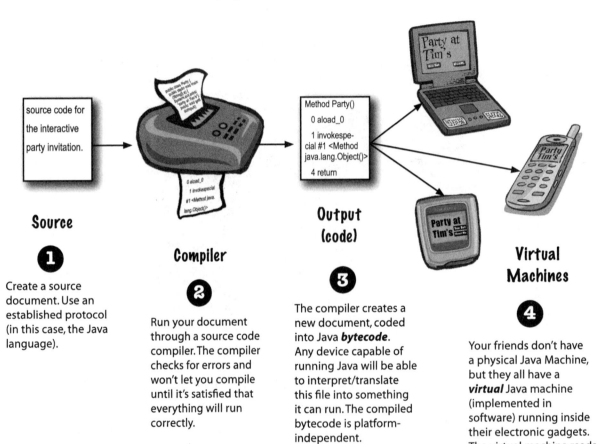

Source

1

Create a source document. Use an established protocol (in this case, the Java language).

Compiler

2

Run your document through a source code compiler. The compiler checks for errors and won't let you compile until it's satisfied that everything will run correctly.

Output (code)

3

The compiler creates a new document, coded into Java *bytecode*. Any device capable of running Java will be able to interpret/translate this file into something it can run. The compiled bytecode is platform-independent.

Virtual Machines

4

Your friends don't have a physical Java Machine, but they all have a *virtual* Java machine (implemented in software) running inside their electronic gadgets. The virtual machine reads and *runs* the bytecode.

What you'll do in Java

You'll type a source code file, compile it using the javac compiler, then run the compiled bytecode on a Java virtual machine.

```
import java.awt.*;
import java.awt.event.*;
class Party {
  public void buildInvite() {

    Frame f = new Frame();
    Label l = new Label("Party at Tim's");
    Button b = new Button("You bet");
    Button c = new Button("Shoot me");
    Panel p = new Panel();
    p.add(l);
  } // more code here...
}
```

Source

Type your source code.

Save as: *Party.java*

```
% javac Party.java
```

Compiler

Compile the *Party.java* file by running `javac` (the compiler application). If you don't have errors, you'll get a second document named *Party.class*

The compiler-generated Party.class file is made up of *bytecodes*.

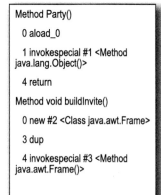

```
Method Party()
  0 aload_0
  1 invokespecial #1 <Method java.lang.Object()>
  4 return
Method void buildInvite()
  0 new #2 <Class java.awt.Frame>
  3 dup
  4 invokespecial #3 <Method java.awt.Frame()>
```

Output (code)

Compiled code: *Party.class*

Virtual Machines

Run the program by starting the Java Virtual Machine (JVM) with the *Party.class* file. The JVM translates the *bytecode* into something the underlying platform understands, and runs your program.

(Note: this is not meant to be a tutorial... you'll be writing real code in a moment, but for now, we just want you to get a feel for how it all fits together.)

A very brief history of Java

Classes in the Java standard library

3500
3000
2500
2000
1500
1000
500
0

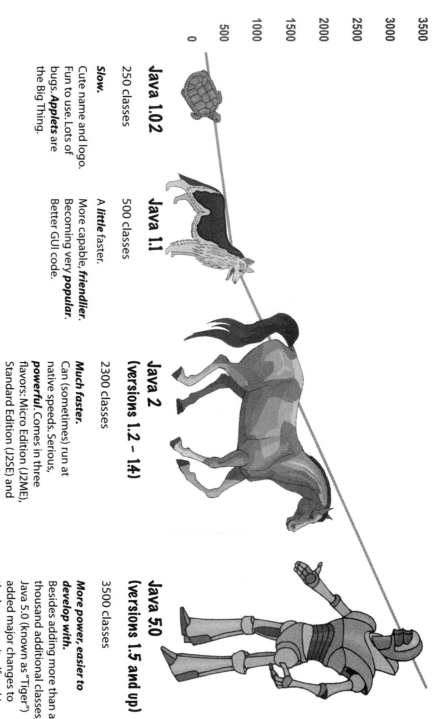

Java 1.02

250 classes

Slow.

Cute name and logo.
Fun to use. Lots of
bugs. *Applets* are
the Big Thing.

Java 1.1

500 classes

A *little* faster.

More capable, *friendlier*.
Becoming very *popular*.
Better GUI code.

**Java 2
(versions 1.2 – 1.4)**

2300 classes

Much faster.
Can (sometimes) run at
native speeds. Serious,
powerful. Comes in three
flavors: Micro Edition (J2ME),
Standard Edition (J2SE) and
Enterprise Edition (J2EE).
Becomes the *language of
choice* for new enterprise
(especially web-based) and
mobile applications.

**Java 5.0
(versions 1.5 and up)**

3500 classes

*More power, easier to
develop with.*
Besides adding more than a
thousand additional classes,
Java 5.0 (known as "Tiger")
added major changes to
the language itself, making
it easier (at least in theory)
for programmers and giving
it new features that were
popular in other languages.

Look how easy it is to write Java.

Try to guess what each line of code is doing...
(answers are on the next page).

```java
int size = 27;
String name = "Fido";
Dog myDog = new Dog(name, size);
x = size - 5;
if (x < 15) myDog.bark(8);

while (x > 3) {
    myDog.play();
}

int[] numList = {2,4,6,8};
System.out.print("Hello");
System.out.print("Dog: " + name);
String num = "8";
int z = Integer.parseInt(num);

try {
    readTheFile("myFile.txt");
}
catch(FileNotFoundException ex) {
    System.out.print("File not found.");
}
```

declare an integer variable named 'size' and give it the value 27

Q: I see Java 2 and Java 5.0, but was there a Java 3 and 4? And why is it Java 5.0 but not Java 2.0?

A: The joys of marketing... when the version of Java shifted from 1.1 to 1.2, the changes to Java were so dramatic that the marketers decided we needed a whole new "name", so they started calling it *Java 2*, even though the actual version of Java was 1.2. But versions 1.3 and 1.4 were still considered *Java 2*. There never *was* a Java 3 or 4. Beginning with Java version 1.5, the marketers decided

once again that the changes were so dramatic that a new name was needed (and most developers agreed), so they looked at the options. The next number in the name sequence would be "3", but calling Java 1.5 *Java 3* seemed more confusing, so they decided to name it *Java 5.0* to match the "5" in version "1.5".

So, the original Java was versions 1.02 (the first official release) through 1.1 were just "Java". Versions 1.2, 1.3, and 1.4 were "Java 2". And beginning with version 1.5, Java is called "Java 5.0." But you'll also see it called "Java 5" (without the ".0") and "Tiger" (its original code-name). We have no idea what will happen with the *next* release...

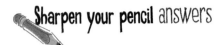

Sharpen your pencil answers

Look how easy it is to write Java.

Don't worry about whether you understand any of this yet!
Everything here is explained in great detail in the book, most within the first 40 pages). If Java resembles a language you've used in the past, some of this will be simple. If not, don't worry about it. *We'll get there...*

```java
int size = 27;
String name = "Fido";
Dog myDog = new Dog(name, size);
x = size - 5;
if (x < 15) myDog.bark(8);


while (x > 3) {
    myDog.play();
}


int[] numList = {2,4,6,8};
System.out.print("Hello");
System.out.print("Dog: " + name);
String num = "8";
int z = Integer.parseInt(num);


try {
    readTheFile("myFile.txt");
}
catch(FileNotFoundException ex) {
    System.out.print("File not found.");
}
```

declare an integer variable named 'size' and give it the value 27

declare a string of characters variable named 'name' and give it the value "Fido"

declare a new Dog variable 'myDog' and make the new Dog using 'name' and 'size'

subtract 5 from 27 (value of 'size') and assign it to a variable named 'x'

if x (value of 22) is less than 15, tell the dog to bark 8 times

keep looping as long as x is greater than 3...

tell the dog to play (whatever THAT means to a dog...)

this looks like the end of the loop -- everything in { } is done in the loop

declare a list of integers variable 'numList', and put 2,4,6,8 into the list

print out "Hello"... probably at the command-line

print out "Hello Fido" (the value of 'name' is "Fido") at the command-line

declare a character string variable 'num' and give it the value of "8"

convert the string of characters "8" into an actual numeric value 8

try to do something...maybe the thing we're trying isn't guaranteed to work...

read a text file named "myFile.txt" (or at least TRY to read the file...)

must be the end of the "things to try", so I guess you could try many things...

this must be where you find out if the thing you tried didn't work...

if the thing we tried failed, print "File not found" out at the command-line

looks like everything in the { } is what to do if the 'try' didn't work...

Code structure in Java

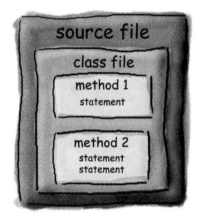

Put a class in a source file.

Put methods in a class.

Put statements in a method.

What goes in a SOURCE file?

A source code file (with the *.java* extension) holds one *class* definition. The class represents a *piece* of your program, although a very tiny application might need just a single class. The class must go within a pair of curly braces.

```
public class Dog {



}                    class
```

What goes in a class?

A class has one or more *methods*. In the Dog class, the *bark* method will hold instructions for how the Dog should bark. Your methods must be declared *inside* a class (in other words, within the curly braces of the class).

```
public class Dog {
    void bark() {


    }
}                 method
```

What goes in a method?

Within the curly braces of a method, write your instructions for how that method should be performed. Method *code* is basically a set of statements, and for now you can think of a method kind of like a function or procedure.

```
public class Dog {
    void bark() {
        statement1;
        statement2;
    }
}            statements
```

Anatomy of a class

When the JVM starts running, it looks for the class you give it at the command line. Then it starts looking for a specially-written method that looks exactly like:

```
public static void main (String[] args) {
    // your code goes here
}
```

Next, the JVM runs everything between the curly braces { } of your main method. Every Java application has to have at least one **class**, and at least one **main** method (not one main per *class*; just one main per *application*).

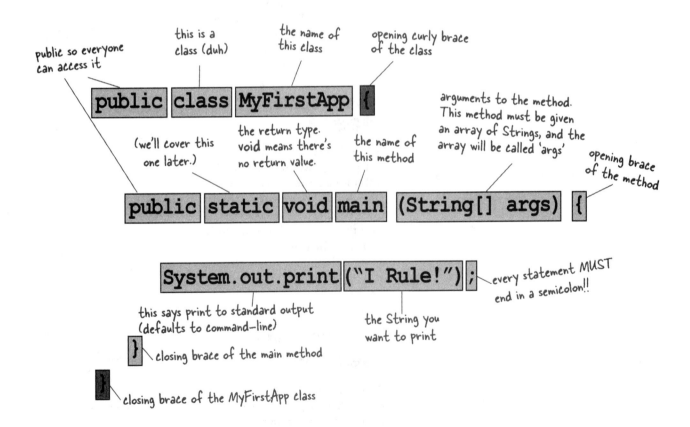

public so everyone can access it

this is a class (duh)

the name of this class

opening curly brace of the class

public **class** **MyFirstApp** **{**

arguments to the method. This method must be given an array of Strings, and the array will be called 'args'

(we'll cover this one later.)

the return type. void means there's no return value.

the name of this method

opening brace of the method

public **static** **void** **main** **(String[] args)** **{**

System.out.print **("I Rule!")** **;**

every statement MUST end in a semicolon!!

this says print to standard output (defaults to command-line)

the String you want to print

} closing brace of the main method

} closing brace of the MyFirstApp class

Don't worry about memorizing anything right now...
this chapter is just to get you started.

Writing a class with a main

In Java, everything goes in a **class**. You'll type your source code file (with a *.java* extension), then compile it into a new class file (with a *.class* extension). When you run your program, you're really running a *class*.

Running a program means telling the Java Virtual Machine (JVM) to "Load the **Hello** class, then start executing its **main()** method. Keep running 'til all the code in main is finished."

In chapter 2, we go deeper into the whole *class* thing, but for now, all you need to think is, *how do I write Java code so that it will run?* And it all begins with **main()**.

The **main()** method is where your program starts running.

No matter how big your program is (in other words, no matter how many *classes* your program uses), there's got to be a **main()** method to get the ball rolling.

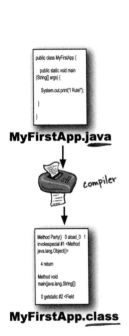

MyFirstApp.java

compiler

MyFirstApp.class

```
public class MyFirstApp {

    public static void main (String[] args) {
        System.out.println("I Rule!");
        System.out.println("The World");
    }

}
```

❶ Save

MyFirstApp.java

❷ Compile

javac MyFirstApp.java

❸ Run

```
File Edit Window Help Scream
%java MyFirstApp
I Rule!
The World
```

What can you say in the main method?

Once you're inside main (or *any* method), the fun begins. You can say all the normal things that you say in most programming languages to *make the computer do something.*

Your code can tell the JVM to:

Syntax Fun

1 **do something**

Statements: declarations, assignments, method calls, etc.

```
int x = 3;
String name = "Dirk";
x = x * 17;
System.out.print("x is " + x);
double d = Math.random();
// this is a comment
```

2 **do something again and again**

Loops: *for* and *while*

```
while (x > 12) {
    x = x -1;
}

for (int x = 0; x < 10; x = x + 1) {
    System.out.print("x is now " + x);
}
```

3 **do something under this condition**

Branching: *if/else* tests

```
if (x == 10) {
    System.out.print("x must be 10");
} else {
    System.out.print("x isn't 10");
}
if ((x < 3) & (name.equals("Dirk"))) {
    System.out.println("Gently");
}
System.out.print("this line runs no matter what");
```

✸ Each statement must end in a semicolon.

```
x = x + 1;
```

✸ A single-line comment begins with two forward slashes.

```
x = 22;
// this line disturbs me
```

✸ Most white space doesn't matter.

```
x      =      3  ;
```

✸ Variables are declared with a **name** and a **type** (you'll learn about all the Java *types* in chapter 3).

```
int weight;
//type: int, name: weight
```

✸ Classes and methods must be defined within a pair of curly braces.

```
public void go() {
    // amazing code here
}
```

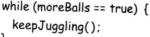

```
while (moreBalls == true) {
    keepJuggling();
}
```

Looping and looping and...

Java has three standard looping constructs: *while*, *do-while*, and *for*. You'll get the full loop scoop later in the book, but not for awhile, so let's do *while* for now.

The syntax (not to mention logic) is so simple you're probably asleep already. As long as some condition is true, you do everything inside the loop *block*. The loop block is bounded by a pair of curly braces, so whatever you want to repeat needs to be inside that block.

The key to a loop is the *conditional test*. In Java, a conditional test is an expression that results in a *boolean* value—in other words, something that is either **true** or **false**.

If you say something like, "While *iceCreamInTheTub is true*, keep scooping", you have a clear boolean test. There either *is* ice cream in the tub or there *isn't*. But if you were to say, "While *Bob* keep scooping", you don't have a real test. To make that work, you'd have to change it to something like, "While Bob is snoring..." or "While Bob is *not* wearing plaid..."

Simple boolean tests

You can do a simple boolean test by checking the value of a variable, using a *comparison operator* including:

< (less than)

> (greater than)

== (equality) (yes, that's *two* equals signs)

Notice the difference between the *assignment* operator (a *single* equals sign) and the *equals* operator (*two* equals signs). Lots of programmers accidentally type **=** when they *want* **==**. (But not you.)

```
int x = 4; // assign 4 to x
while (x > 3) {
    // loop code will run because
    // x is greater than 3
    x = x - 1; // or we'd loop forever
}
int z = 27; //
while (z == 17) {
    // loop code will not run because
    // z is not equal to 17
}
```

Q: Why does everything have to be in a class?

A: Java is an object-oriented (OO) language. It's not like the old days when you had steam-driven compilers and wrote one monolithic source file with a pile of procedures. In chapter 2 you'll learn that a class is a blueprint for an object, and that nearly everything in Java is an object.

Q: Do I have to put a main in every class I write?

A: Nope. A Java program might use dozens of classes (even hundreds), but you might only have *one* with a main method—the one that starts the program running. You might write test classes, though, that have main methods for testing your *other* classes.

Q: In my other language I can do a boolean test on an integer. In Java, can I say something like:

```java
int x = 1;
while (x) { }
```

A: No. A *boolean* and an *integer* are not compatible types in Java. Since the result of a conditional test *must* be a boolean, the only variable you can directly test (without using a comparison operator) is a ***boolean.*** For example, you can say:

```java
boolean isHot = true;
while (isHot) { }
```

Example of a while loop

```java
public class Loopy {
   public static void main (String[] args) {
      int x = 1;
      System.out.println("Before the Loop");
      while (x < 4) {
         System.out.println("In the loop");
         System.out.println("Value of x is " + x);
         x = x + 1;
      }
      System.out.println("This is after the loop");
   }
}
```

```
% java Loopy
Before the Loop
In the loop
Value of x is 1
In the loop
Value of x is 2
In the loop
Value of x is 3
This is after the loop
```

this is the output

BULLET POINTS

- Statements end in a semicolon **;**

- Code blocks are defined by a pair of curly braces **{ }**

- Declare an *int* variable with a name and a type: **int x;**

- The **assignment** operator is *one* equals sign **=**

- The **equals** operator uses *two* equals signs **==**

- A *while* loop runs everything within its block (defined by curly braces) as long as the *conditional test* is **true**.

- If the conditional test is **false**, the *while* loop code block won't run, and execution will move down to the code immediately *after* the loop block.

- Put a boolean test inside parentheses:
  ```java
  while (x == 4) { }
  ```

Conditional branching

In Java, an *if* test is basically the same as the boolean test in a *while* loop – except instead of saying, "*while* there's still beer...", you'll say, "*if* there's still beer..."

```
class IfTest {
  public static void main (String[] args) {
    int x = 3;
    if (x == 3) {
      System.out.println("x must be 3");
    }
    System.out.println("This runs no matter what");
  }
}
```

```
% java IfTest          ← code output
x must be 3
This runs no matter what
```

The code above executes the line that prints "x must be 3" only if the condition (*x* is equal to 3) is true. Regardless of whether it's true, though, the line that prints, "This runs no matter what" will run. So depending on the value of *x*, either one statement or two will print out.

But we can add an *else* to the condition, so that we can say something like, "*If* there's still beer, keep coding, *else* (otherwise) get more beer, and then continue on..."

```
class IfTest2 {
  public static void  main (String[] args) {
    int x = 2;
    if (x == 3) {
      System.out.println("x must be 3");
    } else {
      System.out.println("x is NOT 3");
    }
    System.out.println("This runs no matter what");
  }
}
```

```
% java IfTest2         ← new output
x is NOT 3
This runs no matter what
```

System.out.**print** vs. System.out.print**ln**

If you've been paying attention (of course you have) then you've noticed us switching between **print** and **println**.

Did you spot the difference?

System.out.*println* inserts a newline (think of print*ln* as **print*newline*** while System.out.*print* keeps printing to the *same* line. If you want each thing you print out to be on its own line, use print**ln**. If you want everything to stick together on one line, use print.

Sharpen your pencil

Given the output:

```
% java DooBee
DooBeeDooBeeDo
```

Fill in the missing code:

```
public class DooBee {
  public static void main (String[] args) {
    int x = 1;
    while (x < _3_ ) {
      System.out._print_("Doo");
      System.out._print_("Bee");
      x = x + 1;
    }
    if (x == _3_ ) {
      System.out.print("Do");
    }
  }
}
```

Coding a Serious Business Application

Let's put all your new Java skills to good use with something practical. We need a class with a *main()*, an *int* and a *String* variable, a *while* loop, and an *if* test. A little more polish, and you'll be building that business back-end in no time. But *before* you look at the code on this page, think for a moment about how *you* would code that classic children's favorite, "99 bottles of beer."

```java
public class BeerSong {
    public static void main (String[] args) {
       int beerNum = 99;
       String word = "bottles";

       while (beerNum > 0) {

          if (beerNum == 1) {
            word = "bottle"; // singular, as in ONE bottle.
          }

          System.out.println(beerNum + " " + word + " of beer on the wall");
          System.out.println(beerNum + " " + word + " of beer.");
          System.out.println("Take one down.");
          System.out.println("Pass it around.");
          beerNum = beerNum - 1;

          if (beerNum > 0) {
             System.out.println(beerNum + " " + word + " of beer on the wall");
          } else {
             System.out.println("No more bottles of beer on the wall");
          } // end else
       } // end while loop
    } // end main method
} // end class
```

There's still one little flaw in our code. It compiles and runs, but the output isn't 100% perfect. See if you can spot the flaw , and fix it.

Monday morning at Bob's

Bob's alarm clock rings at 8:30 Monday morning, just like every other weekday. But Bob had a wild weekend, and reaches for the SNOOZE button. And that's when the action starts, and the Java-enabled appliances come to life.

Java inside

First, the alarm clock sends a message to the coffee maker* "Hey, the geek's sleeping in again, delay the coffee 12 minutes."

The coffee maker sends a message to the Motorola™ toaster, "Hold the toast, Bob's snoozing."

Java here too

The alarm clock then sends a message to Bob's Nokia Navigator™ cell phone, "Call Bob's 9 o'clock and tell him we're running a little late."

Finally, the alarm clock sends a message to Sam's (Sam is the dog) wireless collar, with the too-familiar signal that means, "Get the paper, but don't expect a walk."

Java toaster

Sam's collar has Java

A few minutes later, the alarm goes off again. And *again* Bob hits SNOOZE and the appliances start chattering. Finally, the alarm rings a third time. But just as Bob reaches for the snooze button, the clock sends the "jump and bark" signal to Sam's collar. Shocked to full consciousness, Bob rises, grateful that his Java skills and a little trip to Radio Shack™ have enhanced the daily routines of his life.

His toast is toasted.

butter here

His coffee steams.

His paper awaits.

Just another wonderful morning in ***The Java-Enabled House.***

***You* can have a Java-enabled home**. Stick with a sensible solution using Java, Ethernet, and Jini technology. Beware of imitations using other so-called "plug and play" (which actually means "plug and play with it for the next three days trying to get it to work") or "portable" platforms. Bob's sister Betty tried one of those *others*, and the results were, well, not very appealing, or safe. Bit of a shame about her dog, too...

AS IF ON TV

> Could this story be true? Yes and no. While there *are* versions of Java running in devices including PDAs, cell phones (*especially* cell phones), pagers, rings, smart cards, and more –you might not find a Java toaster or dog collar. But even if you can't find a Java-enabled version of your favorite gadget, you can still run it as if it *were* a Java device by controlling it through some other interface (say, your laptop) that *is* running Java. This is known as the Jini *surrogate architecture*. Yes you *can* have that geek dream home.

*IP multicast if you're gonna be all picky about protocol

> Try my new phrase-o-matic and you'll be a slick talker just like the boss or those guys in marketing.

OK, so the beer song wasn't *really* a serious business application. Still need something practical to show the boss? Check out the Phrase-O-Matic code.

note: when you type this into an editor, let the code do its own word/line-wrapping! Never hit the return key when you're typing a String (a thing between "quotes") or it won't compile. So the hyphens you see on this page are real, and you can type them, but don't hit the return key until AFTER you've closed a String.

```java
public class PhraseOMatic {
    public static void main (String[] args) {
```

1   `// make three sets of words to choose from. Add your own!`
```java
        String[] wordListOne = {"24/7","multi-
Tier","30,000 foot","B-to-B","win-win","front-
end", "web-based","pervasive", "smart", "six-
sigma","critical-path", "dynamic"};

        String[] wordListTwo = {"empowered", "sticky",
"value-added", "oriented", "centric", "distributed",
"clustered", "branded","outside-the-box", "positioned",
"networked", "focused", "leveraged", "aligned",
"targeted", "shared", "cooperative", "accelerated"};

        String[] wordListThree = {"process", "tipping-
point", "solution", "architecture", "core competency",
"strategy", "mindshare", "portal", "space", "vision",
"paradigm", "mission"};
```

2   `// find out how many words are in each list`
```java
        int oneLength = wordListOne.length;
        int twoLength = wordListTwo.length;
        int threeLength = wordListThree.length;
```

3   `// generate three random numbers`
```java
        int rand1 = (int) (Math.random() * oneLength);
        int rand2 = (int) (Math.random() * twoLength);
        int rand3 = (int) (Math.random() * threeLength);
```

4   `// now build a phrase`
```java
        String phrase = wordListOne[rand1] + " " +
wordListTwo[rand2] + " " + wordListThree[rand3];
```

5   `// print out the phrase`
```java
        System.out.println("What we need is a " + phrase);
    }
}
```

Phrase-O-Matic

How it works.

In a nutshell, the program makes three lists of words, then randomly picks one word from each of the three lists, and prints out the result. Don't worry if you don't understand *exactly* what's happening in each line. For gosh sakes, you've got the whole book ahead of you, so relax. This is just a quick look from a 30,000 foot outside-the-box targeted leveraged paradigm.

$1.$ The first step is to create three String arrays – the containers that will hold all the words. Declaring and creating an array is easy; here's a small one:

```
String[] pets = {"Fido", "Zeus", "Bin"};
```

Each word is in quotes (as all good Strings must be) and separated by commas.

$2.$ For each of the three lists (arrays), the goal is to pick a random word, so we have to know how many words are in each list. If there are 14 words in a list, then we need a random number between 0 and 13 (Java arrays are zero-based, so the first word is at position 0, the second word position 1, and the last word is position 13 in a 14-element array). Quite handily, a Java array is more than happy to tell you its length. You just have to ask. In the pets array, we'd say:

```
int x = pets.length;
```

and **x** would now hold the value 3.

$3.$ We need three random numbers. Java ships out-of-the-box, off-the-shelf, shrink-wrapped, and core competent with a set of math methods (for now, think of them as functions). The **random()** method returns a random number between 0 and not-quite-1, so we have to multiply it by the number of elements (the array length) in the list we're using. We have to force the result to be an integer (no decimals allowed!) so we put in a cast (you'll get the details in chapter 4). It's the same as if we had any floating point number that we wanted to convert to an integer:

```
int x = (int) 24.6;
```

$4.$ Now we get to build the phrase, by picking a word from each of the three lists, and smooshing them together (also inserting spaces between words). We use the "**+**" operator, which *concatenates* (we prefer the more technical '*smooshes*') the String objects together. To get an element from an array, you give the array the index number (position) of the thing you want using:

```
String s = pets[0]; // s is now the String "Fido"
s = s + " " + "is a dog"; // s is now "Fido is a dog"
```

$5.$ Finally, we print the phrase to the command-line and... voila! *We're in marketing.*

what we need here is a...

pervasive targeted process

dynamic outside-the-box tipping-point

smart distributed core competency

24/7 empowered mindshare

30,000 foot win-win vision

six-sigma networked portal

Fireside Chats

Tonight's Talk: **The compiler and the JVM battle over the question, "Who's more important?"**

The Java Virtual Machine

What, are you kidding? ***HELLO***. I *am* Java. I'm the guy who actually makes a program *run*. The compiler just gives you a *file*. That's it. Just a file. You can print it out and use it for wall paper, kindling, lining the bird cage what*ever*, but the file doesn't *do* anything unless I'm there to run it.

And that's another thing, the compiler has no sense of humor. Then again, if *you* had to spend all day checking nit-picky little syntax violations...

I'm not saying you're, like, *completely* useless. But really, what is it that you do? Seriously. I have no idea. A programmer could just write bytecode by hand, and I'd take it. You might be out of a job soon, buddy.

(I rest my case on the humor thing.) But you still didn't answer my question, what *do* you actually do?

The Compiler

I don't appreciate that tone.

Excuse me, but without *me*, what exactly would you run? There's a *reason* Java was designed to use a bytecode compiler, for your information. If Java were a purely interpreted language, where—at runtime—the virtual machine had to translate straight-from-a-text-editor source code, a Java program would run at a ludicrously glacial pace. Java's had a challenging enough time convincing people that it's finally fast and powerful enough for most jobs.

Excuse me, but that's quite an ignorant (not to mention *arrogant*) perspective. While it *is* true that—*theoretically*—you can run any properly formatted bytecode even if it didn't come out of a Java compiler, in practice that's absurd. A programmer writing bytecode by hand is like doing your word processing by writing raw postscript. And I would appreciate it if you would *not* refer to me as "buddy."

The Java Virtual Machine

But some still get through! I can throw Class-CastExceptions and sometimes I get people trying to put the wrong type of thing in an array that was declared to hold something else, and—

OK. Sure. But what about *security*? Look at all the security stuff I do, and you're like, what, checking for *semicolons*? Oooohhh big security risk! Thank goodness for you!

Whatever. I have to do that same stuff *too*, though, just to make sure nobody snuck in after you and changed the bytecode before running it.

Oh, you can count on it. *Buddy*.

The Compiler

Remember that Java is a strongly-typed language, and that means I can't allow variables to hold data of the wrong type. This is a crucial safety feature, and I'm able to stop the vast majority of violations before they ever get to you. And I also—

Excuse me, but I wasn't done. And yes, there *are* some datatype exceptions that can emerge at runtime, but some of those have to be allowed to support one of Java's other important features—dynamic binding. At runtime, a Java program can include new objects that weren't even *known* to the original programmer, so I have to allow a certain amount of flexibility. But my job is to stop anything that would never—*could* never—succeed at runtime. Usually I can tell when something won't work, for example, if a programmer accidentally tried to use a Button object as a Socket connection, I would detect that and thus protect him from causing harm at runtime.

Excuse me, but I am the first line of defense, as they say. The datatype violations I previously described could wreak havoc in a program if they were allowed to manifest. I am also the one who prevents access violations, such as code trying to invoke a private method, or change a method that – for security reasons – must never be changed. I stop people from touching code they're not meant to see, including code trying to access another class' critical data. It would take hours, perhaps days even, to describe the significance of my work.

Of course, but as I indicated previously, if I didn't prevent what amounts to perhaps 99% of the potential problems, you would grind to a halt. And it looks like we're out of time, so we'll have to revisit this in a later chat.

Code Magnets

A working Java program is all scrambled up on the fridge. Can you rearrange the code snippets to make a working Java program that produces the output listed below? Some of the curly braces fell on the floor and they were too small to pick up, so feel free to add as many of those as you need!

```java
if (x == 1) {
    System.out.print("d");
    x = x - 1;
}
```

```java
if (x == 2) {
    System.out.print("b c");
}
```

```java
class Shuffle1 {
    public static void main(String [] args) {
```

```java
if (x > 2) {
    System.out.print("a");
}
```

```java
int x = 3;
```

```java
x = x - 1;
System.out.print("-");
```

```java
while (x > 0) {
```

Output:

```
File Edit Window Help Sleep
% java Shuffle1
a-b c-d
```

BE the compiler

Each of the Java files on this page represents a complete source file. Your job is to play compiler and determine whether each of these files will compile. If they won't compile, how would you fix them?

B

```java
public static void main(String [] args) {
    int x = 5;
    while ( x > 1 ) {
      x = x - 1;
      if ( x < 3) {
        System.out.println("small x");
      }
    }
}
```

class example B {

Put above here!

}

A

needs
x = x + 1

```java
class Exercise1b {
  public static void main(String [] args) {
    int x = 1;
    while ( x < 10 ) {
      if ( x > 3 ) {
        System.out.println("big x");
      }
    }
  }
}
```

C

```java
class Exercise1b {
    int x = 5;
    while ( x > 1 ) {
      x = x - 1;
      if ( x < 3) {
        System.out.println("small x");
      }
    }
}
```

needs to be in function

JavaCross 7.0

Let's give your right brain something to do.

It's your standard crossword, but almost all of the solution words are from chapter 1. Just to keep you awake, we also threw in a few (non-Java) words from the high-tech world.

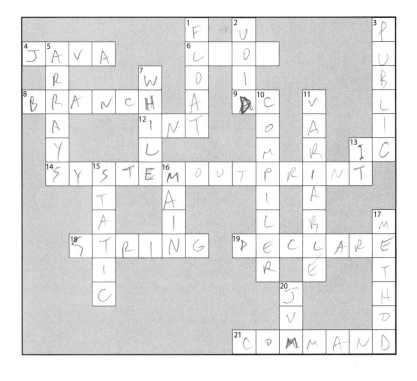

Across

4. Command-line invoker
6. Back again?
8. Can't go both ways
9. Acronym for your laptop's power
12. number variable type
13. Acronym for a chip
14. Say something
18. Quite a crew of characters
19. Announce a new class or method
21. What's a prompt good for?

Down

1. Not an integer (or _____ your boat)
2. Come back empty-handed
3. Open house
5. 'Things' holders
7. Until attitudes improve
10. Source code consumer
11. Can't pin it down
13. Dept. of LAN jockeys
15. Shocking modifier
16. Just gotta have one
17. How to get things done
20. Bytecode consumer

Mixed Messages

A short Java program is listed below. One block of the program is missing. Your challenge is to **match the candidate block of code** (on the left), **with the output** that you'd see if the block were inserted. Not all the lines of output will be used, and some of the lines of output might be used more than once. Draw lines connecting the candidate blocks of code with their matching command-line output. (The answers are at the end of the chapter).

```java
class Test {
  public static void main(String [] args) {
    int x = 0;
    int y = 0;
    while ( x < 5 ) {



      System.out.print(x + "" + y +" ");
      x = x + 1;
    }
  }
}
```

candidate code goes here

Candidates:

match each candidate with one of the possible outputs

```
y = x - y;
```

x y
0 0
1 2
2 3
3 6
4 10

```
y = y + x;
```

x y
0 2
1 4
2 5
3 6
4 7

```
y = y + 2;
if( y > 4 ) {
   y = y - 1;
}
```

x y
1 1
3 4
5 9

```
x = x + 1;
y = y + x;
```

x y
0 2
1 4
3 6
4 8

```
if ( y < 5 ) {
   x = x + 1;
   if ( y < 3 ) {
      x = x - 1;
   }
}
y = y + 2;
```

Possible output:

22 46

11 34 59

02 14 26 38

02 14 36 48

00 11 21 32 42

11 21 32 42 53

00 11 23 36 410

02 14 25 36 47

Pŏŏl Puzzle

Your *job* is to take code snippets from the pool and place them into the blank lines in the code. You may **not** use the same snippet more than once, and you won't need to use all the snippets. Your *goal* is to make a class that will compile and run and produce the output listed. Don't be fooled—this one's harder than it looks.

Output

```
File  Edit  Window  Help  Cheat
%java PoolPuzzleOne
a noise
annoys
an oyster
```

```java
class PoolPuzzleOne {
  public static void main(String [] args) {
    int x = 0;

    while (  x < 4   ) {
      System.out.print("a");
      if ( x < 1 ) {
        System.out.print(" ");
      }
      System.out.print("n");

      if (  x > 1   ) {
        System.out.print(" oyster");

        x = x + 2
      }
      if ( x == 1 ) {
        System.out.print("noys");
      }
      if (  x < 1   ) {
        System.out.print("oise");
      }
      System.out.println("");

      x = x + 1
    }
  }
}
```

Note: Each snippet from the pool can be used only once!

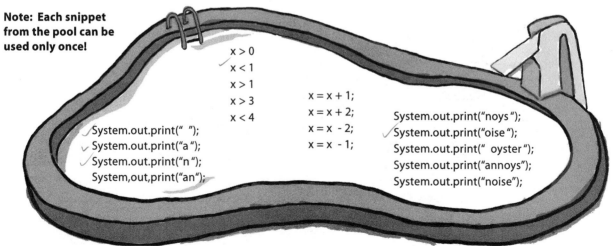

```
x > 0
x < 1
x > 1
x > 3
x < 4
                    x = x + 1;
                    x = x + 2;
                    x = x - 2;
                    x = x - 1;
System.out.print(" ");
System.out.print("a ");
System.out.print("n ");
System,out,print("an");
                              System.out.print("noys ");
                              System.out.print("oise ");
                              System.out.print(" oyster ");
                              System.out.print("annoys");
                              System.out.print("noise");
```

Exercise Solutions

Code Magnets:

```
class Shuffle1 {
  public static void main(String [] args) {

    int x = 3;
    while (x > 0) {

      if (x > 2) {
        System.out.print("a");
      }

      x = x - 1;
      System.out.print("-");

      if (x == 2) {
        System.out.print("b c");
      }

      if (x == 1) {
        System.out.print("d");
        x = x - 1;
      }
    }
  }
}
```

```
File  Edit  Window  Help  Poet
% java Shuffle1
a-b c-d
```

A
```
class Exercise1b {
  public static void main(String [] args) {
    int x = 1;
    while ( x < 10 ) {
      x = x + 1;
      if ( x > 3 ) {
        System.out.println("big x");
      }
    }
  }
}
```
This will compile and run (no output), but without a line added to the program, it would run forever in an infinite 'while' loop!

B
```
class Foo {
  public static void main(String [] args) {
    int x = 5;
    while ( x > 1 ) {
      x = x - 1;
      if ( x < 3 ) {
        System.out.println("small x");
      }
    }
  }
}
```
This file won't compile without a **class declaration, and don't forget** the matching curly brace !

C
```
class Exercise1b {
  public static void main(String [] args) {
    int x = 5;
    while ( x > 1 ) {
      x = x - 1;
      if ( x < 3 ) {
        System.out.println("small x");
      }
    }
  }
}
```
The 'while' loop code must be inside a method. It can't just be hanging out inside the class.

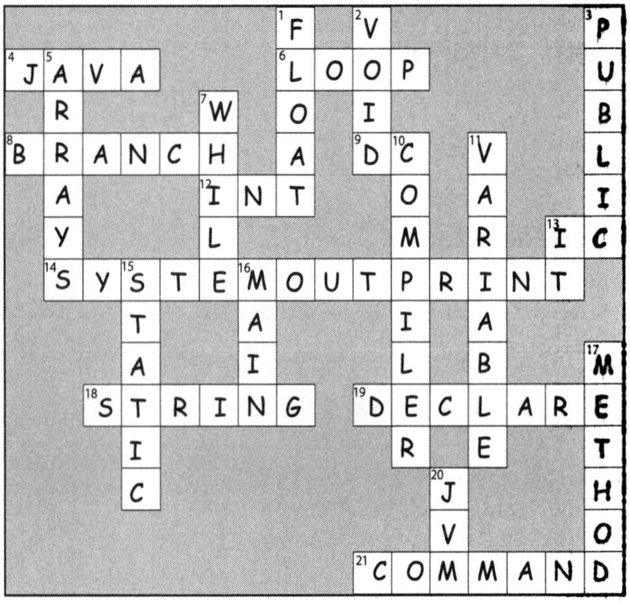

The crossword puzzle (filled in):

```
                          ¹F      ²V              ³P
        ⁴J ⁵A  V  A        ⁶L  O  O  P           U
           R        ⁷W      O     I              B
        ⁸B R  A  N  C  H    A     ⁹D ¹⁰C    ¹¹V  L
           A           ¹²I  N  T      O     A   I
           Y           L              M     R  ¹³I C
        ¹⁴S Y  ⁵S  T  E ¹⁶M  O  U  T  P  R  I  N  T
              T       A             I     A
              A       I             L     B     ¹⁷M
          ¹⁸S T  R  I  N  G      ¹⁹D  E  C  L  A  R  E
              I                   R     E        T
              C                ²⁰J               H
                               V                 O
                         ²¹C  O  M  M  A  N  D
```

```
class PoolPuzzleOne {
  public static void main(String [] args) {
    int x = 0;

    while ( X < 4 ) {

      System.out.print("a");
      if ( x < 1 ) {
        System.out.print(" ");
      }
      System.out.print("n");

      if ( X > 1 ) {

        System.out.print(" oyster");
        x = x + 2;
      }
      if ( x == 1 ) {

        System.out.print("noys");
      }
      if ( X < 1 ) {

        System.out.print("oise");
      }
      System.out.println("");

      X = X + 1;
    }
  }
}
```

```
File  Edit  Window  Help  Cheat
%java PoolPuzzleOne
a noise
annoys
an oyster
```

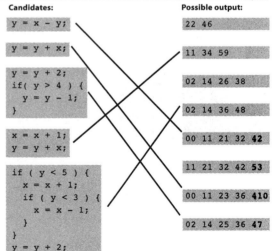

```
class Test {
  public static void main(String [] args) {
    int x = 0;
    int y = 0;
    while ( x < 5 ) {

    ┌─────────────────────────────────┐
    │                                 │
    └─────────────────────────────────┘

      System.out.print(x + "" + y +" ");
      x = x + 1;
    }
  }
}
```

Candidates:

```
y = x - y;
```

```
y = y + x;
```

```
y = y + 2;
if( y > 4 ) {
   y = y - 1;
}
```

```
x = x + 1;
y = y + x;
```

```
if ( y < 5 ) {
   x = x + 1;
   if ( y < 3 ) {
      x = x - 1;
   }
}
y = y + 2;
```

Possible output:

```
22 46
```

```
11 34 59
```

```
02 14 26 38
```

```
02 14 36 48
```

```
00 11 21 32 42
```

```
11 21 32 42 53
```

```
00 11 23 36 410
```

```
02 14 25 36 47
```

A Trip to Objectville

We're going to Objectville! We're leaving this dusty ol' procedural town for good. I'll send you a postcard.

I was told there would be objects. In chapter 1, we put all of our code in the main() method. That's not exactly object-oriented. In fact, that's not object-oriented *at all*. Well, we did *use* a few objects, like the String arrays for the Phrase-O-Matic, but we didn't actually develop any of our own object *types*. So now we've got to leave that procedural world behind, get the heck out of main(), and start making some objects of our own. We'll look at what makes object-oriented (OO) development in Java so much fun. We'll look at the difference between a *class* and an *object*. We'll look at how objects can give you a better life (at least the programming part of your life. Not much we can do about your fashion sense). Warning: once you get to Objectville, you might never go back. Send us a postcard.

Chair Wars
(or How Objects Can Change Your Life)

 nce upon a time in a software shop, two programmers were given the same spec and told to "build it". The Really Annoying Project Manager forced the two coders to compete, by promising that whoever delivers first gets one of those cool Aeron™ chairs all the Silicon Valley guys have. Larry, the procedural programmer, and Brad, the OO guy, both knew this would be a piece of cake.

Larry, sitting in his cube, thought to himself, "What are the things this program has to *do*? What *procedures* do we need?". And he answered himself , "**rotate** and **playSound**." So off he went to build the procedures. After all, what *is* a program if not a pile of procedures?

Brad, meanwhile, kicked back at the cafe and thought to himself, "What are the *things* in this program... who are the key *players*?" He first thought of **The Shapes**. Of course, there were other objects he thought of like the User, the Sound, and the Clicking event. But he already had a library of code for those pieces, so he focused on building Shapes. Read on to see how Brad and Larry built their programs, and for the answer to your burning question, *"So, who got the Aeron?"*

the spec

There will be shapes on a GUI, a square, a circle, and a triangle. When the user clicks on a shape, the shape will rotate clockwise 360º (i.e. all the way around) and play an AIF sound file specific to that particular shape.

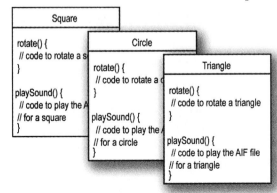

the chair

In Larry's cube

As he had done a gazillion times before, Larry set about writing his **Important Procedures**. He wrote **rotate** and **playSound** in no time.

```
rotate(shapeNum) {
  // make the shape rotate 360°
}
playSound(shapeNum) {
  // use shapeNum to lookup which
  // AIF sound to play, and play it
}
```

At Brad's laptop at the cafe

Brad wrote a *class* for each of the three shapes

```
Square
rotate() {
  // code to rotate a s
}
playSound() {
  // code to play the A
  // for a square
}
```

```
Circle
rotate() {
  // code to rotate a c
}
playSound() {
  // code to play the A
  // for a circle
}
```

```
Triangle
rotate() {
  // code to rotate a triangle
}
playSound() {
  // code to play the AIF file
  // for a triangle
}
```

Larry thought he'd nailed it. He could almost feel the rolled steel of the Aeron beneath his...

But wait! There's been a spec change.

"OK, *technically* you were first, Larry," said the Manager, "but we have to add just one tiny thing to the program. It'll be no problem for crack programmers like you two."

"If I had a dime for every time I've heard that one", thought Larry, knowing that spec-change-no-problem was a fantasy. *"And yet Brad looks strangely serene. What's up with that?"* Still, Larry held tight to his core belief that the OO way, while cute, was just slow. And that if you wanted to change his mind, you'd have to pry it from his cold, dead, carpal-tunnelled hands.

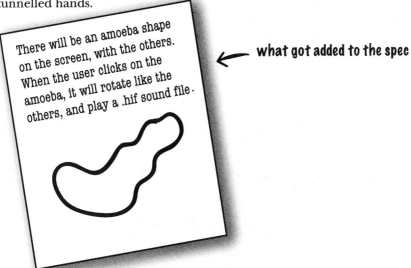

There will be an amoeba shape on the screen, with the others. When the user clicks on the amoeba, it will rotate like the others, and play a .hif sound file.

← **what got added to the spec**

Back in Larry's cube

The rotate procedure would still work; the code used a lookup table to match a shapeNum to an actual shape graphic. But *playSound would have to change.* And what the heck is a .hif file?

```
playSound(shapeNum) {
    // if the shape is not an amoeba,
        // use shapeNum to lookup which
        // AIF sound to play, and play it
    // else
        // play amoeba .hif sound
    }
```

It turned out not to be such a big deal, but *it still made him queasy to touch previously-tested code.* Of *all* people, *he* should know that no matter what the project manager says, *the spec always changes.*

At Brad's laptop at the beach

Brad smiled, sipped his margarita, and *wrote one new class.* Sometimes the thing he loved most about OO was that he didn't have to touch code he'd already tested and delivered. "Flexibility, extensibility,..." he mused, reflecting on the benefits of OO.

Amoeba

rotate() {
  // code to rotate an amoeba
}
playSound() {
  // code to play the new
  // .hif file for an amoeba
}

Larry snuck in just moments ahead of Brad.

(Hah! So much for that foofy OO nonsense). But the smirk on Larry's face melted when the Really Annoying Project Manager said (with that tone of disappointment), "Oh, no, *that's* not how the amoeba is supposed to rotate..."

Turns out, both programmers had written their rotate code like this:

1) determine the rectangle that surrounds the shape

2) calculate the center of that rectangle, and rotate the shape around that point.

But the amoeba shape was supposed to rotate around a point on one *end*, like a clock hand.

"I'm toast." thought Larry, visualizing charred Wonderbread™. "Although, hmmmm. I could just add another if/else to the rotate procedure, and then just hard-code the rotation point code for the amoeba. That probably won't break anything." But the little voice at the back of his head said, *"Big Mistake. Do you honestly think the spec won't change again?"*

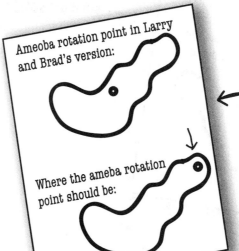

Ameoba rotation point in Larry and Brad's version:

What the spec conveniently forgot to mention

Where the ameba rotation point should be:

Back in Larry's cube

He figured he better add rotation point arguments to the rotate procedure. *A lot of code was affected.* Testing, recompiling, the whole nine yards all over again. Things that used to work, didn't.

```
rotate(shapeNum, xPt, yPt) {
    // if the shape is not an amoeba,
        // calculate the center point
        // based on a rectangle,
        // then rotate
    // else
        // use the xPt and yPt as
        // the rotation point offset
        // and then rotate
}
```

At Brad's laptop on his lawn chair at the Telluride Bluegrass Festival

Without missing a beat, Brad modified the **rotate method**, but only in the Amoeba class. *He never touched the tested, working, compiled code* for the other parts of the program. To give the Amoeba a rotation point, he added an **attribute** that all Amoebas would have. He modified, tested, and delivered (wirelessly) the revised program during a single Bela Fleck set.

Amoeba
int xPoint
int yPoint

rotate() {
  // code to rotate an **amoeba**
  // using amoeba's **x and y**
}

playSound() {
  // code to play the **new**
  // .hif file for an amoeba
}

So, Brad the OO guy got the chair, right?

Not so fast. Larry found a flaw in Brad's approach. And, since he was sure that if he got the chair he'd also get Lucy in accounting, he had to turn this thing around.

LARRY: You've got duplicated code! The rotate procedure is in all four Shape things.

BRAD: It's a *method*, not a *procedure*. And they're *classes*, not *things*.

LARRY: Whatever. It's a stupid design. You have to maintain *four* different rotate "methods". How can that ever be good?

BRAD: Oh, I guess you didn't see the final design. Let me show you how OO **inheritance** works, Larry.

What Larry wanted ⤴
(figured the chair would impress her)

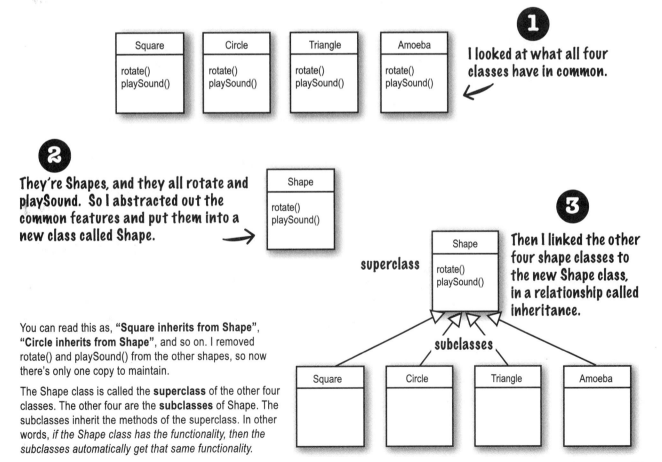

1
I looked at what all four classes have in common.

2
They're Shapes, and they all rotate and playSound. So I abstracted out the common features and put them into a new class called Shape. →

3
Then I linked the other four shape classes to the new Shape class, in a relationship called inheritance.

superclass

subclasses

You can read this as, **"Square inherits from Shape"**, **"Circle inherits from Shape"**, and so on. I removed rotate() and playSound() from the other shapes, so now there's only one copy to maintain.

The Shape class is called the **superclass** of the other four classes. The other four are the **subclasses** of Shape. The subclasses inherit the methods of the superclass. In other words, *if the Shape class has the functionality, then the subclasses automatically get that same functionality.*

What about the Amoeba rotate()?

LARRY: Wasn't that the whole problem here — that the amoeba shape had a completely different rotate and playSound procedure?

BRAD: Method.

LARRY: Whatever. How can amoeba do something different if it "inherits" its functionality from the Shape class?

BRAD: That's the last step. The Amoeba class **overrides** the methods of the Shape class. Then at runtime, the JVM knows exactly which rotate() method to run when someone tells the Amoeba to rotate.

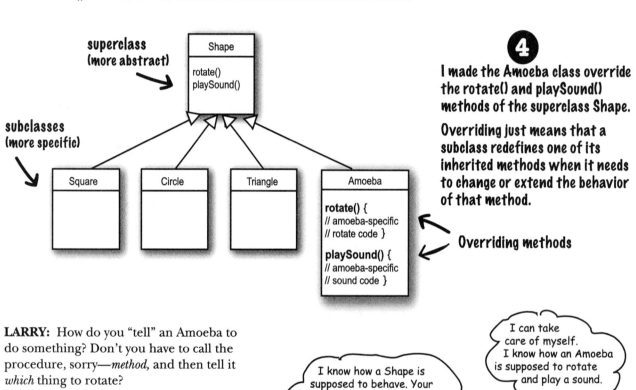

superclass (more abstract)

subclasses (more specific)

Overriding methods

4

I made the Amoeba class override the rotate() and playSound() methods of the superclass Shape.

Overriding just means that a subclass redefines one of its inherited methods when it needs to change or extend the behavior of that method.

LARRY: How do you "tell" an Amoeba to do something? Don't you have to call the procedure, sorry—*method,* and then tell it *which* thing to rotate?

BRAD: That's the really cool thing about OO. When it's time for, say, the triangle to rotate, the program code invokes (calls) the rotate() method *on the triangle object.* The rest of the program really doesn't know or care *how* the triangle does it. And when you need to add something new to the program, you just write a new class for the new object type, so the **new objects will have their own behavior.**

I know how a Shape is supposed to behave. Your job is to tell me **what** to do, and my job is to make it happen. Don't you worry your little programmer head about **how** I do it.

I can take care of myself. I know how an Amoeba is supposed to rotate and play a sound.

The suspense is killing me.
Who got the chair?

Amy from the second floor.

(unbeknownst to all, the Project Manager had given the spec to *three* programmers.)

What do you like about OO?

"It helps me design in a more natural way. Things have a way of evolving."

-Joy, 27, software architect

"Not messing around with code I've already tested, just to add a new feature."

-Brad, 32, programmer

"I like that the data and the methods that operate on that data are together in one class."

-Josh, 22, beer drinker

"Reusing code in other applications. When I write a new class, I can make it flexible enough to be used in something new, later."

-Chris, 39, project manager

"I can't believe Chris just said that. He hasn't written a line of code in 5 years."

-Daryl, 44, works for Chris

"Besides the chair?"

-Amy, 34, programmer

BRAIN POWER

Time to pump some neurons.

You just read a story bout a procedural programmer going head-to-head with an OO programmer. You got a quick overview of some key OO concepts including classes, methods, and attributes. We'll spend the rest of the chapter looking at classes and objects (we'll return to inheritance and overriding in later chapters).

Based on what you've seen so far (and what you may know from a previous OO language you've worked with), take a moment to think about these questions:

What are the fundamental things you need to think about when you design a Java class? What are the questions you need to ask yourself? If you could design a checklist to use when you're designing a class, what would be on the checklist?

---

metacognitive tip

If you're stuck on an exercise, try talking about it out loud. Speaking (and hearing) activates a different part of your brain. Although it works best if you have another person to discuss it with, pets work too. That's how our dog learned polymorphism.

When you design a class, think about the objects that will be created from that class type. Think about:

- things the object **knows**
- things the object **does**

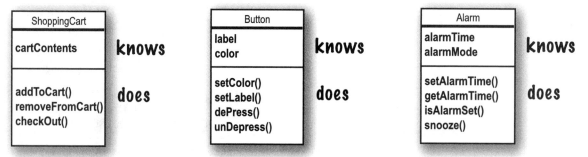

Things an object *knows* about itself are called

- instance variables

Things an object can *do* are called

- methods

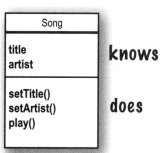

Things an object *knows* about itself are called **instance variables**. They represent an object's state (the data), and can have unique values for each object of that type.

Think of instance as another way of saying object.

Things an object can *do* are called **methods**. When you design a class, you think about the data an object will need to know about itself, and you also design the methods that operate on that data. It's common for an object to have methods that read or write the values of the instance variables. For example, Alarm objects have an instance variable to hold the alarmTime, and two methods for getting and setting the alarmTime.

So objects have instance variables and methods, but those instance variables and methods are designed as part of the class.

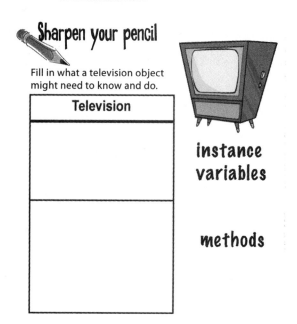

Sharpen your pencil

Fill in what a television object might need to know and do.

Television

instance variables

methods

What's the difference between a class and an object?

one class

many objects

A class is not an object.

(but it's used to construct them)

A class is a *blueprint* **for an object**. It tells the virtual machine *how* to make an object of that particular type. Each object made from that class can have its own values for the instance variables of that class. For example, you might use the Button class to make dozens of different buttons, and each button might have its own color, size, shape, label, and so on.

JVM

class

Look at it this way...

An object is like one entry in your address book.

One analogy for objects is a packet of unused Rolodex™ cards. Each card has the same blank fields (the instance variables). When you fill out a card you are creating an instance (object), and the entries you make on that card represent its state.

The methods of the class are the things you do to a particular card; getName( ), changeName( ), setName( ) could all be methods for class Rolodex.

So, each card can *do* the same things (getName( ), changeName( ), etc.), but each card *knows* things unique to that particular card.

Making your first object

So what does it take to create and use an object? You need *two* classes. One class for the type of object you want to use (Dog, AlarmClock, Television, etc.) and another class to *test* your new class. The *tester* class is where you put the main method, and in that main() method you create and access objects of your new class type. The tester class has only one job: to *try out* the methods and variables of your new object class type.

From this point forward in the book, you'll see two classes in many of our examples. One will be the *real* class – the class whose objects we really want to use, and the other class will be the *tester* class, which we call *<whateverYourClassNameIs>* **TestDrive**. For example, if we make a **Bungee** class, we'll need a **BungeeTestDrive** class as well. Only the *<someClassName>***TestDrive** class will have a main() method, and its sole purpose is to create objects of your new type (the not-the-tester class), and then use the dot operator (.) to access the methods and variables of the new objects. This will all be made stunningly clear by the following examples.

The Dot Operator (.)

The dot operator (.) gives you access to an object's state and behavior (instance variables and methods).

```
// make a new object
```
Dog d = new Dog();

```
// tell it to bark by using the
// dot operator on the
// variable d to call bark()
```
d.bark();

```
// set its size using the
// dot operator
```
d.size = 40;

---

① **Write your class**

```
class Dog {

  int size;
  String breed;
  String name;

  void bark() {
    System.out.println("Ruff! Ruff!");
  }
}
```

instance variables

a method

DOG
size
breed
name
bark()

② **Write a tester (TestDrive) class**

just a main method (we're gonna put code in it in the next step)

```
class DogTestDrive {
  public static void main (String[] args) {
    // Dog test code goes   here
  }
}
```

③ **In your tester, make an object and access the object's variables and methods**

```
class DogTestDrive {
  public static void main (String[] args) {
    Dog d = new Dog();
    d.size = 40;
    d.bark();
  }
}
```

make a Dog object

use the dot operator (.) to set the size of the Dog and to call its bark() method

dot operator

If you already have some OO savvy, you'll know we're not using encapsulation. We'll get there in chapter 4.

Making and testing Movie objects

```
class Movie {
  String title;
  String genre;
  int rating;

  void playIt() {
    System.out.println("Playing the movie");
  }
}

public class MovieTestDrive {
  public static void main(String[] args) {
    Movie one = new Movie();
    one.title = "Gone with the Stock";
    one.genre = "Tragic";
    one.rating = -2;
    Movie two = new Movie();
    two.title = "Lost in Cubicle Space";
    two.genre = "Comedy";
    two.rating = 5;
    two.playIt();
    Movie three = new Movie();
    three.title = "Byte Club";
    three.genre = "Tragic but ultimately uplifting";
    three.rating = 127;
  }
}
```

Sharpen your pencil

```
          MOVIE
        title
        genre
        rating
        playIt()
```

The MovieTestDrive class creates objects (instances) of
the Movie class and uses the dot operator (.) to set the
instance variables to a specific value. The MovieTestDrive
class also invokes (calls) a method on one of the objects.
Fill in the chart to the right with the values the three
objects have at the end of main().

object 1

title
genre
rating

object 2

title
genre
rating

object 3

title
genre
rating

Quick! Get out of main!

As long as you're in main(), you're not really in Objectville. It's fine for a test program to run within the main method, but in a true OO application, you need objects talking to other objects, as opposed to a static main() method creating and testing objects.

The two uses of main:

- to **test** your real class

- to **launch/start** your Java **application**

A real Java application is nothing but objects talking to other objects. In this case, *talking* means objects calling methods on one another. On the previous page, and in chapter 4, we look at using a main() method from a separate TestDrive class to create and test the methods and variables of another class. In chapter 6 we look at using a class with a main() method to start the ball rolling on a *real* Java application (by making objects and then turning those objects loose to interact with other objects, etc.)

As a 'sneak preview', though, of how a real Java application might behave, here's a little example. Because we're still at the earliest stages of learning Java, we're working with a small toolkit, so you'll find this program a little clunky and inefficient. You might want to think about what you could do to improve it, and in later chapters that's exactly what we'll do. Don't worry if some of the code is confusing; the key point of this example is that objects talk to objects.

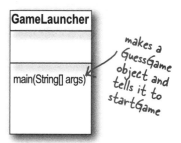

makes a GuessGame object and tells it to startGame

The Guessing Game

Summary:

The guessing game involves a 'game' object and three 'player' objects. The game generates a random number between 0 and 9, and the three player objects try to guess it. (We didn't say it was a really *exciting* game.)

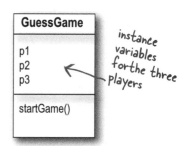

instance variables for the three players

Classes:

`GuessGame.class`   `Player.class`   `GameLauncher.class`

The Logic:

1) The GameLauncher class is where the application starts; it has the main() method.

2) In the main() method, a GuessGame object is created, and its startGame() method is called.

3) The GuessGame object's startGame() method is where the entire game plays out. It creates three players, then "thinks" of a random number (the target for the players to guess). It then asks each player to guess, checks the result, and either prints out information about the winning player(s) or asks them to guess again.

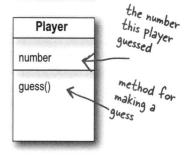

the number this player guessed

method for making a guess

```
public class GuessGame {
    Player p1;                          GuessGame has three instance
    Player p2;              ←           variables for the three Player
    Player p3;                          objects

    public void startGame() {
        p1 = new Player();              create three Player objects and
        p2 = new Player();    ←         assign them to the three Player
        p3 = new Player();              instance variables

        int guessp1 = 0;                declare three variables to hold the
        int guessp2 = 0;      ←         three guesses the Players make
        int guessp3 = 0;

        boolean p1isRight = false;
        boolean p2isRight = false;  ←   declare three variables to hold a true or
        boolean p3isRight = false;      false based on the player's answer

        int targetNumber = (int) (Math.random() * 10);          ←   make a 'target' number that the
        System.out.println("I'm thinking of a number between 0 and 9...");   players have to guess

        while(true) {
            System.out.println("Number to guess is " + targetNumber);

            p1.guess();      ←          call each player's guess() method
            p2.guess();
            p3.guess();

            guessp1 = p1.number;
            System.out.println("Player one guessed " + guessp1);

            guessp2 = p2.number;                                get each player's guess (the result of their
            System.out.println("Player two guessed " + guessp2);   guess() method running) by accessing the
                                                                number variable of each player
            guessp3 = p3.number;
            System.out.println("Player three guessed " + guessp3);

            if (guessp1 == targetNumber) {
                p1isRight = true;
            }                                   check each player's guess to see if it matches
            if (guessp2 == targetNumber) {      the target number. If a player is right,
                p2isRight = true;               then set that player's variable to be true
            }                                   (remember, we set it false by default)
            if (guessp3 == targetNumber) {
                p3isRight = true;
            }

            if (p1isRight || p2isRight || p3isRight) {    if player one OR player two OR player three is right...
                                                          (the || operator means OR)
            System.out.println("We have a winner!");
            System.out.println("Player one got it right? " + p1isRight);
            System.out.println("Player two got it right? " + p2isRight);
            System.out.println("Player three got it right? " + p3isRight);
            System.out.println("Game is over.");
            break; // game over, so break out of the loop

            } else {                                       otherwise, stay in the loop and ask the
                // we must keep going because nobody got it right!   players for another guess.
                System.out.println("Players will have to try again.");
            } // end if/else
        } // end loop
    } // end method
} // end class
```

Running the Guessing Game

```
public class Player {
    int number = 0;  // where the guess goes

    public void guess() {
        number = (int) (Math.random() * 10);
        System.out.println("I'm guessing "
                           + number);
    }
}


public class GameLauncher {
    public static void main (String[] args) {
        GuessGame game = new GuessGame();
        game.startGame();
    }
}
```

Output (it will be different each time you run it)

```
File  Edit  Window  Help  Explode
%java GameLauncher
I'm thinking of a number between 0 and 9...
Number to guess is 7
I'm guessing 1
I'm guessing 9
I'm guessing 9
Player one guessed 1
Player two guessed 9
Player three guessed 9
Players will have to try again.
Number to guess is 7
I'm guessing 3
I'm guessing 0
I'm guessing 9
Player one guessed 3
Player two guessed 0
Player three guessed 9
Players will have to try again.
Number to guess is 7
I'm guessing 7
I'm guessing 5
I'm guessing 0
Player one guessed 7
Player two guessed 5
Player three guessed 0
We have a winner!
Player one got it right? true
Player two got it right? false
Player three got it right? false
Game is over.
```

Java takes out the Garbage

Each time an object is created in Java, it goes into an area of memory known as **The Heap**.

All objects—no matter when, where, or how they're created – live on the heap. But it's not just any old memory heap; the Java heap is actually called the **Garbage-Collectible Heap.** When you create an object, Java allocates memory space on the heap according to how much that particular object needs. An object with, say, 15 instance variables, will probably need more space than an object with only two instance variables. But what happens when you need to reclaim that space? How do you get an object out of the heap when you're done with it? Java manages that memory for you! When the JVM can 'see' that an object can never be used again, that object becomes *eligible for garbage collection*. And if you're running low on memory, the Garbage Collector will run, throw out the unreachable objects, and free up the space, so that the space can be reused. In later chapters you'll learn more about how this works.

there are no Dumb Questions

Q: What if I need global variables and methods? How do I do that if everything has to go in a class?

A: There isn't a concept of 'global' variables and methods in a Java OO program. In practical use, however, there are times when you want a method (or a constant) to be available to any code running in any part of your program. Think of the `random()` method in the Phrase-O-Matic app; it's a method that should be callable from anywhere. Or what about a constant like *pi*? You'll learn in chapter 10 that marking a method as `public` and `static` makes it behave much like a 'global'. Any code, in any class of your application, can access a public static method. And if you mark a variable as `public`, `static`, and `final` – you have essentially made a globally-available *constant*.

Q: Then how is this object-oriented if you can still make global functions and global data?

A: First of all, everything in Java goes in a class. So the constant for *pi* and the method for `random()`, although both public and static, are defined within the `Math` class. And you must keep in mind that these static (global-like) things are the exception rather than the rule in Java. They represent a very special case, where you don't have multiple instances/objects.

Q: What *is* a Java program? What do you actually *deliver*?

A: A Java program is a pile of classes (or at least *one* class). In a Java application, *one* of the classes must have a main method, used to start-up the program. So as a programmer, you write one or more classes. And those classes are what you deliver. If the end-user doesn't have a JVM, then you'll also need to include that with your application's classes, so that they can run your program. There are a number of installer programs that let you bundle your classes with a variety of JVM's (say, for different platforms), and put it all on a CD-ROM. Then the end-user can install the correct version of the JVM (assuming they don't already have it on their machine.)

Q: What if I have a hundred classes? Or a thousand? Isn't that a big pain to deliver all those individual files? Can I bundle them into one *Application Thing*?

A: Yes, it would be a big pain to deliver a huge bunch of individual files to your end-users, but you won't have to. You can put all of your application files into a Java Archive – a *.jar file* – that's based on the pkzip format. In the jar file, you can include a simple text file formatted as something called a *manifest*, that defines which class in that jar holds the main() method that should run.

Make it Stick

A class is like a recipe.
Objects are like cookies.

BULLET POINTS

- Object-oriented programming lets you extend a program without having to touch previously-tested, working code.
- All Java code is defined in a **class**.
- A class describes how to make an object of that class type. **A class is like a blueprint.**
- An object can take care of itself; you don't have to know or care *how* the object does it.
- An object **knows** things and **does** things.
- Things an object knows about itself are called **instance variables**. They represent the *state* of an object.
- Things an object does are called **methods**. They represent the *behavior* of an object.
- When you create a class, you may also want to create a separate test class which you'll use to create objects of your new class type.
- A class can **inherit** instance variables and methods from a more abstract **superclass**.
- At runtime, a Java program is nothing more than objects 'talking' to other objects.

Exercise

BE the compiler

Each of the Java files on this page
represents a complete source file.
Your job is to play compiler and
determine whether each of
these files will compile.
If they won't compile,
how would you fix them,
and if they do compile,
what would be their output?

A

```
class TapeDeck {

  boolean canRecord = false;

  void playTape() {
    System.out.println("tape playing");
  }

  void recordTape() {
    System.out.println("tape recording");
  }
}

class TapeDeckTestDrive {
  public static void main(String [] args) {
    TapeDeck  t = new TapeDeck()
    t.canRecord = true;
    t.playTape();

    if (t.canRecord == true) {
      t.recordTape();
    }

  }

}
```

B

```
class DVDPlayer {

  boolean canRecord = false;

  void recordDVD() {
    System.out.println("DVD recording");
  }
}

class DVDPlayerTestDrive {
  public static void main(String [] args) {

    DVDPlayer d = new DVDPlayer();
    d.canRecord = true;
    d.playDVD();

    if (d.canRecord == true) {
      d.recordDVD();
    }

  }

}
```

Code Magnets

A Java program is all scrambled up on the fridge. Can you reconstruct the code snippets to make a working Java program that produces the output listed below? Some of the curly braces fell on the floor and they were too small to pick up, so feel free to add as many of those as you need.

```
class DrumKit {
    boolean topHat = true;
    boolean snare = true;
    void play TopHat () {

    }
    void play Snare() {

    }

}

class DrumKit TestDrive {

    public static void main (String [] args) {
        DrumKit d = new DrumKit();
        if (d.snare == true) {
            d.playSnare();
        }
        d.snare = false
        d.playSnare()
        d.play TopHat ();
    }
}
```

```
d.playSnare();
```

```
DrumKit d = new DrumKit();
```

```
boolean topHat = true;
```

```
boolean snare = true;
```

```
void playSnare() {
    System.out.println("bang bang ba-bang");
}
```

```
public static void main(String [] args) {
```

```
if (d.snare == true) {
    d.playSnare();
}
```

```
d.snare = false;
```

```
class DrumKitTestDrive {
```

```
d.playTopHat();
```

```
class DrumKit {
```

```
void playTopHat () {
    System.out.println("ding ding da-ding");
}
```

File Edit Window Help Dance

```
% java DrumKitTestDrive
bang bang ba-bang
ding ding da-ding
```

puzzle: Pool Puzzle

x	e1	e2
0	1	0
1	2	2
2	3	5
3	4	10

Pool Puzzle

Your *job* is to take code snippets from the pool and place them into the blank lines in the code. You **may** use the same snippet more than once, and you won't need to use all the snippets. Your *goal* is to make classes that will compile and run and produce the output listed.

Output

```
File  Edit  Window  Help  Implode
%java EchoTestDrive
helloooo...
helloooo...
helloooo...
helloooo...
10
```

Bonus Question !

If the last line of output was **24** instead of **10** how would you complete the puzzle ?

```
public class EchoTestDrive {
   public static void main(String [] args) {
      Echo e1 = new Echo();
      Echo e2 = new Echo();
      int x = 0;
      while (    x < 4    ) {
         e1.hello();
         e1.count = e1.count + 1
         if (    x == 3    ) {
            e2.count = e2.count + 1;
         }
         if (    x > 0    ) {
            e2.count = e2.count + e1.count;
         }
         x = x + 1;
      }
      System.out.println(e2.count);
   }
}
```

```
class    Echo    {
   int    count    = 0;
   void    hello    {
      System.out.println("helloooo... ");
   }
}
```

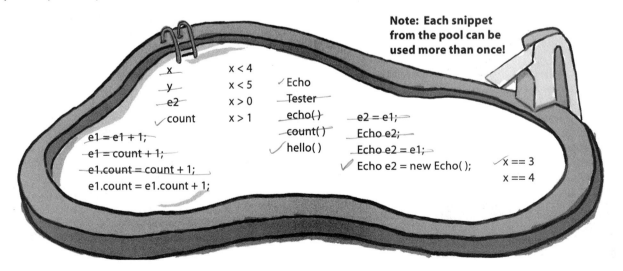

Note: Each snippet from the pool can be used more than once!

```
x          x < 4
y          x < 5        Echo
e2         x > 0        Tester        e2 = e1;
count      x > 1        echo()        Echo e2;
                        count()       Echo e2 = e1;
e1 = e1 + 1;            hello()       Echo e2 = new Echo();    x == 3
e1 = count + 1;                                               x == 4
e1.count = count + 1;
e1.count = e1.count + 1;
```

A bunch of Java components, in full costume, are playing a party game, "Who am I?" They give you a clue, and you try to guess who they are, based on what they say. Assume they always tell the truth about themselves. If they happen to say something that could be true for more than one of them, choose all for whom that sentence can apply. Fill in the blanks next to the sentence with the names of one or more attendees. The first one's on us.

Tonight's attendees:

Class   Method   Object   Instance variable

Who am I?

I am compiled from a .java file. ___class_____

My instance variable values can be different from my buddy's values. _____

I behave like a template. _____

I like to do stuff. _____

I can have many methods. _____

I represent 'state'. _____

I have behaviors. _____

I am located in objects. _____

I live on the heap. _____

I am used to create object instances. _____

My state can change. _____

I declare methods. _____

I can change at runtime. _____

Exercise

Exercise Solutions

Code Magnets:

```
class DrumKit {

  boolean topHat = true;
  boolean snare = true;

  void playTopHat() {
    System.out.println("ding ding da-ding");
  }

  void playSnare() {
    System.out.println("bang bang ba-bang");
  }
}

class DrumKitTestDrive {
  public static void main(String [] args) {

    DrumKit d = new DrumKit();
    d.playSnare();
    d.snare = false;
    d.playTopHat();

    if (d.snare == true) {
      d.playSnare();
    }
  }
}
```

```
File Edit Window Help Dance
% java DrumKitTestDrive
bang bang ba-bang
ding ding da-ding
```

Be the Compiler:

```
class TapeDeck {
  boolean canRecord = false;
  void playTape() {
    System.out.println("tape playing");
  }
  void recordTape() {
    System.out.println("tape recording");
  }
}
```
A

```
class TapeDeckTestDrive {
  public static void main(String [] args) {

    TapeDeck t = new TapeDeck( );
    t.canRecord = true;
    t.playTape();

    if (t.canRecord == true) {
      t.recordTape();
    }
  }
}
```
> We've got the template, now we have to make an object !

```
class DVDPlayer {
  boolean canRecord = false;
  void recordDVD() {
    System.out.println("DVD recording");
  }
  void playDVD ( ) {
    System.out.println("DVD playing");
  }
}
```

```
class DVDPlayerTestDrive {
  public static void main(String [] args) {
    DVDPlayer d = new DVDPlayer();
    d.canRecord = true;
    d.playDVD();
    if (d.canRecord == true) {
      d.recordDVD();
    }
  }
}
```
B

> The line: d.playDVD( ); wouldn't compile without a method !

 Puzzle Solutions

Pool Puzzle

```java
public class EchoTestDrive {
  public static void main(String [] args) {
    Echo e1 = new Echo();
    Echo e2 = new Echo( ); // the correct answer
          - or -
    Echo e2 = e1;   // is the bonus answer!
    int x = 0;
    while ( x < 4 ) {
      e1.hello();
      e1.count = e1.count + 1;
      if ( x == 3 ) {
        e2.count = e2.count + 1;
      }
      if ( x > 0 ) {
        e2.count = e2.count + e1.count;
      }
      x = x + 1;
    }
    System.out.println(e2.count);
  }
}
_____

class Echo {
  int count = 0;
  void hello( ) {
    System.out.println("helloooo... ");
  }
}
```

Who am I?

I am compiled from a .java file.	class
My instance variable values can be different from my buddy's values.	object
I behave like a template.	class
I like to do stuff.	object, method
I can have many methods.	class, object
I represent 'state'.	instance variable
I have behaviors.	object, class
I am located in objects.	method, instance variable
I live on the heap.	object
I am used to create object instances.	class
My state can change.	object, instance variable
I declare methods.	class
I can change at runtime.	object, instance variable

Note: both classes and objects are said to have state and behavior. They're defined in the class, but the object is also said to 'have' them. Right now, we don't care where they *technically* live.

```
 File  Edit  Window  Help  Assimilate
%java EchoTestDrive
helloooo...
helloooo...
helloooo...
helloooo...
10
```

Know Your Variables

Variables come in two flavors: primitive and reference. So far you've used variables in two places—as object **state** (instance variables), and as **local** variables (variables declared within a *method*). Later, we'll use variables as **arguments** (values sent to a method by the calling code), and as **return types** (values sent back to the caller of the method). You've seen variables declared as simple **primitive** integer values (type `int`). You've seen variables declared as something more **complex** like a String or an array. But **there's gotta be more to life** than integers, Strings, and arrays. What if you have a PetOwner object with a Dog instance variable? Or a Car with an Engine? In this chapter we'll unwrap the mysteries of Java types and look at what you can *declare* as a variable, what you can *put* in a variable, and what you can *do* with a variable. And we'll finally see what life is *truly* like on the garbage-collectible heap.

Java cares about type. You can't put a Giraffe in a Rabbit variable.

Rabbit Variable

Declaring a variable

Java cares about type. It won't let you do something bizarre and dangerous like stuff a Giraffe reference into a Rabbit variable—what happens when someone tries to ask the so-called *Rabbit* to hop ()? And it won't let you put a floating point number into an integer variable, unless you *acknowledge to the compiler* that you know you might lose precision (like, everything after the decimal point).

The compiler can spot most problems:

```
Rabbit hopper = new Giraffe();
```

Don't expect that to compile. *Thankfully.*

For all this type-safety to work, you must declare the type of your variable. Is it an integer? a Dog? A single character? Variables come in two flavors: *primitive* and **object reference**. Primitives hold fundamental values (think: simple bit patterns) including integers, booleans, and floating point numbers. Object references hold, well, *references* to *objects* (gee, didn't *that* clear it up.)

We'll look at primitives first and then move on to what an object reference really means. But regardless of the type, you must follow two declaration rules:

---

variables must have a type

Besides a type, a variable needs a name, so that you can use that name in code.

---

variables must have a name

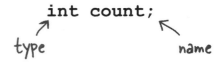

`int count;`

type   name

Note: When you see a statement like: "an object of **type** X", think of *type* and *class* as synonyms. (We'll refine that a little more in later chapters.)

"I'd like a double mocha, no, make it an int."

When you think of Java variables, think of cups. Coffee cups, tea cups, giant cups that hold lots and lots of beer, those big cups the popcorn comes in at the movies, cups with curvy, sexy handles, and cups with metallic trim that you learned can never, ever go in the microwave.

A variable is just a cup. A container. It *holds* something.

It has a size, and a type. In this chapter, we're going to look first at the variables (cups) that hold **primitives**, then a little later we'll look at cups that hold *references to objects*. Stay with us here on the whole cup analogy—as simple as it is right now, it'll give us a common way to look at things when the discussion gets more complex. And that'll happen soon.

Primitives are like the cups they have at the coffeehouse. If you've been to a Starbucks, you know what we're talking about here. They come in different sizes, and each has a name like 'short', 'tall', and, "I'd like a 'grande' mocha half-caff with extra whipped cream".

You might see the cups displayed on the counter, so you can order appropriately:

small   short   tall   grande

And in Java, primitives come in different sizes, and those sizes have names. When you declare a variable in Java, you must declare it with a specific type. The four containers here are for the four integer primitives in Java.

long   int   short   byte

Each cup holds a value, so for Java primitives, rather than saying, "I'd like a tall french roast", you say to the compiler, "I'd like an int variable with the number 90 please." Except for one tiny difference... in Java you also have to give your cup a *name*. So it's actually, "I'd like an int please, with the value of 2486, and name the variable *height*." Each primitive variable has a fixed number of bits (cup size). The sizes for the six numeric primitives in Java are shown below:

byte   short   int   long
8   16   32   64

float   double
32   64

Primitive Types

Type	Bit Depth	Value Range

boolean and char

boolean	(JVM-specific)	***true*** or ***false***
char	16 bits	0 to 65535

numeric (all are signed)

integer

byte	8 bits	-128 to 127
short	16 bits	-32768 to 32767
int	32 bits	-2147483648 to 2147483647
long	64 bits	-huge to huge

floating point

float	32 bits	varies
double	64 bits	varies

Primitive declarations with assignments:

```
int x;
x = 234;
byte b = 89;
boolean isFun = true;
double d = 3456.98;
char c = 'f';
int z = x;
boolean isPunkRock;
isPunkRock = false;
boolean powerOn;
powerOn = isFun;
long big = 3456789;
float f = 32.5f;
```

Note the 'f'. Gotta have that with a float, because Java thinks anything with a floating point is a double, unless you use 'f'.

You *really* don't want to spill that...

Be sure the value can fit into the variable.

You can't put a large value into a small cup.

Well, OK, you can, but you'll lose some. You'll get, as we say, *spillage.* The compiler tries to help prevent this if it can tell from your code that something's not going to fit in the container (variable/cup) you're using.

For example, you can't pour an int-full of stuff into a byte-sized container, as follows:

```
int x = 24;

byte b = x;

//won't work!!
```

Why doesn't this work, you ask? After all, the value of *x* is 24, and 24 is definitely small enough to fit into a byte. *You* know that, and *we* know that, but all the compiler cares about is that you're trying to put a big thing into a small thing, and there's the *possibility* of spilling. Don't expect the compiler to know what the value of *x* is, even if you happen to be able to see it literally in your code.

You can assign a value to a variable in one of several ways including:

- type a *literal* value after the equals sign (x=*12*, isGood = *true*, etc.)
- assign the value of one variable to another (x = y)
- use an expression combining the two (x = y + *43*)

In the examples below, the literal values are in bold italics:

int size = *32*;	declare an int named *size*, assign it the value *32*
char initial = *'j'*;	declare a char named *initial*, assign it the value *'j'*
double d = *456.709*;	declare a double named *d*, assign it the value *456.709*
boolean isCrazy;	declare a boolean named *isCrazy* (no assignment)
isCrazy = *true*;	assign the value *true* to the previously-declared *isCrazy*
int y = x + *456*;	declare an int named *y*, assign it the value that is the sum of whatever *x* is now plus *456*

Sharpen your pencil

The compiler won't let you put a value from a large cup into a small one. But what about the other way—pouring a small cup into a big one? *No problem.*

Based on what you know about the size and type of the primitive variables, see if you can figure out which of these are legal and which aren't. We haven't covered all the rules yet, so on some of these you'll have to use your best judgment. *Tip:* The compiler always errs on the side of safety.

From the following list, ***Circle*** the statements that would be legal if these lines were in a single method:

1. `int x = 34.5;`
2. `boolean boo = x;`
3. `int g = 17;`
4. `int y = g;`
5. `y = y + 10;`
6. `short s;`
7. `s = y;`
8. `byte b = 3;`
9. `byte v = b;`
10. `short n = 12;`
11. `v = n;`
12. `byte k = 128;`

Back away from that keyword!

You know you need a name and a type for your variables.

You already know the primitive types.

But what can you use as names? The rules are simple. You can name a class, method, or variable according to the following rules (the real rules are slightly more flexible, but these will keep you safe):

■ **It must start with a letter, underscore (_), or dollar sign ($). You can't start a name with a number.**

■ **After the first character, you can use numbers as well. Just don't start it with a number.**

■ **It can be anything you like, subject to those two rules, just so long as it isn't one of Java's reserved words.**

are keywords (and other things) that the compiler recognizes. And if you really want to play confuse-a-compiler, then just *try* using a reserved word as a name.

You've already seen some reserved words when we looked at writing our first main class:

```
public    static    void
```

← don't use any of these for your own names.

And the primitive types are reserved as well:

```
boolean char byte short int long float double
```

But there are a lot more we haven't discussed yet. Even if you don't need to know what they mean, you still need to know you can't use 'em yourself. ***Do not***—*under any circumstances*—***try to memorize these now.*** To make room for these in your head, you'd probably have to lose something else. Like where your car is parked. Don't worry, by the end of the book you'll have most of them down cold.

No matter what you hear, do not, I repeat, do **not** let me ingest another large furry dog.

Make it Stick

Java is Pass by value

Wash Cat

threads wait() notify()

The eight primitive types are:

boolean char byte short int long float double

And here's a mnemonic for remembering them:

Be **C**areful! **B**ears **S**houldn't **I**ngest **L**arge **F**urry **D**ogs

If you make up your own, it'll stick even better.

B_ C_ B_ S_ I_ L_ F_ D_

This table reserved.

boolean	byte	char	double	float	int	long	short	public	private
protected	abstract	final	native	static	strictfp	synchronized	transient	volatile	if
else	do	while	switch	case	default	for	break	continue	assert
class	extends	implements	import	instanceof	interface	new	package	super	this
catch	finally	try	throw	throws	return	void	const	goto	enum

Java's keywords and other reserved words (in no useful order). If you use these for names, the compiler will be very, *very* upset.

Controlling your Dog object

You know how to declare a primitive variable and assign it a value. But now what about non-primitive variables? In other words, *what about objects?*

■   **There is actually no such thing as an object variable.**

■   **There's only an object reference variable.**

■   **An object reference variable holds bits that represent a way to access an object.**

■   **It doesn't hold the object itself, but it holds something like a pointer. Or an address. Except, in Java we don't really know *what* is inside a reference variable. We *do* know that whatever it is, it represents one and only one object. And the JVM knows how to use the reference to get to the object.**

You can't stuff an object into a variable. We often think of it that way... we say things like, "I passed the String to the System.out.println() method." Or, "The method returns a Dog", or, "I put a new Foo object into the variable named myFoo."

But that's not what happens. There aren't giant expandable cups that can grow to the size of any object. Objects live in one place and one place only—the garbage collectible heap! (You'll learn more about that later in this chapter.)

Although a primitive variable is full of bits representing the actual *value* of the variable, an object reference variable is full of bits representing *a way to get to the object.*

You use the dot operator (.) on a reference variable to say, "use the thing *before* the dot to get me the thing *after* the dot." For example:

`myDog.bark();`

means, "use the object referenced by the variable myDog to invoke the bark() method." When you use the dot operator on an object reference variable, think of it like pressing a button on the remote control for that object.

Dog d = new Dog(); d.bark();

↖ think of this
like this ↘

Think of a Dog reference variable as a Dog remote control. You use it to get the object to do something (invoke methods).

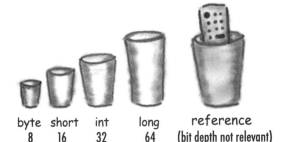

byte short int long reference
8 16 32 64 (bit depth not relevant)

An object reference is just another variable value.

Something that goes in a cup.
Only this time, the value is a remote control.

Primitive Variable

byte x = 7;

The bits representing 7 go into the variable. (00000111).

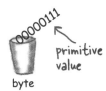

00000111 ← primitive value

byte

Reference Variable

Dog myDog = new Dog();

The bits representing a way to get to the Dog object go into the variable.

The Dog object itself does not go into the variable!

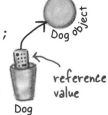

Dog object

reference value

Dog

> With primitive variables, the value of the variable is... the *value* (5, -26.7, 'a').
>
> With reference variables, the value of the variable is... *bits representing a way to get to a specific object.*
>
> You don't know (or care) how any particular JVM implements object references. Sure, they might be a pointer to a pointer to... but even if you *know*, you still can't use the bits for anything other than accessing an object.

We don't care how many 1's and 0's there are in a reference variable. It's up to each JVM and the phase of the moon.

The 3 steps of object declaration, creation and assignment

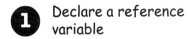

$$\underbrace{\text{Dog myDog}}_{1} \underset{3}{=} \underbrace{\text{new Dog()}}_{2};$$

① Declare a reference variable

Dog myDog = new Dog();

Tells the JVM to allocate space for a reference variable, and names that variable *myDog*. The reference variable is, forever, of type Dog. In other words, a remote control that has buttons to control a Dog, but not a Cat or a Button or a Socket.

myDog

Dog

② Create an object

Dog myDog = **new Dog();**

Tells the JVM to allocate space for a new Dog object on the heap (we'll learn a lot more about that process, especially in chapter 9.)

Dog object

③ Link the object and the reference

Dog myDog **=** new Dog();

Assigns the new Dog to the reference variable myDog. In other words, ***programs the remote control.***

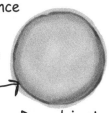

myDog

Dog

Dog object

there are no Dumb Questions

Q: How big is a reference variable?

A: You don't know. Unless you're cozy with someone on the JVM's development team, you don't know how a reference is represented. There are pointers in there somewhere, but you can't access them. You won't need to. (OK, if you insist, you might as well just imagine it to be a 64-bit value.) But when you're talking about memory allocation issues, your Big Concern should be about how many *objects* (as opposed to object *references*) you're creating, and how big *they* (the *objects*) really are.

Q: So, does that mean that all object references are the same size, regardless of the size of the actual objects to which they refer?

A: Yep. All references for a given JVM will be the same size regardless of the objects they reference, but each JVM might have a different way of representing references, so references on one JVM may be smaller or larger than references on another JVM.

Q: Can I do arithmetic on a reference variable, increment it, you know – C stuff?

A: Nope. Say it with me again, "Java is not C."

Java Exposed

This week's interview:
Object Reference

HeadFirst: So, tell us, what's life like for an object reference?

Reference: Pretty simple, really. I'm a remote control and I can be programmed to control different objects.

HeadFirst: Do you mean different objects even while you're running? Like, can you refer to a Dog and then five minutes later refer to a Car?

Reference: Of course not. Once I'm declared, that's it. If I'm a Dog remote control then I'll never be able to point (oops – my bad, we're not supposed to say *point*) I mean *refer* to anything but a Dog.

HeadFirst: Does that mean you can refer to only one Dog?

Reference: No. I can be referring to one Dog, and then five minutes later I can refer to some *other* Dog. As long as it's a Dog, I can be redirected (like reprogramming your remote to a different TV) to it. Unless... no never mind.

HeadFirst: No, tell me. What were you gonna say?

Reference: I don't think you want to get into this now, but I'll just give you the short version – if I'm marked as `final`, then once I am assigned a Dog, I can never be repro-grammed to anything else but *that* one and only Dog. In other words, no other object can be assigned to me.

HeadFirst: You're right, we don't want to talk about that now. OK, so unless you're `final`, then you can refer to one Dog and then refer to a different Dog later. Can you ever refer to *nothing at all*? Is it possible to not be programmed to anything?

Reference: Yes, but it disturbs me to talk about it.

HeadFirst: Why is that?

Reference: Because it means I'm `null`, and that's upsetting to me.

HeadFirst: You mean, because then you have no value?

Reference: Oh, `null` *is* a value. I'm still a remote control, but it's like you brought home a new universal remote control and you don't have a TV. I'm not programmed to control anything. They can press my buttons all day long, but nothing good happens. I just feel so... useless. A waste of bits. Granted, not that many bits, but still. And that's not the worst part. If I am the only reference to a particular object, and then I'm set to `null` (deprogrammed), it means that now *nobody* can get to that object I had been referring to.

HeadFirst: And that's bad because...

Reference: You have to *ask*? Here I've developed a relationship with this object, an intimate connection, and then the tie is suddenly, cruelly, severed. And I will never see that object again, because now it's eligible for [producer, cue tragic music] *garbage collection*. Sniff. But do you think programmers ever consider *that*? Sniff. Why, *why* can't I be a primi-tive? *I hate being a reference.* The responsibility, all the broken attachments...

Life on the garbage-collectible heap

```
Book b = new Book();
```

```
Book c = new Book();
```

Declare two Book reference variables. Create two new Book objects. Assign the Book objects to the reference variables.

The two Book objects are now living on the heap.

References: 2

Objects: 2

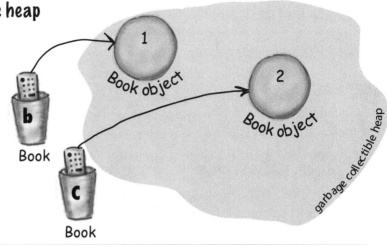

```
Book d = c;
```

Declare a new Book reference variable. Rather than creating a new, third Book object, assign the value of variable *c* to variable *d*. But what does this mean? It's like saying, "Take the bits in *c*, make a copy of them, and stick that copy into *d*."

Both *c* and *d* refer to the same object.

The *c* and *d* variables hold two different copies of the same value. Two remotes programmed to one TV.

References: 3

Objects: 2

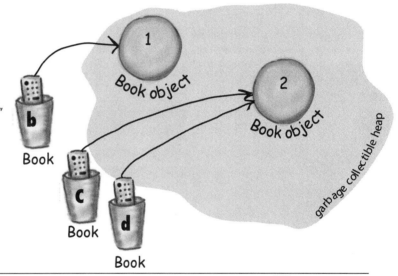

```
c = b;
```

Assign the value of variable *b* to variable *c*. By now you know what this means. The bits inside variable *b* are copied, and that new copy is stuffed into variable *c*.

Both b and c refer to the same object.

References: 3

Objects: 2

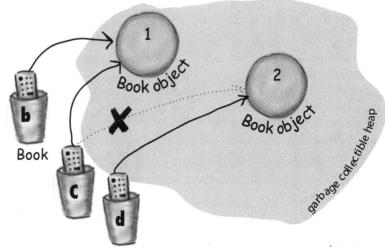

Life and death on the heap

```
Book b = new Book();
```

```
Book c = new Book();
```

Declare two Book reference variables. Create two new Book objects. Assign the Book objects to the reference variables.

The two book objects are now living on the heap.

Active References: 2

Reachable Objects: 2

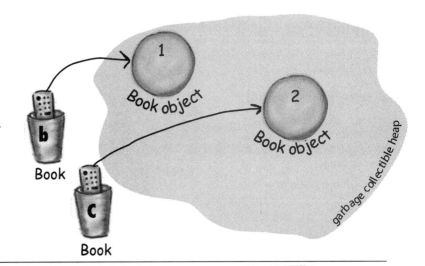

---

b = c;

Assign the value of variable **c** to variable **b**. The bits inside variable **c** are copied, and that new copy is stuffed into variable **b**. Both variables hold identical values.

Both b and c refer to the same object. Object 1 is abandoned and eligible for Garbage Collection (GC).

Active References: 2

Reachable Objects: 1

Abandoned Objects: 1

The first object that **b** referenced, Object 1, has no more references. It's *unreachable*.

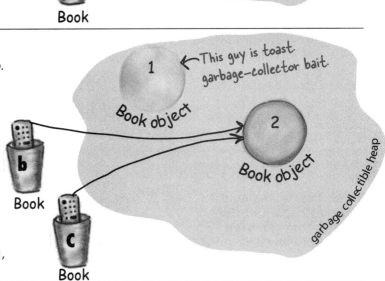

---

c = null;

Assign the value null to variable **c**. This makes **c** a *null reference*, meaning it doesn't refer to anything. But it's still a reference variable, and another Book object can still be assigned to it.

Object 2 still has an active reference (b), and as long as it does, the object is not eligible for GC.

Active References: 1

null References: 1

Reachable Objects: 1

Abandoned Objects: 1

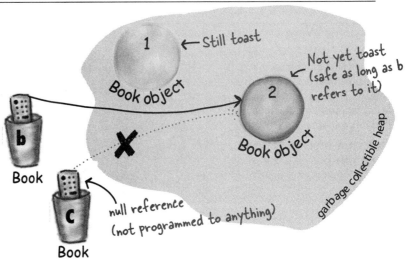

An array is like a tray of cups

① Declare an int array variable. An array variable is a remote control to an array object.

```
int[] nums;
```

② Create a new int array with a length of 7, and assign it to the previously-declared `int[]` variable `nums`

```
nums = new int[7];
```

③ Give each element in the array an int value.
Remember, elements in an int *array* are just int *variables*.

7 int variables
```
nums[0] = 6;
nums[1] = 19;
nums[2] = 44;
nums[3] = 42;
nums[4] = 10;
nums[5] = 20;
nums[6] = 1;
```

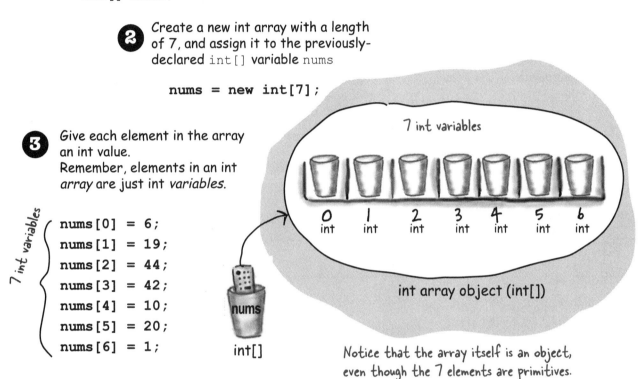

7 int variables

| 0 | 1 | 2 | 3 | 4 | 5 | 6 |
| int | int | int | int | int | int | int |

int array object (int[])

nums

int[]

Notice that the array itself is an object, even though the 7 elements are primitives.

Arrays are objects too

The Java standard library includes lots of sophisticated data structures including maps, trees, and sets (see Appendix B), but arrays are great when you just want a quick, ordered, efficient list of things. Arrays give you fast random access by letting you use an index position to get to any element in the array.

Every element in an array is just a variable. In other words, one of the eight primitive variable types (think: Large Furry Dog) or a

reference variable. Anything you would put in a *variable* of that type can be assigned to an *array element* of that type. So in an array of type int (int[]), each element can hold an int. In a Dog array (Dog[]) each element can hold... a Dog? No, remember that a reference variable just holds a reference (a remote control), not the object itself. So in a Dog array, each element can hold a *remote control* to a Dog. Of course, we still have to make the Dog objects... and you'll see all that on the next page.

Be sure to notice one key thing in the picture above – *the array is an object, even though it's an array of primitives.*

Arrays are always objects, whether they're declared to hold primitives or object references. But you can have an array object that's declared to *hold* primitive values. In other words, the array object can have *elements* which are primitives, but the array itself is *never* a primitive. Regardless of what the array holds, the array itself is always an object!

Make an array of Dogs

1 Declare a Dog array variable

```
Dog[] pets;
```

2 Create a new Dog array with a length of 7, and assign it to the previously-declared Dog[] variable pets

```
pets = new Dog[7];
```

What's missing?

Dogs! We have an array of Dog *references*, but no actual Dog *objects*!

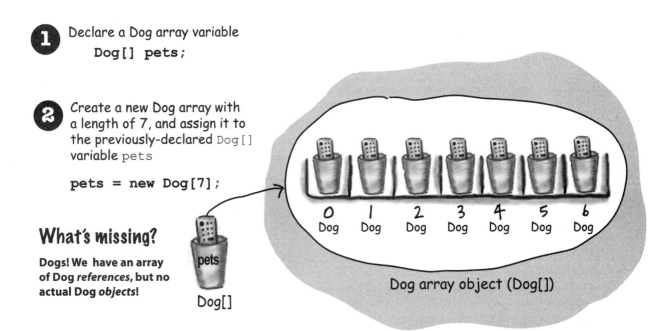

Dog array object (Dog[])

pets
Dog[]

---

3 Create new Dog objects, and assign them to the array elements.
Remember, elements in a Dog *array* are just Dog reference *variables*. We still need Dogs!

```
pets[0] = new Dog();
pets[1] = new Dog();
```

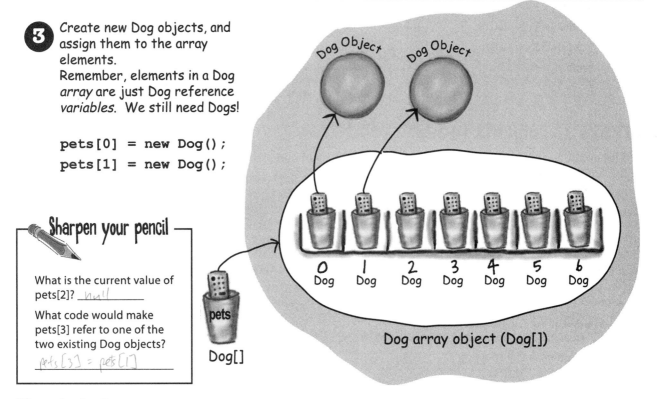

Dog array object (Dog[])

pets
Dog[]

✏ Sharpen your pencil

What is the current value of pets[2]? _null_

What code would make pets[3] refer to one of the two existing Dog objects?

pets[3] = pets[1]

Dog
name
bark()
eat()
chaseCat()

Control your Dog
(with a reference variable)

```
Dog fido = new Dog();
fido.name = "Fido";
```

We created a Dog object and used the dot operator on the reference variable *fido* to access the name variable.*

We can use the *fido* reference to get the dog to bark() or eat() or chaseCat().

```
fido.bark();
fido.chaseCat();
```

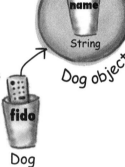

What happens if the Dog is in a Dog array?

We know we can access the Dog's instance variables and methods using the dot operator, but *on what?*

When the Dog is in an array, we don't have an actual variable name (like *fido*). Instead we use array notation and push the remote control button (dot operator) on an object at a particular index (position) in the array:

```
Dog[] myDogs = new Dog[3];
myDogs[0] = new Dog();
myDogs[0].name = "Fido";
myDogs[0].bark();
```

*Yes we know we're not demonstrating encapsulation here, but we're trying to keep it simple. For now. We'll do encapsulation in chapter 4.

Java cares about type.

Once you've declared an array, you can't put anything in it except things that are of the declared array type.

For example, you can't put a Cat into a Dog array (it would be pretty awful if someone thinks that only Dogs are in the array, so they ask each one to bark, and then to their horror discover there's a cat lurking.) And you can't stick a double into an int array (spillage, remember?). You can, however, put a byte into an int array, because a byte will always fit into an int-sized cup. This is known as an implicit widening. We'll get into the details later, for now just remember that the compiler won't let you put the wrong thing in an array, based on the array's declared type.

```
class Dog {
  String name;
  public static void main (String[] args) {
    // make a Dog object and access it
    Dog dog1 = new Dog();
    dog1.bark();
    dog1.name = "Bart";

    // now make a Dog array
    Dog[] myDogs = new Dog[3];
    // and put some dogs in it
    myDogs[0] = new Dog();
    myDogs[1] = new Dog();
    myDogs[2] = dog1;

    // now access the Dogs using the array
    // references
    myDogs[0].name = "Fred";
    myDogs[1].name = "Marge";

    // Hmmmm... what is myDogs[2] name?
    System.out.print("last dog's name is ");
    System.out.println(myDogs[2].name);

    // now loop through the array
    // and tell all dogs to bark
    int x = 0;
    while(x < myDogs.length) {
      myDogs[x].bark();
      x = x + 1;
    }
  }

  public void bark() {
    System.out.println(name + " says Ruff!");
  }
  public void eat() {  }
  public void chaseCat() {  }
}
```

arrays have a variable 'length' that gives you the number of elements in the array

A Dog example

Dog
name
bark() eat() chaseCat()

Output

```
File  Edit  Window  Help  Howl
%java Dog
null says Ruff!
last dog's name is Bart
Fred says Ruff!
Marge says Ruff!
Bart says Ruff!
```

BULLET POINTS

- Variables come in two flavors: primitive and reference.
- Variables must always be declared with a name and a type.
- A primitive variable value is the bits representing the value (5, 'a', true, 3.1416, etc.).
- A reference variable value is the bits representing a way to get to an object on the heap.
- A reference variable is like a remote control. Using the dot operator (.) on a reference variable is like pressing a button on the remote control to access a method or instance variable.
- A reference variable has a value of `null` when it is not referencing any object.
- An array is always an object, even if the array is declared to hold primitives. There is no such thing as a primitive array, only an array that *holds* primitives.

Exercise

BE the compiler

Each of the Java files on this page
represents a complete source file.
Your job is to play compiler and
determine whether each of these files
will compile. If they won't
compile, how would you
fix them?

A

```
class Books {
  String title;
  String author;
}

class BooksTestDrive {
  public static void main(String [] args) {

    Books [] myBooks = new Books[3];
    int x = 0;
    myBooks[0].title = "The Grapes of Java";
    myBooks[1].title = "The Java Gatsby";
    myBooks[2].title = "The Java Cookbook";
    myBooks[0].author = "bob";
    myBooks[1].author = "sue";
    myBooks[2].author = "ian";

    while (x < 3) {
      System.out.print(myBooks[x].title);
      System.out.print(" by ");
      System.out.println(myBooks[x].author);
      x = x + 1;
    }
  }
}
```

(handwritten margin note: need to create Books ; Books[0]=new Books(); Books[0]=new Books();*)*

B

```
class Hobbits {

  String name;

  public static void main(String [] args) {

    Hobbits [] h = new Hobbits[3];
    int z = 0;

    while (z < 4) {
      z = z + 1;
      h[z] = new Hobbits();
      h[z].name = "bilbo";
      if (z == 1) {
        h[z].name = "frodo";
      }
      if (z == 2) {
        h[z].name = "sam";
      }
      System.out.print(h[z].name + " is a ");
      System.out.println("good Hobbit name");
    }
  }
}
```

Code Magnets

A working Java program is all scrambled up on the fridge. Can you reconstruct the code snippets to make a working Java program that produces the output listed below? Some of the curly braces fell on the floor and they were too small to pick up, so feel free to add as many of those as you need!

```
int y = 0;
```

```
ref = index[y];
```

```
islands[0] = "Bermuda";
islands[1] = "Fiji";
islands[2] = "Azores";
islands[3] = "Cozumel";
```

```
int ref;
while (y < 4) {
```

```
System.out.println(islands[ref]);
```

```
index[0] = 1;
index[1] = 3;
index[2] = 0;
index[3] = 2;
```

```
String [] islands = new String[4];
```

```
System.out.print("island = ");
```

```
int [] index = new int[4];
```

```
y = y + 1;
```

```
class TestArrays {

   public static void main(String [] args) {
```

File Edit Window Help Bikini

```
% java TestArrays
island = Fiji
island = Cozumel
island = Bermuda
island = Azores
```

Pool Puzzle

Your **job** is to take code snippets from the pool and place them into the blank lines in the code. You **may** use the same snippet more than once, and you won't need to use all the snippets. Your **goal** is to make a class that will compile and run and produce the output listed.

Output

```
File  Edit  Window  Help  Bermuda
%java Triangle
triangle 0, area = 4.0
triangle 1, area = 10.0
triangle 2, area = 18.0
triangle 3, area = ____   28.0
y = _____   4, t5 area = 343.
```

Bonus Question!

For extra bonus points, use snippets from the pool to fill in the missing output (above).

```
class Triangle {                  (Sometimes we don't use a separate
    double area;                   test class, because we're trying to
    int height;                    save space on the page)
    int length;
    public static void main(String [] args) {
        int x = 0 ;
        Triangle [] ta = new Triangle [4];
        while ( x < 4 ) {
            ta [x] = new Triangle()
            ta [x] .height = (x + 1) * 2;
            ta [x] .length = x + 4;
            ta [x]. setArea();
            System.out.print("triangle "+x+", area");
            System.out.println(" = " + ta[x] .area);
            x = x + 1
        }
        int y = x;
        x = 27;
        Triangle t5 = ta[2];
        ta[2].area = 343;
        System.out.print("y = " + y);
        System.out.println(", t5 area = "+ t5.area);
    }
    void setArea() {
        area = (height * length) / 2;
    }
}
```

Note: Each snippet from the pool can be used more than once!

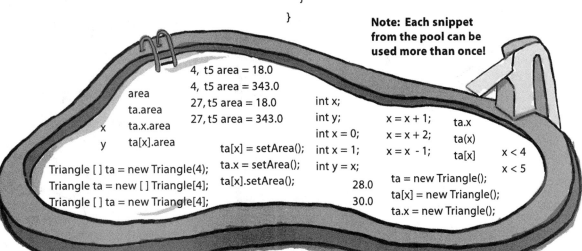

area
ta.area
ta.x.area
ta[x].area

x
y

Triangle [ ] ta = new Triangle(4);
Triangle ta = new [ ] Triangle[4];
Triangle [ ] ta = new Triangle[4];

4, t5 area = 18.0
4, t5 area = 343.0
27, t5 area = 18.0
27, t5 area = 343.0

ta[x] = setArea();
ta.x = setArea();
ta[x].setArea();

int x;
int y;
int x = 0;
int x = 1;
int y = x;

28.0
30.0

x = x + 1;
x = x + 2;
x = x - 1;

ta = new Triangle();
ta[x] = new Triangle();
ta.x = new Triangle();

ta.x
ta(x)
ta[x]

x < 4
x < 5

A Heap o' Trouble

A short Java program is listed to the right. When '// do stuff' is reached, some objects and some reference variables will have been created. Your task is to determine which of the reference variables refer to which objects. Not all the reference variables will be used, and some objects might be referred to more than once. Draw lines connecting the reference variables with their matching objects.

Tip: Unless you're way smarter than us, you probably need to draw diagrams like the ones on page 55 and 56 of this chapter. Use a pencil so you can draw and then erase reference links (the arrows going from a reference remote control to an object).

```java
class HeapQuiz {
  int id = 0;
  public static void main(String [] args) {
    int x = 0;
    HeapQuiz [ ] hq = new HeapQuiz[5];
    while ( x < 3 ) {
      hq[x] = new HeapQuiz();
      hq[x].id = x;
      x = x + 1;
    }
    hq[3] = hq[1];
    hq[4] = hq[1];
    hq[3] = null;
    hq[4] = hq[0];
    hq[0] = hq[3];
    hq[3] = hq[2];
    hq[2] = hq[0];
    // do stuff
  }
}
```

match each reference
variable with matching
object(s)

You might not have to
use every reference.

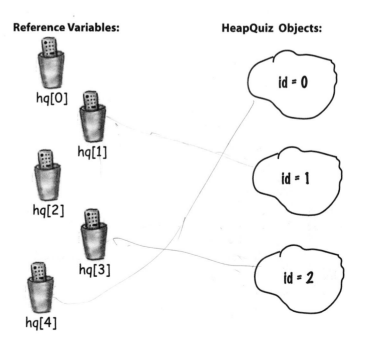

Reference Variables:

hq[0]

hq[1]

hq[2]

hq[3]

hq[4]

HeapQuiz Objects:

id = 0

id = 1

id = 2

The case of the pilfered references

Five-Minute Mystery

It was a dark and stormy night. Tawny strolled into the programmers' bullpen like she owned the place. She knew that all the programmers would still be hard at work, and she wanted help. She needed a new method added to the pivotal class that was to be loaded into the client's new top-secret Java-enabled cell phone. Heap space in the cell phone's memory was as tight as Tawny's top, and everyone knew it. The normally raucous buzz in the bullpen fell to silence as Tawny eased her way to the white board. She sketched a quick overview of the new method's functionality and slowly scanned the room. "Well boys, it's crunch time", she purred. "Whoever creates the most memory efficient version of this method is coming with me to the client's launch party on Maui tomorrow... to help me install the new software."

The next morning Tawny glided into the bullpen wearing her short Aloha dress. "Gentlemen", she smiled, "the plane leaves in a few hours, show me what you've got!". Bob went first; as he began to sketch his design on the white board Tawny said, "Let's get to the point Bob, show me how you handled updating the list of contact objects." Bob quickly drew a code fragment on the board:

```
Contact [] ca = new Contact[10];
while ( x < 10 ) {   // make 10 contact objects
  ca[x] = new Contact();
  x = x + 1;
}
// do complicated Contact list updating stuff with ca
```

"Tawny I know we're tight on memory, but your spec said that we had to be able to access individual contact information for all ten allowable contacts, this was the best scheme I could cook up", said Bob. Kent was next, already imagining coconut cocktails with Tawny, "Bob," he said, "your solution's a bit kludgy don't you think?" Kent smirked, "Take a look at this baby":

```
Contact refc;
while ( x < 10 ) {   // make 10 contact objects
  refc = new Contact();
  x = x + 1;
}
// do complicated Contact list updating stuff with refc
```

"I saved a bunch of reference variables worth of memory, Bob-o-rino, so put away your sunscreen", mocked Kent. "Not so fast Kent!", said Tawny, "you've saved a little memory, but Bob's coming with me.".

Why did Tawny choose Bob's method over Kent's, when Kent's used less memory?

Exercise Solutions

Code Magnets:

```java
class TestArrays {
  public static void main(String [] args) {
    int [] index = new int[4];
    index[0] = 1;
    index[1] = 3;
    index[2] = 0;
    index[3] = 2;
    String [] islands = new String[4];
    islands[0] = "Bermuda";
    islands[1] = "Fiji";
    islands[2] = "Azores";
    islands[3] = "Cozumel";
    int y = 0;
    int ref;
    while (y < 4) {
      ref = index[y];
      System.out.print("island = ");
      System.out.println(islands[ref]);
      y = y + 1;
    }
  }
}
```

```
File Edit Window Help Bikini
% java TestArrays
island = Fiji
island = Cozumel
island = Bermuda
island = Azores
```

```java
class Books {
  String title;
  String author;
}
class BooksTestDrive {
  public static void main(String [] args) {
    Books [] myBooks = new Books[3];
    int x = 0;
    myBooks[0] = new Books();
    myBooks[1] = new Books();
    myBooks[2] = new Books();
    myBooks[0].title = "The Grapes of Java";
    myBooks[1].title = "The Java Gatsby";
    myBooks[2].title = "The Java Cookbook";
    myBooks[0].author = "bob";
    myBooks[1].author = "sue";
    myBooks[2].author = "ian";
    while (x < 3) {
      System.out.print(myBooks[x].title);
      System.out.print(" by ");
      System.out.println(myBooks[x].author);
      x = x + 1;
    }
  }
}
```

A — Remember: We have to actually make the Books objects !

```java
class Hobbits {
  String name;
  public static void main(String [] args) {
    Hobbits [] h = new Hobbits[3];
    int z = -1;
    while (z < 2) {
    z = z + 1;
    h[z] = new Hobbits();
    h[z].name = "bilbo";
    if (z == 1) {
      h[z].name = "frodo";
    }
    if (z == 2) {
      h[z].name = "sam";
    }
    System.out.print(h[z].name + " is a ");
    System.out.println("good Hobbit name");
    }
  }
}
```

B — Remember: arrays start with element 0 !

Puzzle Solutions

```
class Triangle {
  double area;
  int height;
  int length;
  public static void main(String [] args) {
    int x = 0;
    Triangle [ ] ta = new Triangle[4];
    while ( x < 4 ) {
      ta[x] = new Triangle();
      ta[x].height = (x + 1) * 2;
      ta[x].length = x + 4;
      ta[x].setArea();
      System.out.print("triangle "+x+", area");
      System.out.println(" = " + ta[x].area);
      x = x + 1;
    }
    int y = x;
    x = 27;
    Triangle t5 = ta[2];
    ta[2].area = 343;
    System.out.print("y = " + y);
    System.out.println(", t5 area = "+ t5.area);
  }
  void setArea() {
    area = (height * length) / 2;
  }
}
```

```
File Edit Window Help Bermuda
%java Triangle
triangle 0, area = 4.0
triangle 1, area = 10.0
triangle 2, area = 18.0
triangle 3, area = 28.0
y = 4, t5 area = 343
```

The case of the pilfered references

Tawny could see that Kent's method had a serious flaw. It's true that he didn't use as many reference variables as Bob, but there was no way to access any but the last of the Contact objects that his method created. With each trip through the loop, he was assigning a new object to the one reference variable, so the previously referenced object was abandoned on the heap – *unreachable*. Without access to nine of the ten objects created, Kent's method was useless.

(The software was a huge success and the client gave Tawny and Bob an extra week in Hawaii. We'd like to tell you that by finishing this book you too will get stuff like that.)

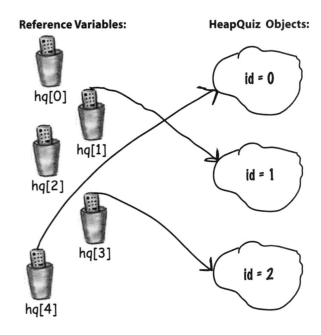

4 methods use instance variables

How Objects Behave

This oughta change her state!

State affects behavior, behavior affects state. We know that objects have **state** and **behavior**, represented by **instance variables** and **methods**. But until now, we haven't looked at how state and behavior are *related*. We already know that each instance of a class (each object of a particular type) can have its own unique values for its instance variables. Dog A can have a *name* "Fido" and a *weight* of 70 pounds. Dog B is "Killer" and weighs 9 pounds. And if the Dog class has a method makeNoise(), well, don't you think a 70-pound dog barks a bit deeper than the little 9-pounder? (Assuming that annoying yippy sound can be considered a *bark*.) Fortunately, that's the whole point of an object—it has *behavior* that acts on its *state*. In other words, *methods use instance variable values*. Like, "if dog is less than 14 pounds, make yippy sound, else..." or "increase weight by 5". *Let's go change some state.*

Remember: a class describes what an object **knows** and what an object **does**

A class is the blueprint for an object. When you write a class, you're describing how the JVM should make an object of that type. You already know that every object of that type can have different *instance variable* values. But what about the methods?

Can every object of that type have different method behavior?

Well... *sort of.**

Every instance of a particular class has the same methods, but the methods can *behave* differently based on the value of the instance variables.

The Song class has two instance variables, *title* and *artist*. The play() method plays a song, but the instance you call play() on will play the song represented by the value of the *title* instance variable for that instance. So, if you call the play() method on one instance you'll hear the song "Politik", while another instance plays "Darkstar". The method code, however, is the same.

```
void play() {
    soundPlayer.playSound(title);
}
```

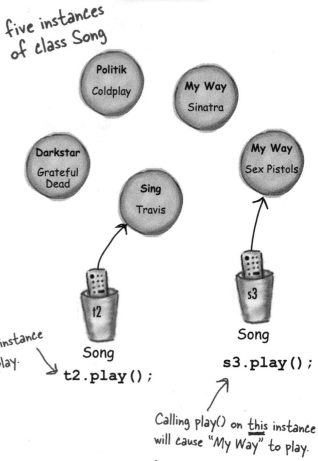

```
Song t2 = new Song();
t2.setArtist("Travis");
t2.setTitle("Sing");
Song s3 = new Song();
s3.setArtist("Sex Pistols");
s3.setTitle("My Way");
```

Calling play() on <u>this</u> instance will cause "Sing" to play.

```
t2.play();
```

```
s3.play();
```

Calling play() on <u>this</u> instance will cause "My Way" to play.

(but not the Sinatra one)

*Yes, another stunningly clear answer!

The size affects the bark

A small Dog's bark is different from a big Dog's bark.

The Dog class has an instance variable *size*, that the *bark()* method uses to decide what kind of bark sound to make.

Bark Different.

```
class Dog {
  int size;
  String name;

  void bark() {
    if (size > 60) {
        System.out.println("Wooof! Wooof!");
    } else if (size > 14) {
        System.out.println("Ruff!   Ruff!");
    } else {
        System.out.println("Yip! Yip!");
    }
  }
}
```

Dog

size
name

bark()

```
class DogTestDrive {

  public static void main (String[] args) {
    Dog one = new Dog();
    one.size = 70;
    Dog two = new Dog();
    two.size = 8;
    Dog three = new Dog();
    three.size = 35;

    one.bark();
    two.bark();
    three.bark();
  }
}
```

```
File Edit  Window  Help Playdead
%java DogTestDrive
Wooof! Wooof!
Yip! Yip!
Ruff!   Ruff!
```

You can send things to a method

Just as you expect from any programming language, you can pass values into your methods. You might, for example, want to tell a Dog object how many times to bark by calling:

d.bark(3);

Depending on your programming background and personal preferences, *you* might use the term *arguments* or perhaps *parameters* for the values passed into a method. Although there *are* formal computer science distinctions that people who wear lab coats and who will almost certainly not read this book, make, we have bigger fish to fry in this book. So *you* can call them whatever you like (arguments, donuts, hairballs, etc.) but we're doing it like this:

A method uses parameters. A caller passes arguments.

Arguments are the things you pass into the methods. An **argument** (a value like 2, "Foo", or a reference to a Dog) lands face-down into a... wait for it... *parameter*. And a parameter is nothing more than a local variable. A variable with a type and a name, that can be used inside the body of the method.

But here's the important part: **If a method takes a parameter, you *must* pass it something.** And that something must be a value of the appropriate type.

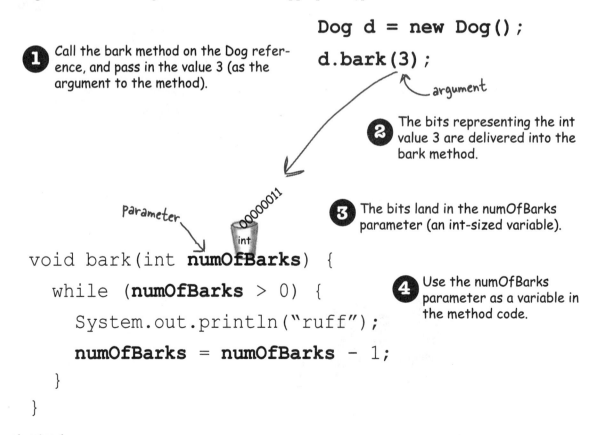

1 Call the bark method on the Dog reference, and pass in the value 3 (as the argument to the method).

```
Dog d = new Dog();
d.bark(3);
```
↖ argument

2 The bits representing the int value 3 are delivered into the bark method.

3 The bits land in the numOfBarks parameter (an int-sized variable).

Parameter

`00000011`
`int`

```
void bark(int numOfBarks) {
    while (numOfBarks > 0) {
        System.out.println("ruff");
        numOfBarks = numOfBarks - 1;
    }
}
```

4 Use the numOfBarks parameter as a variable in the method code.

You can get things *back* from a method.

Methods can return values. Every method is declared with a return type, but until now we've made all of our methods with a **void** return type, which means they don't give anything back.

```
void go() {

}
```

But we can declare a method to give a specific type of value back to the caller, such as:

```
int giveSecret() {

    return 42;

}
```

If you declare a method to return a value, you *must* return a value of the declared type! (Or a value that is *compatible* with the declared type. We'll get into that more when we talk about polymorphism in chapter 7 and chapter 8.)

Whatever you *say* you'll give back, you *better* give back!

> Cute... but not exactly what I was expecting.

The compiler won't let you return the wrong type of thing.

```
int theSecret = life.giveSecret();
```

These types must match

```
int giveSecret() {

    return 42;

}
```

this must fit in an int!

The bits representing 42 are returned from the giveSecret() method, and land in the variable named theSecret.

You can send more than one thing to a method

Methods can have multiple parameters. Separate them with commas when you declare them, and separate the arguments with commas when you pass them. Most importantly, if a method has parameters, you *must* pass arguments of the right type and order.

Calling a two-parameter method, and sending it two arguments.

```
void go() {
   TestStuff t = new TestStuff();
   t.takeTwo(12, 34);
}



void takeTwo(int x, int y) {
   int z = x + y;
   System.out.println("Total is " + z);
}
```

The arguments you pass land in the same order you passed them. First argument lands in the first parameter, second argument in the second parameter, and so on.

You can pass variables into a method, as long as the variable type matches the parameter type.

```
void go() {
   int foo = 7;
   int bar = 3;
   t.takeTwo(foo, bar);
}



void takeTwo(int x, int y) {
   int z = x + y;
   System.out.println("Total is " + z);
}
```

The values of foo and bar land in the x and y parameters. So now the bits in x are identical to the bits in foo (the bit pattern for the integer '7') and the bits in y are identical to the bits in bar.

What's the value of z? It's the same result you'd get if you added foo + bar at the time you passed them into the takeTwo method

Java is pass-by-value.

That means pass-by-copy.

`int x = 7;`

1 Declare an int variable and assign it the value '7'. The bit pattern for 7 goes into the variable named x.

`void go(int z){ }`

2 Declare a method with an int parameter named z.

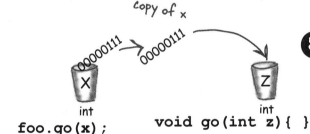

copy of x

`foo.go(x);`   `void go(int z){ }`

3 Call the go() method, passing the variable x as the argument. The bits in x are copied, and the copy lands in z.

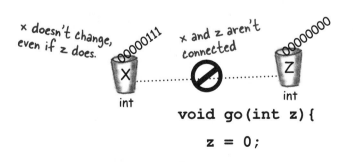

x doesn't change, even if z does.

x and z aren't connected

```
void go(int z){
    z = 0;
}
```

4 Change the value of z inside the method. The value of x doesn't change! The argument passed to the z parameter was only a copy of x.

The method can't change the bits that were in the calling variable x.

there are no Dumb Questions

Q: What happens if the argument you want to pass is an object instead of a primitive?

A: You'll learn more about this in later chapters, but you already *know* the answer. Java passes *everything* by value. ***Everything***. But... value means *bits inside the variable*. And remember, you don't stuff objects into variables; the variable is a remote control—*a reference to an object*. So if you pass a reference to an object into a method, you're passing a *copy of the remote control*. Stay tuned, though, we'll have lots more to say about this.

Q: Can a method declare multiple return values? Or is there some way to return more than one value?

A: Sort of. A method can declare only one return value. BUT... if you want to return, say, three int values, then the declared return type can be an int *array*. Stuff those ints into the array, and pass it on back. It's a little more involved to return multiple values with different types; we'll be talking about that in a later chapter when we talk about ArrayList.

Q: Do I have to return the exact type I declared?

A: You can return anything that can be *implicitly* promoted to that type. So, you can pass a byte where an int is expected. The caller won't care, because the byte fits just fine into the int the caller will use for assigning the result. You must use an *explicit* cast when the declared type is *smaller* than what you're trying to return.

Q: Do I have to do something with the return value of a method? Can I just ignore it?

A: Java doesn't require you to acknowledge a return value. You might want to call a method with a non-void return type, even though you don't care about the return value. In this case, you're calling the method for the work it does *inside* the method, rather than for what the method gives *returns*. In Java, you don't have to assign or use the return value.

Reminder: Java cares about type!

You can't return a Giraffe when the return type is declared as a Rabbit. Same thing with parameters. You can't pass a Giraffe into a method that takes a Rabbit.

BULLET POINTS

- Classes define what an object knows and what an object does.
- Things an object knows are its **instance variables** (state).
- Things an object does are its **methods** (behavior).
- Methods can use instance variables so that objects of the same type can behave differently.
- A method can have parameters, which means you can pass one or more values in to the method.
- The number and type of values you pass in must match the order and type of the parameters declared by the method.
- Values passed in and out of methods can be implicitly promoted to a larger type or explicitly cast to a smaller type.
- The value you pass as an argument to a method can be a literal value (2, 'c', etc.) or a variable of the declared parameter type (for example, *x* where *x* is an int variable). (There are other things you can pass as arguments, but we're not there yet.)
- A method *must* declare a return type. A void return type means the method doesn't return anything.
- If a method declares a non-void return type, it *must* return a value compatible with the declared return type.

Cool things you can do with parameters and return types

Now that we've seen how parameters and return types work, it's time to put them to good use: **Getters** and **Setters**. If you're into being all formal about it, you might prefer to call them *Accessors* and *Mutators*. But that's a waste of perfectly good syllables. Besides, Getters and Setters fits the Java naming convention, so that's what we'll call them.

Getters and Setters let you, well, *get and set things*. Instance variable values, usually. A Getter's sole purpose in life is to send back, as a return value, the value of whatever it is that particular Getter is supposed to be Getting. And by now, it's probably no surprise that a Setter lives and breathes for the chance to take an argument value and use it to *set* the value of an instance variable.

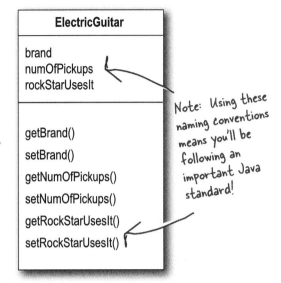

Note: Using these naming conventions means you'll be following an important Java standard!

```java
class ElectricGuitar {

    String brand;
    int numOfPickups;
    boolean rockStarUsesIt;

    String getBrand() {
        return brand;
    }

    void setBrand(String aBrand) {
        brand = aBrand;
    }

    int getNumOfPickups() {
        return numOfPickups;
    }

    void setNumOfPickups(int num) {
        numOfPickups = num;
    }

    boolean getRockStarUsesIt() {
        return rockStarUsesIt;
    }

    void setRockStarUsesIt(boolean yesOrNo) {
        rockStarUsesIt = yesOrNo;
    }
}
```

Encapsulation

Do it or risk humiliation and ridicule.

Until this most important moment, we've been committing one of the worst OO faux pas (and we're not talking minor violation like showing up without the 'B' in BYOB). No, we're talking Faux Pas with a capital 'F'. And 'P'.

Our shameful transgression?

Exposing our data!

Here we are, just humming along without a care in the world leaving our data out there for *anyone* to see and even touch.

You may have already experienced that vaguely unsettling feeling that comes with leaving your instance variables exposed.

Exposed means reachable with the dot operator, as in:

```
theCat.height = 27;
```

Think about this idea of using our remote control to make a direct change to the Cat object's size instance variable. In the hands of the wrong person, a reference variable (remote control) is quite a dangerous weapon. Because what's to prevent:

Jen says you're well-encapsulated...

```
theCat.height = 0;
```
← yikes! We can't let this happen!

This would be a Bad Thing. We need to build setter methods for all the instance variables, and find a way to force other code to call the setters rather than access the data directly.

By forcing everybody to call a setter method, we can protect the cat from unacceptable size changes.

```
public void setHeight(int ht) {
    if (ht > 9) {
        height = ht;
    }
}
```
← We put in checks to guarantee a minimum cat height.

Hide the data

Yes it *is* that simple to go from an implementation that's just begging for bad data to one that protects your data *and* protects your right to modify your implementation later.

OK, so how exactly do you *hide* the data? With the **public** and **private** access modifiers. You're familiar with **public**–we use it with every main method.

Here's an encapsulation *starter* rule of thumb (all standard disclaimers about rules of thumb are in effect): mark your instance variables *private* and provide *public* getters and setters for access control. When you have more design and coding savvy in Java, you will probably do things a little differently, but for now, this approach will keep you safe.

> **Mark instance variables private.**
>
> **Mark getters and setters public.**

"Sadly, Bill forgot to encapsulate his Cat class and ended up with a flat cat."

(overheard at the water cooler).

Java Exposed

**This week's interview:
An Object gets candid about encapsulation.**

HeadFirst: What's the big deal about encapsulation?

Object: OK, you know that dream where you're giving a talk to 500 people when you suddenly realize– you're *naked*?

HeadFirst: Yeah, we've had that one. It's right up there with the one about the Pilates machine and... no, we won't go there. OK, so you feel naked. But other than being a little exposed, is there any danger?

Object: Is there any danger? Is there any *danger*? [starts laughing] Hey, did all you other instances hear that, *"Is there any danger?"* he asks? [falls on the floor laughing]

HeadFirst: What's funny about that? Seems like a reasonable question.

Object: OK, I'll explain it. It's [bursts out laughing again, uncontrollably]

HeadFirst: Can I get you anything? Water?

Object: Whew! Oh boy. No I'm fine, really. I'll be serious. Deep breath. OK, go on.

HeadFirst: So what does encapsulation protect you from?

Object: Encapsulation puts a force-field around my instance variables, so nobody can set them to, let's say, something *inappropriate*.

HeadFirst: Can you give me an example?

Object: Doesn't take a PhD here. Most instance variable values are coded with certain assumptions about the boundaries of the values. Like, think of all the things that would break if negative numbers were allowed. Number of bathrooms in an office. Velocity of an airplane. Birthdays. Barbell weight. Cell phone numbers. Microwave oven power.

HeadFirst: I see what you mean. So how does encapsulation let you set boundaries?

Object: By forcing other code to go through setter methods. That way, the setter method can validate the parameter and decide if it's do-able. Maybe the method will reject it and do nothing, or maybe it'll throw an Exception (like if it's a null social security number for a credit card application), or maybe the method will round the parameter sent in to the nearest acceptable value. The point is, you can do whatever you want in the setter method, whereas you can't do *anything* if your instance variables are public.

HeadFirst: But sometimes I see setter methods that simply set the value without checking anything. If you have an instance variable that doesn't have a boundary, doesn't that setter method create unnecessary overhead? A performance hit?

Object: The point to setters (and getters, too) is that ***you can change your mind later, without breaking anybody else's code!*** Imagine if half the people in your company used your class with public instance variables, and one day you suddenly realized, "Oops– there's something I didn't plan for with that value, I'm going to have to switch to a setter method." You break everyone's code. The cool thing about encapsulation is that *you get to change your mind.* And nobody gets hurt. The performance gain from using variables directly is so miniscule and would rarely—*if ever*— be worth it.

Encapsulating the GoodDog class

Make the instance variable private.

Make the getter and setter methods public.

Even though the methods don't really add new functionality, the cool thing is that you can change your mind later. you can come back and make a method safer, faster, better.

Any place where a particular value can be used, a *method call that returns that type can be used.*

instead of:

int x = 3 + 24;

you can say:

int x = 3 + one.getSize();

```java
class GoodDog {

    private int size;

    public int getSize() {
        return size;
    }

    public void setSize(int s) {
        size = s;
    }

    void bark() {
        if (size > 60) {
            System.out.println("Wooof! Wooof!");
        } else if (size > 14) {
            System.out.println("Ruff!   Ruff!");
        } else {
            System.out.println("Yip! Yip!");
        }
    }
}

class GoodDogTestDrive {

    public static void main (String[] args) {
        GoodDog one = new GoodDog();
        one.setSize(70);
        GoodDog two = new GoodDog();
        two.setSize(8);
        System.out.println("Dog one: " + one.getSize());
        System.out.println("Dog two: " + two.getSize());
        one.bark();
        two.bark();
    }
}
```

GoodDog
size
getSize( )
setSize( )
bark( )

How do objects in an array behave?

Just like any other object. The only difference is how you *get* to them. In other words, how you get the remote control. Let's try calling methods on Dog objects in an array.

1 Declare and create a Dog array, to hold 7 Dog references.

```
Dog[] pets;
pets = new Dog[7];
```

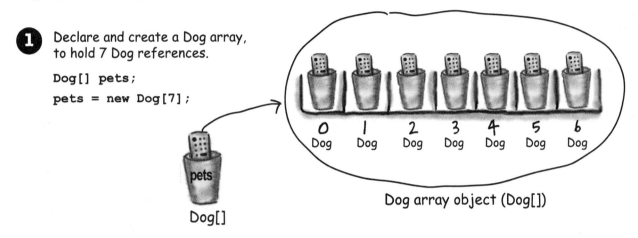

Dog array object (Dog[])

pets

Dog[]

---

2 Create two new Dog objects, and assign them to the first two array elements.

```
pets[0] = new Dog();
pets[1] = new Dog();
```

3 Call methods on the two Dog objects.

```
pets[0].setSize(30);
int x = pets[0].getSize();
pets[1].setSize(8);
```

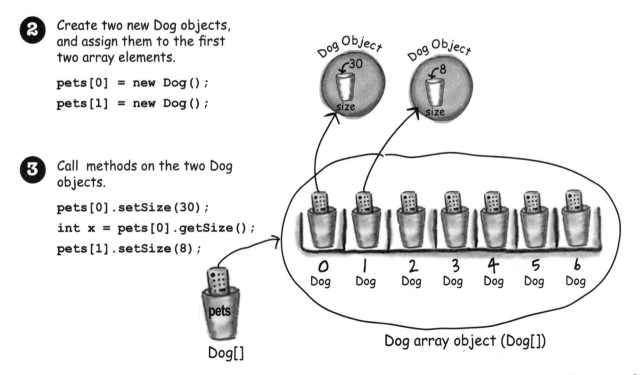

Dog Object

size 30

Dog Object

size 8

Dog array object (Dog[])

pets

Dog[]

Declaring and initializing instance variables

You already know that a variable declaration needs at least a name and a type:

```
int size;
String name;
```

And you know that you can initialize (assign a value) to the variable at the same time:

```
int size = 420;
String name = "Donny";
```

But when you don't initialize an instance variable, what happens when you call a getter method? In other words, what is the *value* of an instance variable *before* you initialize it?

```
class PoorDog {

    private int size;          ← declare two instance variables,
    private String name;         but don't assign a value

    public int getSize() {    ← What will these return??
        return size;
    }
    public String getName() {
        return name;
    }

}

public class PoorDogTestDrive {
    public static void main (String[] args) {
        PoorDog one = new PoorDog();          What do you think? Will
        System.out.println("Dog size is " + one.getSize());   this even compile?
        System.out.println("Dog name is " + one.getName());
    }
}
```

Instance variables always get a default value. If you don't explicitly assign a value to an instance variable, or you don't call a setter method, the instance variable still has a value!

integers	0
floating points	0.0
booleans	false
references	null

```
File Edit Window Help CallVet
% java PoorDogTestDrive
Dog size is 0
Dog name is null
```

You don't have to initialize instance variables, because they always have a default value. Number primitives (including char) get 0, booleans get false, and object reference variables get null.

(Remember, null just means a remote control that isn't controlling / programmed to anything. A reference, but no actual object.

The difference between instance and local variables

1 **Instance** variables are declared inside a class but not within a method.

```
class Horse {
    private double height = 15.2;
    private String breed;
    // more code...
}
```

2 **Local** variables are declared within a method.

```
class AddThing {
    int a;
    int b = 12;

    public int add() {
        int total = a + b;
        return total;
    }
}
```

3 **Local** variables MUST be initialized before use!

```
class Foo {
    public void go() {
        int x;
        int z = x + 3;
    }
}
```

Won't compile!! You can declare x without a value, but as soon as you try to USE it, the compiler freaks out

```
File Edit Window Help Yikes
% javac Foo.java

Foo.java:4: variable x might
not have been initialized

        int z = x + 3;
1 error               ^
```

Local variables do NOT get a default value! The compiler complains if you try to use a local variable before the variable is initialized.

there are no Dumb Questions

Q: What about method parameters? How do the rules about local variables apply to them?

A: Method parameters are virtually the same as local variables—they're declared *inside* the method (well, technically they're declared in the *argument list* of the method rather than within the *body* of the method, but they're still local variables as opposed to instance variables). But method parameters will never be uninitialized, so you'll never get a compiler error telling you that a parameter variable might not have been initialized.

But that's because the compiler will give you an error if you try to invoke a method without sending arguments that the method needs. So parameters are ALWAYS initialized, because the compiler guarantees that methods are always called with arguments that match the parameters declared for the method, and the arguments are assigned (automatically) to the parameters.

Comparing variables (primitives or references)

Sometimes you want to know if two *primitives* are the same. That's easy enough, just use the == operator. Sometimes you want to know if two reference variables refer to a single object on the heap. Easy as well, just use the == operator. But sometimes you want to know if two *objects* are equal. And for that, you need the .equals() method. The idea of equality for objects depends on the type of object. For example, if two different String objects have the same characters (say, "expeditious"), they are meaningfully equivalent, regardless of whether they are two distinct objects on the heap. But what about a Dog? Do you want to treat two Dogs as being equal if they happen to have the same size and weight? Probably not. So whether two different objects should be treated as equal depends on what makes sense for that particular object type. We'll explore the notion of object equality again in later chapters (and appendix B), but for now, we need to understand that the == operator is used *only* to compare the bits in two variables. *What* those bits represent doesn't matter. The bits are either the same, or they're not.

> **Use == to compare two primitives, or to see if two references refer to the *same* object.**
>
> **Use the equals() method to see if two *different* objects are equal.**
>
> **(Such as two different String objects that both represent the characters in "Fred")**

To compare two primitives, use the == operator

The == operator can be used to compare two variables of any kind, and it simply compares the bits.

if (a == b) {...} looks at the bits in a and b and returns true if the bit pattern is the same (although it doesn't care about the size of the variable, so all the extra zeroes on the left end don't matter).

```
int a = 3;

byte b = 3;

if (a == b) { // true }
```

(there are more zeroes on the left side of the int, but we don't care about that here)

the bit patterns are the same, so these two are equal using ==

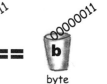

To see if two references are the same (which means they refer to the same object on the heap) use the == operator

Remember, the == operator cares only about the pattern of bits in the variable. The rules are the same whether the variable is a reference or primitive. So the == operator returns true if two reference variables refer to the same object! In that case, we don't know what the bit pattern is (because it's dependent on the JVM, and hidden from us) but we *do* know that whatever it looks like, *it will be the same for two references to a single object.*

```
Foo a = new Foo();

Foo b = new Foo();

Foo c = a;

if (a == b) { // false }

if (a == c) { // true }

if (b == c) { // false }
```

the bit patterns are the same for a and c, so they are equal using ==

a == c is true
a == b is false

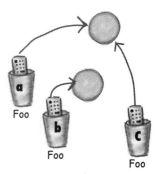

I always keep my variables private. If you want to see them, you have to talk to my methods.

private

Java is Pass by value

Wash Cat

threads wait() notify()

Make it Stick

Roses are red,
this poem is choppy,
passing by value
is passing by copy.

Oh, like you can do better? Try it. Replace our dumb second line with your own. Better yet, replace the whole thing with your own words and you'll *never* forget it.

 Sharpen your pencil

What's legal?

Given the method below, which of the method calls listed on the right are legal?

Put a checkmark next to the ones that are legal. (Some statements are there to assign values used in the method calls).

KEEP ← RIGHT

```
int calcArea(int height, int width) {
    return height * width;
}
```

✓ `int a = calcArea(7, 12);`

✓ `short c = 7;`

✓ `calcArea(c,15);`

`int d = calcArea(57);`

✓ `calcArea(2,3);`

✓ `long t = 42;`

`int f = calcArea(t,17);`

`int g = calcArea();`

`calcArea();`

`byte h = calcArea(4,20);`

`int j = calcArea(2,3,5);`

BE the compiler

Each of the Java files on this page represents a complete source file. Your job is to play compiler and determine whether each of these files will compile. If they won't compile, how would you fix them, and if they do compile, what would be their output?

A

```java
class XCopy {

  public static void main(String [] args) {

    int orig = 42;

    XCopy x = new XCopy();

    int y = x.go(orig);

    System.out.println(orig + " " + y);
  }

  int go(int arg) {

    arg = arg * 2;

    return arg;
  }
}
```

B

```java
class Clock {
  String time;

  void setTime(String t) {
    time = t;
  }

  void getTime() {        // String
    return time;
  }
}

class ClockTestDrive {
  public static void main(String [] args) {

    Clock c = new Clock();

    c.setTime("1245");
    String tod = c.getTime();
    System.out.println("time: " + tod);
  }
}
```

Exercise

A bunch of Java components, in full costume, are playing a party game, "Who am I?" They give you a clue, and you try to guess who they are, based on what they say. Assume they always tell the truth about themselves. If they happen to say something that could be true for more than one guy, then write down all for whom that sentence applies. Fill in the blanks next to the sentence with the names of one or more attendees.

Tonight's attendees:

instance variable, argument, return, getter, setter, encapsulation, public, private, pass by value, method

Who am I?

A class can have any number of these.   _____

A method can have only one of these.   _____

This can be implicitly promoted.   _____

I prefer my instance variables private.   _____

It really means 'make a copy'.   _____

Only setters should update these.   _____

A method can have many of these.   _____

I return something by definition.   _____

I shouldn't be used with instance variables.   _____

I can have many arguments.   _____

By definition, I take one argument.   _____

These help create encapsulation.   _____

I always fly solo.   _____

Mixed Messages

A short Java program is listed to your right. Two blocks of the program are missing. Your challenge is to **match the candidate blocks of code** (below), **with the output** that you'd see if the blocks were inserted.

Not all the lines of output will be used, and some of the lines of output might be used more than once. Draw lines connecting the candidate blocks of code with their matching command-line output.

```java
public class Mix4 {
  int counter = 0;
  public static void main(String [] args) {
    int count = 0;
    Mix4 [] m4a  =new Mix4[20];
    int x = 0;
    while (  ⬚  ) {
      m4a[x] = new Mix4();
      m4a[x].counter = m4a[x].counter + 1;
      count = count + 1;
      count = count + m4a[x].maybeNew(x);
      x = x + 1;
    }
    System.out.println(count + " "
                       + m4a[1].counter);
  }

  public int maybeNew(int index) {
    if (  ⬚  ) {
      Mix4 m4 = new Mix4();
      m4.counter = m4.counter + 1;
      return 1;
    }
    return 0;
  }
}
```

Candidates:

```
x < 9

index < 5
```

```
x < 20

index < 5
```

```
x < 7

index < 7
```

```
x < 19

index < 1
```

Possible output:

```
14 7
```

```
9 5
```

```
19 1
```

```
14 1
```

```
25 1
```

```
7 7
```

```
20 1
```

```
20 5
```

Pool Puzzle

Your **job** is to take code snippets from the pool and place them into the blank lines in the code. You may **not** use the same snippet more than once, and you won't need to use all the snippets. Your **goal** is to make a class that will compile and run and produce the output listed.

Output

```
File  Edit  Window  Help  BellyFlop
%java Puzzle4
result 543345
```

```java
public class Puzzle4 {
   public static void main(String [] args) {

      _____

      int y = 1;
      int x = 0;
      int result = 0;
      while (x < 6) {

         _____

         _____

         y = y * 10;

         _____

      }
      x = 6;
      while (x > 0) {

         _____

         result = result + _____
      }
      System.out.println("result " + result);
   }
}

class _____ {
   int ivar;
   _____  _____ doStuff(int _____) {
      if (ivar > 100) {
         return _____
      } else {
         return _____
      }
   }
}
```

Note: Each snippet from the pool can be used only once!

```
                        doStuff(x);
                        obs.doStuff(x);
                        obs[x].doStuff(factor);
      ivar = x;         obs[x].doStuff(x);        ivar + factor;
      obs.ivar = x;                               ivar * (2 + factor);       Puzzle4
      obs[x].ivar = x;              ivar          ivar * (5 - factor);       Puzzle4b       int
      obs[x].ivar = y;             factor         ivar * factor;             Puzzle4b( )     short
Puzzle4 [ ] obs = new Puzzle4[6];    public                            obs [x] = new Puzzle4b(x);
Puzzle4b [ ] obs = new Puzzle4b[6];  private        x = x + 1;         obs [ ] = new Puzzle4b( );
Puzzle4b [ ] obs = new Puzzle4[6];                  x = x - 1;         obs [x] = new Puzzle4b( );
                                                                       obs = new Puzzle4b( );
```

Fast Times in Stim-City

When Buchanan jammed his twitch-gun into Jai's side, Jai froze. Jai knew that Buchanan was as stupid as he was ugly and he didn't want to spook the big guy. Buchanan ordered Jai into his boss's office, but Jai'd done nothing wrong, (lately), so he figured a little chat with Buchanan's boss Leveler couldn't be too bad. He'd been moving lots of neural-stimmers in the west side lately and he figured Leveler would be pleased. Black market stimmers weren't the best money pump around, but they were pretty harmless. Most of the stim-junkies he'd seen tapped out after a while and got back to life, maybe just a little less focused than before.

Five-Minute Mystery

Leveler's 'office' was a skungy looking skimmer, but once Buchanan shoved him in, Jai could see that it'd been modified to provide all the extra speed and armor that a local boss like Leveler could hope for. "Jai my boy", hissed Leveler, "pleasure to see you again". "Likewise I'm sure...", said Jai, sensing the malice behind Leveler's greeting, "We should be square Leveler, have I missed something?" "Ha! You're making it look pretty good Jai, your volume is up, but I've been experiencing, shall we say, a little 'breach' lately..." said Leveler.

Jai winced involuntarily, he'd been a top drawer jack-hacker in his day. Anytime someone figured out how to break a street-jack's security, unwanted attention turned toward Jai. "No way it's me man", said Jai, "not worth the downside. I'm retired from hacking, I just move my stuff and mind my own business". "Yeah, yeah", laughed Leveler, "I'm sure you're clean on this one, but I'll be losing big margins until this new jack-hacker is shut out!" "Well, best of luck Leveler, maybe you could just drop me here and I'll go move a few more 'units' for you before I wrap up today", said Jai.

"I'm afraid it's not that easy Jai, Buchanan here tells me that word is you're current on J37NE", insinuated Leveler. "Neural Edition? sure I play around a bit, so what?", Jai responded feeling a little queasy. "Neural edition's how I let the stim-junkies know where the next drop will be", explained Leveler. "Trouble is, some stim-junkie's stayed straight long enough to figure out how to hack into my WareHousing database." "I need a quick thinker like yourself Jai, to take a look at my StimDrop J37NE class; methods, instance variables, the whole enchilada, and figure out how they're getting in. It should..", "HEY!", exclaimed Buchanan, "I don't want no scum hacker like Jai nosin' around my code!" "Easy big guy", Jai saw his chance, "I'm sure you did a top rate job with your access modi.. "Don't tell me - bit twiddler!", shouted Buchanan, "I left all of those junkie level methods public, so they could access the drop site data, but I marked all the critical WareHousing methods private. Nobody on the outside can access those methods buddy, nobody!"

"I think I can spot your leak Leveler, what say we drop Buchanan here off at the corner and take a cruise around the block", suggested Jai. Buchanan reached for his twitch-gun but Leveler's stunner was already on Buchanan's neck, "Let it go Buchanan", sneered Leveler, "Drop the twitcher and step outside, I think Jai and I have some plans to make".

What did Jai suspect?

Will he get out of Leveler's skimmer with all his bones intact?

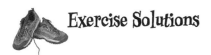

Exercise Solutions

```
class Clock {
  String time;
  void setTime(String t) {
    time = t;
  }
  String getTime() {
    return time;
  }
}
```

B

```
class ClockTestDrive {
  public static void main(String [] args) {
    Clock c = new Clock();
    c.setTime("1245");
    String tod = c.getTime();
    System.out.println("time: " + tod);
  }
}
```

> Note: 'Getter' methods have a return type by definition.

A   Class 'XCopy' compiles and runs as it stands ! The output is: '42 84'. Remember Java is pass by value, (which means pass by copy), the variable 'orig' is not changed by the go( ) method.

A class can have any number of these.	**instance variables, getter, setter, method**
A method can have only one of these.	**return**
This can be implicitly promoted.	**return, argument**
I prefer my instance variables private.	**encapsulation**
It really means 'make a copy'.	**pass by value**
Only setters should update these.	**instance variables**
A method can have many of these.	**argument**
I return something by definition.	**getter**
I shouldn't be used with instance variables	**public**
I can have many arguments.	**method**
By definition, I take one argument.	**setter**
These help create encapsulation.	**getter, setter, public, private**
I always fly solo.	**return**

Puzzle Solutions

```
public class Puzzle4 {
  public static void main(String [] args) {
    Puzzle4b [ ] obs = new Puzzle4b[6];
    int y = 1;
    int x = 0;
    int result = 0;
    while (x < 6) {
      obs[x] = new Puzzle4b( );
      obs[x] . ivar = y;
      y = y * 10;
      x = x + 1;
    }
    x = 6;
    while (x > 0) {
      x = x - 1;
      result = result + obs[x].doStuff(x);
    }
    System.out.println("result " + result);
  }
}
class Puzzle4b {
  int ivar;
  public int doStuff(int factor) {
    if (ivar > 100) {
      return ivar * factor;
    } else {
      return ivar * (5 - factor);
    }
  }
}
```

Output

```
File  Edit  Window  Help  BellyFlop
%java Puzzle4
result 543345
```

Answer to the 5-minute mystery...

Jai knew that Buchanan wasn't the sharpest pencil in the box. When Jai heard Buchanan talk about his code, Buchanan never mentioned his instance variables. Jai suspected that while Buchanan did in fact handle his methods correctly, he failed to mark his instance variables `private`. That slip up could have easily cost Leveler thousands.

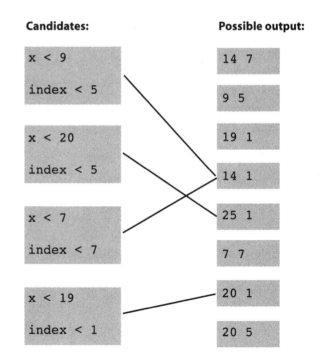

Candidates:

x < 9

index < 5

x < 20

index < 5

x < 7

index < 7

x < 19

index < 1

Possible output:

14 7

9 5

19 1

14 1

25 1

7 7

20 1

20 5

Extra-Strength Methods

I can lift heavy objects.

Let's put some muscle in our methods. We dabbled with variables, played with a few objects, and wrote a little code. But we were weak. We need more tools. Like **operators**. We need more operators so we can do something a little more interesting than, say, *bark*. And **loops**. We need loops, but what's with the wimpy *while* loops? We need *for* loops if we're really serious. Might be useful to **generate random numbers**. And **turn a String into an int**, yeah, that would be cool. Better learn that too. And why don't we learn it all by *building* something real, to see what it's like to write (and test) a program from scratch. **Maybe a game**, like Battleships. That's a heavy-lifting task, so it'll take *two* chapters to finish. We'll build a simple version in this chapter, and then build a more powerful deluxe version in chapter 6.

Let's build a Battleship-style game: "Sink a Dot Com"

It's you against the computer, but unlike the real Battleship game, in this one you don't place any ships of your own. Instead, your job is to sink the computer's ships in the fewest number of guesses.

Oh, and we aren't sinking ships. We're killing Dot Coms. (Thus establishing business relevancy so you can expense the cost of this book).

Goal: Sink all of the computer's Dot Coms in the fewest number of guesses. You're given a rating or level, based on how well you perform.

Setup: When the game program is launched, the computer places three Dot Coms on a **virtual 7 x 7 grid**. When that's complete, the game asks for your first guess.

How you play: We haven't learned to build a GUI yet, so this version works at the command-line. The computer will prompt you to enter a guess (a cell), that you'll type at the command-line as "A3", "C5", etc.). In response to your guess, you'll see a result at the command-line, either "Hit", "Miss", or "You sunk Pets.com" (or whatever the lucky Dot Com of the day is). When you've sent all three Dot Coms to that big 404 in the sky, the game ends by printing out your rating.

You're going to build the Sink a Dot Com **game, with a 7 x 7 grid and three Dot Coms. Each Dot Com takes up three cells.**

part of a game interaction

```
File Edit Window Help Sell
%java DotComBust
Enter a guess   A3
miss
Enter a guess   B2
miss
Enter a guess   C4
miss
Enter a guess   D2
hit
Enter a guess   D3
hit
Enter a guess   D4
Ouch! You sunk Pets.com    : (
kill
Enter a guess   B4
miss
Enter a guess   G3
hit
Enter a guess   G4
hit
Enter a guess   G5
Ouch! You sunk AskMe.com    : (
```

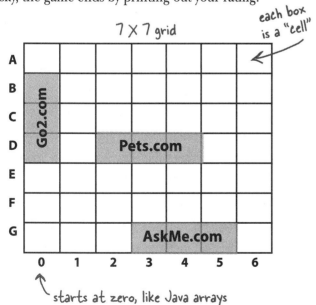

7 X 7 grid

each box is a "cell"

starts at zero, like Java arrays

First, a high-level design

We know we'll need classes and methods, but what should they be? To answer that, we need more information about what the game should do.

First, we need to figure out the general flow of the game. Here's the basic idea:

1 User starts the game

   A Game creates three Dot Coms

   B Game places the three Dot Coms onto a virtual grid

2 Game play begins

Repeat the following until there are no more Dot Coms:

   A Prompt user for a guess ("A2", "C0", etc.)

   B Check the user guess against all Dot Coms to look for a hit, miss, or kill. Take appropriate action: if a hit, delete cell (A2, D4, etc.). If a kill, delete Dot Com.

3 Game finishes

Give the user a rating based on the number of guesses.

Now we have an idea of the kinds of things the program needs to do. The next step is figuring out what kind of **objects** we'll need to do the work. Remember, think like Brad rather than Larry; focus first on the *things* in the program rather than the *procedures*.

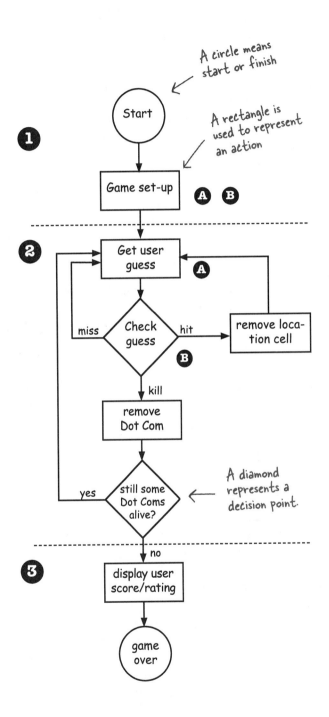

A circle means start or finish

A rectangle is used to represent an action

A diamond represents a decision point.

Whoa. A real flow chart.

The "Simple Dot Com Game"
a gentler introduction

It looks like we're gonna need at least two classes, a Game class and a DotCom class. But before we build the full monty **Sink a Dot Com** game, we'll start with a stripped-down, simplified version, **Simple Dot Com Game.** We'll build the simple version in *this* chapter, followed by the deluxe version that we build in the *next* chapter.

Everything is simpler in this game. Instead of a 2-D grid, we hide the Dot Com in just a single *row.* And instead of *three* Dot Coms, we use *one.*

The goal is the same, though, so the game still needs to make a DotCom instance, assign it a location somewhere in the row, get user input, and when all of the DotCom's cells have been hit, the game is over. This simplified version of the game gives us a big head start on building the full game. If we can get this small one working, we can scale it up to the more complex one later.

In this simple version, the game class has no instance variables, and all the game code is in the main() method. In other words, when the program is launched and main() begins to run, it will make the one and only DotCom instance, pick a location for it (three consecutive cells on the single virtual seven-cell row), ask the user for a guess, check the guess, and repeat until all three cells have been hit.

Keep in mind that the virtual row is... *virtual.* In other words, it doesn't exist anywhere in the program. As long as both the game and the user know that the DotCom is hidden in three consecutive cells out of a possible seven (starting at zero), the row itself doesn't have to be represented in code. You might be tempted to build an array of seven ints and then assign the DotCom to three of the seven elements in the array, but you don't need to. All we need is an array that holds just the three cells the DotCom occupies.

1 **Game starts,** and creates ONE DotCom and gives it a location on three cells in the single row of seven cells.

Instead of "A2", "C4", and so on, the locations are just integers (for example: 1,2,3 are the cell locations in this picture:

| | | | | | | |
|0|1|2|3|4|5|6|

2 **Game play begins.** Prompt user for a guess, then check to see if it hit any of the DotCom's three cells. If a hit, increment the numOfHits variable.

3 **Game finishes** when all three cells have been hit (the numOfHits variable value is 3), and tells the user how many guesses it took to sink the DotCom.

```
┌──────────────────────────────┐
│       SimpleDotComGame        │
├──────────────────────────────┤
│                               │
│  void main                    │
│                               │
└──────────────────────────────┘
```

```
┌──────────────────────────────────────┐
│            SimpleDotCom               │
├──────────────────────────────────────┤
│  int [] locationCells                 │
│  int numOfHits                        │
├──────────────────────────────────────┤
│  String checkYourself(String guess)   │
│  void setLocationCells(int[] loc)     │
└──────────────────────────────────────┘
```

A complete game interaction

```
File Edit Window Help Destroy
%java SimpleDotComGame
enter a number  2
hit
enter a number  3
hit
enter a number  4
miss
enter a number  1
kill
You took 4 guesses
```

Developing a Class

As a programmer, you probably have a methodology/process/approach to writing code. Well, so do we. Our sequence is designed to help you see (and learn) what we're thinking as we work through coding a class. It isn't necessarily the way we (or *you*) write code in the Real World. In the Real World, of course, you'll follow the approach your personal preferences, project, or employer dictate. We, however, can do pretty much whatever we want. And when we create a Java class as a "learning experience", we usually do it like this:

- ☐ Figure out what the class is supposed to *do*.

- ☐ List the **instance variables and methods**.

- ☐ Write **prepcode** for the methods. (You'll see this in just a moment.)

- ☐ Write **test code** for the methods.

- ☐ **Implement** the class.

- ☐ **Test** the methods.

- ☐ **Debug** and **reimplement** as needed.

- ☐ Express gratitude that we don't have to test our so-called *learning experience* app on actual live users.

BRAIN POWER

Flex those dendrites.

How would you decide which class or classes to build *first*, when you're writing a program? Assuming that all but the tiniest programs need more than one class (if you're following good OO principles and not having *one* class do many different jobs), where do you start?

The three things we'll write for each class:

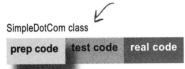

This bar is displayed on the next set of pages to tell you which part you're working on. For example, if you see this picture at the top of a page, it means you're working on prepcode for the SimpleDotCom class.

prep code
A form of pseudocode, to help you focus on the logic without stressing about syntax.

test code
A class or methods that will test the real code and validate that it's doing the right thing.

real code
The actual implementation of the class. This is .... real Java code.

To Do:

SimpleDotCom class
- ☐ write prep code
- ☐ write test code
- ☐ write final Java code

SimpleDotComGame class
- ☐ write prep code
-    write test code [no]
- ☐ write final Java code

SimpleDotCom class

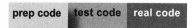 prep code   test code   *real code*

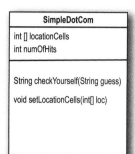

SimpleDotCom
int [] locationCells int numOfHits
String checkYourself(String guess) void setLocationCells(int[] loc)

You'll get the idea of how prepcode (our version of pseudocode) works as you read through this example. It's sort of half-way between real Java code and a plain English description of the class. Most prepcode includes three parts: instance variable declarations, method declarations, method logic. The most important part of prepcode is the method logic, because it defines *what* has to happen, which we later translate into *how*, when we actually write the method code.

DECLARE an *int array* to hold the location cells. Call it *locationCells.*

DECLARE an *int* to hold the number of hits. Call it *numOfHits* and **SET** it to 0.

DECLARE a *checkYourself()* method that takes a *String* for the user's guess ("1", "3", etc.), checks it, and returns a result representing a "hit", "miss", or "kill".

DECLARE a *setLocationCells()* setter method that takes an *int array* (which has the three cell locations as *ints* (2,3,4, etc.).

METHOD: *String checkYourself(String userGuess)*

    GET the user guess as a String parameter

    CONVERT the user guess to an *int*

    REPEAT with each of the location cells in the *int* array

        // COMPARE the user guess to the location cell

        IF the user guess matches

            INCREMENT the number of hits

            // FIND OUT if it was the last location cell:

            IF number of hits is 3, **RETURN** "kill" as the result

            ELSE it was not a kill, so **RETURN** "hit"

            END IF

        ELSE the user guess did not match, so **RETURN** "miss"

        END IF

    END REPEAT

END METHOD

METHOD: *void setLocationCells(int[] cellLocations)*

    GET the cell locations as an *int array* parameter

    ASSIGN the cell locations parameter to the cell locations instance variable

END METHOD

`prep code` `test code` `real code`

Writing the method implementations

let's write the real method code now, and get this puppy working.

Before we start coding the methods, though, let's back up and write some code to *test* the methods. That's right, we're writing the test code *before* there's anything to test!

The concept of writing the test code first is one of the practices of Extreme Programming (XP), and it can make it easier (and faster) for you to write your code. We're not necessarily saying you should use XP, but we do like the part about writing tests first. And XP just *sounds* cool.

Oh my! For a minute there I thought you weren't gonna write your test code first. Whoo! Don't scare me like that.

Extreme Programming (XP)

Extreme Programming(XP) is a newcomer to the software development methodology world. Considered by many to be "the way programmers really want to work", XP emerged in the late 90's and has been adopted by companies ranging from the two-person garage shop to the Ford Motor Company. The thrust of XP is that the customer gets what he wants, when he wants it, even when the spec changes late in the game.

XP is based on a set of proven practices that are all designed to work together, although many folks do pick and choose, and adopt only a portion of XP's rules. These practices include things like:

Make small, but frequent, releases.

Develop in iteration cycles.

Don't put in anything that's not in the spec (no matter how tempted you are to put in functionality "for the future").

Write the test code *first*.

No killer schedules; work regular hours.

Refactor (improve the code) whenever and wherever you notice the opportunity.

Don't release anything until it passes all the tests.

Set realistic schedules, based around small releases.

Keep it simple.

Program in pairs, and move people around so that everybody knows pretty much everything about the code.

prep code | test code | real code

Writing test code for the SimpleDotCom class

We need to write test code that can make a SimpleDotCom object and run its methods. For the SimpleDotCom class, we really care about only the *checkYourself()* method, although we *will* have to implement the *setLocationCells()* method in order to get the *checkYourself()* method to run correctly.

Take a good look at the prepcode below for the *checkYourself()* method (the *setLocationCells()* method is a no-brainer setter method, so we're not worried about it, but in a 'real' application we might want a more robust 'setter' method, which we *would* want to test).

Then ask yourself, "If the checkYourself() method were implemented, what test code could I write that would prove to me the method is working correctly?"

Based on this prepcode:

METHOD *String checkYourself(String userGuess)*

  GET the user guess as a String parameter

  CONVERT the user guess to an *int*

  REPEAT with each of the location cells in the *int* array

    // **COMPARE** the user guess to the location cell

    IF the user guess matches

      INCREMENT the number of hits

      // **FIND OUT** if it was the last location cell:

      IF number of hits is 3, **RETURN** "Kill" as the result

      ELSE it was not a kill, so **RETURN** "Hit"

      END IF

    ELSE the user guess did not match, so **RETURN** "Miss"

    END IF

  END REPEAT

END METHOD

Here's what we should test:

1. Instantiate a SimpleDotCom object.

2. Assign it a location (an array of 3 ints, like {2,3,4}).

3. Create a String to represent a user guess ("2", "0", etc.).

4. Invoke the checkYourself() method passing it the fake user guess.

5. Print out the result to see if it's correct ("passed" or "failed").

prep code | test code | **real code**

there are no
Dumb Questions

Q: Maybe I'm missing something here, but how exactly do you run a test on something that doesn't yet exist!?

A: You don't. We never said you start by *running* the test; you start by *writing* the test. At the time you write the test code, you won't have anything to run it against, so you probably won't be able to compile it until you write 'stub' code that can compile, but that will always cause the test to fail (like, return null.)

Q: Then I still don't see the point. Why not wait until the code is written, and then whip out the test code?

A: The act of thinking through (and writing) the test code helps clarify your thoughts about what the method itself needs to do.

As soon as your implementation code is done, you already have test code just waiting to validate it. Besides, you *know* if you don't do it now, you'll *never* do it. There's always something more interesting to do.

Ideally, write a little test code, then write *only* the implementation code you need in order to pass that test. Then write a little *more* test code and write *only* the new implementation code needed to pass *that* new test. At each test iteration, you run *all* the previously-written tests, so that you always prove that your latest code additions don't break previously-tested code.

Test code for the SimpleDotCom class

```java
public class SimpleDotComTestDrive {

    public static void main (String[] args) {

        SimpleDotCom dot = new SimpleDotCom();

        int[] locations = {2,3,4};

        dot.setLocationCells(locations);

        String userGuess = "2";

        String result = dot.checkYourself(userGuess);

        String testResult = "failed";

        if (result.equals("hit") ) {

            testResult = "passed";

        }

        System.out.println(testResult);

    }
}
```

instantiate a SimpleDotCom object

make an int array for the location of the dot com (3 consecutive ints out of a possible 7).

invoke the setter method on the dot com.

make a fake user guess

invoke the checkYourself() method on the dot com object, and pass it the fake guess.

if the fake guess (2) gives back a "hit", it's working

print out the test result (passed or failed")

Sharpen your pencil

In the next couple of pages we implement the SimpleDotCom class, and then later we return to the test class. Looking at our test code above, what else should be added? What are we *not* testing in this code, that we *should* be testing for? Write your ideas (or lines of code) below:

`prep code`   `test code`   `real code`

The checkYourself() method

There isn't a perfect mapping from prepcode to javacode; you'll see a few adjustments. The prepcode gave us a much better idea of *what* the code needs to do, and now we have to find the Java code that can do the *how*.

In the back of your mind, be thinking about parts of this code you might want (or need) to improve. The numbers ① are for things (syntax and language features) you haven't seen yet. They're explained on the opposite page.

GET the user guess

CONVERT the user guess to an *int*

REPEAT with each cell in the *int* array

IF the user guess matches

INCREMENT the number of hits

// FIND OUT if it was the last cell

IF number of hits is 3,

RETURN "kill" as the result

ELSE it was not a kill, so
RETURN "hit"

ELSE

RETURN "miss"

```java
public String checkYourself(String stringGuess) {

    int guess = Integer.parseInt(stringGuess);   ① ← convert the String to an int

    String result = "miss";   ← make a variable to hold the result we'll return. put "miss" in as the default (i.e. we assume a "miss")

    for (int cell : locationCells) {   ② ← repeat with each cell in the locationCells array (each cell location of the object)

        if (guess == cell) {   ← compare the user guess to this element (cell) in the array

            result = "hit";   ← we got a hit!

            numOfHits++;   ③

            break;   ④ ← get out of the loop, no need to test the other cells

        } // end if

    } // end for

    if (numOfHits == locationCells.length) {

        result = "kill";   ← we're out of the loop, but let's see if we're now 'dead' (hit 3 times) and change the result String to "Kill"

    } // end if

    System.out.println(result);   ← display the result for the user ("Miss", unless it was changed to "Hit" or "Kill")

    return result;   ← return the result back to the calling method

} // end method
```

Just the new stuff

The things we haven't seen before are on this page. Stop worrying! The rest of the details are at the end of the chapter. This is just enough to let you keep going.

A class that ships with Java.

A method in the Integer class that knows how to "parse" a String into the int it represents.

Takes a String.

① Converting a **String to an int**

Integer.parseInt("3")

Read this for loop declaration as "repeat for each element in the 'locationCells' array: take the next element in the array and assign it to the int variable 'cell'."

The colon (:) means "in", so the whole thing means "for each int value IN locationCells..."

New to me!!

② The **for** loop

for (int cell : locationCells) { }

Declare a variable that will hold one element from the array. Each time through the loop, this variable (in this case an int variable named "cell"), will hold a different element from the array, until there are no more elements (or the code does a "break"... see #4 below).

The array to iterate over in the loop. Each time through the loop, the next element in the array will be assigned to the variable "cell". (More on this at the end of this chapter.)

③ The **post-increment operator**

The ++ means add 1 to whatever's there (in other words, increment by 1).

numOfHits++

numOfHits++ is the same (in this case) as saying numOfHits = numOfHits + 1, except slightly more efficient.

④ **break** statement

break;

Gets you out of a loop. Immediately. Right here. No iteration, no boolean test, just get out now!

SimpleDotCom class

`prep code` `test code` `real code`

there are no
Dumb Questions

Q: What happens in Integer.parseInt() if the thing you pass isn't a number? And does it recognize spelled-out numbers, like "three"?

A: Integer.parseInt() works only on Strings that represent the ascii values for digits (0,1,2,3,4,5,6,7,8,9). If you try to parse something like "two" or "blurp", the code will blow up at runtime. (By *blow up*, we actually mean *throw an exception*, but we don't talk about exceptions until the Exceptions chapter. So for now, *blow up* is close enough.)

Q: In the beginning of the book, there was an example of a *for* loop that was really different from this one—are there two different styles of *for* loops?

A: Yes! From the first version of Java there has been a single kind of *for* loop (explained later in this chapter) that looks like this:

```java
for (int i = 0; i < 10; i++) {

    // do something 10 times

}
```

You can use this format for any kind of loop you need. But... beginning with Java 5.0 (Tiger), you can also use the *enhanced* for loop (that's the official description) when your loop needs to iterate over the elements in an array (or *another* kind of collection, as you'll see in the *next* chapter). You can always use the plain old for loop to iterate over an array, but the *enhanced* for loop makes it easier.

Final code for SimpleDotCom and SimpleDotComTester

```java
public class SimpleDotComTestDrive {

    public static void main (String[] args) {
        SimpleDotCom dot = new SimpleDotCom();
        int[] locations = {2,3,4};
        dot.setLocationCells(locations);
        String userGuess = "2";
        String result = dot.checkYourself(userGuess);

    }

}
```

```java
public class SimpleDotCom {

    int[] locationCells;
    int numOfHits = 0;

    public void setLocationCells(int[] locs) {
        locationCells = locs;
    }

    public String checkYourself(String stringGuess) {
        int guess = Integer.parseInt(stringGuess);
        String result = "miss";
        for (int cell : locationCells) {
            if (guess == cell) {
                result = "hit";
                numOfHits++;
                break;
            }
        } // out of the loop

        if (numOfHits ==
                locationCells.length) {
            result = "kill";
        }
        System.out.println(result);
        return result;
    } // close method
} // close class
```

What should we see when we run this code?
The test code makes a SimpleDotCom object and gives it a location at 2,3,4. Then it sends a fake user guess of "2" into the checkYourself() method. If the code is working correctly, we should see the result print out:

```
java SimpleDotComTestDrive
hit
```

There's a little bug lurking here. It compiles and runs, but sometimes... don't worry about it for now, but we *will* have to face it a little later.

prep code | test code | real code

Sharpen your pencil

We built the ⟋ test class, and the SimpleDotCom class. But we still haven't made the actual *game*. Given the code on the opposite page, and the spec for the actual game, write in your ideas for prepcode for the game class. We've given you a few lines here and there to get you started. The actual game code is on the next page, so **don't turn the page until you do this exercise!**

You should have somewhere between 12 and 18 lines (including the ones we wrote, but *not* including lines that have only a curly brace).

METHOD *public static void main (String [] args)*

    DECLARE an int variable to hold the number of user guesses, named *numOfGuesses*

COMPUTE a random number between 0 and 4 that will be the starting location cell position

WHILE the dot com is still alive :

    GET user input from the command line

The SimpleDotComGame needs to do this:

1. Make the single SimpleDotCom Object.

2. Make a location for it (three consecutive cells on a single row of seven virtual cells).

3. Ask the user for a guess.

4. Check the guess.

5. Repeat until the dot com is dead .

6. Tell the user how many guesses it took.

A complete game interaction

```
File  Edit  Window  Help  Runaway
%java SimpleDotComGame
enter a number   2
hit
enter a number   3
hit
enter a number   4
miss
enter a number   1
kill
You took 4 guesses
```

Prepcode for the SimpleDotComGame class
Everything happens in main()

There are some things you'll have to take on faith. For example, we have one line of prepcode that says, "GET user input from command-line". Let me tell you, that's a little more than we want to implement from scratch right now. But happily, we're using OO. And that means you get to ask some *other* class/object to do something for you, without worrying about *how* it does it. When you write prepcode, you should assume that *somehow* you'll be able to do whatever you need to do, so you can put all your brainpower into working out the logic.

```
public static void main (String [] args)

    DECLARE an int variable to hold the number of user guesses, named numOfGuesses, set it to 0.

    MAKE a new SimpleDotCom instance

    COMPUTE a random number between 0 and 4 that will be the starting location cell position

    MAKE an int array with 3 ints using the randomly-generated number, that number incremented by 1,
    and that number incremented by 2 (example: 3,4,5)

    INVOKE the setLocationCells() method on the SimpleDotCom instance

    DECLARE a boolean variable representing the state of the game, named isAlive. SET it to true


    WHILE the dot com is still alive (isAlive == true) :

        GET user input from the command line

        // CHECK the user guess

        INVOKE the checkYourself() method on the SimpleDotCom instance

        INCREMENT numOfGuesses variable

        // CHECK for dot com death

        IF result is "kill"

            SET isAlive to false (which means we won't enter the loop again)

            PRINT the number of user guesses

        END IF
    END WHILE
END METHOD
```

metacognitive tip

Don't work one part of the brain for too long a stretch at one time. Working just the left side of the brain for more than 30 minutes is like working just your left *arm* for 30 minutes. Give each side of your brain a break by switching sides at regular intervals. When you shift to one side, the other side gets to rest and recover. Left-brain activities include things like step-by-step sequences, logical problem-solving, and analysis, while the right-brain kicks in for metaphors, creative problem-solving, pattern-matching, and visualizing.

BULLET POINTS

- Your Java program should start with a high-level design.

- Typically you'll write three things when you create a new class:

    prepcode

    testcode

    real (Java) code

- Prepcode should describe *what* to do, not *how* to do it. Implementation comes later.

- Use the prepcode to help design the test code.

- Write test code *before* you implement the methods.

- Choose *for* loops over *while* loops when you know how many times you want to repeat the loop code.

- Use the pre/post *increment* operator to add 1 to a variable (x++;)

- Use the pre/post *decrement* to subtract 1 from a variable (x--;)

- Use `Integer.parseInt()` to get the int value of a String.

- `Integer.parseInt()` works only if the String represents a digit ("0","1","2", etc.)

- Use *break* to leave a loop early (i.e. even if the boolean test condition is still true).

Howdy from Ghost Town

SimpleDotComGame class

prep code | test code | real code

The game's main() method

Just as you did with the SimpleDotCom class, be thinking about parts of this code you might want (or need) to improve. The numbered things ① are for stuff we want to point out. They're explained on the opposite page. Oh, if you're wondering why we skipped the test code phase for this class, we don't need a test class for the game. It has only one method, so what would you do in your test code? Make a *separate* class that would call *main()* on *this* class? We didn't bother.

```java
public static void main(String[] args) {

    int numOfGuesses = 0;

    GameHelper helper = new GameHelper();

    SimpleDotCom theDotCom = new SimpleDotCom();

    int randomNum = (int) (Math.random() * 5);

    int[] locations = {randomNum, randomNum+1, randomNum+2};

    theDotCom.setLocationCells(locations);

    boolean isAlive = true;

    while(isAlive == true) {

        String guess = helper.getUserInput("enter a number");

        String result = theDotCom.checkYourself(guess);

        numOfGuesses++;

        if (result.equals("kill")) {

            isAlive = false;

            System.out.println("You took " + numOfGuesses + " guesses");

        } // close if

    } // close while

} // close main
```

DECLARE a variable to hold user guess count, set it to 0

MAKE a SimpleDot-Com object

COMPUTE a random number between 0 and 4

MAKE an int array with the 3 cell locations, and

INVOKE setLocationCells on the dot com object

DECLARE a boolean isAlive

WHILE the dot com is still alive

GET user input

// CHECK it

INVOKE checkYourself() on dot com

INCREMENT numOfGuesses

IF result is "kill"

SET gameAlive to false

PRINT the number of user guesses

make a variable to track how many guesses the user makes

this is a special class we wrote that has the method for getting user input. for now, pretend it's part of Java

make the dot com object

① *make a random number for the first cell, and use it to make the cell locations array*

give the dot com its locations (the array)

make a boolean variable to track whether the game is still alive, to use in the while loop test. repeat while game is still alive.

② *get user input String*

ask the dot com to check the guess; save the returned result in a String

increment guess count

was it a "kill"? if so, set isAlive to false (so we won't re-enter the loop) and print user guess count prep code test code **real code**

random() and getUserInput()

Two things that need a bit more explaining, are on this page. This is just a quick look to keep you going; more details on the GameHelper class are at the end of this chapter.

This is a 'cast', and it forces the thing immediately after it to become the type of the cast (i.e. the type in the parens). Math.random returns a double, so we have to cast it to be an int (we want a nice whole number between 0 and 4). In this case, the cast lops off the fractional part of the double.

The Math.random method returns a number from zero to just less than one. So this formula (with the cast), returns a number from 0 to 4. (i.e. 0 – 4.999…, cast to an int)

(1) Make a random number

$$\text{int randomNum} = \text{(int) (Math.random() * 5)}$$

We declare an int variable to hold the random number we get back.

A class that comes with Java.

A method of the Math class.

This method takes a String argument that it uses to prompt the user at the command–line. Whatever you pass in here gets displayed in the terminal just before the method starts looking for user input.

An instance we made earlier, of a class that we built to help with the game. It's called GameHelper and you haven't seen it yet (you will).

(2) Getting user input using the GameHelper class

$$\text{String guess} = \text{helper.getUserInput("enter a number");}$$

We declare a String variable to hold the user input String we get back ("3", "5", etc.).

A method of the GameHelper class that asks the user for command–line input, reads it in after the user hits RETURN, and gives back the result as a String.

prep code | test code | real code

One last class: GameHelper

We made the *dot com* **class.**

We made the *game* **class.**

All that's left is the *helper* **class**— the one with the getUserInput() method. The code to get command-line input is more than we want to explain right now. It opens up way too many topics best left for later. (Later, as in chapter 14.)

Just copy* the code below and compile it into a class named GameHelper. Drop all three classes (SimpleDotCom, SimpleDotComGame, GameHelper) into the same directory, and make it your working directory.

Whenever you see the  logo, you're seeing code that you have to type as-is and take on faith. Trust it. You'll learn how that code works *later*.

> I pre-cooked some code so you don't have to make it yourself.

Ready-bake Code

```java
import java.io.*;
public class GameHelper {
    public String getUserInput(String prompt) {
        String inputLine = null;
        System.out.print(prompt + "  ");
        try {
            BufferedReader is = new BufferedReader(
            new InputStreamReader(System.in));
            inputLine = is.readLine();
            if (inputLine.length() == 0 )   return null;
        } catch (IOException e) {
            System.out.println("IOException: " + e);
        }
        return inputLine;
    }
}
```

*We know how much you enjoy typing, but for those rare moments when you'd rather do something else, we've made the Ready-bake Code available on wickedlysmart.com.

Let's play

Here's what happens when we run it and enter the numbers 1,2,3,4,5,6. Lookin' good.

A complete game interaction
(your mileage may vary)

```
File Edit Window Help Smile
%java SimpleDotComGame
enter a number   1
miss
enter a number   2
miss
enter a number   3
miss
enter a number   4
hit
enter a number   5
hit
enter a number   6
kill
You took 6 guesses
```

What's this? A bug?

Gasp!

Here's what happens when we enter 1,1,1.

A different game interaction
(yikes)

```
File Edit Window Help Faint
%java SimpleDotComGame
enter a number   1
hit
enter a number   1
hit
enter a number   1
kill
You took 3 guesses
```

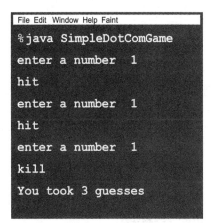

Sharpen your pencil

It's a cliff-hanger!

Will we *find* the bug?

Will we *fix* the bug?

Stay tuned for the next chapter, where we answer these questions and more...

And in the meantime, see if you can come up with ideas for what went wrong and how to fix it.

More about <u>for</u> loops

We've covered all the game code for *this* chapter (but we'll pick it up again to finish the deluxe version of the game in the next chapter). We didn't want to interrupt your work with some of the details and background info, so we put it back here. We'll start with the details of for loops, and if you're a C++ programmer, you can just skim these last few pages...

Regular (non-enhanced) for loops

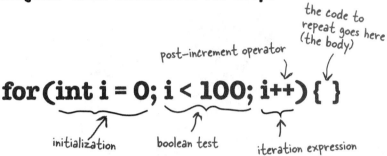

the code to repeat goes here (the body)

post-increment operator

```
for (int i = 0; i < 100; i++) { }
```

initialization   boolean test   iteration expression

repeat for 100 reps:

What it means in plain English: "Repeat 100 times."

How the compiler sees it:

* create a variable *i* and set it to 0.

* repeat while *i* is less than 100.

* at the end of each loop iteration, add 1 to *i*

Part One: *initialization*

Use this part to declare and initialize a variable to use within the loop body. You'll most often use this variable as a counter. You can actually initialize more than one variable here, but we'll get to that later in the book.

Part Two: *boolean test*

This is where the conditional test goes. Whatever's in there, it *must* resolve to a boolean value (you know, **true** or **false**). You can have a test, like (x >= 4), or you can even invoke a method that returns a boolean.

Part Three: *iteration expression*

In this part, put one or more things you want to happen with each trip through the loop. Keep in mind that this stuff happens at the *end* of each loop.

Trips through a loop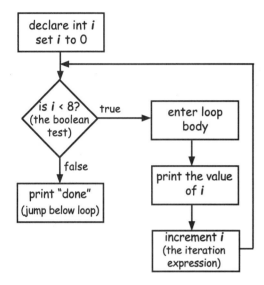

```
for (int i = 0; i < 8; i++) {
    System.out.println(i);
}
System.out.println("done");
```

output:

```
File Edit Window Help Repeat
%java Test
0
1
2
3
4
5
6
7
done
```

declare int *i*
set *i* to 0

is *i* < 8?
(the boolean test) —— true —→ enter loop body

false

print "done"
(jump below loop)

print the value of *i*

increment *i*
(the iteration expression)

Difference between for and while

A *while* loop has only the boolean test; it doesn't have a built-in initialization or iteration expression. A *while* loop is good when you don't know how many times to loop and just want to keep going while some condition is true. But if you *know* how many times to loop (e.g. the length of an array, 7 times, etc.), a *for* loop is cleaner. Here's the loop above rewritten using *while:*

```
int i = 0;       ← we have to declare and
                   initialize the counter
while (i < 8) {
    System.out.println(i);
    i++;         ← we have to increment
                   the counter
}
System.out.println("done");
```

++   --

Pre and Post Increment/Decrement Operator

The shortcut for adding or subtracting 1 from a variable.

```
x++;
```

is the same as:

```
x = x + 1;
```

They both mean the same thing in this context:

"add 1 to the current value of x" or "*increment* x by 1"

And:

```
x--;
```

is the same as:

```
x = x - 1;
```

Of course that's never the whole story. The placement of the operator (either before or after the variable) can affect the result. Putting the operator *before* the variable (for example, ++x), means, "*first*, increment x by 1, and *then* use this new value of x." This only matters when the ++x is part of some larger expression rather than just in a single statement.

```
int x = 0;       int z = ++x;
```

produces: x is 1, z is 1

But putting the ++ *after* the x give you a different result:

```
int x = 0;       int z = x++;
```

produces: x is 1, but *z is 0*! z gets the value of x and *then* x is incremented.

The enhanced for loop

Beginning with Java 5.0 (Tiger), the Java language has a second kind of *for* loop called the *enhanced for*, that makes it easier to iterate over all the elements in an array or other kinds of collections (you'll learn about *other* collections in the next chapter). That's really all that the enhanced for gives you—a simpler way to walk through all the elements in the collection, but since it's the most common use of a *for* loop, it was worth adding it to the language. We'll revisit the *enhanced for loop* in the next chapter, when we talk about collections that *aren't* arrays.

Declare an iteration variable that will hold a single element in the array.

The colon (:) means "IN".

The code to repeat goes here (the body).

for (String name : nameArray) { }

The elements in the array MUST be compatible with the declared variable type.

With each iteration, a different element in the array will be assigned to the variable "name".

The collection of elements that you want to iterate over. Imagine that somewhere earlier, the code said:

String[] nameArray = {"Fred", "Mary", "Bob"};

With the first iteration, the name variable has the value of "Fred", and with the second iteration, a value of "Mary", etc.

What it means in plain English: "For each element in nameArray, assign the element to the 'name' variable, and run the body of the loop."

How the compiler sees it:

* Create a String variable called *name* and set it to null.

* Assign the first value in *nameArray* to name.

* Run the body of the loop (the code block bounded by curly braces).

* Assign the next value in *nameArray* to name.

* Repeat while *there are still elements in the array*.

Note: depending on the programming language they've used in the past, some people refer to the enhanced for as the "for each" or the "for in" loop, because that's how it reads: "for EACH thing IN the collection…"

Part One: *iteration variable declaration*

Use this part to declare and initialize a variable to use within the loop body. With each iteration of the loop, this variable will hold a different element from the collection. The type of this variable must be compatible with the elements in the array! For example, you can't declare an *int* iteration variable to use with a *String[]* array.

Part Two: *the actual collection*

This must be a reference to an array or other collection. Again, don't worry about the *other* non-array kinds of collections yet—you'll see them in the next chapter.

Converting a String to an int

```
int guess = Integer.parseInt(stringGuess);
```

The user types his guess at the command-line, when the game prompts him. That guess comes in as a String ("2","0", etc.), and the game passes that String into the checkYourself() method.

But the cell locations are simply ints in an array, and you can't compare an int to a String.

For example, **this won't work**:

String num = "2";

int x = 2;

if (x == num) // horrible explosion!

Trying to compile that makes the compiler laugh and mock you:

```
operator == cannot be applied to
      int,java.lang.String

    if (x == num) { }
            ^
```

So to get around the whole apples and oranges thing, we have to make the *String* "2" into the *int* 2. Built into the Java class library is a class called Integer (that's right, an Integer *class*, not the int *primitive*), and one of its jobs is to take Strings that *represent* numbers and convert them into *actual* numbers.

a class that ships with Java

takes a String

Integer.parseInt("3")

a method in the Integer class that knows how to "parse" a String into the int it represents.

Casting primitives

long ──can be cast to──▶ short

01011101

but you might lose something

1101

bits on the left side were cut off

In chapter 3 we talked about the sizes of the various primitives, and how you can't shove a big thing directly into a small thing:

```
long y = 42;
int x = y;      // won't compile
```

A *long* is bigger than an *int* and the compiler can't be sure where that *long* has been. It might have been out drinking with the other longs, and taking on really big values. To force the compiler to jam the value of a bigger primitive variable into a smaller one, you can use the **cast** operator. It looks like this:

```
long y = 42;      // so far so good
int x = (int) y; // x = 42 cool!
```

Putting in the cast tells the compiler to take the value of y, chop it down to int size, and set x equal to whatever is left. If the value of y was bigger than the maximum value of x, then what's left will be a weird (but calculable*) number:

```
long y = 40002;
// 40002 exceeds the 16-bit limit of a short
short x = (short) y;  // x now equals -25534!
```

Still, the point is that the compiler lets you do it. And let's say you have a floating point number, and you just want to get at the whole number (*int*) part of it:

```
float f = 3.14f;
int x = (int) f;    //  x will equal 3
```

And don't even *think* about casting anything to a boolean or vice versa—just walk away.

It involves sign bits, binary, 'two's complement' and other geekery, all of which are discussed at the beginning of appendix B.

Exercise

BE the JVM

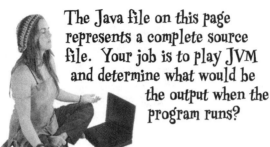

The Java file on this page represents a complete source file. Your job is to play JVM and determine what would be the output when the program runs?

```java
class Output {

  public static void main(String [] args) {
    Output o = new Output();
    o.go();
  }

  void go() {
    int y = 7;
    for(int x = 1; x < 8; x++) {
      y++;
      if (x > 4) {
        System.out.print(++y + " ");
      }
      if (y > 14) {
        System.out.println(" x = " + x);
        break;
      }
    }
  }
}
```

File Edit Window Help OM

% java Output
12 14

-or-

File Edit Window Help Incense

% java Output
12 14 x = 6

-or-

File Edit Window Help Believe

% java Output
13 15 x = 6

Code Magnets

A working Java program is all scrambled up on the fridge. Can you reconstruct the code snippets to make a working Java program that produces the output listed below? Some of the curly braces fell on the floor and they were too small to pick up, so feel free to add as many of those as you need!

```
class MultiFor {

    public static void main(String [] args) {

        for(int x = 0; x < 4; x++) {
            for(int y = 4; y > 2; y--) {


                System.out.println(x+" "+y);

            }
            if(x==1) { x++; }

        }

    }

}
```

```
x++;
```

```
if (x == 1) {
```

```
System.out.println(x + " " + y);
```

```
class MultiFor {
```

```
for(int   y = 4; y > 2; y--) {
```

```
for(int x = 0; x < 4; x++) {
```

```
public static void main(String [] args) {
```

```
File  Edit  Window  Help  Raid
% java MultiFor
0 4
0 3
1 4
1 3
3 4
3 3
```

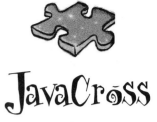

JavaCross

How does a crossword puzzle help you learn Java? Well, all of the words **are** Java related. In addition, the clues provide metaphors, puns, and the like. These mental twists and turns burn alternate routes to Java knowledge, right into your brain!

Across

1. Fancy computer word for build
4. Multi-part loop
6. Test first
7. 32 bits
10. Method's answer
11. Prepcode-esque
13. Change
15. The big toolkit
17. An array unit
18. Instance or local
20. Automatic toolkit
22. Looks like a primitive, but..
25. Un-castable
26. Math method
28. Converter method
29. Leave early

Down

2. Increment type
3. Class's workhorse
5. Pre is a type of _____
6. For's iteration _____
7. Establish first value
8. While or For
9. Update an instance variable
12. Towards blastoff
14. A cycle
16. Talkative package
19. Method messenger (abbrev.)
21. As if
23. Add after
24. Pi house
26. Compile it and ____
27. ++ quantity

Mixed Messages

A short Java program is listed below. One block of the program is missing. Your challenge is to **match the candidate block of code** (on the left), **with the output** that you'd see if the block were inserted. Not all the lines of output will be used, and some of the lines of output might be used more than once. Draw lines connecting the candidate blocks of code with their matching command-line output.

```java
class MixFor5 {
  public static void main(String [] args) {
    int x = 0;
    int y = 30;
    for (int outer = 0; outer < 3; outer++) {
      for(int inner = 4; inner > 1; inner--) {




        y = y - 2;
        if (x == 6) {
          break;
        }
        x = x + 3;
      }
      y = y - 2;
    }
    System.out.println(x + " " + y);
  }
}
```

← candidate code goes here

Candidates:

x = x + 3;
x = x + 6;
x = x + 2;
x++;
x--;
x = x + 0;

Possible output:

45 6
36 6
54 6
60 10
18 6
6 14
12 14

match each candidate with one of the possible outputs

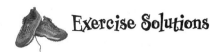 Exercise Solutions

Be the JVM:

```java
class Output {

  public static void main(String [] args) {
    Output o = new Output();
    o.go();
  }
  void go() {
    int y = 7;
    for(int x = 1; x < 8; x++) {
      y++;
      if (x > 4) {
        System.out.print(++y + " ");
      }
      if (y > 14) {
        System.out.println(" x = " + x);
        break;
      }
    }
  }
}
```

> Did you remember to factor in the break statement? How did that affect the output?

```
File  Edit  Window  Help  MotorcycleMaintenance

% java Output
13 15 x = 6
```

Code Magnets:

```java
class MultiFor {

  public static void main(String [] args) {

    for(int x = 0; x < 4; x++) {

      for(int y = 4; y > 2; y--) {
        System.out.println(x + " " + y);
      }

      if (x == 1) {
        x++;
      }
    }
  }
}
```

> What would happen if this code block came before the 'y' for loop?

```
File  Edit  Window  Help  Monopole

% java MultiFor
0 4
0 3
1 4
1 3
3 4
3 3
```

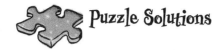
Puzzle Solutions

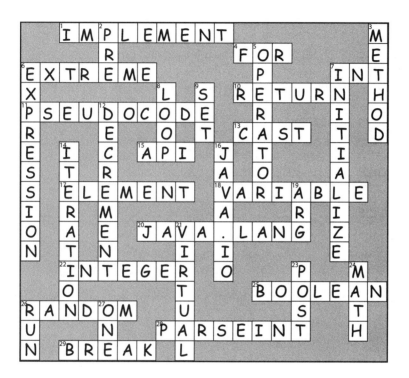

Candidates: **Possible output:**

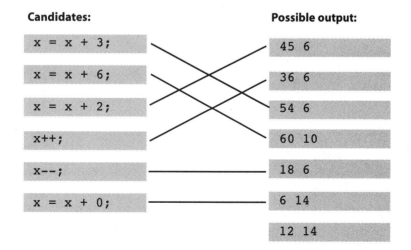

Candidates	Possible output
x = x + 3;	45 6
x = x + 6;	36 6
x = x + 2;	54 6
x++;	60 10
x--;	18 6
x = x + 0;	6 14
	12 14

Using the Java Library

Java ships with hundreds of pre-built classes. You don't have to reinvent the wheel if you know how to find what you need in the Java library, known as the **Java API**. *You've got better things to do.* If you're going to write code, you might as well write *only* the parts that are truly custom for your application. You know those programmers who walk out the door each night at 5 PM? The ones who don't even show *up* until 10 AM? **They use the Java API.** And about eight pages from now, so will you. The core Java library is a giant pile of classes just waiting for you to use like building blocks, to assemble your own program out of largely pre-built code. The Ready-bake Java we use in this book is code you don't have to create from scratch, but you still have to type it. The Java API is full of code you don't even have to *type*. All you need to do is learn to use it.

we still have a **bug**

In our last chapter, we left you with the cliff-hanger. A bug.

How it's supposed to look

Here's what happens when we run it and enter the numbers 1,2,3,4,5,6. Lookin' good.

A complete game interaction
(your mileage may vary)

```
File Edit Window Help Smile
%java SimpleDotComGame
enter a number   1
miss
enter a number   2
miss
enter a number   3
miss
enter a number   4
hit
enter a number   5
hit
enter a number   6
kill
You took 6 guesses
```

How the bug looks

Here's what happens when we enter 2,2,2.

A different game interaction
(yikes)

```
File Edit Window Help Faint
%java SimpleDotComGame
enter a number   2
hit
enter a number   2
hit
enter a number   2
kill
You took 3 guesses
```

In the current version, once you get a hit, you can simply repeat that hit two more times for the kill!

So what happened?

```
public String checkYourself(String stringGuess) {

    int guess = Integer.parseInt(stringGuess);      ← Convert the String
                                                       to an int.

    String result = "miss";      ←      Make a variable to hold the result we'll
                                        return. Put "miss" in as the default
                                        (i.e. we assume a "miss").

    for (int cell : locationCells) {                    ←  Repeat with each
                                                           thing in the array.
        if (guess == cell) {        ←   Compare the user
                                        guess to this element
            result = "hit";  ←          (cell), in the array.
                            we got a hit!
            numOfHits++;  ←

        break;  ←   Get out of the loop, no need
                    to test the other cells.
        } // end if

    } // end for

    if (numOfHits == locationCells.length) {  ←  We're out of the loop, but
                                                 let's see if we're now 'dead'
        result = "kill";                         (hit 3 times) and change the
                                                 result String to "kill".
    } // end if

    System.out.println(result);  ←  Display the result for the user
                                    ("miss", unless it was changed to "hit" or "kill").
    return result;
              ←  Return the result back to
} // end method    the calling method.
```

Here's where it goes wrong. We counted a hit every time the user guessed a cell location, *even if that location had already been hit!*

We need a way to know that when a user makes a hit, he hasn't previously hit that cell. If he has, then we don't want to count it as a hit.

How do we fix it?

We need a way to know whether a cell has already been hit. Let's run through some possibilities, but first, we'll look at what we know so far...

We have a virtual row of 7 cells, and a DotCom will occupy three consecutive cells somewhere in that row. This virtual row shows a DotCom placed at cell locations 4,5 and 6.

The virtual row, with the 3 cell locations for the DotCom object.

The DotCom has an instance variable—an int array—that holds that DotCom object's cell locations.

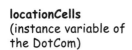

locationCells
(instance variable of the DotCom)

The array instance variable that holds the DotCom's cell locations. This DotCom holds the 3 values of 4, 5, and 6. Those are the numbers the user needs to guess.

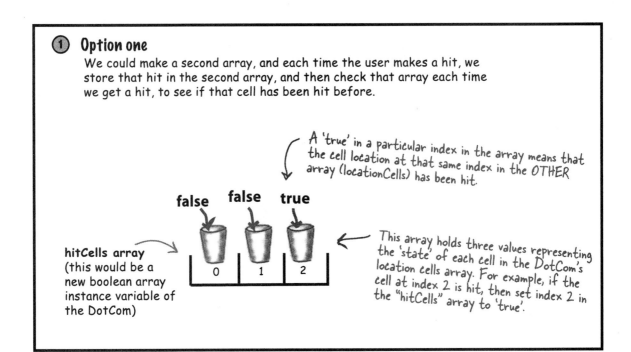

① **Option one**
We could make a second array, and each time the user makes a hit, we store that hit in the second array, and then check that array each time we get a hit, to see if that cell has been hit before.

A 'true' in a particular index in the array means that the cell location at that same index in the OTHER array (locationCells) has been hit.

false   false   true

hitCells array
(this would be a new boolean array instance variable of the DotCom)

This array holds three values representing the 'state' of each cell in the DotCom's location cells array. For example, if the cell at index 2 is hit, then set index 2 in the "hitCells" array to 'true'.

Option one is too clunky

Option one seems like more work than you'd expect. It means that each time the user makes a hit, you have to change the state of the *second* array (the 'hitCells' array), oh -- but first you have to CHECK the 'hitCells' array to see if that cell has already been hit anyway. It would work, but there's got to be something better...

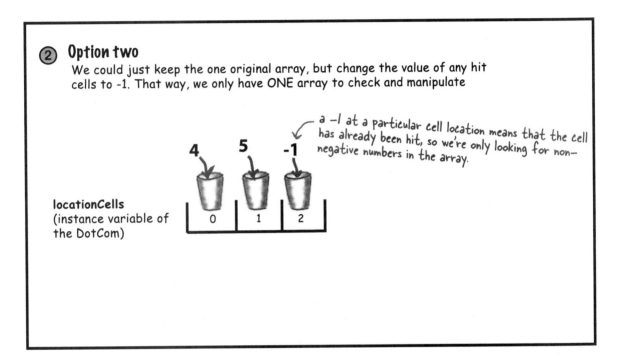

② **Option two**

We could just keep the one original array, but change the value of any hit cells to -1. That way, we only have ONE array to check and manipulate

a –1 at a particular cell location means that the cell has already been hit, so we're only looking for non-negative numbers in the array.

locationCells
(instance variable of the DotCom)

4   5   -1

0   1   2

Option two is a little better, but still pretty clunky

Option two is a little less clunky than option one, but it's not very efficient. You'd still have to loop through all three slots (index positions) in the array, even if one or more are already invalid because they've been 'hit' (and have a -1 value). There has to be something better...

③ **Option three**

We delete each cell location as it gets hit, and then modify the array to be smaller. Except arrays can't change their size, so we have to make a **new** array and copy the remaining cells from the old array into the new smaller array.

4 5 6

locationCells array BEFORE any cells have been hit

The array starts out with a size of 3, and we loop through all 3 cells (positions in the array) to look for a match between the user guess and the cell value (4,5, 6).

4 6

locationCells array AFTER cell '5', which was at index 1 in the array, has been hit

When cell '5' is hit, we make a new, smaller array with only the remaining cell locations, and assign it to the original locationCells reference.

Option three would be much better if the array could shrink, so that we wouldn't have to make a new smaller array, copy the remaining values in, and reassign the reference.

The original prepcode for part of the checkYourself() method:

REPEAT with each of the location cells in the *int* array ➞

    // *COMPARE* the user guess to the location cell

    IF the user guess matches

        INCREMENT the number of hits ➞

        // *FIND OUT* if it was the last location cell:

        IF number of hits is 3, **RETURN** "kill" ➞

        ELSE it was not a kill, so **RETURN** "hit"

        END IF

    ELSE user guess did not match, so **RETURN** "miss"

    END IF

END REPEAT

Life would be good if only we could change it to:

REPEAT with each of the *remaining* location cells

    // *COMPARE* the user guess to the location cell

    IF the user guess matches

        REMOVE this cell from the array

        // *FIND OUT* if it was the last location cell:

        IF the array is now empty, **RETURN** "kill"

        ELSE it was not a kill, so **RETURN** "hit"

        END IF

    ELSE user guess did not match, so **RETURN** "miss"

    END IF

END REPEAT

If only I could find an array that could **shrink** when you **remove** something. And one that you didn't have to loop through to check each element, but instead you could just **ask it if it contains** what you're looking for. And it would let you **get** things out of it, without having to know exactly which slot the things are in. That would be dreamy. But I know it's just a fantasy...

Wake up and smell the library

As if by magic, there really *is* such a thing.

But it's not an *array*, it's an *ArrayList*.

A class in the core Java library (the API).

The Java Standard Edition (which is what you have unless you're working on the Micro Edition for small devices and believe me, *you'd know*) ships with hundreds of pre-built classes. Just like our Ready-Bake code except that these built-in classes are already compiled.

That means no typing.

Just use 'em.

One of a gazillion classes in the Java library.

You can use it in your code as if you wrote it yourself.

ArrayList

add(Object elem)
Adds the object parameter to the list.

remove(int index)
Removes the object at the index parameter.

remove(Object elem)
Removes this object (if it's in the ArrayList).

contains(Object elem)
Returns 'true' if there's a match for the object parameter

isEmpty()
Returns 'true' if the list has no elements

indexOf(Object elem)
Returns either the index of the object parameter, or -1

size()
Returns the number of elements currently in the list

get(int index)
Returns the object currently at the index parameter

This is just a sample of SOME of the methods in ArrayList.

(Note: the add(Object elem) method actually looks a little stranger than the one we've shown here... we'll get to the real one later in the book. For now, just think of it as an add() method that takes the object you want to add.)

Some things you can do with ArrayList

Don't worry about this new <Egg> angle-bracket syntax right now; it just means "make this a list of Egg objects".

(1) Make one

```
ArrayList<Egg> myList = new ArrayList<Egg>();
```

A new ArrayList object is created on the heap. It's little because it's empty.

(2) Put something in it

```
Egg s = new Egg();

myList.add(s);
```

Now the ArrayList grows a "box" to hold the Egg object.

s

(3) Put another thing in it

```
Egg b = new Egg();

myList.add(b);
```

The ArrayList grows again to hold the second Egg object.

s   b

(4) Find out how many things are in it

```
int theSize = myList.size();
```

The ArrayList is holding 2 objects so the size() method returns 2

(5) Find out if it contains something

```
boolean isIn = myList.contains(s);
```

The ArrayList DOES contain the Egg object referenced by 's', so contains() returns **true**

(6) Find out where something is (i.e. its index)

```
int idx = myList.indexOf(b);
```

ArrayList is zero-based (means first index is 0) and since the object referenced by 'b' was the second thing in the list, indexOf() returns **1**

(7) Find out if it's empty

```
boolean empty = myList.isEmpty();
```

it's definitely NOT empty, so isEmpty() returns **false**

(8) Remove something from it

```
myList.remove(s);
```

Hey look — it shrank!

b

when arrays aren't enough

Sharpen your pencil

Fill in the rest of the table below by looking at the ArrayList code on the left and putting in what you think the code might be if it were using a regular array instead. We don't expect you to get all of them exactly right, so just make your best guess.

ArrayList	regular array
`ArrayList<String> myList = new` `ArrayList<String>();`	String [] myList = new String[2];
`String a = new String("whoohoo");`	String a = new String("whoohoo");
`myList.add(a);`	int x=0
	my List [x] = a ;
`String b = new String("Frog");`	String b = new String("Frog");
`myList.add(b);`	x++ ;
	myList [x] = b
`int theSize = myList.size();`	int theSize = myList.length
`Object o = myList.get(1);`	Object o = myList [1] ;
`myList.remove(1);`	
`boolean isIn = myList.contains(b);`	

there are no Dumb Questions

Q: So ArrayList is cool, but how would I know it exists?

A: The question is really, "How do I *know* what's in the API?" and that's the key to your success as a Java programmer. Not to mention your key to being as lazy as possible while still managing to build software. You might be amazed at how much time you can save when somebody else has already done most of the heavy lifting, and all you have to do is step in and create the fun part.

But we digress... the short answer is that you spend some time learning what's in the core API. The long answer is at the end of this chapter, where you'll learn *how* to do that.

Q: But that's a pretty big issue. Not only do I need to know that the Java library comes with ArrayList, but more importantly I have to know that ArrayList is the thing that can do what I want! So how do I go from a need-to-do-something to a-way-to-do-it using the API?

A: Now you're really at the heart of it. By the time you've finished this book, you'll have a good grasp of the language, and the rest of your learning curve really is about knowing how to get from a problem to a solution, with you writing the least amount of code. If you can be patient for a few more pages, we start talking about it at the end of this chapter.

Java Exposed

This week's interview:
ArrayList, on arrays

HeadFirst: So, ArrayLists are like arrays, right?

ArrayList: In their dreams! *I* am an *object* thank you very much.

HeadFirst: If I'm not mistaken, arrays are objects too. They live on the heap right there with all the other objects.

ArrayList: Sure arrays go on the heap, *duh*, but an array is still a wanna-be ArrayList. A poser. Objects have state *and* behavior, right? We're clear on that. But have you actually tried calling a method on an array?

HeadFirst: Now that you mention it, can't say I have. But what method would I call, anyway? I only care about calling methods on the stuff I put *in* the array, not the array itself. And I can use array syntax when I want to put things in and take things out of the array.

ArrayList: Is that so? You mean to tell me you actually *removed* something from an array? (Sheesh, where do they *train* you guys? McJava's?)

HeadFirst: Of *course* I take something out of the array. I say Dog d = dogArray[1] and I get the Dog object at index 1 out of the array.

ArrayList: Allright, I'll try to speak slowly so you can follow along. You were *not*, I repeat *not*, removing that Dog from the array. All you did was make a copy of the *reference to the Dog* and assign it to another Dog variable.

HeadFirst: Oh, I see what you're saying. No I didn't actually remove the Dog object from the array. It's still there. But I can just set its reference to null, I guess.

ArrayList: But I'm a first-class object, so I have methods and I can actually, you know, *do* things like remove the Dog's reference from myself, not just set it to null. And I can change my size, *dynamically* (look it up). Just try to get an *array* to do that!

HeadFirst: Gee, hate to bring this up, but the rumor is that you're nothing more than a glorified but less-efficient array. That in fact you're just a wrapper for an array, adding extra methods for things like resizing that I would have had to write myself. And while we're at it, *you can't even hold primitives!* Isn't that a big limitation?

ArrayList: I can't *believe* you buy into that urban legend. No, I am *not* just a less-efficient array. I will admit that there are a few *extremely* rare situations where an array might be just a tad, I repeat, *tad* bit faster for certain things. But is it worth the *miniscule* performance gain to give up all this *power*. Still, look at all this *flexibility*. And as for the primitives, of *course* you can put a primtive in an ArrayList, as long as it's wrapped in a primitive wrapper class (you'll see a lot more on that in chapter 10). And as of Java 5.0, that wrapping (and unwrapping when you take the primitive out again) happens automatically. And allright, I'll *acknowledge* that yes, if you're using an ArrayList of *primitives*, it probably is faster with an array, because of all the wrapping and unwrapping, but still... who really uses primitives *these* days?

Oh, look at the time! *I'm late for Pilates.* We'll have to do this again sometime.

Comparing ArrayList to a regular array

ArrayList	regular array
`ArrayList<String> myList = new` `ArrayList<String>();`	`String [] myList = new String[2];`
`String a = new String("whoohoo");` `myList.add(a);`	`String a = new String("whoohoo");` `myList[0] = a;`
`String b = new String("Frog");` `myList.add(b);`	`String b = new String("Frog");` `myList[1] = b;`
`int theSize = myList.size();`	`int theSize = myList.length;`
`Object o = myList.get(1);`	`String o = myList[1];`
`myList.remove(1);`	`myList[1] = null;`

`boolean isIn = myList.contains(b);`	`boolean isIn = false;`
	
	`    for (String item : myList) {`
	
	`        if (b.equals(item)) {`
	
	`            isIn = true;`
	
	`            break;`
	
	`        }`
	
	`    }`

Here's where it starts to look really different...

Notice how with ArrayList, you're working with an object of type ArrayList, so you're just invoking regular old methods on a regular old object, using the regular old dot operator.

With an *array*, you use *special array syntax* (like myList[0] = foo) that you won't use anywhere else except with arrays. Even though an array *is* an object, it lives in its own special world and you can't invoke any methods on it, although you can access its one and only instance variable, *length*.

Comparing ArrayList to a regular array

(1) A plain old array has to know its size at the time it's created.

But for ArrayList, you just make an object of type ArrayList. Every time. It never needs to know how big it should be, because it grows and shrinks as objects are added or removed.

```
new String[2]    Needs a size.
```

```
new ArrayList<String>()
```
No size required (although you can give it a size if you want to).

(2) To put an object in a regular array, you must assign it to a specific location.

(An index from 0 to one less than the length of the array.)

```
myList[1] = b;
```
Needs an index.

If that index is outside the boundaries of the array (like, the array was declared with a size of 2, and now you're trying to assign something to index 3), it blows up at runtime.

With ArrayList, you can specify an index using the *add(anInt, anObject)* method, or you can just keep saying *add(anObject)* and the ArrayList will keep growing to make room for the new thing.

```
myList.add(b);
```
No index.

(3) Arrays use array syntax that's not used anywhere else in Java.

But ArrayLists are plain old Java objects, so they have no special syntax.

```
myList[1]
```
The array brackets [ ] are special syntax used only for arrays.

(4) ArrayLists in Java 5.0 are parameterized.

We just said that unlike arrays, ArrayLists have no special syntax. But they *do* use something special that was added to Java 5.0 Tiger—*parameterized types*.

```
ArrayList<String>
```
The <String> in angle brackets is a "type parameter". ArrayList<String> means simply "a list of Strings", as opposed to ArrayList<Dog> which means, "a list of Dogs".

Prior to Java 5.0, there was no way to declare the *type* of things that would go in the ArrayList, so to the compiler, all ArrayLists were simply heterogenous collections of objects. But now, using the <typeGoesHere> syntax, we can declare and create an ArrayList that knows (and restricts) the types of objects it can hold. We'll look at the details of parameterized types in ArrayLists in the Collections chapter, so for now, don't think too much about the angle bracket <> syntax you see when we use ArrayLists. Just know that it's a way to force the compiler to allow only a specific type of object (*the type in angle brackets*) in the ArrayList.

Let's fix the DotCom code.

Remember, this is how the buggy version looks:

We've renamed the class DotCom now (instead of SimpleDotCom), for the new advanced version, but this is the same code you saw in the last chapter.

```java
public class DotCom {

    int[] locationCells;
    int numOfHits = 0;

    public void setLocationCells(int[] locs) {
        locationCells = locs;
    }

    public String checkYourself(String stringGuess) {
        int guess = Integer.parseInt(stringGuess);
        String result = "miss";

        for (int cell : locationCells) {
            if (guess == cell) {

                result = "hit";
                numOfHits++;

                break;
            }
        } // out of the loop

        if (numOfHits == locationCells.length) {
            result = "kill";
        }
        System.out.println(result);
            return result;
    } // close method
} // close class
```

Where it all went wrong. We counted each guess as a hit, without checking whether that cell had already been hit.

New and improved DotCom class

Now with ArrayList power!

```java
import java.util.ArrayList;
```
Ignore this line for now; we talk about it at the end of the chapter.

```java
public class DotCom {

    private ArrayList<String> locationCells;
    // private int numOfHits;
    // don't need that now
```
Change the String array to an ArrayList that holds Strings.

```java
    public void setLocationCells(ArrayList<String> loc) {
        locationCells = loc;
    }
```
New and improved argument name.

```java
    public String checkYourself(String userInput) {

        String result = "miss";
```
Find out if the user guess is in the ArrayList, by asking for its index. If it's not in the list, then indexOf() returns a –1.

```java
        int index = locationCells.indexOf(userInput);

        if (index >= 0) {
```
If index is greater than or equal to zero, the user guess is definitely in the list, so remove it.

```java
            locationCells.remove(index);

            if (locationCells.isEmpty()) {
```
If the list is empty, this was the killing blow!

```java
                result = "kill";
            } else {
                result = "hit";
            } // close if

        } // close outer if

        return result;
    } // close method
} // close class
```

Let's build the REAL game: "Sink a Dot Com"

We've been working on the 'simple' version, but now let's build the real one. Instead of a single row, we'll use a grid. And instead of one DotCom, we'll use three.

Goal: Sink all of the computer's Dot Coms in the fewest number of guesses. You're given a rating level based on how well you perform.

Setup: When the game program is launched, the computer places three Dot Coms, randomly, on the **virtual 7 x 7 grid**. When that's complete, the game asks for your first guess.

How you play: We haven't learned to build a GUI yet, so this version works at the command-line. The computer will prompt you to enter a guess (a cell), which you'll type at the command-line (as "A3", "C5", etc.). In response to your guess, you'll see a result at the command-line, either "hit", "miss", or "You sunk Pets.com" (or whatever the lucky Dot Com of the day is). When you've sent all three Dot Coms to that big 404 in the sky, the game ends by printing out your rating.

You're going to build the Sink a Dot Com game, with a 7 x 7 grid and three Dot Coms. Each Dot Com takes up three cells.

part of a game interaction

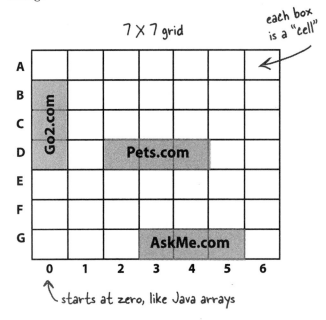

7 X 7 grid

each box is a "cell"

starts at zero, like Java arrays

```
File  Edit  Window  Help  Sell
%java DotComBust
Enter a guess   A3
miss
Enter a guess   B2
miss
Enter a guess   C4
miss
Enter a guess   D2
hit
Enter a guess   D3
hit
Enter a guess   D4
Ouch! You sunk Pets.com    : (
kill
Enter a guess   B4
miss
Enter a guess   G3
hit
Enter a guess   G4
hit
Enter a guess   G5
Ouch! You sunk AskMe.com    : (
```

What needs to change?

We have three classes that need to change: the DotCom class (which is now called DotCom instead of SimpleDotCom), the game class (DotComBust) and the game helper class (which we won't worry about now).

Ⓐ DotCom class

⊙ **Add a *name* variable**
to hold the name of the DotCom ("Pets.com", "Go2.com", etc.) so each Dot-Com can print its name when it's killed (see the output screen on the opposite page).

Ⓑ DotComBust class (the game)

⊙ **Create *three* DotComs instead of one.**

⊙ **Give each of the three DotComs a *name*.**
Call a setter method on each DotCom instance, so that the DotCom can assign the name to its name instance variable.

DotComBust class continued...

⊙ **Put the DotComs on a grid rather than just a single row, and do it for all three DotComs.**
This step is now way more complex than before, if we're going to place the DotComs randomly. Since we're not here to mess with the math, we put the algorithm for giving the DotComs a location into the GameHelper (Ready-bake) class.

⊙ **Check each user guess *with all three DotComs*, instead of just one.**

⊙ **Keep playing the game** (i.e accepting user guesses and checking them with the remaining DotComs) *until there are no more live DotComs.*

⊙ **Get out of main.** We kept the simple one in main just to... keep it simple. But that's not what we want for the *real* game.

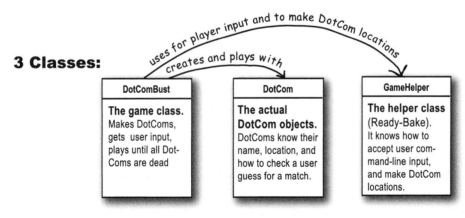

3 Classes:

uses for player input and to make DotCom locations

creates and plays with

DotComBust	DotCom	GameHelper
The game class. Makes DotComs, gets user input, plays until all Dot-Coms are dead	**The actual DotCom objects.** DotComs know their name, location, and how to check a user guess for a match.	**The helper class** (Ready-Bake). It knows how to accept user com-mand-line input, and make DotCom locations.

5 Objects:

DotComBust

Do
Do
DotCom

GameHelper

Plus 4 ArrayLists: 1 for the DotComBust and 1 for each of the 3 DotCom objects.

Who does what in the DotComBust game (and when)

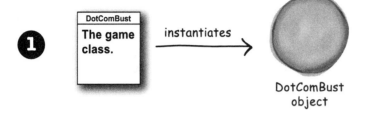

1 The main() method in the DotComBust class instantiates the DotComBust object that does all the game stuff.

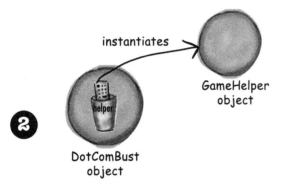

2 The DotComBust (game) object instantiates an instance of GameHelper, the object that will help the game do its work.

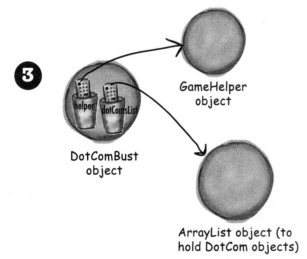

3 The DotComBust object instantiates an ArrayList that will hold the 3 DotCom objects.

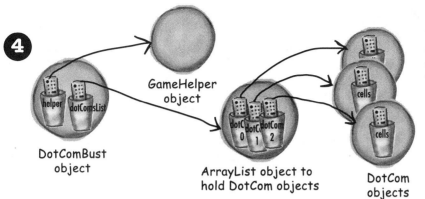

4 The DotComBust object creates three DotCom objects (and puts them in the ArrayList)

GameHelper object

DotComBust object

ArrayList object to hold DotCom objects

DotCom objects

The DotComBust object asks the helper object for a location for a DotCom (does this 3 times, one for each DotCom)

The DotComBust object gives each of the Dot-Com objects a location (which the DotComBust got from the helper object) like "A2", "B2", etc. Each DotCom object puts his own three location cells in an ArrayList

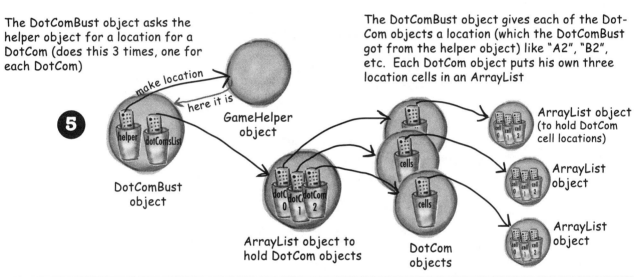

5

make location
here it is
GameHelper object

DotComBust object

ArrayList object to hold DotCom objects

DotCom objects

ArrayList object (to hold DotCom cell locations)

ArrayList object

ArrayList object

The DotComBust object asks the helper object for a user guess (the helper prompts the user and gets input from the command-line)

The DotComBust object loops through the list of DotComs, and asks each one to check the user guess for a match. The DotCom checks its locations ArrayList and returns a result ("hit", "miss", etc.)

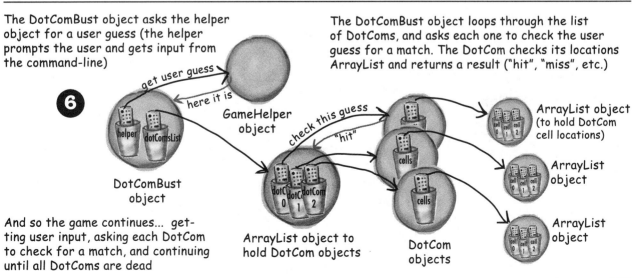

6

get user guess
here it is
GameHelper object

check this guess
"hit"

DotComBust object

And so the game continues... getting user input, asking each DotCom to check for a match, and continuing until all DotComs are dead

ArrayList object to hold DotCom objects

DotCom objects

ArrayList object (to hold DotCom cell locations)

ArrayList object

ArrayList object

prep code | test code | real code

DotComBust
GameHelper helper ArrayList dotComsList int numOfGuesses
setUpGame() startPlaying() checkUserGuess() finishGame()

Prep code for the real DotComBust class

The DotComBust class has three main jobs: set up the game, play the game until the DotComs are dead, and end the game. Although we could map those three jobs directly into three methods, we split the middle job (play the game) into *two* methods, to keep the granularity smaller. Smaller methods (meaning smaller chunks of functionality) help us test, debug, and modify the code more easily.

Variable Declarations

DECLARE and instantiate the *GameHelper* instance variable, named *helper.*

DECLARE and instantiate an *ArrayList* to hold the list of DotComs (initially three) Call it *dotComsList.*

DECLARE an int variable to hold the number of user guesses (so that we can give the user a score at the end of the game). Name it *numOfGuesses* and set it to 0.

Method Declarations

DECLARE a *setUpGame()* method to create and initialize the DotCom objects with names and locations. Display brief instructions to the user.

DECLARE a *startPlaying()* method that asks the player for guesses and calls the checkUserGuess() method until all the DotCom objects are removed from play.

DECLARE a *checkUserGuess()* method that loops through all remaining DotCom objects and calls each DotCom object's checkYourself() method.

DECLARE a *finishGame()* method that prints a message about the user's performance, based on how many guesses it took to sink all of the DotCom objects.

Method Implementations

METHOD: *void setUpGame()*

    // make three DotCom objects and name them

    CREATE three DotCom objects.

    SET a name for each DotCom.

    ADD the DotComs to the *dotComsList* (the ArrayList).

    REPEAT with each of the DotCom objects in the *dotComsList* array

        CALL the *placeDotCom()* method on the helper object, to get a randomly-selected location for this DotCom (three cells, vertically or horizontally aligned, on a 7 X 7 grid).

        SET the location for each DotCom based on the result of the *placeDotCom()* call.

    END REPEAT

END METHOD

prep code | test code | real code

Method implementations continued:

METHOD: *void startPlaying()*

    REPEAT while any DotComs exist

        GET user input by calling the helper *getUserInput()* method

        EVALUATE the user's guess by *checkUserGuess()* method

    END REPEAT

END METHOD

METHOD: *void checkUserGuess(String userGuess)*

    // find out if there's a hit (and kill) on any DotCom

    INCREMENT the number of user guesses in the *numOfGuesses* variable

    SET the local *result* variable (a *String*) to "miss", assuming that the user's guess will be a miss.

    REPEAT with each of the DotObjects in the *dotComsList* array

        EVALUATE the user's guess by calling the DotCom object's *checkYourself()* method

        SET the result variable to "hit" or "kill" if appropriate

        IF the result is "kill", **REMOVE** the DotCom from the *dotComsList*

    END REPEAT

    DISPLAY the *result* value to the user

END METHOD

METHOD: *void finishGame()*

    DISPLAY a generic "game over" message, then:

        IF number of user guesses is small,

            DISPLAY a congratulations message

        ELSE

            DISPLAY an insulting one

        END IF

END METHOD

Sharpen your pencil

How should we go from prep code to the final code? First we start with test code, and then test and build up our methods bit by bit. We won't keep showing you test code in this book, so now it's up to you to think about what you'd need to know to test these methods. And which method do you test and write first? See if you can work out some prep code for a set of tests. Prep code or even bullet points are good enough for this exercise, but if you want to try to write the *real* test code (in Java), knock yourself out.

the DotComBust code (the game)

prep code   test code   real code

Sharpen your pencil

Annotate the code yourself!

Match the annotations at the bottom of each page with the numbers in the code. Write the number in the slot in front of the corresponding annotation.

You'll use each annotation just once, and you'll need all of the annotations.

```java
import java.util.*;
public class DotComBust {

    private GameHelper helper = new GameHelper();
    private ArrayList<DotCom> dotComsList = new ArrayList<DotCom>();
    private int numOfGuesses = 0;

    private void setUpGame() {
        // first make some dot coms and give them locations
        DotCom one = new DotCom();
        one.setName("Pets.com");
        DotCom two = new DotCom();
        two.setName("eToys.com");
        DotCom three = new DotCom();
        three.setName("Go2.com");
        dotComsList.add(one);
        dotComsList.add(two);
        dotComsList.add(three);

        System.out.println("Your goal is to sink three dot coms.");
        System.out.println("Pets.com, eToys.com, Go2.com");
        System.out.println("Try to sink them all in the fewest number of guesses");

        for (DotCom dotComToSet : dotComsList) {
            ArrayList<String> newLocation = helper.placeDotCom(3);
            dotComToSet.setLocationCells(newLocation);
        } // close for loop
    } // close setUpGame method

    private void startPlaying() {
        while(!dotComsList.isEmpty()) {
            String userGuess = helper.getUserInput("Enter a guess");
            checkUserGuess(userGuess);
        } // close while
        finishGame();
    } // close startPlaying method
```

① declare and initialize the variables we'll need

⑧ get user input

③ ask the helper for a DotCom location

④ repeat with each DotCom in the list

③ print brief instructions for user

⑥ call the setter method on this DotCom to give it the location you just got from the helper

⑨ call our own checkUserGuess method

⑩ call our own finishGame method

② make three DotCom objects, give 'em names, and stick 'em in the ArrayList

⑦ as long as the DotCom list is NOT empty

Whatever you do,
DON'T turn the
page!

Not until you've
finished this
exercise.

Our version is on
the next page.
→

prep code	test code	real code

```
private void checkUserGuess(String userGuess) {

    numOfGuesses++; (11)
    String result  = "miss"; (12)

    for (DotCom dotComToTest : dotComsList) { (13)
       result = dotComToTest.checkYourself(userGuess); (14)
       if (result.equals("hit")) {
           break; (15)
       }
       if (result.equals("kill")) {
           dotComsList.remove(dotComToTest); (16)
           break;
       }
    } // close for
    System.out.println(result); (17)
} // close method


private void finishGame() {
    System.out.println("All Dot Coms are dead! Your stock is now worthless.");
    if (numOfGuesses <= 18) {
       System.out.println("It only took you " + numOfGuesses + " guesses.");
       System.out.println(" You got out before your options sank.");    (18)
    } else {
       System.out.println("Took you long enough. "+ numOfGuesses + " guesses.");
       System.out.println("Fish are dancing with your options.");
    }
} // close method

public static void main (String[] args) {
    DotComBust game = new DotComBust(); (19)
    game.setUpGame(); (20)
    game.startPlaying(); (21)
} // close method
}
```

(13) repeat with all DotComs in the list

(18) print a message telling the user how he did in the game

(17) print the result for the user

(16) this guy's dead, so take him out of the DotComs list then get out of the loop

(11) increment the number of guesses the user has made

(20) tell the game object to set up the game

(12) assume it's a 'miss', unless told otherwise

(15) get out of the loop early, no point in testing the others

(21) tell the game object to start the main game play loop (keeps asking for user input and checking the guess)

(14) ask the DotCom to check the user guess, looking for a hit (or kill)

(19) create the game object

the DotComBust code (the game)

`prep code` `test code` **real code**

```java
import java.util.*;
public class DotComBust {

    private GameHelper helper = new GameHelper();
    private ArrayList<DotCom> dotComsList = new ArrayList<DotCom>();
    private int numOfGuesses = 0;

    private void setUpGame() {
        // first make some dot coms and give them locations
        DotCom one = new DotCom();
        one.setName("Pets.com");
        DotCom two = new DotCom();
        two.setName("eToys.com");
        DotCom three = new DotCom();
        three.setName("Go2.com");
        dotComsList.add(one);
        dotComsList.add(two);
        dotComsList.add(three);

        System.out.println("Your goal is to sink three dot coms.");
        System.out.println("Pets.com, eToys.com, Go2.com");
        System.out.println("Try to sink them all in the fewest number of guesses");

        for (DotCom dotComToSet : dotComsList) {

            ArrayList<String> newLocation = helper.placeDotCom(3);

            dotComToSet.setLocationCells(newLocation);

        } // close for loop
    } // close setUpgame method

    private void startPlaying() {

        while(!dotComsList.isEmpty()) {

            String userGuess = helper.getUserInput("Enter a guess");
            checkUserGuess(userGuess);

        } // close while
        finishGame();
    } // close startPlaying method
```

Declare and initialize the variables we'll need.

Make an ArrayList of DotCom objects (in other words, a list that will hold ONLY DotCom objects, just as DotCom[] would mean an array of DotCom objects).

Make three DotCom objects, give 'em names, and stick 'em in the ArrayList.

Print brief instructions for user.

← Repeat with each DotCom in the list.

Ask the helper for a DotCom location (an ArrayList of Strings).

Call the setter method on this DotCom to give it the location you just got from the helper.

As long as the DotCom list is NOT empty (the ! means NOT, it's the same as (dotComsList.isEmpty() == false).

← Get user input.

Call our own checkUserGuess method.

← Call our own finishGame method.

prep code   test code   real code

```java
private void checkUserGuess (String userGuess) {

    numOfGuesses++;                                    ← increment the number of guesses the user has made

    String result  = "miss";                           ← assume it's a 'miss', unless told otherwise

    for (DotCom dotComToTest : dotComsList) {           ← repeat with all DotComs in the list

        result = dotComToTest.checkYourself(userGuess);  ← ask the DotCom to check the user
                                                            guess, looking for a hit (or kill)
        if (result.equals("hit")) {
                                                    ← get out of the loop early, no point
            break;                                     in testing the others
        }
        if (result.equals("kill")) {

            dotComsList.remove(dotComToTest);           ← this guy's dead, so take him out of the
            break;                                         DotComs list then get out of the loop
        }

    } // close for

    System.out.println(result);  ←  print the result for the user
} // close method


private void finishGame() {                                              print a message telling the
    System.out.println("All Dot Coms are dead! Your stock is now worthless.");  user how he did in the game
    if (numOfGuesses <= 18) {
        System.out.println("It only took you " + numOfGuesses + " guesses.");
        System.out.println(" You got out before your options sank.");
    } else {
        System.out.println("Took you long enough. "+ numOfGuesses + " guesses.");
        System.out.println("Fish are dancing with your options");
    }
} // close method


public static void main (String[] args) {
    DotComBust game = new DotComBust();  ←  create the game object
    game.setUpGame();                    ←  tell the game object to set up the game
    game.startPlaying();                 ←  tell the game object to start the main
} // close method                            game play loop (keeps asking for user
}                                            input and checking the guess)
```

prep code   test code   real code

The final version of the DotCom class

```java
import java.util.*;

public class DotCom {
    private ArrayList<String> locationCells;
    private String name;
```

DotCom's instance variables:
- an ArrayList of cell locations
- the DotCom's name

```java
    public void setLocationCells(ArrayList<String> loc) {
        locationCells = loc;
    }
```

← A setter method that updates the DotCom's location. (Random location provided by the GameHelper placeDotCom( ) method.)

```java
    public void setName(String n)
        name = n;
    }
```

← Your basic setter method

```java
    public String checkYourself(String userInput) {
        String result = "miss";
        int index = locationCells.indexOf(userInput);
```

The ArrayList indexOf( ) method in action! If the user guess is one of the entries in the ArrayList, indexOf( ) will return its ArrayList location. If not, indexOf( ) will return −1.

```java
        if (index >= 0) {
            locationCells.remove(index);
```

← Using ArrayList's remove( ) method to delete an entry.

```java
            if (locationCells.isEmpty()) {
```

← Using the isEmpty( ) method to see if all of the locations have been guessed

```java
                result = "kill";
                System.out.println("Ouch! You sunk " + name + "   : ( ");
            } else {
                result = "hit";
            }  // close if
        } // close if
        return result;
```

↖ Tell the user when a DotCom has been sunk.

← Return: 'miss' or 'hit' or 'kill'.

```java
    } // close method
} // close class
```

Super Powerful Boolean Expressions

So far, when we've used boolean expressions for our loops or `if` tests, they've been pretty simple. We will be using more powerful boolean expressions in some of the Ready-Bake code you're about to see, and even though we know you wouldn't peek, we thought this would be a good time to discuss how to energize your expressions.

'And' and 'Or' Operators (&&, ||)

Let's say you're writing a chooseCamera( ) method, with lots of rules about which camera to select. Maybe you can choose cameras ranging from $50 to $1000, but in some cases you want to limit the price range more precisely. You want to say something like:

'If the price *range* is between $300 **and** $400 then choose X.'

```
if (price >= 300 && price < 400) {
    camera = "X";
}
```

Let's say that of the ten camera brands available, you have some logic that applies to only a *few* of the list:

```
if (brand.equals("A") || brand.equals("B") ) {
    // do stuff for only brand A or brand B
}
```

Boolean expressions can get really big and complicated:

```
if ((zoomType.equals("optical") &&
    (zoomDegree >= 3 && zoomDegree <= 8)) ||
    (zoomType.equals("digital") &&
    (zoomDegree >= 5 && zoomDegree <= 12))) {
    // do appropriate zoom stuff
}
```

If you want to get *really* technical, you might wonder about the *precedence* of these operators. Instead of becoming an expert in the arcane world of precedence, we recommend that you **use parentheses** to make your code clear.

Not equals (!= and !)

Let's say that you have a logic like, "of the ten available camera models, a certain thing is *true for all but one*."

```
if (model != 2000) {
    // do non-model 2000 stuff
}
```

or for comparing objects like strings...

```
if (!brand.equals("X")) {
    // do non-brand X stuff
}
```

Short Circuit Operators (&& , ||)

The operators we've looked at so far, && and ||, are known as **short circuit** operators. In the case of &&, the expression will be true only if *both* sides of the && are true. So if the JVM sees that the left side of a && expression is false, it stops right there! Doesn't even bother to look at the right side.

Similarly, with ||, the expression will be true if *either* side is true, so if the JVM sees that the left side is true, it declares the entire statement to be true and doesn't bother to check the right side.

Why is this great? Let's say that you have a reference variable and you're not sure whether it's been assigned to an object. If you try to call a method using this null reference variable (i.e. no object has been assigned), you'll get a NullPointerException. So, try this:

```
if (refVar != null &&
    refVar.isValidType() ) {
    // do 'got a valid type' stuff
}
```

Non Short Circuit Operators (& , |)

When used in boolean expressions, the & and | operators act like their && and || counterparts, except that they force the JVM to *always* check *both* sides of the expression. Typically, & and | are used in another context, for manipulating bits.

Ready-bake: GameHelper

Ready-bake Code

This is the helper class for the game. Besides the user input method (that prompts the user and reads input from the command-line), the helper's Big Service is to create the cell locations for the DotComs. If we were you, we'd just back away slowly from this code, except to type it in and compile it. We tried to keep it fairly small to you wouldn't have to type so much, but that means it isn't the most readable code. And remember, you won't be able to compile the DotComBust game class until you have *this* class.

```java
import java.io.*;
import java.util.*;

public class GameHelper {

   private static final String alphabet = "abcdefg";
   private int gridLength = 7;
   private int gridSize = 49;
   private int [] grid = new int[gridSize];
   private int comCount = 0;

   public String getUserInput(String prompt) {
      String inputLine = null;
      System.out.print(prompt + "  ");
      try {
        BufferedReader is = new BufferedReader(
         new InputStreamReader(System.in));
        inputLine = is.readLine();
        if (inputLine.length() == 0 )  return null;
      } catch (IOException e) {
        System.out.println("IOException: " + e);
      }
      return inputLine.toLowerCase();
   }

   public ArrayList<String> placeDotCom(int comSize) {
      ArrayList<String> alphaCells = new ArrayList<String>();
      String [] alphacoords = new String [comSize];      // holds 'f6' type coords
      String temp = null;                                // temporary String for concat
      int [] coords = new int[comSize];                  // current candidate coords
      int attempts = 0;                                  // current attempts counter
      boolean success = false;                           // flag = found a good location ?
      int location = 0;                                  // current starting location

      comCount++;                                        // nth dot com to place
      int incr = 1;                                      // set horizontal increment
      if ((comCount % 2) == 1) {                         // if odd dot com (place vertically)
        incr = gridLength;                               // set vertical increment
      }

      while ( !success & attempts++ < 200 ) {            // main search loop  (32)
        location = (int) (Math.random() * gridSize);     // get random starting point
         //System.out.print(" try " + location);
        int x = 0;                                       // nth position in dotcom to place
         success = true;                                 // assume success
         while (success && x < comSize) {                // look for adjacent unused spots
            if (grid[location] == 0) {                   // if not already used
```

Note: For extra credit, you might try 'un-commenting' the System.out.print(ln)'s in the placeDotCom( ) method, just to watch it work! These print statements will let you "cheat" by giving you the location of the DotComs, but it will help you test it.

Ready-bake Code

GameHelper class code continued...

```java
      coords[x++] = location;                        // save location
      location += incr;                              // try 'next' adjacent
      if (location >= gridSize){                     // out of bounds - 'bottom'
        success = false;                             // failure
      }
      if (x>0 && (location % gridLength == 0)) {     // out of bounds - right edge
        success = false;                             // failure
      }
    } else {                                         // found already used location
        // System.out.print(" used " + location);
        success = false;                             // failure
    }
  }
}                                                    // end while

int x = 0;                                           // turn location into alpha coords
int row = 0;
int column = 0;
// System.out.println("\n");
while (x < comSize) {
  grid[coords[x]] = 1;                               // mark master grid pts. as 'used'
  row = (int) (coords[x] / gridLength);              // get row value
  column = coords[x] % gridLength;                   // get numeric column value
  temp = String.valueOf(alphabet.charAt(column));    // convert to alpha

  alphaCells.add(temp.concat(Integer.toString(row)));
  x++;
  // System.out.print("  coord "+x+" = " + alphaCells.get(x-1));
}

// System.out.println("\n");

  return alphaCells;
  }
}
```

This is the statement that tells you exactly where the DotCom is located.

Using the Library (the Java API)

You made it all the way through the DotComBust game, thanks to the help of ArrayList. And now, as promised, it's time to learn how to fool around in the Java library.

In the Java API, classes are grouped into packages.

To use a class in the API, you have to know which package the class is in.

Every class in the Java library belongs to a package. The package has a name, like **javax.swing** (a package that holds some of the Swing GUI classes you'll learn about soon). ArrayList is in the package called **java.util**, which surprise surprise, holds a pile of *utility* classes. You'll learn a lot more about packages in chapter 16, including how to put your *own* classes into your *own* packages. For now though, we're just looking to *use* some of the classes that come with Java.

Using a class from the API, in your own code, is simple. You just treat the class as though you wrote it yourself... as though you compiled it, and there it sits, waiting for you to use it. With one big difference: somewhere in your code you have to indicate the *full* name of the library class you want to use, and that means package name + class name.

Even if you didn't know it, *you've already been using classes from a package.* System (System.out.println), String, and Math (Math.random()), all belong to the **java.lang** package.

You have to know the __full__ name* of the class you want to use in your code.

ArrayList is not the *full* name of ArrayList, just as 'Kathy' isn't a full name (unless it's like Madonna or Cher, but we won't go there). The full name of ArrayList is actually:

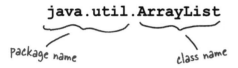

You have to tell Java which ArrayList you want to use. You have two options:

 IMPORT

Put an import statement at the top of your source code file:

```
import java.util.ArrayList;
public class MyClass {... }
```

OR

 TYPE

Type the full name everywhere in your code. Each time you use it. *Anywhere* you use it.

When you declare and/or instantiate it:

```
java.util.ArrayList<Dog> list = new java.util.ArrayList<Dog>();
```

When you use it as an argument type:

```
public void go(java.util.ArrayList<Dog> list) { }
```

When you use it as a return type:

```
public java.util.ArrayList<Dog> foo() {...}
```

*Unless the class is in the java.lang package.

---

there are no
Dumb Questions

Q: Why does there have to be a full name? Is that the only purpose of a package?

A: Packages are important for three main reasons. First, they help the overall organization of a project or library. Rather than just having one horrendously large pile of classes, they're all grouped into packages for specific kinds of functionality (like GUI, or data structures, or database stuff, etc.)

Second, packages give you a name-scoping, to help prevent collisions if you and 12 other programmers in your company all decide to make a class with the same name. If you have a class named Set and someone else (including the Java API) has a class named Set, you need some way to tell the JVM *which* Set class you're trying to use.

Third, packages provide a level of security, because you can restrict the code you write so that only other classes in the same package can access it. You'll learn all about that in chapter 16.

Q: OK, back to the name collision thing. How does a full name really help? What's to prevent two people from giving a class the same package name?

A: Java has a naming convention that usually prevents this from happening, as long as developers adhere to it. We'll get into that in more detail in chapter 16.

Where'd that 'x' come from?

(or, what does it mean when a package starts with javax?)

Geek Bits

In the first and second versions of Java (1.02 and 1.1), all classes that shipped with Java (in other words, the standard library) were in packages that began with *java*. There was always *java.lang*, of course — the one you don't have to import. And there was *java.net, java.io, java.util* (although there was no such thing as ArrayList way back then), and a few others, including the *java.awt* package that held GUI-related classes.

Looming on the horizon, though, were other packages not included in the standard library. These classes were known as *extensions,* and came in two main flavors: *standard*, and *not* standard. Standard extensions were those that Sun considered official, as opposed to experimental, early access, or beta packages that might or might not ever see the light of day.

Standard extensions, by convention, all began with an 'x' appended to the regular *java* package starter. The mother of all standard extensions was the Swing library. It included several packages, all of which began with *javax.swing*.

But standard extensions can get promoted to first-class, ships-with-Java, standard-out-of-the-box library packages. And that's what happened to Swing, beginning with version 1.2 (which eventually became the first version dubbed 'Java 2').

"Cool", everyone thought (including us). "Now everyone who has Java will have the Swing classes, and we won't have to figure out how to get those classes installed with our end-users."

Trouble was lurking beneath the surface, however, because when packages get promoted, well of COURSE they have to start with *java,* not *javax*. Everyone KNOWS that packages in the standard library don't have that "x", and that only extensions have the "x". So, just (and we mean just) before version 1.2 went final, Sun changed the package names and deleted the "x" (among other changes). Books were printed and in stores featuring Swing code with the new names. Naming conventions were intact. All was right with the Java world.

Except the 20,000 or so screaming developers who realized that with that simple name change came disaster! All of their Swing-using code had to be changed! The horror! Think of all those import statements that started with *javax*...

And in the final hour, desperate, as their hopes grew thin, the developers convinced Sun to "screw the convention, save our code". The rest is history. So when you see a package in the library that begins with *javax*, you know it started life as an extension, and then got a promotion.

BULLET POINTS

- **ArrayList** is a class in the Java API.

- To put something into an ArrayList, use **add()**.

- To remove something from an ArrayList use **remove()**.

- To find out where something is (and if it is) in an ArrayList, use i**ndexOf()**.

- To find out if an ArrayList is empty, use **isEmpty()**.

- To get the size (number of elements) in an ArrayList, use the **size()** *method*.

- To get the **length** (number of elements) in a regular old array, remember, you use the length **variable**.

- An ArrayList **resizes dynamically** to what-ever size is needed. It grows when objects are added, and it **shrinks** when objects are removed.

- You declare the type of the array using a **type parameter**, which is a type name in angle brackets. Example: ArrayList<Button> means the ArrayList will be able to hold only objects of type Button (or subclasses of Button as you'll learn in the next couple of chapters).

- Although an ArrayList holds objects and not primitives, the compiler will automatically "wrap" (and "unwrap" when you take it out) a primitive into an Object, and place that object in the ArrayList instead of the primitive. (More on this feature later in the book.)

- Classes are grouped into packages.

- A class has a full name, which is a combination of the package name and the class name. Class ArrayList is really java.util.ArrayList.

- To use a class in a package other than java.lang, you must tell Java the full name of the class.

- You use either an import statement at the top of your source code, or you can type the full name every place you use the class in your code.

there are no Dumb Questions

Q: Does `import` **make my class bigger? Does it actually compile the imported class or package into *my* code?**

A: Perhaps you're a C programmer? An `import` is not the same as an `include`. So the answer is no and no. Repeat after me: "an `import` statement saves you from typing." That's really it. You don't have to worry about your code becoming bloated, or slower, from too many imports. An `import` is simply the way you give Java the *full name of a class*.

Q: **OK, how come I never had to import the String class? Or System?**

A: Remember, you get the java.lang package sort of "pre-imported" for free. Because the classes in java.lang are so fundamental, you don't have to use the full name. There is only one java.lang.String class, and one java.lang.System class, and Java darn well knows where to find them.

Q: **Do I have to put my own classes into packages? How do I do that? *Can* I do that?**

A: In the real world (which you should try to avoid), yes, you *will* want to put your classes into packages. We'll get into that in detail in chapter 16. For now, we won't put our code examples in a package.

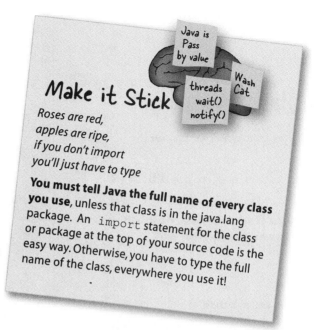

Make it Stick

Roses are red,
apples are ripe,
if you don't import
you'll just have to type

You must tell Java the full name of every class you use, unless that class is in the java.lang package. An `import` statement for the class or package at the top of your source code is the easy way. Otherwise, you have to type the full name of the class, everywhere you use it!

[notes: Java is Pass by value; threads wait() notify(); Wash Cat]

One more time, in the unlikely event that you don't already have this down:

import

or

"Good to know there's an ArrayList in the java.util package. But by myself, how would I have figured that out?"

- Julia, 31, hand model

How to play with the API

Two things you want to know:

1 **What classes are in the library?**

2 **Once you find a class, how do you know what it can do?**

1 **Browse a Book**

2 **Use the HTML API docs**

1 Browse a Book

Flipping through a reference book is the best way to find out what's in the Java library. You can easily stumble on a class that looks useful, just by browsing pages.

class name

package name

class description

methods (and other things we'll talk about later)

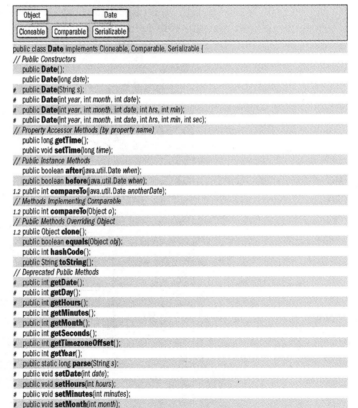

java.util.Currency

Returned By: java.text.DecimalFormat.getCurrency(), java.text.DecimalFormatSymbols.getCurrency(), java.text.NumberFormat.getCurrency(), Currency.getInstance()

Date   Java 1.0
java.util   *cloneable serializable comparable*

This class represents dates and times and lets you work with them in a system-independent way. You can create a **Date** by specifying the number of milliseconds from the epoch (midnight GMT, January 1st, 1970) or the year, month, date, and, optionally, the hour, minute, and second. Years are specified as the number of years since 1900. If you call the **Date** constructor with no arguments, the **Date** is initialized to the current time and date. The instance methods of the class allow you to get and set the various date and time fields, to compare dates and times, and to convert dates to and from string representations. As of Java 1.1, many of the date methods have been deprecated in favor of the methods of the **Calendar** class.

```
Object ———————— Date
Cloneable   Comparable   Serializable
```

```
public class Date implements Cloneable, Comparable, Serializable {
// Public Constructors
    public Date();
    public Date(long date);
#   public Date(String s);
#   public Date(int year, int month, int date);
#   public Date(int year, int month, int date, int hrs, int min);
#   public Date(int year, int month, int date, int hrs, int min, int sec);
// Property Accessor Methods (by property name)
    public long getTime();
    public void setTime(long time);
// Public Instance Methods
    public boolean after(java.util.Date when);
    public boolean before(java.util.Date when);
1.2 public int compareTo(java.util.Date anotherDate);
// Methods Implementing Comparable
1.2 public int compareTo(Object o);
// Public Methods Overriding Object
1.2 public Object clone();
    public boolean equals(Object obj);
    public int hashCode();
    public String toString();
// Deprecated Public Methods
#   public int getDate();
#   public int getDay();
#   public int getHours();
#   public int getMinutes();
#   public int getMonth();
#   public int getSeconds();
#   public int getTimezoneOffset();
#   public int getYear();
#   public static long parse(String s);
#   public void setDate(int date);
#   public void setHours(int hours);
#   public void setMinutes(int minutes);
#   public void setMonth(int month);
```

Use the HTML API docs

Java comes with a fabulous set of online docs called, strangely, the Java API. They're part of a larger set called the Java 5 Standard Edition Documentation (which, depending on what day of the week you look, Sun may be referring to as "Java 2 Standard Edition 5.0"), and you have to download the docs separately; they don't come shrink-wrapped with the Java 5 download. If you have a high-speed internet connection, or tons of patience, you can also browse them at java.sun.com. Trust us, you probably want these on your hard drive.

The API docs are the best reference for getting more details about a class and its methods. Let's say you were browsing through the reference book and found a class called Calendar, in java.util. The book tells you a little about it, enough to know that this is indeed what you want to use, but you still need to know more about the methods.

The reference book, for example, tells you what the methods take, as arguments, and what they return. Look at ArrayList, for example. In the reference book, you'll find the method indexOf(), that we used in the DotCom class. But if all you knew is that there is a method called indexOf() that takes an object and returns the index (an int) of that object, you still need to know one crucial thing: what happens if the object is not in the ArrayList? Looking at the method signature alone won't tell you how that works. But the API docs will (most of the time, anyway). The API docs tell you that the indexOf() method returns a -1 if the object parameter is not in the ArrayList. That's how we knew we could use it both as a way to check if an object is even *in* the ArrayList, and to get its index at the same time, if the object was there. But without the API docs, we might have thought that the indexOf() method would blow up if the object wasn't in the ArrayList.

① Scroll through the packages and select one (click it) to restrict the list in the lower frame to only classes from that package.

② Scroll through the classes and select one (click it) to choose the class that will fill the main browser frame.

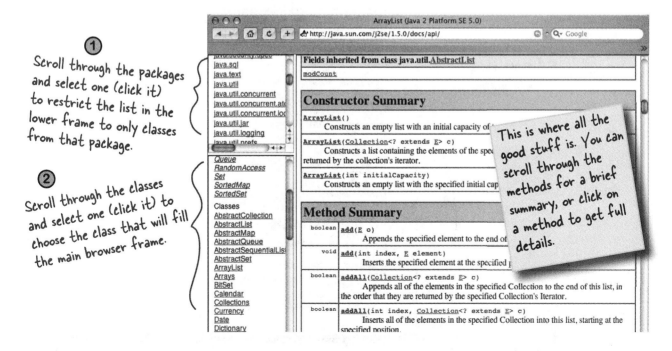

This is where all the good stuff is. You can scroll through the methods for a brief summary, or click on a method to get full details.

Code Magnets

Can you reconstruct the code snippets to make a working Java program that produces the output listed below? **NOTE:** To do this exercise, you need one NEW piece of info—if you look in the API for ArrayList, you'll find a *second* add method that takes two arguments:

add(int index, Object o)

It lets you specify to the ArrayList *where* to put the object you're adding.

```
a.remove(2);
```

```
printAL(a);
```

```
printAL(a);
```

```
a.add(0,"zero");
a.add(1,"one");
```

```
public static void printAL(ArrayList<String> al) {
```

```
if (a.contains("two")) {
    a.add("2.2");
}
```

```
a.add(2,"two");
```

```
public static void main (String[] args) {
```

```
System.out.print(element + "   ");
}
System.out.println(" ");
```

```
if (a.contains("three")) {
    a.add("four");
}
```

```
public class ArrayListMagnet {
```

```
if (a.indexOf("four") != 4) {
    a.add(4, "4.2");
}
```

```
}
```

```
}
```

```
import java.util.*;
```

```
}
```

```
printAL(a);
```

```
ArrayList<String> a = new ArrayList<String>();
```

```
for (String element : al) {
```

```
a.add(3,"three");
printAL(a);
```

```
File Edit Window Help Dance
% java ArrayListMagnet
zero   one    two    three
zero   one    three  four
zero   one    three  four   4.2
zero   one    three  four   4.2
```

JavaCross 7.0

How does this crossword puzzle help you learn Java? Well, all of the words **are** Java related (except one red herring).

Hint: When in doubt, remember ArrayList.

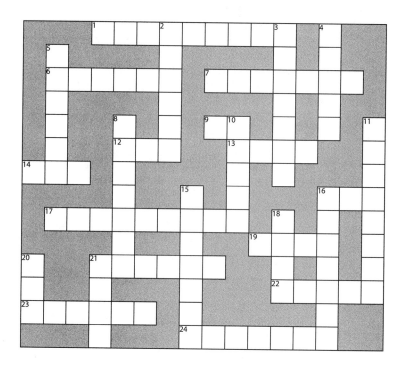

Across

1. I can't behave

6. Or, in the courtroom

7. Where it's at baby

9. A fork's origin

12. Grow an ArrayList

13. Wholly massive

14. Value copy

16. Not an object

17. An array on steroids

19. Extent

21. 19's counterpart

22. Spanish geek snacks   (Note: This has nothing to do with Java.)

23. For lazy fingers

24. Where packages roam

Down

2. Where the Java action is.

3. Addressable unit

4. 2nd smallest

5. Fractional default

8. Library's grandest

10. Must be low density

11. He's in there somewhere

15. As if

16. dearth method

18. What shopping and arrays have in common

20. Library acronym

21. What goes around

More Hints:

Down	Across
2. What's overridable?	1. 8 varieties
3. Think ArrayList	7. Think ArrayList
4. & 10. Primitive	16. Common primitive
16. Think ArrayList	21. Array's extent
18. He's making a _____	22. Not about Java - Spanish appetizers

Exercise Solutions

```java
import java.util.*;

public class ArrayListMagnet {

    public static void main (String[] args) {

        ArrayList<String> a = new ArrayList<String>();

        a.add(0,"zero");
        a.add(1,"one");

        a.add(2,"two");

        a.add(3,"three");
        printAL(a);

        if (a.contains("three")) {
            a.add("four");
        }

        a.remove(2);

        printAL(a);

        if (a.indexOf("four") != 4) {
            a.add(4, "4.2");
        }

        printAL(a);

        if (a.contains("two")) {
            a.add("2.2");
        }
        printAL(a);
    }

    public static void printAL(ArrayList<String> al) {

        for (String element : al) {

            System.out.print(element + "   ");
        }
        System.out.println(" ");
    }
}
```

```
File Edit Window Help Dance

% java ArrayListMagnet
zero   one   two   three
zero   one   three   four
zero   one   three   four   4.2
zero   one   three   four   4.2
```

JavaCross answers

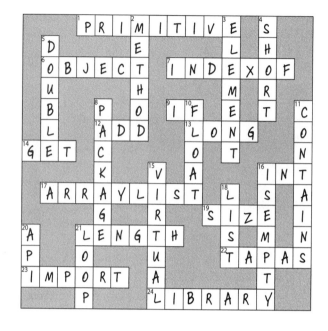

Sharpen your pencil

Write your OWN set of clues! Look at each word, and try to write your own clues. Try making them easier, or harder, or more technical than the ones we have.

Across

1. _____

6. _____

7. _____

9. _____

12. _____

13. _____

14. _____

16. _____

17. _____

19. _____

21. _____

22. _____

23. _____

24. _____

Down

2. _____

3. _____

4. _____

5. _____

8. _____

10. _____

11. _____

15. _____

16. _____

18. _____

20. _____

21. _____

Better Living in Objectville

We were underpaid, overworked coders 'till we tried the Polymorphism Plan. But thanks to the Plan, our future is bright. Yours can be too!

Plan your programs with the future in mind. If there were a way to write Java code such that you could take more vacations, how much would it be worth to you? What if you could write code that someone *else* could extend, **easily**? And if you could write code that was flexible, for those pesky last-minute spec changes, would that be something you're interested in? Then this is your lucky day. For just three easy payments of 60 minutes time, you can have all this. When you get on the Polymorphism Plan, you'll learn the 5 steps to better class design, the 3 tricks to polymorphism, the 8 ways to make flexible code, and if you act now—a bonus lesson on the 4 tips for exploiting inheritance. Don't delay, an offer this good will give you the design freedom and programming flexibility you deserve. It's quick, it's easy, and it's available now. Start today, and we'll throw in an extra level of abstraction!

Chair Wars Revisited...

Remember way back in chapter 2, when Larry (procedural guy) and Brad (OO guy) were vying for the Aeron chair? Let's look at a few pieces of that story to review the basics of inheritance.

LARRY: You've got duplicated code! The rotate procedure is in all four Shape things. It's a stupid design. You have to maintain four different rotate "methods". How can that ever be good?

BRAD: Oh, I guess you didn't see the final design. Let me show you how OO **inheritance** works, Larry.

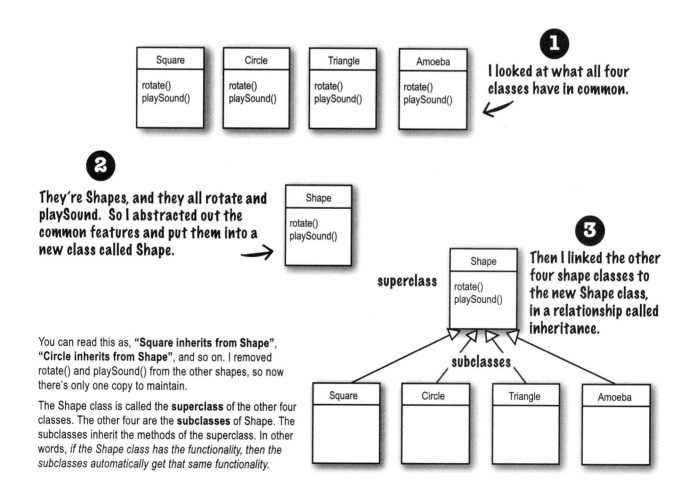

1 I looked at what all four classes have in common.

2 They're Shapes, and they all rotate and playSound. So I abstracted out the common features and put them into a new class called Shape.

3 Then I linked the other four shape classes to the new Shape class, in a relationship called inheritance.

superclass

subclasses

You can read this as, **"Square inherits from Shape"**, **"Circle inherits from Shape"**, and so on. I removed rotate() and playSound() from the other shapes, so now there's only one copy to maintain.

The Shape class is called the **superclass** of the other four classes. The other four are the **subclasses** of Shape. The subclasses inherit the methods of the superclass. In other words, *if the Shape class has the functionality, then the subclasses automatically get that same functionality.*

What about the Amoeba rotate()?

LARRY: Wasn't that the whole problem here — that the amoeba shape had a completely different rotate and playSound procedure?

How can amoeba do something different if it *inherits* its functionality from the Shape class?

BRAD: That's the last step. The Amoeba class *overrides* the methods of the Shape class. Then at runtime, the JVM knows exactly which *rotate()* method to run when someone tells the Amoeba to rotate.

Override Now
Ask Me How

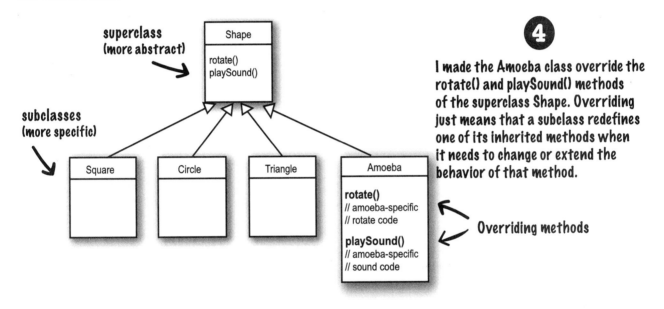

superclass
(more abstract)

Shape

rotate()
playSound()

subclasses
(more specific)

Square

Circle

Triangle

Amoeba

rotate()
// amoeba-specific
// rotate code

playSound()
// amoeba-specific
// sound code

4

I made the Amoeba class override the rotate() and playSound() methods of the superclass Shape. Overriding just means that a subclass redefines one of its inherited methods when it needs to change or extend the behavior of that method.

Overriding methods

BRAIN POWER

How would you represent a house cat and a tiger, in an inheritance structure. Is a domestic cat a specialized version of a tiger? Which would be the subclass and which would be the superclass? Or are they both subclasses to some *other* class?

How would you design an inheritance structure? What methods would be overridden?

Think about it. *Before* you turn the page.

Understanding Inheritance

When you design with inheritance, you put common code in a class and then tell other more specific classes that the common (more abstract) class is their superclass. When one class inherits from another, **the subclass inherits from the superclass.**

In Java, we say that the **subclass *extends* the superclass**. An inheritance relationship means that the subclass inherits the **members** of the superclass. When we say "members of a class" we mean the instance variables and methods.

For example, if PantherMan is a subclass of SuperHero, the PantherMan class automatically inherits the instance variables and methods common to all superheroes including `suit`, `tights`, `specialPower`, `useSpecialPower()` and so on. But the PantherMan **subclass can add new methods and instance variables** of its own, and it **can override the methods it inherits from the superclass** SuperHero.

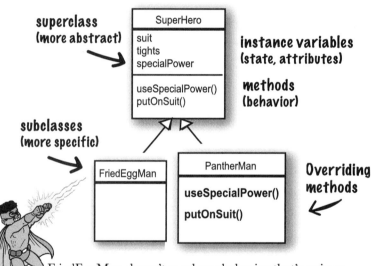

FriedEggMan doesn't need any behavior that's unique, so he doesn't override any methods. The methods and instance variables in SuperHero are sufficient.

PantherMan, though, has specific requirements for his suit and special powers, so `useSpecialPower()` and `putOnSuit()` are both overridden in the PantherMan class.

Instance variables are not overridden because they don't need to be. They don't define any special behavior, so a subclass can give an inherited instance variable any value it chooses. PantherMan can set his inherited `tights` to purple, while FriedEggMan sets his to white.

An inheritance example:

```java
public class Doctor {

    boolean worksAtHospital;

    void treatPatient() {
      // perform a checkup

    }
}

public class FamilyDoctor extends Doctor {

    boolean makesHouseCalls;
    void giveAdvice() {
      // give homespun advice
    }

}

public class Surgeon extends Doctor{

    void treatPatient() {
      // perform surgery
    }

    void makeIncision() {
      // make incision (yikes!)
    }
}
```

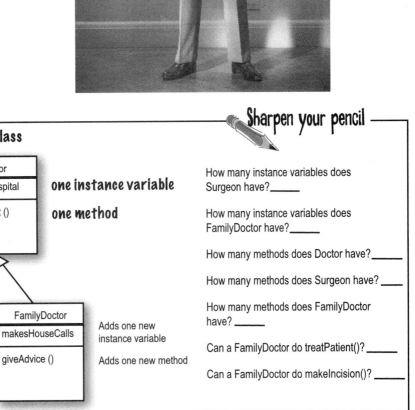

> I inherited my procedures so I didn't bother with medical school. Relax, this won't hurt a bit. (now where did I put that power saw...)

Sharpen your pencil

superclass

Doctor
worksAtHospital
treatPatient ()

one instance variable

one method

subclasses

Overrides the inherited treatPatient() method

Adds one new method

Surgeon
treatPatient ()
makeIncision()

FamilyDoctor
makesHouseCalls
giveAdvice ()

Adds one new instance variable

Adds one new method

How many instance variables does Surgeon have?_____

How many instance variables does FamilyDoctor have?_____

How many methods does Doctor have?_____

How many methods does Surgeon have?_____

How many methods does FamilyDoctor have? _____

Can a FamilyDoctor do treatPatient()? _____

Can a FamilyDoctor do makeIncision()? _____

Let's design the inheritance tree for an Animal simulation program

Imagine you're asked to design a simulation program that lets the user throw a bunch of different animals into an environment to see what happens. We don't have to code the thing now, we're mostly interested in the design.

We've been given a list of *some* of the animals that will be in the program, but not all. We know that each animal will be represented by an object, and that the objects will move around in the environment, doing whatever it is that each particular type is programmed to do.

And we want other programmers to be able to add new kinds of animals to the program at any time.

First we have to figure out the common, abstract characteristics that all animals have, and build those characteristics into a class that all animal classes can extend.

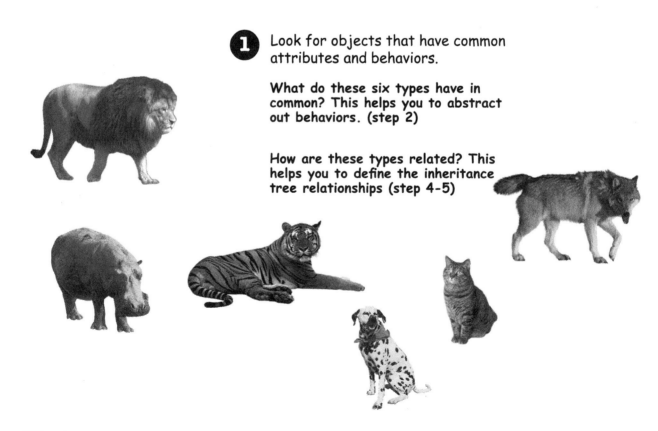

1 Look for objects that have common attributes and behaviors.

What do these six types have in common? This helps you to abstract out behaviors. (step 2)

How are these types related? This helps you to define the inheritance tree relationships (step 4-5)

Using inheritance to avoid duplicating code in subclasses

We have five *instance variables:*

picture – the file name representing the JPEG of this animal

food – the type of food this animal eats. Right now, there can be only two values: *meat* or *grass*.

hunger – an int representing the hunger level of the animal. It changes depending on when (and how much) the animal eats.

boundaries – values representing the height and width of the 'space' (for example, 640 x 480) that the animals will roam around in.

location – the X and Y coordinates for where the animal is in the space.

We have four *methods:*

makeNoise () – behavior for when the animal is supposed to make noise.

eat() – behavior for when the animal encounters its preferred food source, *meat* or *grass*.

sleep() – behavior for when the animal is considered asleep.

roam() – behavior for when the animal is not eating or sleeping (probably just wandering around waiting to bump into a food source or a boundary).

Design a class that represents the common state and behavior.

These objects are all animals, so we'll make a common superclass called Animal.

We'll put in methods and instance variables that all animals might need.

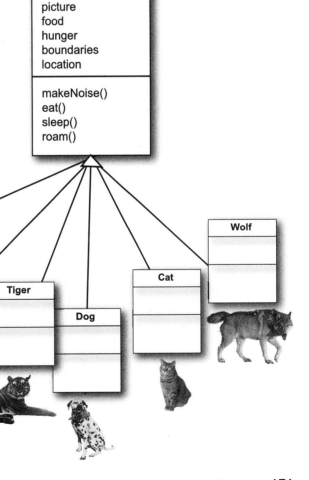

Do all animals eat the same way?

Assume that we all agree on one thing: the instance variables will work for *all* Animal types. A lion will have his own value for picture, food (we're thinking *meat*), hunger, boundaries, and location. A hippo will have different *values* for his instance variables, but he'll still have the same variables that the other Animal types have. Same with dog, tiger, and so on. But what about *behavior*?

Which methods should we override?

Does a lion make the same **noise** as a dog? Does a cat **eat** like a hippo? Maybe in *your* version, but in ours, eating and making noise are Animal-type-specific. We can't figure out how to code those methods in such a way that they'd work for any animal. OK, that's not true. We could write the makeNoise() method, for example, so that all it does is play a sound file defined in an instance variable for that type, but that's not very specialized. Some animals might make different noises for different situations (like one for eating, and another when bumping into an enemy, etc.)

So just as with the Amoeba overriding the Shape class rotate() method, to get more amoeba-specific (in other words, *unique*) behavior, we'll have to do the same for our Animal subclasses.

3 Decide if a subclass needs behaviors (method implementations) that are specific to that particular subclass type.

Looking at the Animal class, we decide that eat() and makeNoise() should be overridden by the individual subclasses.

> I'm one bad*ss plant-eater.

> In the dog community, barking is an important part of our cultural identity. We have a unique sound, and we want that diversity to be recognized and respected.

Animal
picture
food
hunger
boundaries
location
makeNoise()
eat()
sleep()
roam()

We better override these two methods, eat() and makeNoise(), so that each animal type can define its own specific behavior for eating and making noise. For now, it looks like sleep() and roam() can stay generic.

Looking for more inheritance opportunities

The class hierarchy is starting to shape up. We have each subclass override the *makeNoise()* and *eat()* methods, so that there's no mistaking a Dog bark from a Cat meow (quite insulting to both parties). And a Hippo won't eat like a Lion.

But perhaps there's more we can do. We have to look at the subclasses of Animal, and see if two or more can be grouped together in some way, and given code that's common to only *that* new group. Wolf and Dog have similarities. So do Lion, Tiger, and Cat.

Look for more opportunities to use abstraction, by finding two or more *subclasses* that might need common behavior.

We look at our classes and see that Wolf and Dog might have some behavior in common, and the same goes for Lion, Tiger, and Cat.

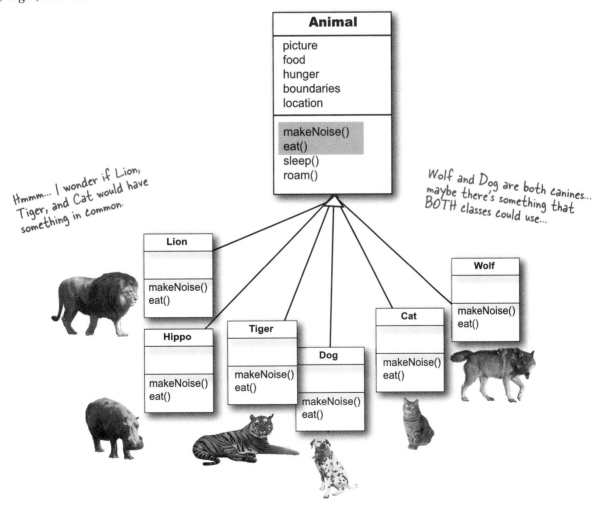

Hmmm... I wonder if Lion, Tiger, and Cat would have something in common.

Wolf and Dog are both canines... maybe there's something that BOTH classes could use...

Animal

picture
food
hunger
boundaries
location

makeNoise()
eat()
sleep()
roam()

Lion

makeNoise()
eat()

Hippo

makeNoise()
eat()

Tiger

makeNoise()
eat()

Dog

makeNoise()
eat()

Cat

makeNoise()
eat()

Wolf

makeNoise()
eat()

5 Finish the class hierarchy

Since animals already have an organizational hierarchy (the whole kingdom, genus, phylum thing), we can use the level that makes the most sense for class design. We'll use the biological "families" to organize the animals by making a Feline class and a Canine class.

We decide that Canines could use a common roam() method, because they tend to move in packs. We also see that Felines could use a common roam() method, because they tend to avoid others of their own kind. We'll let Hippo continue to use its inherited roam() method— the generic one it gets from Animal.

So we're done with the design for now; we'll come back to it later in the chapter.

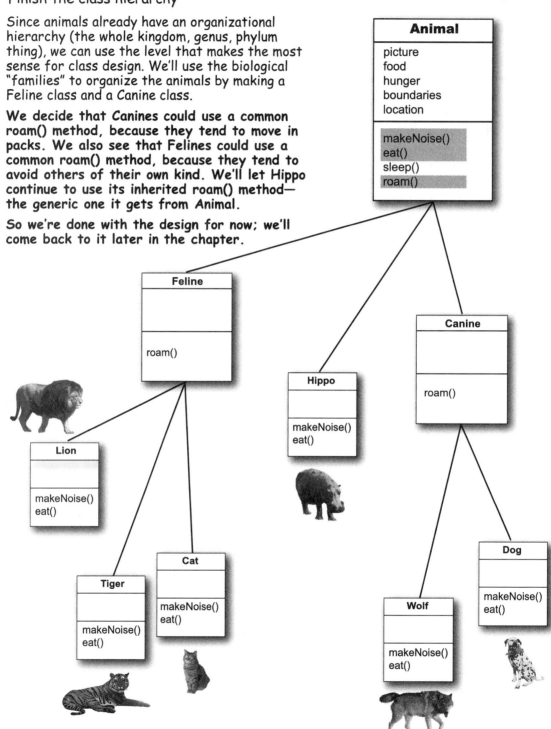

Which method is called?

The Wolf class has four methods. One inherited from Animal, one inherited from Canine (which is actually an overridden version of a method in class Animal), and two overridden in the Wolf class. When you create a Wolf object and assign it to a variable, you can use the dot operator on that reference variable to invoke all four methods. But which *version* of those methods gets called?

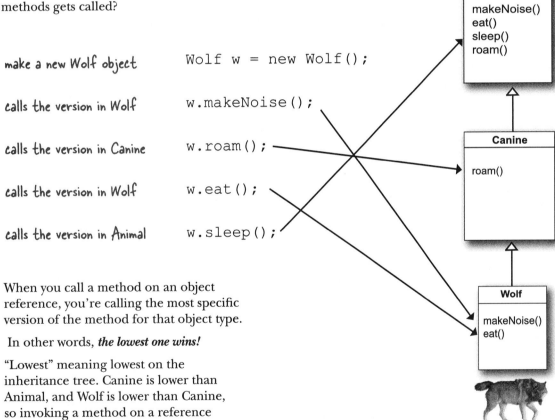

make a new Wolf object

`Wolf w = new Wolf();`

calls the version in Wolf

`w.makeNoise();`

calls the version in Canine

`w.roam();`

calls the version in Wolf

`w.eat();`

calls the version in Animal

`w.sleep();`

Animal

makeNoise()
eat()
sleep()
roam()

Canine

roam()

Wolf

makeNoise()
eat()

When you call a method on an object reference, you're calling the most specific version of the method for that object type.

In other words, *the lowest one wins!*

"Lowest" meaning lowest on the inheritance tree. Canine is lower than Animal, and Wolf is lower than Canine, so invoking a method on a reference to a Wolf object means the JVM starts looking first in the Wolf class. If the JVM doesn't find a version of the method in the Wolf class, it starts walking back up the inheritance hierarchy until it finds a match.

Designing an Inheritance Tree

Class	Superclasses	Subclasses
Clothing	---	Boxers, Shirt
Boxers	Clothing	
Shirt	Clothing	

Inheritance Table

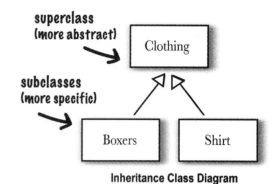

superclass
(more abstract)

subclasses
(more specific)

Inheritance Class Diagram

Sharpen your pencil

Find the relationships that make sense. Fill in the last two columns

Class	Superclasses	Subclasses
Musician		
Rock Star		
Fan		
Bass Player		
Concert Pianist		

Hint: not everything can be connected to something else.
Hint: you're allowed to add to or change the classes listed.

Draw an inheritance diagram here.

there are no Dumb Questions

Q: You said that the JVM starts walking up the inheritance tree, starting at the class type you invoked the method on (like the Wolf example on the previous page). But what happens if the JVM doesn't ever find a match?

A: Good question! But you don't have to worry about that. The compiler guarantees that a particular method is callable for a specific reference type, but it doesn't say (or care) from which *class* that method actually comes from at runtime. With the Wolf example, the compiler checks for a sleep() method, but doesn't care that sleep() is actually defined in (and inherited from) class Animal. Remember that if a class *inherits* a method, it *has* the method.

Where the inherited method is defined (in other words, in which superclass it is defined) makes no difference to the compiler. But at runtime, **the JVM will always pick the right one**. And the right one means, ***the most specific version for that particular object.***

Using IS-A and HAS-A

Remember that when one class inherits from another, we say that the subclass *extends* the superclass. When you want to know if one thing should extend another, apply the IS-A test.

Triangle IS-A Shape, yeah, that works.

Cat IS-A Feline, that works too.

Surgeon IS-A Doctor, still good.

Tub extends Bathroom, sounds reasonable.
Until you apply the IS-A test.

To know if you've designed your types correctly, ask, "Does it make sense to say type X IS-A type Y?" If it doesn't, you know there's something wrong with the design, so if we apply the IS-A test, Tub IS-A Bathroom is definitely false.

What if we reverse it to Bathroom extends Tub? That still doesn't work, Bathroom IS-A Tub doesn't work.

Tub and Bathroom *are* related, but not through inheritance. Tub and Bathroom are joined by a HAS-A relationship. Does it make sense to say "Bathroom HAS-A Tub"? If yes, then it means that Bathroom has a Tub instance variable. In other words, Bathroom has a *reference* to a Tub, but Bathroom does not *extend* Tub and vice-versa.

> Does it make sense to say a Tub IS-A Bathroom? Or a Bathroom IS-A Tub? Well it doesn't to me. The relationship between my Tub and my Bathroom is HAS-A. Bathroom HAS-A Tub. That means Bathroom has a Tub instance variable.

Tub
int size; Bubbles b;

Bathroom
Tub bathtub; Sink theSink;

Bubbles
int radius; int colorAmt;

Bathroom HAS-A Tub and Tub HAS-A Bubbles.
But nobody inherits from (extends) anybody else.

But wait! There's more!

The IS-A test works *anywhere* in the inheritance tree. If your inheritance tree is well-designed, the IS-A test should make sense when you ask *any* subclass if it IS-A *any* of its supertypes.

If class B extends class A, class B IS-A class A.

This is true anywhere in the inheritance tree. If class C extends class B, class C passes the IS-A test for both B *and* A.

Canine extends Animal

Wolf extends Canine

Wolf extends Animal

Canine IS-A Animal

Wolf IS-A Canine

Wolf IS-A Animal

Animal

makeNoise()
eat()
sleep()
roam()

Canine

roam()

Wolf

makeNoise()
eat()

With an inheritance tree like the one shown here, you're *always* allowed to say **"Wolf extends Animal"** or "Wolf IS-A Animal". It makes no difference if Animal is the superclass of the superclass of Wolf. In fact, **as long as Animal is *somewhere* in the inheritance hierarchy above Wolf, Wolf IS-A Animal will always be true.**

The structure of the Animal inheritance tree says to the world:

"Wolf IS-A Canine, so Wolf can do anything a Canine can do. And Wolf IS-A Animal, so Wolf can do anything an Animal can do."

It makes no difference if Wolf overrides some of the methods in Animal or Canine. As far as the world (of other code) is concerned, a Wolf can do those four methods. *How* he does them, or *in which class they're overridden* makes no difference. A Wolf can makeNoise(), eat(), sleep(), and roam() because a Wolf extends from class Animal.

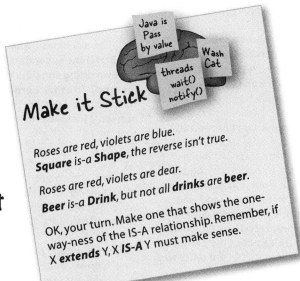

Java is
Pass
by value

Wash
Cat

threads
wait()
notify()

Roses are red, violets are blue.
Square is-a **Shape**, the reverse isn't true.

Roses are red, violets are dear.
Beer is-a **Drink**, but not all **drinks** are **beer**.

OK, your turn. Make one that shows the one-way-ness of the IS-A relationship. Remember, if X **extends** Y, X **IS-A** Y must make sense.

How do you know if you've got your inheritance right?

There's obviously more to it than what we've covered so far, but we'll look at a lot more OO issues in the next chapter (where we eventually refine and improve on some of the design work we did in *this* chapter).

For now, though, a good guideline is to use the IS-A test. If "X IS-A Y" makes sense, both classes (X and Y) should probably live in the same inheritance hierarchy. Chances are, they have the same or overlapping behaviors.

Keep in mind that the inheritance IS-A relationship works in only *one* direction!

Triangle IS-A Shape makes sense, so you can have Triangle extend Shape.

But the reverse—Shape IS-A Triangle—does *not* make sense, so Shape should not extend Triangle. Remember that the IS-A relationship implies that if X IS-A Y, then X can do anything a Y can do (and possibly more).

Sharpen your pencil

Put a check next to the relationships that make sense.

☐ **Oven extends Kitchen**

☐ **Guitar extends Instrument**

☐ **Person extends Employee**

☐ **Ferrari extends Engine**

☐ **FriedEgg extends Food**

☐ **Beagle extends Pet**

☐ **Container extends Jar**

☐ **Metal extends Titanium**

☐ **GratefulDead extends Band**

☐ **Blonde extends Smart**

☐ **Beverage extends Martini**

Hint: apply the IS-A test

there are no
Dumb Questions

Q: So we see how a subclass gets to inherit a superclass method, but what if the superclass wants to use the subclass version of the method?

A: A superclass won't necessarily *know* about any of its subclasses. You might write a class and much later someone else comes along and extends it. But even if the superclass creator does know about (and wants to use) a subclass version of a method, there's no sort of *reverse* or *backwards* inheritance. Think about it, children inherit from parents, not the other way around.

Q: In a subclass, what if I want to use BOTH the superclass version and my overriding subclass version of a method? In other words, I don't want to completely *replace* the superclass version, I just want to add more stuff to it.

A: You can do this! And it's an important design feature. Think of the word "extends" as meaning, "I want to *extend* the functionality of the superclass".

```
public void roam() {
    super.roam();
    // my own roam stuff
}
```

this calls the inherited version of roam(), then comes back to do your own subclass-specific code

You can design your superclass methods in such a way that they contain method implementations that will work for any subclass, even though the subclasses may still need to 'append' more code. In your subclass overriding method, you can call the superclass version using the keyword **super**. It's like saying, "first go run the superclass version, then come back and finish with my own code..."

Who gets the Porsche, who gets the porcelain?
(how to know what a subclass can inherit from its superclass)

A subclass inherits members of the superclass. Members include instance variables and methods, although later in this book we'll look at other inherited members. A superclass can choose whether or not it wants a subclass to inherit a particular member by the level of access the particular member is given.

There are four access levels that we'll cover in this book. Moving from most restrictive to least, the four access levels are:

private   default   protected   public

Access levels control *who sees what,* and are crucial to having well-designed, robust Java code. For now we'll focus just on public and private. The rules are simple for those two:

> **public** members *are* inherited
> **private** members are *not* inherited

When a subclass inherits a member, it is ***as if the subclass defined the member itself***. In the Shape example, Square inherited the `rotate()` and `playSound()` methods and to the outside world (other code) the Square class simply *has* a `rotate()` and `playSound()` method.

The members of a class include the variables and methods defined in the class plus anything inherited from a superclass.

Note: get more details about default and protected in chapter 16 (deployment) and appendix B.

When designing with inheritance, are you USING or abusing?

Although some of the reasons behind these rules won't be revealed until later in this book, for now, simply *knowing* a few rules will help you build a better inheritance design.

DO use inheritance when one class is a more specific type of a superclass. Example: Willow *is a* more specific type of Tree, so Willow *extends* Tree makes sense.

DO consider inheritance when you have behavior (implemented code) that should be shared among multiple classes of the same general type. Example: Square, Circle, and Triangle all need to rotate and play sound, so putting that functionality in a superclass Shape might make sense, and makes for easier maintenance and extensibility. Be aware, however, that while inheritance is one of the key features of object-oriented programming, it's not necessarily the best way to achieve behavior reuse. It'll get you started, and often it's the right design choice, but design patterns will help you see other more subtle and flexible options. If you don't know about design patterns, a good follow-on to this book would be *Head First Design Patterns*.

DO NOT use inheritance just so that you can reuse code from another class, if the relationship between the superclass and subclass violate either of the above two rules. For example, imagine you wrote special printing code in the Alarm class and now you need printing code in the Piano class, so you have Piano extend Alarm so that Piano inherits the printing code. That makes no sense! A Piano is *not* a more specific type of Alarm. (So the printing code should be in a Printer class, that all printable objects can take advantage of via a HAS-A relationship.)

DO NOT use inheritance if the subclass and superclass do not pass the IS-A test. Always ask yourself if the subclass IS-A more specific type of the superclass. Example: Tea IS-A Beverage makes sense. Beverage IS-A Tea does not.

BULLET POINTS

- A subclass *extends* a superclass.

- A subclass inherits all *public* instance variables and methods of the superclass, but does not inherit the *private* instance variables and methods of the superclass.

- Inherited methods *can* be overridden; instance variables *cannot* be overridden (although they can be *redefined* in the subclass, but that's not the same thing, and there's almost never a need to do it.)

- Use the IS-A test to verify that your inheritance hierarchy is valid. If X *extends* Y, then X *IS-A* Y must make sense.

- The IS-A relationship works in only one direction. A Hippo is an Animal, but not all Animals are Hippos.

- When a method is overridden in a subclass, and that method is invoked on an instance of the subclass, the overridden version of the method is called. (*The lowest one wins.*)

- If class B extends A, and C extends B, class B IS-A class A, and class C IS-A class B, and class C also IS-A class A.

So what does all this inheritance really buy you?

You get a lot of OO mileage by designing with inheritance. You can get rid of duplicate code by abstracting out the behavior common to a group of classes, and sticking that code in a superclass. That way, when you need to modify it, you have only one place to update, and *the change is magically reflected in all the classes that inherit that behavior.* Well, there's no magic involved, but it *is* pretty simple: make the change and compile the class again. That's it. **You don't have to touch the subclasses!**

Just deliver the newly-changed superclass, and all classes that extend it will automatically use the new version.

A Java program is nothing but a pile of classes, so the subclasses don't have to be recompiled in order to use the new version of the superclass. As long as the superclass doesn't *break* anything for the subclass, everything's fine. (We'll discuss what the word 'break' means in this context, later in the book. For now, think of it as modifying something in the superclass that the subclass is depending on, like a particular method's arguments or return type, or method name, etc.)

① **You avoid duplicate code.**

Put common code in one place, and let the subclasses inherit that code from a superclass. When you want to change that behavior, you have to modify it in only one place, and everybody else (i.e. all the subclasses) see the change.

② **You define a common protocol for a group of classes.**

Um, what the heck does THAT mean?

Inheritance lets you guarantee that all classes grouped under a certain supertype have all the methods that the supertype has.*

In other words, you define a common protocol for a set of classes related through inheritance.

When you define methods in a superclass, that can be inherited by subclasses, you're announcing a kind of protocol to other code that says, "All my subtypes (i.e. subclasses) can do these things, with these methods that look like this..."

In other words, you establish a *contract*.

Class Animal establishes a common protocol for all Animal subtypes:

```
Animal

makeNoise()
eat()
sleep()
roam()
```

You're telling the world that any Animal can do these four things. That includes the method arguments and return types.

And remember, when we say *any Animal,* we mean Animal *and any class that extends from Animal.* Which again means, *any class that has Animal somewhere above it in the inheritance hierarchy.*

But we're not even at the really cool part yet, because we saved the best—*polymorphism*—for last.

When you define a supertype for a group of classes, *any subclass of that supertype can be substituted where the supertype is expected.*

Say, what?

Don't worry, we're nowhere near done explaining it. Two pages from now, you'll be an expert.

And I care because...

Because you get to take advantage of polymorphism.

Which matters to me because...

Because you get to refer to a subclass object using a reference declared as the supertype.

And that means to me...

You get to write really flexible code. Code that's cleaner (more efficient, simpler). Code that's not just easier to *develop,* but also much, much easier to *extend,* in ways you never imagined at the time you originally wrote your code.

That means you can take that tropical vacation while your co-workers update the program, and your co-workers might not even need your source code.

You'll see how it works on the next page.

We don't know about you, but personally, we find the whole tropical vacation thing particularly motivating.

*When we say "all the methods" we mean "all the *inheritable* methods", which for now actually means, "all the *public* methods", although later we'll refine that definition a bit more.

The 3 steps of object declaration and assignment

$$\overbrace{\text{Dog}\ \underbrace{\text{myDog}}_{3}}^{1} = \overbrace{\text{new Dog}()}^{2};$$

1 Declare a reference variable

Dog myDog = new Dog();

Tells the JVM to allocate space for a reference variable. The reference variable is, forever, of type Dog. In other words, a remote control that has buttons to control a Dog, but not a Cat or a Button or a Socket.

Dog

To see how polymorphism works, we have to step back and look at the way we *normally* declare a reference and create an object...

2 Create an object

Dog myDog = **new Dog()**;

Tells the JVM to allocate space for a new Dog object on the garbage collectible heap.

Dog object

3 Link the object and the reference

Dog myDog **=** new Dog();

Assigns the new Dog to the reference variable myDog. In other words, ***program the remote control.***

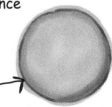

Dog object

Dog

The important point is that the reference type AND the object type are the same.

In this example, both are <u>Dog</u>.

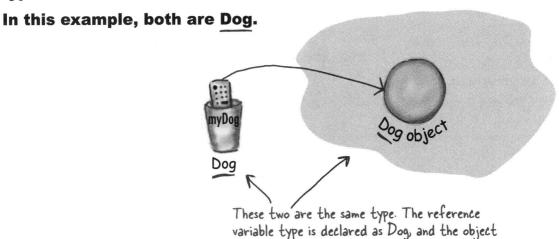

These two are the same type. The reference variable type is declared as Dog, and the object is created as new Dog().

But with polymorphism, the reference and the object can be _different_.

```
Animal myDog = new Dog();
```

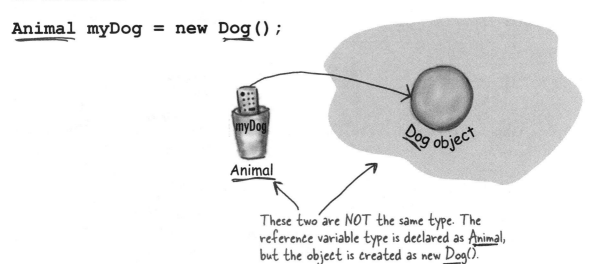

These two are NOT the same type. The reference variable type is declared as <u>Animal</u>, but the object is created as new <u>Dog()</u>.

With polymorphism, the reference type can be a superclass of the actual object type.

When you declare a reference variable, any object that passes the IS-A test for the declared type of the reference variable can be assigned to that reference. In other words, anything that *extends* the declared reference variable type can be *assigned* to the reference variable. **This lets you do things like make polymorphic arrays.**

uh... nope. Still not gettin' it.

OK, OK maybe an example will help.

Declare an array of type Animal. In other words, an array that will hold objects of type Animal.

```
Animal[] animals = new Animal[5];

animals [0] = new Dog();

animals [1] = new Cat();

animals [2] = new Wolf();

animals [3] = new Hippo();

animals [4] = new Lion();


for (int i = 0; i < animals.length; i++) {

    animals[i].eat();

    animals[i].roam();
}
```

But look what you get to do... you can put ANY subclass of Animal in the Animal array!

And here's the best polymorphic part (the raison d'être for the whole example), you get to loop through the array and call one of the Animal-class methods, and every object does the right thing!

When 'i' is 0, a Dog is at index 0 in the array, so you get the Dog's eat() method. When 'i' is 1, you get the Cat's eat() method

Same with roam().

But wait! There's more!

You can have polymorphic arguments and return types.

If you can declare a reference variable of a supertype, say, Animal, and assign a subclass object to it, say, Dog, think of how that might work when the reference is an argument to a method...

```
class Vet {

    public void giveShot(Animal a) {

        // do horrible things to the Animal at

        // the other end of the 'a' parameter

        a.makeNoise();

    }

}
```

The Animal parameter can take ANY Animal type as the argument. And when the Vet is done giving the shot, it tells the Animal to makeNoise(), and whatever Animal is really out there on the heap, that's whose makeNoise() method will run.

```
class PetOwner {

    public void start() {

        Vet v = new Vet();

        Dog d = new Dog();

        Hippo h = new Hippo();

        v.giveShot(d);

        v.giveShot(h);

    }

}
```

The Vet's giveShot() method can take any Animal you give it. As long as the object you pass in as the argument is a subclass of Animal, it will work.

← *Dog's makeNoise() runs*

← *Hippo's makeNoise() runs*

> NOW I get it! If I write my code using polymorphic arguments, where I declare the method parameter as a superclass type, I can pass in any subclass object at runtime. Cool. Because that also means I can write my code, go on vacation, and someone else can add new subclass types to the program and my methods will still work... (the only downside is I'm just making life easier for that idiot Jim).

With polymorphism, you can write code that doesn't have to change when you introduce new subclass types into the program.

Remember that Vet class? If you write that Vet class using arguments declared as type *Animal*, your code can handle any Animal *subclass*. That means if others want to take advantage of your Vet class, all they have to do is make sure *their* new Animal types extend class Animal. The Vet methods will still work, even though the Vet class was written without any knowledge of the new Animal subtypes the Vet will be working on.

BRAIN POWER

Why is polymorphism guaranteed to work this way? Why is it always safe to assume that any *subclass* type will have the methods you think you're calling on the *superclass* type (the superclass reference type you're using the dot operator on)?

there are no
Dumb Questions

Q: **Are there any practical limits on the levels of subclassing? How deep can you go?**

A: If you look in the Java API, you'll see that most inheritance hierarchies are wide but not deep. Most are no more than one or two levels deep, although there are exceptions (especially in the GUI classes). You'll come to realize that it usually makes more sense to keep your inheritance trees shallow, but there isn't a hard limit (well, not one that you'd ever run into).

Q: **Hey, I just thought of something... if you don't have access to the source code for a class, but you want to change the way a method of that class works, could you use subclassing to do that? To extend the "bad" class and override the method with your own better code?**

A: Yep. That's one cool feature of OO, and sometimes it saves you from having to rewrite the class from scratch, or track down the programmer who hid the source code.

Q: **Can you extend *any* class? Or is it like class members where if the class is private you can't inherit it...**

A: There's no such thing as a private class, except in a very special case called an *inner* class, that we haven't looked at yet. But there *are* three things that can prevent a class from being subclassed.

The first is access control. Even though a class *can't* be marked `private`, a class *can* be non-public (what you get if you don't declare the class as `public`). A non-public class can be subclassed only by classes in the same package as the class. Classes in a different package won't be able to subclass (or even *use*, for that matter) the non-public class.

The second thing that stops a class from being subclassed is the keyword modifier `final`. A final class means that it's the end of the inheritance line. Nobody, ever, can extend a final class.

The third issue is that if a class has only `private` constructors (we'll look at constructors in chapter 9), it can't be subclassed.

Q: **Why would you ever want to make a final class? What advantage would there be in preventing a class from being subclassed?**

A: Typically, you won't make your classes final. But if you need security — the security of knowing that the methods will always work the way that you wrote them (because they can't be overridden), a final class will give you that. A lot of classes in the Java API are final for that reason. The String class, for example, is final because, well, imagine the havoc if somebody came along and changed the way Strings behave!

Q: **Can you make a *method* final, without making the whole *class* final?**

A: If you want to protect a specific method from being overridden, mark the *method* with the `final` modifier. Mark the whole *class* as final if you want to guarantee that *none* of the methods in that class will ever be overridden.

Keeping the contract: rules for overriding

When you override a method from a superclass, you're agreeing to fulfill the contract. The contract that says, for example, "I take no arguments and I return a boolean." In other words, the arguments and return types of your overriding method must look to the outside world *exactly* like the overridden method in the superclass.

The methods *are* the contract.

If polymorphism is going to work, the Toaster's version of the overridden method from Appliance has to work at runtime. Remember, the compiler looks at the reference type to decide whether you can call a particular method on that reference. With an Appliance reference to a Toaster, the compiler cares only if class *Appliance* has the method you're invoking on an Appliance reference. But at runtime, the JVM looks not at the *reference* type (Appliance) but at the actual *Toaster* object on the heap. So if the compiler has already *approved* the method call, the only way it can work is if the overriding method has the same arguments and return types. Otherwise, someone with an Appliance reference will call turnOn() as a no-arg method, even though there's a version in Toaster that takes an int. Which one is called at runtime? The one in Appliance. In other words, *the turnOn(int level) method in Toaster is not an override!*

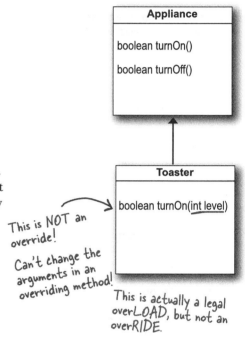

This is NOT an override!

Can't change the arguments in an overriding method!

This is actually a legal overLOAD, but not an overRIDE.

① Arguments must be the same, and return types must be compatible.

The contract of superclass defines how other code can use a method. Whatever the superclass takes as an argument, the subclass overriding the method must use that same argument. And whatever the superclass declares as a return type, the overriding method must declare either the same type, or a subclass type. Remember, a subclass object is guaranteed to be able to do anything its superclass declares, so it's safe to return a subclass where the superclass is expected.

② The method can't be less accessible.

That means the access level must be the same, or friendlier. That means you can't, for example, override a public method and make it private. What a shock that would be to the code invoking what it *thinks* (at compile time) is a public method, if suddenly at runtime the JVM slammed the door shut because the overriding version called at runtime is private!

So far we've learned about two access levels: private and public. The other two are in the deployment chapter (Release your Code) and appendix B. There's also another rule about overriding related to exception handling, but we'll wait until the chapter on exceptions (Risky Behavior) to cover that.

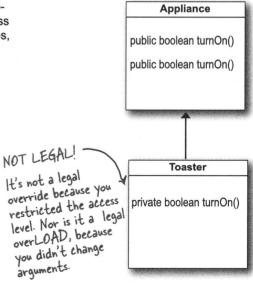

NOT LEGAL!

It's not a legal override because you restricted the access level. Nor is it a legal overLOAD, because you didn't change arguments.

Overloading a method

Method overloading is nothing more than having two methods with the same name but different argument lists. Period. There's no polymorphism involved with overloaded methods!

Overloading lets you make multiple versions of a method, with different argument lists, for convenience to the callers. For example, if you have a method that takes only an int, the calling code has to convert, say, a double into an int before calling your method. But if you overloaded the method with another version that takes a double, then you've made things easier for the caller. You'll see more of this when we look into constructors in the object lifecycle chapter.

Since an overloading method isn't trying to fulfill the polymorphism contract defined by its superclass, overloaded methods have much more flexibility.

> An overloaded method is just a different method that happens to have the same method name. It has nothing to do with inheritance and polymorphism. An overloaded method is NOT the same as an overridden method.

① **The return types can be different.**

You're free to change the return types in overloaded methods, as long as the argument lists are different.

② **You can't change ONLY the return type.**

If only the return type is different, it's not a valid over*load*—the compiler will assume you're trying to over*ride* the method. And even *that* won't be legal unless the return type is a subtype of the return type declared in the superclass. To overload a method, you MUST change the argument list, although you *can* change the return type to anything.

③ **You *can* vary the access levels in any direction.**

You're free to overload a method with a method that's more restrictive. It doesn't matter, since the new method isn't obligated to fulfill the contract of the overloaded method.

Legal examples of method overloading:

```
public class Overloads {

    String uniqueID;

    public int addNums(int a, int b) {
        return a + b;
    }

    public double addNums(double a, double b) {
        return a + b;
    }

    public void setUniqueID(String theID) {
        // lots of validation code, and then:
        uniqueID = theID;
    }

    public void setUniqueID(int ssNumber) {
        String numString = "" + ssNumber;
        setUniqueID(numString);
    }
}
```

Exercise

Mixed Messages

```
a = 6;        56
b = 5;        11
a = 5;        65
```

A short Java program is listed below. One block of the program is missing! Your challenge is to match the candidate block of code (on the left), with the output that you'd see if the block were inserted. Not all the lines of output will be used, and some of the lines of output might be used more than once. Draw lines connecting the candidate blocks of code with their matching command-line output.

the program:

```java
class A {
  int ivar = 7;
  void m1() {
    System.out.print("A's m1, ");
  }
  void m2() {
    System.out.print("A's m2, ");
  }
  void m3() {
    System.out.print("A's m3, ");
  }
}

class B extends A {
  void  m1() {
    System.out.print("B's m1, ");
  }
}
```

```java
class C extends B {
  void m3() {
    System.out.print("C's m3, "+(ivar + 6));
  }
}

public class Mixed2 {
  public static void main(String [] args) {
    A a = new A();
    B b = new B();
    C c = new C();
    A a2 = new C();

    [                    ]
  }
}
```

candidate code goes here
(three lines)

code candidates:

```
b.m1();
c.m2();   }
a.m3();
───────
c.m1();
c.m2();   }
c.m3();
───────
a.m1();
b.m2();   }
c.m3();
───────
a2.m1();
a2.m2();  }
a2.m3();
```

output:

A's m1, A's m2, C's m3, 6

B's m1, A's m2, A's m3,

A's m1, B's m2, A's m3,

B's m1, A's m2, C's m3, 13

B's m1, C's m2, A's m3,

B's m1, A's m2, C's m3, 6

A's m1, A's m2, C's m3, 13

BE the Compiler

Which of the A-B pairs of methods listed on the right, if inserted into the classes on the left, would compile and produce the output shown? (The A method inserted into class Monster, the B method inserted into class Vampire.)

```java
public class MonsterTestDrive {
  public static void main(String [] args) {
    Monster [] ma = new Monster[3];
    ma[0] = new Vampire();
    ma[1] = new Dragon();
    ma[2] = new Monster();
    for(int x = 0; x < 3; x++) {
      ma[x].frighten(x);
    }
  }
}


class Monster {

  A

}


class Vampire extends Monster {

  B

}


class Dragon extends Monster {
  boolean frighten(int degree) {
    System.out.println("breath fire");
    return true;
  }
}
```

File Edit Window Help SaveYourself

```
% java MonsterTestDrive
a bite?
breath fire
arrrgh
```

1

A
```java
boolean frighten(int d) {
   System.out.println("arrrgh");
   return true;
}
```
B
```java
boolean frighten(int x) {
   System.out.println("a bite?");
   return false;
}
```

2

A
```java
boolean frighten(int x) {
   System.out.println("arrrgh");
   return true;
}
```
B
```java
int frighten(int f) {
   System.out.println("a bite?");
   return 1;
}
```

3

A
```java
boolean frighten(int x) {
   System.out.println("arrrgh");
   return false;
}
```
B
```java
boolean scare(int x) {
   System.out.println("a bite?");
   return true;
}
```

4

A
```java
boolean frighten(int z) {
   System.out.println("arrrgh");
   return true;
}
```
B
```java
boolean frighten(byte b) {
   System.out.println("a bite?");
   return true;
}
```

Pool Puzzle

Your *job* is to take code snippets from the pool and place them into the blank lines in the code. You may use the same snippet more than once, and you might not need to use all the snippets. Your *goal* is to make a set of classes that will compile and run together as a program. Don't be fooled – this one's harder than it looks.

```
public class Rowboat _____ _____ {

   public _____ rowTheBoat() {

      System.out.print("stroke natasha");

   }
}
_____
public class _____ {

   private int _____ ;

   _____ void _____ ( _____ ) {

      length = len;

   }
   public int getLength() {

      _____ _____ ;

   }
   public _____ move() {

      System.out.print("_____");

   }
}
```

```
public class TestBoats {

   _____ _____ _____ main(String[] args){

      _____ b1 = new Boat();

      Sailboat b2 = new _____();

      Rowboat _____ = new Rowboat();

      b2.setLength(32);

      b1._____();

      b3._____();

      _____.move();

   }
}
_____
public class _____ _____ Boat {

   public _____ _____() {

      System.out.print("_____");

   }
}
```

OUTPUT: `drift   drift   hoist sail`

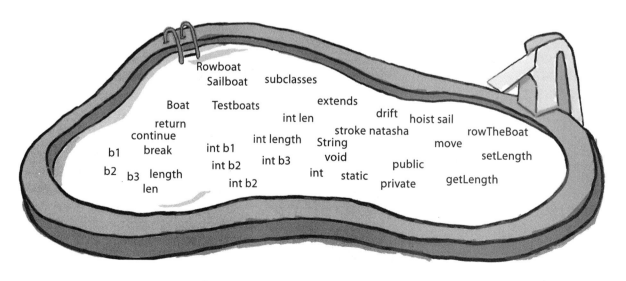

Rowboat
Sailboat   subclasses
Boat   Testboats   extends   drift   hoist sail   rowTheBoat
return   int len   stroke natasha   move
continue   int length   String   setLength
b1   break   int b1   int b3   void   public   getLength
b2   b3   length   int b2   int   static   private
   len

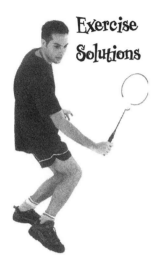

Exercise
Solutions

BE the Compiler

Set 1 will work.

Set 2 will not compile because of Vampire's return type (int).

The Vampire's frighten() method (B) is not a legal override OR overload of Monster's frighten() method. Changing ONLY the return type is not enough to make a valid overload, and since an int is not compatible with a boolean, the method is not a valid override. (Remember, if you change ONLY the return type, it must be to a return type that is compatible with the superclass version's return type, and then it's an over*ride*.)

Sets 3 and 4 will compile, but produce:

arrrgh

breath fire

arrrgh

Remember, class Vampire did not over*ride* class Monster's frighten() method. (The frighten() method in Vampire's set 4 takes a byte, not an int.)

---

code candidates:

Mixed Messages

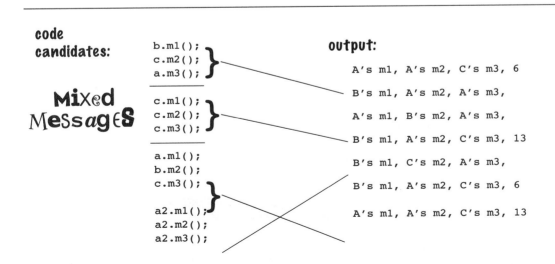

```
b.m1();
c.m2();
a.m3();
```
```
c.m1();
c.m2();
c.m3();
```
```
a.m1();
b.m2();
c.m3();
```
```
a2.m1();
a2.m2();
a2.m3();
```

output:

```
A's m1, A's m2, C's m3, 6
B's m1, A's m2, A's m3,
A's m1, B's m2, A's m3,
B's m1, A's m2, C's m3, 13
B's m1, C's m2, A's m3,
B's m1, A's m2, C's m3, 6
A's m1, A's m2, C's m3, 13
```

```
public class Rowboat extends Boat {
    public void rowTheBoat() {
        System.out.print("stroke natasha");
    }
}
public class Boat {
    private int length ;
    public void setLength ( int len ) {
        length = len;
    }
    public int getLength() {
        return length ;
    }
    public void move() {
        System.out.print("drift ");
    }
}
```

```
public class TestBoats {
    public static void main(String[] args){
        Boat b1 = new Boat();
        Sailboat b2 = new Sailboat();
        Rowboat b3 = new Rowboat();
        b2.setLength(32);
        b1.move();
        b3.move();
        b2.move();
    }
}
public class Sailboat extends Boat {
    public void move() {
        System.out.print("hoist sail ");
    }
}
```

OUTPUT: `drift  drift  hoist sail`

Serious Polymorphism

Inheritance is just the beginning. To exploit polymorphism, we need interfaces (and not the GUI kind). We need to go beyond simple inheritance to a level of flexibility and extensibility you can get only by designing and coding to interface specifications. Some of the coolest parts of Java wouldn't even be possible without interfaces, so even if you don't design with them yourself, you still have to use them. But you'll *want* to design with them. You'll *need* to design with them. ***You'll wonder how you ever lived without them***. What's an interface? It's a 100% abstract class. What's an abstract class? It's a class that can't be instantiated. What's that good for? You'll see in just a few moments. But if you think about the end of the last chapter, and how we used polymorphic arguments so that a single Vet method could take Animal subclasses of all types, well, that was just scratching the surface. Interfaces are the ***poly*** in polymorphism. The ***ab*** in abstract. The ***caffeine*** in Java.

Did we forget about something when we designed this?

The class structure isn't too bad. We've designed it so that duplicate code is kept to a minimum, and we've overridden the methods that we think should have subclass-specific implementations. We've made it nice and flexible from a polymorphic perspective, because we can design Animal-using programs with Animal arguments (and array declarations), so that any Animal subtype—*including those we never imagined at the time we wrote our code*—can be passed in and used at runtime. We've put the common protocol for all Animals (the four methods that we want the world to know all Animals have) in the Animal superclass, and we're ready to start making new Lions and Tigers and Hippos.

Animal

picture
food
hunger
boundaries
location

makeNoise()
eat()
sleep()
roam()

Feline

roam()

Hippo

makeNoise()
eat()

Canine

roam()

Lion

makeNoise()
eat()

Tiger

makeNoise()
eat()

Cat

makeNoise()
eat()

Wolf

makeNoise()
eat()

Dog

makeNoise()
eat()

We know we can say:

```
Wolf aWolf = new Wolf();
```

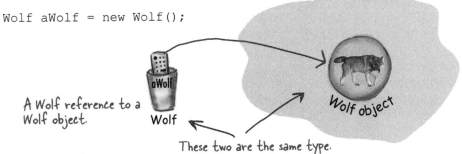

A Wolf reference to a
Wolf object.

Wolf

These two are the same type.

And we know we can say:

```
Animal aHippo = new Hippo();
```

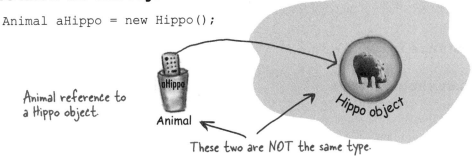

Animal reference to
a Hippo object.

Animal

These two are NOT the same type.

But here's where it gets weird:

```
Animal anim = new Animal();
```

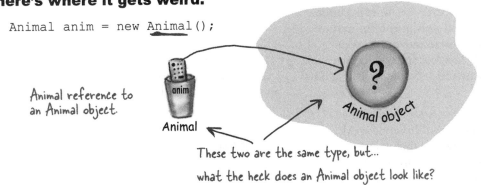

Animal reference to
an Animal object.

Animal

These two are the same type, but...

what the heck does an Animal object look like?

What does a new Animal() object *look* like?

scary objects

What are the instance variable values?

Some classes just should **not** be instantiated!

It makes sense to create a Wolf object or a Hippo object or a Tiger object, but what exactly *is* an Animal object? What shape is it? What color, size, number of legs...

Trying to create an object of type Animal is like **a nightmare Star Trek™ transporter accident.** The one where somewhere in the beam-me–up process something bad happened to the buffer.

But how do we deal with this? We *need* an Animal class, for inheritance and polymorphism. But we want programmers to instantiate only the less abstract *subclasses* of class Animal, not Animal itself. We want Tiger objects and Lion objects, *not Animal objects*.

Fortunately, there's a simple way to prevent a class from ever being instantiated. In other words, to stop anyone from saying "**new**" on that type. By marking the class as **abstract**, the compiler will stop any code, anywhere, from ever creating an instance of that type.

You can still use that abstract type as a reference type. In fact, that's a big part of why you have that abstract class in the first place (to use it as a polymorphic argument or return type, or to make a polymorphic array).

When you're designing your class inheritance structure, you have to decide which classes are *abstract* and which are *concrete*. Concrete classes are those that are specific enough to be instantiated. A *concrete* class just means that it's OK to make objects of that type.

Making a class abstract is easy—put the keyword **abstract** before the class declaration:

```
abstract class Canine extends Animal {
    public void roam() { }
}
```

The compiler won't let you instantiate an abstract class

An abstract class means that nobody can ever make a new instance of that class. You can still use that abstract class as a declared reference type, for the purpose of polymorphism, but you don't have to worry about somebody making objects of that type. The compiler *guarantees* it.

```
abstract public class Canine extends Animal
{
    public void roam() { }

}
```
```
public class MakeCanine {
    public void go() {
        Canine c;

        c = new Dog();

        c = new Canine();

        c.roam();

    }

}
```

This is OK, because you can always assign a subclass object to a superclass reference, even if the superclass is abstract.

class Canine is marked abstract, so the compiler will NOT let you do this.

```
File Edit Window Help BeamMeUp
% javac MakeCanine.java

MakeCanine.java:5: Canine is abstract;
cannot be instantiated
        c = new Canine();
            ^
1 error
```

An **abstract class** has virtually* no use, no value, no purpose in life, unless it is ***extended.***

With an abstract class, the guys doing the work at runtime are **instances of a *subclass*** of your abstract class.

*There is an exception to this—an abstract class can have static members (see chapter 10).

Abstract vs. Concrete

A class that's not abstract is called a *concrete* class. In the Animal inheritance tree, if we make Animal, Canine, and Feline abstract, that leaves Hippo, Wolf, Dog, Tiger, Lion, and Cat as the concrete subclasses.

Flip through the Java API and you'll find a lot of abstract classes, especially in the GUI library. What does a GUI Component look like? The Component class is the superclass of GUI-related classes for things like buttons, text areas, scrollbars, dialog boxes, you name it. You don't make an instance of a generic *Component* and put it on the screen, you make a JButton. In other words, you instantiate only a *concrete subclass* of Component, but never Component itself.

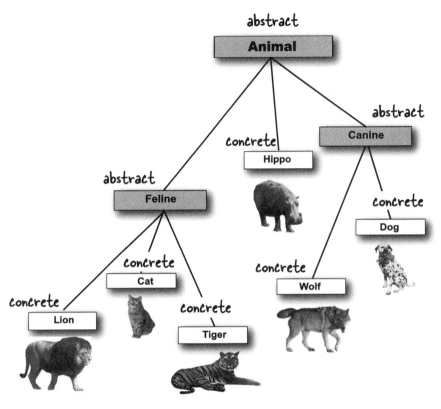

BRAIN POWER

Hmmmm... do I feel like red or white tonight?

Hmmmm... the Camelot Vineyards 1997 Pinot Noir was a pretty decent year...

abstract or concrete?

How do you know when a class should be abstract? **Wine** is probably abstract. But what about **Red** and **White**? Again probably abstract (for some of us, anyway). But at what point in the hierarchy do things become concrete?

Do you make **PinotNoir** concrete, or is it abstract too? It looks like the Camelot Vineyards 1997 Pinot Noir is probably concrete no matter what. But how do you know for sure?

Look at the Animal inheritance tree above. Do the choices we've made for which classes are abstract and which are concrete seem appropriate? Would you change anything about the Animal inheritance tree (other than adding more Animals, of course)?

Abstract methods

Besides classes, you can mark *methods* abstract, too. An abstract class means the class must be *extended*; an abstract method means the method must be *overridden*. You might decide that some (or all) behaviors in an abstract class don't make any sense unless they're implemented by a more specific subclass. In other words, you can't think of any generic method implementation that could possibly be useful for subclasses. What would a generic *eat()* method look like?

An abstract method has no body!

Because you've already decided there isn't any code that would make sense in the abstract method, you won't put in a method body. So no curly braces— just end the declaration with a semicolon.

```
public abstract void eat();
```

No method body!
End it with a semicolon.

It really sucks to be an abstract method. You don't have a body.

If you declare an abstract *method*, you MUST mark the *class* abstract as well. You can't have an abstract method in a non-abstract class.

If you put even a single abstract method in a class, you have to make the class abstract. But you *can* mix both abstract and non-abstract methods in the abstract class.

---

there are no Dumb Questions

Q: What is the *point* of an abstract method? I thought the whole point of an abstract class was to have common code that could be inherited by subclasses.

A: Inheritable method implementations (in other words, methods with actual *bodies*) are A Good Thing to put in a superclass. *When it makes sense.* And in an abstract class, it often *doesn't* make sense, because you can't come up with any generic code that subclasses would find useful. The point of an abstract method is that even though you haven't put in any actual method code, you've still defined part of the *protocol* for a group of subtypes (subclasses).

Q: Which is good because...

A: Polymorphism! Remember, what you want is the ability to use a superclass type (often abstract) as a method argument, return type, or array type. That way, you get to add new subtypes (like a new Animal subclass) to your program without having to rewrite (or add) new methods to deal with those new types. Imagine how you'd have to change the Vet class, if it didn't use Animal as its argument type for methods. You'd have to have a separate method for every single Animal subclass! One that takes a Lion, one that takes a Wolf, one that takes a... you get the idea. So with an abstract method, you're saying, "All subtypes of this type have THIS method." for the benefit of polymorphism.

You MUST implement all abstract methods

I have wonderful news, mother. Joe finally implemented all his abstract methods! Now everything is working just the way we planned...

***Implementing* an abstract method is just like *overriding* a method.**

Abstract methods don't have a body; they exist solely for polymorphism. That means the first concrete class in the inheritance tree must implement *all* abstract methods.

You can, however, pass the buck by being abstract yourself. If both Animal and Canine are abstract, for example, and both have abstract methods, class Canine does not have to implement the abstract methods from Animal. But as soon as we get to the first concrete subclass, like Dog, that subclass must implement *all* of the abstract methods from both Animal and Canine.

But remember that an abstract class can have both abstract and *non*-abstract methods, so Canine, for example, could implement an abstract method from Animal, so that Dog didn't have to. But if Canine says nothing about the abstract methods from Animal, Dog has to implement all of Animal's abstract methods.

When we say "you must implement the abstract method", that means you *must provide a body*. That means you must create a non-abstract method in your class with the same method signature (name and arguments) and a return type that is compatible with the declared return type of the abstract method. What you put *in* that method is up to you. All Java cares about is that the method is *there*, in your concrete subclass.

 **Sharpen your pencil**

Abstract vs. Concrete Classes

Let's put all this abstract rhetoric into some concrete use. In the middle column we've listed some classes. Your job is to imagine applications where the listed class might be concrete, and applications where the listed class might be abstract. We took a shot at the first few to get you going. For example, class Tree would be abstract in a tree nursery program, where differences between an Oak and an Aspen matter. But in a golf simulation program, Tree might be a concrete class (perhaps a subclass of Obstacle), because the program doesn't care about or distinguish between different types of trees. (There's no one right answer; it depends on your design.)

Concrete	Sample class	Abstract
golf course simulation	Tree	tree nursery application
_____	House	architect application
satellite photo application	Town	_____
_____	Football Player	coaching application
_____	Chair	_____
_____	Customer	_____
_____	Sales Order	_____
_____	Book	_____
_____	Store	_____
_____	Supplier	_____
_____	Golf Club	_____
_____	Carburetor	_____
_____	Oven	_____

Polymorphism in action

Let's say that we want to write our *own* kind of list class, one that will hold Dog objects, but pretend for a moment that we don't know about the ArrayList class. For the first pass, we'll give it just an *add()* method. We'll use a simple Dog array (Dog []) to keep the added Dog objects, and give it a length of 5. When we reach the limit of 5 Dog objects, you can still call the *add()* method but it won't do anything. If we're *not* at the limit, the *add()* method puts the Dog in the array at the next available index position, then increments that next available index (nextIndex).

Building our own Dog-specific list

(Perhaps the world's worst attempt at making our own ArrayList kind of class, from scratch.)

```
public class MyDogList {

    private Dog [] dogs = new Dog[5];          Use a plain old Dog array
                                               behind the scenes.

    private int nextIndex = 0;      We'll increment this each
                                    time a new Dog is added.

    public void add(Dog d) {
                                               If we're not already at the limit
        if (nextIndex < dogs.length) {         of the dogs array, add the Dog
                                               and print a message.
            dogs[nextIndex] = d;

            System.out.println("Dog added at " + nextIndex);

            nextIndex++;        increment, to give us the
                                next index to use
        }
    }
}
```

version
1

MyDogList

Dog[] dogs
int nextIndex

add(Dog d)

Uh-oh, now we need to keep Cats, too.

We have a few options here:

1) Make a separate class, MyCatList, to hold Cat objects. Pretty clunky.

2) Make a single class, DogAndCatList, that keeps two different arrays as instance variables and has two different add() methods: addCat(Cat c) and addDog(Dog d). Another clunky solution.

3) Make heterogeneous AnimalList class, that takes *any* kind of Animal subclass (since we know that if the spec changed to add Cats, sooner or later we'll have some *other* kind of animal added as well). We like this option best, so let's change our class to make it more generic, to take Animals instead of just Dogs. We've highlighted the key changes (the logic is the same, of course, but the type has changed from Dog to Animal everywhere in the code.

Building our own <u>Animal</u>-specific list

Don't panic. We're not making a new Animal object; we're making a new array object, of type Animal. (Remember, you cannot make a new instance of an abstract type, but you CAN make an array object declared to HOLD that type.)

version 2

MyAnimalList

Animal[] animals
int nextIndex

add(**Animal** a)

```java
public class MyAnimalList {

    private Animal[] animals = new Animal[5];
    private int nextIndex = 0;

    public void add(Animal a) {
        if (nextIndex < animals.length) {
            animals[nextIndex] = a;
            System.out.println("Animal added at " + nextIndex);
            nextIndex++;
        }
    }
}
```

```java
public class AnimalTestDrive{
    public static void main (String[] args) {
        MyAnimalList list = new MyAnimalList();
        Dog a = new Dog();
        Cat c = new Cat();
        list.add(a);
        list.add(c);
    }
}
```

```
File Edit Window Help Harm

% java AnimalTestDrive

Animal added at 0

Animal added at 1
```

What about non-Animals? Why not make a class generic enough to take anything?

You know where this is heading. We want to change the type of the array, along with the *add()* method argument, to something *above* Animal. Something even *more* generic, *more* abstract than Animal. But how can we do it? We don't *have* a superclass for Animal.

Then again, maybe we do...

Remember those methods of ArrayList? Look how the remove, contains, and indexOf method all use an object of type... *Object!*

Every class in Java extends class Object.

Class Object is the mother of all classes; it's the superclass of *everything*.

Even if you take advantage of polymorphism, you still have to create a class with methods that take and return *your* polymorphic type. Without a common superclass for everything in Java, there'd be no way for the developers of Java to create classes with methods that could take *your* custom types... *types they never knew about when they wrote the ArrayList class.*

So you were making subclasses of class Object from the very beginning and you didn't even know it. *Every class you write extends Object,* without your ever having to say it. But you can think of it as though a class you write looks like this:

```
public class Dog extends Object { }
```

But wait a minute, Dog *already* extends something, *Canine.* That's OK. The compiler will make *Canine* extend Object instead. Except *Canine* extends Animal. No problem, then the compiler will just make *Animal* extend Object.

Any class that doesn't *explicitly* extend another class, *implicitly* extends Object.

So, since Dog extends Canine, it doesn't *directly* extend Object (although it does extend it indirectly), and the same is true for Canine, but Animal *does* directly extend Object.

 version 3

(These are just a few of the methods in ArrayList...there are many more.)

ArrayList

boolean remove(Object elem)
Removes the object at the index parameter. Returns 'true' if the element was in the list.

boolean contains(Object elem)
Returns 'true' if there's a match for the object parameter.

boolean isEmpty()
Returns 'true' if the list has no elements.

int indexOf(Object elem)
Returns either the index of the object parameter, or -1.

Object get(int index)
Returns the element at this position in the list.

boolean add(Object elem)
Adds the element to the list (returns 'true').

// more

Many of the ArrayList methods use the ultimate polymorphic type, Object. Since every class in Java is a subclass of Object, these ArrayList methods can take anything!

(Note: as of Java 5.0, the get() and add() methods actually look a little different than the ones shown here, but for now this is the way to think about it. We'll get into the full story a little later.)

So what's in this ultra-super-megaclass Object?

If you were Java, what behavior would you want *every* object to have? Hmmmm... let's see... how about a method that lets you find out if one object is equal to another object? What about a method that can tell you the actual class type of that object? Maybe a method that gives you a hashcode for the object, so you can use the object in hashtables (we'll talk about Java's hashtables in chapter 17 and appendix B). Oh, here's a good one—a method that prints out a String message for that object.

And what do you know? As if by magic, class Object does indeed have methods for those four things. That's not all, though, but these are the ones we really care about.

Object

boolean equals()
Class getClass()
int hashCode()
String toString()

Just SOME of the methods of class Object.

YourClassHere

Every class you write inherits all the methods of class Object. The classes you've written inherited methods you didn't even know you had.

---

(1) equals(Object o)

```
Dog a = new Dog();
Cat c = new Cat();

if (a.equals(c)) {
    System.out.println("true");
} else {
    System.out.println("false");
}
```

File Edit Window Help Stop

```
% java TestObject
false
```

Tells you if two objects are considered 'equal' (we'll talk about what 'equal' really means in appendix B).

(2) getClass()

```
Cat c = new Cat();
System.out.println(c.getClass());
```

File Edit Window Help Faint

```
% java TestObject
class Cat
```

Gives you back the class that object was instantiated from.

(3) hashCode()

```
Cat c = new Cat();
System.out.println(c.hashCode());
```

File Edit Window Help Drop

```
% java TestObject
8202111
```

Prints out a hashcode for the object (for now, think of it as a unique ID).

(4) toString()

```
Cat c = new Cat();
System.out.println(c.toString());
```

File Edit Window Help LapseIntoComa

```
% java TestObject
Cat@7d277f
```

Prints out a String message with the name of the class and some other number we rarely care about.

Object and abstract classes

Q: Is class Object abstract?

A: No. Well, not in the formal Java sense anyway. Object is a non-abstract class because it's got method implementation code that all classes can inherit and use out-of-the-box, without having to override the methods.

Q: Then *can* you override the methods in Object?

A: Some of them. But some of them are marked `final`, which means you can't override them. You're encouraged (strongly) to override hashCode(), equals(), and toString() in your own classes, and you'll learn how to do that a little later in the book. But some of the methods, like getClass(), do things that must work in a specific, guaranteed way.

Q: If ArrayList methods are generic enough to use Object, then what does it mean to say ArrayList<DotCom>? I thought I was restricting the ArrayList to hold only DotCom objects?

A: You *were* restricting it. Prior to Java 5.0, ArrayLists couldn't be restricted. They were all essentially what you get in Java 5.0 today if you write ArrayList<Object>. In other words, **an ArrayList restricted to anything that's an Object,** which means *any* object in Java, instantiated from *any* class type! We'll cover the details of this new <type> syntax later in the book.

Q: OK, back to class Object being non-abstract (so I guess that means it's concrete), HOW can you let somebody make an Object object? Isn't that just as weird as making an Animal object?

A: Good question! Why is it acceptable to make a new Object instance? Because sometimes you just want a generic object to use as, well, as an object. A *lightweight* object. By far, the most common use of an instance of type Object is for thread synchronization (which you'll learn about in chapter 15). For now, just stick that on the back burner and assume that you will rarely make objects of type Object, even though you *can*.

Q: So is it fair to say that the main purpose for type Object is so that you can use it for a polymorphic argument and return type? Like in ArrayList?

A: The Object class serves *two* main purposes: to act as a polymorphic type for methods that need to work on any class that you or anyone else makes, and to provide *real* method code that all objects in Java need at runtime (and putting them in class Object means all other classes inherit them). Some of the most important methods in Object are related to threads, and we'll see those later in the book.

Q: If it's so good to use polymorphic types, why don't you just make ALL your methods take and return type Object?

A: Ahhhh... think about what would happen. For one thing, you would defeat the whole point of 'type-safety', one of Java's greatest protection mechanisms for your code. With type-safety, Java guarantees that you won't ask the wrong object to do something you *meant* to ask of another object type. Like, ask a *Ferrari* (which you think is a *Toaster*) to *cook itself*. But the truth is, you *don't* have to worry about that fiery Ferrari scenario, even if you *do* use Object references for everything. Because when objects are referred to by an Object reference type, Java *thinks* it's referring to an instance of type Object. And that means the only methods you're allowed to call on that object are the ones declared in class Object! So if you were to say:

```
Object o = new Ferrari();
o.goFast(); //Not legal!
```

You wouldn't even make it past the compiler.

Because Java is a strongly-typed language, the compiler checks to make sure that you're calling a method on an object that's actually capable of *responding*. In other words, you can call a method on an object reference *only* if the class of the reference type actually *has* the method. We'll cover this in much greater detail a little later, so don't worry if the picture isn't crystal clear.

Using polymorphic references of type Object has a price...

Before you run off and start using type Object for all your ultra-flexible argument and return types, you need to consider a little issue of using type Object as a reference. And keep in mind that we're not talking about making instances of type Object; we're talking about making instances of some other type, but using a reference of type Object.

When you put an object into an ArrayList**<Dog>**, it goes in as a Dog, and comes out as a Dog:

```
ArrayList<Dog> myDogArrayList = new ArrayList<Dog>();
```
← *Make an ArrayList declared to hold Dog objects.*
```
Dog aDog = new Dog();
```
←*Make a Dog.*
```
myDogArrayList.add(aDog);
```
←*Add the Dog to the list.*
```
Dog d = myDogArrayList.get(0);
```
← *Assign the Dog from the list to a new Dog reference variable. (Think of it as though the get() method declares a Dog return type because you used ArrayList<Dog>.)*

But what happens when you declare it as ArrayList**<Object>**? If you want to make an ArrayList that will literally take *any* kind of Object, you declare it like this:

```
ArrayList<Object> myDogArrayList = new ArrayList<Object>();
```
← *Make an ArrayList declared to hold any type of Object.*
```
Dog aDog = new Dog();
```
←*Make a Dog.*
```
myDogArrayList.add(aDog);
```
←*Add the Dog to the list.*

(These two steps are the same.)

But what happens when you try to get the Dog object and assign it to a Dog reference?

Dog d = myDogArrayList.get(0); *NO!! Won't compile!! When you use ArrayList<Object>, the get() method returns type Object. The Compiler knows only that the object inherits from Object (somewhere in its inheritance tree) but it doesn't know it's a Dog!!*

Everything comes out of an ArrayList<Object> as a reference of type **Object**, *regardless of what the actual object is, or what the reference type was when you added the object to the list.*

The objects go IN as SoccerBall, Fish, Guitar, and Car.

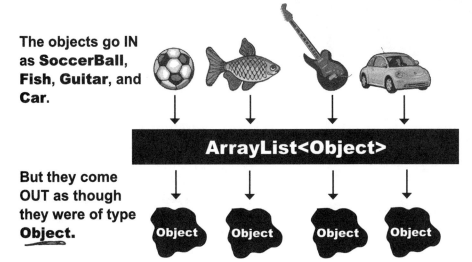

ArrayList<Object>

But they come OUT as though they were of type Object.

Object   Object   Object   Object

Objects come out of an ArrayList<Object> acting like they're generic instances of class Object. The Compiler cannot assume the object that comes out is of any type other than Object.

When a Dog won't act like a Dog

The problem with having everything treated polymorphically as an Object is that the objects *appear* to lose (but not permanently) their true essence. *The Dog appears to lose its dogness.* Let's see what happens when we pass a Dog to a method that returns a reference to the same Dog object, but declares the return type as type Object rather than Dog.

I don't know what you're talking about. Sit? Stay? bark? Hmmmm... I don't recall knowing those.

BAD
☹

```
public void go() {
    Dog aDog = new Dog();
    Dog sameDog = getObject(aDog);
}
```

This line won't work! Even though the method returned a reference to the very same Dog the argument referred to, the return type Object means the compiler won't let you assign the returned reference to anything but Object.

```
public Object getObject(Object o) {
    return o;
}
```

We're returning a reference to the same Dog, but as a return type of Object. This part is perfectly legal. Note: this is similar to how the get() method works when you have an ArrayList<Object> rather than an ArrayList<Dog>.

```
File  Edit  Window  Help  Remember
DogPolyTest.java:10: incompatible types
found    : java.lang.Object
required: Dog
        Dog sameDog = takeObjects(aDog);
1 error                              ^
```

The compiler doesn't know that the thing returned from the method is actually a Dog, so it won't let you assign it to a Dog reference. (You'll see why on the next page.)

GOOD
☺

```
public void go() {
    Dog aDog = new Dog();
    Object sameDog = getObject(aDog);
}
```

This works (although it may not be very useful, as you'll see in a moment) because you can assign ANYTHING to a reference of type Object, since every class passes the IS-A test for Object. Every object in Java is an instance of type Object, because every class in Java has Object at the top of its inheritance tree.

```
public Object getObject(Object o) {
    return o;

}
```

Objects don't bark.

So now we know that when an object is referenced by a variable declared as type Object, it can't be assigned to a variable declared with the actual object's type. And we know that this can happen when a return type or argument is declared as type Object, as would be the case, for example, when the object is put into an ArrayList of type Object using ArrayList<Object>. But what are the implications of this? Is it a problem to have to use an Object reference variable to refer to a Dog object? Let's try to call Dog methods on our Dog-That-Compiler-Thinks-Is-An-Object:

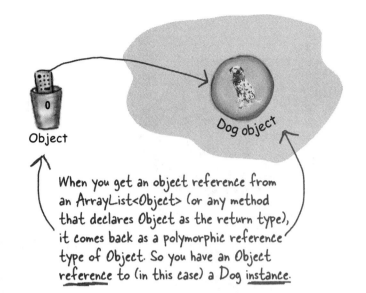

Object

When you get an object reference from an ArrayList<Object> (or any method that declares Object as the return type), it comes back as a polymorphic reference type of Object. So you have an Object reference to (in this case) a Dog instance.

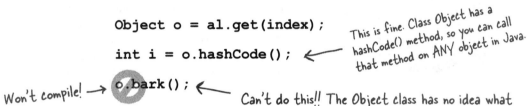

```
Object o = al.get(index);

int i = o.hashCode();

o.bark();
```

Won't compile! →

This is fine. Class Object has a hashCode() method, so you can call that method on ANY object in Java.

Can't do this!! The Object class has no idea what it means to bark(). Even though YOU know it's really a Dog at that index, the compiler doesn't..

> **The compiler decides whether you can call a method based on the *reference* type, not the actual *object* type.**

Even if you *know* the object is capable ("...but it really *is* a Dog, honest..."), the compiler sees it only as a generic Object. For all the compiler knows, you put a Button object out there. Or a Microwave object. Or some other thing that really doesn't know how to bark.
The compiler checks the class of the *reference* type—not the *object* type—to see if you can call a method using that reference.

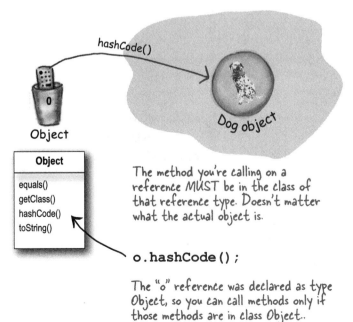

hashCode()

Object

Object
equals()
getClass()
hashCode()
toString()

The method you're calling on a reference MUST be in the class of that reference type. Doesn't matter what the actual object is.

`o.hashCode();`

The "o" reference was declared as type Object, so you can call methods only if those methods are in class Object..

He treats me like an Object. But I can do so much more...if only he'd see me for what I *really* am.

Get in touch with your inner Object.

An object contains *everything* it inherits from each of its superclasses. That means *every* object—regardless of its actual class type—is *also* an instance of class Object. That means any object in Java can be treated not just as a Dog, Button, or Snowboard, but also as an Object. When you say **new Snowboard()**, you get a single object on the heap—a Snowboard object—but that Snowboard wraps itself around an inner core representing the Object (capital "O") portion of itself.

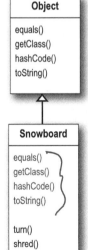

```
Object
equals()
getClass()
hashCode()
toString()
```

```
Snowboard
equals()
getClass()
hashCode()
toString()

turn()
shred()
getAir()
loseControl()
```

Snowboard inherits methods from superclass Object, and adds four more.

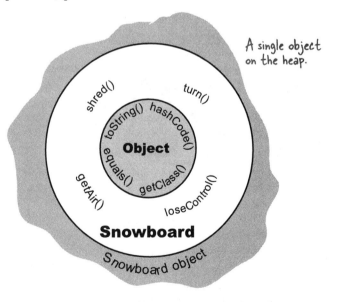

A single object on the heap.

There is only ONE object on the heap here. A Snowboard object. But it contains both the <u>Snowboard</u> class parts of itself and the <u>Object</u> class parts of itself.

'Polymorphism' means 'many forms'.

You can treat a Snowboard as a Snowboard or as an Object.

If a reference is like a remote control, the remote control takes on more and more buttons as you move down the inheritance tree. A remote control (reference) of type Object has only a few buttons—the buttons for the exposed methods of class Object. But a remote control of type Snowboard includes all the buttons from class Object, plus any new buttons (for new methods) of class Snowboard. The more specific the class, the more buttons it may have.

Of course that's not always true; a subclass might not add any new methods, but simply override the methods of its superclass. The key point is that even if the *object* is of type Snowboard, an Object *reference* to the Snowboard object can't see the Snowboard-specific methods.

> When you put an object in an ArrayList<Object>, you can treat it only as an Object, regardless of the type it was when you put it in.
>
> When you get a reference from an ArrayList<Object>, the reference is always of type *Object*.
>
> That means you get an *Object* remote control.

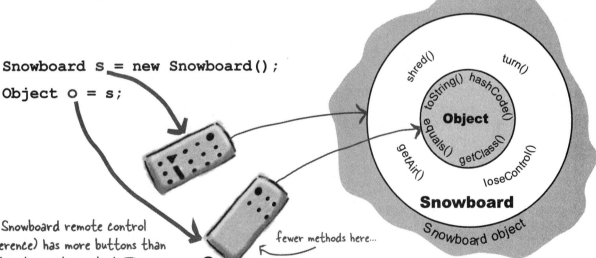

```
Snowboard s = new Snowboard();
Object o = s;
```

shred() *turn()*
toString() *hashCode()*
Object
equals() *getClass()*
getAir() *loseControl()*
Snowboard
Snowboard object

fewer methods here...

o

The Snowboard remote control (reference) has more buttons than an Object remote control. The Snowboard remote can see the full Snowboardness of the Snowboard object. It can access all the methods in Snowboard, including both the inherited Object methods and the methods from class Snowboard.

The Object reference can see <u>only</u> the Object parts of the Snowboard object. It can access only the methods of class Object. It has fewer buttons than the Snowboard remote control.

Wait a minute... what good is a Dog if it comes out of an ArrayList<Object> and it can't do any Dog things? There's gotta be a way to get the Dog back to a state of Dogness...

I hope it doesn't hurt. And what's so wrong with staying an Object? OK, I can't fetch, sure, but I can give you a real nice hashcode.

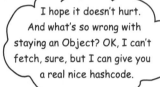

Cast the so-called 'Object' (but we know he's actually a Dog) to type Dog, so that you can treat him like the Dog he really is.

Casting an object reference back to its *real* type.

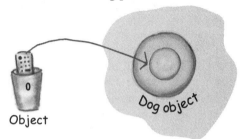

Object

Dog object

It's really still a Dog *object*, but if you want to call Dog-specific methods, you need a *reference* declared as type Dog. If you're *sure** the object is really a Dog, you can make a new Dog reference to it by copying the Object reference, and forcing that copy to go into a Dog reference variable, using a cast (Dog). You can use the new *Dog* reference to call *Dog* methods.

```
Object o = al.get(index);
Dog d = (Dog) o;          cast the Object back to
d.roam();                 a Dog we know is there.
```

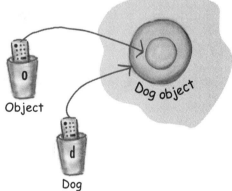

Object

Dog object

Dog

*If you're *not* sure it's a Dog, you can use the **instanceof** operator to check. Because if you're wrong when you do the cast, you'll get a ClassCastException at runtime and come to a grinding halt.

```
if (o instanceof Dog) {
    Dog d = (Dog) o;
}
```

So now you've seen how much Java cares about the methods in the class of the reference variable.

You can call a method on an object *only* if the class of the reference variable has that method.

Think of the public methods in your class as your contract, your promise to the outside world about the things you can do.

When you write a class, you almost always *expose* some of the methods to code outside the class. To *expose* a method means you make a method *accessible*, usually by marking it public.

Imagine this scenario: you're writing code for a small business accounting program. A custom application for "Simon's Surf Shop". The good re-user that you are, you found an Account class that appears to meet your needs perfectly, according to its documentation, anyway. Each account instance represents an individual customer's account with the store. So there you are minding your own business invoking the *credit()* and *debit()* methods on an account object when you realize you need to get a balance on an account. No problem—there's a *getBalance()* method that should do nicely.

Account
debit(double amt)
credit(double amt)
double getBalance()

Except... when you invoke the *getBalance()* method, the whole thing blows up at runtime. Forget the documentation, the class does not have that method. Yikes!

But that won't happen to you, because everytime you use the dot operator on a reference (a.doStuff()), the compiler looks at the *reference* type (the type 'a' was declared to be) and checks that class to guarantee the class has the method, and that the method does indeed take the argument you're passing and return the kind of value you're expecting to get back.

Just remember that the compiler checks the class of the *reference* variable, not the class of the actual *object* at the other end of the reference.

What if you need to change the contract?

OK, pretend you're a Dog. Your Dog class isn't the *only* contract that defines who you are. Remember, you inherit accessible (which usually means *public*) methods from all of your superclasses.

True, your Dog class defines a contract.

But not *all* of your contract.

Everything in class *Canine* is part of your contract.

Everything in class *Animal* is part of your contract.

Everything in class *Object* is part of your contract.

According to the IS-A test, you *are* each of those things—Canine, Animal, and Object.

But what if the person who designed your class had in mind the Animal simulation program, and now he wants to use you (class Dog) for a Science Fair Tutorial on Animal objects.

That's OK, you're probably reusable for that.

But what if later he wants to use you for a PetShop program? *You don't have any Pet behaviors.* A Pet needs methods like *beFriendly()* and *play().*

OK, now pretend you're the Dog class programmer. No problem, right? Just add some more methods to the Dog class. You won't be breaking anyone else's code by *adding* methods, since you aren't touching the *existing* methods that someone else's code might be calling on Dog objects.

Can you see any drawbacks to that approach (adding Pet methods to the Dog class)?

BRAIN POWER

Think about what **YOU** would do if **YOU** were the Dog class programmer and needed to modify the Dog so that it could do Pet things, too. We know that simply adding new Pet behaviors (methods) to the Dog class will work, and won't break anyone else's code.

But... this is a PetShop program. It has more than just Dogs! And what if someone wants to use your Dog class for a program that has *wild* Dogs? What do you think your options might be, and without worrying about how Java handles things, just try to imagine how you'd *like* to solve the problem of modifying some of your Animal classes to include Pet behaviors.

Stop right now and think about it, **before you look at the next page** where we begin to reveal *everything.*

(thus rendering the whole exercise completely useless, robbing you of your One Big Chance to burn some brain calories)

Let's explore some design options for reusing some of our existing classes in a PetShop program.

On the next few pages, we're going to walk through some possibilities. We're not yet worried about whether Java can actually *do* what we come up with. We'll cross that bridge once we have a good idea of some of the tradeoffs.

① **Option one**

We take the easy path, and put pet methods in class Animal.

Pros:

All the Animals will instantly inherit the pet behaviors. We won't have to touch the existing Animal subclasses at all, and any Animal subclasses created in the future will also get to take advantage of inheriting those methods. That way, class Animal can be used as the polymorphic type in any program that wants to treat the Animals as pets

Cons:

So... when was the last time you saw a Hippo at a pet shop? Lion? Wolf? Could be dangerous to give non-pets pet methods.

Also, we almost certainly WILL have to touch the pet classes like Dog and Cat, because (in our house, anyway) Dogs and Cats tend to implement pet behaviors VERY differently.

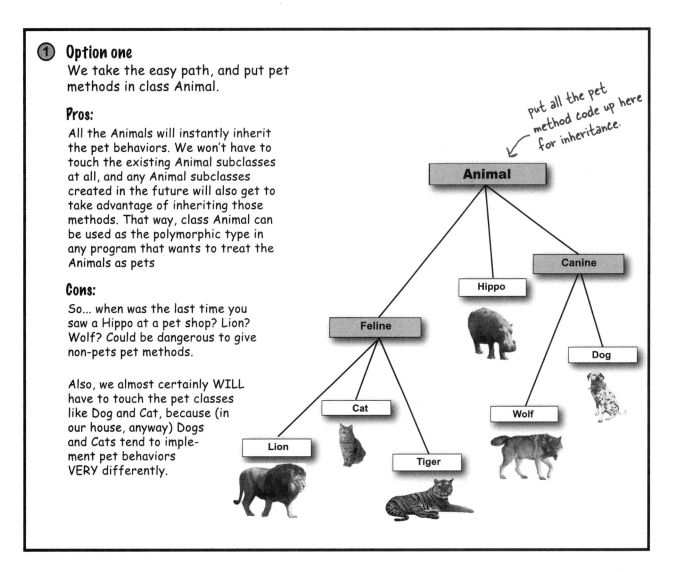

put all the pet method code up here for inheritance.

Option two

We start with Option One, putting the pet methods in class Animal, but we make the methods abstract, forcing the Animal subclasses to override them.

Pros:

That would give us all the benefits of Option One, but without the drawback of having non-pet Animals running around with pet methods (like beFriendly()). All Animal classes would have the method (because it's in class Animal), but because it's abstract the non-pet Animal classes won't inherit any functionality. All classes MUST override the methods, but they can make the methods "do-nothings".

Cons:

Because the pet methods in the Animal class are all abstract, the concrete Animal subclasses are forced to implement all of them. (Remember, all abstract methods MUST be implemented by the first concrete subclass down the inheritance tree.) What a waste of time! You have to sit there and type in each and every pet method into each and every concrete non-pet class, and all future subclasses as well. And while this does solve the problem of non-pets actually DOING pet things (as they would if they inherited pet functionality from class Animal), the contract is bad. Every *non*-pet class would be announcing to the world that it, too, has those pet methods, even though the methods wouldn't actually DO anything when called.

This approach doesn't look good at all. It just seems wrong to stuff everything into class Animal that more than one Animal type might need, UNLESS it applies to ALL Animal subclasses.

put all the pet methods up here, but with no implementations. Make all pet methods abstract.

Animal

Hippo

Canine

Dog

Feline

Cat

Wolf

Lion

Tiger

> Ask me to be friendly. No, seriously... ask me. I have the method.

③ Option three

Put the pet methods ONLY in the classes where they belong.

Pros:

No more worries about Hippos greeting you at the door or licking your face. The methods are where they belong, and ONLY where they belong. Dogs can implement the methods and Cats can implement the methods, but nobody else has to know about them.

Cons:

Two Big Problems with this approach. First off, you'd have to agree to a protocol, and all programmers of pet Animal classes now and in the future would have to KNOW about the protocol. By protocol, we mean the exact methods that we've decided all pets should have. The pet contract without anything to back it up. But what if one of the programmers gets it just a tiny bit wrong? Like, a method takes a String when it was supposed to take an int? Or they named it *do*Friendly() instead of *be*Friendly()? Since it isn't in a contract, the compiler has no way to check you to see if you've implemented the methods correctly. Someone could easily come along to use the pet Animal classes and find that not all of them work quite right.

And second, you don't get to use polymorphism for the pet methods. Every class that needs to use pet behaviors would have to know about each and every class! In other words, you can't use Animal as the polymorphic type now, because the compiler won't let you call a Pet method on an Animal reference (even if it's really a Dog object) because class Animal doesn't have the method.

☆ Put the pet methods ONLY in the Animal classes that can be pets, instead of in Animal.

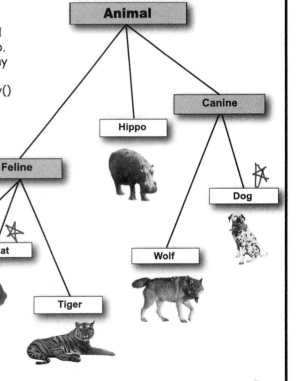

So what we REALLY need is:

* A way to have pet behavior in **just** the pet classes

* A way to guarantee that all pet classes have all of the same methods defined (same name, same arguments, same return types, no missing methods, etc.), without having to cross your fingers and hope all the programmers get it right.

* A way to take advantage of polymorphism so that all pets can have their pet methods called, without having to use arguments, return types, and arrays for each and every pet class.

It looks like we need TWO superclasses at the top

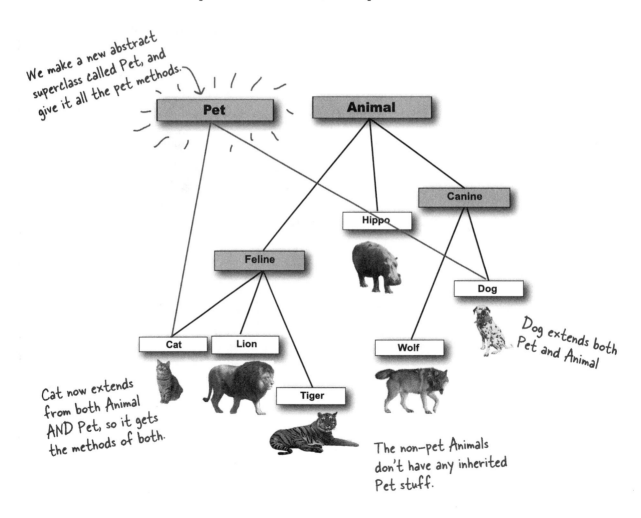

We make a new abstract superclass called Pet, and give it all the pet methods.

Cat now extends from both Animal AND Pet, so it gets the methods of both.

Dog extends both Pet and Animal

The non-pet Animals don't have any inherited Pet stuff.

There's just one problem with the "two superclasses" approach...

It's called "multiple inheritance" and it can be a Really Bad Thing.

That is, if it were possible to do in Java.

But it isn't, because multiple inheritance has a problem known as The Deadly Diamond of Death.

Deadly Diamond of Death

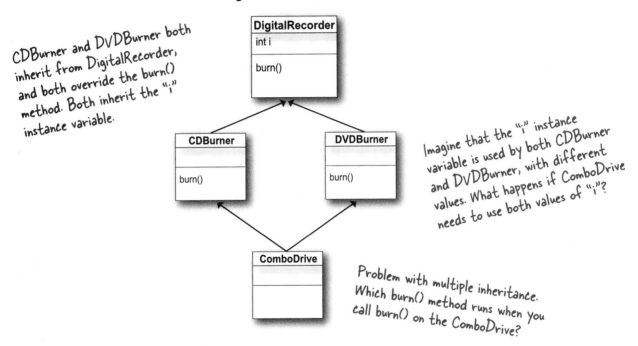

CDBurner and DVDBurner both inherit from DigitalRecorder, and both override the burn() method. Both inherit the "i" instance variable.

Imagine that the "i" instance variable is used by both CDBurner and DVDBurner, with different values. What happens if ComboDrive needs to use both values of "i"?

Problem with multiple inheritance. Which burn() method runs when you call burn() on the ComboDrive?

A language that allows the Deadly Diamond of Death can lead to some ugly complexities, because you have to have special rules to deal with the potential ambiguities. And extra rules means extra work for you both in *learning* those rules and watching out for those "special cases". Java is supposed to be *simple*, with consistent rules that don't blow up under some scenarios. So Java (unlike C++) protects you from having to think about the Deadly Diamond of Death. But that brings us back to the original problem! *How do we handle the Animal/Pet thing?*

Interface to the rescue!

Java gives you a solution. An *interface*. Not a *GUI* interface, not the generic use of the *word* interface as in, "That's the public interface for the Button class API," but the Java *keyword* **interface**.

A Java interface solves your multiple inheritance problem by giving you much of the polymorphic *benefits* of multiple inheritance without the pain and suffering from the Deadly Diamond of Death (DDD).

The way in which interfaces side-step the DDD is surprisingly simple: **make all the methods abstract!** That way, the subclass **must** implement the methods (remember, abstract methods *must* be implemented by the first concrete subclass), so at runtime the JVM isn't confused about *which* of the two inherited versions it's supposed to call.

```
                 Pet
    ┌─────────────────────────────┐
    ├─────────────────────────────┤
    │                             │
    ├─────────────────────────────┤
    │ abstract void beFriendly();  │
    │                             │
    │ abstract void play();        │
    │                             │
    └─────────────────────────────┘
```

A Java interface is like a 100% pure abstract class.

All methods in an interface are abstract, so any class that IS-A Pet MUST implement (i.e. override) the methods of Pet.

To DEFINE an interface:

```
public interface Pet {...}
```

Use the keyword "interface" instead of "class"

To IMPLEMENT an interface:

```
public class Dog extends Canine implements Pet {...}
```

Use the keyword "implements" followed by the interface name. Note that when you implement an interface you still get to extend a class

Making and Implementing the Pet interface

interface methods are implicitly public and abstract, so typing in 'public' and 'abstract' is optional (in fact, it's not considered 'good style' to type the words in, but we did here just to reinforce it, and because we've never been slaves to fashion...)

You say 'interface' instead of 'class' here

```
public interface Pet {
    (public abstract) void beFriendly();
    (public abstract) void play();
}
```

All interface methods are abstract, so they MUST end in semicolons. Remember, they have no body!

Dog IS-A Animal and Dog IS-A Pet

You say 'implements' followed by the name of the interface.

```
public class Dog extends Canine implements Pet {
    public void beFriendly() {...}
    public void play() {..}

    public void roam() {...}
    public void eat() {...}
}
```

You SAID you are a Pet, so you MUST implement the Pet methods. It's your contract. Notice the curly braces instead of semicolons.

These are just normal overriding methods.

there are no Dumb Questions

Q: Wait a minute, interfaces don't really give you multiple inheritance, because you can't put any implementation code in them. If all the methods are abstract, what does an interface really buy you?

A: Polymorphism, polymorphism, polymorphism. Interfaces are the ultimate in flexibility, because if you use interfaces instead of concrete subclasses (or even abstract superclass types) as arguments and return types, you can pass anything that implements that interface. And think about it—with an interface, a class doesn't have to come from just one inheritance tree. A class can extend one class, and implement an interface. But another class might implement the same interface, yet come from a completely different inheritance tree! So you get to treat an object by the role it plays, rather than by the class type from which it was instantiated.

In fact, if you wrote your code to use interfaces, you wouldn't even have to give anyone a superclass that they had to extend. You could just give them the interface and say, "Here,' I don't care what kind of class inheritance structure you come from, just implement this interface and you'll be good to go."

The fact that you can't put in implementation code turns out not to be a problem for most good designs, because most interface methods wouldn't make sense if implemented in a generic way. In other words, most interface methods would need to be overridden even if the methods weren't _forced_ to be abstract.

Classes from *different* inheritance trees can implement the *same* interface.

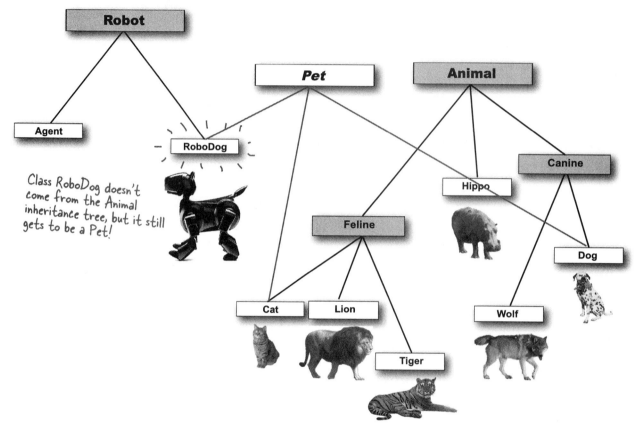

Class RoboDog doesn't come from the Animal inheritance tree, but it still gets to be a Pet!

When you use a *class* as a polymorphic type (like an array of type Animal or a method that takes a Canine argument), the objects you can stick in that type must be from the same inheritance tree. But not just anywhere in the inheritance tree; the objects must be from a class that is a subclass of the polymorphic type. An argument of type Canine can accept a Wolf and a Dog, but not a Cat or a Hippo.

But when you use an *interface* as a polymorphic type (like an array of Pets), the objects can be from *anywhere* in the inheritance tree. The only requirement is that the objects are from a class that *implements* the interface. Allowing classes in different inheritance trees to implement a common interface is crucial in the Java API. Do you want an object to be able to save its state to a file? Implement the Serializable interface. Do you need objects to run

their methods in a separate thread of execution? Implement Runnable. You get the idea. You'll learn more about Serializable and Runnable in later chapters, but for now, remember that classes from *any* place in the inheritance tree might need to implement those interfaces. Nearly *any* class might want to be saveable or runnable.

Better still, a class can implement *multiple* interfaces!

A Dog object IS-A Canine, and IS-A Animal, and IS-A Object, all through inheritance. But a Dog IS-A Pet through interface implementation, and the Dog might implement other interfaces as well. You could say:

```
public class Dog extends Animal implements
Pet, Saveable, Paintable { ... }
```

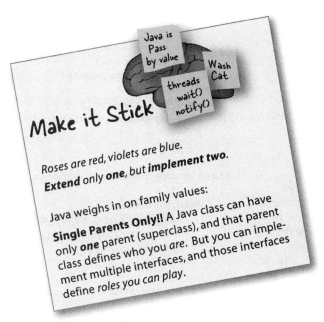

Make it Stick

Roses are red, violets are blue.
Extend *only* **one**, *but* **implement two**.

Java weighs in on family values:

Single Parents Only!! A Java class can have only **one** parent (superclass), and that parent class defines who you *are*. But you can implement multiple interfaces, and those interfaces define *roles you can play*.

How do you know whether to make a class, a subclass, an *abstract* class, or an interface?

▶ Make a class that doesn't extend anything (other than Object) when your new class doesn't pass the IS-A test for any other type.

▶ Make a subclass (in other words, *extend* a class) only when you need to make a **more specific** version of a class and need to override or add new behaviors.

▶ Use an abstract class when you want to define a **template** for a group of subclasses, and you have at least *some* implementation code that all subclasses could use. Make the class abstract when you want to guarantee that nobody can make objects of that type.

▶ Use an interface when you want to define a **role** that other classes can play, regardless of where those classes are in the inheritance tree.

Invoking the superclass version of a method

Q: What if you make a concrete subclass and you need to override a method, but you want the behavior in the superclass version of the method? In other words, what if you don't need to *replace* the method with an override, but you just want to *add* to it with some additional specific code.

A: Ahhh... think about the meaning of the word 'extends'. One area of good OO design looks at how to design concrete code that's *meant* to be overridden. In other words, you write method code in, say, an abstract class, that does work that's generic enough to support typical concrete implementations. But, the concrete code isn't enough to handle *all* of the subclass-specific work. So the subclass overrides the method and *extends* it by adding the rest of the code. The keyword super lets you invoke a superclass version of an overridden method, from within the subclass.

superclass version of the method does important stuff that subclasses could use

```java
abstract class Report {
    void runReport() {
        // set-up report
    }
    void printReport() {
        // generic printing
    }
}

class BuzzwordsReport extends Report {

    void runReport() {
        super.runReport();
        buzzwordCompliance();
        printReport();
    }
    void buzzwordCompliance() {...}
}
```

call superclass version, then come back and do some subclass-specific stuff

If method code inside a BuzzwordReport subclass says:

super.runReport();

the runReport() method inside the superclass Report will run

subclass method (overrides the superclass version)

superclass methods (including the overridden runReport()

runReport()
buzzwordCompliance()

runReport()
printReport()
Report

BuzzwordReport

super.runReport();

A reference to the subclass object (BuzzwordReport) will always call the subclass version of an overridden method. That's polymorphism. But the subclass code can call super.runReport() to invoke the superclass version.

The super keyword is really a reference to the superclass portion of an object. When subclass code uses super, as in super.runReport(), the superclass version of the method will run.

BULLET POINTS

- When you don't want a class to be instantiated (in other words, you don't want anyone to make a new object of that class type) mark the class with the `abstract` keyword.

- An abstract class can have both abstract and non-abstract methods.

- If a class has even *one* abstract method, the class must be marked abstract.

- An abstract method has no body, and the declaration ends with a semicolon (no curly braces).

- All abstract methods must be implemented in the first concrete subclass in the inheritance tree.

- Every class in Java is either a direct or indirect subclass of class **Object** (java.lang.Object).

- Methods can be declared with Object arguments and/or return types.

- You can call methods on an object *only* if the methods are in the class (or interface) used as the *reference* variable type, regardless of the actual *object* type. So, a reference variable of type Object can be used only to call methods defined in class Object, regardless of the type of the object to which the reference refers.

- A reference variable of type Object can't be assigned to any other reference type without a *cast*. A cast can be used to assign a reference variable of one type to a reference variable of a subtype, but at runtime the cast will fail if the object on the heap is NOT of a type compatible with the cast.
  Example: `Dog d = (Dog) x.getObject(aDog);`

- All objects come out of an ArrayList<Object> as type Object (meaning, they can be referenced only by an Object reference variable, unless you use a *cast*).

- Multiple inheritance is not allowed in Java, because of the problems associated with the "Deadly Diamond of Death". That means you can extend only one class (i.e. you can have only one immediate superclass).

- An interface is like a 100% pure abstract class. It defines *only* abstract methods.

- Create an interface using the `interface` keyword instead of the word `class`.

- Implement an interface using the keyword `implements`
  Example: `Dog implements Pet`

- Your class can implement multiple interfaces.

- A class that implements an interface *must* implement all the methods of the interface, since *all interface methods are implicitly public and abstract*.

- To invoke the superclass version of a method from a subclass that's overridden the method, use the `super` keyword. Example: `super.runReport();`

Q: **There's still something strange here... you never explained how it is that ArrayList<Dog> gives back Dog references that don't need to be cast, yet the ArrayList class uses Object in its methods, not Dog (or DotCom or anything else). What's the special trick going on when you say ArrayList<Dog>?**

A: You're right for calling it a special trick. In fact it is a special trick that ArrayList<Dog> gives back Dogs without you having to do any cast, since it looks like ArrayList methods don't know anything about Dogs, or any type besides Object.

The short answer is that *the compiler puts in the cast for you!* When you say ArrayList<Dog>, there is no special class that has methods to take and return Dog objects, but instead the <Dog> is a signal to the compiler that you want the compiler to let you put ONLY Dog objects in and to stop you if you try to add any other type to the list. And since the compiler stops you from adding anything but Dogs to the ArrayList, the compiler also knows that its safe to cast anything that comes out of that ArrayList do a Dog reference. In other words, using ArrayList<Dog> saves you from having to cast the Dog you get back. But it's much more important than that... because remember, a cast can fail at runtime, and wouldn't you rather have your errors happen at compile time rather than, say, when your customer is using it for something critical?

But there's a lot more to this story, and we'll get into all the details in the Collections chapter.

Exercise

Here's your chance to demonstrate your artistic abilities. On the left you'll find sets of class and interface declarations. Your job is to draw the associated class diagrams on the right. We did the first one for you. Use a dashed line for "implements" and a solid line for "extends".

Given:

What's the Picture?

1)
```
public interface Foo { }
public class Bar implements Foo { }
```

2)
```
public interface Vinn { }
public abstract class Vout implements Vinn { }
```

3)
```
public abstract class Muffie implements Whuffie { }
public class Fluffie extends Muffie { }
public interface Whuffie { }
```

4)
```
public class Zoop { }
public class Boop extends Zoop { }
public class Goop extends Boop { }
```

5)
```
public class Gamma extends Delta implements Epsilon { }
public interface Epsilon { }
public interface Beta { }
public class Alpha extends Gamma implements Beta { }
public class Delta { }
```

1)

┌─────────────┐
│ (interface) │
│   Foo   │
│   │
└─────────────┘
      △
      ┆
┌─────────────┐
│   Bar   │
│   │
└─────────────┘

2)

3)

4)

5)

Exercise

On the left you'll find sets of class diagrams. Your job is to turn these into valid Java declarations. We did number 1 for you (and it was a tough one).

What's the Declaration?

Given:

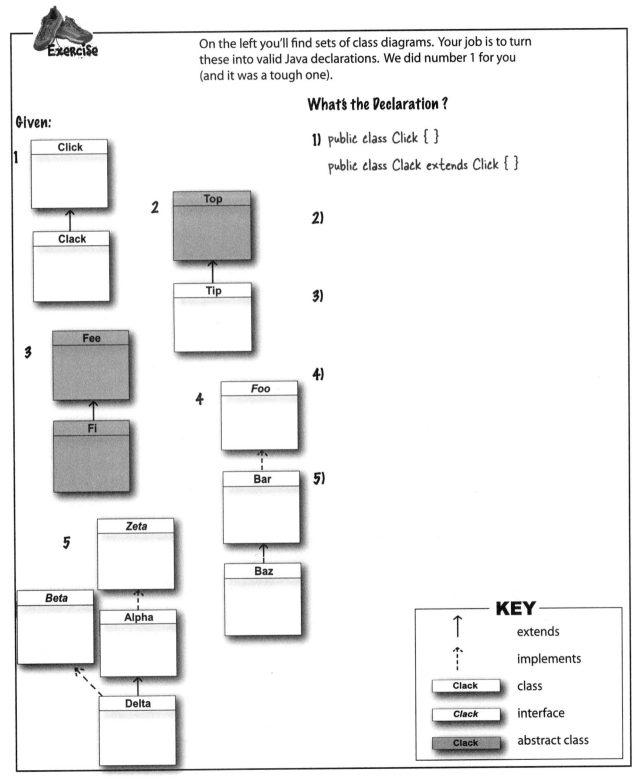

1) public class Click { }

public class Clack extends Click { }

2)

3)

4)

5)

KEY

↑	extends
⇡	implements
Clack	class
Clack	interface
Clack	abstract class

Pŏŏl Puzzle

Your **job** is to take code snippets from the pool and place them into the blank lines in the code and output. You **may** use the same snippet more than once, and you won't need to use all the snippets. Your **goal** is to make a set of classes that will compile and run and produce the output listed.

```
_____ Nose {

   _____

}


abstract class Picasso implements _____ {

   _____

      return 7;

   }

}


class _____  _____  _____ { }


class _____  _____  _____ {

   _____

      return 5;

   }

}
```

```
public _____  _____ extends Clowns {

   public static void main(String [] args) {

      _____

      i[0] = new _____

      i[1] = new _____

      i[2] = new _____

      for(int x = 0; x < 3; x++) {

         System.out.println(_____

               + " " + _____.getClass( ) );

      }

   }

}
```

Output

```
File  Edit  Window  Help  BeAfraid
%java _____
5 class Acts
7 class Clowns
        _____Of76
```

Note: Each snippet from the pool can be used more than once!

```
                          class
    Acts( );              extends       i
    Nose( );              interface     i( )
    Of76( );              implements    i(x)
    Clowns( );                          i[x]
    Picasso( );                i[x]           class
                                              5 class
                                              7 class
                                              7 public class          Acts
                                                                      Nose
    Of76 [ ] i = new Nose[3];   public int iMethod( );                Of76
    Of76 [ 3 ] i;               public int iMethod { }                Clowns
    Nose [ ] i = new Nose( );   public int iMethod ( ) {      i.iMethod(x)    Picasso
    Nose [ ] i = new Nose[3];   public int iMethod ( ) { }    i(x).iMethod[ ]
                                                              i[x].iMethod( )
                                                              i[x].iMethod[ ]
```

Exercise Solutions

What's the Picture?

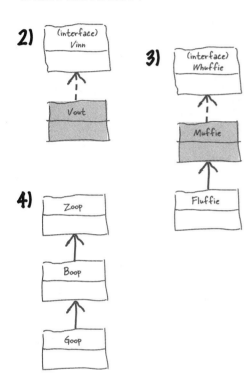

2)
(interface)
Vinn

Vout

3)
(interface)
Whuffie

Muffie

Fluffie

4)
Zoop

Boop

Goop

5)
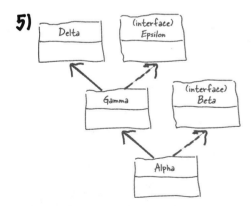

Delta

(interface)
Epsilon

Gamma

(interface)
Beta

Alpha

What's the Declaration?

2) public abstract class Top { }
public class Tip extends Top { }

3) public abstract class Fee { }
public abstract class Fi extends Fee { }

4) public interface Foo { }
public class Bar implements Foo { }
public class Baz extends Bar { }

5) public interface Zeta { }
public class Alpha implements Zeta { }
public interface Beta { }
public class Delta extends Alpha implements Beta { }

```
interface Nose {
   public int iMethod( );
}
abstract class Picasso implements Nose {
   public int iMethod( ) {
      return 7;
   }
}
class Clowns extends Picasso { }

class Acts extends Picasso {
   public int iMethod( ) {
      return 5;
   }
}
```

```
public class Of76 extends Clowns {
   public static void main(String [] args) {
      Nose [ ] i = new Nose [3];
      i[0] = new Acts( );
      i[1] = new Clowns( );
      i[2] = new Of76( );
      for(int x = 0; x < 3; x++) {
         System.out.println( i [x]. iMethod( )
                  + " " + i [x].getClass( ) );
      }
   }
}
```

Output

```
 File  Edit  Window  Help  KillTheMime
%java Of76
5 class Acts
7 class Clowns
7 class  Of76
```

Life and Death of an Object

...then he said, "I can't feel my legs!" and I said "Joe! Stay with me Joe!" But it was... too late. The garbage collector came and... he was gone. Best object I ever had.

Objects are born and objects die. You're in charge of an object's lifecycle. You decide when and how to **construct** it. You decide when to **destroy** it. Except you don't actually *destroy* the object yourself, you simply *abandon* it. But once it's abandoned, the heartless **Garbage Collector (gc)** can vaporize it, reclaiming the memory that object was using. If you're gonna write Java, you're gonna create objects. Sooner or later, you're gonna have to let some of them go, or risk running out of RAM. In this chapter we look at how objects are created, where they live while they're alive, and how to keep or abandon them efficiently. That means we'll talk about the heap, the stack, scope, constructors, super constructors, null references, and more. Warning: this chapter contains material about object death that some may find disturbing. Best not to get too attached.

The Stack and the Heap: where things live

Before we can understand what really happens when you create an object, we have to step back a bit. We need to learn more about where everything lives (and for how long) in Java. That means we need to learn more about the Stack and the Heap. In Java, we (programmers) care about two areas of memory—the one where objects live (the heap), and the one where method invocations and local variables live (the stack). When a JVM starts up, it gets a chunk of memory from the underlying OS, and uses it to run your Java program. How *much* memory, and whether or not you can tweak it, is dependent on which version of the JVM (and on which platform) you're

running. But usually you *won't* have anything to say about it. And with good programming, you probably won't care (more on that a little later).

We know that all *objects* live on the garbage-collectible heap, but we haven't yet looked at where *variables* live. And where a variable lives depends on what *kind* of variable it is. And by "kind", we don't mean *type* (i.e. primitive or object reference). The two *kinds* of variables whose lives we care about now are *instance* variables and *local* variables. Local variables are also known as *stack* variables, which is a big clue for where they live.

The Stack

Where method invocations and local variables live

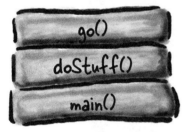

go()

doStuff()

main()

The Heap

Where **ALL** objects live

also known as "The Garbage-Collectible Heap"

Duck object

Snowboard object

Button object

Instance Variables

Instance variables are declared inside a *class* but *not* inside a method. They represent the "fields" that each individual object has (which can be filled with different values for each instance of the class). Instance variables live inside the object they belong to.

```
public class Duck {
    int size;
}
```

← Every Duck has a "size" instance variable.

Local Variables

Local variables are declared inside a *method*, including method parameters. They're temporary, and live only as long as the method is on the stack (in other words, as long as the method has not reached the closing curly brace).

```
public void foo(int x) {
    int i = x + 3;
    boolean b = true;
}
```

The parameter x and the variables i and b are all local variables.

Methods are stacked

When you call a method, the method lands on the top of a call stack. That new thing that's actually pushed onto the stack is the stack *frame*, and it holds the state of the method including which line of code is executing, and the values of all local variables.

The method at the *top* of the stack is always the currently-running method for that stack (for now, assume there's only one stack, but in chapter 14 we'll add more.) A method stays on the stack until the method hits its closing curly brace (which means the method's done). If method *foo()* calls method *bar()*, method *bar()* is stacked on top of method *foo()*.

A call stack with two methods

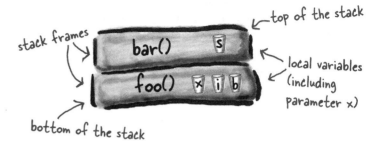

The method on the top of the stack is always the currently-executing method.

```
public void doStuff() {
    boolean b = true;
    go(4);
}
public void go(int x) {
    int z = x + 24;
    crazy();
    // imagine more code here
}
public void crazy() {
    char c = 'a';
}
```

A stack scenario

The code on the left is a snippet (we don't care what the rest of the class looks like) with three methods. The first method (*doStuff()*) calls the second method (*go()*), and the second method calls the third (*crazy()*). Each method declares one local variable within the body of the method, and method *go()* also declares a parameter variable (which means *go()* has two local variables).

① Code from another class calls **doStuff()**, and **doStuff()** goes into a stack frame at the top of the stack. The boolean variable named 'b' goes on the **doStuff()** stack frame.

② **doStuff()** calls **go()**, **go()** is *pushed* on top of the stack. Variables 'x' and 'z' are in the **go()** stack frame.

③ **go()** calls **crazy()**, **crazy()** is now on the top of the stack, with variable 'c' in the frame.

④ **crazy()** completes, and its stack frame is *popped* off the stack. Execution goes back to the **go()** method, and picks up at the line following the call to **crazy()**.

What about local variables that are objects?

Remember, a non-primitive variable holds a *reference* to an object, not the object itself. You already know where objects live—on the heap. It doesn't matter where they're declared or created. *If the local variable is a reference to an object, only the variable (the reference/remote control) goes on the stack.*

The object itself still goes in the heap.

barf() declares and creates a new Duck reference variable 'd' (since it's declared inside the method, it's a local variable and goes on the stack.

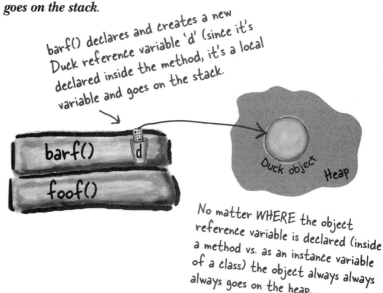

```java
public class StackRef {
    public void foof() {
        barf();
    }

    public void barf() {
        Duck d = new Duck(24);
    }
}
```

No matter WHERE the object reference variable is declared (inside a method vs. as an instance variable of a class) the object always always always goes on the heap.

there are no Dumb Questions

Q: One more time, WHY are we learning the whole stack/heap thing? How does this help me? Do I really need to learn about it?

A: Knowing the fundamentals of the Java Stack and Heap is crucial if you want to understand variable scope, object creation issues, memory management, threads, and exception handling. We cover threads and exception handling in later chapters but the others you'll learn in this one. You do not need to know anything about *how* the Stack and Heap are implemented in any particular JVM and/or platform. Everything you need to know about the Stack and Heap is on this page and the previous one. If you nail these pages, all the other topics that depend on your knowing this stuff will go much, much, much easier. Once again, some day you will SO thank us for shoving Stacks and Heaps down your throat.

BULLET POINTS

- ▶ Java has two areas of memory we care about: the Stack and the Heap.

- ▶ Instance variables are variables declared inside a class but outside any method.

- ▶ Local variables are variables declared inside a method or method parameter.

- ▶ All local variables live on the stack, in the frame corresponding to the method where the variables are declared.

- ▶ Object reference variables work just like primitive variables—if the reference is declared as a local variable, it goes on the stack.

- ▶ All objects live in the heap, regardless of whether the reference is a local or instance variable.

If local variables live on the stack, where do instance variables live?

When you say new CellPhone(), Java has to make space on the Heap for that CellPhone. But how *much* space? Enough for the object, which means enough to house all of the object's instance variables. That's right, instance variables live on the Heap, inside the object they belong to.

Remember that the *values* of an object's instance variables live inside the object. If the instance variables are all primitives, Java makes space for the instance variables based on the primitive type. An int needs 32 bits, a long 64 bits, etc. Java doesn't care about the value inside primitive variables; the bit-size of an int variable is the same (32 bits) whether the value of the int is 32,000,000 or 32.

But what if the instance variables are *objects*? What if CellPhone HAS-A Antenna? In other words, CellPhone has a reference variable of type Antenna.

When the new object has instance variables that are object references rather than primitives, the real question is: does the object need space for all of the objects it holds references to? The answer is, *not exactly*. No matter what, Java has to make space for the instance variable *values*. But remember that a reference variable value is not the whole *object*, but merely a *remote control* to the object. So if CellPhone has an instance variable declared as the non-primitive type Antenna, Java makes space within the CellPhone object only for the Antenna's *remote control* (i.e. reference variable) but not the Antenna *object*.

Well then when does the Antenna *object* get space on the Heap? First we have to find out *when* the Antenna object itself is created. That depends on the instance variable declaration. If the instance variable is declared but no object is assigned to it, then only the space for the reference variable (the remote control) is created.

```
private Antenna ant;
```

No actual Antenna object is made on the heap unless or until the reference variable is assigned a new Antenna object.

```
private Antenna ant = new Antenna();
```

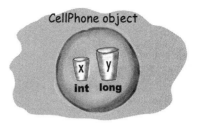

Object with two primitive instance variables. Space for the variables lives in the object.

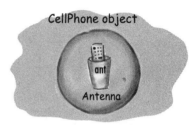

Object with one non-primitive instance variable— a reference to an Antenna object, but no actual Antenna object. This is what you get if you declare the variable but don't initialize it with an actual Antenna object.

```
public class CellPhone {
    private Antenna ant;
}
```

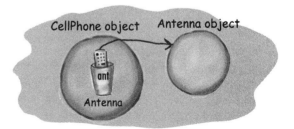

Object with one non-primitive instance variable, and the Antenna variable is assigned a new Antenna object.

```
public class CellPhone {
    private Antenna ant = new Antenna();
}
```

The miracle of object creation

Now that you know where variables and objects live, we can dive into the mysterious world of object creation. Remember the three steps of object declaration and assignment: declare a reference variable, create an object, and assign the object to the reference.

But until now, step two—where a miracle occurs and the new object is "born"—has remained a Big Mystery. Prepare to learn the facts of object life. *Hope you're not squeamish.*

Review the 3 steps of object declaration, creation and assignment:

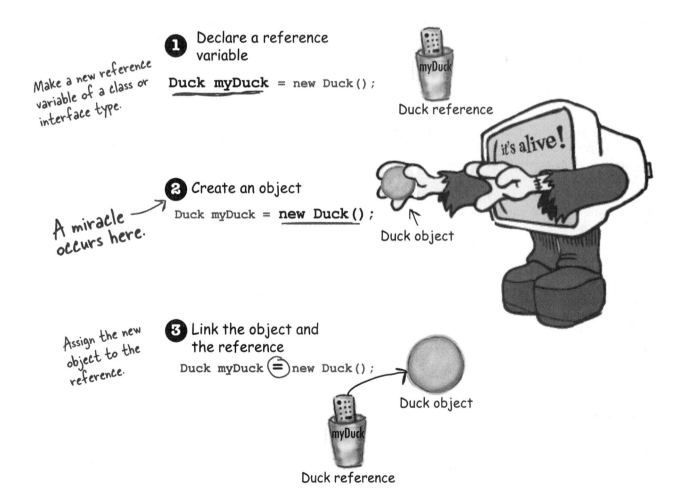

Make a new reference variable of a class or interface type.

1 Declare a reference variable

`Duck myDuck = new Duck();`

Duck reference

A miracle occurs here.

2 Create an object

`Duck myDuck = new Duck();`

Duck object

it's alive!

Assign the new object to the reference.

3 Link the object and the reference

`Duck myDuck (=)new Duck();`

Duck object

myDuck

Duck reference

Are we calling a method named Duck()?
Because it sure *looks* like it.

$$Duck\ myDuck\ =\ new\ Duck();$$

It looks like we're calling a method named Duck(), because of the parentheses.

No.

We're calling the Duck *constructor*.

A constructor *does* look and feel a lot like a method, but it's not a method. It's got the code that runs when you say **new**. In other words, *the code that runs when you instantiate an object*.

The only way to invoke a constructor is with the keyword **new** followed by the class name. The JVM finds that class and invokes the constructor in that class. (OK, technically this isn't the *only* way to invoke a constructor. But it's the only way to do it from *outside* a constructor. You *can* call a constructor from within another constructor, with restrictions, but we'll get into all that later in the chapter.)

But where is the constructor?

If we didn't write it, who did?

You can write a constructor for your class (we're about to do that), but if you don't, *the compiler writes one for you!*

Here's what the compiler's default constructor looks like:

```java
public  Duck() {

}
```

Notice something missing? How is this
different from a method?

Its name is the same as the class name. That's mandatory.

```java
public  Duck() {
    // constructor code goes here
}
```

Where's the return type? If this were a method, you'd need a return type between "public" and "Duck()".

> **A constructor** has the code that runs when you instantiate an object. In other words, the code that runs when you say new on a class type.
>
> Every class you create has a constructor, even if you don't write it yourself.

Construct a Duck

The key feature of a constructor is that it runs *before* the object can be assigned to a reference. That means you get a chance to step in and do things to get the object ready for use. In other words, before anyone can use the remote control for an object, the object has a chance to help construct itself. In our Duck constructor, we're not doing anything useful, but it still demonstrates the sequence of events.

If it Quacks like a constructor...

```java
public class Duck {

    public Duck() {
        System.out.println("Quack");
    }
}
```
← Constructor code.

The constructor gives you a chance to step into the middle of new.

```java
public class UseADuck {

    public static void main (String[] args) {
        Duck d = new Duck();
    }
}
```
← This calls the Duck constructor.

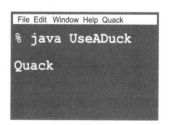

```
File Edit Window Help Quack
% java UseADuck

Quack
```

✎ Sharpen your pencil

A constructor lets you jump into the middle of the object creation step—into the middle of **new**. Can you imagine conditions where that would be useful? Which of these might be useful in a Car class constructor, if the Car is part of a Racing Game? Check off the ones that you came up with a scenario for.

- ☐ Increment a counter to track how many objects of this class type have been made.
- ☐ Assign runtime-specific state (data about what's happening NOW).
- ☐ Assign values to the object's important instance variables.
- ☐ Get and save a reference to the object that's *creating* the new object.
- ☐ Add the object to an ArrayList.
- ☐ Create HAS-A objects.
- ☐ _____ (your idea here)

Initializing the state of a new Duck

Most people use constructors to initialize the state of an object. In other words, to make and assign values to the object's instance variables.

```java
public Duck() {
    size = 34;
}
```

That's all well and good when the Duck class *developer* knows how big the Duck object should be. But what if we want the programmer who is *using* Duck to decide how big a particular Duck should be?

Imagine the Duck has a size instance variable, and you want the programmer using your Duck class to set the size of the new Duck. How could you do it?

Well, you could add a setSize() setter method to the class. But that leaves the Duck temporarily without a size*, and forces the Duck user to write *two* statements—one to create the Duck, and one to call the setSize() method. The code below uses a setter method to set the initial size of the new Duck.

```java
public class Duck {
    int size;   ← instance variable

    public Duck() {
        System.out.println("Quack");   ← constructor
    }

    public void setSize(int newSize) {   ← setter method
        size = newSize;
    }
}
```

```java
public class UseADuck {

    public static void main (String[] args) {
        Duck d = new Duck();

        d.setSize(42);
    }
}
```

There's a bad thing here. The Duck is alive at this point in the code, but without a size!* And then you're relying on the Duck-user to KNOW that Duck creation is a two-part process: one to call the constructor and one to call the setter.

*Instance variables do have a default value. 0 or 0.0 for numeric primitives, false for booleans, and null for references.

Q: Why do you need to write a constructor if the compiler writes one for you?

A: If you need code to help initialize your object and get it ready for use, you'll have to write your own constructor. You might, for example, be dependent on input from the user before you can finish making the object ready. There's another reason you might have to write a constructor, even if you don't need any constructor code yourself. It has to do with your superclass constructor, and we'll talk about that in a few minutes.

Q: How can you tell a constructor from a method? Can you also have a method that's the same name as the class?

A: Java lets you declare a method with the same name as your class. That doesn't make it a constructor, though. The thing that separates a method from a constructor is the return type. Methods *must* have a return type, but constructors *cannot* have a return type.

Q: Are constructors inherited? If you don't provide a constructor but your superclass does, do you get the superclass constructor instead of the default?

A: Nope. Constructors are not inherited. We'll look at that in just a few pages.

Using the constructor to initialize important Duck state*

If an object shouldn't be used until one or more parts of its state (instance variables) have been initialized, don't let anyone get ahold of a Duck object until you're finished initializing! It's usually way too risky to let someone make— and get a reference to—a new Duck object that isn't quite ready for use until that someone turns around and calls the *setSize()* method. How will the Duck-user even *know* that he's required to call the setter method after making the new Duck?

The best place to put initialization code is in the constructor. And all you need to do is make a constructor with arguments.

> Let the user make a new Duck *and* set the Duck's size all in one call. The call to new. The call to the Duck constructor.

```java
public class Duck {
    int size;

    public Duck(int duckSize) {
        System.out.println("Quack");

        size = duckSize;

        System.out.println("size is " + size);
    }
}
```

Add an int parameter to the Duck constructor.

Use the argument value to set the size instance variable.

```java
public class UseADuck {

    public static void main (String[] args) {
        Duck d = new Duck(42);
    }
}
```

This time there's only one statement. We make the new Duck and set its size in one statement.

Pass a value to the constructor.

```
File Edit Window Help Honk
% java UseADuck
Quack
size is 42
```

*Not to imply that not all Duck state is not unimportant.

Make it easy to make a Duck
Be sure you have a no-arg constructor

What happens if the Duck constructor takes an argument? Think about it. On the previous page, there's only *one* Duck constructor—and it takes an int argument for the *size* of the Duck. That might not be a big problem, but it does make it harder for a programmer to create a new Duck object, especially if the programmer doesn't *know* what the size of a Duck should be. Wouldn't it be helpful to have a default size for a Duck, so that if the user doesn't know an appropriate size, he can still make a Duck that works?

Imagine that you want Duck users to have TWO options for making a Duck—one where they supply the Duck size (as the constructor argument) and one where they don't specify a size and thus get your default Duck size.

You can't do this cleanly with just a single constructor. Remember, if a method (or constructor—same rules) has a parameter, you *must* pass an appropriate argument when you invoke that method or constructor. You can't just say, "If someone doesn't pass anything to the constructor, then use the default size", because they won't even be able to compile without sending an int argument to the constructor call. You *could* do something clunkly like this:

```
public class Duck {
   int size;

   public Duck(int newSize) {
      if (newSize == 0) {
         size = 27;
      } else {
         size = newSize;
      }
   }
}
```

If the parameter value is zero, give the new Duck a default size, otherwise use the parameter value for the size. NOT a very good solution.

But that means the programmer making a new Duck object has to *know* that passing a "0" is the protocol for getting the default Duck size. Pretty ugly. What if the other programmer doesn't know that? Or what if he really *does* want a zero-size Duck? (Assuming a zero-sized Duck is allowed. If you don't want zero-sized Duck objects, put validation code in the constructor to prevent it.) The point is, it might not always be possible to distinguish between a genuine "I want zero for the size" constructor argument and a "I'm sending zero so you'll give me the default size, whatever that is" constructor argument.

You really want TWO ways to make a new Duck:

```
public class Duck2 {
   int size;

   public Duck2() {
      // supply default size
      size = 27;
   }

   public Duck2(int duckSize) {
      // use duckSize parameter
      size = duckSize;
   }
}
```

To make a Duck when you know the size:

```
Duck2 d = new Duck2(15);
```

To make a Duck when you do *not* know the size:

```
Duck2 d2 = new Duck2();
```

So this two-options-to-make-a-Duck idea needs *two* constructors. One that takes an int and one that doesn't. *If you have more than one constructor in a class, it means you have overloaded constructors.*

Doesn't the compiler <u>always</u> make a no-arg constructor for you? No!

You might think that if you write *only* a constructor with arguments, the compiler will see that you don't have a no-arg constructor, and stick one in for you. But that's not how it works. The compiler gets involved with constructor-making *only if you don't say anything at all about constructors.*

If you write a constructor that takes arguments, and you *still* want a no-arg constructor, you'll have to build the no-arg constructor yourself!

As soon as *you* provide a constructor, ANY kind of constructor, the compiler backs off and says, "OK Buddy, looks like you're in charge of constructors now."

If you have more than one constructor in a class, the constructors MUST have different argument lists.

The argument list includes the order and types of the arguments. As long as they're different, you can have more than one constructor. You can do this with methods as well, but we'll get to that in another chapter.

OK, let's see here... "You have the right to your own constructor." Makes sense.

"If you cannot afford a constructor, one will be provided for you by the compiler." Good to know.

Overloaded constructors means you have more than one constructor in your class.

To compile, each constructor must have a *different* argument list!

The class below is legal because all four constructors have different argument lists. If you had two constructors that took only an int, for example, the class wouldn't compile. What you name the parameter variable doesn't count. It's the variable *type* (int, Dog, etc.) and *order* that matters. You *can* have two constructors that have identical types, *as long as the order is different*. A constructor that takes a String followed by an int, is *not* the same as one that takes an int followed by a String.

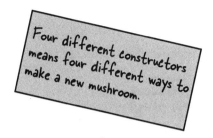

Four different constructors means four different ways to make a new mushroom.

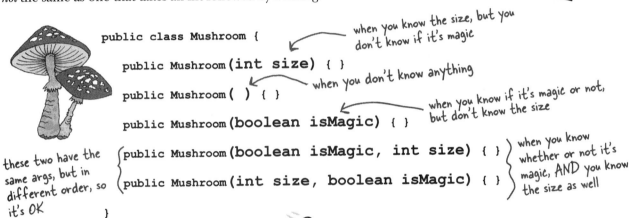

```
public class Mushroom {

    public Mushroom (int size) { }

    public Mushroom ( ) { }

    public Mushroom (boolean isMagic) { }

    public Mushroom (boolean isMagic, int size) { }

    public Mushroom (int size, boolean isMagic) { }

}
```

when you know the size, but you don't know if it's magic

when you don't know anything

when you know if it's magic or not, but don't know the size

when you know whether or not it's magic, AND you know the size as well

these two have the same args, but in different order, so it's OK

BULLET POINTS

► Instance variables live within the object they belong to, on the Heap.

► If the instance variable is a reference to an object, both the reference and the object it refers to are on the Heap.

► A constructor is the code that runs when you say **new** on a class type.

► A constructor must have the same name as the class, and must *not* have a return type.

► You can use a constructor to initialize the state (i.e. the instance variables) of the object being constructed.

► If you don't put a constructor in your class, the compiler will put in a default constructor.

► The default constructor is always a no-arg constructor.

► If you put a constructor—any constructor—in your class, the compiler will not build the default constructor.

► If you want a no-arg constructor, and you've already put in a constructor with arguments, you'll have to build the no-arg constructor yourself.

► Always provide a no-arg constructor if you can, to make it easy for programmers to make a working object. Supply default values.

► Overloaded constructors means you have more than one constructor in your class.

► Overloaded constructors must have different argument lists.

► You cannot have two constructors with the same argument lists. An argument list includes the order and/or type of arguments.

► Instance variables are assigned a default value, even when you don't explicitly assign one. The default values are 0/0.0/false for primitives, and null for references.

Sharpen your pencil

Match the `new Duck()` call with the constructor that runs when that Duck is instantiated. We did the easy one to get you started.

```java
public class TestDuck {

  public static void main(String[] args) {

    int weight = 8;
    float density = 2.3F;
    String name = "Donald";
    long[] feathers = {1,2,3,4,5,6};
    boolean canFly = true;
    int airspeed = 22;

    Duck[] d = new Duck[7];

    d[0] = new Duck();

    d[1] = new Duck(density, weight);

    d[2] = new Duck(name, feathers);

    d[3] = new Duck(canFly);

    d[4] = new Duck(3.3F, airspeed);

    d[5] = new Duck(false);

    d[6] = new Duck(airspeed, density);
  }
}
```

```java
class Duck {

  int pounds = 6;
  float floatability = 2.1F;
  String name = "Generic";
  long[] feathers = {1,2,3,4,5,6,7};
  boolean canFly = true;
  int maxSpeed = 25;

  public Duck() {
    System.out.println("type 1 duck");
  }

  public Duck(boolean fly) {
    canFly = fly;
    System.out.println("type 2 duck");
  }

  public Duck(String n, long[] f) {
    name = n;
    feathers = f;
    System.out.println("type 3 duck");
  }

  public Duck(int w, float f) {
    pounds = w;
    floatability = f;
    System.out.println("type 4 duck");
  }

  public Duck(float density, int max) {
    floatability = density;
    maxSpeed = max;
    System.out.println("type 5 duck");
  }
}
```

Q: Earlier you said that it's good to have a no-argument constructor so that if people call the no-arg constructor, we can supply default values for the "missing" arguments. But aren't there times when it's impossible to come up with defaults? Are there times when you should not have a no-arg constructor in your class?

A: You're right. There are times when a no-arg constructor doesn't make sense. You'll see this in the Java API—some classes don't have a no-arg constructor. The Color class, for example, represents a... color. Color objects are used to, for example, set or change the color of a screen font or GUI button. When you make a Color instance, that instance is of a particular color (you know, Death-by-Chocolate Brown, Blue-Screen-of-Death Blue, Scandalous Red, etc.). If you make a Color object, you must specify the color in some way.

```java
Color c = new Color(3,45,200);
```

(We're using three ints for RGB values here. We'll get into using Color later, in the Swing chapters.) Otherwise, what would you get? The Java API programmers *could* have decided that if you call a no-arg Color constructor you'll get a lovely shade of mauve. But good taste prevailed.

If you try to make a Color without supplying an argument:

```java
Color c = new Color();
```

The compiler freaks out because it can't find a matching no-arg constructor in the Color class.

```
File Edit Window Help StopBeingStupid
cannot resolve symbol
:constructor Color()
location: class
java.awt.Color
Color c = new Color();
          ^
1 error
```

Nanoreview: four things to remember about constructors

(1) A constructor is the code that runs when somebody says **new** on a class type

```
Duck d = new Duck();
```

(2) A constructor must have the same name as the class, and *no* return type

```
public Duck(int size) { }
```

(3) If you don't put a constructor in your class, the compiler puts in a default constructor. The default constructor is always a no-arg constructor.

```
public Duck() { }
```

(4) You can have more than one constructor in your class, as long as the argument lists are different. Having more than one constructor in a class means you have overloaded constructors.

```
public Duck() { }

public Duck(int size) { }

public Duck(String name) { }

public Duck(String name, int size) { }
```

Doing all the Brain Barbells has been shown to produce a 42% increase in neuron size. And you know what they say, "Big neurons..."

What about superclasses?

When you make a Dog, should the Canine constructor run too?

If the superclass is abstract, should it even *have* a constructor?

We'll look at this on the next few pages, so stop now and think about the implications of constructors and superclasses.

there are no Dumb Questions

Q: Do constructors have to be `public`?

A: No. Constructors can be `public`, `private`, or *default* (which means no access modifier at all). We'll look more at *default* access in chapter 16 and appendix B.

Q: How could a private constructor ever be useful? Nobody could ever call it, so nobody could ever make a new object!

A: But that's not exactly right. Marking something `private` doesn't mean *nobody* can access it, it just means that *nobody outside the class* can access it. Bet you're thinking "Catch 22". Only code from the *same* class as the class-with-private-constructor can make a new object from that class, but without first making an object, how do you ever get to run code from that class in the first place? How do you ever get to anything in that class? *Patience grasshopper.* We'll get there in the next chapter.

Wait a minute... we never DID talk about superclasses and inheritance and how that all fits in with constructors.

Here's where it gets fun. Remember from the last chapter, the part where we looked at the Snowboard object wrapping around an inner core representing the Object portion of the Snowboard class? The Big Point there was that every object holds not just its *own* declared instance variables, but also *everything from its superclasses* (which, at a minimum, means class Object, since *every* class extends Object).

So when an object is created (because somebody said **new**; there is *no other way* to create an object other than someone, somewhere saying **new** on the class type), the object gets space for *all* the instance variables, from all the way up the inheritance tree. Think about it for a moment... a superclass might have setter methods encapsulating a private variable. But that variable has to live *somewhere*. When an object is created, it's almost as though *multiple* objects materialize—the object being new'd and one object per each superclass. Conceptually, though, it's much better to think of it like the picture below, where the object being created has *layers* of itself representing each superclass.

A single object on the heap

There is only ONE object on the heap here. A Snowboard object. But it contains both the Snowboard parts of itself and the Object parts of itself. All instance variables from both classes have to be here.

Object

Foo a; int b; int c;
equals() getClass() hashCode() toString()

Object has instance variables encapsulated by access methods. Those instance variables are created when any subclass is instantiated. (These aren't the REAL Object variables, but we don't care what they are since they're encapsulated)

Snowboard

Foo x Foo y int z
turn() shred() getAir() loseControl()

Snowboard also has instance variables of its own, so to make a Snowboard object we need space for the instance variables of <u>both</u> classes.

The role of superclass constructors in an object's life.

All the constructors in an object's inheritance tree must run when you make a new object.

Let that sink in.

That means every superclass has a constructor (because every class has a constructor), and each constructor up the hierarchy runs at the time an object of a subclass is created.

Saying **new** is a Big Deal. It starts the whole constructor chain reaction. And yes, even abstract classes have constructors. Although you can never say new on an abstract class, an abstract class is still a superclass, so its constructor runs when someone makes an instance of a concrete subclass.

The super constructors run to build out the superclass parts of the object. Remember, a subclass might inherit methods that depend on superclass state (in other words, the value of instance variables in the superclass). For an object to be fully-formed, all the superclass parts of itself must be fully-formed, and that's why the super constructor *must* run. All instance variables from every class in the inheritance tree have to be declared and initialized. Even if Animal has instance variables that Hippo doesn't inherit (if the variables are private, for example), the Hippo still depends on the Animal methods that *use* those variables.

When a constructor runs, it immediately calls its superclass constructor, all the way up the chain until you get to the class Object constructor.

On the next few pages, you'll learn how superclass constructors are called, and how you can call them yourself. You'll also learn what to do if your superclass constructor has arguments!

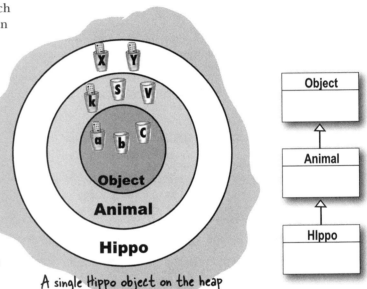

A single Hippo object on the heap

A new Hippo object also IS-A Animal and IS-A Object. If you want to make a Hippo, you must also make the Animal and Object parts of the Hippo.

This all happens in a process called Constructor Chaining.

object construction

Making a Hippo means making the Animal and Object parts too...

```java
public class Animal {
    public Animal() {
        System.out.println("Making an Animal");
    }
}
```

```java
public class Hippo extends Animal {
    public Hippo() {
        System.out.println("Making a Hippo");
    }
}
```

```java
public class TestHippo {
    public static void main (String[] args) {
        System.out.println("Starting...");
        Hippo h = new Hippo();
    }
}
```

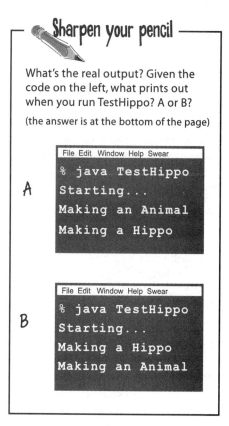

Sharpen your pencil

What's the real output? Given the code on the left, what prints out when you run TestHippo? A or B?

(the answer is at the bottom of the page)

A
```
% java TestHippo
Starting...
Making an Animal
Making a Hippo
```

B
```
% java TestHippo
Starting...
Making a Hippo
Making an Animal
```

① Code from another class says **new Hippo ()** and the **Hippo()** constructor goes into a stack frame at the top of the stack.

② **Hippo()** invokes the superclass constructor which pushes the **Animal()** constructor onto the top of the stack.

③ **Animal()** invokes the superclass constructor which pushes the **Object()** constructor onto the top of the stack, since Object is the superclass of Animal.

④ **Object()** completes, and its stack frame is *popped* off the stack. Execution goes back to the **Animal()** constructor, and picks up at the line following Animal's call to its superclass constructor

The first one, A. The Hippo() constructor is invoked first, but it's the Animal constructor that finishes first.

252 chapter 9

How do you invoke a superclass constructor?

You might think that somewhere in, say, a Duck constructor, if Duck extends Animal you'd call Animal(). But that's not how it works:

```
public class Duck extends Animal {
    int size;

    public Duck(int newSize) {
        Animal();
        size = newSize;
    }
}
```

BAD! → `Animal();` ← NO! This is not legal!

The only way to call a super constructor is by calling *super()*. That's right—*super()* calls the **super constructor**.

What are the odds?

```
public class Duck extends Animal {
    int size;

    public Duck(int newSize) {
        super();
        size = newSize;
    }
}
```

`super();` ← you just say super()

A call to *super()* in your constructor puts the superclass constructor on the top of the Stack. And what do you think that superclass constructor does? *Calls its superclass constructor.* And so it goes until the Object constructor is on the top of the Stack. Once *Object()* finishes, it's popped off the Stack and the next thing down the Stack (the subclass constructor that called *Object()*) is now on top. *That* constructor finishes and so it goes until the original constructor is on the top of the Stack, where *it* can now finish.

And how is it that we've gotten away without doing it?

You probably figured that out.

Our good friend the compiler puts in a call to *super()* if you don't.

So the compiler gets involved in constructor-making in *two* ways:

① If you *don't* provide a constructor
The compiler puts one in that looks like:

```
public ClassName() {
    super();
}
```

② If you *do* provide a constructor but you do *not* put in the call to super()

The compiler will put a call to super() in each of your overloaded constructors.* The compiler-supplied call looks like:

`super();`

It always looks like that. The compiler-inserted call to *super()* is always a no-arg call. If the superclass has overloaded constructors, only the no-arg one is called.

*Unless the constructor calls another overloaded constructor (you'll see that in a few pages).

Can the child exist before the parents?

If you think of a superclass as the parent to the subclass child, you can figure out which has to exist first. *The superclass parts of an object have to be fully-formed (completely built) before the subclass parts can be constructed.* Remember, the subclass object might depend on things it inherits from the superclass, so it's important that those inherited things be finished. No way around it. The superclass constructor must finish before its subclass constructor.

Look at the Stack series on page 248 again, and you can see that while the Hippo constructor is the *first* to be invoked (it's the first thing on the Stack), it's the *last* one to complete! Each subclass constructor immediately invokes its own superclass constructor, until the Object constructor is on the top of the Stack. Then Object's constructor completes and we bounce back down the Stack to Animal's constructor. Only after Animal's constructor completes do we finally come back down to finish the rest of the Hippo constructor. For that reason:

> Eewwww... that is SO creepy. There's **no** way I could have been born before my parents. That's just *wrong.*

The call to super() must be the *first* statement in each constructor!*

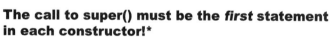

```
┌── Possible constructors for class Boop ─────────────────────────────────┐
│                                          ☑ public Boop() {              │
│  ☑ public Boop() {                          }          ←                │
│       super();    ←                                                     │
│     }                                     ☑ public Boop(int i) {        │
│                                                size = i;  ←             │
│  ☑ public Boop(int i) {                      }                          │
│       super();    ←                                                     │
│       size = i;                           ⊘ public Boop(int i) {        │
│     }                                          size = i;                │
│                                                super();  ←              │
│                                              }                          │
└─────────────────────────────────────────────────────────────────────────┘
```

These are OK because the programmer explicitly coded the call to super(), as the first statement.

These are OK because the compiler will put a call to super() in as the first statement.

BAD!! This won't compile! You can't explicitly put the call to super() below anything else.

*There's an exception to this rule; you'll learn it on page 252.

Superclass constructors with arguments

What if the superclass constructor has arguments? Can you pass something in to the *super()* call? Of course. If you couldn't, you'd never be able to extend a class that didn't have a no-arg constructor. Imagine this scenario: all animals have a name. There's a *getName()* method in class Animal that returns the value of the *name* instance variable. The instance variable is marked private, but the subclass (in this case, Hippo) inherits the *getName()* method. So here's the problem: Hippo has a *getName()* method (through inheritance), but does not have the *name* instance variable. Hippo has to depend on the Animal part of himself to keep the name instance variable, and return it when someone calls *getName()* on a Hippo object. But... how does the Animal part get the name? The only reference Hippo has to the Animal part of himself is through *super()*, so that's the place where Hippo sends the Hippo's name up to the Animal part of himself, so that the Animal part can store it in the private *name* instance variable.

```
Animal
-----------------------------
private String name
-----------------------------
Animal(String n)

String getName()
```

```
Hippo
-----------------------------

-----------------------------
Hippo(String n)

[other Hippo-spe-
cific methods]
```

```java
public abstract class Animal {
    private String name;          // All animals (including
                                  //   subclasses) have a name

    public String getName() {     // A getter method that
        return name;              //   Hippo inherits
    }

    public Animal(String theName) {    // The constructor that
        name = theName;                //   takes the name and assigns
    }                                  //   it the name instance
}                                      //   variable
```

The Animal part of me needs to know my name, so I take a name in my own Hippo constructor, then pass the name to super()

```java
public class Hippo extends Animal {

    public Hippo(String name) {    // Hippo constructor takes a name
        super(name);               // it sends the name up the Stack to
    }                              //   the Animal constructor
}
```

```java
public class MakeHippo {
    public static void main(String[] args) {    // Make a Hippo, passing the
        Hippo h = new Hippo("Buffy");            //   name "Buffy", passing the
        System.out.println(h.getName());         //   constructor. Then call the
    }                                            //   Hippo's inherited getName()
}
```

```
File Edit Window Help Hide
%java MakeHippo
Buffy
```

Invoking one overloaded constructor from another

What if you have overloaded constructors that, with the exception of handling different argument types, all do the same thing? You know that you don't want *duplicate* code sitting in each of the constructors (pain to maintain, etc.), so you'd like to put the bulk of the constructor code (including the call to super()) in only *one* of the overloaded constructors. You want whichever constructor is first invoked to call The Real Constructor and let The Real Constructor finish the job of construction. It's simple: just say *this()*. Or *this(aString)*. Or *this(27, x)*. In other words, just imagine that the keyword *this* is a reference to **the current object**

You can say *this()* only within a constructor, and it must be the first statement in the constructor!

But that's a problem, isn't it? Earlier we said that super() must be the first statement in the constructor. Well, that means you get a choice.

Every constructor can have a call to super() or this(), but never both!

> Use this() to call a constructor from another overloaded constructor in the same class.
>
> The call to this() can be used only in a constructor, and must be the first statement in a constructor.
>
> A constructor can have a call to super() OR this(), but never both!

```
class Mini extends Car {

    Color color;

    public Mini() {
        this(Color.Red);
    }

    public Mini(Color c) {
        super("Mini");
        color = c;
        // more initialization
    }

    public Mini(int size) {
        this(Color.Red);
        super(size);
    }
}
```

The no-arg constructor supplies a default Color and calls the overloaded Real Constructor (the one that calls super()).

This is The Real Constructor that does The Real Work of initializing the object (including the call to super())

Won't work!! Can't have super() and this() in the same constructor, because they each must be the first statement!

```
File Edit Window Help Drive
javac Mini.java
Mini.java:16: call to super must
be first statement in constructor

        super();
        ^
```

Sharpen your pencil

Some of the constructors in the SonOfBoo class will not compile. See if you can recognize which constructors are not legal. Match the compiler errors with the SonOfBoo constructors that caused them, by drawing a line from the compiler error to the "bad" constructor.

```java
public class Boo {
    public Boo(int i) { }
    public Boo(String s) { }
    public Boo(String s, int i) { }
}
```

```java
class SonOfBoo extends Boo {

    public SonOfBoo() {
        super("boo");
    }

    public SonOfBoo(int i) {
        super("Fred");
    }

    public SonOfBoo(String s) {
        super(42);
    }

    public SonOfBoo(int i, String s) {
    }

    public SonOfBoo(String a, String b, String c) {
        super(a,b);
    }

    public SonOfBoo(int i, int j) {
        super("man", j);
    }

    public SonOfBoo(int i, int x, int y) {
        super(i, "star");
    }
}
```

Make it Stick

Java is Pass by value

threads wait() notify()

Wash Cat

Roses are red, violets are blue.
Your parents come first, way before you.
The superclass parts of an object must be fully-formed before the new subclass object can exist. Just like there's no way you could have been born before your parents.

```
File Edit Window Help
%javac SonOfBoo.java
cannot resolve symbol
symbol : constructor Boo
(java.lang.String,java.la
ng.String)
```

```
File Edit Window Help Yadayadayada
%javac SonOfBoo.java
cannot resolve symbol
symbol   : constructor Boo
(int,java.lang.String)
```

```
File Edit Window Help ImNotListening
%javac SonOfBoo.java
cannot resolve symbol
symbol:constructor Boo()
```

Now we know how an object is born, but how long does an object *live*?

An *object's* life depends entirely on the life of references referring to it. If the reference is considered "alive", the object is still alive on the Heap. If the reference dies (and we'll look at what that means in just a moment), the object will die.

So if an object's life depends on the reference variable's life, how long does a *variable* live?

That depends on whether the variable is a *local* variable or an *instance* variable. The code below shows the life of a local variable. In the example, the variable is a primitive, but variable lifetime is the same whether it's a primitive or reference variable.

```java
public class TestLifeOne {

    public void read() {
        int s = 42;
        sleep();
    }

    public void sleep() {
        s = 7;
    }
}
```

's' is scoped to the read() method, so it can't be used anywhere else

BAD!! Not legal to use 's' here!

sleep() can't see the 's' variable. Since it's not in sleep()'s own Stack frame, sleep() doesn't know anything about it.

The variable 's' is alive, but in scope only within the read() method. When sleep() completes and read() is on top of the Stack and running again, read() can still see 's'. When read() completes and is popped off the Stack, 's' is dead. Pushing up digital daisies.

① A <u>local</u> variable lives only within the method that declared the variable.

```java
public void read() {
    int s = 42;
    // 's' can be used only
    // within this method.
    // When this method ends,
    // 's' disappears completely.
}
```

Variable '**s**' can be used *only* within the *read()* method. In other words, **the variable is in scope only within its own method**. No other code in the class (or any other class) can see '**s**'.

② An <u>instance</u> variable lives as long as the object does. If the object is still alive, so are its instance variables.

```java
public class Life {
    int size;

    public void setSize(int s) {
        size = s;
        // 's' disappears at the
        // end of this method,
        // but 'size' can be used
        // anywhere in the class
    }
}
```

Variable '**s**' (this time a method parameter) is in scope only within the setSize() method. But instance variable size is scoped to the life of the *object* as opposed to the life of the *method*.

The difference between **life** and **scope** for local variables:

Life

A local variable is *alive* as long as its Stack frame is on the Stack. In other words, *until the method completes.*

Scope

A local variable is in *scope* only within the method in which the variable was declared. When its own method calls another, the variable is alive, but not in scope until its method resumes. *You can use a variable only when it is in scope.*

```java
public void doStuff() {
    boolean b = true;
    go(4);
}
public void go(int x) {
    int z = x + 24;
    crazy();
    // imagine more code here
}
public void crazy() {
    char c = 'a';
}
```

1 *doStuff()* goes on the Stack. Variable 'b' is alive and in scope.

2 *go()* plops on top of the Stack. 'x' and 'z' are alive and in scope, and 'b' is alive but *not* in scope.

3 *crazy()* is pushed onto the Stack, with 'c' now alive and in scope. The other three variables are alive but out of scope.

4 *crazy()* completes and is popped off the Stack, so 'c' is out of scope *and dead.* When go() resumes where it left off, 'x' and 'z' are both alive and back in scope. Variable 'b' is still alive but out of scope (until go() completes).

While a local variable is alive, its state persists. As long as method doStuff() is on the Stack, for example, the 'b' variable keeps its value. But the 'b' variable can be used only while doStuff()'s Stack frame is at the top. In other words, you can use a local variable *only* while that local variable's method is actually running (as opposed to waiting for higher Stack frames to complete).

What about reference variables?

The rules are the same for primtives and references. A reference variable can be used only when it's in scope, which means you can't use an object's remote control unless you've got a reference variable that's in scope. The *real* question is,

"How does *variable* life affect *object* life?"

An object is alive as long as there are live references to it. If a reference variable goes out of scope but is still alive, the object it *refers* to is still alive on the Heap. And then you have to ask... "What happens when the Stack frame holding the reference gets popped off the Stack at the end of the method?"

If that was the *only* live reference to the object, the object is now abandoned on the Heap. The reference variable disintegrated with the Stack frame, so the abandoned object is now, *officially*, toast. The trick is to know the point at which an object becomes *eligible for garbage collection*.

Once an object is eligible for garbage collection (GC), you don't have to worry about reclaiming the memory that object was using. If your program gets low on memory, GC will destroy some or all of the eligible objects, to keep you from running out of RAM. You can still run out of memory, but *not* before all eligible objects have been hauled off to the dump. Your job is to make sure that you abandon objects (i.e, make them eligible for GC) when you're done with them, so that the garbage collector has something to reclaim. If you hang on to objects, GC can't help you and you run the risk of your program dying a painful out-of-memory death.

An object's life has no value, no meaning, no point, unless somebody has a reference to it.

If you can't get to it, you can't ask it to do anything and it's just a big fat waste of bits.

But if an object is unreachable, the Garbage Collector will figure that out. Sooner or later, that object's goin' down.

An object becomes eligible for GC when its last live reference disappears.

Three ways to get rid of an object's reference:

(1) The reference goes out of scope, permanently

```
void go() {
    Life z = new Life();
}
```
reference 'z' dies at end of method

(2) The reference is assigned another object

```
Life z = new Life();
z = new Life();
```
the first object is abandoned when z is 'reprogrammed' to a new object.

(3) The reference is explicitly set to null

```
Life z = new Life();
z = null;
```
the first object is abandoned when z is 'deprogrammed'.

Object-killer #1

**Reference goes
out of scope,
permanently.**

```java
public class StackRef  {
   public void foof() {
      barf();
   }

   public void barf() {
      Duck d = new Duck();
   }
}
```

I don't like where this is headed.

1 *foof()* is pushed onto the Stack, no variables are declared.

The new Duck goes on the Heap, and as long as barf() is running, the 'd' reference is alive and in scope, so the Duck is considered alive.

2 *barf()* is pushed onto the Stack, where it declares a reference variable, and creates a new object assigned to that reference. The object is created on the Heap, and the reference is alive and in scope.

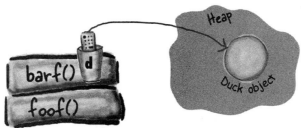

3 *barf()* completes and pops off the Stack. Its frame disintegrates, so 'd' is now dead and gone. Execution returns to *foof()*, but *foof()* can't use 'd' .

Uh-oh. The 'd' variable went away when the barf() Stack frame was blown off the stack, so the Duck is abandoned. Garbage-collector bait.

Object-killer #2

Assign the reference to another object

```
public class ReRef {

    Duck d = new Duck();

    public void go() {
      d = new Duck();
    }
}
```

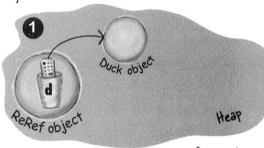

1

Duck object

d

ReRef object   Heap

The new Duck goes on the Heap, referenced by 'd'. Since 'd' is an instance variable, the Duck will live as long as the ReRef object that instantiated it is alive. Unless...

When someone calls the go() method, this Duck is abandoned. His only reference has been reprogrammed for a different Duck

2

Duck object

d

ReRef object   Duck object   Heap

'd' is assigned a new Duck object, leaving the original (first) Duck object abandoned. That first Duck is now as good as dead.

Dude, all you had to do was reset the reference. Guess they didn't have memory management back then.

Object-killer #3

Explicitly set the reference to null

```
public class ReRef {

    Duck d = new Duck();

    public void go() {
      d = null;
    }
}
```

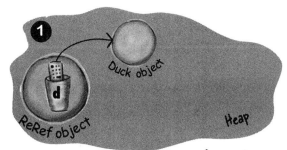

The new Duck goes on the Heap, referenced by 'd'. Since 'd' is an instance variable, the Duck will live as long as the ReRef object that instantiated it is alive. Unless...

The meaning of null

When you set a reference to **null**, you're deprogramming the remote control. In other words, you've got a remote control, but no TV at the other end. A null reference has bits representing 'null' (*we* don't know or care what those bits are, as long as the JVM knows).

If you have an unprogrammed remote control, in the real world, the buttons don't do anything when you press them. But in Java, you can't press the buttons (i.e. use the dot operator) on a null reference, because the JVM knows (this is a runtime issue, not a compiler error) that you're expecting a bark but there's no Dog there to do it!

If you use the dot operator on a null reference, you'll get a NullPointerException at runtime. You'll learn all about Exceptions in the Risky Behavior chapter.

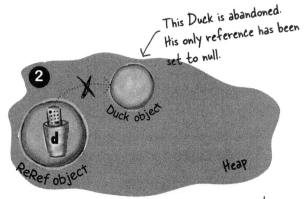

This Duck is abandoned. His only reference has been set to null.

'd' is set to null, which is just like having a remote control that isn't programmed to anything. You're not even allowed to use the dot operator on 'd' until it's reprogrammed (assigned an object).

Fireside Chats

Tonight's Talk: **An instance variable and a local variable discuss life and death (with remarkable civility)**

Instance Variable	Local Variable
I'd like to go first, because I tend to be more important to a program than a local variable. I'm there to support an object, usually throughout the object's entire life. After all, what's an object without *state*? And what is state? Values kept in ***instance variables***.	
	I appreciate your point of view, and I certainly appreciate the value of object state and all, but I don't want folks to be misled. Local variables are *really* important. To use your phrase, "After all, what's an object without *behavior*?" And what is behavior? Algorithms in methods. And you can bet your bits there'll be some *local variables* in there to make those algorithms work.
No, don't get me wrong, I do understand your role in a method, it's just that your life is so short. So temporary. That's why they call you guys "temporary variables".	
	Within the local-variable community, the phrase "temporary variable" is considered derogatory. We prefer "local", "stack", "automatic", or "Scope-challenged".
My apologies. I understand completely.	
	Anyway, it's true that we don't have a long life, and it's not a particularly *good* life either. First, we're shoved into a Stack frame with all the other local variables. And then, if the method we're part of calls another method, another frame is pushed on top of us. And if *that* method calls *another* method... and so on. Sometimes we have to wait forever for all the other methods on top of the Stack to complete so that our method can run again.
I never really thought about it like that. What are you doing while the other methods are running and you're waiting for your frame to be the top of the Stack again?	
	Nothing. Nothing at all. It's like being in stasis—that thing they do to people in science fiction movies when they have to travel long distances. Suspended animation, really. We just sit there on hold. As long as our frame is still there, we're safe and the value we hold is secure, but it's a mixed blessing when our

Instance Variable

Local Variable

frame gets to run again. On the one hand, we get to be active again. On the other hand, the clock starts ticking again on our short lives. The more time our method spends running, the closer we get to the end of the method. We *all* know what happens then.

We saw an educational video about it once. Looks like a pretty brutal ending. I mean, when that method hits its ending curly brace, the frame is literally *blown* off the Stack! Now *that's* gotta hurt.

Tell me about it. In computer science they use the term *popped* as in "the frame was popped off the Stack". That makes it sound fun, or maybe like an extreme sport. But, well, you saw the footage. So why don't we talk about you? I know what my little Stack frame looks like, but where do *you* live?

I live on the Heap, with the objects. Well, not *with* the objects, actually *in* an object. The object whose state I store. I have to admit life can be pretty luxurious on the Heap. A lot of us feel guilty, especially around the holidays.

But you don't *always* live as long as the object who declared you, right? Say there's a Dog object with a Collar instance variable. Imagine *you're* an instance variable of the *Collar* object, maybe a reference to a Buckle or something, sitting there all happy inside the *Collar* object who's all happy inside the *Dog* object. But... what happens if the Dog wants a new Collar, or *nulls* out its Collar instance variable? That makes the Collar object eligible for GC. So... if *you're* an instance variable inside the Collar, and the whole *Collar* is abandoned, what happens to *you*?

OK, hypothetically, yes, if I'm an instance variable of the Collar and the Collar gets GC'd, then the Collar's instance variables would indeed be tossed out like so many pizza boxes. But I was told that this almost never happens.

And you believed it? That's what they say to keep us motivated and productive. But aren't you forgetting something else? What if you're an instance variable inside an object, and that object is referenced *only* by a *local* variable? If I'm the only reference to the object you're in, when I go, you're coming with me. Like it or not, our fates may be connected. So I say we forget about all this and go get drunk while we still can. Carpe RAM and all that.

They let us *drink*?

BE the Garbage Collector

Which of the lines of code on the right, if added to the class on the left at point A, would cause exactly one additional object to be eligible for the Garbage Collector? (Assume that point A (//call more methods) will execute for a long time, giving the Garbage Collector time to do its stuff.)

```
public class GC {
  public static GC doStuff() {
    GC newGC = new GC();
    doStuff2(newGC);
    return newGC;
  }


  public static void main(String [] args) {
    GC gc1;
    GC gc2 = new GC();
    GC gc3 = new GC();
    GC gc4 = gc3;
    gc1 = doStuff();

    A

    // call more methods
  }


  public static void doStuff2(GC copyGC) {
    GC localGC
  }
}
```

1	copyGC = null;
2	gc2 = null;
3	newGC = gc3;
4	gc1 = null;
5	newGC = null;
6	gc4 = null;
7	gc3 = gc2;
8	gc1 = gc4;
9	gc3 = null;

Popular Objects

In this code example, several new objects are created. Your challenge is to find the object that is 'most popular', i.e. the one that has the most reference variables referring to it. Then list how *many* total references there are for that object, and what they are! We'll start by pointing out one of the new objects, and its reference variable.

Good Luck !

```java
class Bees {
   Honey [] beeHA;
}

class Raccoon {
   Kit k;
   Honey rh;
}

class Kit {
   Honey kh;
}

class Bear {
   Honey hunny;
}

public class Honey {
   public static void main(String [] args) {
      Honey honeyPot = new Honey();
      Honey [] ha = {honeyPot, honeyPot, honeyPot, honeyPot};
      Bees b1 = new Bees();
      b1.beeHA = ha;
      Bear [] ba = new Bear[5];
      for (int x=0; x < 5; x++) {
         ba[x] = new Bear();
         ba[x].hunny = honeyPot;
      }
      Kit k = new Kit();
      k.kh = honeyPot;
      Raccoon r = new Raccoon();

      r.rh = honeyPot;
      r.k = k;
      k = null;
   }   //  end of main
}
```

Here's a new Raccoon object!

Here's its reference variable 'r'.

Five-Minute
Mystery

"We've run the simulation four times, and the main module's temperature consistently drifts out of nominal towards cold", Sarah said, exasperated. "We installed the new temp-bots last week. The readings on the radiator bots, designed to cool the living quarters, seem to be within spec, so we've focused our analysis on the heat retention bots, the bots that help to warm the quarters." Tom sighed, at first it had seemed that nano-technology was going to really put them ahead of schedule. Now, with only five weeks left until launch, some of the orbiter's key life support systems were still not passing the simulation gauntlet.

"What ratios are you simulating?", Tom asked.

"Well if I see where you're going, we already thought of that", Sarah replied. "Mission control will not sign off on critical systems if we run them out of spec. We are required to run the v3 radiator bot's SimUnits in a 2:1 ratio with the v2 radiator's SimUnits", Sarah continued. "Overall, the ratio of retention bots to radiator bots is supposed to run 4:3."

"How's power consumption Sarah?", Tom asked. Sarah paused, "Well that's another thing, power consumption is running higher than anticipated. We've got a team tracking that down too, but because the nanos are wireless it's been hard to isolate the power consumption of the radiators from the retention bots." "Overall power consumption ratios", Sarah continued, "are designed to run 3:2 with the radiators pulling more power from the wireless grid."

"OK Sarah", Tom said "Let's take a look at some of the simulation initiation code. We've got to find this problem, and find it quick!"

```java
import java.util.*;
class V2Radiator {
  V2Radiator(ArrayList list) {
    for(int x=0; x<5; x++) {
      list.add(new SimUnit("V2Radiator"));
    }
  }
}


class V3Radiator extends V2Radiator {
  V3Radiator(ArrayList lglist) {
    super(lglist);
    for(int g=0; g<10; g++) {
      lglist.add(new SimUnit("V3Radiator"));
    }
  }
}


class RetentionBot {
  RetentionBot(ArrayList rlist) {
    rlist.add(new SimUnit("Retention"));
  }
}
```

```
public class TestLifeSupportSim {
  public static void main(String [] args) {
    ArrayList aList = new ArrayList();
    V2Radiator v2 = new V2Radiator(aList);
    V3Radiator v3 = new V3Radiator(aList);
    for(int z=0; z<20; z++) {
      RetentionBot ret = new RetentionBot(aList);
    }
  }
}

class SimUnit {
  String botType;
  SimUnit(String type) {
    botType = type;
  }
  int powerUse() {
    if ("Retention".equals(botType)) {
      return 2;
    } else {
      return 4;
    }
  }
}
```

Tom gave the code a quick look and a small smile creeped across his lips. I think I've found the problem Sarah, and I bet I know by what percentage your power usage readings are off too!

What did Tom suspect? How could he guess the power readings errors, and what few lines of code could you add to help debug this program?

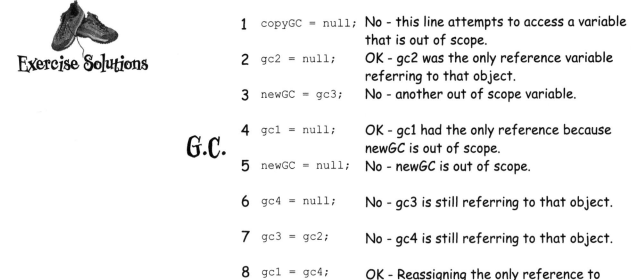

Exercise Solutions

G.C.

1 `copyGC = null;` No - this line attempts to access a variable that is out of scope.

2 `gc2 = null;` OK - gc2 was the only reference variable referring to that object.

3 `newGC = gc3;` No - another out of scope variable.

4 `gc1 = null;` OK - gc1 had the only reference because newGC is out of scope.

5 `newGC = null;` No - newGC is out of scope.

6 `gc4 = null;` No - gc3 is still referring to that object.

7 `gc3 = gc2;` No - gc4 is still referring to that object.

8 `gc1 = gc4;` OK - Reassigning the only reference to that object.

9 `gc3 = null;` No - gc4 is still referring to that object.

Popular Objects

It probably wasn't too hard to figure out that the Honey object first referred to by the honeyPot variable is by far the most 'popular' object in this class. But maybe it was a little trickier to see that all of the variables that point from the code to the Honey object refer to the ***same object***! There are a total of 12 active references to this object right before the main( ) method completes. The *k.kh* variable is valid for a while, but k gets nulled at the end. Since *r.k* still refers to the Kit object, *r.k.kh* (although never explicitly declared), refers to the object!

```
public class Honey {
    public static void main(String [] args) {
        Honey honeyPot = new Honey();
        Honey [] ha = {honeyPot, honeyPot,
                       honeyPot, honeyPot};
        Bees b1 = new Bees();
        b1.beeHA = ha;
        Bear [] ba = new Bear[5];
        for (int x=0; x < 5; x++) {
            ba[x] = new Bear();
            ba[x].hunny = honeyPot;
        }
        Kit k = new Kit();
        k.kh = honeyPot;
        Raccoon r = new Raccoon();

        r.rh = honeyPot;
        r.k = k;
        k = null;
    } }    // end of main
}
```

Honey Object

(ends up null)

Five-Minute Mystery Solution

Tom noticed that the constructor for the V2Radiator class took an ArrayList. That meant that every time the *V3*Radiator constructor was called, it passed an ArrayList in its super() call to the *V2*Radiator constructor. That meant that an extra five V2Radiator SimUnits were created. If Tom was right, total power use would have been 120, not the 100 that Sarah's expected ratios predicted.

Since all the Bot classes create SimUnits, writing a constructor for the SimUnit class, that printed out a line everytime a SimUnit was created, would have quickly highlighted the problem!

Numbers Matter

Do the Math. But there's more to working with numbers than just doing primitive arithmetic. You might want to get the absolute value of a number, or round a number, or find the larger of two numbers. You might want your numbers to print with exactly two decimal places, or you might want to put commas into your large numbers to make them easier to read. And what about working with dates? You might want to print dates in a variety of ways, or even *manipulate* dates to say things like, "add three weeks to today's date". And what about parsing a String into a number? Or turning a number into a String? You're in luck. The Java API is full of handy number-tweaking methods ready and easy to use. But most of them are **static**, so we'll start by learning what it means for a variable or method to be static, including constants in Java—static *final* variables.

MATH methods: as close as you'll ever get to a *global* method

Except there's no global *anything* in Java. But think about this: what if you have a method whose behavior doesn't depend on an instance variable value. Take the round() method in the Math class, for example. It does the same thing every time—rounds a floating point number(the argument to the method) to the nearest integer. Every time. If you had 10,000 instances of class Math, and ran the round(42.2) method, you'd get an integer value of 42. Every time. In other words, the method acts on the argument, but is never affected by an instance variable state. The only value that changes the way the round() method runs is the argument passed to the method!

Doesn't it seem like a waste of perfectly good heap space to make an instance of class Math simply to run the round() method? And what about *other* Math methods like min(), which takes two numerical primitives and returns the smaller of the two. Or max(). Or abs(), which returns the absolute value of a number.

These methods never use instance variable values. In fact the Math class doesn't *have* any instance variables. So there's nothing to be gained by making an instance of class Math. So guess what? You don't have to. As a matter of fact, you can't.

Methods in the Math class don't use any instance variable values. And because the methods are 'static', you don't need to have an instance of Math. All you need is the Math <u>class</u>.

```java
int x = Math.round(42.2);
int y = Math.min(56,12);
int z = Math.abs(-343);
```

↑
These methods never use instance variables, so their behavior doesn't need to know about a specific object.

If you try to make an instance of class Math:

```java
Math mathObject = new Math();
```

You'll get this error:

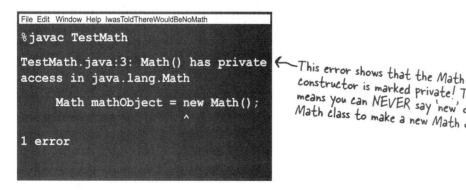

```
File Edit Window Help IwasToldThereWouldBeNoMath
%javac TestMath

TestMath.java:3: Math() has private
access in java.lang.Math

     Math mathObject = new Math();
                       ^
1 error
```

← This error shows that the Math constructor is marked private! That means you can NEVER say 'new' on the Math class to make a new Math object.

The difference between regular (non-static) and static methods

Java is object-oriented, but once in a while you have a special case, typically a utility method (like the Math methods), where there is no need to have an instance of the class. The keyword **static** lets a method run *without any instance of the class*. A static method means "behavior not dependent on an instance variable, so no instance/object is required. Just the class."

regular (non-static) method

```
public class Song {
    String title;
    public Song(String t) {
        title = t;
    }
    public void play() {
        SoundPlayer player = new SoundPlayer();
        player.playSound(title);
    }
}
```

Instance variable value affects the behavior of the play() method.

The current value of the 'title' instance variable is the song that plays when you call play().

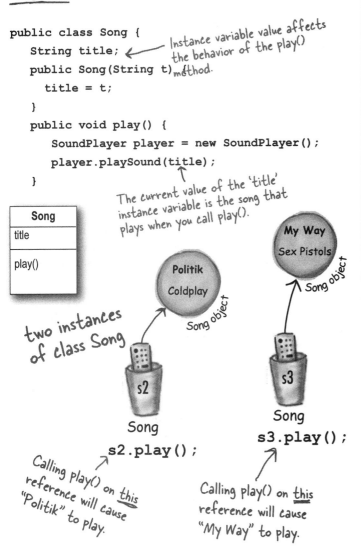

two instances of class Song

Song
s2.play();

Calling play() on this reference will cause "Politik" to play.

Song
s3.play();

Calling play() on this reference will cause "My Way" to play.

static method

```
public static int min(int a, int b){
    //returns the lesser of a and b
}
```

Math
min()
max()
abs()
...

No instance variables. The method behavior doesn't change with instance variable state.

`Math.min(42,36);`

Use the Class name, rather than a reference variable name.

NO OBJECTS!! Absolutely NO OBJECTS anywhere in this picture!

Call a static method using a class name

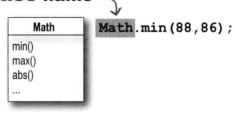

```
Math.min(88,86);
```

Call a non-static method using a reference variable name

```
Song t2 = new Song();

t2.play();
```

What it means to have a class with static methods.

Often (although not always), a class with static methods is not meant to be instantiated. In Chapter 8 we talked about abstract classes, and how marking a class with the **abstract** modifier makes it impossible for anyone to say 'new' on that class type. In other words, *it's impossible to instantiate an abstract class.*

But you can restrict other code from instantiating a *non*-abstract class by marking the constructor **private**. Remember, a *method* marked private means that only code from within the class can invoke the method. A *constructor* marked private means essentially the same thing—only code from within the class can invoke the constructor. Nobody can say 'new' from *outside* the class. That's how it works with the Math class, for example. The constructor is private, you cannot make a new instance of Math. The compiler knows that your code doesn't have access to that private constructor.

This does *not* mean that a class with one or more static methods should never be instantiated. In fact, every class you put a main() method in is a class with a static method in it!

Typically, you make a main() method so that you can launch or test another class, nearly always by instantiating a class in main, and then invoking a method on that new instance.

So you're free to combine static and non-static methods in a class, although even a single non-static method means there must be *some* way to make an instance of the class. The only ways to get a new object are through 'new' or deserialization (or something called the Java Reflection API that we don't go into). No other way. But exactly *who* says new can be an interesting question, and one we'll look at a little later in this chapter.

Static methods can't use non-static (instance) variables!

Static methods run without knowing about any particular instance of the static method's class. And as you saw on the previous pages, there might not even *be* any instances of that class. Since a static method is called using the *class* (*Math*.random()) as opposed to an *instance reference* (*t2*.play()), a static method can't refer to any instance variables of the class. The static method doesn't know *which* instance's variable value to use.

If you try to use an instance variable from inside a static method, the compiler thinks, "I don't know *which* object's instance variable you're talking about!" If you have ten Duck objects on the heap, a static method doesn't know about any of them.

If you try to compile this code:

```java
public class Duck {

   private int size;

   public static void main (String[] args) {
      System.out.println("Size of duck is " + size);
   }

   public void setSize(int s) {
      size = s;
   }
   public int getSize() {
      return size;
   }
}
```

Which Duck? Whose size?

If there's a Duck on the heap somewhere, we don't know about it.

You'll get this error:

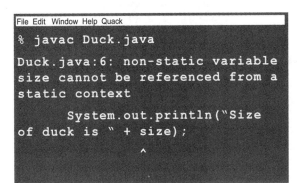

```
File Edit Window Help Quack
% javac Duck.java
Duck.java:6: non-static variable
size cannot be referenced from a
static context
      System.out.println("Size
of duck is " + size);
        ^
```

I'm sure they're talking about MY size variable.

No, I'm pretty sure they're talking about MY size variable.

Static methods can't use non-static methods, either!

What do non-static methods do? *They usually use instance variable state to affect the behavior of the method.* A getName() method returns the value of the name variable. Whose name? The object used to invoke the getName() method.

This won't compile:

Calling getSize() just postpones the inevitable—getSize() uses the size instance variable.

```
public class Duck {

   private int size;

   public static void main (String[] args) {
      System.out.println("Size is " + getSize());
   }

   public void setSize(int s) {
      size = s;
   }
   public int getSize() {
      return size;
   }
}
```

Back to the same problem... whose size?

```
File Edit  Window Help Jack-in

% javac Duck.java

Duck.java:6: non-static method
getSize() cannot be referenced
from a static context

        System.out.println("Size
of duck is " + getSize());
        ^
```

Make it Stick

Java is Pass by value

threads wait() notify()

Wash Cat

Roses are red,
and known to bloom late

Statics can't see instance variable state

---

there are no
Dumb Questions

Q: What if you try to call a non-static method from a static method, but the non-static method doesn't use any instance variables. Will the compiler allow that?

A: No. The compiler knows that whether you do or do not use instance variables in a non-static method, you *can*. And think about the implications... if you were allowed to compile a scenario like that, then what happens if in the future you want to change the implementation of that non-static method so that one day it *does* use an instance variable? Or worse, what happens if a subclass *overrides* the method and uses an instance variable in the overriding version?

Q: I could swear I've seen code that calls a static method using a reference variable instead of the class name.

A: You *can* do that, but as your mother always told you, "Just because it's legal doesn't mean it's good." Although it *works* to call a static method using any instance of the class, it makes for misleading (less-readable) code. You *can* say,

```
Duck d = new Duck();
String[] s = {};
d.main(s);
```

This code is legal, but the compiler just resolves it back to the real class anyway ("OK, *d* is of type Duck, and main() is static, so I'll call the static main() in class Duck"). In other words, using *d* to invoke main() doesn't imply that main() will have any special knowledge of the object that *d* is referencing. It's just an alternate *way* to invoke a static method, but the method is still static!

Static variable:
value is the same for ALL instances of the class

Imagine you wanted to count how many Duck instances are being created while your program is running. How would you do it? Maybe an instance variable that you increment in the constructor?

```
class Duck {
   int duckCount = 0;
    public Duck() {
        duckCount++;
    }
}
```

this would always set duckCount to 1 each time a Duck was made

No, that wouldn't work because duckCount is an instance variable, and starts at 0 for each Duck. You could try calling a method in some other class, but that's kludgey. You need a class that's got only a single copy of the variable, and all instances share that one copy.

That's what a static variable gives you: a value shared by all instances of a class. In other words, one value per *class*, instead of one value per *instance*.

The static duckCount variable is initialized ONLY when the class is first loaded, NOT each time a new instance is made.

```
public class Duck {

   private int size;
   private static int duckCount = 0;

   public Duck() {
       duckCount++;
   }

   public void setSize(int s) {
       size = s;
   }
   public int getSize() {
       return size;
   }
}
```

Now it will keep incrementing each time the Duck constructor runs, because duckCount is static and won't be reset to 0.

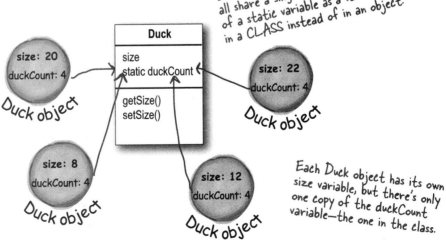

A Duck object doesn't keep its own copy of duckCount.

Because duckCount is static, Duck objects all share a single copy of it. You can think of a static variable as a variable that lives in a CLASS instead of in an object.

Each Duck object has its own size variable, but there's only one copy of the duckCount variable—the one in the class.

kid instance one

static variable: iceCream

kid instance two

Static variables are shared.

All instances of the same class share a single copy of the static variables.

instance variables: 1 per **instance**

static variables: 1 per **class**

Brain Barbell

Earlier in this chapter, we saw that a private constructor means that the class can't be instantiated from code running outside the class. In other words, only code from within the class can make a new instance of a class with a private constructor. (There's a kind of chicken-and-egg problem here.)

What if you want to write a class in such a way that only ONE instance of it can be created, and anyone who wants to use an instance of the class will always use that one, single instance?

Initializing a static variable

Static variables are initialized when a *class is loaded*. A class is loaded because the JVM decides it's time to load it. Typically, the JVM loads a class because somebody's trying to make a new instance of the class, for the first time, or use a static method or variable of the class. As a programmer, you also have the option of telling the JVM to load a class, but you're not likely to need to do that. In nearly all cases, you're better off letting the JVM decide when to *load* the class.

And there are two guarantees about static initialization:

Static variables in a class are initialized before any *object* of that class can be created.

Static variables in a class are initialized before any *static method* of the class runs.

> **All static variables in a class are initialized *before* any object of that class can be created.**

```
class Player {

    static int playerCount = 0;

    private String name;

    public Player(String n) {

        name = n;

        playerCount++;

    }

}


public class PlayerTestDrive {

    public static void main(String[] args) {

        System.out.println(Player.playerCount);

        Player one = new Player("Tiger Woods");

        System.out.println(Player.playerCount);

    }

}
```

The playerCount is initialized when the class is loaded. We explicitly initialized it to 0, but we don't need to since 0 is the default value for ints. Static variables get default values just like instance variables.

Default values for declared but uninitialized static and instance variables are the same:
Primitive integers (long, short, etc.): 0
Primitive floating points (float, double): 0.0
boolean: false
object references: null

Access a static variable just like a static method—with the class name.

Static variables are initialized when the class is loaded. If you don't explicitly initialize a static variable (by assigning it a value at the time you declare it), it gets a default value, so int variables are initialized to zero, which means we didn't need to explicitly say "playerCount = 0". Declaring, but not initializing, a static variable means the static variable will get the default value for that variable type, in exactly the same way that instance variables are given default values when declared.

```
File Edit Window Help What?

% java PlayerTestDrive

0

1
```

← before any instances are made

← after an object is created

static <u>final</u> variables are constants

A variable marked **final** means that—once initialized—it can never change. In other words, the value of the static final variable will stay the same as long as the class is loaded. Look up Math.PI in the API, and you'll find:

```
public static final double PI = 3.141592653589793;
```

The variable is marked **public** so that any code can access it.

The variable is marked **static** so that you don't need an instance of class Math (which, remember, you're not allowed to create).

The variable is marked **final** because PI doesn't change (as far as Java is concerned).

There is no other way to designate a variable as a constant, but there is a naming convention that helps you to recognize one.
Constant variable names should be in all caps!

> A **static initializer** is a block of code that runs when a class is loaded, before any other code can use the class, so it's a great place to initialize a static final variable.
> ```
> class Foo {
>     final static int x;
>     static {
>         x = 42;
>     }
> }
> ```

Initialize a *final* static variable:

1 **At the time you declare it:**

```
public class Foo {
    public static final int FOO_X = 25;
}
```

notice the naming convention -- static final variables are constants, so the name should be all uppercase, with an underscore separating the words

OR

2 **In a static initializer:**

```
public class Bar {
    public static final double BAR_SIGN;

    static {
        BAR_SIGN = (double) Math.random();
    }
}
```

this code runs as soon as the class is loaded, before any static method is called and even before any static variable can be used.

If you don't give a value to a final variable in one of those two places:

```
public class Bar {
    public static final double BAR_SIGN;

}
```
no initialization!

The compiler will catch it:

```
File Edit Window Help Jack-in
% javac Bar.java
Bar.java:1: variable BAR_SIGN
might not have been initialized
1 error
```

final isn't just for static variables...

You can use the keyword **final** to modify non-static variables too, including instance variables, local variables, and even method parameters. In each case, it means the same thing: the value can't be changed. But you can also use final to stop someone from overriding a method or making a subclass.

non-static final **variables**

```
class Foof {
    final int size = 3; ← now you can't change size
    final int whuffie;

    Foof() {
        whuffie = 42; ← now you can't change whuffie
    }

    void doStuff(final int x) {
        // you can't change x
    }

    void doMore() {
        final int z = 7;
        // you can't change z
    }
}
```

final **method**

```
class Poof {
    final void calcWhuffie() {
        // important things
        // that must never be overridden
    }
}
```

final **class**

```
final class MyMostPerfectClass {
    // cannot be extended
}
```

A final **variable** means you can't **change** its value.

A final **method** means you can't **override** the method.

A final **class** means you can't **extend** the class (i.e. you can't make a subclass).

It's all so... so *final*. I mean, if I'd *known* I wouldn't be able to change things...

there are no
Dumb Questions

Q: **A static method can't access a non-static variable. But can a non-static method access a static variable?**

A: Of course. A non-static method in a class can always call a static method in the class or access a static variable of the class.

Q: **Why would I want to make a class final? Doesn't that defeat the whole purpose of OO?**

A: Yes and no. A typical reason for making a class final is for security. You can't, for example, make a subclass of the String class. Imagine the havoc if someone extended the String class and substituted their own String subclass objects, polymorphically, where String objects are expected. If you need to count on a particular implementation of the methods in a class, make the class final.

Q: **Isn't it redundant to have to mark the methods final if the class is final?**

A: If the class is final, you don't need to mark the methods final. Think about it—if a class is final it can never be subclassed, so none of the methods can ever be overridden.

On the other hand, if you *do* want to allow others to extend your class, and you want them to be able to override some, but not all, of the methods, then don't mark the class final but go in and selectively mark specific methods as final. A final method means that a subclass can't override that particular method.

BULLET POINTS

- A *static method* should be called using the class name rather than an object reference variable: `Math.random()` vs. `myFoo.go()`

- A static method can be invoked without any instances of the method's class on the heap.

- A static method is good for a utility method that does not (and will never) depend on a particular instance variable value.

- A static method is not associated with a particular instance—only the class—so it cannot access any instance variable values of its class. It wouldn't know *which* instance's values to use.

- A static method cannot access a non-static method, since non-static methods are usually associated with instance variable state.

- If you have a class with only static methods, and you do not want the class to be instantiated, you can mark the constructor private.

- A *static variable* is a variable shared by all members of a given class. There is only one copy of a static variable in a class, rather than one copy per each individual instance for instance variables.

- A static method can access a static variable.

- To make a constant in Java, mark a variable as both static and final.

- A final static variable must be assigned a value either at the time it is declared, or in a static initializer.
  ```
  static {
      DOG_CODE = 420;
  }
  ```

- The naming convention for constants (final static variables) is to make the name all uppercase.

- A final variable value cannot be changed once it has been assigned.

- Assigning a value to a final *instance* variable must be either at the time it is declared, or in the constructor.

- A final method cannot be overridden.

- A final class cannot be extended (subclassed).

Sharpen your pencil

What's Legal?

Given everything you've just learned about static and final, which of these would compile?

KEEP
←
RIGHT

(1)
```java
public class Foo {
    static int x;

    public void go() {
        System.out.println(x);
    }
}
```

(4)
```java
public class Foo4 {
    static final int x = 12;

    public void go() {
        System.out.println(x);
    }
}
```

(2)
```java
public class Foo2 {
    int x;

    public static void go() {
        System.out.println(x);
    }
}
```

(5)
```java
public class Foo5 {
    static final int x = 12;

    public void go(final int x) {
        System.out.println(x);
    }
}
```

(3)
```java
public class Foo3 {
    final int x;

    public void go() {
        System.out.println(x);
    }
}
```

(6)
```java
public class Foo6 {
    int x = 12;

    public static void go(final int x) {
        System.out.println(x);
    }
}
```

Math methods

Now that we know how static methods work, let's look at some static methods in class Math. This isn't all of them, just the highlights. Check your API for the rest including sqrt(), tan(), ceil(), floor(), and asin().

Math.random()

Returns a double between 0.0 through (but not including) 1.0.

```
double r1 = Math.random();
int r2 = (int) (Math.random() * 5);
```

Math.abs()

Returns a double that is the absolute value of the argument. The method is overloaded, so if you pass it an int it returns an int. Pass it a double it returns a double.

```
int x = Math.abs(-240);  // returns 240
double d = Math.abs(240.45);  // returns  240.45
```

Math.round()

Returns an int or a long (depending on whether the argument is a float or a double) rounded to the nearest integer value.

```
int x = Math.round(-24.8f);  // returns -25
int y = Math.round(24.45f);  // returns 24
```

↑
Remember, floating point literals are assumed to be doubles unless you add the 'f'.

Math.min()

Returns a value that is the minimum of the two arguments. The method is overloaded to take ints, longs, floats, or doubles.

```
int x = Math.min(24,240);  // returns 24
double y = Math.min(90876.5, 90876.49);  // returns 90876.49
```

Math.max()

Returns a value that is the maximum of the two arguments. The method is overloaded to take ints, longs, floats, or doubles.

```
int x = Math.max(24,240);  // returns 240
double y = Math.max(90876.5, 90876.49);  // returns 90876.5
```

Wrapping a primitive

Sometimes you want to treat a primitive like an object. For example, in all versions of Java prior to 5.0, you cannot put a primitive directly into a collection like ArrayList or HashMap:

```
int x = 32;
ArrayList list = new ArrayList();
list.add(x);
```

This won't work unless you're using Java 5.0 or greater!! There's no add(int) method in ArrayList that takes an int! (ArrayList only has add() methods that take object references, not primitives.)

There's a wrapper class for every primitive type, and since the wrapper classes are in the java. lang package, you don't need to import them. You can recognize wrapper classes because each one is named after the primitive type it wraps, but with the first letter capitalized to follow the class naming convention.

Oh yeah, for reasons absolutely nobody on the planet is certain of, the API designers decided not to map the names *exactly* from primitive type to class type. You'll see what we mean:

Boolean

Character

Byte

Short

Integer

Long

Float

Double

Watch out! The names aren't mapped exactly to the primitive types. The class names are fully spelled out.

wrapping a value

```
int i = 288;
Integer iWrap = new Integer(i);
```

Give the primitive to the wrapper constructor. That's it.

_un_wrapping a value

```
int unWrapped = iWrap.intValue();
```

All the wrappers work like this. Boolean has a booleanValue(), Character has a charValue(), etc.

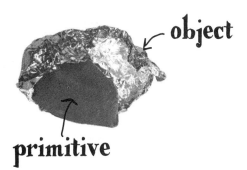

object

primitive

When you need to treat a primitive like an object, wrap it. If you're using any version of Java before 5.0, you'll do this when you need to store a primitive value inside a collection like ArrayList or HashMap.

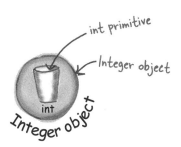

int primitive

Integer object

int

Integer object

Note: the picture at the top is a chocolate in a foil wrapper. Get it? Wrapper? Some people think it looks like a baked potato, but that works too.

> This is stupid. You mean I can't just make an ArrayList of ints??? I have to wrap every single frickin' one in a new Integer object, then unwrap it when I try to access that value in the ArrayList? That's a waste of time and an error waiting to happen...

Before Java 5.0, YOU had to do the work...

She's right. In all versions of Java prior to 5.0, primitives were primitives and object references were object references, and they were NEVER treated interchangeably. It was always up to you, the programmer, to do the wrapping and unwrapping. There was no way to pass a primitive to a method expecting an object reference, and no way to assign the result of a method returning an object reference directly to a primitive variable—even when the returned reference is to an Integer and the primitive variable is an int. There was simply no relationship between an Integer and an int, other than the fact that Integer has an instance variable of type int (to hold the primitive the Integer wraps). All the work was up to you.

An ArrayList of primitive ints

Without autoboxing (Java versions *before* 5.0)

```
public void doNumsOldWay() {

    ArrayList listOfNumbers = new ArrayList();

    listOfNumbers.add(new Integer(3));

    Integer one = (Integer) listOfNumbers.get(0);

    int intOne = one.intValue();
}
```

Make an ArrayList (Remember, before 5.0 you could not specify the TYPE, so all ArrayLists were lists of Objects.)

You can't add the primitive '3' to the list, so you have to wrap it in an Integer first.

It comes out as type Object, but you can cast the Object to an Integer.

Finally you can get the primitive out of the Integer.

Autoboxing: blurring the line between primitive and object

The autoboxing feature added to Java 5.0 does the conversion from primitive to wrapper object *automatically!*

Let's see what happens when we want to make an ArrayList to hold ints.

An ArrayList of primitive ints

With autoboxing (Java versions 5.0 or greater)

```
public void doNumsNewWay() {

    ArrayList<Integer> listOfNumbers = new ArrayList<Integer>();

    listOfNumbers.add(3);   Just add it!

    int num = listOfNumbers.get(0);

}
```

Make an ArrayList of type Integer.

And the compiler automatically unwraps (unboxes) the Integer object so you can assign the int value directly to a primitive without having to call the intValue() method on the Integer object.

Although there is NOT a method in ArrayList for add(int), the compiler does all the wrapping (boxing) for you. In other words, there really IS an Integer object stored in the ArrayList, but you get to "pretend" that the ArrayList takes ints. (You can add both ints and Integers to an ArrayList<Integer>.)

Q: Why not declare an ArrayList<int> if you want to hold ints?

A: Because... *you can't.* Remember, the rule for generic types is that you can specify only class or interface types, *not primitives*. So ArrayList<int> will not compile. But as you can see from the code above, it doesn't really matter, since the compiler lets you put ints into the ArrayList<Integer>. In fact, there's really no way to *prevent* you from putting primitives into an ArrayList where the type of the list is the type of that primitive's wrapper, if you're using a Java 5.0-compliant compiler, since autoboxing will happen automatically. So, you can put boolean primitives in an ArrayList<Boolean> and chars into an ArrayList<Character>.

Autoboxing works almost everywhere

Autoboxing lets you do more than just the obvious wrapping and unwrapping to use primitives in a collection... it also lets you use either a primitive or its wrapper type virtually anywhere one or the other is expected. Think about that!

Fun with autoboxing

Method arguments

If a method takes a wrapper type, you can pass a reference to a wrapper or a primitive of the matching type. And of course the reverse is true—if a method takes a primitive, you can pass in either a compatible primitive or a reference to a wrapper of that primitive type.

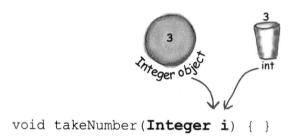

```
void takeNumber(Integer i) { }
```

Return values

If a method declares a primitive return type, you can return either a compatible primitive or a reference to the wrapper of that primitive type. And if a method declares a wrapper return type, you can return either a reference to the wrapper type or a primitive of the matching type.

```
int giveNumber() {
    return x;
}
```

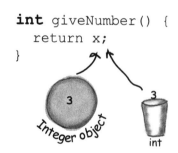

Boolean expressions

Any place a boolean value is expected, you can use either an expression that evaluates to a boolean (4 > 2), or a primitive boolean, or a reference to a Boolean wrapper.

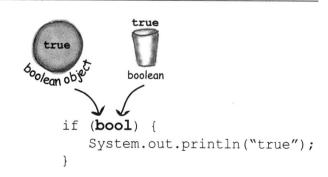

```
if (bool) {
    System.out.println("true");
}
```

Operations on numbers

This is probably the strangest one—yes, you can now use a wrapper type as an operand in operations where the primitive type is expected. That means you can apply, say, the increment operator against a reference to an Integer object!

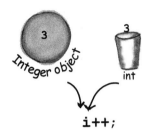

i++;

But don't worry—this is just a compiler trick. The language wasn't modified to make the operators work on objects; the compiler simply converts the object to its primitive type before the operation. It sure looks weird, though.

```
Integer i = new Integer(42);
i++;
```

And that means you can also do things like:

```
Integer j = new Integer(5);
Integer k = j + 3;
```

Assignments

You can assign either a wrapper or primitive to a variable declared as a matching wrapper or primitive. For example, a primitive int variable can be assigned to an Integer reference variable, and vice-versa—a reference to an Integer object can be assigned to a variable declared as an int primitive.

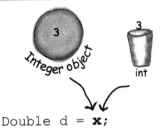

Double d = x;

Sharpen your pencil

Will this code compile? Will it run? If it runs, what will it do?

Take your time and think about this one; it brings up an implication of autoboxing that we didn't talk about.

You'll have to go to your compiler to find the answers. (Yes, we're forcing you to experiment, for your own good of course.)

```
public class TestBox {

    Integer i;
    int j;

    public static void main (String[] args) {
        TestBox t = new TestBox();
        t.go();
    }

    public void go() {
        j=i;
        System.out.println(j);
        System.out.println(i);
    }
}
```

But wait! There's more! Wrappers have static utility methods too!

Besides acting like a normal class, the wrappers have a bunch of really useful static methods. We've used one in this book before—Integer.parseInt().

The parse methods take a String and give you back a primitive value.

Converting a String to a primitive value is easy:

No problem to parse "2" into 2.

```
String s = "2";
int x = Integer.parseInt(s);
double d = Double.parseDouble("420.24");

boolean b = new Boolean("true").booleanValue();
```

You'd think there would be a Boolean.parseBoolean() wouldn't you? But there isn't. Fortunately there's a Boolean constructor that takes (and parses) a String, and then you just get the primitive value by unwrapping it.

But if you try to do this:

```
String t = "two";
int y = Integer.parseInt(t);
```

Uh-oh. This compiles just fine, but at runtime it blows up. Anything that can't be parsed as a number will cause a NumberFormatException

You'll get a runtime exception:

```
File Edit Window Help Clue
% java Wrappers
Exception in thread "main"
java.lang.NumberFormatException: two
at java.lang.Integer.parseInt(Integer.java:409)
at java.lang.Integer.parseInt(Integer.java:458)
at Wrappers.main(Wrappers.java:9)
```

Every method or constructor that parses a String can throw a NumberFormatException. It's a runtime exception, so you don't have to handle or declare it. But you might want to.

(We'll talk about Exceptions in the next chapter.)

And now in reverse... turning a primitive number into a String

There are several ways to turn a number into a String.
The easiest is to simply concatenate the number to an
existing String.

```
double d = 42.5;
String doubleString = "" + d;
```

Remember the '+' operator is overloaded
in Java (the only overloaded operator) as a
String concatenator. Anything added to a
String becomes Stringified.

```
double d = 42.5;
String doubleString = Double.toString(d);
```

Another way to do it using a static
method in class Double.

> Yeah,
> but how do I make it
> look like money? With a dollar
> sign and two decimal places
> like $56.87 or what if I want
> commas like 45,687,890 or
> what if I want it in...

> Where's my printf
> like I have in C? Is
> number formatting part of
> the I/O classes?

Number formatting

In Java, formatting numbers and dates doesn't have to be coupled with I/O. Think about it. One of the most typical ways to display numbers to a user is through a GUI. You put Strings into a scrolling text area, or maybe a table. If formatting was built only into print statements, you'd never be able to format a number into a nice String to display in a GUI. Before Java 5.0, most formatting was handled through classes in the java.text package that we won't even look at in this version of the book, now that things have changed.

In Java 5.0, the Java team added more powerful and flexible formatting through a Formatter class in java.util. But you don't need to create and call methods on the Formatter class yourself, because Java 5.0 added convenience methods to some of the I/O classes (including printf()) and the String class. So it's a simple matter of calling a static String.format() method and passing it the thing you want formatted along with formatting instructions.

Of course, you do have to know how to supply the formatting instructions, and that takes a little effort unless you're familiar with the **printf()** function in C/C++. Fortunately, even if you *don't* know printf() you can simply follow recipes for the most basic things (that we're showing in this chapter). But you *will* want to learn how to format if you want to mix and match to get *anything* you want.

We'll start here with a basic example, then look at how it works. (Note: we'll revisit formatting again in the I/O chapter.)

Formatting a number to use commas

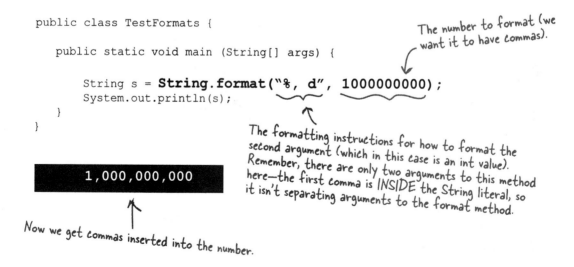

```
public class TestFormats {

    public static void main (String[] args) {

        String s = String.format("%, d", 1000000000);
        System.out.println(s);
    }
}
```

The number to format (we want it to have commas).

The formatting instructions for how to format the second argument (which in this case is an int value). Remember, there are only two arguments to this method here—the first comma is INSIDE the String literal, so it isn't separating arguments to the format method.

```
1,000,000,000
```

Now we get commas inserted into the number.

Formatting deconstructed...

At the most basic level, formatting consists of two main parts (there is more, but we'll start with this to keep it cleaner):

① **Formatting instructions**

You use special format specifiers that describe how the argument should be formatted.

② **The argument to be formatted.**

Although there can be more than one argument, we'll start with just one. The argument type can't be just *anything*... it has to be something that can be formatted using the format specifiers in the formatting instructions. For example, if your formatting instructions specify a *floating point number*, you can't pass in a Dog or even a String that looks like a floating point number.

Note: if you already know printf() from c/C++, you can probably just skim the next few pages. Otherwise, read carefully!

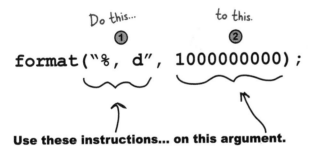

Do this...   to this.
①   **②**

```
format("%, d", 1000000000);
```

Use these instructions... on this argument.

What do these instructions actually say?

"Take the second argument to this method, and format it as a **d**ecimal integer and insert **commas**."

How do they say that?

On the next page we'll look in more detail at what the syntax "%, d" actually means, but for starters, any time you see the percent sign (%) in a format String (which is always the first argument to a format() method), think of it as representing a variable, and the variable is the other argument to the method. The rest of the characters after the percent sign describe the formatting instructions for the argument.

The percent (%) says, "insert argument here" (and format it using these instructions)

The first argument to a format() method is called the format String, and it can actually include characters that you just want printed as-is, without extra formatting. When you see the % sign, though, think of the percent sign as a variable that represents the other argument to the method.

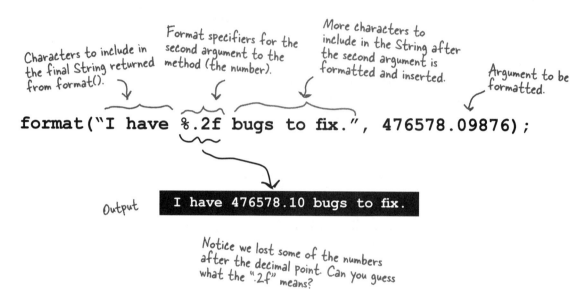

Characters to include in the final String returned from format().

Format specifiers for the second argument to the method (the number).

More characters to include in the String after the second argument is formatted and inserted.

Argument to be formatted.

```
format("I have %.2f bugs to fix.", 476578.09876);
```

Output

```
I have 476578.10 bugs to fix.
```

Notice we lost some of the numbers after the decimal point. Can you guess what the ".2f" means?

The "%" sign tells the formatter to insert the other method argument (the second argument to format(), the number) here, AND format it using the ".2f" characters after the percent sign. Then the rest of the format String, "bugs to fix", is added to the final output.

Adding a comma

```
format("I have %,.2f bugs to fix.", 476578.09876);
```

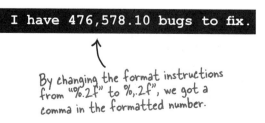

```
I have 476,578.10 bugs to fix.
```

By changing the format instructions from "%.2f" to %,.2f", we got a comma in the formatted number.

> But how does it even KNOW where the instructions end and the rest of the characters begin? How come it doesn't print out the "f" in "%.2f"? Or the "2"? How does it know that the .2f was part of the instructions and NOT part of the String?

The format String uses its own little language syntax

You obviously can't put just *anything* after the "%" sign. The syntax for what goes after the percent sign follows very specific rules, and describes how to format the argument that gets inserted at that point in the result (formatted) String.

You've already seen two examples:

%, d means "insert commas and format the number as a decimal integer."

and

%.2f means "format the number as a floating point with a precision of two decimal places."

and

%,.2f means "insert commas and format the number as a floating point with a precision of two decimal places."

The real question is really, "How do I know what to put after the percent sign to get it to do what I want?" And that includes knowing the symbols (like "d" for decimal and "f" for floating point) as well as the order in which the instructions must be placed following the percent sign. For example, if you put the comma after the "d" like this: "%d," instead of "%,d" it won't work!

Or will it? What do you think this will do:

```
String.format("I  have %.2f, bugs to fix.", 476578.09876);
```

(We'll answer that on the next page.)

The format specifier

Everything after the percent sign up to and including the type indicator (like "d" or "f") are part of the formatting instructions. After the type indicator, the formatter assumes the next set of characters are meant to be part of the output String, until or unless it hits another percent (%) sign. Hmmmm... is that even possible? Can you have more than one formatted argument variable? Put that thought on hold for right now; we'll come back to it in a few minutes. For now, let's look at the syntax for the format specifiers—the things that go after the percent (%) sign and describe how the argument should be formatted.

A format specifier can have up to five different parts (not including the "%"). Everything in brackets [ ] below is optional, so only the percent (%) and the type are required. But the order is also mandatory, so any parts you DO use must go in this order.

`%[argument number][flags][width][.precision]`**`type`**

We'll get to this later... it lets you say WHICH argument if there's more than one. (Don't worry about it just yet.)

These are for special formatting options like inserting commas, or putting negative numbers in parentheses, or to make the numbers left justified.

This defines the MINIMUM number of characters that will be used. That's *minimum* not TOTAL. If the number is longer than the width, it'll still be used in full, but if it's less than the width, it'll be padded with zeroes.

You already know this one...it defines the precision. In other words, it sets the number of decimal places. Don't forget to include the "." in there.

Type is mandatory (see the next page) and will usually be "d" for a decimal integer or "f" for a floating point number.

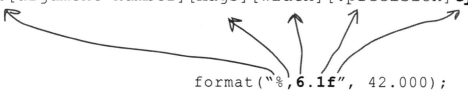

`%[argument number][flags][width][.precision]`**`type`**

`format("%,6.1f", 42.000);`

There's no "argument number" specified in this format String, but all the other pieces are there.

The only required specifier is for TYPE

Although type is the only required specifier, remember that if you *do* put in anything else, type must always come last! There are more than a dozen different type modifiers (not including dates and times; they have their own set), but most of the time you'll probably use %d (decimal) or %f (floating point). And typically you'll combine %f with a precision indicator to set the number of decimal places you want in your output.

The TYPE is mandatory, everything else is optional.

%d   *decimal*

```
format("%d", 42);
```

> A 42.25 would not work! It would be the same as trying to directly assign a double to an int variable.

```
42
```

The argument must be compatible with an int, so that means only byte, short, int, and char (or their wrapper types).

%f   *floating point*

```
format("%.3f", 42.000000);
```

> Here we combined the "f" with a precision indicator ".3" so we ended up with three zeroes.

```
42.000
```

The argument must be of a floating point type, so that means only a float or double (primitive or wrapper) as well as something called BigDecimal (which we don't look at in this book).

%x   *hexadecimal*

```
format("%x", 42);
```

```
2a
```

The argument must be a byte, short, int, long (including both primitive and wrapper types), and BigInteger.

%c   *character*

```
format("%c", 42);
```

> The number 42 represents the char "*".

```
*
```

The argument must be a byte, short, char, or int (including both primitive and wrapper types).

> You must include a type in your format instructions, and if you specify things besides type, the type must always come <u>last</u>. Most of the time, you'll probably format numbers using either "d" for decimal or "f" for floating point.

What happens if I have more than one argument?

Imagine you want a String that looks like this:

"The rank is *20,456,654* out of *100,567,890.24*."

But the numbers are coming from variables. What do you do? You simply add *two* arguments after the format String (first argument), so that means your call to format() will have three arguments instead of two. And inside that first argument (the format String), you'll have two different format specifiers (two things that start with "%"). The first format specifier will insert the second argument to the method, and the second format specifier will insert the third argument to the method. In other words, the variable insertions in the format String use the order in which the other arguments are passed into the format() method.

```
int one = 20456654;
double two = 100567890.248907;
String s = String.format("The rank is %,d out of %,.2f", one, two);
```

```
The rank is 20,456,654 out of 100,567,890.25
```

We added commas to both variables, and restricted the floating point number (the second variable) to two decimal places.

When you have more than one argument, they're inserted using the order in which you pass them to the format() method.

As you'll see when we get to date formatting, you might actually want to apply different formatting specifiers to the same argument. That's probably hard to imagine until you see how *date* formatting (as opposed to the *number* formating we've been doing) works. Just know that in a minute, you'll see how to be more specific about which format specifiers are applied to which arguments.

Q: Um, there's something REALLY strange going on here. Just how many arguments *can* I pass? I mean, how many overloaded format() methods are IN the String class? So, what happens if I want to pass, say, ten different arguments to be formatted for a single output String?

A: Good catch. Yes, there *is* something strange (or at least new and different) going on, and no there are *not* a bunch of overloaded format() methods to take a different number of possible arguments. In order to support this new formatting (printf-like) API in Java, the language needed another new feature—*variable argument lists* (called *varargs* for short). We'll talk about varargs only in the appendix because outside of formatting, you probably won't use them much in a well-designed system.

So much for numbers, what about dates?

Imagine you want a String that looks like this: "Sunday, Nov 28 2004"

Nothing special there, you say? Well, imagine that all you have to start with is a variable of type Date—A Java class that can represent a timestamp, and now you want to take that object (as opposed to a number) and send it through the formatter.

The main difference between number and date formatting is that date formats use a two-character type that starts with "t" (as opposed to the single character "f" or "d", for example). The examples below should give you a good idea of how it works:

The complete date and time   %tc

```
String.format("%tc", new Date());
```

```
Sun Nov 28 14:52:41 MST 2004
```

Just the time   %tr

```
String.format("%tr", new Date());
```

```
03:01:47 PM
```

Day of the week, month and day   %tA %tB %td

There isn't a single format specifier that will do exactly what we want, so we have to combine three of them for day of the week (%tA), month (%tB), and day of the month (%td).

```
Date today = new Date();
String.format("%tA, %tB %td",today,today,today)
```

The comma is not part of the formatting... it's just the character we want printed after the first inserted formatted argument.

But that means we have to pass the Date object in three times, one for each part of the format that we want. In other words, the %tA will give us just the day of the week, but then we have to do it again to get just the month and again for the day of the month.

```
Sunday, November 28
```

Same as above, but *without duplicating the arguments*   %tA %tB %td

```
Date today = new Date();
String.format("%tA, %<tB %<td",today);
```

You can think of this as kind of like calling three different getter methods on the Date object, to get three different pieces of data from it.

The angle-bracket "<" is just another flag in the specifier that tells the formatter to "use the previous argument again." So it saves you from repeating the arguments, and instead you format the same argument three different ways.

Let's see... how many work days will there be if the project starts on Feb 27th and ends on August 5th?

Working with Dates

You need to do more with dates than just get *today's* date. You need your programs to adjust dates, find elapsed times, prioritize schedules, heck, make schedules. You need industrial strength date manipulation capabilities.

You could make your own date routines of course... (and don't forget about leap years!) And, ouch, those occasional, pesky leap-*seconds*. Wow, this could get complicated. The good news is that the Java API is rich with classes that can help you manipulate dates. Sometimes it feels a little *too* rich...

Moving backward and forward in time

Let's say your company's work schedule is Monday through Friday. You've been assigned the task of figuring out the last work day in each calendar month this year...

It seems that java.util.Date is actually... out of date

Earlier we used java.util.Date to find today's date, so it seems logical that this class would be a good place to start looking for some handy date manipulation capabilities, but when you check out the API you'll find that most of Date's methods have been deprecated!

The Date class is still great for getting a "time stamp"—an object that represents the current date and time, so use it when you want to say, "give me NOW".

The good news is that the API recommends **java.util.Calendar** instead, so let's take a look:

Use java.util.Calendar for your date *manipulation*

The designers of the Calendar API wanted to think globally, literally. The basic idea is that when you want to work with dates, you ask for a Calendar (through a static method of the Calendar class that you'll see on the next page), and the JVM hands you back an instance of a concrete subclass of Calendar. (Calendar is actually an abstract class, so you're always working with a concrete subclass.)

More interesting, though, is that the *kind* of calendar you get back will be *appropriate for your locale.* Much of the world uses the Gregorian calendar, but if you're in an area that doesn't use a Gregorian calendar you can get Java libraries to handle other calendars such as Buddhist, or Islamic or Japanese.

The standard Java API ships with **java.util.GregorianCalendar**, so that's what we'll be using here. For the most part, though, you don't even have to think about the kind of Calendar subclass you're using, and instead focus only on the methods of the Calendar class.

For a time-stamp of "now", use Date. But for everything else, use Calendar.

Getting an object that extends Calendar

How in the world do you get an "instance" of an abstract class?
Well you don't of course, this won't work:

This WON'T work:

```
Calendar cal = new Calendar();
```

The compiler won't allow this!

Instead, use the static "getInstance()" method:

```
Calendar cal = Calendar.getInstance();
```

This syntax should look familiar at this point — we're invoking a static method.

> Wait a minute. If you can't make an instance of the Calendar class, what exactly are you assigning to that Calendar reference?

You can't get an instance of Calendar, but you can can get an instance of a concrete Calendar subclass.

Obviously you can't get an instance of Calendar, because Calendar is abstract. But you're still free to call static methods on Calendar, since *static* methods are called on the *class*, rather than on a particular instance. So you call the static getInstance() on Calendar and it gives you back... an instance of a concrete subclass. Something that extends Calendar (which means it can be polymorphically assigned to Calendar) and which—by contract—can respond to the methods of class Calendar.

In most of the world, and by default for most versions of Java, you'll be getting back a **java.util.GregorianCalendar** instance.

Working with Calendar objects

There are several key concepts you'll need to understand in
order to work with Calendar objects:

- **Fields hold** *state* - A Calendar object has many fields that are used to
  represent aspects of its ultimate state, its date and time. For instance, you
  can get and set a Calendar's *year* or *month*.

- **Dates and Times can be** *incremented* - The Calendar class has methods that
  allow you to add and subtract values from various fields, for example "add
  one to the month", or "subtract three years".

- **Dates and Times can be represented in** *milliseconds* - The Calendar class
  lets you convert your dates into and out of a millisecond representation.
  (Specifically, the number of milliseconds that have occured since January
  1st, 1970.) This allows you to perform precise calculations such as "elapsed
  time between two times" or "add 63 hours and 23 minutes and 12 seconds
  to this time".

An example of working with a Calendar object:

```
Calendar c = Calendar.getInstance();
c.set(2004,0,7,15,40);
long day1 = c.getTimeInMillis();
day1 += 1000 * 60 * 60;
c.setTimeInMillis(day1);
System.out.println("new hour " + c.get(c.HOUR_OF_DAY));
c.add(c.DATE, 35);
System.out.println("add 35 days " + c.getTime());
c.roll(c.DATE, 35);
System.out.println("roll 35 days " + c.getTime());
c.set(c.DATE, 1);
System.out.println("set to 1 " + c.getTime());
```

Set time to Jan. 7, 2004 at 15:40.
(Notice the month is zero-based.)

Convert this to a big ol'
amount of milliseconds.

Add an hour's worth of millis, then update the time.
(Notice the "+=", it's like day1 = day1 + ...).

Add 35 days to the date, which
should move us into February.

"Roll" 35 days onto this date. This
"rolls" the date ahead 35 days, but
DOES NOT change the month!

We're not incrementing here, just
doing a "set" of the date.

```
File  Edit  Window  Help  Time-Flies
new hour 16
add 35 days Wed Feb 11 16:40:41 MST 2004
roll 35 days Tue Feb 17 16:40:41 MST 2004
set to 1 Sun Feb 01 16:40:41 MST 2004
```

This output confirms how millis,
add, roll, and set work.

Highlights of the Calendar API

We just worked through using a few of the fields and methods in the Calendar class. This is a big API, so we're showing only a few of the most common fields and methods that you'll use. Once you get a few of these it should be pretty easy to bend the rest of the this API to your will.

Key Calendar Methods

add(int field, int amount)
    Adds or subtracts time from the calendar's field.

get(int field)
    Returns the value of the given calendar field.

getInstance()
    Returns a Calendar, you can specify a locale.

getTimeInMillis()
    Returns this Calendar's time in millis, as a long.

roll(int field, boolean up)
    Adds or subtracts time without changing larger fields.

set(int field, int value)
    Sets the value of a given Calendar field.

set(year, month, day, hour, minute) (all ints)
    A common variety of set to set a complete time.

setTimeInMillis(long millis)
    Sets a Calendar's time based on a long milli-time.

// more...

Key Calendar Fields

DATE / DAY_OF_MONTH
    Get / set the day of month

HOUR / HOUR _OF_DAY
    Get / set the 12 hour or 24 hour value.

MILLISECOND
    Get / set the milliseconds.

MINUTE
    Get / set the minute.

MONTH
    Get / set the month.

YEAR
    Get / set the year.

ZONE_OFFSET
    Get / set raw offset of GMT in millis.

// more...

Even more Statics!... static <u>imports</u>

New to Java 5.0... a real mixed blessing. Some people love this idea, some people hate it. Static imports exist only to save you some typing. If you hate to type, you might just like this feature. The downside to static imports is that - if you're not careful - using them can make your code a lot harder to read.

The basic idea is that whenever you're using a static class, a static variable, or an enum (more on those later), you can import them, and save yourself some typing.

Use Carefully:

static imports can make your code confusing to read

Some old-fashioned code:

```java
import java.lang.Math;

class NoStatic {

  public static void main(String [] args) {

    System.out.println("sqrt " + Math.sqrt(2.0));

    System.out.println("tan " + Math.tan(60));

  }

}
```

The syntax to use when declaring static imports.

Same code, with static imports:

```java
import static java.lang.System.out;

import static java.lang.Math.*;

class WithStatic {

  public static void main(String [] args) {

    out.println("sqrt " + sqrt(2.0));

    out.println("tan " + tan(60));

  }

}
```

Static imports in action.

 **Caveats & Gotchas**

- If you're only going to use a static member a few times, we think you should avoid static imports, to help keep the code more readable.

- If you're going to use a static member a lot, (like doing lots of Math calculations), then it's probably OK to use the static import.

- Notice that you can use wildcards (.*), in your static import declaration.

- A big issue with static imports is that it's not too hard to create naming conflicts. For example, if you have two different classes with an "add()" method, how will you and the compiler know which one to use?

Fireside Chats

Tonight's Talk: **An instance variable takes cheap shots at a static variable**

Instance Variable

I don't even know why we're doing this. Everyone knows static variables are just used for constants. And how many of those are there? I think the whole API must have, what, four? And it's not like anybody ever uses them.

Static Variable

You really should check your facts. When was the last time you looked at the API? It's frickin' loaded with statics! It even has entire classes dedicated to holding constant values. There's a class called SwingConstants, for example, that's just full of them.

Full of it. Yeah, you can say that again. OK, so there are a few in the Swing library, but everybody knows Swing is just a special case.

It might be a special case, but it's a really important one! And what about the Color class? What a pain if you had to remember the RGB values to make the standard colors? But the color class already has constants defined for blue, purple, white, red, etc. Very handy.

Ok, but besides a few GUI things, give me an example of just one static variable that anyone would actually use. In the real world.

How's System.out for starters? The out in System.out is a static variable of the System class. You personally don't make a new instance of the System, you just ask the System class for its out variable.

Well, that's another special case. And nobody uses that except for debugging anyway.

Oh, like debugging isn't important?

And here's something that probably never crossed your narrow mind—let's face it, static variables are more efficient. One per class instead of one per instance. The memory savings might be huge!

Instance Variable

Um, aren't you forgetting something?

Static variables are about as un-OO as it gets!! Gee why not just go take a giant backwards step and do some procedural programming while we're at it.

You're like a global variable, and any programmer worth his PDA knows that's usually a Bad Thing.

Yeah you live in a class, but they don't call it *Class*-Oriented programming. That's just stupid. You're a relic. Something to help the old-timers make the leap to java.

Well, OK, every once in a while sure, it makes sense to use a static, but let me tell you, abuse of static variables (and methods) is the mark of an immature OO programmer. A designer should be thinking about *object* state, not *class* state.

Static methods are the worst things of all, because it usually means the programmer is thinking procedurally instead of about objects doing things based on their unique object state.

Riiiiight. Whatever you need to tell yourself...

Static Variable

What?

What do you mean *un*-OO?

I am NOT a global variable. There's no such thing. I live in a class! That's pretty OO you know, a CLASS. I'm not just sitting out there in space somewhere; I'm a natural part of the state of an object; the only difference is that I'm shared by all instances of a class. Very efficient.

Alright just stop right there. THAT is definitely not true. Some static variables are absolutely crucial to a system. And even the ones that aren't crucial sure are handy.

Why do you say that? And what's wrong with static methods?

Sure, I know that objects should be the focus of an OO design, but just because there are some clueless programmers out there... don't throw the baby out with the bytecode. There's a time and place for statics, and when you need one, nothing else beats it.

Exercise

BE the compiler

The Java file on this page represents a complete program. Your job is to play compiler and determine whether this file will compile. If it won't compile, how would you fix it, and if it does compile, what would be its output?

```java
class StaticSuper{

  static {
    System.out.println("super static block");
  }

  StaticSuper{
    System.out.println(
      "super constructor");
  }
}


public class StaticTests extends StaticSuper {
  static int rand;

  static {
    rand = (int) (Math.random() * 6);
    System.out.println("static block " + rand);
  }

  StaticTests() {
    System.out.println("constructor");
  }

  public static void main(String [] args) {
    System.out.println("in main");
    StaticTests st = new StaticTests();
  }
}
```

If it compiles, which of these is the output?

Possible Output

```
File  Edit  Window  Help  Cling
%java StaticTests
static block 4
in main
super static block
super constructor
constructor
```

Possible Output

```
File  Edit  Window  Help  Electricity
%java StaticTests
super static block
static block 3
in main
super constructor
constructor
```

Exercise

This chapter explored the wonderful, static, world of Java. Your job is to decide whether each of the following statements is true or false.

TRUE OR FALSE

1. To use the Math class, the first step is to make an instance of it.

2. You can mark a constructor with the **static** keyword.

3. Static methods don't have access to instance variable state of the 'this' object.

4. It is good practice to call a static method using a reference variable.

5. Static variables could be used to count the instances of a class.

6. Constructors are called before static variables are initialized.

7. MAX_SIZE would be a good name for a static final variable.

8. A static initializer block runs before a class's constructor runs.

9. If a class is marked final, all of its methods must be marked final.

10. A final method can only be overridden if its class is extended.

11. There is no wrapper class for boolean primitives.

12. A wrapper is used when you want to treat a primitive like an object.

13. The parseXxx methods always return a String.

14. Formatting classes (which are decoupled from I/O), are in the java.format package.

Lunar Code Magnets

This one might actually be useful! In addition to what you've learned in the last few pages about manipulating dates, you'll need a little more information... First, full moons happen every 29.52 days or so. Second, there was a full moon on Jan. 7th, 2004. Your job is to reconstruct the code snippets to make a working Java program that produces the output listed below (plus more full moon dates). (You might not need all of the magnets, and add all the curly braces you need.) Oh, by the way, your output will be different if you don't live in the mountain time zone.

```
long day1 = c.getTimeInMillis();
```

```
c.set(2004,1,7,15,40);
```

```
import static java.lang.System.out;
```

```
static int DAY_IM = 60 * 60 * 24;
```

```
("full moon on %tc", c));
```

```
(c.format
```

```
Calendar c = new Calendar();
```

```
class FullMoons {
```

```
public static void main(String [] args) {
```

```
day1 += (DAY_IM * 29.52);
```

```
for (int x = 0; x < 60; x++) {
```

```
static int DAY_IM = 1000 * 60 * 60 * 24;
```

```
println
```

```
import java.io.*;
```

```
("full moon on %t", c));
```

```
import java.util.*;
```

```
static import java.lang.System.out;
```

```
c.set(2004,0,7,15,40);
```

```
out.println
```

```
c.setTimeInMillis(day1);
```

```
(String.format
```

```
Calendar c = Calendar.getInstance();
```

File Edit Window Help Howl

```
% java FullMoons
full moon on Fri Feb 06 04:09:35 MST 2004
full moon on Sat Mar 06 16:38:23 MST 2004
full moon on Mon Apr 05 06:07:11 MDT 2004
```

Exercise Solutions

BE the compiler

```
StaticSuper( ) {
  System.out.println(
    "super constructor");
}
```

StaticSuper is a constructor, and must have ( ) in its signature. Notice that as the output below demonstrates, the static blocks for both classes run before either of the constructors run.

Possible Output

```
File  Edit  Window  Help  Cling
%java StaticTests
super static block
static block 3
in main
super constructor
constructor
```

True or False

1. To use the Math class, the first step is to make an instance of it.	**False**
2. You can mark a constructor with the keyword 'static'.	**False**
3. Static methods don't have access to an object's instance variables.	**True**
4. It is good practice to call a static method using a reference variable.	**False**
5. Static variables could be used to count the instances of a class.	**True**
6. Constructors are called before static variables are initialized.	**False**
7. MAX_SIZE would be a good name for a static final variable.	**True**
8. A static initializer block runs before a class's constructor runs.	**True**
9. If a class is marked final, all of its methods must be marked final.	**False**
10. A final method can only be overridden if its class is extended.	**False**
11. There is no wrapper class for boolean primitives.	**False**
12. A wrapper is used when you want to treat a primitive like an object.	**True**
13. The parseXxx methods always return a String.	**False**
14. Formatting classes (which are decoupled from I/O), are in the java.format package.	**False**

Exercise Solutions

```java
import java.util.*;

import static java.lang.System.out;

class FullMoons {

  static int DAY_IM = 1000 * 60 * 60 * 24;

  public static void main(String [] args) {

    Calendar c = Calendar.getInstance();

    c.set(2004,0,7,15,40);

    long day1 = c.getTimeInMillis();

    for (int x = 0; x < 60; x++) {

      day1 += (DAY_IM * 29.52)

      c.setTimeInMillis(day1);

      out.println(String.format("full moon on %tc", c));

    }

  }

}
```

Notes on the Lunar Code Magnet:

You might discover that a few of the dates produced by this program are off by a day. This astronomical stuff is a little tricky, and if we made it perfect, it would be too complex to make an exercise here.

Hint: one problem you might try to solve is based on differences in time zones. Can you spot the issue?

```
File  Edit  Window  Help  Howl
% java FullMoons
full moon on Fri Feb 06 04:09:35 MST 2004
full moon on Sat Mar 06 16:38:23 MST 2004
full moon on Mon Apr 05 06:07:11 MDT 2004
```

Risky Behavior

Sure it's risky, but I can **handle** it if something goes wrong.

Stuff happens. The file isn't there. The server is down. No matter how good a programmer you are, you can't control everything. Things can go wrong. *Very* wrong. When you write a risky method, you need code to handle the bad things that might happen. But how do you *know* when a method is risky? And where do you put the code to *handle* the *exceptional* situation? So far in this book, we haven't *really* taken any risks. We've certainly had things go wrong at runtime, but the problems were mostly flaws in our own code. Bugs. And those we should fix at development time. No, the problem-handling code we're talking about here is for code that you *can't* guarantee will work at runtime. Code that expects the file to be in the right directory, the server to be running, or the Thread to stay asleep. And we have to do this *now*. Because in *this* chapter, we're going to build something that uses the risky JavaSound API. We're going to build a MIDI Music Player.

Let's make a Music Machine

Over the next three chapters, we'll build a few different sound applications, including a BeatBox Drum Machine. In fact, before the book is done, we'll have a multi-player version so you can send your drum loops to another player, kind of like a chat room. You're going to write the whole thing, although you can choose to use Ready-bake code for the GUI parts. OK, so not every IT department is looking for a new BeatBox server, but we're doing this to *learn* more about *Java*. Building a BeatBox is just a way to have fun *while* we're learning Java.

The finished BeatBox looks something like this:

You make a beatbox loop (a 16-beat drum pattern) by putting checkmarks in the boxes.

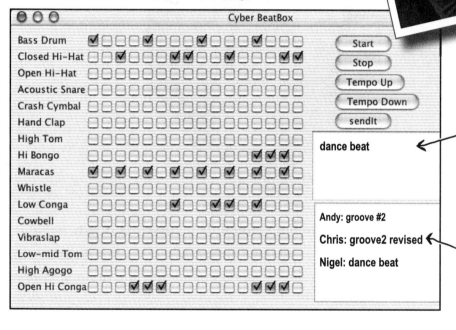

your message, that gets sent to the other players, along with your current beat pattern, when you hit "SendIt"

incoming messages from other players. Click one to load the pattern that goes with it, and then click 'Start' to play it.

Put checkmarks in the boxes for each of the 16 'beats'. For example, on beat 1 (of 16) the Bass drum and the Maracas will play, on beat 2 nothing, and on beat 3 the Maracas and Closed Hi-Hat... you get the idea. When you hit 'Start', it plays your pattern in a loop until you hit 'Stop'. At any time, you can "capture" one of your own patterns by sending it to the BeatBox server (which means any other players can listen to it). You can also load any of the incoming patterns by clicking on the message that goes with it.

We'll start with the basics

Obviously we've got a few things to learn before the whole program is finished, including how to build a Swing GUI, how to *connect* to another machine via networking, and a little I/O so we can *send* something to the other machine.

Oh yeah, and the JavaSound API. *That's* where we'll start in this chapter. For now, you can forget the GUI, forget the networking and the I/O, and focus only on getting some MIDI-generated sound to come out of your computer. And don't worry if you don't know a thing about MIDI, or a thing about reading or making music. Everything you need to learn is covered here. You can almost smell the record deal.

The JavaSound API

JavaSound is a collection of classes and interfaces added to Java starting with version 1.3. These aren't special add-ons; they're part of the standard J2SE class library. JavaSound is split into two parts: MIDI and Sampled. We use only MIDI in this book. MIDI stands for Musical Instrument Digital Interface, and is a standard protocol for getting different kinds of electronic sound equipment to communicate. But for our BeatBox app, you can think of MIDI as *a kind of sheet music* that you feed into some device you can think of like a high-tech 'player piano'. In other words, MIDI data doesn't actually include any *sound*, but it does include the *instructions* that a MIDI-reading instrument can play back. Or for another analogy, you can think of a MIDI file like an HTML document, and the instrument that renders the MIDI file (i.e. *plays* it) is like the Web browser.

MIDI data says *what* to do (play middle C, and here's how hard to hit it, and here's how long to hold it, etc.) but it doesn't say anything at all about the actual *sound* you hear. MIDI doesn't know how to make a flute, piano, or Jimmy Hendrix guitar sound. For the actual sound, we need an instrument (a MIDI device) that can read and play a MIDI file. But the device is usually more like an *entire band or orchestra* of instruments. And that instrument might be a physical device, like the electronic keyboard synthesizers the rock musicians play, or it could even be an instrument built entirely in software, living in your computer.

For our BeatBox, we use only the built-in, software-only instrument that you get with Java. It's called a *synthesizer* (some folks refer to it as a *software synth*) because it *creates* sound. Sound that you *hear*.

MIDI file

play high C, hit it hard and hold it for 2 beats

MIDI file has information about how a song should be played, but it doesn't have any actual sound data. It's kind of like sheet music instructions for a player-piano.

MIDI-capable Instrument

Speaker

MIDI device knows how to 'read' a MIDI file and play back the sound. The device might be a synthesizer keyboard or some other kind of instrument. Usually, a MIDI instrument can play a LOT of different sounds (piano, drums, violin, etc.), and all at the same time. So a MIDI file isn't like sheet music for just one musician in the band -- it can hold the parts for ALL the musicians playing a particular song.

First we need a Sequencer

Before we can get any sound to play, we need a Sequencer object. The sequencer is the object that takes all the MIDI data and sends it to the right instruments. It's the thing that *plays* the music. A sequencer can do a lot of different things, but in this book, we're using it strictly as a playback device. Like a CD-player on your stereo, but with a few added features. The Sequencer class is in the javax.sound.midi package (part of the standard Java library as of version 1.3). So let's start by making sure we can make (or get) a Sequencer object.

```java
import javax.sound.midi.*;

public class MusicTest1 {

    public void play() {

        Sequencer sequencer = MidiSystem.getSequencer();

        System.out.println("We got a sequencer");

    } // close play

    public static void main(String[] args) {

        MusicTest1 mt = new MusicTest1();

        mt.play();

    } // close main

} // close class
```

← import the javax.sound.midi package

We need a Sequencer object. It's the main part of the MIDI device/instrument we're using. It's the thing that, well, sequences all the MIDI information into a 'song'. But we don't make a brand new one ourselves -- we have to ask the MidiSystem to give us one.

Something's wrong!

This code won't compile! The compiler says there's an 'unreported exception' that must be caught or declared.

```
File Edit Window Help SayWhat?

% javac MusicTest1.java

MusicTest1.java:13: unreported exception javax.sound.midi.
MidiUnavailableException; must be caught or declared to be
thrown

    Sequencer sequencer = MidiSystem.getSequencer();
                                    ^


1 errors
```

What happens when a method you want to call (probably in a class you didn't write) is risky?

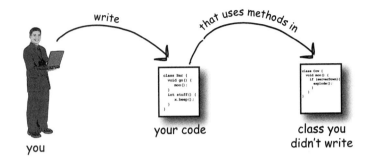

1 Let's say you want to call a method in a class that you didn't write.

you

your code

class you didn't write

write • that uses methods in

2 That method does something risky, something that might not work at runtime.

class you didn't write

```
void moo() {
    if (serverDown) {
        explode();
    }
}
```

3 You need to *know* that the method you're calling is risky.

I wonder if that method could blow up...

My moo() method will explode if the server is down.

class you didn't write

you

Now that I know, I can take precautions.

write safely

4 You then write code that can handle the failure if it *does* happen. You need to be prepared, just in case.

your code

you

Methods in Java use *exceptions* to tell the calling code, "Something Bad Happened. I failed."

Java's exception-handling mechanism is a clean, well-lighted way to handle "exceptional situations" that pop up at runtime; it lets you put all your error-handling code in one easy-to-read place. It's based on you *knowing* that the method you're calling is risky (i.e. that the method *might* generate an exception), so that you can write code to deal with that possibility. If you *know* you might get an exception when you call a particular method, you can be *prepared* for—possibly even *recover* from—the problem that caused the exception.

So, how *do* you know if a method throws an exception? You find a **throws** clause in the risky method's declaration.

The `getSequencer()` **method takes a risk. It can fail at runtime. So it must 'declare' the risk *you* take when you call it.**

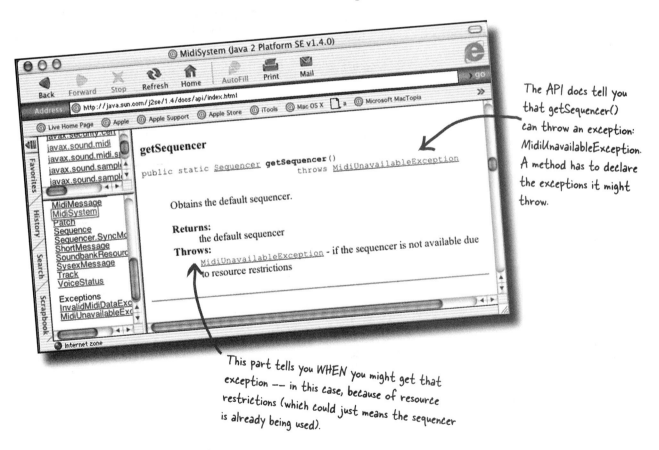

The API does tell you that getSequencer() can throw an exception: MidiUnavailableException. A method has to declare the exceptions it might throw.

This part tells you WHEN you might get that exception -- in this case, because of resource restrictions (which could just means the sequencer is already being used).

The compiler needs to know that YOU know you're calling a risky method.

If you wrap the risky code in something called a **try/catch**, the compiler will relax.

A try/catch block tells the compiler that you *know* an exceptional thing could happen in the method you're calling, and that you're prepared to handle it. That compiler doesn't care *how* you handle it; it cares only that you say you're taking care of it.

Dear Compiler,

I know I'm taking a risk here, but don't you think it's worth it? What should I do?

signed, geeky in Waikiki

Dear geeky,

Life is short (especially on the heap). Take the risk. try it. But just in case things don't work out, be sure to catch any problems before all hell breaks loose.

```java
import javax.sound.midi.*;

public class MusicTest1 {
    public void play() {

        try {
            Sequencer sequencer = MidiSystem.getSequencer();
            System.out.println("Successfully got a sequencer");
        } catch(MidiUnavailableException ex) {
            System.out.println("Bummer");
        }
    } // close play

    public static void main(String[] args) {
        MusicTest1 mt = new MusicTest1();
        mt.play();
    } // close main
} // close class
```

put the risky thing in a 'try' block.

make a 'catch' block for what to do if the exceptional situation happens —— in other words, a MidiUnavailableException is thrown by the call to getSequencer().

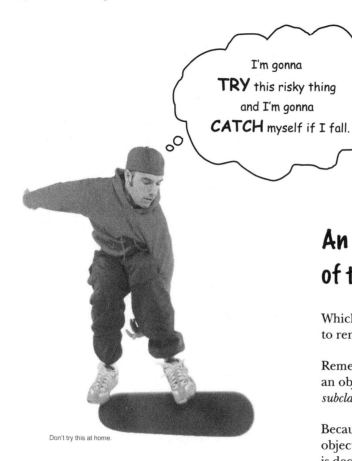

I'm gonna **TRY** this risky thing and I'm gonna **CATCH** myself if I fall.

Don't try this at home.

Part of the Exception class hierarchy. They all extend class Throwable and inherit two key methods.

Throwable

getMessage()
printStackTrace()

Exception

IOException

InterruptedException

An exception is an object... of type Exception.

Which is fortunate, because it would be much harder to remember if exceptions were of type Broccoli.

Remember from your polymorphism chapters that an object of type Exception *can* be an instance of any *subclass* of Exception.

Because an *Exception* is an object, what you *catch* is an object. In the following code, the **catch** argument is declared as type Exception, and the parameter reference variable is *ex*.

```
try {

    // do risky thing

} catch(Exception ex) {

    // try to recover

}
```

it's just like declaring a method argument.

This code only runs if an Exception is thrown.

What you write in a catch block depends on the exception that was thrown. For example, if a server is down you might use the catch block to try another server. If the file isn't there, you might ask the user for help finding it.

If it's *your* code that catches the exception, then whose code throws it?

You'll spend much more of your Java coding time *handling* exceptions than you'll spend *creating* and *throwing* them yourself. For now, just know that when your code *calls* a risky method—a method that declares an exception—it's the risky method that *throws* the exception back to *you*, the caller.

In reality, it might be you who wrote both classes. It really doesn't matter who writes the code... what matters is knowing which method *throws* the exception and which method *catches* it.

When somebody writes code that could throw an exception, they must *declare* the exception.

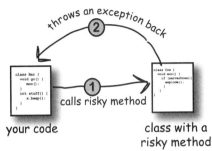

throws an exception back

calls risky method

your code   class with a risky method

---

① **Risky, exception-throwing code:**

this method MUST tell the world (by declaring) that it throws a BadException

```java
public void takeRisk() throws BadException {
    if (abandonAllHope) {
        throw new BadException();
    }
}
```

create a new Exception object and throw it.

> One method will catch what another method throws. An exception is always thrown back to the caller.
>
> The method that throws has to declare that it might throw the exception.

② **Your code that *calls* the risky method:**

```java
public void crossFingers() {
    try {
        anObject.takeRisk();
    } catch (BadException ex) {
        System.out.println("Aaargh!");
        ex.printStackTrace();
    }
}
```

If you can't recover from the exception, at LEAST get a stack trace using the printStackTrace() method that all exceptions inherit.

The compiler checks for everything except RuntimeExceptions.

The compiler guarantees:

Exceptions that are NOT subclasses of RuntimeException are checked for by the compiler. They're called "checked exceptions"

① If you *throw* an exception in your code you *must* declare it using the *throws* keyword in your method declaration.

② If you *call* a method that throws an exception (in other words, a method that *declares* it throws an exception), you must *acknowledge* that you're aware of the exception possibility. One way to satisfy the compiler is to wrap the call in a try/catch. (There's a second way we'll look at a little later in this chapter.)

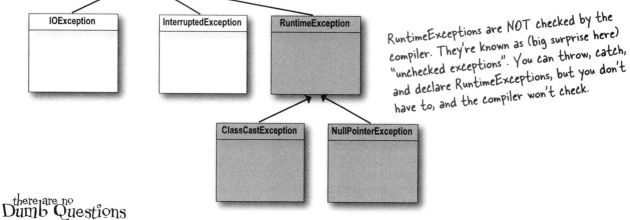

RuntimeExceptions are NOT checked by the compiler. They're known as (big surprise here) "unchecked exceptions". You can throw, catch, and declare RuntimeExceptions, but you don't have to, and the compiler won't check.

there are no Dumb Questions

Q: Wait just a minute! How come this is the FIRST time we've had to try/catch an Exception? What about the exceptions I've already gotten like NullPointerException and the exception for DivideByZero. I even got a NumberFormatException from the Integer.parseInt() method. How come we didn't have to catch those?

A: The compiler cares about all subclasses of Exception, *unless* they are a special type, RuntimeException. Any exception class that extends RuntimeException gets a free pass. RuntimeExceptions can be thrown anywhere, with or without throws declarations or try/catch blocks. The compiler doesn't bother checking whether a method declares that it throws a RuntimeException, or whether the caller acknowledges that they might get that exception at runtime.

Q: I'll bite. WHY doesn't the compiler care about those runtime exceptions? Aren't they just as likely to bring the whole show to a stop?

A: Most RuntimeExceptions come from a problem in your code logic, rather than a condition that fails at runtime in ways that you cannot predict or prevent. You *cannot* guarantee the file is there. You *cannot* guarantee the server is up. But you *can* make sure your code doesn't index off the end of an array (that's what the .length attribute is for).

You WANT RuntimeExceptions to happen at development and testing time. You don't want to code in a try/catch, for example, and have the overhead that goes with it, to catch something that shouldn't happen in the first place.

A try/catch is for handling exceptional situations, not flaws in your code. Use your catch blocks to try to recover from situations you can't guarantee will succeed. Or at the very least, print out a message to the user and a stack trace, so somebody can figure out what happened.

BULLET POINTS

- A method can throw an exception when something fails at runtime.

- An exception is always an object of type Exception. (Which, as you remember from the polymorphism chapters means the object is from a class that has Exception somewhere up its inheritance tree.)

- The compiler does NOT pay attention to exceptions that are of type **RuntimeException**. A RuntimeException does not have to be declared or wrapped in a try/catch (although you're free to do either or both of those things)

- All Exceptions the compiler cares about are called 'checked exceptions' which really means *compiler*-checked exceptions. Only RuntimeExceptions are excluded from compiler checking. All other exceptions must be acknowledged in your code, according to the rules.

- A method throws an exception with the keyword **throw**, followed by a new exception object:

  ```
  throw new NoCaffeineException();
  ```

- Methods that *might* throw a checked exception ***must*** announce it with a **throws Exception** declaration.

- If your code calls a checked-exception-throwing method, it must reassure the compiler that precautions have been taken.

- If you're prepared to handle the exception, wrap the call in a try/catch, and put your exception handling/recovery code in the catch block.

- If you're not prepared to handle the exception, you can still make the compiler happy by officially 'ducking' the exception. We'll talk about ducking a little later in this chapter.

metacoGNitive tiP

If you're trying to learn something new, make that the *last* thing you try to learn before going to sleep. So, once you put this book down (assuming you can tear yourself away from it) don't read anything else more challenging than the back of a Cheerios™ box. Your brain needs time to process what you've read and learned. That could take a few *hours*. If you try to shove something new in right on top of your Java, some of the Java might not 'stick.'

Of course, this doesn't rule out learning a physical skill. Working on your latest Ballroom KickBoxing routine probably won't affect your Java learning.

For the best results, read this book (or at least look at the pictures) right before going to sleep.

Sharpen your pencil

Which of these do you think might throw an exception that the compiler would care about? We're only looking for the things that you can't control in your code. We did the first one.

(Because it was the easiest.)

Things you want to do

✔ connect to a remote server

___ access an array beyond its length

___ display a window on the screen

✔ retrieve data from a database

✔ see if a text file is where you *think* it is

✔ create a new file

___ read a character from the command-line

What might go wrong

the server is down

_____

_____

database goes down

file is not there

filesystem is not writeable

_____

Flow control in try/catch blocks

When you call a risky method, one of two things can happen. The risky method either succeeds, and the try block completes, or the risky method throws an exception back to your calling method.

If the try **succeeds**

(doRiskyThing() does *not* throw an exception)

```
try {
①  Foo f = x.doRiskyThing();
    int b = f.getNum();

} catch (Exception ex) {
    System.out.println("failed");
}
②  System.out.println("We made it!");
```

First the try block runs, then the code below the catch runs.

The code in the catch block never runs.

```
File Edit Window Help RiskAll
%java Tester

We made it!
```

If the try **fails**

(because doRiskyThing() *does* throw an exception)

```
try {
①  Foo f = x.doRiskyThing();
    int b = f.getNum();

} catch (Exception ex) {
②  System.out.println("failed");
}
③  System.out.println("We made it!");
```

The try block runs, but the call to doRiskyThing() throws an exception, so the rest of the try block doesn't run.

The catch block runs, then the method continues on.

The rest of the try block never runs, which is a Good Thing because the rest of the try depends on the success of the call to doRiskyThing().

```
File Edit Window Help RiskAll
%java Tester

failed

We made it!
```

Finally: for the things you want to do *no matter what.*

If you try to cook something, you start by turning on the oven.

If the thing you try is a complete **failure**, *you have to turn off the oven.*

If the thing you try **succeeds**, *you have to turn off the oven.*

You have to turn off the oven no matter what!

A finally block is where you put code that must run *regardless* of an exception.

```
try {
    turnOvenOn();
    x.bake();
} catch (BakingException ex) {
    ex.printStackTrace();
} finally {
    turnOvenOff();
}
```

Without finally, you have to put the turnOvenOff() in *both* the try and the catch because *you have to turn off the oven no matter what.* A finally block lets you put all your important cleanup code in *one* place instead of duplicating it like this:

```
try {
    turnOvenOn();
    x.bake();
    turnOvenOff();
} catch (BakingException ex) {
    ex.printStackTrace();
    turnOvenOff();
}
```

Are you sure you want to try this?

No matter what, do NOT let me forget to turn off the oven! Last time I torched half the neighborhood.

If the try block fails (an exception), flow control immediately moves to the catch block. When the catch block completes, the finally block runs. When the finally block completes, the rest of the method continues on.

If the try block succeeds (*no exception*), flow control skips over the catch block and moves to the finally block. When the finally block completes, the rest of the method continues on.

If the try or catch block has a return statement, finally will still run! Flow jumps to the finally, then back to the return.

Sharpen your pencil

Flow Control

Look at the code to the left. What do you think the output of this program would be? What do you think it would be if the third line of the program were changed to: `String test = "yes"; ?`
Assume ScaryException extends Exception.

```java
public class TestExceptions {

  public static void main(String [] args) {

    String test = "no";
    try {
      System.out.println("start try");
      doRisky(test);
      System.out.println("end try");
    } catch ( ScaryException se) {
        System.out.println("scary exception");
    } finally {
        System.out.println("finally");
    }
    System.out.println("end of main");
  }

  static void doRisky(String test) throws ScaryException {
    System.out.println("start risky");
    if ("yes".equals(test)) {

      throw new ScaryException();
    }
    System.out.println("end risky");
    return;
  }
}
```

Output when test = "no"

Output when test = "yes"

When test = "no": start try - start risky - end risky - end try - finally - end of main
When test = "yes": start try - start risky - scary exception - finally - end of main

Did we mention that a method can throw more than one exception?

A method can throw multiple exceptions if it darn well needs to. But a method's declaration must declare *all* the checked exceptions it can throw (although if two or more exceptions have a common superclass, the method can declare just the superclass.)

Catching multiple exceptions

The compiler will make sure that you've handled *all* the checked exceptions thrown by the method you're calling. Stack the *catch* blocks under the *try*, one after the other. Sometimes the order in which you stack the catch blocks matters, but we'll get to that a little later.

```
public class Laundry {
    public void doLaundry() throws PantsException, LingerieException {
        // code that could throw either exception
    }
}
```

This method declares two, count 'em, TWO exceptions.

```
public class Foo {
    public void go() {
        Laundry laundry = new Laundry();
        try {
            laundry.doLaundry();
        } catch(PantsException pex) {
            // recovery code
        } catch(LingerieException lex) {
            // recovery code
        }
    }
}
```

if doLaundry() throws a PantsException, it lands in the PantsException catch block.

if doLaundry() throws a LingerieException, it lands in the LingerieException catch block.

Exceptions are polymorphic

Exceptions are objects, remember. There's nothing all that special about one, except that it is *a thing that can be **thrown***. So like all good objects, Exceptions can be referred to polymorphically. A LingerieException *object*, for example, could be assigned to a ClothingException *reference*. A PantsException could be assigned to an Exception reference. You get the idea. The benefit for exceptions is that a method doesn't have to explicitly declare every possible exception it might throw; it can declare a superclass of the exceptions. Same thing with catch blocks—you don't have to write a catch for each possible exception as long as the catch (or catches) you have can handle any exception thrown.

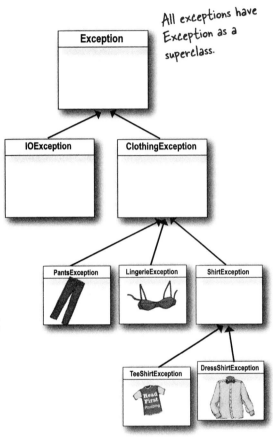

All exceptions have Exception as a superclass.

① You can DECLARE exceptions using a supertype of the exceptions you throw.

```
public void doLaundry() throws ClothingException {
```

Declaring a ClothingException lets you throw any subclass of ClothingException. That means doLaundry() can throw a PantsException, LingerieException, TeeShirtException, and DressShirtException without explicitly declaring them individually.

② You can CATCH exceptions using a supertype of the exception thrown.

```
try {

    laundry.doLaundry();

} catch(ClothingException cex) {

    // recovery code

}
```

can catch any ClothingException subclass

```
try {

    laundry.doLaundry();

} catch(ShirtException sex) {

    // recovery code

}
```

can catch only TeeShirtException and DressShirtException

Just because you CAN catch everything with one big super polymorphic catch, doesn't always mean you SHOULD.

You *could* write your exception-handling code so that you specify only *one* catch block, using the supertype Exception in the catch clause, so that you'll be able to catch *any* exception that might be thrown.

```
try {

    laundry.doLaundry();

} catch(Exception ex) {

    // recovery code...

}
```

← *Recovery from WHAT? This catch block will catch ANY and all exceptions, so you won't automatically know what went wrong.*

Write a different catch block for each exception that you need to handle uniquely.

For example, if your code deals with (or recovers from) a TeeShirtException differently than it handles a LingerieException, write a catch block for each. But if you treat all other types of ClothingException in the same way, then add a ClothingException catch to handle the rest.

```
try {

    laundry.doLaundry();

} catch(TeeShirtException tex) {

    // recovery from TeeShirtException

} catch(LingerieException lex) {

    // recovery from LingerieException

} catch(ClothingException cex) {

    // recovery from all others

}
```

← *TeeShirtExceptions and LingerieExceptions need different recovery code, so you should use different catch blocks.*

← *All other ClothingExceptions are caught here.*

Multiple catch blocks must be ordered from smallest to biggest

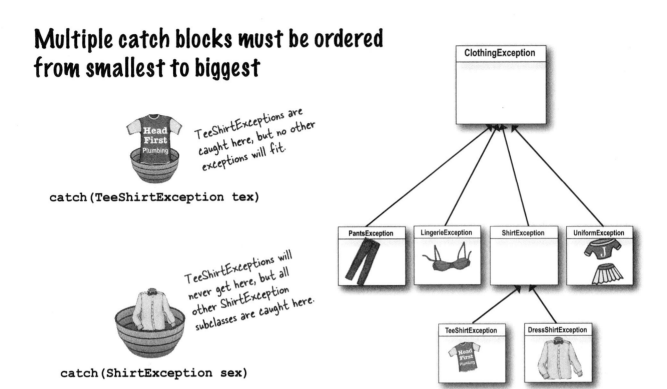

TeeShirtExceptions are caught here, but no other exceptions will fit.

`catch(TeeShirtException tex)`

TeeShirtExceptions will never get here, but all other ShirtException subclasses are caught here.

`catch(ShirtException sex)`

All ClothingExceptions are caught here, although TeeShirtException and ShirtException will never get this far.

`catch(ClothingException cex)`

The higher up the inheritance tree, the bigger the catch 'basket'. As you move down the inheritance tree, toward more and more specialized Exception classes, the catch 'basket' is smaller. It's just plain old polymorphism.

A ShirtException catch is big enough to take a TeeShirtException or a DressShirtException (and any future subclass of anything that extends ShirtException). A ClothingException is even bigger (i.e. there are more things that can be referenced using a ClothingException type). It can take an exception of type ClothingException(duh), and any ClothingException subclasses: PantsException, UniformException, LingerieException, and ShirtException. The mother of all catch arguments is type **Exception**; it will catch *any* exception, including runtime (unchecked) exceptions, so you probably won't use it outside of testing.

You can't put bigger baskets above smaller baskets.

Well, you *can* but it won't compile. Catch blocks are not like overloaded methods where the best match is picked. With catch blocks, the JVM simply starts at the first one and works its way down until it finds a catch that's broad enough (in other words, high enough on the inheritance tree) to handle the exception. If your first catch block is **catch(Exception ex)**, the compiler knows there's no point in adding any others—they'll never be reached.

> Size matters when you have multiple catch blocks. The one with the biggest basket has to be on the bottom. Otherwise, the ones with smaller baskets are useless.

Don't do this!

```
try {
    laundry.doLaundry();
```

```
} catch(ClothingException cex) {
    // recovery from ClothingException
```

```
} catch(LingerieException lex) {
    // recovery from LingerieException
```

```
} catch(ShirtException sex) {
    // recovery from ShirtException
}
```

Siblings can be in any order, because they can't catch one another's exceptions.

You could put ShirtException above LingerieException and nobody would mind. Because even though ShirtException is a bigger (broader) type because it can catch other classes (its own subclasses), ShirtException can't catch a LingerieException so there's no problem.

polymorphic puzzle

Assume the try/catch block here is legally coded. Your task is to draw two different class diagrams that can accurately reflect the Exception classes. In other words, what class inheritance structures would make the try/catch blocks in the sample code legal?

```
try {
  x.doRisky();
} catch(AlphaEx a) {
   // recovery from AlphaEx
} catch(BetaEx b) {
  // recovery from BetaEx
} catch(GammaEx c) {
   // recovery from GammaEx
} catch(DeltaEx d) {
   // recovery from DeltaEx
}
```

Your task is to create two different *legal* try / catch structures (similar to the one above left), to accurately represent the class diagram shown on the left. Assume ALL of these exceptions might be thrown by the method with the try block.

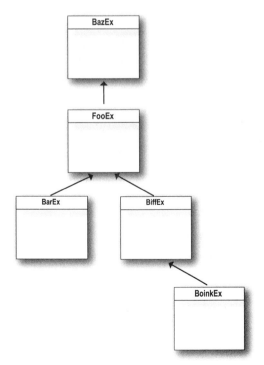

When you don't want to handle an exception...

just duck it

What the...?

There is NO way I'm catching that thing. I'm gettin' out of the way-- somebody behind me can handle it.

If you don't want to handle an exception, you can duck it by declaring it.

When you call a risky method, the compiler needs you to acknowledge it. Most of the time, that means wrapping the risky call in a try/ catch. But you have another alternative, simply *duck* it and let the method that called *you* catch the exception.

It's easy—all you have to do is *declare* that *you* throw the exceptions. Even though, technically, *you* aren't the one doing the throwing, it doesn't matter. You're still the one letting the exception whiz right on by.

But if you duck an exception, then you don't have a try/catch, so what happens when the risky method (doLaundry()) *does* throw the exception?

When a method throws an exception, that method is popped off the stack immediately, and the exception is thrown to the next method down the stack—the *caller*. But if the *caller* is a *ducker*, then there's no catch for it so the *caller* pops off the stack immediately, and the exception is thrown to the next method and so on... where does it end? You'll see a little later.

```
public void foo() throws ReallyBadException {
    // call risky method without a try/catch
    laundry.doLaundry();
}
```

You don't REALLY throw it, but since you don't have a try/catch for the risky method you call, YOU are now the "risky method". Because now, whoever calls YOU has to deal with the exception.

Ducking (by declaring) only delays the inevitable

Sooner or later, *somebody* has to deal with it. But what if *main()* ducks the exception?

```
public class Washer {
    Laundry laundry = new Laundry();

    public void foo() throws ClothingException {
        laundry.doLaundry();
    }

    public static void main (String[] args) throws ClothingException {
        Washer a = new Washer();
        a.foo();
    }
}
```

Both methods duck the exception (by declaring it) so there's nobody to handle it! This compiles just fine.

1 doLaundry() throws a ClothingException	**2** foo() ducks the exception	**3** main() ducks the exception	**4** The JVM shuts down

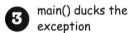

main() calls foo()

foo() calls doLaundry()

doLaundry() is running and throws a ClothingException

doLaundry() pops off the stack immediately and the exception is thrown back to foo().

But foo() doesn't have a try/catch, so...

foo() pops off the stack immediately and the exception is thrown back to... who? What? There's nobody left but the JVM, and it's thinking, "Don't expect ME to get you out of this."

 We're using the tee-shirt to represent a Clothing Exception. We know, we know... you would have preferred the blue jeans.

Handle or Declare. It's the law.

So now we've seen both ways to satisfy the compiler when you call a risky (exception-throwing) method.

① HANDLE

Wrap the risky call in a try/catch

```
try {
    laundry.doLaundry();
} catch(ClothingException cex) {
    // recovery code
}
```

This had better be a big enough catch to handle all exceptions that doLaundry() might throw. Or else the compiler will still complain that you're not catching all of the exceptions.

② DECLARE (duck it)

Declare that YOUR method throws the same exceptions as the risky method you're calling.

```
void foo() throws ClothingException {
    laundry.doLaundry();
}
```

The doLaundry() method throws a ClothingException, but by declaring the exception, the foo() method gets to duck the exception. No try/catch.

But now this means that whoever calls the foo() method has to follow the Handle or Declare law. If foo() ducks the exception (by declaring it), and main() calls foo(), then main() has to deal with the exception.

```
public class Washer {
    Laundry laundry = new Laundry();

    public void foo() throws ClothingException {
        laundry.doLaundry();
    }

    public static void main (String[] args) {
        Washer a = new Washer();
        a.foo();
    }
}
```

TROUBLE!!
Now main() won't compile, and we get an "unreported exception" error. As far as the compiler's concerned, the foo() method throws an exception.

Because the foo() method ducks the ClothingException thrown by doLaundry(), main() has to wrap a.foo() in a try/catch, or main() has to declare that it, too, throws ClothingException!

Getting back to our music code...

Now that you've completely forgotten, we started this chapter with a first look at some JavaSound code. We created a Sequencer object but it wouldn't compile because the method Midi.getSequencer() declares a checked exception (MidiUnavailableException). But we can fix that now by wrapping the call in a try/catch.

```
public void play() {
    try {

        Sequencer sequencer = MidiSystem.getSequencer();
        System.out.println("Successfully got a sequencer");

    } catch(MidiUnavailableException ex) {
        System.out.println("Bummer");

    }
} // close play
```

No problem calling getSequencer(), now that we've wrapped it in a try/catch block.

The catch parameter has to be the 'right' exception. If we said 'catch(FileNotFoundException f), the code would not compile, because polymorphically a MidiUnavilableException won't fit into a FileNotFoundException. Remember it's not enough to have a catch block... you have to catch the thing being thrown!

Exception Rules

① You cannot have a catch or finally without a try

```
void go() {
    Foo f = new Foo();
    f.foof();
    catch(FooException ex) { }
}
```
NOT LEGAL! Where's the try?

② You cannot put code between the try and the catch

```
try {
    x.doStuff();
}
int y = 43;
} catch(Exception ex) { }
```
NOT LEGAL! You can't put code between the try and the catch.

③ A try MUST be followed by either a catch or a finally

```
try {
    x.doStuff();
} finally {
    // cleanup
}
```
LEGAL because you have a finally, even though there's no catch. But you cannot have a try by itself.

④ A try with only a finally (no catch) must still declare the exception.

```
void go() throws FooException {
    try {
        x.doStuff();
    } finally { }
}
```
A try without a catch doesn't satisfy the handle or declare law

Code Kitchen

But why don't you just use Ready-bake code?

There is NO way I'm letting Betty win the code-off this year, so I'm gonna make it myself from scratch.

You don't have to do it yourself, but it's a lot more fun if you do.

The rest of this chapter is optional; you can use Ready-bake code for all the music apps.

But if you want to learn more about JavaSound, turn the page.

Making actual sound

Remember near the beginning of the chapter, we looked at how MIDI data holds the instructions for *what* should be played (and *how* it should be played) and we also said that MIDI data doesn't actually *create any sound that you hear*. For sound to come out of the speakers, the MIDI data has to be sent through some kind of MIDI device that takes the MIDI instructions and renders them in sound, either by triggering a hardware instrument or a 'virtual' instrument (software synthesizer). In this book, we're using only software devices, so here's how it works in JavaSound:

You need FOUR things:

① The thing that plays the music

② The music to be played...a song.

③ The part of the Sequence that holds the actual information

④ The actual music information: notes to play, how long, etc.

Sequencer —plays→ **Sequence** —has a→ **Track** —holds→

Midi Event

Midi Event

Midi Event

Midi Event

The Sequencer is the thing that actually causes a song to be played. Think of it like a **music CD player.**

The Sequence is the song, the musical piece that the Sequencer will play. For this book, think of the Sequence as a music CD, but **the whole CD plays just one song.**

For this book, we only need one Track, so just imagine a a music CD with only one song. A single Track. This Track is where all the song data (MIDI information) lives.

A MIDI event is a message that the Sequencer can understand. A MIDI event might say (if it spoke English), "At this moment in time, play middle C, play it this fast and this hard, and hold it for this long."

A MIDI event might also say something like, "Change the current instrument to Flute."

For this book, think of the Sequence as a single-song CD (has only one Track). The information about how to play the song lives on the Track, and the Track is part of the Sequence.

And you need FIVE steps:

(1) Get a **Sequencer** and open it

```
Sequencer player = MidiSystem.getSequencer();
player.open();
```

(2) Make a new **Sequence**

```
Sequence seq = new Sequence(timing,4);
```

(3) Get a new **Track** from the Sequence

```
Track t = seq.createTrack();
```

(4) Fill the Track with **MidiEvents** and give the Sequence to the Sequencer

```
t.add(myMidiEvent1);
player.setSequence(seq);
```

> Uh, hate to break it to you, but that's only FOUR steps.

> Ahhhh. We forgot to push the PLAY button. You have to start() the Sequencer!

```
player.start();
```

Your very first sound player app

Type it in and run it. You'll hear the sound of someone playing a single note on a piano! (OK, maybe not some*one*, but some*thing*.)

```java
import javax.sound.midi.*;    ← Don't forget to import the midi package

public class MiniMiniMusicApp {

    public static void main(String[] args) {
        MiniMiniMusicApp mini = new MiniMiniMusicApp();
        mini.play();
    } // close main

    public void play() {

        try {

            Sequencer player = MidiSystem.getSequencer();
            player.open();


            Sequence seq = new Sequence(Sequence.PPQ, 4);


            Track track = seq.createTrack();


            ShortMessage a = new ShortMessage();
            a.setMessage(144, 1, 44, 100);
            MidiEvent noteOn = new MidiEvent(a, 1);
            track.add(noteOn);


            ShortMessage b = new ShortMessage();
            b.setMessage(128, 1, 44, 100);
            MidiEvent noteOff = new MidiEvent(b, 16);
            track.add(noteOff);

            player.setSequence(seq);

            player.start();

        } catch (Exception ex) {
            ex.printStackTrace();
        }
    } // close play
} // close class
```

① — get a Sequencer and open it (so we can use it... a Sequencer doesn't come already open)

② — Don't worry about the arguments to the Sequence constructor. Just copy these (think of 'em as Ready-bake arguments).

③ — Ask the Sequence for a Track. Remember, the Track lives in the Sequence, and the MIDI data lives in the Track.

④ — Put some MidiEvents into the Track. This part is mostly Ready-bake code. The only thing you'll have to care about are the arguments to the setMessage() method, and the arguments to the MidiEvent constructor. We'll look at those arguments on the next page.

Give the Sequence to the Sequencer (like putting the CD in the CD player)

Start() the Sequencer (like pushing PLAY)

Making a MidiEvent (song data)

A MidiEvent is an instruction for part of a song. A series of MidiEvents is kind of like sheet music, or a player piano roll. Most of the MidiEvents we care about describe *a thing to do* and the *moment in time to do it*. The moment in time part matters, since timing is everything in music. This note follows this note and so on. And because MidiEvents are so detailed, you have to say at what moment to *start* playing the note (a NOTE ON event) and at what moment to *stop* playing the notes (NOTE OFF event). So you can imagine that firing the "stop playing note G" (NOTE OFF message) *before* the "start playing Note G" (NOTE ON) message wouldn't work.

The MIDI instruction actually goes into a Message object; the MidiEvent is a combination of the Message plus the moment in time when that message should 'fire'. In other words, the Message might say, "Start playing Middle C" while the MidiEvent would say, "Trigger this message at beat 4".

So we always need a Message and a MidiEvent.

The Message says *what* to do, and the MidiEvent says *when* to do it.

> A MidiEvent says **what to do** and **when to do it**.
>
> Every instruction must include the **timing** for that instruction.
>
> In other words, at which **beat** that thing should happen.

① Make a **Message**

```
ShortMessage a = new ShortMessage();
```

② Put the **Instruction** in the Message

```
a.setMessage(144, 1, 44, 100);
```

This message says, "start playing note 44" (we'll look at the other numbers on the next page)

③ Make a new **MidiEvent** using the Message

```
MidiEvent noteOn = new MidiEvent(a, 1);
```

The instructions are in the message, but the MidiEvent adds the moment in time when the instruction should be triggered. This MidiEvent says to trigger message 'a' at the first beat (beat 1).

④ Add the MidiEvent to the **Track**

```
track.add(noteOn);
```

A Track holds all the MidiEvent objects. The Sequence organizes them according to when each event is supposed to happen, and then the Sequencer plays them back in that order. You can have lots of events happening at the exact same moment in time. For example, you might want two notes played simultaneously, or even different instruments playing different sounds at the same time.

MIDI message: the heart of a MidiEvent

A MIDI message holds the part of the event that says *what* to do. The actual instruction you want the sequencer to execute. The first argument of an instruction is always the type of the message. The values you pass to the other three arguments depend on the type of message. For example, a message of type 144 means "NOTE ON". But in order to carry out a NOTE ON, the sequencer needs to know a few things. Imagine the sequencer saying, "OK, I'll play a note, but *which channel?* In other words, do you want me to play a Drum note or a Piano note? And *which note?* Middle-C? D Sharp? And while we're at it, at *which velocity* should I play the note?

To make a MIDI message, make a ShortMessage instance and invoke setMessage(), passing in the four arguments for the message. But remember, the message says only *what* to do, so you still need to stuff the message into an event that adds *when* that message should 'fire'.

Anatomy of a message

The *first* argument to setMessage() always represents the message 'type', while the *other three* arguments represent different things depending on the message type.

```
                    message type
                         channel
                              note to play
                                   velocity
a.setMessage(144,   1,   44,   100);
```

The last 3 args vary depending on the message type. This is a NOTE ON message, so the other args are for things the Sequencer needs to know in order to play a note.

> **The *Message* says what to do, the *MidiEvent* says when to do it.**

① Message type

144 means
NOTE ON

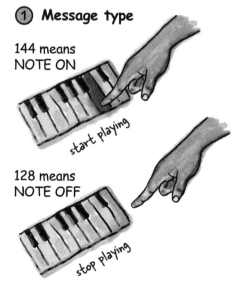

start playing

128 means
NOTE OFF

stop playing

② Channel

Think of a channel like a musician in a band. Channel 1 is musician 1 (the keyboard player), channel 9 is the drummer, etc.

③ Note to play

A number from 0 to 127, going from low to high notes.

7 127

④ Velocity

How fast and hard did you press the key? 0 is so soft you probably won't hear anything, but 100 is a good default.

Change a message

Now that you know what's in a Midi message, you can start experimenting. You can change the note that's played, how long the note is held, add more notes, and even change the instrument.

① Change the note

Try a number between 0 and 127 in the note on and note off messages.

```
a.setMessage(144, 1, 20, 100);
```

② Change the duration of the note

Change the note off event (not the *message*) so that it happens at an earlier or later beat.

```
b.setMessage(128, 1, 44, 100);
MidiEvent noteOff = new MidiEvent(b, 3);
```

③ Change the instrument

Add a new message, BEFORE the note-playing message, that sets the instrument in channel 1 to something other than the default piano. The change-instrument message is '192', and the third argument represents the actual instrument (try a number between 0 and 127)

```
first.setMessage(192, 1, 102, 0);
```

change-instrument message
in channel 1 (musician 1)
to instrument 102

Version 2: Using command-line args to experiment with sounds

This version still plays just a single note, but you get to use command-line arguments to change the instrument and note. Experiment by passing in two int values from 0 to 127. The first int sets the instrument, the second int sets the note to play.

```java
import javax.sound.midi.*;

public class MiniMusicCmdLine {   // this is the first one

    public static void main(String[] args) {
        MiniMusicCmdLine mini = new MiniMusicCmdLine();
        if (args.length < 2) {
            System.out.println("Don't forget the instrument and note args");
        } else {
            int instrument = Integer.parseInt(args[0]);
            int note = Integer.parseInt(args[1]);
            mini.play(instrument, note);
        }
    } // close main

    public void play(int instrument, int note) {

      try {

         Sequencer player = MidiSystem.getSequencer();
         player.open();
         Sequence seq = new Sequence(Sequence.PPQ, 4);
         Track track = seq.createTrack();

         MidiEvent event = null;

         ShortMessage first = new ShortMessage();
         first.setMessage(192, 1, instrument, 0);
         MidiEvent changeInstrument = new MidiEvent(first, 1);
         track.add(changeInstrument);

         ShortMessage a = new ShortMessage();
         a.setMessage(144, 1, note, 100);
         MidiEvent noteOn = new MidiEvent(a, 1);
         track.add(noteOn);

         ShortMessage b = new ShortMessage();
         b.setMessage(128, 1, note, 100);
         MidiEvent noteOff = new MidiEvent(b, 16);
         track.add(noteOff);
         player.setSequence(seq);
         player.start();

      } catch (Exception ex) {ex.printStackTrace();}
    } // close play
} // close class
```

Run it with two int args from 0 to 127. Try these for starters:

```
File Edit Window Help Attenuate
%java MiniMusicCmdLine 102 30

%java MiniMusicCmdLine 80 20

%java MiniMusicCmdLine 40 70
```

Where we're headed with the rest of the CodeKitchens

Chapter 15: the goal

When we're done, we'll have a working BeatBox that's also a Drum Chat Client. We'll need to learn about GUIs (including event handling), I/O, networking, and threads. The next three chapters (12, 13, and 14) will get us there.

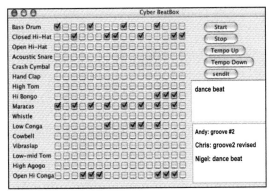

Chapter 12: MIDI events

This CodeKitchen lets us build a little "music video" (bit of a stretch to call it that...) that draws random rectangles to the beat of the MIDI music. We'll learn how to construct and play a lot of MIDI events (instead of just a couple, as we do in the current chapter).

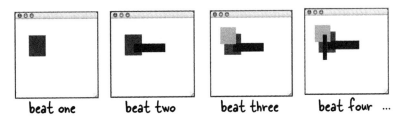

beat one   beat two   beat three   beat four ...

Chapter 13: Stand-alone BeatBox

Now we'll actually build the real BeatBox, GUI and all. But it's limited—as soon as you change a pattern, the previous one is lost. There's no Save and Restore feature, and it doesn't communicate with the network. (But you can still use it to work on your drum pattern skills.)

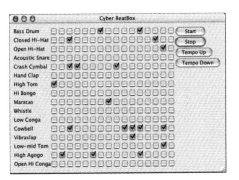

Chapter 14: Save and Restore

You've made the perfect pattern, and now you can save it to a file, and reload it when you want to play it again. This gets us ready for the final version (chapter 15), where instead of writing the pattern to a file, we send it over a network to the chat server.

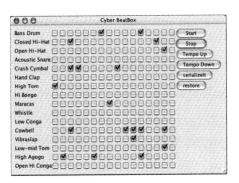

This chapter explored the wonderful world of exceptions. Your job is to decide whether each of the following exception-related statements is true or false.

👍 TRUE OR FALSE 👎

1. A try block must be followed by a catch *and* a finally block.

2. If you write a method that might cause a compiler-checked exception, you *must* wrap that risky code in a try / catch block.

3. Catch blocks can be polymorphic.

4. Only 'compiler checked' exceptions can be caught.

5. If you define a try / catch block, a matching finally block is optional.

6. If you define a try block, you can pair it with a matching catch or finally block, or both.

7. If you write a method that declares that it can throw a compiler-checked exception, you must also wrap the exception throwing code in a try / catch block.

8. The main( ) method in your program must handle all unhandled exceptions thrown to it.

9. A single try block can have many different catch blocks.

10. A method can only throw one kind of exception.

11. A finally block will run regardless of whether an exception is thrown.

12. A finally block can exist without a try block.

13. A try block can exist by itself, without a catch block or a finally block.

14. Handling an exception is sometimes referred to as 'ducking'.

15. The order of catch blocks never matters.

16. A method with a try block and a finally block, can optionally declare the exception.

17. Runtime exceptions must be *handled* or *declared*.

Code Magnets

A working Java program is scrambled up on the fridge. Can you reconstruct all the code snippets to make a working Java program that produces the output listed below? Some of the curly braces fell on the floor and they were too small to pick up, so feel free to add as many of those as you need!

```
System.out.print("r");
```

```
try {
```

```
System.out.print("t");
```

```
doRisky(test);
```

```
System.out.println("s");
```

```
} finally {
```

```
System.out.print("o");
```

```
class MyEx extends Exception { }

public class ExTestDrive {
```

```
System.out.print("w");
```

```
if ("yes".equals(t)) {
```

```
System.out.print("a");
```

```
throw new MyEx();
```

```
} catch (MyEx e) {
```

```
static void doRisky(String t) throws MyEx {
    System.out.print("h");
```

```
public static void main(String [] args) {
    String test = args[0];
```

```
File Edit Window Help ThrowUp
% java ExTestDrive yes
thaws

% java ExTestDrive no
throws
```

JavaCross 7.0

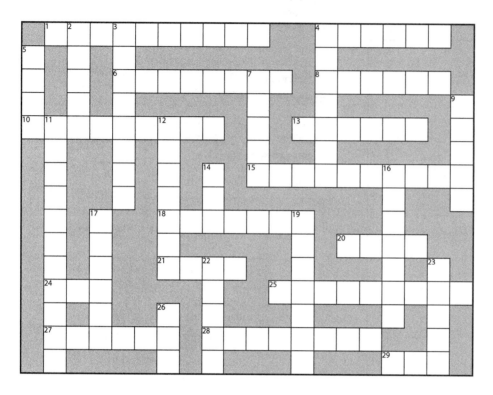

You know what to do!

Across

1. To give value
4. Flew off the top
6. All this and more!
8. Start
10. The family tree
13. No ducking
15. Problem objects
18. One of Java's '49'
20. Class hierarchy
21. Too hot to handle
24. Common primitive
25. Code recipe
27. Unruly method action
28. No Picasso here
29. Start a chain of events

Down

2. Currently usable
3. Template's creation
4. Don't show the kids
5. Mostly static API class
7. Not about behavior
9. The template
11. Roll another one off the line
12. Javac saw it coming
14. Attempt risk
16. Automatic acquisition
17. Changing method
19. Announce a duck
22. Deal with it
23. Create bad news
26. One of my roles

More Hints:

Across
6. A Java child
8. Start a method
13. Instead of declare
20. Also a type of collection
21. Quack
27. Starts a problem
28. Not Abstract

Down
2. Or a mouthwash
3. For _____ (not example)
5. Numbers …
9. Only public or default
16. _____ the family fortune
17. Not a 'getter'

 Exercise Solutions

Code Magnets

```java
class MyEx extends Exception { }

public class ExTestDrive {

  public static void main(String [] args) {
    String test = args[0];
    try {

      System.out.print("t");

      doRisky(test);

      System.out.print("o");

    } catch ( MyEx e) {

      System.out.print("a");

    } finally {

      System.out.print("w");
    }
    System.out.println("s");
  }

  static void doRisky(String t) throws MyEx {
    System.out.print("h");

    if ("yes".equals(t)) {

      throw new MyEx();
    }

    System.out.print("r");

  }
}
```

TRUE OR FALSE

1. False, either or both.

2. False, you can declare the exception.

3. True.

4. False, runtime exception can be caught.

5. True.

6. True, both are acceptable.

7. False, the declaration is sufficient.

8. False, but if it doesn't the JVM may shut down.

9. True.

10. False.

11. True. It's often used to clean-up partially completed tasks.

12. False.

13. False.

14. False, ducking is synonomous with declaring.

15. False, broadest exceptions must be caught by the last catch blocks.

16. False, if you don't have a catch block, you *must* declare.

17. False.

```
File Edit Window Help Chill
% java ExTestDrive yes
thaws

% java ExTestDrive no
throws
```

JavaCross Answers

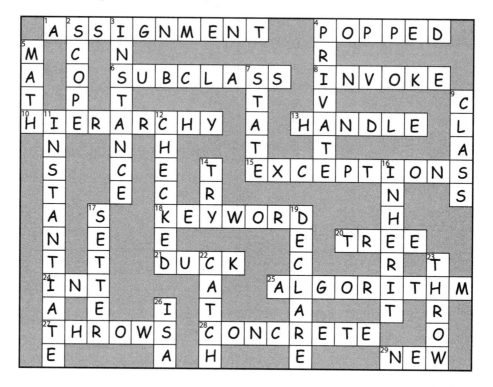

A Very Graphic Story

Face it, you need to make GUIs. If you're building applications that other people are going to use, you *need* a graphical interface. If you're building programs for yourself, you *want* a graphical interface. Even if you believe that the rest of your natural life will be spent writing server-side code, where the client user interface is a web page, sooner or later you'll need to write tools, and you'll want a graphical interface. Sure, command-line apps are retro, but not in a good way. They're weak, inflexible, and unfriendly. We'll spend two chapters working on GUIs, and learn key Java language features along the way including **Event Handling** and **Inner Classes**. In this chapter, we'll put a button on the screen, and make it do something when you click it. We'll paint on the screen, we'll display a jpeg image, and we'll even do some animation.

It all starts with a window

A JFrame is the object that represents a window on the screen. It's where you put all the interface things like buttons, checkboxes, text fields, and so on. It can have an honest-to-goodness menu bar with menu items. And it has all the little windowing icons for whatever platform you're on, for minimizing, maximizing, and closing the window.

The JFrame looks different depending on the platform you're on. This is a JFrame on Mac OS X:

"If I see one more command-line app, you're fired."

a JFrame with a menu bar and two 'widgets' (a button and a radio button)

Put widgets in the window

Once you have a JFrame, you can put things ('widgets') in it by adding them to the JFrame. There are a ton of Swing components you can add; look for them in the javax.swing package. The most common include JButton, JRadioButton, JCheckBox, JLabel, JList, JScrollPane, JSlider, JTextArea, JTextField, and JTable. Most are really simple to use, but some (like JTable) can be a bit more complicated.

Making a GUI is easy:

① Make a frame (a JFrame)
```
JFrame frame = new JFrame();
```

② Make a widget (button, text field, etc.)
```
JButton button = new JButton("click me");
```

③ Add the widget to the frame
```
frame.getContentPane().add(button);
```

You don't add things to the frame directly. Think of the frame as the trim around the window, and you add things to the window pane.

④ Display it (give it a size and make it visible)
```
frame.setSize(300,300);
frame.setVisible(true);
```

Your first GUI: a button on a frame

```
import javax.swing.*;
```
← don't forget to import this swing package

```
public class SimpleGui1 {
    public static void main (String[] args) {
```
make a frame and a button
```
        JFrame frame = new JFrame();
        JButton button = new JButton("click me");
```
← ← (you can pass the button constructor the text you want on the button)

```
        frame.setDefaultCloseOperation(JFrame.EXIT_ON_CLOSE);
```
← this line makes the program quit as soon as you close the window (if you leave this out it will just sit there on the screen forever)

```
        frame.getContentPane().add(button);
```
add the button to the frame's content pane

```
        frame.setSize(300,300);
```
← give the frame a size, in pixels

```
        frame.setVisible(true);
    }
}
```
finally, make it visible!! (if you forget this step, you won't see anything when you run this code)

Let's see what happens when we run it:

%java SimpleGui1

Whoa! That's a Really Big Button.

The button fills all the available space in the frame. Later we'll learn to control where (and how big) the button is on the frame.

But nothing happens when I click it...

That's not exactly true. When you press the button it shows that 'pressed' or 'pushed in' look (which changes depending on the platform look and feel, but it always does *something* to show when it's being pressed).

The real question is, "How do I get the button to do something specific when the user clicks it?"

We need two things:

① A **method** to be called when the user clicks (the thing you want to happen as a result of the button click).

② A way to **know** when to trigger that method. In other words, a way to know when the user clicks the button!

When the user clicks, we want to know.

We're interested in the user-takes-action-on-a-button event.

Q: Will a button look like a Windows button when you run on Windows?

A: If you want it to. You can choose from a few "look and feels"—classes in the core library that control what the interface looks like. In most cases you can choose between at least two different looks: the standard Java look and feel, also known as *Metal*, and the native look and feel for your platform. The Mac OS X screens in this book use either the OS X *Aqua* look and feel, or the *Metal* look and feel.

Q: Can I make a program look like Aqua all the time? Even when it's running under Windows?

A: Nope. Not all look and feels are available on every platform. If you want to be safe, you can either explicitly set the look and feel to Metal, so that you know exactly what you get regardless of where the app is running, or don't specify a look and feel and accept the defaults.

Q: I heard Swing was dog-slow and that nobody uses it.

A: This was true in the past, but isn't a given anymore. On weak machines, you might feel the pain of Swing. But on the newer desktops, and with Java version 1.3 and beyond, you might not even notice the difference between a Swing GUI and a native GUI. Swing is used heavily today, in all sorts of applications.

Getting a user event

Imagine you want the text on the button to change from *click me* to *I've been clicked* when the user presses the button. First we can write a method that changes the text of the button (a quick look through the API will show you the method):

```java
public void changeIt() {
    button.setText("I've been clicked!");
}
```

But *now* what? How will we *know* when this method should run? **How will we know when the button is clicked?**

In Java, the process of getting and handling a user event is called *event-handling*. There are many different event types in Java, although most involve GUI user actions. If the user clicks a button, that's an event. An event that says "The user wants the action of this button to happen." If it's a "Slow Tempo" button, the user wants the slow-tempo action to occur. If it's a Send button on a chat client, the user wants the send-my-message action to happen. So the most straightforward event is when the user clicked the button, indicating they want an action to occur.

With buttons, you usually don't care about any intermediate events like button-is-being-pressed and button-is-being-released. What you want to say to the button is, "I don't care how the user plays with the button, how long they hold the mouse over it, how many times they change their mind and roll off before letting go, etc. *Just tell me when the user means business!* In other words, don't call me unless the user clicks in a way that indicates he wants the darn button to do what it says it'll do!"

First, the button needs to know that we care.

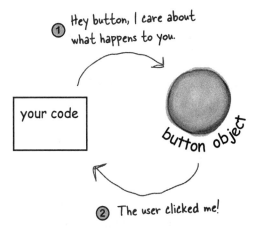

① Hey button, I care about what happens to you.

your code

button object

② The user clicked me!

Second, the button needs a way to call us back when a button-clicked event occurs.

BRAIN POWER

1) How could you tell a button object that you care about its events? That you're a concerned listener?

2) How will the button call you back? Assume that there's no way for you to tell the button the name of your unique method (changeIt()). So what else can we use to reassure the button that we have a specific method it can call when the event happens? [hint: think Pet]

If you care about the button's events, **implement an interface** that says, "I'm *listening* for your events."

A listener interface is the bridge between the listener (you) and event source (the button).

The Swing GUI components are event sources. In Java terms, an event source is an object that can turn user actions (click a mouse, type a key, close a window) into events. And like virtually everything else in Java, an event is represented as an object. An object of some event class. If you scan through the java.awt.event package in the API, you'll see a bunch of event classes (easy to spot—they all have *Event* in the name). You'll find MouseEvent, KeyEvent, WindowEvent, ActionEvent, and several others.

An event *source* (like a button) creates an *event object* when the user does something that matters (like *click* the button). Most of the code you write (and all the code in this book) will *receive* events rather than *create* events. In other words, you'll spend most of your time as an event *listener* rather than an event *source*.

Every event type has a matching listener interface. If you want MouseEvents, implement the MouseListener interface. Want WindowEvents? Implement WindowListener. You get the idea. And remember your interface rules—to implement an interface you *declare* that you implement it (class Dog implements Pet), which means you must *write implementation methods* for every method in the interface.

Some interfaces have more than one method because the event itself comes in different flavors. If you implement MouseListener, for example, you can get events for mousePressed, mouseReleased, mouseMoved, etc. Each of those mouse events has a separate method in the interface, even though they all take a MouseEvent. If you implement MouseListener, the mousePressed() method is called when the user (you guessed it) presses the mouse. And when the user lets go, the mouseReleased() method is called. So for mouse events, there's only one event *object*, MouseEvent, but several different event *methods*, representing the different *types* of mouse events.

When you implement a listener interface, you give the button a way to call you back. The interface is where the call-back method is declared.

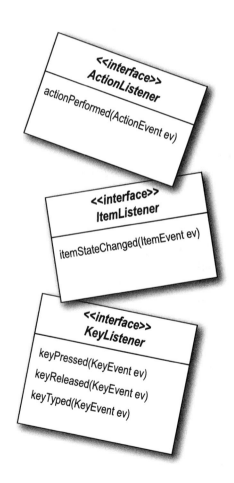

How the listener and source communicate:

"Button, please add me to your list of listeners and call my actionPerformed() method when the user clicks you."

"OK, you're an ActionListener, so I know how to call you back when there's an event -- I'll call the actionPerformed() method that I *know* you have."

button.addActionListener(this)

actionPerformed(theEvent)

The Listener

If your class wants to know about a button's ActionEvents, you implement the ActionListener interface. The button needs to know you're interested, so you register with the button by calling its addActionListener(this) and passing an ActionListener reference to it (in this case, *you* are the ActionListener so you pass *this*). The button needs a way to call you back when the event happens, so it calls the method in the listener interface. As an ActionListener, you *must* implement the interface's sole method, actionPerformed(). The compiler guarantees it.

The Event Source

A button is a source of ActionEvents, so it has to know which objects are interested listeners. The button has an addActionListener() method to give interested objects (listeners) a way to *tell* the button they're interested.

When the button's addActionListener() runs (because a potential listener invoked it), the button takes the parameter (a reference to the listener object) and stores it in a list. When the user clicks the button, the button 'fires' the event by calling the actionPerformed() method on each listener in the list.

Getting a button's ActionEvent

① Implement the ActionListener interface

② Register with the button (tell it you want to listen for events)

③ Define the event-handling method (implement the actionPerformed() method from the ActionListener interrface)

```
import javax.swing.*;
import java.awt.event.*;
```
← *a new import statement for the package that ActionListener and ActionEvent are in.*

①

```
public class SimpleGui1B implements ActionListener {
    JButton button;

    public static void main (String[] args) {
        SimpleGui1B gui = new SimpleGui1B();
        gui.go();
    }

    public void go() {
        JFrame frame = new JFrame();
        button = new JButton("click me");
```

Implement the interface. This says, "an instance of SimpleGui1B IS-A ActionListener".

(The button will give events only to ActionListener implementers)

② —
```
        button.addActionListener(this);
```
← *register your interest with the button. This says to the button, "Add me to your list of listeners". The argument you pass MUST be an object from a class that implements ActionListener!!*

```
        frame.getContentPane().add(button);
        frame.setDefaultCloseOperation(JFrame.EXIT_ON_CLOSE);
        frame.setSize(300,300);
        frame.setVisible(true);
    }
```

Implement the ActionListener interface's actionPerformed() method.. This is the actual event-handling method!

③
```
    public void actionPerformed(ActionEvent event) {
        button.setText("I've been clicked!");
    }
}
```

The button calls this method to let you know an event happened. It sends you an ActionEvent object as the argument, but we don't need it. Knowing the event happened is enough info for us.

Listeners, Sources, and Events

For most of your stellar Java career, *you* will not be the *source* of events.

(No matter how much you fancy yourself the center of your social universe.)

Get used to it. ***Your job is to be a good listener.***

(Which, if you do it sincerely, *can* improve your social life.)

As a listener, my job is to **implement** the interface, **register** with the button, and **provide** the event-handling.

As an event source, my job is to **accept** registrations (from listeners), **get** events from the user. and **call** the listener's event-handling method (when the user clicks me)

Source SENDS the event

Listener GETS the event

Hey, what about me? I'm a player too, you know! As an event object, I'm the **argument** to the event call-back method (from the interface) and my job is to **carry data** about the event back to the listener.

Event object

Event object HOLDS DATA about the event

there are no
Dumb Questions

Q: **Why can't I be a source of events?**

A: You CAN. We just said that *most* of the time you'll be the receiver and not the originator of the event (at least in the *early* days of your brilliant Java career). Most of the events you might care about are 'fired' by classes in the Java API, and all you have to do is be a listener for them. You might, however, design a program where you need a custom event, say, StockMarketEvent thrown when your stock market watcher app finds something it deems important. In that case, you'd make the StockWatcher object be an event source, and you'd do the same things a button (or any other source) does—make a listener interface for your custom event, provide a registration method (addStockListener()), and when somebody calls it, add the caller (a listener) to the list of listeners. Then, when a stock event happens, instantiate a StockEvent object (another class you'll write) and send it to the listeners in your list by calling their stockChanged(StockEvent ev) method. And don't forget that for every *event type* there must be a *matching listener interface* (so you'll create a StockListener interface with a stockChanged() method).

Q: **I don't see the importance of the event object that's passed to the event call-back methods. If somebody calls my mousePressed method, what other info would I need?**

A: A lot of the time, for most designs, you don't need the event object. It's nothing more than a little data carrier, to send along more info about the event. But sometimes you might need to query the event for specific details about the event. For example, if your mousePressed() method is called, you know the mouse was pressed. But what if you want to know exactly where the mouse was pressed? In other words, what if you want to know the X and Y screen coordinates for where the mouse was pressed?

Or sometimes you might want to register the *same* listener with *multiple* objects. An onscreen calculator, for example, has 10 numeric keys and since they all do the same thing, you might not want to make a separate listener for every single key. Instead, you might register a single listener with each of the 10 keys, and when you get an event (because your event call-back method is called) you can call a method on the event object to find out *who* the real event source was. In other words, *which key sent this event*.

Sharpen your pencil

Each of these widgets (user interface objects) are the source of one or more events. Match the widgets with the events they might cause. Some widgets might be a source of more than one event, and some events can be generated by more than one widget.

Widgets	Event methods
check box	windowClosing()
text field	actionPerformed()
scrolling list	itemStateChanged()
button	mousePressed()
dialog box	keyTyped()
radio button	mouseExited()
menu item	focusGained()

How do you KNOW if an object is an event source?

Look in the API.

OK. Look for what?

A method that starts with 'add', ends with 'Listener', and takes a listener interface argument. If you see:

addKeyListener(KeyListener k)

you know that a class with this method is a source of KeyEvents. There's a naming pattern.

Getting back to graphics...

Now that we know a little about how events work (we'll learn more later), let's get back to putting stuff on the screen. We'll spend a few minutes playing with some fun ways to get graphic, before returning to event handling.

Three ways to put things on your GUI:

① **Put widgets on a frame**

   Add buttons, menus, radio buttons, etc.

```
frame.getContentPane().add(myButton);
```

The javax.swing package has more than a dozen widget types.

② **Draw 2D graphics on a widget**

Use a graphics object to paint shapes.

```
graphics.fillOval(70,70,100,100);
```

You can paint a lot more than boxes and circles; the Java2D API is full of fun, sophisticated graphics methods.

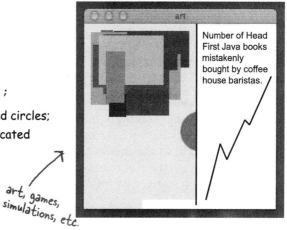

art, games, simulations, etc.

charts, business graphics, etc.

③ **Put a JPEG on a widget**

You can put your own images on a widget.

```
graphics.drawImage(myPic,10,10,this);
```

Make your own drawing widget

If you want to put your own graphics on the screen, your best bet is to make your own paintable widget. You plop that widget on the frame, just like a button or any other widget, but when it shows up it will have your images on it. You can even make those images move, in an animation, or make the colors on the screen change every time you click a button.

It's a piece of cake.

Make a subclass of JPanel and override one method, paintComponent().

All of your graphics code goes inside the paintComponent() method. Think of the paintComponent() method as the method called by the system to say, "Hey widget, time to paint yourself." If you want to draw a circle, the paintComponent() method will have code for drawing a circle. When the frame holding your drawing panel is displayed, paintComponent() is called and your circle appears. If the user iconifies/minimizes the window, the JVM knows the frame needs "repair" when it gets de-iconified, so it calls paintComponent() again. Anytime the JVM thinks the display needs refreshing, your paintComponent() method will be called.

One more thing, *you never call this method yourself!* The argument to this method (a Graphics object) is the actual drawing canvas that gets slapped onto the *real* display. You can't get this by yourself; it must be handed to you by the system. You'll see later, however, that you *can* ask the system to refresh the display (repaint()), which ultimately leads to paintComponent() being called.

```java
import java.awt.*;
import javax.swing.*;

class MyDrawPanel extends JPanel {

    public void paintComponent(Graphics g) {

        g.setColor(Color.orange);

        g.fillRect(20,50,100,100);
    }
}
```

you need both of these

Make a subclass of JPanel, a widget that you can add to a frame just like anything else. Except this one is your own customized widget.

This is the Big Important Graphics method. You will NEVER call this yourself. The system calls it and says, "Here's a nice fresh drawing surface, of type Graphics, that you may paint on now.".

Imagine that 'g' is a painting machine. You're telling it what color to paint with and then what shape to paint (with coordinates for where it goes and how big it is)

Fun things to do in paintComponent()

Let's look at a few more things you can do in paintComponent().
The most fun, though, is when you start experimenting yourself.
Try playing with the numbers, and check the API for class
Graphics (later we'll see that there's even *more* you can do besides
what's in the Graphics class).

Display a JPEG

```
public void paintComponent(Graphics g) {

    Image image = new ImageIcon("catzilla.jpg").getImage();

    g.drawImage(image,3,4,this);

}
```

your file name goes here

The x,y coordinates for where the picture's top left corner should go. This says "3 pixels from the left edge of the panel and 4 pixels from the top edge of the panel". These numbers are always relative to the widget (in this case your JPanel subclass), not the entire frame.

Paint a randomly-colored circle on a black background

```
public void paintComponent(Graphics g) {

    g.fillRect(0,0,this.getWidth(), this.getHeight());



    int red = (int) (Math.random() * 255);
    int green = (int) (Math.random() * 255);
    int blue = (int) (Math.random() * 255);

    Color randomColor = new Color(red, green, blue);
    g.setColor(randomColor);
    g.fillOval(70,70,100,100);
}
```

fill the entire panel with black (the default color)

The first two args define the (x,y) upper left corner, relative to the panel, for where drawing starts, so 0, 0 means "start 0 pixels from the left edge and 0 pixels from the top edge." The other two args say, "Make the width of this rectangle as wide as the panel (this.width()), and make the height as tall as the panel (this.height)"

You can make a color by passing in 3 ints to represent the RGB values.

start 70 pixels from the left, 70 from the top, make it 100 pixels wide, and 100 pixels tall.

drawing gradients with Graphics2D

Behind every good Graphics reference is a Graphics2D object.

The argument to paintComponent() is declared as type Graphics (java.awt.Graphics).

```
public void paintComponent(Graphics g) { }
```

So the parameter 'g' IS-A Graphics object. Which means it *could* be a *subclass* of Graphics (because of polymorphism). And in fact, it *is*.

The object referenced by the 'g' parameter is actually an instance of the* Graphics2D *class.

Why do you care? Because there are things you can do with a Graphics2D reference that you can't do with a Graphics reference. A Graphics2D object can do more than a Graphics object, and it really is a Graphics2D object lurking behind the Graphics reference.

Remember your polymorphism. The compiler decides which methods you can call based on the reference type, not the object type. If you have a Dog object referenced by an Animal reference variable:

```
Animal a = new Dog();
```

You can NOT say:

```
a.bark();
```

Even though you know it's really a Dog back there. The compiler looks at 'a', sees that it's of type Animal, and finds that there's no remote control button for bark() in the Animal class. But you can still get the object back to the Dog it really *is* by saying:

```
Dog d = (Dog) a;
d.bark();
```

So the bottom line with the Graphics object is this:

If you need to use a method from the Graphics2D class, you can't *use* the the paintComponent parameter ('g') straight from the method. But you can *cast* it with a new Graphics2D variable.

```
Graphics2D g2d = (Graphics2D) g;
```

Methods you can call on a Graphics reference:

    drawImage()

    drawLine()

    drawPolygon

    drawRect()

    drawOval()

    fillRect()

    fillRoundRect()

    setColor()

To cast the Graphics2D *object* to a Graphics2D *reference*:

```
Graphics2D g2d = (Graphics2D) g;
```

Methods you can call on a Graphics2D reference:

    fill3DRect()

    draw3DRect()

    rotate()

    scale()

    shear()

    transform()

    setRenderingHints()

(these are not complete method lists, check the API for more)

Because life's too short to paint the circle a solid color when there's a gradient blend waiting for you.

it's really a Graphics2D object masquerading as a mere Graphics object.

```
public void paintComponent(Graphics g) {

    Graphics2D g2d = (Graphics2D) g;
```

cast it so we can call something that Graphics2D has but Graphics doesn't

```
    GradientPaint gradient = new GradientPaint(70,70,Color.blue, 150,150, Color.orange);
```

starting point • starting color • ending point • ending color

this sets the virtual paint brush to a gradient instead of a solid color

```
    g2d.setPaint(gradient);

    g2d.fillOval(70,70,100,100);

}
```

the fillOval() method really means "fill the oval with whatever is loaded on your paintbrush (i.e. the gradient)"

```
public void paintComponent(Graphics g) {
    Graphics2D g2d = (Graphics2D) g;

    int red = (int) (Math.random() * 255);
    int green = (int) (Math.random() * 255);
    int blue = (int) (Math.random() * 255);
    Color startColor = new Color(red, green, blue);

    red = (int) (Math.random() * 255);
    green = (int) (Math.random() * 255);
    blue = (int) (Math.random() * 255);
    Color endColor = new Color(red, green, blue);

    GradientPaint gradient = new GradientPaint(70,70,startColor, 150,150, endColor);
    g2d.setPaint(gradient);
    g2d.fillOval(70,70,100,100);
}
```

this is just like the one above, except it makes random colors for the start and stop colors of the gradient. Try it!

BULLET POINTS

EVENTS

- To make a GUI, start with a window, usually a JFrame
  ```
  JFrame frame = new JFrame();
  ```

- You can add widgets (buttons, text fields, etc.) to the JFrame using:
  ```
  frame.getContentPane().add(button);
  ```

- Unlike most other components, the JFrame doesn't let you add to it directly, so you must add to the JFrame's content pane.

- To make the window (JFrame) display, you must give it a size and tell it be visible:
  ```
  frame.setSize(300,300);
  frame.setVisible(true);
  ```

- To know when the user clicks a button (or takes some other action on the user interface) you need to listen for a GUI event.

- To listen for an event, you must register your interest with an event source. An event source is the thing (button, checkbox, etc.) that 'fires' an event based on user interaction.

- The listener interface gives the event source a way to call you back, because the interface defines the method(s) the event source will call when an event happens.

- To register for events with a source, call the source's registration method. Registration methods always take the form of: **add<EventType>Listener**. To register for a button's ActionEvents, for example, call:
  ```
  button.addActionListener(this);
  ```

- Implement the listener interface by implementing all of the interface's event-handling methods. Put your event-handling code in the listener call-back method. For ActionEvents, the method is:
  ```
  public void actionPerformed(ActionEvent
                              event) {
      button.setText("you clicked!");
  }
  ```

- The event object passed into the event-handler method carries information about the event, including the source of the event.

GRAPHICS

- You can draw 2D graphics directly on to a widget.

- You can draw a .gif or .jpeg directly on to a widget.

- To draw your own graphics (including a .gif or .jpeg), make a subclass of JPanel and override the paintComponent() method.

- The paintComponent() method is called by the GUI system. YOU NEVER CALL IT YOURSELF. The argument to paintComponent() is a Graphics object that gives you a surface to draw on, which will end up on the screen. You cannot construct that object yourself.

- Typical methods to call on a Graphics object (the paintComponent paramenter) are:
  ```
  graphics.setColor(Color.blue);
  g.fillRect(20,50,100,120);
  ```

- To draw a .jpg, construct an Image using:
  ```
  Image image = new ImageIcon("catzilla.
  jpg").getImage();
  ```
  and draw the imagine using:
  ```
  g.drawImage(image,3,4,this);
  ```

- The object referenced by the Graphics parameter to paintComponent() is actually an instance of the Graphics2D class. The Graphics 2D class has a variety of methods including:
  fill3DRect(), draw3DRect(), rotate(), scale(), shear(), transform()

- To invoke the Graphics2D methods, you must cast the parameter from a Graphics object to a Graphics2D object:
  ```
  Graphics2D g2d = (Graphics2D) g;
  ```

We can get an event.
We can paint graphics.
But can we paint graphics *when* we get an event?

Let's hook up an event to a change in our drawing panel. We'll make the circle change colors each time you click the button. Here's how the program flows:

Start the app

1 The frame is built with the two widgets (your drawing panel and a button). A listener is created and registered with the button. Then the frame is displayed and it just waits for the user to click.

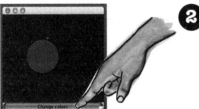

2 The user clicks the button and the button creates an event object and calls the listener's event handler.

3 The event handler calls repaint() on the frame. The system calls paintComponent() on the drawing panel.

4 Voila! A new color is painted because paintComponent() runs again, filling the circle with a random color.

Wait a minute...how do you put TWO things on a frame?

GUI layouts: putting more than one widget on a frame

We cover GUI layouts in the *next* chapter, but we'll do a quickie lesson here to get you going. By default, a frame has five regions you can add to. You can add only *one* thing to each region of a frame, but don't panic! That one thing might be a panel that holds three other things including a panel that holds two more things and... you get the idea. In fact, we were 'cheating' when we added a button to the frame using:

```
frame.getContentPane().add(button);
```

This isn't really the way you're supposed to do it (the one-arg add method).

This is the better (and usually mandatory) way to add to a frame's default content pane. Always specify WHERE (which region) you want the widget to go.

When you call the single-arg add method (the one we shouldn't use) the widget will automatically land in the center regsion.

```
frame.getContentPane().add(BorderLayout.CENTER, button);
```

we call the two-argument add method, that takes a region (using a constant) and the widget to add to that region.

default region

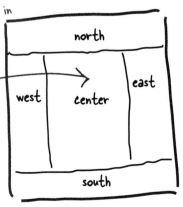

north

west | center | east

south

Sharpen your pencil

Given the pictures on page 351, write the code that adds the button and the panel to the frame.

The circle changes color each time you click the button.

The custom drawing panel (instance of MyDrawPanel) is in the CENTER region of the frame.

```java
import javax.swing.*;
import java.awt.*;
import java.awt.event.*;


public class SimpleGui3C implements ActionListener {

    JFrame frame;

    public static void main (String[] args) {
        SimpleGui3C gui = new SimpleGui3C();
        gui.go();
    }

    public void go() {
        frame = new JFrame();
        frame.setDefaultCloseOperation(JFrame.EXIT_ON_CLOSE);

        JButton button = new JButton("Change colors");
        button.addActionListener(this);

        MyDrawPanel drawPanel = new MyDrawPanel();

        frame.getContentPane().add(BorderLayout.SOUTH, button);
        frame.getContentPane().add(BorderLayout.CENTER, drawPanel);
        frame.setSize(300,300);
        frame.setVisible(true);
    }

    public void actionPerformed(ActionEvent event) {
        frame.repaint();
    }
}
```

Button is in the SOUTH region of the frame

Add the listener (this) to the button.

Add the two widgets (button and drawing panel) to the two regions of the frame.

When the user clicks, tell the frame to repaint() itself. That means paintComponent() is called on every widget in the frame!

```java
class MyDrawPanel extends JPanel {

    public void paintComponent(Graphics g) {
        // Code to fill the oval with a random color
        // See page 347 for the code
    }

}
```

The drawing panel's paintComponent() method is called every time the user clicks.

Let's try it with TWO buttons

The south button will act as it does now, simply calling repaint on the frame. The second button (which we'll stick in the east region) will change the text on a label. (A label is just text on the screen.)

So now we need FOUR widgets

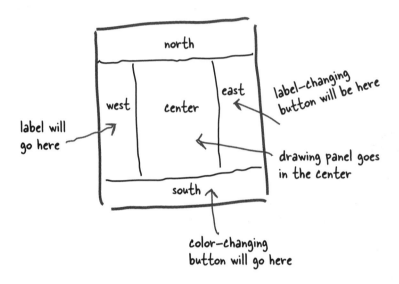

label will go here

label-changing button will be here

drawing panel goes in the center

color-changing button will go here

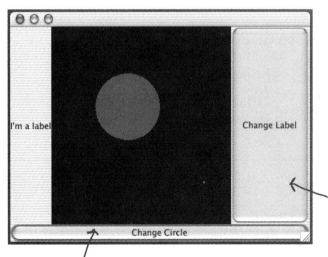

And we need to get TWO events

Uh-oh.

Is that even possible? How do you get *two* events when you have only *one* actionPerformed() method?

This button changes the text on the opposite side

This button changes the color of the circle

How do you get action events for two different buttons, when each button needs to do something different?

---

① *option one*
Implement <u>two</u> actionPerformed() methods

```
class MyGui implements ActionListener {
    // lots of code here and then:

    public void actionPerformed(ActionEvent event) {
        frame.repaint();
    }

    public void actionPerformed(ActionEvent event) {
        label.setText("That hurt!");
    }
}
```

↖ *But this is impossible!*

Flaw: You can't! You can't implement the same method twice in a Java class. It won't compile. And even if you *could*, how would the event source know *which* of the two methods to call?

---

② *option two*
Register the same listener with <u>both</u> buttons.

```
class MyGui implements ActionListener {
    // declare a bunch of instance variables here

    public void go() {
        // build gui
        colorButton = new JButton();
        labelButton = new JButton();
        colorButton.addActionListener(this);
        labelButton.addActionListener(this);
        // more gui code here ...
    }

    public void actionPerformed(ActionEvent event) {
        if (event.getSource() == colorButton) {
            frame.repaint();
        } else {
            label.setText("That hurt!");
        }
    }
}
```

Register the same listener with both buttons

Query the event object to find out which button actually fired it, and use that to decide what to do.

Flaw: this does work, but in most cases it's not very OO. One event handler doing many different things means that you have a single method doing many different things. If you need to change how *one* source is handled, you have to mess with *everybody's* event handler. Sometimes it *is* a good solution, but usually it hurts maintainability and extensibility.

How do you get action events for two different buttons, when each button needs to do something different?

③ *option three*
Create two separate ActionListener classes

```
class MyGui  {
   JFrame frame;
   JLabel label;
   void gui() {
       // code to instantiate the two listeners and register one
       // with the color button and the other with the label button
   }
} // close class
```

```
class ColorButtonListener implements ActionListener {
   public void actionPerformed(ActionEvent event) {
       frame.repaint();
   }
}
```
↖ Won't work! This class doesn't have a reference to the 'frame' variable of the MyGui class

```
class LabelButtonListener implements ActionListener {
   public void actionPerformed(ActionEvent event) {
       label.setText("That hurt!");
   }
}
```
↖ Problem! This class has no reference to the variable 'label'

Flaw: these classes won't have access to the variables they need to act on, 'frame' and 'label'. You could fix it, but you'd have to give each of the listener classes a reference to the main GUI class, so that inside the actionPerformed() methods the listener could use the GUI class reference to access the variables of the GUI class. But that's breaking encapsulation, so we'd probably need to make getter methods for the gui widgets (getFrame(), getLabel(), etc.). And you'd probably need to add a constructor to the listener class so that you can pass the GUI reference to the listener at the time the listener is instantiated. And, well, it gets messier and more complicated.

There has got to be a better way!

Wouldn't it be wonderful if you could have two different listener classes, but the listener classes could access the instance variables of the main GUI class, almost as if the listener classes *belonged* to the other class. Then you'd have the best of both worlds. Yeah, that would be dreamy. But it's just a fantasy...

Inner class to the rescue!

You *can* have one class nested inside another. It's easy. Just make sure that the definition for the inner class is *inside* the curly braces of the outer class.

Simple inner class:

```
class MyOuterClass   {

    class MyInnerClass {
        void go() {
        }
    }

}
```

Inner class is fully enclosed by outer class

An inner class gets a special pass to use the outer class's stuff. *Even the private stuff.* And the inner class can use those private variables and methods of the outer class as if the variables and members were defined in the inner class. That's what's so handy about inner classes—they have most of the benefits of a normal class, but with special access rights.

> An inner class can use all the methods and variables of the outer class, even the private ones.
>
> The inner class gets to use those variables and methods just as if the methods and variables were declared within the inner class.

Inner class using an outer class variable

```
class MyOuterClass   {

    private int x;

    class MyInnerClass {
        void go() {
            x = 42;
        }
    } // close inner class

} // close outer class
```

use 'x' as if it were a variable of the inner class!

An inner class instance must be tied to an outer class instance*.

Remember, when we talk about an inner *class* accessing something in the outer class, we're really talking about an *instance* of the inner class accessing something in an *instance* of the outer class. But *which* instance?

Can *any* arbitrary instance of the inner class access the methods and variables of *any* instance of the outer class? **No!**

*An **inner** object must be tied to a specific **outer** object on the heap.*

Over 65,536 copies sold!

Getting in touch with your inner class

Dr. Poly Morphism

The new bestseller from the author of "Who Moved my Char?"

An inner object shares a special bond with an outer object. ♥

① Make an instance of the outer class

MyOuter object

② Make an instance of the inner class, by using the instance of the outer class.

MyInner object

③ The outer and inner objects are now intimately linked.

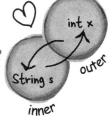

These two objects on the heap have a special bond. The inner can use the outer's variables (and vice-versa).

int x

outer

String s

inner

*There's an exception to this, for a very special case—an inner class defined within a static method. But we're not going there, and you might go your entire Java life without ever encountering one of these.

How to make an instance of an inner class

If you instantiate an inner class from code *within* an outer class, the instance of the outer class is the one that the inner object will 'bond' with. For example, if code within a method instantiates the inner class, the inner object will bond to the instance whose method is running.

Code in an outer class can instantiate one of its own inner classes, in exactly the same way it instantiates any other class... **new MyInner()**

```
class MyOuter   {

    private int x;

    MyInner inner = new MyInner();

    public void doStuff() {
        inner.go();
    }

    class MyInner {
        void go() {
            x = 42;
        }
    } // close inner class

} // close outer class
```

The outer class has a private instance variable 'x'

Make an instance of the inner class

call a method on the inner class

The method in the inner class uses the outer class instance variable 'x', as if 'x' belonged to the inner class.

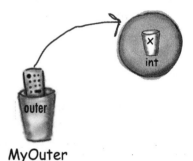

MyOuter

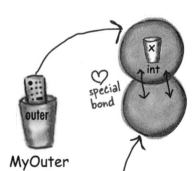

MyOuter

MyInner

Side bar

You *can* instantiate an inner instance from code running *outside* the outer class, but you have to use a special syntax. Chances are you'll go through your entire Java life and never need to make an inner class from outside, but just in case you're interested...

```
class Foo {
    public static void main (String[] args) {
        MyOuter outerObj = new MyOuter();
        MyOuter.MyInner innerObj = outerObj.new MyInner();
    }
}
```

Now we can get the two-button code working

```
public class TwoButtons {          the main GUI class doesn't
                                   implement ActionListener now

    JFrame frame;
    JLabel label;

    public static void main (String[] args) {
        TwoButtons gui = new TwoButtons ();
        gui.go();
    }

    public void go() {
        frame = new JFrame();
        frame.setDefaultCloseOperation(JFrame.EXIT_ON_CLOSE);

        JButton labelButton = new JButton("Change Label");
        labelButton.addActionListener(new LabelListener());

        JButton colorButton = new JButton("Change Circle");
        colorButton.addActionListener(new ColorListener());

        label = new JLabel("I'm a label");
        MyDrawPanel drawPanel = new MyDrawPanel();

        frame.getContentPane().add(BorderLayout.SOUTH, colorButton);
        frame.getContentPane().add(BorderLayout.CENTER, drawPanel);
        frame.getContentPane().add(BorderLayout.EAST, labelButton);
        frame.getContentPane().add(BorderLayout.WEST, label);

        frame.setSize(300,300);
        frame.setVisible(true);
    }

    class LabelListener implements ActionListener {
        public void actionPerformed(ActionEvent event) {
            label.setText("Ouch!");
        }
    } // close inner class

    class ColorListener implements ActionListener {
        public void actionPerformed(ActionEvent event) {
            frame.repaint();
        }
    }  // close inner class

}
```

instead of passing (this) to the button's listener registration method, pass a new instance of the appropriate listener class.

Now we get to have TWO ActionListeners in a single class!

inner class knows about 'label'

the inner class gets to use the 'frame' instance variable, without having an explicit reference to the outer class object.

TwoButtons object

inner → outer

LabelListener object   inner

ColorListener object

Java Exposed

This weeks interview:
Instance of an Inner Class

HeadFirst: What makes inner classes important?

Inner object: Where do I start? We give you a chance to implement the same interface more than once in a class. Remember, you can't implement a method more than once in a normal Java class. But using *inner* classes, each inner class can implement the *same* interface, so you can have all these *different* implementations of the very same interface methods.

HeadFirst: Why would you ever *want* to implement the same method twice?

Inner object: Let's revisit GUI event handlers. Think about it... if you want *three* buttons to each have a different event behavior, then use *three* inner classes, all implementing ActionListener—which means each class gets to implement its own actionPerformed method.

HeadFirst: So are event handlers the only reason to use inner classes?

Inner object: Oh, gosh no. Event handlers are just an obvious example. Anytime you need a separate class, but still want that class to behave as if it were part of *another* class, an inner class is the best—and sometimes *only*—way to do it.

HeadFirst: I'm still confused here. If you want the inner class to *behave* like it belongs to the outer class, why have a separate class in the first place? Why wouldn't the inner class code just be *in* the outer class in the first place?

Inner object: I just *gave* you one scenario, where you need more than one implementation of an interface. But even when you're not using interfaces, you might need two different *classes* because those classes represent two different *things*. It's good OO.

HeadFirst: Whoa. Hold on here. I thought a big part of OO design is about reuse and maintenance. You know, the idea that if you have two separate classes, they can each be modified and used independently, as opposed to stuffing it all into one class yada yada yada. But with an *inner* class, you're still just working with one *real* class in the end, right? The enclosing class is the only one that's reusable and

separate from everybody else. Inner classes aren't exactly reusable. In fact, I've heard them called "Reuseless—useless over and over again."

Inner object: Yes it's true that the inner class is not *as* reusable, in fact sometimes not reusable at all, because it's intimately tied to the instance variables and methods of the outer class. But it—

HeadFirst: —which only proves my point! If they're not reusable, why bother with a separate class? I mean, other than the interface issue, which sounds like a workaround to me.

Inner object: As I was saying, you need to think about IS-A and polymorphism.

HeadFirst: OK. And I'm thinking about them because...

Inner object: Because the outer and inner classes might need to pass *different* IS-A tests! Let's start with the polymorphic GUI listener example. What's the declared argument type for the button's listener registration method? In other words, if you go to the API and check, what kind of *thing* (class or interface type) do you have to pass to the addActionListener() method?

HeadFirst: You have to pass a listener. Something that implements a particular listener interface, in this case ActionListener. Yeah, we know all this. What's your point?

Inner object: My point is that polymorphically, you have a method that takes only one particular *type*. Something that passes the IS-A test for ActionListener. But—and here's the big thing—what if your class needs to be an IS-A of something that's a *class* type rather than an interface?

HeadFirst: Wouldn't you have your class just *extend* the class you need to be a part of? Isn't that the whole point of how subclassing works? If B is a subclass of A, then anywhere an A is expected a B can be used. The whole pass-a-Dog-where-an-Animal-is-the-declared-type thing.

Inner object: Yes! Bingo! So now what happens if you need to pass the IS-A test for two different classes? Classes that aren't in the same inheritance hierarchy?

HeadFirst: Oh, well you just... hmmm. I think I'm getting it. You can always *implement* more than one interface, but you can *extend* only *one* class. You can only be one kind of IS-A when it comes to *class* types.

Inner object: Well done! Yes, you can't be both a Dog and a Button. But if you're a Dog that needs to sometimes be a Button (in order to pass yourself to methods that take a Button), the Dog class (which extends Animal so it can't extend Button) can have an *inner* class that acts on the Dog's behalf as a Button, by extending Button, and thus wherever a Button is required the Dog can pass his inner Button instead of himself. In other words, instead of saying x.takeButton(this), the Dog object calls x.takeButton(new MyInnerButton()).

HeadFirst: Can I get a clear example?

Inner object: Remember the drawing panel we used, where we made our own subclass of JPanel? Right now, that class is a separate, non-inner, class. And that's fine, because the class doesn't need special access to the instance variables of the main GUI. But what if it did? What if we're doing an animation on that panel, and it's getting its coordinates from the main application (say, based on something the user does elsewhere in the GUI). In that case, if we make the drawing panel an inner class, the drawing panel class gets to be a subclass of JPanel, while the outer class is still free to be a subclass of something else.

HeadFirst: Yes I see! And the drawing panel isn't reusable enough to be a separate class anyway, since what it's actually painting is specific to this one GUI application.

Inner object: Yes! You've got it!

HeadFirst: Good. Then we can move on to the nature of the *relationship* between you and the outer instance.

Inner object: What is it with you people? Not enough sordid gossip in a serious topic like polymorphism?

HeadFirst: Hey, you have no idea how much the public is willing to pay for some good old tabloid dirt. So, someone creates you and becomes instantly bonded to the outer object, is that right?

Inner object: Yes that's right. And yes, some have compared it to an arranged marriage. We don't have a say in which object we're bonded to.

HeadFirst: Alright, I'll go with the marriage analogy. Can you get a *divorce* and remarry something *else*?

Inner object: No, it's for life.

HeadFirst: Whose life? Yours? The outer object? Both?

Inner object: Mine. I can't be tied to any other outer object. My only way out is garbage collection.

HeadFirst: What about the outer object? Can it be associated with any other inner objects?

Inner object: So now we have it. This is what you *really* wanted. Yes, yes. My so-called 'mate' can have as many inner objects as it wants.

HeadFirst: Is that like, serial monogamy? Or can it have them all at the same time?

Inner object: All at the same time. There. Satisfied?

HeadFirst: Well, it does make sense. And let's not forget, it was *you* extolling the virtues of "multiple implementations of the same interface". So it makes sense that if the outer class has three buttons, it would need three different inner classes (and thus three different inner class objects) to handle the events. Thanks for everything. Here's a tissue.

He thinks he's got it made, having *two* inner class objects. But *we* have access to all his private data, so just imagine the damage we could do...

Using an inner class for animation

We saw why inner classes are handy for event listeners, because you get to implement the same event-handling method more than once. But now we'll look at how useful an inner class is when used as a subclass of something the outer class doesn't extend. In other words, when the outer class and inner class are in different inheritance trees!

Our goal is to make a simple animation, where the circle moves across the screen from the upper left down to the lower right.

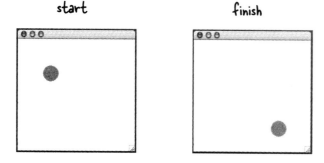

start   finish

How simple animation works

1 Paint an object at a particular x and y coordinate

```
g.fillOval(20,50,100,100);
```

> 20 pixels from the left,
> 50 pixels from the top

2 Repaint the object at a <u>different</u> x and y coordinate

```
g.fillOval(25,55,100,100);
```

> 25 pixels from the left, 55
> pixels from the top
>
> (the object moved a little
> down and to the right)

3 Repeat the previous step with changing x and y values for as long as the animation is supposed to continue.

---

there are no Dumb Questions

Q: Why are we learning about animation here? I doubt if I'm going to be making games.

A: You might not be making games, but you might be creating simulations, where things change over time to show the results of a process. Or you might be building a visualization tool that, for example, updates a graphic to show how much memory a program is using, or to show you how much traffic is coming through your load-balancing server. Anything that needs to take a set of continuously-changing numbers and translate them into something useful for getting information out of the numbers.

Doesn't that all sound business-like? That's just the "official justification", of course. The real reason we're covering it here is just because it's a simple way to demonstrate another use of inner classes. (And because we just *like* animation, and our next Head First book is about J2EE and we *know* we can't get animation in that one.)

What we <u>really</u> want is something like...

```
class MyDrawPanel extends JPanel {
    public void paintComponent(Graphics g) {
        g.setColor(Color.orange);
        g.fillOval(x,y,100,100);
    }
}
```

each time paintComponent() is called, the oval gets painted at a different location

---

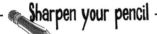 **Sharpen your pencil**

But where do we get the new x and y coordinates?

And who calls repaint()?

See if you can **design a simple solution** to get the ball to animate from the top left of the drawing panel down to the bottom right. Our answer is on the next page, so don't turn this page until you're done!

Big Huge Hint: make the drawing panel an inner class.

Another Hint: don't put any kind of repeat loop in the paintComponent() method.

Write your ideas (or the code) here:

The complete simple animation code

```
import javax.swing.*;
import java.awt.*;


public class SimpleAnimation {

    int x = 70;
    int y = 70;
```
make two instance variables in the main GUI class, for the x and y coordinates of the circle.

```
    public static void main (String[] args) {
        SimpleAnimation gui = new SimpleAnimation ();
        gui.go();
    }

    public void go() {
        JFrame frame = new JFrame();
        frame.setDefaultCloseOperation(JFrame.EXIT_ON_CLOSE);

        MyDrawPanel drawPanel = new MyDrawPanel();

        frame.getContentPane().add(drawPanel);
        frame.setSize(300,300);
        frame.setVisible(true);
```
Nothing new here. Make the widgets and put them in the frame.

This is where the action is!

```
        for (int i = 0; i < 130; i++) {
```
repeat this 130 times

```
            x++;
            y++;
```
increment the x and y coordinates

```
            drawPanel.repaint();
```
tell the panel to repaint itself (so we can see the circle in the new location)

```
            try {
                Thread.sleep(50);
            } catch(Exception ex) { }
        }
```
Slow it down a little (otherwise it will move so quickly you won't SEE it move). Don't worry, you weren't supposed to already know this. We'll get to threads in chapter 15.

```
    }// close go() method
```

Now it's an inner class.
```
class MyDrawPanel extends JPanel {

        public void paintComponent(Graphics g) {
            g.setColor(Color.green);
            g.fillOval(x,y,40,40);
```
Use the continually-updated x and y coordinates of the outer class.
```
        }
    } // close inner class
} // close outer class
```

Uh-oh. It didn't move... it *smeared*.

What did we do wrong?

There's one little flaw in the paintComponent() method.

We forgot to <u>erase</u> what was already there! So we got trails.

Not exactly the look we were going for.

To fix it, all we have to do is fill in the entire panel with the background color, before painting the circle each time. The code below adds two lines at the start of the method: one to set the color to white (the background color of the drawing panel) and the other to fill the entire panel rectangle with that color. In English, the code below says, "Fill a rectangle starting at x and y of 0 (0 pixels from the left and 0 pixels from the top) and make it as wide and as high as the panel is currently.

```
public void paintComponent(Graphics g) {
    g.setColor(Color.white);
    g.fillRect(0,0,this.getWidth(), this.getHeight());

    g.setColor(Color.green);
    g.fillOval(x,y,40,40);

}
```

getWidth() and getHeight() are methods inherited from JPanel.

Sharpen your pencil (optional, just for fun)

What changes would you make to the x and y coordinates to produce the animations below? (assume the first one example moves in 3 pixel increments)

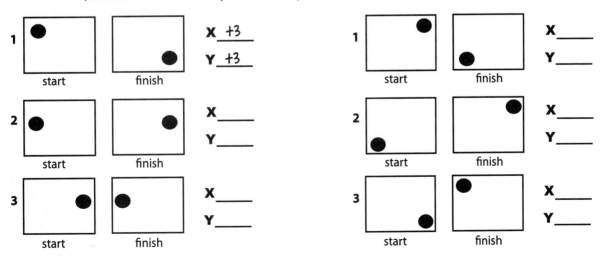

1 start finish X **+3** Y **+3**

2 start finish X_____ Y_____

3 start finish X_____ Y_____

1 start finish X_____ Y_____

2 start finish X_____ Y_____

3 start finish X_____ Y_____

Code Kitchen

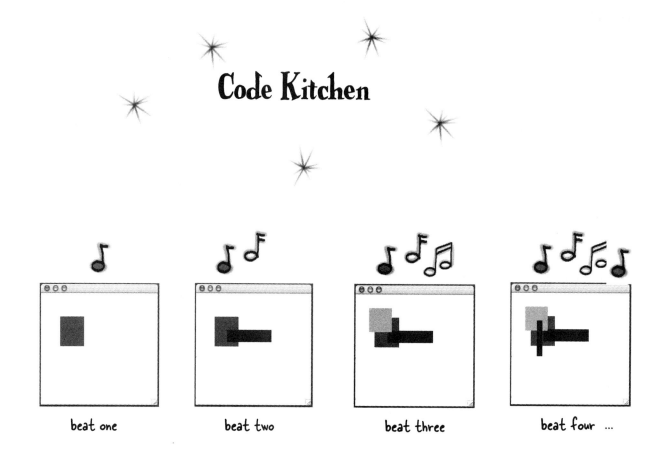

beat one   beat two   beat three   beat four ...

Let's make a music video. We'll use Java-generated random graphics that keep time with the music beats.

Along the way we'll register (and listen for) a new kind of non-**GUI** event, triggered by the music itself.

Remember, this part is all optional. But we think it's good for you. And you'll like it. And you can use it to impress people.

(Ok, sure, it might work only on people who are really easy to impress, but still...)

Listening for a non-GUI event

OK, maybe not a music video, but we *will* make a program that draws random graphics on the screen with the beat of the music. In a nutshell, the program listens for the beat of the music and draws a random graphic rectangle with each beat.

That brings up some new issues for us. So far, we've listened for only GUI events, but now we need to listen for a particular kind of MIDI event. Turns out, listening for a non-GUI event is just like listening for GUI events: you implement a listener interface, register the listener with an event source, then sit back and wait for the event source to call your event-handler method (the method defined in the listener interface).

The simplest way to listen for the beat of the music would be to register and listen for the actual MIDI events, so that whenever the sequencer gets the event, our code will get it too and can draw the graphic. But... there's a problem. A bug, actually, that won't let us listen for the MIDI events *we're* making (the ones for NOTE ON).

So we have to do a little work-around. There is another type of MIDI event we can listen for, called a ControllerEvent. Our solution is to register for ControllerEvents, and then make sure that for every NOTE ON event, there's a matching ControllerEvent fired at the same 'beat'. How do we make sure the ControllerEvent is fired at the same time? We add it to the track just like the other events! In other words, our music sequence goes like this:

BEAT 1 - NOTE ON, CONTROLLER EVENT

BEAT 2 - NOTE OFF

BEAT 3 - NOTE ON, CONTROLLER EVENT

BEAT 4 - NOTE OFF

and so on.

Before we dive into the full program, though, let's make it a little easier to make and add MIDI messages/events since in *this* program, we're gonna make a lot of them.

What the music art program needs to do:

1 Make a series of MIDI messages/events to play random notes on a piano (or whatever instrument you choose)

2 Register a listener for the events

3 Start the sequencer playing

4 Each time the listener's event handler method is called, draw a random rectangle on the drawing panel, and call repaint.

We'll build it in three iterations:

1 Version One: Code that simplifies making and adding MIDI events, since we'll be making a lot of them.

2 Version Two: Register and listen for the events, but without graphics. Prints a message at the command-line with each beat.

3 Version Three: The real deal. Adds graphics to version two.

An easier way to make messages / events

Right now, making and adding messages and events to a track is tedious. For each message, we have to make the message instance (in this case, ShortMessage), call setMessage(), make a MidiEvent for the message, and add the event to the track. In last chapter's code, we went through each step for every message. That means eight lines of code just to make a note play and then stop playing! Four lines to add a NOTE ON event, and four lines to add a NOTE OFF event.

```
ShortMessage a = new ShortMessage();
a.setMessage(144, 1, note, 100);
MidiEvent noteOn = new MidiEvent(a, 1);
track.add(noteOn);

ShortMessage b = new ShortMessage();
b.setMessage(128, 1, note, 100);
MidiEvent noteOff = new MidiEvent(b, 16);
track.add(noteOff);
```

Things that have to happen for each event:

1. Make a message instance
```
ShortMessage first = new ShortMessage();
```

2. Call setMessage() with the instructions
```
first.setMessage(192, 1, instrument, 0)
```

3. Make a MidiEvent instance for the message
```
MidiEvent noteOn = new MidiEvent(first, 1);
```

4. Add the event to the track
```
track.add(noteOn);
```

Let's build a static utility method that makes a message and returns a MidiEvent

the four arguments for the message

The event 'tick' for WHEN this message should happen

```
public static MidiEvent makeEvent(int comd, int chan, int one, int two, int tick) {
    MidiEvent event = null;
    try {
        ShortMessage a = new ShortMessage();
        a.setMessage(comd, chan, one, two);
        event = new MidiEvent(a, tick);

    }catch(Exception e) { }
    return event;
}
```

whoo! A method with five parameters.

make the message and the event, using the method parameters

return the event (a MidiEvent all loaded up with the message)

Example: how to use the new static makeEvent() method

There's no event handling or graphics here, just a sequence of 15 notes that go up the scale. The point of this code is simply to learn how to use our new makeEvent() method. The code for the next two versions is much smaller and simpler thanks to this method.

```java
import javax.sound.midi.*;          ←——— don't forget the import

public class MiniMusicPlayer1 {

    public static void main(String[] args) {

        try {

            Sequencer sequencer = MidiSystem.getSequencer();   ←— make (and open) a sequencer
            sequencer.open();
            ←————————————

            Sequence seq = new Sequence(Sequence.PPQ, 4);   ←— make a sequence
            Track track = seq.createTrack();                ←———— and a track

        for (int i = 5; i < 61; i+= 4) {  ←—— make a bunch of events to make the notes keep
                                              going up (from piano note 5 to piano note 61)

            track.add(makeEvent(144,1,i,100,i));
            track.add(makeEvent(128,1,i,100,i + 2));

        } // end loop                                    call our new makeEvent() method to make the
                                                         message and event, then add the result (the
            sequencer.setSequence(seq);                  MidiEvent returned from makeEvent()) to
            sequencer.setTempoInBPM(220);   } start it running   the track. These are NOTE ON (144) and
            sequencer.start();                           NOTE OFF (128) pairs
        } catch (Exception ex) {ex.printStackTrace();}
    } // close main


    public static MidiEvent makeEvent(int comd, int chan, int one, int two, int tick) {
        MidiEvent event = null;
        try {
            ShortMessage a = new ShortMessage();
            a.setMessage(comd, chan, one, two);
          event = new MidiEvent(a, tick);

        }catch(Exception e) { }
      return event;
    }
} // close class
```

Version Two: registering and getting ControllerEvents

We need to listen for ControllerEvents, so we implement the listener interface

```java
import javax.sound.midi.*;
public class MiniMusicPlayer2 implements ControllerEventListener {

    public static void main(String[] args) {
        MiniMusicPlayer2 mini = new MiniMusicPlayer2();
        mini.go();
    }
    public void go() {

        try {
            Sequencer sequencer = MidiSystem.getSequencer();
            sequencer.open();

            int[] eventsIWant = {127};
            sequencer.addControllerEventListener(this, eventsIWant);

            Sequence seq = new Sequence(Sequence.PPQ, 4);
            Track track = seq.createTrack();

            for (int i = 5; i < 60; i+= 4) {
                track.add(makeEvent(144,1,i,100,i));

                track.add(makeEvent(176,1,127,0,i));

                track.add(makeEvent(128,1,i,100,i + 2));
            } // end loop

            sequencer.setSequence(seq);
            sequencer.setTempoInBPM(220);
            sequencer.start();
        } catch (Exception ex) {ex.printStackTrace();}
    } // close

    public void controlChange(ShortMessage event) {
        System.out.println("la");
    }

    public MidiEvent makeEvent(int comd, int chan, int one, int two, int tick) {
        MidiEvent event = null;
        try {
            ShortMessage a = new ShortMessage();
            a.setMessage(comd, chan, one, two);
            event = new MidiEvent(a, tick);

        }catch(Exception e) { }
        return event;
    }
} // close class
```

Register for events with the sequencer. The event registration method takes the listener AND an int array representing the list of ControllerEvents you want. We want only one event, #127.

Here's how we pick up the beat -- we insert our OWN ControllerEvent (176 says the event type is ControllerEvent) with an argument for event number #127. This event will do NOTH-ING! We put it in JUST so that we can get an event each time a note is played. In other words, its sole purpose is so that something will fire that WE can listen for (we can't listen for NOTE ON/OFF events). Note that we're making this event happen at the SAME tick as the NOTE ON. So when the NOTE ON event happens, we'll know about it because OUR event will fire at the same time.

The event handler method (from the Controller-Event listener interface). Each time we get the event, we'll print "la" to the command-line.

Code that's different from the previous version is highlighted in gray. (and we're not running it all within main() this time)

Version Three: drawing graphics in time with the music

This final version builds on version two by adding the GUI parts. We build a frame, add a drawing panel to it, and each time we get an event, we draw a new rectangle and repaint the screen. The only other change from version two is that the notes play randomly as opposed to simply moving up the scale.

The most important change to the code (besides building a simple GUI) is that we make the drawing panel implement the ControllerEventListener rather than the program itself. So when the drawing panel (an inner class) gets the event, it knows how to take care of itself by drawing the rectangle.

Complete code for this version is on the next page.

The drawing panel inner class:

The drawing panel is a listener

```
class MyDrawPanel extends JPanel implements ControllerEventListener {

    boolean msg = false;    // We set a flag to false, and we'll set it
                            // to true only when we get an event.
    public void controlChange(ShortMessage event) {
        msg = true;         // We got an event, so we set the flag to
        repaint();          // true and call repaint()
    }

    public void paintComponent(Graphics g) {
      if (msg) {            // We have to use a flag because OTHER things might trigger a repaint(),
                            // and we want to paint ONLY when there's a ControllerEvent

        Graphics2D g2 = (Graphics2D) g;

        int r = (int) (Math.random() * 250);
        int gr = (int) (Math.random() * 250);
        int b = (int) (Math.random() * 250);
                                              // The rest is code to generate
                                              // a random color and paint a
        g.setColor(new Color(r,gr,b));        // semi-random rectangle.

        int ht = (int) ((Math.random() * 120) + 10);
        int width = (int) ((Math.random() * 120) + 10);
        int x = (int) ((Math.random() * 40) + 10);
        int y = (int) ((Math.random() * 40) + 10);
        g.fillRect(x,y,ht, width);
        msg = false;

      } // close if
    } // close method
  } // close inner class
```

Sharpen your pencil

This is the complete code listing for Version Three. It builds directoy on Version Two. Try to annotate it yourself, without looking at the previous pages.

```java
import javax.sound.midi.*;
import java.io.*;
import javax.swing.*;
import java.awt.*;

public class MiniMusicPlayer3 {

    static JFrame f = new JFrame("My First Music Video");
    static MyDrawPanel ml;

    public static void main(String[] args) {
        MiniMusicPlayer3 mini = new MiniMusicPlayer3();
        mini.go();
    } // close method


    public  void setUpGui() {
        ml = new MyDrawPanel();
        f.setContentPane(ml);
        f.setBounds(30,30, 300,300);
        f.setVisible(true);
    } // close method

    public void go() {
        setUpGui();

        try {

            Sequencer sequencer = MidiSystem.getSequencer();
            sequencer.open();
            sequencer.addControllerEventListener(ml, new int[] {127});
            Sequence seq = new Sequence(Sequence.PPQ, 4);
            Track track = seq.createTrack();

            int r = 0;
            for (int i = 0; i < 60; i+= 4) {

                r = (int) ((Math.random() * 50) + 1);
                track.add(makeEvent(144,1,r,100,i));
                track.add(makeEvent(176,1,127,0,i));
                track.add(makeEvent(128,1,r,100,i + 2));
            } // end loop

            sequencer.setSequence(seq);
            sequencer.start();
            sequencer.setTempoInBPM(120);
        } catch (Exception ex) {ex.printStackTrace();}
    } // close method
```

A bunch of Java hot-shots, in full costume, are playing the party game "Who am I?" They give you a clue, and you try to guess who they are, based on what they say. Assume they always tell the truth about themselves. If they happen to say something that could be true for more than one guy, then write down all for whom that sentence applies. Fill in the blanks next to the sentence with the names of one or more attendees.

Tonight's attendees:

Any of the charming personalities from this chapter just might show up!

I got the whole GUI, in my hands.   _____

Every event type has one of these.   _____

The listener's key method.   _____

This method gives JFrame its size.   _____

You add code to this method but never call it.   _____

When the user actually does something, it's an _____ .   _____

Most of these are event sources.   _____

I carry data back to the listener.   _____

An addXxxListener( ) method says an object is an _____ .   _____

How a listener signs up.   _____

The method where all the graphics code goes.   _____

I'm typically bound to an instance.   _____

The 'g' in (Graphics g), is really of class.   _____

The method that gets paintComponent( ) rolling.   _____

The package where most of the Swingers reside.   _____

Exercise

BE the compiler

The Java file on this page represents a complete source file. Your job is to play compiler and determine whether this file will compile. If it won't compile, how would you fix it, and if it does compile, what would it do?

```java
import javax.swing.*;
import java.awt.event.*;
import java.awt.*;

class InnerButton {

  JFrame frame;
  JButton b;

  public static void main(String [] args) {
    InnerButton gui = new InnerButton();
    gui.go();
  }

  public void go() {
    frame = new JFrame();
    frame.setDefaultCloseOperation(
                JFrame.EXIT_ON_CLOSE);

    b = new JButton("A");
    b.addActionListener();

    frame.getContentPane().add(
                BorderLayout.SOUTH, b);
    frame.setSize(200,100);
    frame.setVisible(true);
  }

  class BListener extends ActionListener {
    public void actionPerformed(ActionEvent e) {
      if (b.getText().equals("A")) {
        b.setText("B");
      } else {
        b.setText("A");
      }
    }
  }
}
```

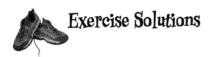

Exercise Solutions

Who am I?

I got the whole GUI, in my hands.	JFrame
Every event type has one of these.	listener interface
The listener's key method.	actionPerformed( )
This method gives JFrame its size.	setSize( )
You add code to this method but never call it.	paintComponent( )
When the user actually does something, it's an ____	event
Most of these are event sources.	swing components
I carry data back to the listener.	event object
An addXxxListener( ) method says an object is an ____	event source
How a listener signs up.	addActionListener( )
The method where all the graphics code goes.	paintComponent( )
I'm typically bound to an instance.	inner class
The 'g' in (Graphics g), is really of this class.	Graphics2d
The method that gets paintComponent( ) rolling.	repaint( )
The package where most of the Swingers reside.	javax.swing

BE the compiler

> Once this code is fixed, it will create a GUI with a button that toggles between A and B when you click it.

```
import javax.swing.*;
import java.awt.event.*;
import java.awt.*;

class InnerButton {

  JFrame frame;
  JButton b;

  public static void main(String [] args) {
    InnerButton gui = new InnerButton();
    gui.go();
  }

  public void go() {
    frame = new JFrame();
    frame.setDefaultCloseOperation(
              JFrame.EXIT_ON_CLOSE);
```

> The addActionListener( ) method takes a class that implements the ActionListener interface

```
    b = new JButton("A");
    b.addActionListener( new BListener() );

    frame.getContentPane().add(
              BorderLayout.SOUTH, b);
    frame.setSize(200,100);
    frame.setVisible(true);
  }

  class BListener implements ActionListener {
    public void actionPerformed(ActionEvent e) {
      if (b.getText().equals("A")) {
        b.setText("B");
      } else {
        b.setText("A");
      }
    }
  }
}
```

> ActionListener is an interface, interfaces are implemented, not extended

Pool Puzzle

```java
import javax.swing.*;
import java.awt.*;
public class Animate {
    int x = 1;
    int y = 1;
    public static void main (String[] args) {
        Animate gui = new Animate ();
        gui.go();
    }
    public void go() {
        JFrame frame = new JFrame();
        frame.setDefaultCloseOperation(
                      JFrame.EXIT_ON_CLOSE);
        MyDrawP drawP = new MyDrawP();
        frame.getContentPane().add(drawP);
        frame.setSize(500,270);
        frame.setVisible(true);
        for (int i = 0; i < 124; i++,x++,y++ ) {
            x++;
            drawP.repaint();
            try {
                Thread.sleep(50);
            } catch(Exception ex) { }
        }
    }
class MyDrawP extends JPanel {
    public void paintComponent(Graphics g ) {
        g.setColor(Color.white);
        g.fillRect(0,0,500,250);
        g.setColor(Color.blue);
        g.fillRect(x,y,500-x*2,250-y*2);
    }
  }
}
```

The Amazing, Shrinking, Blue Rectangle.

Work on Your Swing

Why won't the ball go where *I* want it to go? (like, smack in Suzy Smith's face) I've gotta learn to control it.

Swing is easy. Unless you actually *care* where things end up on the screen. Swing code *looks* easy, but then you compile it, run it, look at it and think, "hey, *that's* not supposed to go *there*." The thing that makes it *easy* to code is the thing that makes it *hard* to *control*—the **Layout Manager**. Layout Manager objects control the size and location of the widgets in a Java GUI. They do a ton of work on your behalf, but you won't always like the results. You want two buttons to be the same size, but they aren't. You want the text field to be three inches long, but it's nine. Or one. And *under* the label instead of *next* to it. But with a little work, you can get layout managers to submit to your will. In this chapter, we'll work on our Swing and in addition to layout managers, we'll learn more about widgets. We'll make them, display them (where *we* choose), and use them in a program. It's not looking too good for Suzy.

Swing components

Component is the more correct term for what we've been calling a *widget*. The *things* you put in a GUI. *The things a user sees and interacts with.* Text fields, buttons, scrollable lists, radio buttons, etc. are all components. In fact, they all extend `javax.swing.JComponent`.

Components can be nested

In Swing, virtually *all* components are capable of holding other components. In other words, *you can stick just about anything into anything else.* But most of the time, you'll add *user interactive* components such as buttons and lists into *background* components such as frames and panels. Although it's *possible* to put, say, a panel inside a button, that's pretty weird, and won't win you any usability awards.

With the exception of JFrame, though, the distinction between *interactive* components and *background* components is artificial. A JPanel, for example, is usually used as a background for grouping other components, but even a JPanel can be interactive. Just as with other components, you can register for the JPanel's events including mouse clicks and keystrokes.

> A widget is technically a Swing Component. Almost every thing you can stick in a GUI extends from javax.swing.JComponent.

Four steps to making a GUI (review)

1 Make a window (a JFrame)
```
JFrame frame = new JFrame();
```

2 Make a component (button, text field, etc.)
```
JButton button = new JButton("click me");
```

3 Add the component to the frame
```
frame.getContentPane().add(BorderLayout.EAST, button);
```

4 Display it (give it a size and make it visible)
```
frame.setSize(300,300);
frame.setVisible(true);
```

Put interactive components:

press here   JButton

choose me   JCheckBox

This is a text field.   JTextField

Into background components:

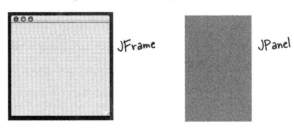

JFrame

JPanel

Layout Managers

A layout manager is a Java object associated with a particular component, almost always a *background* component. The layout manager controls the components contained *within* the component the layout manager is associated with. In other words, if a frame holds a panel, and the panel holds a button, the panel's layout manager controls the size and placement of the button, while the frame's layout manager controls the size and placement of the panel. The button, on the other hand, doesn't need a layout manager because the button isn't holding other components.

> As a layout manager, I'm in charge of the size and placement of your components. In this GUI, I'm the one who decided how big these buttons should be, and where they are relative to each other and the frame.

If a panel holds five things, even if those five things each have their own layout managers, the size and location of the five things in the panel are all controlled by the panel's layout manager. If those five things, in turn, hold *other* things, then those *other* things are placed according to the layout manager of the thing holding them.

When we say *hold* we really mean *add* as in, a panel *holds* a button because the button was *added* to the panel using something like:

myPanel.add(button);

Layout managers come in several flavors, and each background component can have its own layout manager. Layout managers have their own policies to follow when building a layout. For example, one layout manager might insist that all components in a panel must be the same size, arranged in a grid, while another layout manager might let each component choose its own size, but stack them vertically. Here's an example of nested layouts:

```
JPanel panelA = new JPanel();
JPanel panelB = new JPanel();
panelB.add(new JButton("button 1"));
panelB.add(new JButton("button 2"));
panelB.add(new JButton("button 3"));
panelA.add(panelB);
```

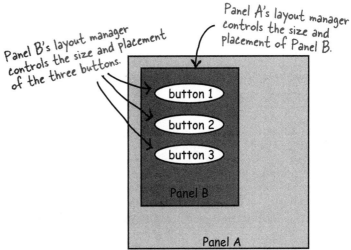

Panel B's layout manager controls the size and placement of the three buttons.

Panel A's layout manager controls the size and placement of Panel B.

Panel A's layout manager has NOTHING to say about the three buttons. The hierarchy of control is only one level—Panel A's layout manager controls only the things added directly to Panel A, and does not control anything nested within those added components.

How does the layout manager decide?

Different layout managers have different policies for arranging components (like, arrange in a grid, make them all the same size, stack them vertically, etc.) but the components being layed out do get at least *some* small say in the matter. In general, the process of laying out a background component looks something like this:

A layout scenario:

① Make a panel and add three buttons to it.

② The panel's layout manager asks each button how big that button prefers to be.

③ The panel's layout manager uses its layout policies to decide whether it should respect all, part, or none of the buttons' preferences.

④ Add the panel to a frame.

⑤ The frame's layout manager asks the panel how big the panel prefers to be.

⑥ The frame's layout manager uses its layout policies to decide whether it should respect all, part, or none of the panel's preferences.

Let's see here... the first button wants to be 30 pixels wide, and the text field needs 50, and the frame is 200 pixels wide and I'm supposed to arrange everything vertically...

layout manager

Different layout managers have different policies

Some layout managers respect the size the component wants to be. If the button wants to be 30 pixels by 50 pixels, that's what the layout manager allocates for that button. Other layout managers respect only part of the component's preferred size. If the button wants to be 30 pixels by 50 pixels, it'll be 30 pixels by however wide the button's background *panel* is. Still other layout managers respect the preference of only the *largest* of the components being layed out, and the rest of the components in that panel are all made that same size. In some cases, the work of the layout manager can get very complex, but most of the time you can figure out what the layout manager will probably do, once you get to know that layout manager's policies.

The Big Three layout managers: border, flow, and box.

BorderLayout

A BorderLayout manager divides a background component into five regions. You can add only one component per region to a background controlled by a BorderLayout manager. Components laid out by this manager usually don't get to have their preferred size. **BorderLayout is the default layout manager for a frame!**

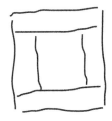

one component per region

FlowLayout

A FlowLayout manager acts kind of like a word processor, except with components instead of words. Each component is the size it wants to be, and they're laid out left to right in the order that they're added, with "word-wrap" turned on. So when a component won't fit horizontally, it drops to the next "line" in the layout. **FlowLayout is the default layout manager for a panel!**

components added left to right, wrapping to a new line when needed

BoxLayout

A BoxLayout manager is like FlowLayout in that each component gets to have its own size, and the components are placed in the order in which they're added. But, unlike FlowLayout, a BoxLayout manager can stack the components vertically (or horizontally, but usually we're just concerned with vertically). It's like a FlowLayout but instead of having automatic 'component wrapping', you can insert a sort of 'component return key' and **force** the components to start a new line.

components added top to bottom, one per 'line'

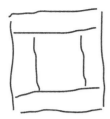 **BorderLayout cares about five regions:**
east, west, north, south, and center

Let's add a button to the <u>east</u> region:

```
import javax.swing.*;
import java.awt.*;  ← — BorderLayout is in java.awt package

public class Button1 {

    public static void main (String[] args) {
        Button1 gui = new Button1();
        gui.go();
    }

    public void go() {
        JFrame frame = new JFrame();
        JButton button = new JButton("click me"); ↓ — specify the region
        frame.getContentPane().add(BorderLayout.EAST, button);
        frame.setSize(200,200);
        frame.setVisible(true);
    }
}
```

Brain Barbell

How did the BorderLayout manager come up with this size for the button?

What are the factors the layout manager has to consider?

Why isn't it wider or taller?

Watch what happens when we give the button more characters...

We changed only the text on the button

```
public void go() {
    JFrame frame = new JFrame();
    JButton button = new JButton("click like you mean it");
    frame.getContentPane().add(BorderLayout.EAST, button);
    frame.setSize(200,200);
    frame.setVisible(true);
}
```

First, I ask the button for its preferred size.

I have a lot of words now, so I'd prefer to be 60 pixels wide and 25 pixels tall.

Button object

Since it's in the east region of a border layout, I'll respect its preferred width. But I don't care how tall it wants to be; it's gonna be as tall as the frame, because that's my policy.

Next time I'm goin' with flow layout. Then I get EVERYTHING I want.

Button object

click like you mean it

The button gets its preferred width, but not height.

Let's try a button in the NORTH region

```
public void go() {
    JFrame frame = new JFrame();
    JButton button = new JButton("There is no spoon...");
    frame.getContentPane().add(BorderLayout.NORTH, button);
    frame.setSize(200,200);
    frame.setVisible(true);
}
```

← *The button is as tall as it wants to be, but as wide as the frame.*

Now let's make the button ask to be <u>taller</u>

How do we do that? The button is already as wide
as it can ever be—as wide as the frame. But we
can try to make it taller by giving it a bigger font.

```
public void go() {
    JFrame frame = new JFrame();
    JButton button = new JButton("Click This!");
    Font bigFont = new Font("serif", Font.BOLD, 28);
    button.setFont(bigFont);
    frame.getContentPane().add(BorderLayout.NORTH, button);
    frame.setSize(200,200);
    frame.setVisible(true);
}
```

A bigger font will force the frame to allocate more space for the button's height.

← *The width stays the same, but now the button is taller. The north region stretched to accommodate the button's new preferred height.*

I think I'm getting it... if I'm in **east** or **west**, I get my preferred width but the height is up to the layout manager. And if I'm in **north** or **south**, it's just the opposite—I get my preferred height, but not width.

Button object

But what happens in the center region?

The center region gets whatever's left!

(except in one special case we'll look at later)

```
public void go() {
    JFrame frame = new JFrame();

    JButton east = new JButton("East");
    JButton west = new JButton("West");
    JButton north = new JButton("North");
    JButton south = new JButton("South");
    JButton center = new JButton("Center");

    frame.getContentPane().add(BorderLayout.EAST, east);
    frame.getContentPane().add(BorderLayout.WEST, west);
    frame.getContentPane().add(BorderLayout.NORTH, north);
    frame.getContentPane().add(BorderLayout.SOUTH, south);
    frame.getContentPane().add(BorderLayout.CENTER, center);

    frame.setSize(300,300);
    frame.setVisible(true);
}
```

Components in the center get whatever space is left over, based on the frame dimensions (300 x 300 in this code).

Components in the east and west get their preferred width.

Components in the north and south get their preferred height.

When you put something in the north or south, it goes all the way across the frame, so the things in the east and west won't be as tall as they would be if the north and south regions were empty.

300 pixels

300 pixels

FlowLayout cares about the <u>flow</u> of the components:

left to right, top to bottom, in the order they were added.

Let's add a panel to the east region:

A JPanel's layout manager is FlowLayout, by default. When we add a panel to a frame, the size and placement of the panel is still under the BorderLayout manager's control. But anything *inside* the *panel* (in other words, components added to the panel by calling **panel.add(aComponent)**) are under the panel's FlowLayout manager's control. We'll start by putting an empty panel in the frame's east region, and on the next pages we'll add things to the panel.

The panel doesn't have anything in it, so it doesn't ask for much width in the east region.

```java
import javax.swing.*;
import java.awt.*;

public class Panel1 {

    public static void main (String[] args) {
        Panel1 gui = new Panel1();
        gui.go();
    }

    public void go() {
        JFrame frame = new JFrame();
        JPanel panel = new JPanel();
        panel.setBackground(Color.darkGray);
        frame.getContentPane().add(BorderLayout.EAST, panel);
        frame.setSize(200,200);
        frame.setVisible(true);
    }
}
```

Make the panel gray so we can see where it is on the frame.

Let's add a button to the panel

```
public void go() {
    JFrame frame = new JFrame();
    JPanel panel = new JPanel();
    panel.setBackground(Color.darkGray);

    JButton button = new JButton("shock me");

    panel.add(button);
    frame.getContentPane().add(BorderLayout.EAST, panel);

    frame.setSize(250,200);
    frame.setVisible(true);
}
```

Add the button to the panel and add the panel to the frame. The panel's layout manager (flow) controls the button, and the frame's layout manager (border) controls the panel.

panel

panel

The panel expanded!

And the button got its preferred size in both dimensions, because the panel uses flow layout, and the button is part of the panel (not the frame).

> Ok... I need to know how big the **panel** wants to be...

> I need to know how big the **button** wants to

> I have a button now, so my layout manager's gonna have to figure out how big I need to be...

> Based on my font size and the number of characters, I want to be 70 pixels wide and 20 pixels tall.

controls → *Panel object*

controls → *Button object*

The frame's
BorderLayout manager

The panel's
FlowLayout manager

What happens if we add TWO buttons to the panel?

```
public void go() {
    JFrame frame = new JFrame();
    JPanel panel = new JPanel();
    panel.setBackground(Color.darkGray);

    JButton button = new JButton("shock me");      ← make TWO buttons
    JButton buttonTwo = new JButton("bliss");      ←

    panel.add(button);         ←
    panel.add(buttonTwo);      ← add BOTH to the panel

    frame.getContentPane().add(BorderLayout.EAST, panel);
    frame.setSize(250,200);
    frame.setVisible(true);
}
```

what we *wanted*:

We want the buttons stacked on top of each other

what we *got*:

The panel expanded to fit both buttons side by side.

notice that the 'bliss' button is smaller than the 'shock me' button... that's how flow layout works. The button gets just what it needs (and no more).

✎ Sharpen your pencil

If the code above were modified to the code below, what would the GUI look like?

```
JButton button = new JButton("shock me");
JButton buttonTwo = new JButton("bliss");
JButton buttonThree = new JButton("huh?");
panel.add(button);
panel.add(buttonTwo);
panel.add(buttonThree);
```

Draw what you think the GUI would look like if you ran the code to the left.

(Then try it!)

BoxLayout to the rescue!

It keeps components stacked, even if there's room to put them side by side.

Unlike FlowLayout, BoxLayout can force a 'new line' to make the components wrap to the next line, even if there's room for them to fit horizontally.

But now you'll have to change the panel's layout manager from the default FlowLayout to BoxLayout.

```
public void go() {
    JFrame frame = new JFrame();
    JPanel panel = new JPanel();
    panel.setBackground(Color.darkGray);

    panel.setLayout(new BoxLayout(panel, BoxLayout.Y_AXIS));

    JButton button = new JButton("shock me");
    JButton buttonTwo = new JButton("bliss");
    panel.add(button);
    panel.add(buttonTwo);
    frame.getContentPane().add(BorderLayout.EAST, panel);
    frame.setSize(250,200);
    frame.setVisible(true);
}
```

Change the layout manager to be a new instance of BoxLayout.

The BoxLayout constructor needs to know the component its laying out (i.e., the panel) and which axis to use (we use Y_AXIS for a vertical stack).

Notice how the panel is narrower again, because it doesn't need to fit both buttons horizontally. So the panel told the frame it needed enough room for only the largest button, 'shock me'.

Dumb Questions
there are no

Q: How come you can't add directly to a frame the way you can to a panel?

A: A JFrame is special because it's where the rubber meets the road in making something appear on the screen. While all your Swing components are pure Java, a JFrame has to connect to the underlying OS in order to access the display. Think of the content pane as a 100% pure Java layer that sits on *top* of the JFrame. Or think of it as though JFrame is the window frame and the content pane is the... glass. You know, the window *pane*. And you can even *swap* the content pane with your own JPanel, to make your JPanel the frame's content pane, using,

```
myFrame.setContentPane(myPanel);
```

Q: Can I change the layout manager of the frame? What if I want the frame to use flow instead of border?

A: The easiest way to do this is to make a panel, build the GUI the way you want in the panel, and then make that panel the frame's content pane using the code in the previous answer (rather than using the default content pane).

Q: What if I want a different preferred size? Is there a setSize() method for components?

A: Yes, there is a setSize(), but the layout managers will ignore it. There's a distinction between the *preferred size* of the component and the size *you* want it to be. The preferred size is based on the size the component actually *needs* (the component makes that decision for itself). The layout manager calls the component's getPreferredSize() method, and *that* method doesn't *care* if you've previously called setSize() on the component.

Q: Can't I just put things where I want them? Can I turn the layout managers off?

A: Yep. On a component by component basis, you can call `setLayout(null)` and then it's up to you to hard-code the exact screen locations and dimensions. In the long run, though, it's almost always easier to use layout managers.

BULLET POINTS

- Layout managers control the size and location of components nested within other components.
- When you add a component to another component (sometimes referred to as a *background* component, but that's not a technical distinction), the added component is controlled by the layout manager of the *background* component.
- A layout manager asks components for their preferred size, before making a decision about the layout. Depending on the layout manager's policies, it might respect all, some, or none of the component's wishes.
- The BorderLayout manager lets you add a component to one of five regions. You must specify the region when you add the component, using the following syntax:
  ```
  add(BorderLayout.EAST, panel);
  ```
- With BorderLayout, components in the north and south get their preferred height, but not width. Components in the east and west get their preferred width, but not height. The component in the center gets whatever is left over (unless you use **pack()**).
- The pack() method is like shrink-wrap for the components; it uses the full preferred size of the center component, then determines the size of the frame using the center as a starting point, building the rest based on what's in the other regions.
- FlowLayout places components left to right, top to bottom, in the order they were added, wrapping to a new line of components only when the components won't fit horizontally.
- FlowLayout gives components their preferred size in both dimensions.
- BoxLayout lets you align components stacked vertically, even if they could fit side-by-side. Like FlowLayout, BoxLayout uses the preferred size of the component in both dimensions.
- BorderLayout is the default layout manager for a frame; FlowLayout is the default for a panel.
- If you want a panel to use something other than flow, you have to call **setLayout()** on the panel.

Playing with Swing components

You've learned the basics of layout managers, so now let's try out a few of the most common components: a text field, scrolling text area, checkbox, and list. We won't show you the whole darn API for each of these, just a few highlights to get you started.

JTextField

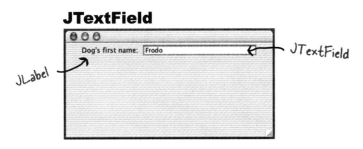

JLabel

JTextField

Constructors

20 means 20 columns, not 20 pixels. This defines the preferred width of the text field.

```
JTextField field = new JTextField(20);

JTextField field = new JTextField("Your name");
```

How to use it

① Get text out of it

```
System.out.println(field.getText());
```

② Put text in it

```
field.setText("whatever");
field.setText("");
```
This clears the field

③ Get an ActionEvent when the user presses return or enter

You can also register for key events if you really want to hear about it every time the user presses a key.

```
field.addActionListener(myActionListener);
```

④ Select/Highlight the text in the field

```
field.selectAll();
```

⑤ Put the cursor back in the field (so the user can just start typing)

```
field.requestFocus();
```

JTextArea

Unlike JTextField, JTextArea can have more than one line of text. It takes a little configuration to make one, because it doesn't come out of the box with scroll bars or line wrapping. To make a JTextArea scroll, you have to stick it in a ScrollPane. A ScrollPane is an object that really loves to scroll, and will take care of the text area's scrolling needs.

10 means 10 lines (sets the preferred height)
20 means 20 columns (sets the preferred width)

Constructor

```
JTextArea text = new JTextArea(10,20);
```

How to use it

① Make it have a vertical scrollbar only

Make a JScrollPane and give it the text area that it's going to scroll for.

```
JScrollPane scroller = new JScrollPane(text);
text.setLineWrap(true);
```
← *Turn on line wrapping*

Tell the scroll pane to use only a vertical scrollbar

```
scroller.setVerticalScrollBarPolicy(ScrollPaneConstants.VERTICAL_SCROLLBAR_ALWAYS);
scroller.setHorizontalScrollBarPolicy(ScrollPaneConstants.HORIZONTAL_SCROLLBAR_NEVER);

panel.add(scroller);
```

Important!! You give the text area to the scroll pane (through the scroll pane constructor), then add the scroll pane to the panel. You don't add the text area directly to the panel!

② Replace the text that's in it

```
text.setText("Not all who are lost are wandering");
```

③ Append to the text that's in it

```
text.append("button clicked");
```

④ Select/Highlight the text in the field

```
text.selectAll();
```

⑤ Put the cursor back in the field (so the user can just start typing)

```
text.requestFocus();
```

JTextArea example

```java
import javax.swing.*;
import java.awt.*;
import java.awt.event.*;


public class TextArea1 implements ActionListener {

    JTextArea text;

    public static void main (String[] args) {
        TextArea1 gui = new TextArea1();
        gui.go();
    }


    public void go() {
        JFrame frame = new JFrame();
        JPanel panel = new JPanel();
        JButton button = new JButton("Just Click It");
        button.addActionListener(this);
        text = new JTextArea(10,20);
        text.setLineWrap(true);

        JScrollPane scroller = new JScrollPane(text);
        scroller.setVerticalScrollBarPolicy(ScrollPaneConstants.VERTICAL_SCROLLBAR_ALWAYS);
        scroller.setHorizontalScrollBarPolicy(ScrollPaneConstants.HORIZONTAL_SCROLLBAR_NEVER);

        panel.add(scroller);

        frame.getContentPane().add(BorderLayout.CENTER, panel);
        frame.getContentPane().add(BorderLayout.SOUTH, button);

        frame.setSize(350,300);
        frame.setVisible(true);
    }

    public void actionPerformed(ActionEvent ev) {
        text.append("button clicked \n ");
    }
}
```

Insert a new line so the words go on a separate line each time the button is clicked. Otherwise, they'll run together.

JCheckBox

Constructor

```
JCheckBox check = new JCheckBox("Goes to 11");
```

How to use it

① Listen for an item event (when it's selected or deselected)

```
check.addItemListener(this);
```

② Handle the event (and find out whether or not it's selected)

```
public void itemStateChanged(ItemEvent ev) {
   String onOrOff = "off";
   if (check.isSelected()) onOrOff = "on";
   System.out.println("Check box is " + onOrOff);
}
```

③ Select or deselect it in code

```
check.setSelected(true);
check.setSelected(false);
```

there are no Dumb Questions

Q: Aren't the layout managers just more trouble than they're worth? If I have to go to all this trouble, I might as well just hard-code the size and coordinates for where everything should go.

A: Getting the exact layout you want from a layout manager can be a challenge. But think about what the layout manager is really doing for you. Even the seemingly simple task of figuring out where things should go on the screen can be complex. For example, the layout manager takes care of keeping your components from overlapping one another. In other words, it knows how to manage the spacing between components (and between the edge of the frame). Sure you can do that yourself, but what happens if you want components to be very tightly packed? You might get them placed just right, by hand, but that's only good for your JVM!

Why? Because the components can be slightly different from platform to platform, especially if they use the underlying platform's native 'look and feel'. Subtle things like the bevel of the buttons can be different in such a way that components that line up neatly on one platform suddenly squish together on another.

And we're still not at the really Big Thing that layout managers do. Think about what happens when the user resizes the window! Or your GUI is dynamic, where components come and go. If you had to keep track of re-laying out all the components every time there's a change in the size or contents of a background component...yikes!

JList

Constructor

```
String [] listEntries = {"alpha", "beta", "gamma", "delta",
                         "epsilon", "zeta", "eta", "theta "};

list = new JList(listEntries);
```

JList constructor takes an array of any object type. They don't have to be Strings, but a String representation will appear in the list.

How to use it

This is just like with JTextArea -- you make a JScrollPane (and give it the list), then add the scroll pane (NOT the list) to the panel.

① Make it have a vertical scrollbar

```
JScrollPane scroller = new JScrollPane(list);
scroller.setVerticalScrollBarPolicy(ScrollPaneConstants.VERTICAL_SCROLLBAR_ALWAYS);
scroller.setHorizontalScrollBarPolicy(ScrollPaneConstants.HORIZONTAL_SCROLLBAR_NEVER);

panel.add(scroller);
```

② Set the number of lines to show before scrolling

```
list.setVisibleRowCount(4);
```

③ Restrict the user to selecting only ONE thing at a time

```
list.setSelectionMode(ListSelectionModel.SINGLE_SELECTION);
```

④ Register for list selection events

```
list.addListSelectionListener(this);
```

⑤ Handle events (find out which thing in the list was selected)

You'll get the event TWICE if you don't put in this if test.

```
public void valueChanged(ListSelectionEvent lse) {
    if( !lse.getValueIsAdjusting()) {
        String selection = (String) list.getSelectedValue();
        System.out.println(selection);
    }
}
```

getSelectedValue() actually returns an Object. A list isn't limited to only String objects.

Code Kitchen

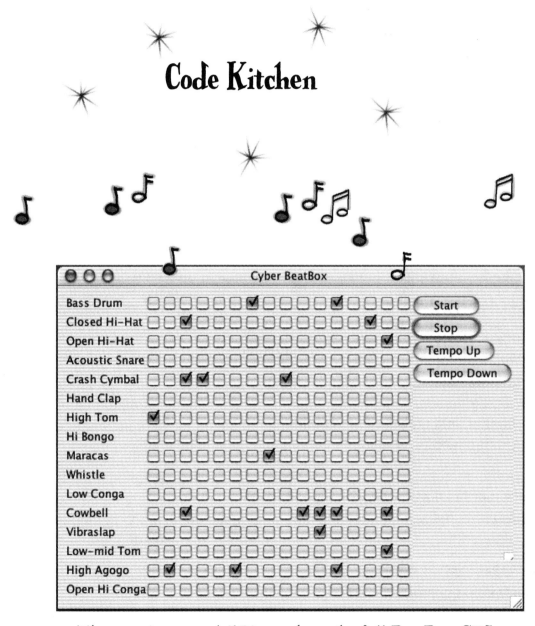

This part's optional. We're making the full BeatBox, GUI and all. In the Saving Objects chapter, we'll learn how to save and restore drum patterns. Finally, in the networking chapter (Make a Connection), we'll turn the BeatBox into a working chat client.

Making the BeatBox

This is the full code listing for this version of the BeatBox, with buttons for starting, stopping, and changing the tempo. The code listing is complete, and fully-annotated, but here's the overview:

① Build a GUI that has 256 checkboxes (JCheckBox) that start out unchecked, 16 labels (JLabel) for the instrument names, and four buttons.

② Register an ActionListener for each of the four buttons. We don't need listeners for the individual checkboxes, because we aren't trying to change the pattern sound dynamically (i.e. as soon as the user checks a box). Instead, we wait until the user hits the 'start' button, and then walk through all 256 checkboxes to get their state and make a MIDI track.

③ Set-up the MIDI system (you've done this before) including getting a Sequencer, making a Sequence, and creating a track. We are using a sequencer method that's new to Java 5.0, setLoopCount(). This method allows you to specify how many times you want a sequence to loop. We're also using the sequence's tempo factor to adjust the tempo up or down, and maintain the new tempo from one iteration of the loop to the next.

④ When the user hits 'start', the real action begins. The event-handling method for the 'start' button calls the buildTrackAndStart() method. In that method, we walk through all 256 checkboxes (one row at a time, a single instrument across all 16 beats) to get their state, then use the information to build a MIDI track (using the handy makeEvent() method we used in the previous chapter). Once the track is built, we start the sequencer, which keeps playing (because we're looping it) until the user hits 'stop'.

BeatBox code

```java
import java.awt.*;
import javax.swing.*;
import javax.sound.midi.*;
import java.util.*;
import java.awt.event.*;


public class BeatBox {

    JPanel mainPanel;
    ArrayList<JCheckBox> checkboxList;
    Sequencer sequencer;
    Sequence sequence;
    Track track;
    JFrame theFrame;

    String[] instrumentNames = {"Bass Drum", "Closed Hi-Hat",
        "Open Hi-Hat","Acoustic Snare", "Crash Cymbal", "Hand Clap",
        "High Tom", "Hi Bongo", "Maracas", "Whistle", "Low Conga",
        "Cowbell", "Vibraslap", "Low-mid Tom", "High Agogo",
        "Open Hi Conga"};
    int[] instruments = {35,42,46,38,49,39,50,60,70,72,64,56,58,47,67,63};


    public static void main (String[] args) {
        new BeatBox2().buildGUI();
    }

    public void buildGUI() {
        theFrame = new JFrame("Cyber BeatBox");
        theFrame.setDefaultCloseOperation(JFrame.EXIT_ON_CLOSE);
        BorderLayout layout = new BorderLayout();
        JPanel background = new JPanel(layout);
        background.setBorder(BorderFactory.createEmptyBorder(10,10,10,10));

        checkboxList = new ArrayList<JCheckBox>();
        Box buttonBox = new Box(BoxLayout.Y_AXIS);

        JButton start = new JButton("Start");
        start.addActionListener(new MyStartListener());
        buttonBox.add(start);

        JButton stop = new JButton("Stop");
        stop.addActionListener(new MyStopListener());
        buttonBox.add(stop);

        JButton upTempo = new JButton("Tempo Up");
        upTempo.addActionListener(new MyUpTempoListener());
        buttonBox.add(upTempo);

        JButton downTempo = new JButton("Tempo Down");
```

We store the checkboxes in an ArrayList

These are the names of the instruments, as a String array, for building the GUI labels (on each row)

These represent the actual drum 'keys'. The drum channel is like a piano, except each 'key' on the piano is a different drum. So the number '35' is the key for the Bass drum, 42 is Closed Hi-Hat, etc.

An 'empty border' gives us a margin between the edges of the panel and where the components are placed. Purely aesthetic.

Nothing special here, just lots of GUI code. You've seen most of it before.

```
        downTempo.addActionListener(new MyDownTempoListener());
        buttonBox.add(downTempo);

        Box nameBox = new Box(BoxLayout.Y_AXIS);
        for (int i = 0; i < 16; i++) {
            nameBox.add(new Label(instrumentNames[i]));
        }

        background.add(BorderLayout.EAST, buttonBox);
        background.add(BorderLayout.WEST, nameBox);

        theFrame.getContentPane().add(background);

        GridLayout grid = new GridLayout(16,16);
        grid.setVgap(1);
        grid.setHgap(2);
        mainPanel = new JPanel(grid);
        background.add(BorderLayout.CENTER, mainPanel);

        for (int i = 0; i < 256; i++) {
            JCheckBox c = new JCheckBox();
            c.setSelected(false);
            checkboxList.add(c);
            mainPanel.add(c);
        } // end loop

        setUpMidi();

        theFrame.setBounds(50,50,300,300);
        theFrame.pack();
        theFrame.setVisible(true);
} // close method


public void setUpMidi() {
    try {
        sequencer = MidiSystem.getSequencer();
        sequencer.open();
        sequence = new Sequence(Sequence.PPQ,4);
        track = sequence.createTrack();
        sequencer.setTempoInBPM(120);

    } catch(Exception e) {e.printStackTrace();}
} // close method
```

Still more GUI set-up code. Nothing remarkable.

Make the checkboxes, set them to 'false' (so they aren't checked) and add them to the ArrayList AND to the GUI panel.

The usual MIDI set-up stuff for getting the Sequencer, the Sequence, and the Track. Again, nothing special.

This is where it all happens! Where we turn checkbox state into MIDI events, and add them to the Track.

We'll make a 16-element array to hold the values for one instrument, across all 16 beats. If the instrument is supposed to play on that beat, the value at that element will be the key. If that instrument is NOT supposed to play on that beat, put in a zero.

```java
public void buildTrackAndStart() {
    int[] trackList = null;

    sequence.deleteTrack(track);
    track = sequence.createTrack();

    for (int i = 0; i < 16; i++) {
        trackList = new int[16];

        int key = instruments[i];

        for (int j = 0; j < 16; j++ ) {

            JCheckBox jc = (JCheckBox) checkboxList.get(j + (16*i));
            if ( jc.isSelected()) {
                trackList[j] = key;
            } else {
                trackList[j] = 0;
            }
        } // close inner loop

        makeTracks(trackList);
        track.add(makeEvent(176,1,127,0,16));
    } // close outer

    track.add(makeEvent(192,9,1,0,15));
    try {

        sequencer.setSequence(sequence);
        sequencer.setLoopCount(sequencer.LOOP_CONTINUOUSLY);
        sequencer.start();
        sequencer.setTempoInBPM(120);
    } catch(Exception e) {e.printStackTrace();}
} // close buildTrackAndStart method

public class MyStartListener implements ActionListener {
    public void actionPerformed(ActionEvent a) {
        buildTrackAndStart();
    }
} // close inner class
```

get rid of the old track, make a fresh one.

do this for each of the 16 ROWS (i.e. Bass, Congo, etc.)

Set the 'key' that represents which instrument this is (Bass, Hi-Hat, etc. The instruments array holds the actual MIDI numbers for each instrument.)

Do this for each of the BEATS for this row

Is the checkbox at this beat selected? If yes, put the key value in this slot in the array (the slot that represents this beat). Otherwise, the instrument is NOT supposed to play at this beat, so set it to zero.

For this instrument, and for all 16 beats, make events and add them to the track.

We always want to make sure that there IS an event at beat 16 (it goes 0 to 15). Otherwise, the BeatBox might not go the full 16 beats before it starts over.

Let's you specify the number of loop iterations, or in this case, continuous looping.

NOW PLAY THE THING!!

First of the inner classes, listeners for the buttons. Nothing special here.

```
public class MyStopListener implements ActionListener {
    public void actionPerformed(ActionEvent a) {
        sequencer.stop();
    }
} // close inner class

public class MyUpTempoListener implements ActionListener {
    public void actionPerformed(ActionEvent a) {
        float tempoFactor = sequencer.getTempoFactor();
        sequencer.setTempoFactor((float)(tempoFactor * 1.03));
    }
} // close inner class

public class MyDownTempoListener implements ActionListener {
    public void actionPerformed(ActionEvent a) {
        float tempoFactor = sequencer.getTempoFactor();
        sequencer.setTempoFactor((float)(tempoFactor * .97));
    }
} // close inner class
```

The other inner class listeners for the buttons

The Tempo Factor scales the sequencer's tempo by the factor provided. The default is 1.0, so we're adjusting +/- 3% per click.

```
public void makeTracks(int[] list) {

    for (int i = 0; i < 16; i++) {
        int key = list[i];

        if (key != 0) {
            track.add(makeEvent(144,9,key, 100, i));
            track.add(makeEvent(128,9,key, 100, i+1));
        }
    }
}
```

This makes events for one instrument at a time, for all 16 beats. So it might get an int[ ] for the Bass drum, and each index in the array will hold either the key of that instrument, or a zero. If it's a zero, the instrument isn't supposed to play at that beat. Otherwise, make an event and add it to the track.

Make the NOTE ON and NOT OFF events, and add them to the Track.

```
public  MidiEvent makeEvent(int comd, int chan, int one, int two, int tick) {
    MidiEvent event = null;
    try {
        ShortMessage a = new ShortMessage();
        a.setMessage(comd, chan, one, two);
        event = new MidiEvent(a, tick);

    } catch(Exception e) {e.printStackTrace(); }
    return event;
}

} // close class
```

This is the utility method from last chapter's CodeKitchen. Nothing new.

Exercise

Which code goes with which layout?

Five of the six screens below were made from one of the code fragments on the opposite page. Match each of the five code fragments with the layout that fragment would produce.

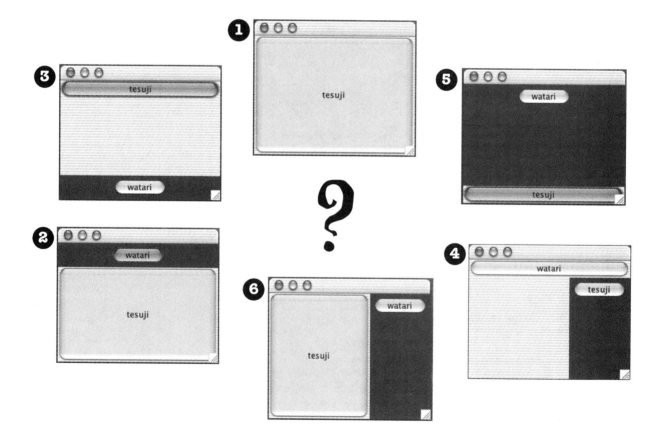

Code Fragments

D
```
JFrame frame = new JFrame();
JPanel panel = new JPanel();
panel.setBackground(Color.darkGray);
JButton button = new JButton("tesuji");
JButton buttonTwo = new JButton("watari");
frame.getContentPane().add(BorderLayout.NORTH,panel);
panel.add(buttonTwo);
frame.getContentPane().add(BorderLayout.CENTER,button);
```

B
```
JFrame frame = new JFrame();
JPanel panel = new JPanel();
panel.setBackground(Color.darkGray);
JButton button = new JButton("tesuji");
JButton buttonTwo = new JButton("watari");
panel.add(buttonTwo);
frame.getContentPane().add(BorderLayout.CENTER,button);
frame.getContentPane().add(BorderLayout.EAST, panel);
```

C
```
JFrame frame = new JFrame();
JPanel panel = new JPanel();
panel.setBackground(Color.darkGray);
JButton button = new JButton("tesuji");
JButton buttonTwo = new JButton("watari");
panel.add(buttonTwo);
frame.getContentPane().add(BorderLayout.CENTER,button);
```

A
```
JFrame frame = new JFrame();
JPanel panel = new JPanel();
panel.setBackground(Color.darkGray);
JButton button = new JButton("tesuji");
JButton buttonTwo = new JButton("watari");
panel.add(button);
frame.getContentPane().add(BorderLayout.NORTH,buttonTwo);
frame.getContentPane().add(BorderLayout.EAST, panel);
```

E
```
JFrame frame = new JFrame();
JPanel panel = new JPanel();
panel.setBackground(Color.darkGray);
JButton button = new JButton("tesuji");
JButton buttonTwo = new JButton("watari");
frame.getContentPane().add(BorderLayout.SOUTH,panel);
panel.add(buttonTwo);
frame.getContentPane().add(BorderLayout.NORTH,button);
```

GUI-Cross 7.0

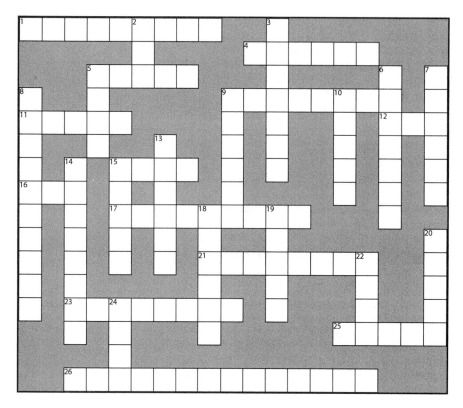

You can do it.

Across

1. Artist's sandbox
4. Border's catchall
5. Java look
9. Generic waiter
11. A happening
12. Apply a widget
15. JPanel's default
16. Polymorphic test
17. Shake it baby
21. Lots to say
23. Choose many
25. Button's pal
26. Home of actionPerformed

Down

2. Swing's dad
3. Frame's purview
5. Help's home
6. More fun than text
7. Component slang
8. Romulin command
9. Arrange
10. Border's top
13. Manager's rules
14. Source's behavior
15. Border by default
18. User's behavior
19. Inner's squeeze
20. Backstage widget
22. Mac look
24. Border's right

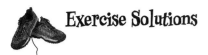

Exercise Solutions

C
```
JFrame frame = new JFrame();
JPanel panel = new JPanel();
panel.setBackground(Color.darkGray);
JButton button = new JButton("tesuji");
JButton buttonTwo = new JButton("watari");
panel.add(buttonTwo);
frame.getContentPane().add(BorderLayout.CENTER,button);
```

D
```
JFrame frame = new JFrame();
JPanel panel = new JPanel();
panel.setBackground(Color.darkGray);
JButton button = new JButton("tesuji");
JButton buttonTwo = new JButton("watari");
frame.getContentPane().add(BorderLayout.NORTH,panel);
panel.add(buttonTwo);
frame.getContentPane().add(BorderLayout.CENTER,button);
```

E
```
JFrame frame = new JFrame();
JPanel panel = new JPanel();
panel.setBackground(Color.darkGray);
JButton button = new JButton("tesuji");
JButton buttonTwo = new JButton("watari");
frame.getContentPane().add(BorderLayout.SOUTH,panel);
panel.add(buttonTwo);
frame.getContentPane().add(BorderLayout.NORTH,button);
```

A
```
JFrame frame = new JFrame();
JPanel panel = new JPanel();
panel.setBackground(Color.darkGray);
JButton button = new JButton("tesuji");
JButton buttonTwo = new JButton("watari");
panel.add(button);
frame.getContentPane().add(BorderLayout.NORTH,buttonTwo);
frame.getContentPane().add(BorderLayout.EAST, panel);
```

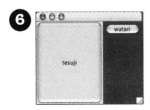

B
```
JFrame frame = new JFrame();
JPanel panel = new JPanel();
panel.setBackground(Color.darkGray);
JButton button = new JButton("tesuji");
JButton buttonTwo = new JButton("watari");
panel.add(buttonTwo);
frame.getContentPane().add(BorderLayout.CENTER,button);
frame.getContentPane().add(BorderLayout.EAST, panel);
```

Puzzle Answers
GUI-Cross 7.0

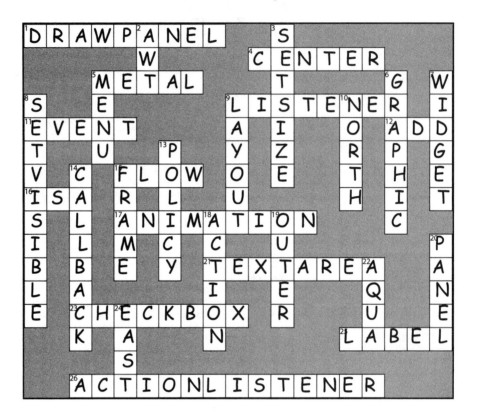

Saving Objects

If I have to read one more file full of data, I think I'll have to kill him. He knows I can save whole objects, but does he let me? NO, that would be too easy. Well, we'll just see how he feels after I...

Objects can be flattened and inflated. Objects have state and behavior. *Behavior* lives in the *class*, but *state* lives within each individual *object*. So what happens when it's time to *save* the state of an object? If you're writing a game, you're gonna need a Save/Restore Game feature. If you're writing an app that creates charts, you're gonna need a Save/Open File feature. If your program needs to save state, *you can do it the hard way*, interrogating each object, then painstakingly writing the value of each instance variable to a file, in a format you create. Or, **you can do it the easy OO way**—you simply freeze-dry/flatten/persist/dehydrate the object itself, and reconstitute/inflate/restore/rehydrate it to get it back. But you'll still have to do it the hard way *sometimes*, especially when the file your app saves has to be read by some other non-Java application, so we'll look at both in this chapter.

Capture the Beat

You've *made* the perfect pattern. You want to *save* the pattern. You could grab a piece of paper and start scribbling it down, but instead you hit the **Save** button (or choose Save from the File menu). Then you give it a name, pick a directory, and exhale knowing that your masterpiece won't go out the window with the blue screen of death.

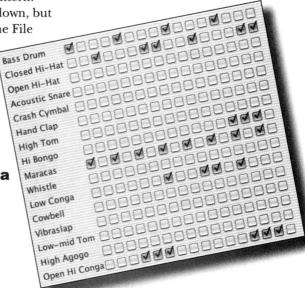

You have lots of options for how to save the state of your Java program, and what you choose will probably depend on how you plan to *use* the saved state. Here are the options we'll be looking at in this chapter.

If your data will be used by only the Java program that generated it:

① Use serialization

Write a file that holds flattened (serialized) objects. Then have your program read the serialized objects from the file and inflate them back into living, breathing, heap-inhabiting objects.

If your data will be used by *other* programs:

② Write a plain text file

Write a file, with delimiters that other programs can parse. For example, a tab-delimited file that a spreadsheet or database application can use.

These aren't the only options, of course. You can save data in any format you choose. Instead of writing characters, for example, you can write your data as bytes. Or you can write out any kind of Java primitive *as* a Java primitive—there are methods to write ints, longs, booleans, etc. But regardless of the method you use, the fundamental I/O techniques are pretty much the same: write some data to *something*, and usually that something is either a file on disk or a stream coming from a network connection. Reading the data is the same process in reverse: read some data from either a file on disk or a network connection. And of course everything we talk about in this part is for times when you aren't using an actual database.

Saving State

Imagine you have a program, say, a fantasy adventure game, that takes more than one session to complete. As the game progresses, characters in the game become stronger, weaker, smarter, etc., and gather and use (and lose) weapons. You don't want to start from scratch each time you launch the game—it took you forever to get your characters in top shape for a spectacular battle. So, you need a way to save the state of the characters, and a way to restore the state when you resume the game. And since you're also the game programmer, you want the whole save and restore thing to be as easy (and foolproof) as possible.

Imagine you have three game characters to save...

```
GameCharacter

int power
String type
Weapon[]  weapons

getWeapon()
useWeapon()
increasePower()
// more
```

power: 50
type: Elf
weapons: bow, sword, dust

object

power: 200
type: Troll
weapons: bare hands, big ax

object

power: 120
type: Magician
weapons: spells, invisibility

object

① Option one

Write the three serialized character objects to a file

Create a file and write three serialized character objects. The file won't make sense if you try to read it as text:

    ¨ÌsrGameCharacter
    ¨%gê8MÛIpowerLjava/lang/
    String;[weaponst[Ljava/lang/
    String;xp♀tlfur[Ljava.lang.String;≠"VÁ
    È{Gxptbowtswordtdustsq˜»tTrolluq˜tb
    are handstbig axsq˜xtMagicianuq˜tspe
    llstinvisibility

② Option two

Write a plain text file

Create a file and write three lines of text, one per character, separating the pieces of state with commas:

    50,Elf,bow, sword,dust
    200,Troll,bare hands,big ax
    120,Magician,spells,invisibility

The serialized file is much harder for humans to read, but it's much easier (and safer) for your program to restore the three objects from serialization than from reading in the object's variable values that were saved to a text file. For example, imagine all the ways in which you could accidentally read back the values in the wrong order! The type might become "dust" instead of "Elf", while the Elf becomes a weapon...

Writing a serialized object to a file

Here are the steps for serializing (saving) an object. Don't bother
memorizing all this; we'll go into more detail later in this chapter.

If the file "MyGame.ser" doesn't exist, it will be created automatically.

1 **Make a FileOutputStream**

```
FileOutputStream fileStream = new FileOutputStream("MyGame.ser");
```

Make a FileOutputStream object. FileOutputStream knows how to connect to (and create) a file.

2 **Make an ObjectOutputStream**

```
ObjectOutputStream os = new ObjectOutputStream(fileStream);
```

ObjectOutputStream lets you write objects, but it can't directly connect to a file. It needs to be fed a 'helper'. This is actually called 'chaining' one stream to another.

3 **Write the object**

```
os.writeObject(characterOne);
os.writeObject(characterTwo);
os.writeObject(characterThree);
```

serializes the objects referenced by character-One, characterTwo, and characterThree, and writes them to the file "MyGame.ser".

4 **Close the ObjectOutputStream**

```
os.close();
```

Closing the stream at the top closes the ones underneath, so the FileOutputStream (and the file) will close automatically.

Data moves in streams from one place to another.

Connection streams represent a connection to a source or destination (file, socket, etc.) while **chain** streams can't connect on their own and must be chained to a connection stream.

The Java I/O API has *connection* streams, that represent connections to destinations and sources such as files or network sockets, and *chain* streams that work only if chained to other streams.

Often, it takes at least two streams hooked together to do something useful—*one* to represent the connection and *another* to call methods on. Why two? Because *connection* streams are usually too low-level. FileOutputStream (a connection stream), for example, has methods for writing *bytes*. But we don't want to write *bytes*! We want to write *objects*, so we need a higher-level *chain* stream.

OK, then why not have just a single stream that does *exactly* what you want? One that lets you write objects but underneath converts them to bytes? Think good OO. Each class does *one* thing well. FileOutputStreams write bytes to a file. ObjectOutputStreams turn objects into data that can be written to a stream. So we make a FileOutputStream that lets us write to a file, and we hook an ObjectOutputStream (a chain stream) on the end of it. When we call writeObject() on the ObjectOutputStream, the object gets pumped into the stream and then moves to the FileOutputStream where it ultimately gets written as bytes to a file.

The ability to mix and match different combinations of connection and chain streams gives you tremendous flexibility! If you were forced to use only a *single* stream class, you'd be at the mercy of the API designers, hoping they'd thought of *everything* you might ever want to do. But with chaining, you can patch together your own *custom* chains.

destination

| Object | is written to | object is flattened (serialized) ObjectOutputStream (a chain stream) | is chained to | object is written as bytes to 011010010110111001 FileOutputStream (a connection stream) | 01101001 01101110 01 File |

What really happens to an object when it's serialized?

1 Object on the heap

2 Object serialized

Objects on the heap have state—the value of the object's instance variables. These values make one instance of a class different from another instance of the same class.

Serialized objects **save the values of the instance variables**, so that an identical instance (object) can be brought back to life on the heap.

Object with two primitive instance variables.

00100101

01000110

width   height

The values are sucked out and pumped into the stream.

00100101

01000110

foo.ser

The instance variable values for width and height are saved to the file "foo.ser", along with a little more info the JVM needs to restore the object (like what its class type is).

```
Foo myFoo = new Foo();
myFoo.setWidth(37);
myFoo.setHeight(70);
```

```
FileOutputStream fs = new FileOutputStream("foo.ser");
ObjectOutputStream os = new ObjectOutputStream(fs);
os.writeObject(myFoo);
```

Make a FileOutputStream that connects to the file "foo.ser", then chain an ObjectOutputStream to it, and tell the ObjectOutputStream to write the object.

But what exactly <u>IS</u> an object's state? What needs to be saved?

Now it starts to get interesting. Easy enough to save the *primitive* values 37 and 70. But what if an object has an instance variable that's an object *reference*? What about an object that has five instance variables that are object references? What if those object instance variables themselves have instance variables?

Think about it. What part of an object is potentially unique? Imagine what needs to be restored in order to get an object that's identical to the one that was saved. It will have a different memory location, of course, but we don't care about that. All we care about is that out there on the heap, we'll get an object that has the same state the object had when it was saved.

Brain Barbell

What has to happen for the Car object to be saved in such a way that it can be restored back to its original state?

Think of what—and how—you might need to save the Car.

And what happens if an Engine object has a reference to a Carburetor? And what's inside the Tire [] array object?

The Car object has two instance variables that reference two other objects.

Engine object

Tire [] array object

Car object

Engine   Tire []

What does it take to save a Car object?

When an object is serialized, all the objects it refers to from instance variables are *also* serialized. And all the objects *those* objects refer to are serialized. And all the objects *those* objects refer to are serialized... and the best part is, it happens automatically!

This Kennel object has a reference to a Dog [] array object. The Dog [] holds references to two Dog objects. Each Dog object holds a reference to a String and a Collar object. The String objects have a collection of characters and the Collar objects have an int.

When you save the Kennel, <u>all</u> of this is saved!

> Serialization saves the entire **object graph**. All objects referenced by instance variables, starting with the object being serialized.

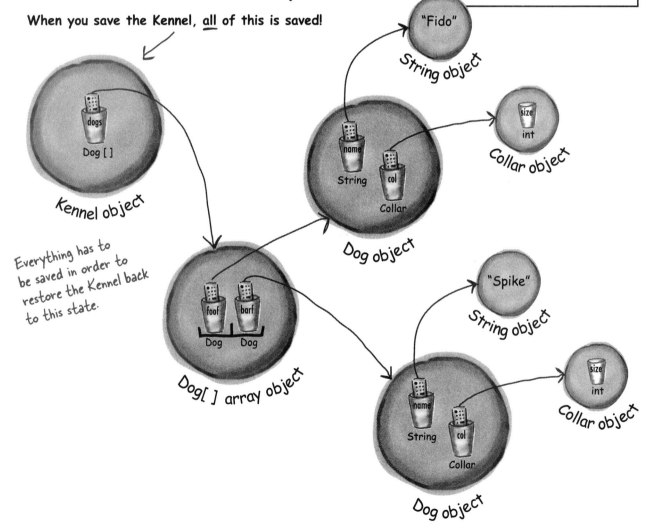

Everything has to be saved in order to restore the Kennel back to this state.

If you want your class to be serializable, implement Serializable

The Serializable interface is known as a *marker* or *tag* interface, because the interface doesn't have any methods to implement. Its sole purpose is to announce that the class implementing it is, well, *serializable*. In other words, objects of that type are saveable through the serialization mechanism. If any superclass of a class is serializable, the subclass is automatically serializable even if the subclass doesn't explicitly declare *implements Serializable*. (This is how interfaces always *work*. If your superclass "IS-A" Serializable, you are too).

```
objectOutputStream.writeObject(myBox);
```

Whatever goes here MUST implement Serializable or it will fail at runtime.

Serializable is in the java.io package, so you need the import.

```java
import java.io.*;

public class Box implements Serializable {
```

No methods to implement, but when you say "implements Serializable", it says to the JVM, "it's OK to serialize objects of this type."

```java
    private int width;
    private int height;
```

← these two values will be saved

```java
    public void setWidth(int w) {
        width = w;
    }

    public void setHeight(int h) {
        height = h;
    }

    public static void main (String[] args) {

        Box myBox = new Box();
        myBox.setWidth(50);
        myBox.setHeight(20);
```

I/O operations can throw exceptions.

```java
        try {
            FileOutputStream fs = new FileOutputStream("foo.ser");
            ObjectOutputStream os = new ObjectOutputStream(fs);
            os.writeObject(myBox);
            os.close();
        } catch(Exception ex) {
            ex.printStackTrace();
        }
    }
}
```

Connect to a file named "foo.ser" if it exists. If it doesn't, make a new file named "foo.ser".

Make an ObjectOutputStream chained to the connection stream.

Tell it to write the object.

Serialization is all or nothing.

Can you imagine what would happen if some of the object's state didn't save correctly?

> Eeewww! That creeps me out just thinking about it! Like, what if a Dog comes back with no weight. Or no ears. Or the collar comes back size 3 instead of 30. That just can't be allowed!

Either the entire object graph is serialized correctly or serialization fails.

You can't serialize a Pond object if its Duck instance variable refuses to be serialized (by not implementing Serializable).

```
import java.io.*;

public class Pond implements Serializable {        ← Pond objects can be serialized.

    private Duck duck = new Duck();        ← Class Pond has one instance
                                              variable, a Duck.

    public static void main (String[] args) {
        Pond myPond = new Pond();
        try {
            FileOutputStream fs = new FileOutputStream("Pond.ser");
            ObjectOutputStream os = new ObjectOutputStream(fs);

            os.writeObject(myPond);        When you serialize myPond (a Pond
            os.close();                    object), its Duck instance variable
                                           automatically gets serialized.

        } catch(Exception ex) {
            ex.printStackTrace();
        }
    }
}

public class Duck {        Yikes!! Duck is not serializable!
    // duck code here      It doesn't implement Serializable,
}                          so when you try to serialize a
                           Pond object, it fails because the
                           Pond's Duck instance variable
                           can't be saved.
```

When you try to run the main in class Pond:

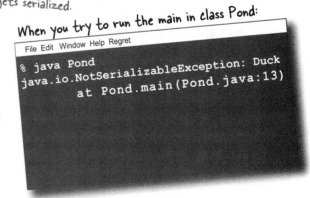

```
File Edit Window Help Regret
% java Pond
java.io.NotSerializableException: Duck
        at Pond.main(Pond.java:13)
```

It's hopeless, then? I'm completely screwed if the idiot who wrote the class for my instance variable forgot to make it Serializable?

Mark an instance variable as <u>transient</u> if it can't (or shouldn't) be saved.

If you want an instance variable to be skipped by the serialization process, mark the variable with the **transient** keyword.

transient says, "don't save this variable during serialization, just skip it."

```
import java.net.*;
class Chat implements Serializable {
   transient String currentID;

   String userName;

   // more code

}
```

userName variable will be saved as part of the object's state during serialization.

If you have an instance variable that can't be saved because it isn't serializable, you can mark that variable with the transient keyword and the serialization process will skip right over it.

So why would a variable not be serializable? It could be that the class designer simply *forgot* to make the class implement Serializable. Or it might be because the object relies on runtime-specific information that simply can't be saved. Although most things in the Java class libraries are serializable, you can't save things like network connections, threads, or file objects. They're all dependent on (and specific to) a particular runtime 'experience'. In other words, they're instantiated in a way that's unique to a particular run of your program, on a particular platform, in a particular JVM. Once the program shuts down, there's no way to bring those things back to life in any meaningful way; they have to be created from scratch each time.

there are no
Dumb Questions

Q: **If serialization is so important, why isn't it the default for all classes? Why doesn't class Object implement Serializable, and then all subclasses will be automatically Serializable.**

A: Even though most classes will, and should, implement Serializable, you always have a choice. And you must make a conscious decision on a class-by-class basis, for each class you design, to 'enable' serialization by implementing Serializable. First of all, if serialization were the default, how would you turn it off? Interfaces indicate functionality, not a *lack* of functionality, so the model of polymorphism wouldn't work correctly if you had to say, "implements NonSerializable" to tell the world that you cannot be saved.

Q: **Why would I ever write a class that *wasn't* serializable?**

A: There are very few reasons, but you might, for example, have a security issue where you don't want a password object stored. Or you might have an object that makes no sense to save, because its key instance variables are themselves not serializable, so there's no useful way for you to make *your* class serializable.

Q: **If a class I'm using isn't serializable, but there's no good reason (except that the designer just forgot or was stupid), can I subclass the 'bad' class and make the *subclass* serializable?**

A: Yes! If the class itself is extendable (i.e. not final), you can make a serializable subclass, and just substitute the subclass everywhere your code is expecting the superclass type. (Remember, polymorphism allows this.) Which brings up another interesting issue: what does it *mean* if the superclass is not serializable?

Q: **You brought it up: what *does* it mean to have a serializable subclass of a non-serializable superclass?**

A: First we have to look at what happens when a class is deserialized, (we'll talk about that on the next few pages). In a nutshell, when an object is deserialized and its superclass is *not* serializable, the superclass constructor will run just as though a new object of that type were being created. If there's no decent reason for a class to not be serializable, making a serializable subclass might be a good solution.

Q: **Whoa! I just realized something big... if you make a variable 'transient', this means the variable's value is skipped over during serialization. Then what happens to it? We solve the problem of having a non-serializable instance variable by making the instance variable transient, but don't we NEED that variable when the object is brought back to life? In other words, isn't the whole point of serialization to preserve an object's state?**

A: Yes, this is an issue, but fortunately there's a solution. If you serialize an object, a transient reference instance variable will be brought back as *null*, regardless of the value it had at the time it was saved. That means the entire object graph connected to that particular instance variable won't be saved. This could be bad, obviously, because you probably need a non-null value for that variable.

You have two options:

1) When the object is brought back, reinitialize that null instance variable back to some default state. This works if your deserialized object isn't dependent on a particular value for that transient variable. In other words, it might be important that the Dog have a Collar, but perhaps all Collar objects are the same so it doesn't matter if you give the resurrected Dog a brand new Collar; nobody will know the difference.

2) If the value of the transient variable *does* matter (say, if the color and design of the transient Collar are unique for each Dog) then you need to save the key values of the Collar and use them when the Dog is brought back to essentially re-create a brand new Collar that's identical to the original.

Q: **What happens if two objects in the object graph are the same object? Like, if you have two different Cat objects in the Kennel, but both Cats have a reference to the same Owner object. Does the Owner get saved twice? I'm hoping not.**

A: Excellent question! Serialization is smart enough to know when two objects in the graph are the same. In that case, only *one* of the objects is saved, and during deserialization, any references to that single object are restored.

Deserialization: restoring an object

The whole point of serializing an object is so that you can restore it back to its original state at some later date, in a different 'run' of the JVM (which might not even be the same JVM that was running at the time the object was serialized). Deserialization is a lot like serialization in reverse.

serialized

deserialized

1 **Make a FileInputStream**

If the file "MyGame.ser" doesn't exist, you'll get an exception.

```
FileInputStream fileStream = new FileInputStream("MyGame.ser");
```

Make a FileInputStream object. The FileInputStream knows how to connect to an existing file.

2 **Make an ObjectInputStream**

```
ObjectInputStream os = new ObjectInputStream(fileStream);
```

ObjectInputStream lets you read objects, but it can't directly connect to a file. It needs to be chained to a connection stream, in this case a FileInputStream.

3 **read the objects**

```
Object one = os.readObject();
Object two = os.readObject();
Object three = os.readObject();
```

Each time you say readObject(), you get the next object in the stream. So you'll read them back in the same order in which they were written. You'll get a big fat exception if you try to read more objects than you wrote.

4 **Cast the objects**

```
GameCharacter elf = (GameCharacter) one;
GameCharacter troll = (GameCharacter) two;
GameCharacter magician = (GameCharacter) three;
```

The return value of readObject() is type Object (just like with ArrayList), so you have to cast it back to the type you know it really is.

5 **Close the ObjectInputStream**

```
os.close();
```

Closing the stream at the top closes the ones underneath, so the FileInputStream (and the file) will close automatically.

What happens during deserialization?

When an object is deserialized, the JVM attempts to bring the object back to life by making a new object on the heap that has the same state the serialized object had at the time it was serialized. Well, except for the transient variables, which come back either null (for object references) or as default primitive values.

This step will throw an exception if the JVM can't find or load the class!

class is found and loaded, saved instance variables reassigned

01101001 01101110 01	is read by →	011010010110111001	is chained to		→	Object

File

object is read as bytes

FileInputStream
(a connection stream)

ObjectInputStream
(a chain stream)

1 The object is **read** from the stream.

2 The JVM determines (through info stored with the serialized object) the object's **class type**.

3 The JVM attempts to **find and load** the object's **class**. If the JVM can't find and/or load the class, the JVM throws an exception and the deserialization fails.

4 A new object is given space on the heap, but the **serialized object's constructor does NOT run!** Obviously, if the constructor ran, it would restore the state of the object back to its original 'new' state, and that's not what we want. We want the object to be restored to the state it had *when it was serialized*, not when it was first created.

5 If the object has a non-serializable class somewhere up its inheritance tree, the **constructor for that non-serializable class will run** along with any constructors above that (even if they're serializable). Once the constructor chaining begins, you can't stop it, which means all superclasses, beginning with the first non-serializable one, will reinitialize their state.

6 The object's **instance variables are given the values from the serialized state**. Transient variables are given a value of null for object references and defaults (0, false, etc.) for primitives.

there are no Dumb Questions

Q: Why doesn't the class get saved as part of the object? That way you don't have the problem with whether the class can be found.

A: Sure, they could have made serialization work that way. But what a tremendous waste and overhead. And while it might not be such a hardship when you're using serialization to write objects to a file on a local hard drive, serialization is also used to send objects over a network connection. If a class was bundled with each serialized (shippable) object, bandwidth would become a much larger problem than it already is.

For objects serialized to ship over a network, though, there actually *is* a mechanism where the serialized object can be 'stamped' with a URL for where its class can be found. This is used in Java's Remote Method Invocation (RMI) so that you can send a serialized object as part of, say, a method argument, and if the JVM receiving the call doesn't have the class, it can use the URL to fetch the class from the network and load it, all automatically. (We'll talk about RMI in chapter 17.)

Q: What about static variables? Are they serialized?

A: Nope. Remember, static means "one per class" not "one per object". Static variables are not saved, and when an object is deserialized, it will have whatever static variable its class *currently* has. The moral: don't make serializable objects dependent on a dynamically-changing static variable! It might not be the same when the object comes back.

Saving and restoring the game characters

```java
import java.io.*;

public class GameSaverTest {
    public static void main(String[] args) {
        GameCharacter one = new GameCharacter(50, "Elf", new String[] {"bow", "sword", "dust"});
        GameCharacter two = new GameCharacter(200, "Troll", new String[] {"bare hands", "big ax"});
        GameCharacter three = new GameCharacter(120, "Magician", new String[] {"spells", "invisibility"});

        // imagine code that does things with the characters that might change their state values

        try {
            ObjectOutputStream os = new ObjectOutputStream(new FileOutputStream("Game.ser"));
            os.writeObject(one);
            os.writeObject(two);
            os.writeObject(three);
            os.close();
        } catch(IOException ex) {
            ex.printStackTrace();
        }
        one = null;
        two = null;
        three = null;

        try {
            ObjectInputStream is = new ObjectInputStream(new FileInputStream("Game.ser"));
            GameCharacter oneRestore = (GameCharacter) is.readObject();
            GameCharacter twoRestore = (GameCharacter) is.readObject();
            GameCharacter threeRestore = (GameCharacter) is.readObject();

            System.out.println("One's type: " + oneRestore.getType());
            System.out.println("Two's type: " + twoRestore.getType());
            System.out.println("Three's type: " + threeRestore.getType());
        } catch(Exception ex) {
            ex.printStackTrace();
        }
    }
}
```

Make some characters...

We set them to null so we can't access the objects on the heap.

Now read them back in from the file...

Check to see if it worked.

```
File Edit Window Help Resuscitate
% java GameSaver

Elf

Troll

Magician
```

power: 50
type: Elf
weapons: bow, sword, dust

object

power: 200
type: Troll
weapons: bare hands, big ax

object

power: 120
type: Magician
weapons: spells, invisibility

object

The GameCharacter class

```java
import java.io.*;

public class GameCharacter implements Serializable {
    int power;
    String type;
    String[] weapons;

    public GameCharacter(int p, String t, String[] w) {
        power = p;
        type = t;
        weapons = w;
    }

    public int getPower() {
      return power;
    }

    public String getType() {
        return type;
    }

    public String getWeapons() {
        String weaponList = "";

        for (int i = 0; i < weapons.length; i++) {
            weaponList += weapons[i] + " ";
        }
        return weaponList;
    }
}
```

This is a basic class just for testing Serialization, and we don't have an actual game, but we'll leave that to you to experiment.

Object Serialization

BULLET POINTS

- ► You can save an object's state by serializing the object.
- ► To serialize an object, you need an ObjectOutputStream (from the java.io package)
- ► Streams are either connection streams or chain streams
- ► Connection streams can represent a connection to a source or destination, typically a file, network socket connection, or the console.
- ► Chain streams cannot connect to a source or destination and must be chained to a connection (or other) stream.
- ► To serialize an object to a file, make a FileOuputStream and chain it into an ObjectOutputStream.
- ► To serialize an object, call *writeObject(theObject)* on the ObjectOutputStream. You do not need to call methods on the FileOutputStream.
- ► To be serialized, an object must implement the Serializable interface. If a superclass of the class implements Serializable, the subclass will automatically be serializable even if it does not specifically declare *implements Serializable.*
- ► When an object is serialized, its entire object graph is serialized. That means any objects referenced by the serialized object's instance variables are serialized, and any objects referenced by those objects...and so on.
- ► If any object in the graph is not serializable, an exception will be thrown at runtime, unless the instance variable referring to the object is skipped.
- ► Mark an instance variable with the *transient* keyword if you want serialization to skip that variable. The variable will be restored as null (for object references) or default values (for primitives).
- ► During deserialization, the class of all objects in the graph must be available to the JVM.
- ► You read objects in (using readObject()) in the order in which they were originally written.
- ► The return type of readObject() is type Object, so deserialized objects must be cast to their real type.
- ► Static variables are not serialized! It doesn't make sense to save a static variable value as part of a specific object's state, since all objects of that type share only a single value—the one in the class.

Writing a String to a Text File

Saving objects, through serialization, is the easiest way to save and restore data between runnings of a Java program. But sometimes you need to save data to a plain old text file. Imagine your Java program has to write data to a simple text file that some other (perhaps non-Java) program needs to read. You might, for example, have a servlet (Java code running within your web server) that takes form data the user typed into a browser, and writes it to a text file that somebody else loads into a spreadsheet for analysis.

Writing text data (a String, actually) is similar to writing an object, except you write a String instead of an object, and you use a FileWriter instead of a FileOutputStream (and you don't chain it to an ObjectOutputStream).

What the game character data might look like if you wrote it out as a human-readable text file.

```
50,Elf,bow, sword,dust
200,Troll,bare hands,big ax
120,Magician,spells,invisibility
```

To write a serialized object:

```
objectOutputStream.writeObject(someObject);
```

To write a String:

```
fileWriter.write("My first String to save");
```

```
import java.io.*;        ← We need the java.io package for FileWriter

class WriteAFile {
    public static void main (String[] args) {
                                                      If the file "Foo.txt" does not
                                                      exist, FileWriter will create it.
        try {
            FileWriter writer = new FileWriter("Foo.txt");

            writer.write("hello foo!"); ←  The write() method takes
                                            a String
            writer.close(); ← Close it when you're done!

        } catch(IOException ex) {
            ex.printStackTrace();
        }
    }
}
```

ALL the I/O stuff must be in a try/catch. Everything can throw an IOException!!

Text File Example: e-Flashcards

Remember those flashcards you used in school? Where you had a question on one side and the answer on the back? They aren't much help when you're trying to understand something, but nothing beats 'em for raw drill-and-practice and rote memorization. *When you have to burn in a fact.* And they're also great for trivia games.

We're going to make an electronic version that has three classes:

1) *QuizCardBuilder*, a simple authoring tool for creating and saving a set of e-Flashcards.

2) *QuizCardPlayer*, a playback engine that can load a flashcard set and play it for the user.

3) *QuizCard*, a simple class representing card data. We'll walk through the code for the builder and the player, and have you make the QuizCard class yourself, using this ⟶

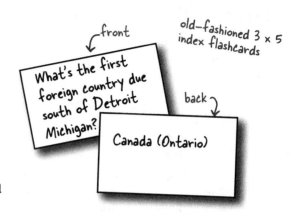

old-fashioned 3 x 5 index flashcards

front

What's the first foreign country due south of Detroit Michigan?

back

Canada (Ontario)

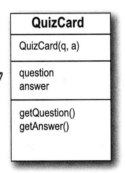

QuizCard
QuizCard(q, a)
question answer
getQuestion() getAnswer()

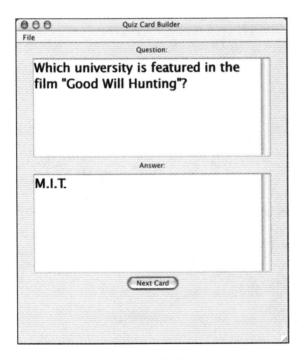

QuizCardBuilder

Has a File menu with a "Save" option for saving the current set of cards to a text file.

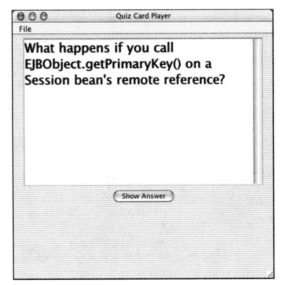

QuizCardPlayer

Has a File menu with a "Load" option for loading a set of cards from a text file.

Quiz Card Builder (code outline)

public class QuizCardBuilder {

   public void **go()** {   *Builds and displays the GUI, including*
      // build and display gui   *making and registering event listeners.*
   }

                Inner class
   private class **NextCardListener** implements ActionListener {
      public void actionPerformed(ActionEvent ev) {   *Triggered when user hits 'Next Card' button;*
         // add the current card to the list and clear the text areas   *means the user wants to store that card in*
      }   *the list and start a new card.*
   }

                Inner class
   private class **SaveMenuListener** implements ActionListener {
      public void actionPerformed(ActionEvent ev) {   *Triggered when use chooses 'Save' from the*
         // bring up a file dialog box   *File menu; means the user wants to save all*
         // let the user name and save the set   *the cards in the current list as a 'set' (like,*
      }   *Quantum Mechanics Set, Hollywood Trivia,*
   }   *Java Rules, etc.).*

                Inner class
   private class **NewMenuListener** implements ActionListener {
      public void actionPerformed(ActionEvent ev) {   *Triggered by choosing 'New' from the File*
         // clear out the card list, and clear out the text areas   *menu; means the user wants to start a*
      }   *brand new set (so we clear out the card*
   }   *list and the text areas).*

   private void **saveFile(File file)** {
      // iterate through the list of cards, and write each one out to a text file
      // in a parseable way (in other words, with clear separations between parts)
   }
}

Called by the SaveMenuListener;
does the actual file writing.

Quiz Card Builder code

```java
import java.util.*;
import java.awt.event.*;
import javax.swing.*;
import java.awt.*;
import java.io.*;

public class QuizCardBuilder {

    private JTextArea question;
    private JTextArea answer;
    private ArrayList<QuizCard> cardList;
    private JFrame frame;

    public static void main (String[] args) {
        QuizCardBuilder builder = new QuizCardBuilder();
        builder.go();
    }


    public void go() {
        // build gui

        frame = new JFrame("Quiz Card Builder");
        JPanel mainPanel = new JPanel();
        Font bigFont = new Font("sanserif", Font.BOLD, 24);
        question = new JTextArea(6,20);
        question.setLineWrap(true);
        question.setWrapStyleWord(true);
        question.setFont(bigFont);

        JScrollPane qScroller = new JScrollPane(question);
        qScroller.setVerticalScrollBarPolicy(ScrollPaneConstants.VERTICAL_SCROLLBAR_ALWAYS);
        qScroller.setHorizontalScrollBarPolicy(ScrollPaneConstants.HORIZONTAL_SCROLLBAR_NEVER);

        answer = new JTextArea(6,20);
        answer.setLineWrap(true);
        answer.setWrapStyleWord(true);
        answer.setFont(bigFont);

        JScrollPane aScroller = new JScrollPane(answer);
        aScroller.setVerticalScrollBarPolicy(ScrollPaneConstants.VERTICAL_SCROLLBAR_ALWAYS);
        aScroller.setHorizontalScrollBarPolicy(ScrollPaneConstants.HORIZONTAL_SCROLLBAR_NEVER);

        JButton nextButton = new JButton("Next Card");

        cardList = new ArrayList<QuizCard>();

        JLabel qLabel = new JLabel("Question:");
        JLabel aLabel = new JLabel("Answer:");

        mainPanel.add(qLabel);
        mainPanel.add(qScroller);
        mainPanel.add(aLabel);
        mainPanel.add(aScroller);
        mainPanel.add(nextButton);
        nextButton.addActionListener(new NextCardListener());
        JMenuBar menuBar = new JMenuBar();
        JMenu fileMenu = new JMenu("File");
        JMenuItem newMenuItem = new JMenuItem("New");
```

This is all GUI code here. Nothing special, although you might want to look at the MenuBar, Menu, and MenuItems code.

```
        JMenuItem saveMenuItem = new JMenuItem("Save");
        newMenuItem.addActionListener(new NewMenuListener());

        saveMenuItem.addActionListener(new SaveMenuListener());
        fileMenu.add(newMenuItem);
        fileMenu.add(saveMenuItem);
        menuBar.add(fileMenu);
        frame.setJMenuBar(menuBar);
        frame.getContentPane().add(BorderLayout.CENTER, mainPanel);
        frame.setSize(500,600);
        frame.setVisible(true);
    }
```

We make a menu bar, make a File menu, then put 'new' and 'save' menu items into the File menu. We add the menu to the menu bar, then tell the frame to use this menu bar. Menu items can fire an ActionEvent

```
    public class NextCardListener implements ActionListener {
        public void actionPerformed(ActionEvent ev) {

            QuizCard card = new QuizCard(question.getText(), answer.getText());
            cardList.add(card);
            clearCard();
        }
    }

    public class SaveMenuListener implements ActionListener {
        public void actionPerformed(ActionEvent ev) {
            QuizCard card = new QuizCard(question.getText(), answer.getText());
            cardList.add(card);

            JFileChooser fileSave = new JFileChooser();
            fileSave.showSaveDialog(frame);
            saveFile(fileSave.getSelectedFile());
        }
    }
```

Brings up a file dialog box and waits on this line until the user chooses 'Save' from the dialog box. All the file dialog navigation and selecting a file, etc. is done for you by the JFileChooser! It really is this easy.

```
    public class NewMenuListener implements ActionListener {
        public void actionPerformed(ActionEvent ev) {
            cardList.clear();
            clearCard();
        }
    }

    private void clearCard() {
        question.setText("");
        answer.setText("");
        question.requestFocus();
    }
```

The method that does the actual file writing (called by the SaveMenuListener's event handler). The argument is the 'File' object the user is saving. We'll look at the File class on the next page.

```
    private void saveFile(File file) {
        try {
            BufferedWriter writer = new BufferedWriter(new FileWriter(file));

            for(QuizCard card:cardList) {
                writer.write(card.getQuestion() + "/");
                writer.write(card.getAnswer() + "\n");
            }
            writer.close();

        } catch(IOException ex) {
            System.out.println("couldn't write the cardList out");
            ex.printStackTrace();
        }
    }
}
```

We chain a BufferedWriter on to a new FileWriter to make writing more efficient. (We'll talk about that in a few pages).

Walk through the ArrayList of cards and write them out, one card per line, with the question and answer separated by a "/", and then add a newline character ("\n")

The java.io.File class

The java.io.File class *represents* a file on disk, but doesn't actually represent the *contents* of the file. What? Think of a File object as something more like a *pathname* of a file (or even a *directory*) rather than The Actual File Itself. The File class does not, for example, have methods for reading and writing. One VERY useful thing about a File object is that it offers a much safer way to represent a file than just using a String file name. For example, most classes that take a String file name in their constructor (like FileWriter or FileInputStream) can take a File object instead. You can construct a File object, verify that you've got a valid path, etc. and then give that File object to the FileWriter or FileInputStream.

Some things you can do with a File object:

① **Make a File object representing an existing file**
```
File f = new File("MyCode.txt");
```

② **Make a new directory**
```
File dir = new File("Chapter7");
dir.mkdir();
```

③ **List the contents of a directory**
```
if (dir.isDirectory()) {
    String[] dirContents = dir.list();
    for (int i = 0; i < dirContents.length; i++) {
        System.out.println(dirContents[i]);
    }
}
```

④ **Get the absolute path of a file or directory**
```
System.out.println(dir.getAbsolutePath());
```

⑤ **Delete a file or directory (returns true if successful)**
```
boolean isDeleted = f.delete();
```

A File object represents the name and path of a file or directory on disk, for example:

/Users/Kathy/Data/GameFile.txt

But it does NOT represent, or give you access to, the data *in* the file!

An address is NOT the same as the actual house! A File object is like a street address... it ~~represents~~ the name and location of a particular file, but it isn't the file itself.

A File object represents the filename "GameFile.txt"

GameFile.txt

50,Elf,bow,sword,dust
200,Troll,bare hands,big ax
120,Magician,spells,invisibility

A File object does NOT represent (or give you direct access to) the data inside the file!

The beauty of buffers

If there were no buffers, it would be like shopping without a cart. You'd have to carry each thing out to your car, one soup can or toilet paper roll at a time.

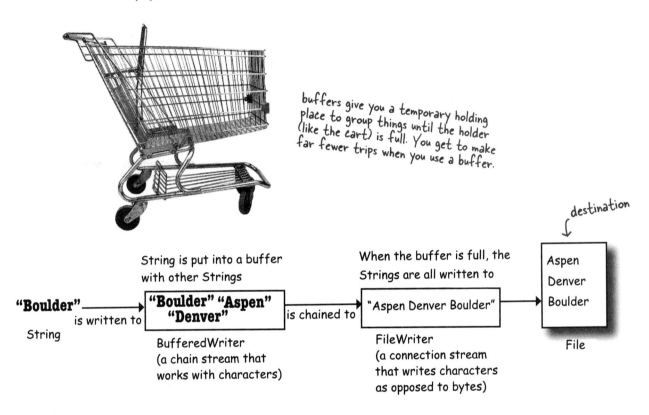

buffers give you a temporary holding place to group things until the holder (like the cart) is full. You get to make far fewer trips when you use a buffer.

destination

String is put into a buffer with other Strings	When the buffer is full, the Strings are all written to	Aspen Denver Boulder

"Boulder" → is written to → **"Boulder" "Aspen" "Denver"** → is chained to → "Aspen Denver Boulder" → Aspen Denver Boulder

String

BufferedWriter (a chain stream that works with characters)

FileWriter (a connection stream that writes characters as opposed to bytes)

File

```
BufferedWriter writer = new BufferedWriter(new FileWriter(aFile));
```

Notice that we don't even need to keep a reference to the FileWriter object. The only thing we care about is the BufferedWriter, because that's the object we'll call methods on, and when we close the BufferedWriter, it will take care of the rest of the chain.

The cool thing about buffers is that they're *much* more efficient than working without them. You can write to a file using FileWriter alone, by calling write(someString), but FileWriter writes each and every thing you pass to the file each and every time. That's overhead you don't want or need, since every trip to the disk is a Big Deal compared to manipulating data in memory. By chaining a BufferedWriter onto a FileWriter, the BufferedWriter will hold all the stuff you write to it until it's full. *Only when the buffer is full will the FileWriter actually be told to write to the file on disk.*

If you do want to send data *before* the buffer is full, you do have control. ***Just Flush It***. Calls to writer.flush() say, "send whatever's in the buffer, ***now!***"

Reading from a Text File

Reading text from a file is simple, but this time we'll use a File object to represent the file, a FileReader to do the actual reading, and a BufferedReader to make the reading more efficient.

The read happens by reading lines in a *while* loop, ending the loop when the result of a readLine() is null. That's the most common style for reading data (pretty much anything that's not a Serialized object): read stuff in a while loop (actually a while loop *test*), terminating when there's nothing left to read (which we know because the result of whatever read method we're using is null).

A file with two lines of text.

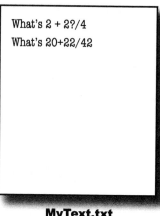

What's 2 + 2?/4
What's 20+22/42

MyText.txt

```
import java.io.*;      Don't forget the import.

class ReadAFile {
    public static void main (String[] args) {

        try {
            File myFile = new File("MyText.txt");
            FileReader fileReader = new FileReader(myFile);

            BufferedReader reader = new BufferedReader(fileReader);

            String line = null;

            while ((line = reader.readLine()) != null) {
                System.out.println(line);
            }
            reader.close();

        } catch(Exception ex) {
            ex.printStackTrace();
        }
    }
}
```

A FileReader is a connection stream for characters, that connects to a text file

Chain the FileReader to a BufferedReader for more efficient reading. It'll go back to the file to read only when the buffer is empty (because the program has read everything in it).

Make a String variable to hold each line as the line is read

This says, "Read a line of text, and assign it to the String variable 'line'. While that variable is not null (because there WAS something to read) print out the line that was just read."

Or another way of saying it, "While there are still lines to read, read them and print them."

Quiz Card Player (code outline)

```java
public class QuizCardPlayer {

  public void go() {
    // build and display gui
  }

  class NextCardListener implements ActionListener {
    public void actionPerformed(ActionEvent ev) {
      // if this is a question, show the answer, otherwise show next question
      // set a flag for whether we're viewing a question or answer
    }
  }

  class OpenMenuListener implements ActionListener {
    public void actionPerformed(ActionEvent ev) {
      // bring up a file dialog box
      // let the user navigate to and choose a card set to open
    }
  }

  private void loadFile(File file) {
    // must build an ArrayList of cards, by reading them from a text file
    // called from the OpenMenuListener event handler, reads the file one line at a time
    // and tells the makeCard() method to make a new card out of the line
    // (one line in the file holds both the question and answer, separated by a "/")
  }

  private void makeCard(String lineToParse) {
    // called by the loadFile method, takes a line from the text file
    // and parses into two pieces—question and answer—and creates a new QuizCard
    // and adds it to the ArrayList called CardList
  }

}
```

Quiz Card Player code

```java
import java.util.*;
import java.awt.event.*;
import javax.swing.*;
import java.awt.*;
import java.io.*;

public class QuizCardPlayer {

    private JTextArea display;
    private JTextArea answer;
    private ArrayList<QuizCard> cardList;
    private QuizCard currentCard;
    private int currentCardIndex;
    private JFrame frame;
    private JButton nextButton;
    private boolean isShowAnswer;


    public static void main (String[] args) {
        QuizCardPlayer reader = new QuizCardPlayer();
        reader.go();
    }

    public void go() {

        // build gui

        frame = new JFrame("Quiz Card Player");
        JPanel mainPanel = new JPanel();
        Font bigFont = new Font("sanserif", Font.BOLD, 24);

        display = new JTextArea(10,20);
        display.setFont(bigFont);

        display.setLineWrap(true);
        display.setEditable(false);

        JScrollPane qScroller = new JScrollPane(display);
        qScroller.setVerticalScrollBarPolicy(ScrollPaneConstants.VERTICAL_SCROLLBAR_ALWAYS);
        qScroller.setHorizontalScrollBarPolicy(ScrollPaneConstants.HORIZONTAL_SCROLLBAR_NEVER);
        nextButton = new JButton("Show Question");
        mainPanel.add(qScroller);
        mainPanel.add(nextButton);
        nextButton.addActionListener(new NextCardListener());

        JMenuBar menuBar = new JMenuBar();
        JMenu fileMenu = new JMenu("File");
        JMenuItem loadMenuItem = new JMenuItem("Load card set");
        loadMenuItem.addActionListener(new OpenMenuListener());
        fileMenu.add(loadMenuItem);
        menuBar.add(fileMenu);
        frame.setJMenuBar(menuBar);
        frame.getContentPane().add(BorderLayout.CENTER, mainPanel);
        frame.setSize(640,500);
        frame.setVisible(true);

    } // close go
```

Just GUI code on this page; nothing special

```
public class NextCardListener implements ActionListener {
    public void actionPerformed(ActionEvent ev) {
        if (isShowAnswer) {
            // show the answer because they've seen the question
            display.setText(currentCard.getAnswer());
            nextButton.setText("Next Card");
            isShowAnswer = false;
        } else {
            // show the next question
            if (currentCardIndex < cardList.size()) {

                showNextCard();

            } else {
                // there are no more cards!
                display.setText("That was last card");
                nextButton.setEnabled(false);
            }
        }
    }
}
```

Check the isShowAnswer boolean flag to see if they're currently viewing a question or an answer, and do the appropriate thing depending on the answer.

```
public class OpenMenuListener implements ActionListener {
    public void actionPerformed(ActionEvent ev) {
        JFileChooser fileOpen = new JFileChooser();
        fileOpen.showOpenDialog(frame);
        loadFile(fileOpen.getSelectedFile());
    }
}
```

Bring up the file dialog box and let them navigate to and choose the file to open.

```
private void loadFile(File file) {

    cardList = new ArrayList<QuizCard>();
    try {
        BufferedReader reader = new BufferedReader(new FileReader(file));
        String line = null;
        while ((line = reader.readLine()) != null) {
            makeCard(line);
        }
        reader.close();

    } catch(Exception ex) {
        System.out.println("couldn't read the card file");
        ex.printStackTrace();
    }

    // now time to start by showing the first card
    showNextCard();
}
```

Make a BufferedReader chained to a new FileReader, giving the FileReader the File object the user chose from the open file dialog.

Read a line at a time, passing the line to the makeCard() method that parses it and turns it into a real QuizCard and adds it to the ArrayList.

```
private void makeCard(String lineToParse) {
    String[] result = lineToParse.split("/");
    QuizCard card = new QuizCard(result[0], result[1]);
    cardList.add(card);
    System.out.println("made a card");
}
```

Each line of text corresponds to a single flashcard, but we have to parse out the question and answer as separate pieces. We use the String split() method to break the line into two tokens (one for the question and one for the answer). We'll look at the split() method on the next page.

```
private void showNextCard() {
    currentCard = cardList.get(currentCardIndex);
    currentCardIndex++;
    display.setText(currentCard.getQuestion());
    nextButton.setText("Show Answer");
    isShowAnswer = true;
}
} // close class
```

Parsing with String split()

Imagine you have a flashcard like this:

Saved in a question file like this:

question

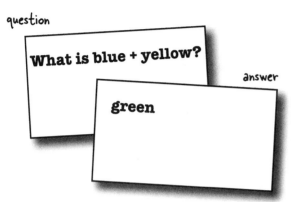

What is blue + yellow?

answer

green

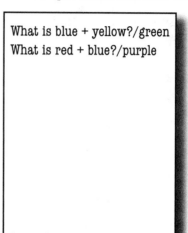

What is blue + yellow?/green
What is red + blue?/purple

How do you separate the question and answer?

When you read the file, the question and answer are smooshed together in one line, separated by a forward slash "/" (because that's how we wrote the file in the QuizCardBuilder code).

String split() lets you break a String into pieces.

The split() method says, "give me a separator, and I'll break out all the pieces of this String for you and put them in a String array."

token 1   separator   token 2

```
String toTest = "What is blue + yellow?/green";

String[] result = toTest.split("/");

for (String token:result) {

    System.out.println(token);

}
```

In the QuizCardPlayer app, this is what a single line looks like when it's read in from the file.

The split() method takes the "/" and uses it to break apart the String into (in this case) two pieces. (Note: split() is FAR more powerful than what we're using it for here. It can do extremely complex parsing with filters, wildcards, etc.)

Loop through the array and print each token (piece). In this example, there are only two tokens: "What is blue + yellow?" and "green".

Q: OK, I look in the API and there are about five million classes in the java.io package. How the heck do you know which ones to use?

A: The I/O API uses the modular 'chaining' concept so that you can hook together connection streams and chain streams (also called 'filter' streams) in a wide range of combinations to get just about anything you could want.

The chains don't have to stop at two levels; you can hook multiple chain streams to one another to get just the right amount of processing you need.

Most of the time, though, you'll use the same small handful of classes. If you're writing text files, BufferedReader and BufferedWriter (chained to FileReader and FileWriter) are probably all you need. If you're writing serialized objects, you can use ObjectOutputStream and ObjectInputStream (chained to FileInputStream and FileOutputStream).

In other words, 90% of what you might typically do with Java I/O can use what we've already covered.

Q: What about the new I/O nio classes added in 1.4?

A: The java.nio classes bring a big performance improvement and take greater advantage of native capabilities of the machine your program is running on. One of the key new features of nio is that you have direct control of buffers. Another new feature is non-blocking I/O, which means your I/O code doesn't just sit there, waiting, if there's nothing to read or write. Some of the existing classes (including FileInputStream and FileOutputStream) take advantage of some of the new features, under the covers. The nio classes are more complicated to use, however, so unless you *really* need the new features, you might want to stick with the simpler versions we've used here. Plus, if you're not careful, nio can lead to a performance *loss*. Non-nio I/O is probably right for 90% of what you'll normally do, especially if you're just getting started in Java.

But you *can* ease your way into the nio classes, by using FileInputStream and accessing its *channel* through the getChannel() method (added to FileInputStream as of version 1.4).

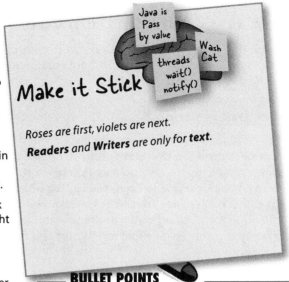

Make it Stick

Roses are first, violets are next.
Readers *and* ***Writers*** *are only for* ***text.***

BULLET POINTS

- To write a text file, start with a FileWriter connection stream.
- Chain the FileWriter to a BufferedWriter for efficiency.
- A File object represents a file at a particular path, but does not represent the actual contents of the file.
- With a File object you can create, traverse, and delete directories.
- Most streams that can use a String filename can use a File object as well, and a File object can be safer to use.
- To read a text file, start with a FileReader connection stream.
- Chain the FileReader to a BufferedReader for efficiency.
- To parse a text file, you need to be sure the file is written with some way to recognize the different elements. A common approach is to use some kind of character to separate the individual pieces.
- Use the String split() method to split a String up into individual tokens. A String with one separator will have two tokens, one on each side of the separator. *The separator doesn't count as a token.*

Version ID: A Big Serialization Gotcha

Now you've seen that I/O in Java is actually pretty simple, especially if you stick to the most common connection/chain combinations. But there's one issue you might *really* care about.

Version Control is crucial!

If you serialize an object, you must have the class in order to deserialize and use the object. OK, that's obvious. But what might be less obvious is what happens if you *change the class* in the meantime? Yikes. Imagine trying to bring back a Dog object when one of its instance variables (non-transient) has changed from a double to a String. That violates Java's type-safe sensibilities in a Big Way. But that's not the only change that might hurt compatibility. Think about the following:

Changes to a class that can hurt deserialization:

Deleting an instance variable

Changing the declared type of an instance variable

Changing a non-transient instance variable to transient

Moving a class up or down the inheritance hierarchy

Changing a class (anywhere in the object graph) from Serializable to not Serializable (by removing 'implements Serializable' from a class declaration)

Changing an instance variable to static

Changes to a class that are usually OK:

Adding new instance variables to the class (existing objects will deserialize with default values for the instance variables they didn't have when they were serialized)

Adding classes to the inheritance tree

Removing classes from the inheritance tree

Changing the access level of an instance variable has no affect on the ability of deserialization to assign a value to the variable

Changing an instance variable from transient to non-transient (previously-serialized objects will simply have a default value for the previously-transient variables)

① You write a Dog class

class version ID #343

Dog.class

② You serialize a Dog object using that class

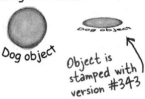

Dog object

Object is stamped with version #343

③ You change the Dog class

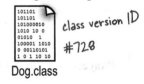

class version ID #728

Dog.class

④ You deserialize a Dog object using the changed class

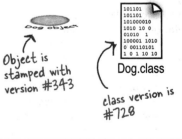

Object is stamped with version #343

Dog.class

class version is #728

⑤ Serailization fails!!

The JVM says, "you can't teach an old Dog new code".

Using the serialVersionUID

Each time an object is serialized, the object (including every object in its graph) is 'stamped' with a version ID number for the object's class. The ID is called the serialVersionUID, and it's computed based on information about the class structure. As an object is being deserialized, if the class has changed since the object was serialized, the class could have a different serialVersionUID, and deserialization will fail! But you can control this.

If you think there is ANY possibility that your class might *evolve*, put a serial version ID in your class.

When Java tries to deserialize an object, it compares the serialized object's serialVersionUID with that of the class the JVM is using for deserializing the object. For example, if a Dog instance was serialized with an ID of, say 23 (in reality a serialVersionUID is much longer), when the JVM deserializes the Dog object it will first compare the Dog object serialVersionUID with the Dog class serialVersionUID. If the two numbers don't match, the JVM assumes the class is not compatible with the previously-serialized object, and you'll get an exception during deserialization.

So, the solution is to put a serialVersionUID in your class, and then as the class evolves, the serialVersionUID will remain the same and the JVM will say, "OK, cool, the class is compatible with this serialized object." even though the class has actually changed.

This works *only* if you're careful with your class changes! In other words, *you* are taking responsibility for any issues that come up when an older object is brought back to life with a newer class.

To get a serialVersionUID for a class, use the serialver tool that ships with your Java development kit.

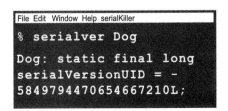

```
File Edit Window Help serialKiller
% serialver Dog
Dog: static final long
serialVersionUID = -
5849794470654667210L;
```

When you think your class might evolve after someone has serialized objects from it...

(1) Use the serialver command-line tool to get the version ID for your class

```
File Edit Window Help serialKiller
% serialver Dog
Dog: static final long
serialVersionUID = -
5849794470654667210L;
```

(2) Paste the output into your class

```
public class Dog {

    static final long serialVersionUID =
                    -6849794470754667710L;

    private String name;
    private int size;

    // method code here
}
```

(3) Be sure that when you make changes to the class, you take responsibility in your code for the consequences of the changes you made to the class! For example, be sure that your new Dog class can deal with an old Dog being deserialized with default values for instance variables added to the class *after* the Dog was serialized.

Code Kitchen

When you click "serializeIt", the current pattern will be saved.

"restore" loads the saved pattern back in, and resets the checkboxes.

Let's make the BeatBox save and restore our favorite pattern

Saving a BeatBox pattern

Remember, in the BeatBox, a drum pattern is nothing more than a bunch of checkboxes. When it's time to play the sequence, the code walks through the checkboxes to figure out which drums sounds are playing at each of the 16 beats. So to save a pattern, all we need to do is save the state of the checkboxes.

We can make a simple boolean array, holding the state of each of the 256 checkboxes. An array object is serializable as long as the things *in* the array are serializable, so we'll have no trouble saving an array of booleans.

To load a pattern back in, we read the single boolean array object (deserialize it), and restore the checkboxes. Most of the code you've already seen, in the Code Kitchen where we built the BeatBox GUI, so in this chapter, we look at only the save and restore code.

This CodeKitchen gets us ready for the next chapter, where instead of writing the pattern to a *file*, we send it over the *network* to the server. And instead of loading a pattern *in* from a file, we get patterns from the *server*, each time a participant sends one to the server.

Serializing a pattern

This is an inner class inside the BeatBox code.

```java
public class MySendListener implements ActionListener {

    public void actionPerformed(ActionEvent a) {

        boolean[] checkboxState = new boolean[256];

        for (int i = 0; i < 256; i++) {

            JCheckBox check = (JCheckBox) checkboxList.get(i);
            if (check.isSelected()) {
                checkboxState[i] = true;
            }
        }

        try {
            FileOutputStream fileStream = new FileOutputStream(new File("Checkbox.ser"));
            ObjectOutputStream os = new ObjectOutputStream(fileStream);
            os.writeObject(checkboxState);
        } catch(Exception ex) {
            ex.printStackTrace();
        }

    } // close method
} // close inner class
```

It all happens when the user clicks the button and the ActionEvent fires.

Make a boolean array to hold the state of each checkbox.

Walk through the checkboxList (ArrayList of checkboxes), and get the state of each one, and add it to the boolean array.

This part's a piece of cake. Just write/serialize the one boolean array!

Restoring a BeatBox pattern

This is pretty much the save in reverse... read the boolean array and use it to restore the state of the GUI checkboxes. It all happens when the user hits the "restore" 'button.

Restoring a pattern

This is another inner class inside the BeatBox class.

```java
public class MyReadInListener implements ActionListener {

    public void actionPerformed(ActionEvent a) {
        boolean[] checkboxState = null;
        try {
            FileInputStream fileIn = new FileInputStream(new File("Checkbox.ser"));
            ObjectInputStream is = new ObjectInputStream(fileIn);
            checkboxState = (boolean[]) is.readObject();
        } catch(Exception ex) {ex.printStackTrace();}


        for (int i = 0; i < 256; i++) {
            JCheckBox check = (JCheckBox) checkboxList.get(i);
            if (checkboxState[i]) {
                check.setSelected(true);
            } else {
                check.setSelected(false);
            }
        }

        sequencer.stop();
        buildTrackAndStart();

    } // close method
} // close inner class
```

Read the single object in the file (the boolean array) and cast it back to a boolean array (remember, readObject() returns a reference of type __Object__.

Now restore the state of each of the checkboxes in the ArrayList of actual JCheckBox objects (checkboxList).

Now stop whatever is currently playing, and rebuild the sequence using the new state of the checkboxes in the ArrayList.

> ### Sharpen your pencil
>
> This version has a huge limitation! When you hit the "serializeIt" button, it serializes automatically, to a file named "Checkbox.ser" (which gets created if it doesn't exist). But each time you save, you overwrite the previously-saved file.
>
> Improve the save and restore feature, by incorporating a JFileChooser so that you can name and save as many different patterns as you like, and load/restore from *any* of your previously-saved pattern files.

 Sharpen your pencil

Can they be saved?

Which of these do you think are, or should be, serializable? If not, why not? Not meaningful? Security risk? Only works for the current execution of the JVM? Make your best guess, without looking it up in the API.

Object type	Serializable?	If not, why not?
Object	Yes / No	_____
String	Yes / No	_____
File	Yes / No	_____
Date	Yes / No	_____
OutputStream	Yes / No	_____
JFrame	Yes / No	_____
Integer	Yes / No	_____
System	Yes / No	_____

What's Legal?

Circle the code fragments that would compile (assuming they're within a legal class).

```
FileReader fileReader = new FileReader();
BufferedReader reader = new BufferedReader(fileReader);
```

```
FileOutputStream f = new FileOutputStream(new File("Foo.ser"));
ObjectOutputStream os = new ObjectOutputStream(f);
```

```
BufferedReader reader = new BufferedReader(new FileReader(file));
String line = null;
while ((line = reader.readLine()) != null) {
    makeCard(line);
}
```

```
ObjectInputStream is = new ObjectInputStream(new FileOutputStream("Game.ser"));
GameCharacter oneAgain = (GameCharacter) is.readObject();
```

This chapter explored the wonerful world of
Java I/O. Your job is to decide whether each
of the following I/O-related statements is
true or false.

TRUE OR FALSE

1. Serialization is appropriate when saving data for non-Java programs to use.

2. Object state can be saved only by using serialization.

3. ObjectOutputStream is a class used to save serialized objects.

4. Chain streams can be used on their own or with connection streams.

5. A single call to writeObject() can cause many objects to be saved.

6. All classes are serializable by default.

7. The transient modifier allows you to make instance variables serializable.

8. If a superclass is not serializable then the subclass can't be serializable.

9. When objects are deserialized, they are read back in last-in, first out sequence.

10. When an object is deserialized, its constructor does not run.

11. Both serialization and saving to a text file can throw exceptions.

12. BufferedWriters can be chained to FileWriters.

13. File objects represent files, but not directories.

14. You can't force a buffer to send its data before it's full.

15. Both file readers and file writers can be buffered.

16. The String split() method includes separators as tokens in the result array.

17. *Any* change to a class breaks previously serialized objects of that class.

Code Magnets

This one's tricky, so we promoted it from an Exercise to full Puzzle status.
Reconstruct the code snippets to make a working Java program that
produces the output listed below? (You might not need all of the magnets,
and you may reuse a magnet more than once.)

```
class DungeonGame implements Serializable {

                                                    try {

FileOutputStream fos = new
    FileOutputStream("dg.ser");          short getZ() {

                                             return z;

    e.printStackTrace();

                                       oos.close();

ObjectInputStream ois = new
    ObjectInputStream(fis);              int getX() {

                                             return x;

System.out.println(d.getX()+d.getY()+d.getZ());

FileInputStream fis = new              public int x = 3;
    FileInputStream("dg.ser");         transient long y = 4;

                                       private short z = 5;

long getY() {
    return y;                     class DungeonTest {

    ois.close();
                                   import java.io.*;

fos.writeObject(d);
                                   } catch (Exception e) {

    d = (DungeonGame) ois.readObject();

ObjectOutputStream oos = new
    ObjectOutputStream(fos);               oos.writeObject(d);

    public static void main(String [] args) {
        DungeonGame d = new DungeonGame();
```

```
File Edit Window Help Torture
% java DungeonTest
12
8
```

Exercise Solutions

1. Serialization is appropriate when saving data for non-Java programs to use. **False**

2. Object state can be saved only by using serialization. **False**

3. ObjectOutputStream is a class used to save serialized objects. **True**

4. Chain streams can be usedon their own or with connection streams. **False**

5. A single call to writeObject() can cause many objects to be saved. **True**

6. All classes are serializable by default. **False**

7. The transient modifier allows you to make instance variables serializable. **False**

8. If a superclass is not serializable then the subclass can't be serializable. **False**

9. When objects are deserialized they are read back in last-in, first out sequence. **False**

10. When an object is deserialized, its constructor does not run. **True**

11. Both serialization and saving to a text file can throw exceptions. **True**

12. BufferedWriters can be chained to FileWriters. **True**

13. File objects represent files, but not directories. **False**

14. You can't force a buffer to send its data before it's full. **False**

15. Both file readers and file writers can optionally be buffered. **True**

16. The String split() method includes separators as tokens in the result array. **False**

17. *Any* change to a class breaks previously serialized objects of that class. **False**

Good thing we're finally at the answers. I was gettin' kind of tired of this chapter.

```java
import java.io.*;

class DungeonGame implements Serializable {
  public int x = 3;
  transient long y = 4;
  private short z = 5;
  int getX() {
    return x;
  }
  long getY() {
    return y;
  }
  short getZ() {
    return z;
  }
}

class DungeonTest {
  public static void main(String [] args) {
    DungeonGame d = new DungeonGame();
    System.out.println(d.getX() + d.getY() + d.getZ());
    try {
      FileOutputStream fos = new FileOutputStream("dg.ser");
      ObjectOutputStream oos = new ObjectOutputStream(fos);
      oos.writeObject(d);
      oos.close();
      FileInputStream fis = new FileInputStream("dg.ser");
      ObjectInputStream ois = new ObjectInputStream(fis);
      d = (DungeonGame) ois.readObject();
      ois.close();
    } catch (Exception e) {
      e.printStackTrace();
    }
    System.out.println(d.getX() + d.getY() + d.getZ());
  }
}
```

```
File Edit Window Help Escape
% java DungeonTest
12
8
```

Make a Connection

Connect with the outside world. Your Java program can reach out and touch a program on another machine. It's easy. All the low-level networking details are taken care of by classes in the java.net library. One of Java's big benefits is that sending and receiving data over a network is just I/O with a slightly different connection stream at the end of the chain. If you've got a BufferedReader, you can *read*. And the BufferedReader could care less if the data came out of a file or flew down an ethernet cable. In this chapter we'll connect to the outside world with sockets. We'll make *client* sockets. We'll make *server* sockets. We'll make *clients* and *servers*. And we'll make them talk to each other. Before the chapter's done, you'll have a fully-functional, multithreaded chat client. Did we just say *multithreaded*? Yes, now you *will* learn the secret of how to talk to Bob while simultaneously listening to Suzy.

Real-time Beat Box Chat

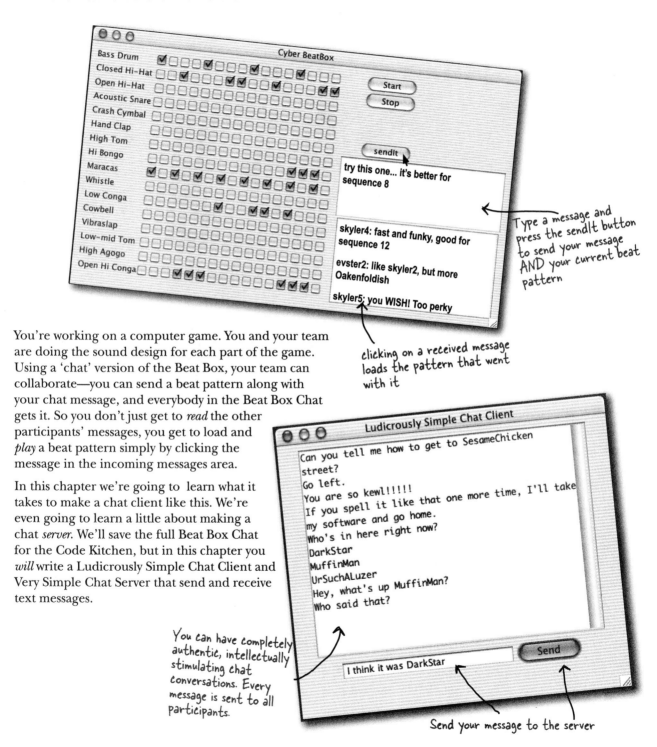

Type a message and press the sendIt button to send your message AND your current beat pattern

clicking on a received message loads the pattern that went with it

You're working on a computer game. You and your team are doing the sound design for each part of the game. Using a 'chat' version of the Beat Box, your team can collaborate—you can send a beat pattern along with your chat message, and everybody in the Beat Box Chat gets it. So you don't just get to *read* the other participants' messages, you get to load and *play* a beat pattern simply by clicking the message in the incoming messages area.

In this chapter we're going to learn what it takes to make a chat client like this. We're even going to learn a little about making a chat *server*. We'll save the full Beat Box Chat for the Code Kitchen, but in this chapter you *will* write a Ludicrously Simple Chat Client and Very Simple Chat Server that send and receive text messages.

You can have completely authentic, intellectually stimulating chat conversations. Every message is sent to all participants.

Send your message to the server

Chat Program Overview

The Client has to know about the Server.

The Server has to know about ALL the Clients.

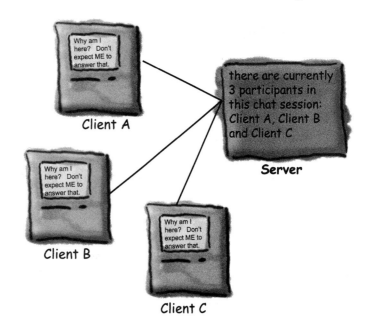

How it Works:

1 Client connects to the server

2 The server makes a connection and adds the client to the list of participants

3 Another client connects

4 Client A sends a message to the chat service

5 The server distributes the message to ALL participants (including the original sender)

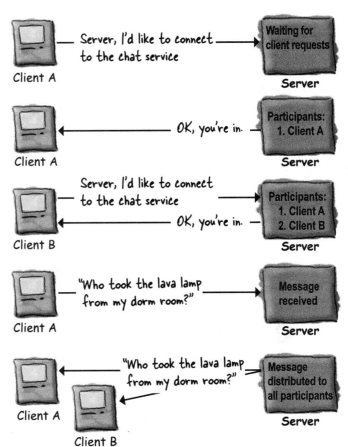

Connecting, Sending, and Receiving

The three things we have to learn to get the client working are :

1) How to establish the initial **connection** between the client and server

2) How to **send** messages *to* the server

3) How to **receive** messages *from* the server

There's a lot of low-level stuff that has to happen for these things to work. But we're lucky, because the Java API networking package (java.net) makes it a piece of cake for programmers. You'll see a lot more GUI code than networking and I/O code.

And that's not all.

Lurking within the simple chat client is a problem we haven't faced so far in this book: doing two things at the same time. Establishing a connection is a one-time operation (that either works or fails). But after that, a chat participant wants to *send outgoing messages* and **simultaneously** *receive incoming messages* from the other participants (via the server). Hmmmm... that one's going to take a little thought, but we'll get there in just a few pages.

❶ Connect

Client connects to the server by establishing a **Socket** connection.

Make a socket connection to 196.164.1.103 at port 5000

Client A

chat server at 196.164.1.103, port 5000

Server

❷ Send

Client **sends** a message to the server

writer.println(aMessage)

Client A

Server machine at 196.164.1.103

Server

❸ Receive

Client **gets** a message from the server

String s = reader.readLine()

Client A

Server machine at 196.164.1.103

Server

Make a network Socket connection

To connect to another machine, we need a Socket connection. A Socket (java.net.Socket class) is an object that represents a network connection between two machines. What's a connection? A *relationship* between two machines, where **two pieces of software know about each other**. Most importantly, those two pieces of software know how to *communicate* with each other. In other words, how to send *bits* to each other.

We don't care about the low-level details, thankfully, because they're handled at a much lower place in the 'networking stack'. If you don't know what the 'networking stack' is, don't worry about it. It's just a way of looking at the layers that information (bits) must travel through to get from a Java program running in a JVM on some OS, to physical hardware (ethernet cables, for example), and back again on some other machine. *Somebody* has to take care of all the dirty details. But not you. That somebody is a combination of OS-specific software and the Java networking API. The part that you have to worry about is high-level—make that *very* high-level—and shockingly simple. Ready?

To make a Socket connection, you need to know two things about the server: who it is, and which port it's running on.

In other words,

IP address and TCP port number.

TCP port number

```
Socket chatSocket = new Socket("196.164.1.103", 5000);
```

IP address for the server

The chat server is at 196.164.1.103, port 5000. When I need to talk to him, that's where I'll send the message.

Socket connection to port 5000 on the server at 196.164.1.103

Socket connection back to the client at 196.164.1.100, port 4242

This client is at 196.164.1.100, port 4242. When I need to talk to him, that's where I'll send the message.

Client

Server

A Socket connection means the two machines have information about each other, including network location (IP address) and TCP port.

A TCP port is just a number. A 16-bit number that identifies a specific program on the server.

Your internet web (HTTP) server runs on port 80. That's a standard. If you've got a Telnet server, its running on port 23. FTP? 20. POP3 mail server? 110. SMTP? 25. The Time server sits at 37. Think of port numbers as unique identifiers. They represent a logical connection to a particular piece of software running on the server. That's it. You can't spin your hardware box around and find a TCP port. For one thing, you have 65536 of them on a server (0 - 65535). So they obviously don't represent a place to plug in physical devices. They're just a number representing an application.

Without port numbers, the server would have no way of knowing which application a client wanted to connect to. And since each application might have its own unique protocol, think of the trouble you'd have without these identifiers. What if your web browser, for example, landed at the POP3 mail server instead of the HTTP server? The mail server won't know how to parse an HTTP request! And even if it did, the POP3 server doesn't know anything about servicing the HTTP request.

When you write a server program, you'll include code that tells the program which port number you want it to run on (you'll see how to do this in Java a little later in this chapter). In the Chat program we're writing in this chapter, we picked 5000. Just because we wanted to. And because it met the criteria that it be a number between 1024 and 65535. Why 1024? Because 0 through 1023 are reserved for the well-known services like the ones we just talked about.

And if you're writing services (server programs) to run on a company network, you should check with the sys-admins to find out which ports are already taken. Your sys-admins might tell you, for example, that you can't use any port number below, say, 3000. In any case, if you value your limbs, you won't assign port numbers with abandon. Unless it's your *home* network. In which case you just have to check with your *kids*.

Well-known TCP port numbers for common server applications

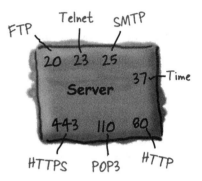

A server can have up to 65536 different server apps running, one per port.

The TCP port numbers from 0 to 1023 are reserved for well-known services. Don't use them for your own server programs!*

The chat server we're writing uses port 5000. We just picked a number between 1024 and 65535.

*Well, you *might* be able to use one of these, but the sys-admin where you work will probably kill you.

there are no Dumb Questions

Q: How do you know the port number of the server program you want to talk to?

A: That depends on whether the program is one of the well-known services. If you're trying to connect to a well-known service, like the ones on the opposite page (HTTP, SMTP, FTP, etc.) you can look these up on the internet (Google "Well-Known TCP Port"). Or ask your friendly neighborhood sys-admin.

But if the program isn't one of the well-known services, you need to find out from whoever is deploying the service. Ask him. Or her. Typically, if someone writes a network service and wants others to write clients for it, they'll publish the IP address, port number, and protocol for the service. For example, if you want to write a client for a GO game server, you can visit one of the GO server sites and find information about how to write a client for that particular server.

Q: Can there ever be more than one program running on a single port? In other words, can two applications on the same server have the same port number?

A: No! If you try to bind a program to a port that is already in use, you'll get a BindException. To *bind* a program to a port just means starting up a server application and telling it to run on a particular port. Again, you'll learn more about this when we get to the server part of this chapter.

IP address is the <u>mall</u>

Port number is the specific store in the mall

IP address is like specifying a particular shopping mall, say, "Flatirons Marketplace"

Port number is like naming a specific store, say, "Bob's CD Shop"

Brain Barbell

OK, you got a Socket connection. The client and the server know the IP address and TCP port number for each other. Now what? How do you communicate over that connection? In other words, how do you move bits from one to the other? Imagine the kinds of messages your chat client needs to send and receive.

How do these two actually talk to each other?

Client   Server

To read data from a Socket, use a BufferedReader

To communicate over a Socket connection, you use streams. Regular old I/O streams, just like we used in the last chapter. One of the coolest features in Java is that most of your I/O work won't care what your high-level chain stream is actually connected to. In other words, you can use a BufferedReader just like you did when you were writing to a file, the difference is that the underlying connection stream is connected to a *Socket* rather than a *File!*

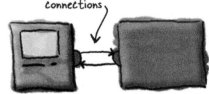

input and output streams to and from the Socket connections

1 **Make a Socket connection to the server**

The port number, which you know because we TOLD you that 5000 is the port number for our chat server.

```
Socket chatSocket = new Socket("127.0.0.1", 5000);
```

127.0.0.1 is the IP address for "localhost", in other words, the one this code is running on. You can use this when you're testing your client and server on a single, stand-alone machine.

2 **Make an InputStreamReader chained to the Socket's low-level (connection) input stream**

```
InputStreamReader stream = new InputStreamReader(chatSocket.getInputStream());
```

InputStreamReader is a 'bridge' between a low-level byte stream (like the one coming from the Socket) and a high-level character stream (like the BufferedReader we're after as our top of the chain stream).

All we have to do is ASK the socket for an input stream! It's a low-level connection stream, but we're just gonna chain it to something more text-friendly.

3 **Make a BufferedReader and read!**

Chain the BufferedReader to the InputStreamReader(which was chained to the low-level connection stream we got from the Socket.)

```
BufferedReader reader = new BufferedReader(stream);
String message = reader.readLine();
```

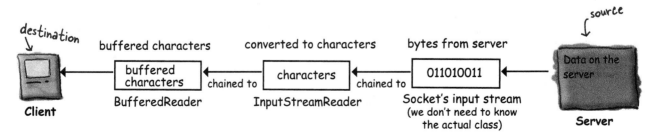

destination

buffered characters   *converted to characters*   *bytes from server*   *source*

| | buffered characters | | characters | | 011010011 | | Data on the server |

Client   BufferedReader   InputStreamReader   Socket's input stream (we don't need to know the actual class)   Server

To write data to a Socket, use a PrintWriter

We didn't use PrintWriter in the last chapter, we used BufferedWriter. We have a choice here, but when you're writing one String at a time, PrintWriter is the standard choice. And you'll recognize the two key methods in PrintWriter, print() and println()! Just like good ol' System.out.

1 **Make a <u>Socket</u> connection to the server**

this part's the same as it was on the opposite page —— to write to the server, we still have to connect to it.

```
Socket chatSocket = new Socket("127.0.0.1", 5000);
```

2 **Make a <u>PrintWriter</u> chained to the Socket's low-level (connection) output stream**

```
PrintWriter writer = new PrintWriter(chatSocket.getOutputStream());
```

PrintWriter acts as its own bridge between character data and the bytes it gets from the Socket's low-level output stream. By chaining a PrintWriter to the Socket's output stream, we can write Strings to the Socket connection.

The Socket gives us a low-level connection stream and we chain it to the PrintWriter by giving it to the PrintWriter constructor.

3 **Write (print) something**

```
writer.println("message to send");
writer.print("another message");
```
← *println() adds a new line at the end of what it sends.*
← *print() doesn't add the new line.*

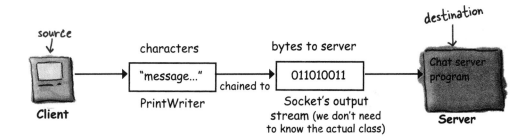

destination

source	characters	bytes to server	
Client	"message..." PrintWriter	011010011 Socket's output stream (we don't need to know the actual class)	Chat server program Server

chained to

The DailyAdviceClient

Before we start building the Chat app, let's start with something a little smaller. The Advice Guy is a server program that offers up practical, inspirational tips to get you through those long days of coding.

We're building a client for The Advice Guy program, which pulls a message from the server each time it connects.

What are you waiting for? Who *knows* what opportunities you've missed without this app.

The Advice Guy

❶ Connect

Client connects to the server and gets an input stream from it

❷ Read

Client reads a message from the server

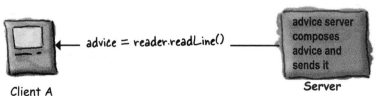

DailyAdviceClient code

This program makes a Socket, makes a BufferedReader (with the
help of other streams), and reads a single line from the server
application (whatever is running at port 4242).

```java
import java.io.*;
import java.net.*;        ← class Socket is in java.net

public class DailyAdviceClient {

    public void go() {
        try {              ← a lot can go wrong here
            Socket s = new Socket("127.0.0.1", 4242);

            InputStreamReader streamReader = new InputStreamReader(s.getInputStream());
            BufferedReader reader = new BufferedReader(streamReader);

            String advice = reader.readLine();
            System.out.println("Today you should: " + advice);

            reader.close();   ← this closes ALL the streams

        } catch(IOException ex) {
            ex.printStackTrace();
        }
    }

    public static void main(String[] args) {
        DailyAdviceClient client = new DailyAdviceClient();
        client.go();
    }
}
```

make a Socket connection to whatever is running on port 4242, on the same host this code is running on. (The 'localhost')

chain a BufferedReader to an InputStreamReader to the input stream from the Socket.

this readLine() is EXACTLY the same as if you were using a BufferedReader chained to a FILE.. In other words, by the time you call a BufferedWriter method, the writer doesn't know or care where the characters came from.

Sharpen your pencil

Test your memory of the streams/classes for reading and writing from a Socket. Try not to look at the opposite page!

To **read** text from a Socket:

source

Client

write/draw in the chain of streams the client uses to read from the server

Server

To **send** text to a Socket:

destination

Client

write/draw in the chain of streams the client uses to send something to the server

Server

Sharpen your pencil

Fill in the blanks:

What two pieces of information does the client need in order to make a
Socket connection with a server? _____   _____

Which TCP port numbers are reserved for 'well-known services' like HTTP and FTP? _____

TRUE or FALSE: The range of valid TCP port numbers can be represented
by a short primitive? _____

Writing a simple server

So what's it take to write a server application? Just a couple of Sockets. Yes, a couple as in *two*. A ServerSocket, which waits for client requests (when a client makes a new Socket()) and a plain old Socket socket to use for communication with the client.

How it Works:

1 Server application makes a ServerSocket, on a specific port

```
ServerSocket serverSock = new ServerSocket(4242);
```

This starts the server application listening for client requests coming in for port 4242.

2 Client makes a Socket connection to the server application

```
Socket sock = new Socket("190.165.1.103", 4242);
```

Client knows the IP address and port number (published or given to him by whomever configures the server app to be on that port)

3 Server makes a new Socket to communicate with this client

```
Socket sock = serverSock.accept();
```

The accept() method blocks (just sits there) while it's waiting for a client Socket connection. When a client finally tries to connect, the method returns a plain old Socket (on a *different* port) that knows how to communicate with the client (i.e., knows the *client's* IP address and port number). The Socket is on a different port than the ServerSocket, so that the ServerSocket can go back to waiting for other clients.

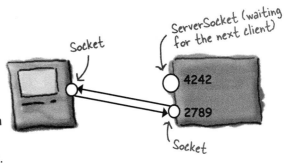

DailyAdviceServer code

This program makes a ServerSocket and waits for client requests. When it gets a client request (i.e. client said new Socket() for this application), the server makes a new Socket connection to that client. The server makes a PrintWriter (using the Socket's output stream) and sends a message to the client.

remember the imports

daily advice comes from this array

(remember, these Strings were word-wrapped by the code editor. Never hit return in the middle of a String!)

```java
import java.io.*;
import java.net.*;

public class DailyAdviceServer {

    String[] adviceList = {"Take smaller bites", "Go for the tight jeans. No they do NOT
make you look fat.", "One word: inappropriate", "Just for today, be honest. Tell your
boss what you *really* think", "You might want to rethink that haircut."};

    public void go() {

        try {
            ServerSocket serverSock = new ServerSocket(4242);

            while(true) {

                Socket sock = serverSock.accept();

                PrintWriter writer = new PrintWriter(sock.getOutputStream());
                String advice = getAdvice();
                writer.println(advice);
                writer.close();
                System.out.println(advice);
            }

        } catch(IOException ex) {
            ex.printStackTrace();
        }
    } // close go

    private String getAdvice() {
        int random = (int) (Math.random() * adviceList.length);
        return adviceList[random];
    }

    public static void main(String[] args) {
        DailyAdviceServer server = new DailyAdviceServer();
        server.go();
    }
}
```

ServerSocket makes this server application 'listen' for client requests on port 4242 on the machine this code is running on.

The server goes into a permanent loop, waiting for (and servicing) client requests

the accept method blocks (just sits there) until a request comes in, and then the method returns a Socket (on some anonymous port) for communicating with the client

now we use the Socket connection to the client to make a PrintWriter and send it (println()) a String advice message. Then we close the Socket because we're done with this client.

Brain Barbell

How does the server know how to communicate with the client?

The client knows the IP address and port number of the server, but how is the server able to make a Socket connection with the client (and make input and output streams)?

Think about how / when / where the server gets knowledge about the client.

there are no Dumb Questions

Q: The advice server code on the opposite page has a VERY serious limitation—it looks like it can handle only one client at a time!

A: Yes, that's right. It can't accept a request from a client until it has finished with the current client and started the next iteration of the infinite loop (where it sits at the accept() call until a request comes in, at which time it makes a Socket with the new client and starts the process over again).

Q: Let me rephrase the problem: how can you make a server that can handle multiple clients concurrently??? This would *never* work for a chat server, for instance.

A: Ah, that's simple, really. Use separate threads, and give each new client Socket to a new thread. We're just about to learn how to do that!

BULLET POINTS

- Client and server applications communicate over a Socket connection.

- A Socket represents a connection between two applications which may (or may not) be running on two different physical machines.

- A client must know the IP address (or domain name) and TCP port number of the server application.

- A TCP port is a 16-bit unsigned number assigned to a specific server application. TCP port numbers allow different clients to connect to the same machine but communicate with different applications running on that machine.

- The port numbers from 0 through 1023 are reserved for 'well-known services' including HTTP, FTP, SMTP, etc.

- A client connects to a server by making a Server socket
  `Socket s = new Socket("127.0.0.1", 4200);`

- Once connected, a client can get input and output streams from the socket. These are low-level 'connection' streams.
  `sock.getInputStream();`

- To read text data from the server, create a BufferedReader, chained to an InputStreamReader, which is chained to the input stream from the Socket.

- InputStreamReader is a 'bridge' stream that takes in bytes and converts them to text (character) data. It's used primarily to act as the middle chain between the high-level BufferedReader and the low-level Socket input stream.

- To write text data to the server, create a PrintWriter chained directly to the Socket's output stream. Call the print() or println() methods to send Strings to the server.

- Servers use a ServerSocket that waits for client requests on a particular port number.

- When a ServerSocket gets a request, it 'accepts' the request by making a Socket connection with the client.

Writing a Chat Client

We'll write the Chat client application in two stages. First we'll make a send-only version that sends messages to the server but doesn't get to read any of the messages from other participants (an exciting and mysterious twist to the whole chat room concept).

Then we'll go for the full chat monty and make one that both sends *and* receives chat messages.

Version One: send-only

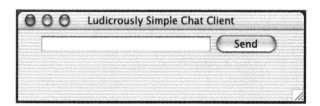

Type a message, then press 'Send' to send it to the server. We won't get any messages FROM the server in this version, so there's no scrolling text area.

Code outline

```
public class SimpleChatClientA {

    JTextField outgoing;
    PrintWriter writer;
    Socket sock;

    public void go() {
        // make gui and register a listener with the send button
        // call the setUpNetworking() method
    }

    private void setUpNetworking() {
        // make a Socket, then make a PrintWriter
        // assign the PrintWriter to writer instance variable
    }

    public class SendButtonListener implements ActionListener {
        public void actionPerformed(ActionEvent ev) {
            // get the text from the text field and
            // send it to the server using the writer (a PrintWriter)
        }
    }  // close SendButtonListener inner class

} // close outer class
```

```
import java.io.*;
import java.net.*;                    imports for the streams (java.io),
import javax.swing.*;                 Socket (java.net) and the GUI
import java.awt.*;                    stuff
import java.awt.event.*;

public class SimpleChatClientA {

    JTextField outgoing;
    PrintWriter writer;
    Socket sock;

    public void go() {
        JFrame frame = new JFrame("Ludicrously Simple Chat Client");
        JPanel mainPanel = new JPanel();
        outgoing = new JTextField(20);
        JButton sendButton = new JButton("Send");               build the GUI, nothing new
        sendButton.addActionListener(new SendButtonListener());  here, and nothing related to
        mainPanel.add(outgoing);                                networking or I/O.
        mainPanel.add(sendButton);
        frame.getContentPane().add(BorderLayout.CENTER, mainPanel);
        setUpNetworking();
        frame.setSize(400,500);
        frame.setVisible(true);
    } // close go
                                         we're using localhost so
                                         you can test the client
    private void setUpNetworking() {     and server on one machine
        try {
            sock = new Socket("127.0.0.1", 5000);              This is where we make the Socket
            writer = new PrintWriter(sock.getOutputStream());   and the PrintWriter (it's called
            System.out.println("networking established");      from the go() method right before
        } catch(IOException ex) {                              displaying the app GUI)
            ex.printStackTrace();
        }
    } // close setUpNetworking

    public class SendButtonListener implements ActionListener {
        public void actionPerformed(ActionEvent ev) {
            try {
                writer.println(outgoing.getText());      Now we actually do the writing.
                writer.flush();                          Remember, the writer is chained to
                                                         the input stream from the Socket, so
            } catch(Exception ex) {                      whenever we do a println(), it goes
                ex.printStackTrace();                    over the network to the server!
            }
            outgoing.setText("");
            outgoing.requestFocus();
        }
    } // close SendButtonListener inner class

    public static void main(String[] args) {
        new SimpleChatClientA().go();
    }
} // close outer class
```

> If you want to try this now, type in
> the Ready-bake chat server code
> listed at the end of this chapter.
> First, start the server in one terminal.
> Next, use another terminal to start
> this client.

Version Two: send and receive

Ludicrously Simple Chat Client

Can you tell me how to get to SesameChicken
street?
Go left.
You are so kewl!!!!!
If you spell it like that one more time, I'll take
my software and go home.
Who's in here right now?
DarkStar
MuffinMan
UrSuchALuzer
Hey, what's up MuffinMan?
Who said that?

incoming messages

I think it was DarkStar

Send

outgoing message

The Server sends a message to all client participants, as soon as the message is received by the server. When a client sends a message, it doesn't appear in the incoming message display area until the server sends it to everyone.

Big Question: *HOW* do you get messages from the server?

Should be easy; when you set up the networking make an input stream as well (probably a BufferedReader). Then read messages using readLine().

Bigger Question: *WHEN* do you get messages from the server?

Think about that. What are the options?

① Option One: Poll the server every 20 seconds

Pros: Well, it's do-able

Cons: How does the server know what you've seen and what you haven't? The server would have to store the messages, rather than just doing a distribute-and-forget each time it gets one. And why 20 seconds? A delay like this affects usability, but as you reduce the delay, you risk hitting your server needlessly. Inefficient.

② Option Two: Read something in from the server each time the user sends a message.

Pros: Do-able, very easy

Cons: Stupid. Why choose such an arbitrary time to check for messages? What if a user is a lurker and doesn't send anything?

③ Option Three: Read messages as soon as they're sent from the server

Pros: Most efficient, best usability

Cons: How do you do you do two things at the same time? Where would you put this code? You'd need a loop somewhere that was always waiting to read from the server. But where would that go? Once you launch the GUI, nothing happens until an event is fired by a GUI component.

In Java you really CAN walk and chew gum at the same time.

You know by now that we're going with option three.

We want something to run continuously, checking for messages from the server, but *without interrupting the user's ability to interact with the GUI!* So while the user is happily typing new messages or scrolling through the incoming messages, we want something *behind the scenes* to keep reading in new input from the server.

That means we finally need a new thread. A new, separate stack

We want everything we did in the Send-Only version (version one) to work the same way, while a new *process* runs along side that reads information from the server and displays it in the incoming text area.

Well, not quite. Unless you have multiple processors on your computer, each new Java thread is not actually a separate process running on the OS. But it almost *feels* as though it is.

Multithreading in Java

Java has multiple threading built right into the fabric of the language. And it's a snap to make a new thread of execution:

```
Thread t = new Thread();
t.start();
```

That's it. By creating a new Thread *object*, you've launched a separate *thread of execution*, with its very own call stack.

Except for one problem.

That thread doesn't actually *do* anything, so the thread "dies" virtually the instant it's born. When a thread dies, its new stack disappears again. End of story.

So we're missing one key component—the thread's *job*. In other words, we need the code that you want to have run by a separate thread.

Multiple threading in Java means we have to look at both the *thread* and the *job* that's *run* by the thread. And we'll also have to look at the Thread *class* in the java.lang package. (Remember, java.lang is the package you get imported for free, implicitly, and it's where the classes most fundamental to the language live, including String and System.)

Java has multiple threads but only one Thread class

We can talk about *thread* with a lower-case 't' and **Thread** with a capital 'T'. When you see *thread*, we're talking about a separate thread of execution. In other words, a separate call stack. When you see **Thread**, think of the Java naming convention. What, in Java, starts with a capital letter? Classes and interfaces. In this case, **Thread** is a class in the java.lang package. A **Thread** object represents a *thread of execution*; you'll create an instance of class **Thread** each time you want to start up a new *thread* of execution.

> A thread is a separate 'thread of execution'. In other words, a separate call stack.
>
> A Thread is a Java class that represents a thread.
>
> To make a thread, make a Thread.

thread

main thread

another thread started by the code

A thread (lower-case 't') is a separate thread of execution. That means a separate call stack. Every Java application starts up a main thread—the thread that puts the main() method on the bottom of the stack. The JVM is responsible for starting the main thread (and other threads, as it chooses, including the garbage collection thread). As a programmer, you can write code to start other threads of your own.

Thread

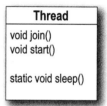

java.lang.Thread class

Thread (capital 'T') is a class that represents a thread of execution. It has methods for starting a thread, joining one thread with another, and putting a thread to sleep. (It has more methods; these are just the crucial ones we need to use now).

What does it mean to have more than one call stack?

With more than one call stack, you get the *appearance* of having multiple things happen at the same time. In reality, only a true multiprocessor system can actually do more than one thing at a time, but with Java threads, it can *appear* that you're doing several things simultaneously. In other words, execution can move back and forth between stacks so rapidly that you feel as though all stacks are executing at the same time. Remember, Java is just a process running on your underlying OS. So first, Java *itself* has to be 'the currently executing process' on the OS. But once Java gets its turn to execute, exactly *what* does the JVM *run*? Which bytecodes execute? Whatever is on the top of the currently-running stack! And in 100 milliseconds, the currently executing code might switch to a *different* method on a *different* stack.

One of the things a thread must do is keep track of which statement (of which method) is currently executing on the thread's stack.

It might look something like this:

the active thread

1 **The JVM calls the main() method.**

```
public static void main(String[] args) {
    ...
}
```

```
main()
```
main thread

---

a new thread starts and becomes the active thread

2 **main() starts a new thread. The main thread is temporarily frozen while the new thread starts running.**

```
Runnable r = new MyThreadJob();
Thread t = new Thread(r);
t.start();
Dog d = new Dog();
```
you'll learn what this means in just a moment...

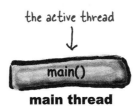

```
t.start()
```
```
main()
```
main thread

```
run()
```
user thread A

---

the active thread again

3 **The JVM switches between the new thread (user thread A) and the original main thread, until both threads complete.**

```
Dog()
```
```
main()
```
main thread

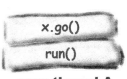

```
x.go()
```
```
run()
```
user thread A

How to launch a new thread:

❶ Make a Runnable object (the thread's job)

```
Runnable threadJob = new MyRunnable();
```

Runnable is an interface you'll learn about on the next page. You'll write a class that implements the Runnable interface, and that class is where you'll define the work that a thread will perform. In other words, the method that will be run from the thread's new call stack.

❷ Make a Thread object (the worker) and give it a Runnable (the job)

```
Thread myThread = new Thread(threadJob);
```

Pass the new Runnable object to the Thread constructor. This tells the new Thread object which method to put on the bottom of the new stack—the Runnable's run() method.

❸ Start the Thread

```
myThread.start();
```

Nothing happens until you call the Thread's start() method. That's when you go from having just a Thread instance to having a new thread of execution. When the new thread starts up, it takes the Runnable object's run() method and puts it on the bottom of the new thread's stack.

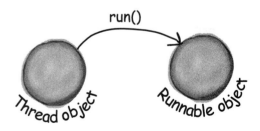

Every Thread needs a job to do.
A method to put on the new thread stack.

All I need is a real job. Just give me a Runnable and I'll get to work!

Thread

Runnable is to a Thread what a job is to a worker. A Runnable is the job a thread is supposed to run.

A Runnable holds the method that goes on the bottom of the new thread's stack: run().

A Thread object needs a job. A job the thread will run when the thread is started. That job is actually the first method that goes on the new thread's stack, and it must always be a method that looks like this:

```
public void run() {
    // code that will be run by the new thread
}
```

The Runnable interface defines only one method, public void run(). (Remember, it's an interface so the method is public regardless of whether you type it in that way.)

How does the thread know which method to put at the bottom of the stack? Because Runnable defines a contract. Because Runnable is an interface. A thread's job can be defined in any class that implements the Runnable interface. The thread cares only that you pass the Thread constructor an object of a class that implements Runnable.

When you pass a Runnable to a Thread constructor, you're really just giving the Thread a way to get to a run() method. You're giving the Thread its job to do.

To make a job for your thread, implement the Runnable interface

Runnable is in the java.lang package, so you don't need to import it.

```java
public class MyRunnable implements Runnable {

    public void run() {
        go();
    }

    public void go() {
        doMore();
    }

    public void doMore() {
        System.out.println("top o' the stack");
    }
}
```

② *Runnable has only one method to implement: public void run() (with no arguments). This is where you put the JOB the thread is supposed to run. This is the method that goes at the bottom of the new stack.*

```java
class ThreadTester {

    public static void main (String[] args) {

        Runnable threadJob = new MyRunnable();
        Thread myThread = new Thread(threadJob);

        myThread .start();

        System.out.println("back in main");
    }
}
```

Pass the new Runnable instance into the new Thread constructor. This tells the thread what method to put on the bottom of the new stack. In other words, the first method that the new thread will run.

①

You won't get a new thread of execution until you call start() on the Thread instance. A thread is not really a thread until you start it. Before that, it's just a Thread instance, like any other object, but it won't have any real 'threadness'.

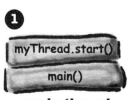

①

| myThread.start() |
| main() |

main thread

②

| doMore() |
| go() |
| run() |

new thread

Brain Barbell

What do you think the output will be if you run the ThreadTester class? (we'll find out in a few pages)

The three states of a new thread

this is where a thread wants to be!

`Thread t = new Thread(r);`

NEW	**RUNNABLE**	**RUNNING**

t.start();

Selected to run

"I'm waiting to get started."

"I'm good to go!"

"Can I supersize that for you?"

Thread t = new Thread(r);

A Thread instance has been created but not started. In other words, there is a Thread *object*, but no *thread of execution*.

t.start();

When you start the thread, it moves into the runnable state. This means the thread is ready to run and just waiting for its Big Chance to be selected for execution. At this point, there is a new call stack for this thread.

This is the state all threads lust after! To be The Chosen One. The Currently Running Thread. Only the JVM thread scheduler can make that decision. You can sometimes *influence* that decision, but you cannot force a thread to move from runnable to running. In the running state, a thread (and ONLY this thread) has an active call stack, and the method on the top of the stack is executing.

But there's more. Once the thread becomes runnable, it can move back and forth between runnable, running, and an additional state: *temporarily not runnable* (also known as 'blocked').

Typical runnable/running loop

RUNNABLE   **RUNNING**

Typically, a thread moves back and forth between runnable and running, as the JVM thread scheduler selects a thread to run and then kicks it back out so another thread gets a chance.

Selected to run

Sent back to runnable so another thread can have a chance

A thread can be made temporarily not-runnable

RUNNABLE   **RUNNING**

The thread scheduler can move a running thread into a blocked state, for a variety of reasons. For example, the thread might be executing code to read from a Socket input stream, but there isn't any data to read. The scheduler will move the thread out of the running state until something becomes available. Or the executing code might have told the thread to put itself to sleep (sleep()). Or the thread might be waiting because it tried to call a method on an object, and that object was 'locked'. In that case, the thread can't continue until the object's lock is freed by the thread that has it.

All of those conditions (and more) cause a thread to become temporarily not-runnable.

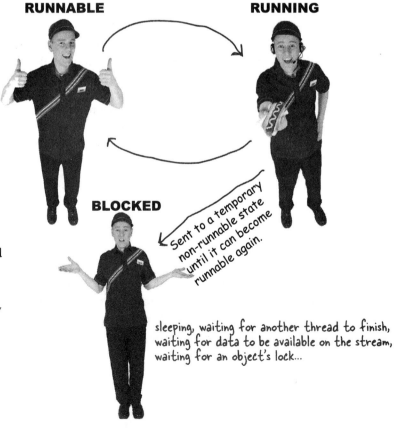

BLOCKED

Sent to a temporary non-runnable state until it can become runnable again.

sleeping, waiting for another thread to finish, waiting for data to be available on the stream, waiting for an object's lock...

The Thread Scheduler

The thread scheduler makes all the decisions about who moves from runnable to running, and about when (and under what circumstances) a thread leaves the running state. The scheduler decides who runs, and for how long, and where the threads go when the scheduler decides to kick them out of the currently-running state.

You can't control the scheduler. There is no API for calling methods on the scheduler. Most importantly, there are no guarantees about scheduling! (There are a few *almost*-guarantees, but even those are a little fuzzy.)

The bottom line is this: *do not base your program's correctness on the scheduler working in a particular way!* The scheduler implementations are different for different JVM's, and even running the same program on the same machine can give you different results. One of the worst mistakes new Java programmers make is to test their multi-threaded program on a single machine, and assume the thread scheduler will always work that way, regardless of where the program runs.

So what does this mean for write-once-run-anywhere? It means that to write platform-independent Java code, your multi-threaded program must work no matter *how* the thread scheduler behaves. That means that you can't be dependent on, for example, the scheduler making sure all the threads take nice, perfectly fair and equal turns at the running state. Although highly unlikely today, your program might end up running on a JVM with a scheduler that says, "OK thread five, you're up, and as far as I'm concerned, you can stay here until you're done, when your run() method completes."

The secret to almost everything is *sleep*. That's right, *sleep*. Putting a thread to sleep, even for a few milliseconds, forces the currently-running thread to leave the running state, thus giving another thread a chance to run. The thread's sleep() method does come with *one* guarantee: a sleeping thread will *not* become the currently-running thread before the the length of its sleep time has expired. For example, if you tell your thread to sleep for two seconds (2,000 milliseconds), that thread can never become the running thread again until sometime *after* the two seconds have passed.

Number four, you've had enough time. Back to runnable. Number two, looks like you're up!

Oh, now it looks like you're gonna have to sleep. Number five, come take his place. Number two, you're still sleeping...

The thread scheduler makes all the decisions about who runs and who doesn't. He usually makes the threads take turns, nicely. But there's no guarantee about that. He might let one thread run to its heart's content while the other threads 'starve'.

An example of how unpredictable the scheduler can be...

Running this code on one machine:

```java
public class MyRunnable implements Runnable {

    public void run() {
        go();
    }

    public void go() {
        doMore();
    }

    public void doMore() {
        System.out.println("top o' the stack");
    }
}


class ThreadTestDrive {

    public static void main (String[] args) {

        Runnable threadJob = new MyRunnable();
        Thread myThread = new Thread(threadJob);

        myThread.start();

        System.out.println("back in main");
    }
}
```

Notice how the order changes randomly. Sometimes the new thread finishes first, and sometimes the main thread finishes first.

Produced this output:

```
File Edit Window Help PickMe
% java ThreadTestDrive
back in main
top o' the stack
% java ThreadTestDrive
top o' the stack
back in main
% java ThreadTestDrive
top o' the stack
back in main
% java ThreadTestDrive
top o' the stack
back in main
% java ThreadTestDrive
top o' the stack
back in main
% java ThreadTestDrive
top o' the stack
back in main
% java ThreadTestDrive
back in main
top o' the stack
```

How did we end up with different results?

Sometimes it runs like this:

main() starts the new thread	The scheduler sends the main thread out of running and back to runnable, so that the new thread can run.	The scheduler lets the new thread run to completion, printing out "top o' the stack"	The new thread goes away, because its run() completed. The main thread once again becomes the running thread, and prints "back in main"

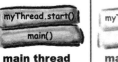

main thread

main thread

new thread

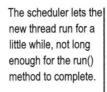

main thread

time

And sometimes it runs like this:

main() starts the new thread	The scheduler sends the main thread out of running and back to runnable, so that the new thread can run.	The scheduler lets the new thread run for a little while, not long enough for the run() method to complete.	The scheduler sends the new thread back to runnable.	The scheduler selects the main thread to be the running thread again. Main prints out "back in main"	The new thread returns to the running state and prints out "top o' the stack".

main thread

main thread

new thread

new thread

main thread

new thread

time

there are no Dumb Questions

Q: I've seen examples that don't use a separate Runnable implementation, but instead just make a subclass of Thread and override the Thread's run() method. That way, you call the Thread's no-arg constructor when you make the new thread;

Thread t = new Thread(); // no Runnable

A: Yes, that *is* another way of making your own thread, but think about it from an OO perspective. What's the purpose of subclassing? Remember that we're talking about two different things here—the *Thread* and the thread's *job*. From an OO view, those two are very separate activities, and belong in separate classes. The only time you want to subclass/extend the Thread class, is if you are making a new and more specific type of Thread. In other words, if you think of the Thread as the worker, don't extend the Thread class unless you need more specific *worker* behaviors. But if all you need is a new *job* to be run by a Thread/worker, then implement Runnable in a separate, *job*-specific (not *worker*-specific) class.

This is a design issue and not a performance or language issue. It's perfectly legal to subclass Thread and override the run() method, but it's rarely a good idea.

Q: Can you reuse a Thread object? Can you give it a new job to do and then restart it by calling start() again?

A: No. Once a thread's run() method has completed, the thread can never be restarted. In fact, at that point the thread moves into a state we haven't talked about—**dead**. In the dead state, the thread has finished its run() method and can never be restarted. The Thread object might still be on the heap, as a living object that you can call other methods on (if appropriate), but the Thread object has permanently lost its 'threadness'. In other words, there is no longer a separate call stack, and the Thread object is no longer a *thread*. It's just an object, at that point, like all other objects.

But, there are design patterns for making a pool of threads that you can keep using to perform different jobs. But you don't do it by restarting() a dead thread.

BULLET POINTS

- A thread with a lower-case 't' is a separate thread of execution in Java.

- Every thread in Java has its own call stack.

- A Thread with a capital 'T' is the java.lang.Thread class. A Thread object represents a thread of execution.

- A Thread needs a job to do. A Thread's job is an instance of something that implements the Runnable interface.

- The Runnable interface has just a single method, run(). This is the method that goes on the bottom of the new call stack. In other words, it is the first method to run in the new thread.

- To launch a new thread, you need a Runnable to pass to the Thread's constructor.

- A thread is in the NEW state when you have instantiated a Thread object but have not yet called start().

- When you start a thread (by calling the Thread object's start() method), a new stack is created, with the Runnable's run() method on the bottom of the stack. The thread is now in the RUNNABLE state, waiting to be chosen to run.

- A thread is said to be RUNNING when the JVM's thread scheduler has selected it to be the currently-running thread. On a single-processor machine, there can be only one currently-running thread.

- Sometimes a thread can be moved from the RUNNING state to a BLOCKED (temporarily non-runnable) state. A thread might be blocked because it's waiting for data from a stream, or because it has gone to sleep, or because it is waiting for an object's lock.

- Thread scheduling is not guaranteed to work in any particular way, so you cannot be certain that threads will take turns nicely. You can help influence turn-taking by putting your threads to sleep periodically.

Putting a thread to sleep

One of the best ways to help your threads take turns is to put them to sleep periodically. All you need to do is call the static sleep() method, passing it the sleep duration, in milliseconds.

For example:

```
Thread.sleep(2000);
```

will knock a thread out of the running state, and keep it out of the runnable state for two seconds. The thread *can't* become the running thread again until after at least two seconds have passed.

A bit unfortunately, the sleep method throws an InterruptedException, a checked exception, so all calls to sleep must be wrapped in a try/catch (or declared). So a sleep call really looks like this:

```
try {
   Thread.sleep(2000);
} catch(InterruptedException ex) {
    ex.printStackTrace();
}
```

Your thread will probably *never* be interrupted from sleep; the exception is in the API to support a thread communication mechanism that almost nobody uses in the Real World. But, you still have to obey the handle or declare law, so you need to get used to wrapping your sleep() calls in a try/catch.

Now you know that your thread won't wake up *before* the specified duration, but is it possible that it will wake up some time *after* the 'timer' has expired? Yes and no. It doesn't matter, really, because when the thread wakes up, **it always goes back to the runnable state!** The thread won't automatically wake up at the designated time and become the currently-running thread. When a thread wakes up, the thread is once again at the mercy of the thread scheduler. Now, for applications that don't require perfect timing, and that have only a few threads, it might appear as though the thread wakes up and resumes running right on schedule (say, after the 2000 milliseconds). But don't bet your program on it.

> Put your thread to sleep if you want to be sure that other threads get a chance to run.
>
> When the thread wakes up, it always goes back to the runnable state and waits for the thread scheduler to choose it to run again.

Using sleep to make our program more predictable.

Remember our earlier example that kept giving us different results each time we ran it? Look back and study the code and the sample output. Sometimes main had to wait until the new thread finished (and printed "top o' the stack"), while other times the new thread would be sent back to runnable before it was finished, allowing the main thread to come back in and print out "back in main". How can we fix that? Stop for a moment and answer this question: "Where can you put a sleep() call, to make sure that "back in main" always prints before "top o' the stack"?

We'll wait while you work out an answer (there's more than one answer that would work).

Figure it out?

This is what we want—a consistent order of print statements:

```
File Edit Window Help SnoozeButton
% java ThreadTestDrive
back in main
top o' the stack
% java ThreadTestDrive
back in main
top o' the stack
% java ThreadTestDrive
back in main
top o' the stack
% java ThreadTestDrive
back in main
top o' the stack
% java ThreadTestDrive
back in main
top o' the stack
```

```java
public class MyRunnable implements Runnable {

   public void run() {
      go();
   }

   public void go() {

      try {
        Thread.sleep(2000);
      } catch(InterruptedException ex) {
        ex.printStackTrace();
      }

      doMore();
   }

   public void doMore() {
      System.out.println("top o' the stack");
   }
}

class ThreadTestDrive {
   public static void main (String[] args) {
      Runnable theJob = new MyRunnable();
      Thread t = new Thread(theJob);
      t.start();
      System.out.println("back in main");
   }
}
```

Calling sleep here will force the new thread to leave the currently-running state!

The main thread will become the currently-running thread again, and print out "back in main". Then there will be a pause (for about two seconds) before we get to this line, which calls doMore() and prints out "top o' the stack"

Making and starting *two* threads

Threads have names. You can give your threads a name of your choosing, or you can accept their default names. But the cool thing about names is that you can use them to tell which thread is running. The following example starts two threads. Each thread has the same job: run in a loop, printing the currently-running thread's name with each iteration.

```java
public class RunThreads implements Runnable {

    public static void main(String[] args) {
        RunThreads runner = new RunThreads();
        Thread alpha = new Thread(runner);
        Thread beta = new Thread(runner);
        alpha.setName("Alpha thread");
        beta.setName("Beta thread");
        alpha.start();
        beta.start();
    }

    public void run() {
        for (int i = 0; i < 25; i++) {
            String threadName = Thread.currentThread().getName();
            System.out.println(threadName + " is running");
        }
    }
}
```

Make one Runnable instance.

Make two threads, with the same Runnable (the same job—we'll talk more about the "two threads and one Runnable" in a few pages).

Name the threads.

Start the threads.

Each thread will run through this loop, printing its name each time.

What will happen?

Part of the output when the loop iterates 25 times.

Will the threads take turns? Will you see the thread names alternating? How often will they switch? With each iteration? After five iterations?

You already know the answer: *we don't know!* It's up to the scheduler. And on your OS, with your particular JVM, on your CPU, you might get very different results.

Running under OS X 10.2 (Jaguar), with five or fewer iterations, the Alpha thread runs to completion, then the Beta thread runs to completion. Very consistent. Not guaranteed, but very consistent.

But when you up the loop to 25 or more iterations, things start to wobble. The Alpha thread might not get to complete all 25 iterations before the scheduler sends it back to runnable to let the Beta thread have a chance.

```
File  Edit  Window  Help  Centauri
Alpha thread is running
Alpha thread is running
Alpha thread is running
Beta thread is running
Alpha thread is running
Beta thread is running
Beta thread is running
Beta thread is running
Beta thread is running
Beta thread is running
Beta thread is running
Beta thread is running
Beta thread is running
Beta thread is running
Beta thread is running
Beta thread is running
Beta thread is running
Beta thread is running
Beta thread is running
Alpha thread is running
```

Wow! Threads are the greatest thing since the MINI Cooper! I can't think of a single downside to using threads, can you?

Um, yes. There IS a dark side.
Threads can lead to concurrency 'issues.'

Concurrency issues lead to race conditions. Race conditions lead to data corruption. Data corruption leads to fear... you know the rest.

It all comes down to one potentially deadly scenario: two or more threads have access to a single object's *data*. In other words, methods executing on two different stacks are both calling, say, getters or setters on a single object on the heap.

It's a whole 'left-hand-doesn't-know-what-the-right-hand-is-doing' thing. Two threads, without a care in the world, humming along executing their methods, each thread thinking that he is the One True Thread. The only one that matters. After all, when a thread is not running, and in runnable (or blocked) it's essentially knocked unconscious. When it becomes the currently-running thread again, it doesn't know that it ever stopped.

Marriage in Trouble.
Can this couple be saved?

Next, on a very special Dr. Steve Show

[Transcript from episode #42]

Welcome to the Dr. Steve show.

We've got a story today that's centered around the top two reasons why couples split up—finances and sleep.

Today's troubled pair, Ryan and Monica, share a bed and a bank account. But not for long if we can't find a solution. The problem? The classic "two people—one bank account" thing.

Here's how Monica described it to me:

"Ryan and I agreed that neither of us will overdraw the checking account. So the procedure is, whoever wants to withdraw money *must* check the balance in the account *before* making the withdrawal. It all seemed so simple. But suddenly we're bouncing checks and getting hit with overdraft fees!

Ryan and Monica: victims of the "two people, one account" problem.

I thought it wasn't possible, I thought our procedure was safe. But then *this* happened:

Ryan needed $50, so he checked the balance in the account, and saw that it was $100. No problem. So, he plans to withdraw the money. **But first he falls asleep!**

Ryan falls asleep after he checks the balance but before he makes the withdrawal. When he wakes up, he immediately makes the withdrawl without checking the balance again.

And that's where *I* come in, while Ryan's still asleep, and now *I* want to withdraw $100. I check the balance, and it's $100 (because Ryan's still asleep and hasn't yet made his withdrawal), so I think, no problem. So I make the withdrawal, and again no problem. But then Ryan wakes up, completes *his* withdrawal, and we're suddenly overdrawn! He didn't even know that he fell asleep, so he just went ahead and completed his transaction without checking the balance again. You've got to help us Dr. Steve!"

Is there a solution? Are they doomed? We can't stop Ryan from falling asleep, but can we make sure that Monica can't get her hands on the bank account until after he wakes up?

Take a moment and think about that while we go to a commercial break.

The Ryan and Monica problem, in code

The following example shows what can happen when *two* threads (Ryan and Monica) share a *single* object (the bank account).

The code has two classes, BankAccount, and MonicaAndRyanJob. The MonicaAndRyanJob class implements Runnable, and represents the behavior that Ryan and Monica both have—checking the balance and making withdrawals. But of course, each thread falls asleep *in between* checking the balance and actually making the withdrawal.

The MonicaAndRyanJob class has an instance variable of type BankAccount., that represents their shared account.

The code works like this:

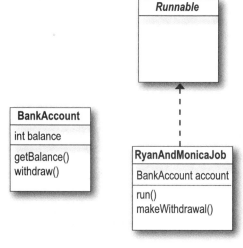

(1) Make one instance of RyanAndMonicaJob.

The RyanAndMonicaJob class is the Runnable (the job to do), and since both Monica and Ryan do the same thing (check balance and withdraw money), we need only one instance.

```
RyanAndMonicaJob  theJob = new RyanAndMonicaJob();
```

(2) Make two threads with the same Runnable (the RyanAndMonicaJob instance)

```
Thread one = new Thread(theJob);
Thread two = new Thread(theJob);
```

(3) Name and start the threads
```
one.setName("Ryan");
two.setName("Monica");
one.start();
two.start();
```

(4) Watch both threads execute the run() method (check the balance and make a withdrawal)

One thread represents Ryan, the other represents Monica. Both threads continually check the balance and then make a withdrawal, but only if it's safe!
```
if (account.getBalance() >= amount) {
   try {
      Thread.sleep(500);
   } catch(InterruptedException ex) {ex.printStackTrace(); }
}
```

In the run() method, do exactly what Ryan and Monica would do—check the balance and, if there's enough money, make the withdrawal.

This should protect against overdrawing the account.

Except... Ryan and Monica always fall asleep <u>after</u> they check the balance but <u>before</u> they finish the withdrawal.

The Ryan and Monica example

```java
class BankAccount {
   private int balance = 100;
```
← The account starts with a balance of $100.

```java
   public int getBalance() {
      return balance;
   }
   public void withdraw(int amount) {
      balance = balance - amount;
   }
}


 public class RyanAndMonicaJob implements Runnable {

   private BankAccount account = new BankAccount();
```
← There will be only ONE instance of the RyanAndMonicaJob. That means only ONE instance of the bank account. Both threads will access this one account.

```java
   public static void main (String [] args) {
      RyanAndMonicaJob   theJob = new RyanAndMonicaJob();
```
← Instantiate the Runnable (job)

```java
      Thread one = new Thread(theJob);
      Thread two = new Thread(theJob);
```
← Make two threads, giving each thread the same Runnable job. That means both threads will be accessing the one account instance variable in the Runnable class.

```java
      one.setName("Ryan");
      two.setName("Monica");
      one.start();
      two.start();
   }

   public void run() {
    for (int x = 0; x < 10; x++) {
       makeWithdrawl(10);
       if (account.getBalance() < 0) {
         System.out.println("Overdrawn!");
       }
    }
   }
```
In the run() method, a thread loops through and tries to make a withdrawal with each iteration. After the withdrawal, it checks the balance once again to see if the account is overdrawn.

```java
   private void makeWithdrawal(int amount) {
      if (account.getBalance() >= amount) {
      System.out.println(Thread.currentThread().getName() + " is about to withdraw");
       try {
         System.out.println(Thread.currentThread().getName() + " is going to sleep");
         Thread.sleep(500);
       } catch(InterruptedException ex) {ex.printStackTrace(); }
       System.out.println(Thread.currentThread().getName() + " woke up.");
       account.withdraw(amount);
       System.out.println(Thread.currentThread().getName() + " completes the withdrawl");
       }
      else {
       System.out.println("Sorry, not enough for " + Thread.currentThread().getName());
      }
   }
}
```
Check the account balance, and if there's not enough money, we just print a message. If there IS enough, we go to sleep, then wake up and complete the withdrawal, just like Ryan did.

We put in a bunch of print statements so we can see what's happening as it runs.

Ryan and Monica output

```
File Edit Window Help Visa
Ryan is about to withdraw
Ryan is going to sleep
Monica woke up.
Monica completes the withdrawl
Monica is about to withdraw
Monica is going to sleep
Ryan woke up.
Ryan completes the withdrawl
Ryan is about to withdraw
Ryan is going to sleep
Monica woke up.
Monica completes the withdrawl
Monica is about to withdraw
Monica is going to sleep
Ryan woke up.
Ryan completes the withdrawl
Ryan is about to withdraw
Ryan is going to sleep
Monica woke up.
Monica completes the withdrawl
Sorry, not enough for Monica
Sorry, not enough for Monica
Sorry, not enough for Monica
Sorry, not enough for Monica
Sorry, not enough for Monica
Ryan woke up.
Ryan completes the withdrawl
Overdrawn!
Sorry, not enough for Ryan
Overdrawn!
Sorry, not enough for Ryan
Overdrawn!
Sorry, not enough for Ryan
Overdrawn!
```

How did this happen? →

The makeWithdrawal() method always checks the balance before making a withdrawal, but still we overdraw the account.

Here's one scenario:

Ryan checks the balance, sees that there's enough money, and then falls asleep.

Meanwhile, Monica comes in and checks the balance. She, too, sees that there's enough money. She has no idea that Ryan is going to wake up and complete a withdrawal.

Monica falls asleep.

Ryan wakes up and completes his withdrawal.

Monica wakes up and completes her withdrawal. Big Problem! In between the time when she checked the balance and made the withdrawal, Ryan woke up and pulled money from the account.

Monica's check of the account was not valid, because Ryan had already checked and was still in the middle of making a withdrawal.

Monica must be stopped from getting into the account until Ryan wakes up and finishes his transaction. And vice-versa.

They need a lock for account access!

The lock works like this:

(1) There's a lock associated with the bank account transaction (checking the balance and withdrawing money). There's only one key, and it stays with the lock until somebody wants to access the account.

The bank account transaction is unlocked when nobody is using the account.

(2) When Ryan wants to access the bank account (to check the balance and withdraw money), he locks the lock and puts the key in his pocket. Now nobody else can access the account, since the key is gone.

When Ryan wants to access the account, he secures the lock and takes the key.

(3) **Ryan keeps the key in his pocket until he finishes the transaction.** He has the only key, so Monica can't access the account (or the checkbook) until Ryan unlocks the account and returns the key.

Now, even if Ryan falls asleep after he checks the balance, he has a guarantee that the balance will be the same when he wakes up, because he kept the key while he was asleep!

When Ryan is finished, he unlocks the lock and returns the key. Now the key is available for Monica (or Ryan again) to access the account.

We need the makeWithdrawal() method to run as one atomic thing.

We need to make sure that once a thread enters the makeWithdrawal() method, *it must be allowed to finish the method* before any other thread can enter.

In other words, we need to make sure that once a thread has checked the account balance, that thread has a guarantee that it can wake up and finish the withdrawal *before any other thread can check the account balance!*

Use the **synchronized** keyword to modify a method so that only one thread at a time can access it.

That's how you protect the bank account! You don't put a lock on the bank account itself; you lock the method that does the banking transaction. That way, one thread gets to complete the whole transaction, start to finish, even if that thread falls asleep in the middle of the method!

So if you don't lock the back account, then what exactly *is* locked? Is it the method? The Runnable object? The thread itself?

We'll look at that on the next page. In code, though, it's quite simple—just add the synchronized modifier to your method declaration:

The synchronized **keyword means that a thread needs a key in order to access the synchronized code.**

To protect your *data* (like the bank account), synchronize the *methods* that act on that data.

```
private synchronized void makeWithdrawal(int amount) {

    if (account.getBalance() >= amount) {
        System.out.println(Thread.currentThread().getName() + " is about to withdraw");
        try {
            System.out.println(Thread.currentThread().getName() + " is going to sleep");
            Thread.sleep(500);
        } catch(InterruptedException ex) {ex.printStackTrace(); }
        System.out.println(Thread.currentThread().getName() + " woke up.");
        account.withdraw(amount);
        System.out.println(Thread.currentThread().getName() + " completes the withdrawl");
    } else {
        System.out.println("Sorry, not enough for " + Thread.currentThread().getName());
    }
}
```

(Note for you physics-savvy readers: yes, the convention of using the word 'atomic' here does not reflect the whole subatomic particle thing. Think Newton, not Einstein, when you hear the word 'atomic' in the context of threads or transactions. Hey, it's not OUR convention. If WE were in charge, we'd apply Heisenberg's Uncertainty Principle to pretty much everything related to threads.)

Using an object's lock

Every object has a lock. Most of the time, the lock is unlocked, and you can imagine a virtual key sitting with it. Object locks come into play only when there are synchronized methods. When an object has one or more synchronized methods, *a thread can enter a synchronized method only if the thread can get the key to the object's lock!*

The locks are not per *method*, they are per *object*. If an object has two synchronized methods, it does not simply mean that you can't have two threads entering the same method. It means you can't have two threads entering *any* of the synchronized methods.

Think about it. If you have multiple methods that can potentially act on an object's instance variables, all those methods need to be protected with synchronized.

The goal of synchronization is to protect critical data. But remember, you don't lock the data itself, you synchronize the methods that *access* that data.

So what happens when a thread is cranking through its call stack (starting with the run() method) and it suddenly hits a synchronized method? The thread recognizes that it needs a key for that object before it can enter the method. It looks for the key (this is all handled by the JVM; there's no API in Java for accessing object locks), and if the key is available, the thread grabs the key and enters the method.

From that point forward, the thread hangs on to that key like the thread's life depends on it. The thread won't give up the key until it completes the synchronized method. So while that thread is holding the key, no other threads can enter *any* of that object's synchronized methods, because the one key for that object won't be available.

> Hey, this object's takeMoney() method is synchronized. I need to get this object's key before I can go in...

Every Java object has a lock. A lock has only one key.

Most of the time, the lock is unlocked and nobody cares.

But if an object has synchronized methods, a thread can enter one of the synchronized methods ONLY if the key for the object's lock is available. In other words, only if another thread hasn't already grabbed the one key.

The dreaded "Lost Update" problem

Here's another classic concurrency problem, that comes from the database world. It's closely related to the Ryan and Monica story, but we'll use this example to illustrate a few more points.

The lost update revolves around one process:

Step 1: Get the balance in the account

```
int i = balance;
```

Step 2: Add 1 to that balance

```
balance = i + 1;
```

The trick to showing this is to force the computer to take two steps to complete the change to the balance. In the real world, you'd do this particular move in a single statement:
balance++;

But by forcing it into *two* steps, the problem with a non-atomic process will become clear. So imagine that rather than the trivial "get the balance and then add 1 to the current balance" steps, the two (or more) steps in this method are much more complex, and couldn't be done in one statement.

In the "Lost Update" problem, we have two threads, both trying to increment the balance.

```
class TestSync implements Runnable {

    private int balance;

    public void run() {
        for(int i = 0; i < 50; i++) {
            increment();
            System.out.println("balance is " + balance);
        }
    }

    public void increment() {
        int i = balance;
        balance = i + 1;
    }
}
```

each thread runs 50 times, incrementing the balance on each iteration

Here's the crucial part! We increment the balance by adding 1 to whatever the value of balance was AT THE TIME WE READ IT (rather than adding 1 to whatever the CURRENT value is)

```
public class TestSyncTest {
    public static void main (String[] args) {
        TestSync job = new TestSync();
        Thread a = new Thread(job);
        Thread b = new Thread(job);
        a.start();
        b.start();
    }
}
```

Let's run this code...

① Thread A runs for awhile

Put the value of balance into variable i.
Balance is 0, so i is now 0.
Set the value of balance to the result of i + 1.
Now balance is 1.
Put the value of balance into variable i.
Balance is 1, so i is now 1.
Set the value of balance to the result of i + 1.
Now balance is 2.

② Thread B runs for awhile

Put the value of balance into variable i.
Balance is 2, so i is now 2.
Set the value of balance to the result of i + 1.
Now balance is 3.
Put the value of balance into variable i.
Balance is 3, so i is now 3.

[now thread B is sent back to runnable,
***before** it sets the value of balance to 4]*

③ Thread A runs again, picking up where it left off

Put the value of balance into variable i.
Balance is 3, so i is now 3.
Set the value of balance to the result of i + 1.
Now balance is 4.
Put the value of balance into variable i.
Balance is 4, so i is now 4.
Set the value of balance to the result of i + 1.
Now balance is 5.

④ Thread B runs again, and picks up exactly where it left off!

Set the value of balance to the result of i + 1.
Now balance is 4.

Yikes!!

Thread A updated it to 5, but
now B came back and stepped
on top of the update A made,
as if A's update never happened.

**We lost the last updates
that Thread A made!
Thread B had previously
done a 'read' of the value
of balance, and when B
woke up, it just kept going
as if it never missed a beat.**

Make the increment() method atomic. Synchronize it!

Synchronizing the increment() method solves the "Lost Update" problem, because it keeps the two steps in the method as one unbreakable unit.

```
public synchronized void increment() {
    int i = balance;
    balance = i + 1;
}
```

Once a thread enters the method, we have to make sure that all the steps in the method complete (as one atomic process) before any other thread can enter the method.

---

there are no Dumb Questions

Q: Sounds like it's a good idea to synchronize everything, just to be thread-safe.

A: Nope, it's not a good idea. Synchronization doesn't come for free. First, a synchronized method has a certain amount of overhead. In other words, when code hits a synchronized method, there's going to be a performance hit (although typically, you'd never notice it) while the matter of "is the key available?" is resolved.

Second, a synchronized method can slow your program down because synchronization restricts concurrency. In other words, a synchronized method forces other threads to get in line and wait their turn. This might not be a problem in your code, but you have to consider it.

Third, and most frightening, synchronized methods can lead to deadlock! (See page 516.)

A good rule of thumb is to synchronize only the bare minimum that should be synchronized. And in fact, you can synchronize at a granularity that's even smaller than a method. We don't use it in the book, but you can use the synchronized keyword to synchronize at the more fine-grained level of one or more statements, rather than at the whole-method level.

doStuff() doesn't need to be synchronized, so we don't synchronize the whole method.

```
public void go() {
    doStuff();

    synchronized(this) {
        criticalStuff();
        moreCriticalStuff();
    }
}
```

Now, only these two method calls are grouped into one atomic unit. When you use the synchronized keyword WITHIN a method, rather than in a method declaration, you have to provide an argument that is the object whose key the thread needs to get.

Although there are other ways to do it, you will almost always synchronize on the current object (this). That's the same object you'd lock if the whole method were synchronized.

① Thread A runs for awhile

Attempt to enter the increment() method.

The method is synchronized, so **get the key** for this object
Put the value of balance into variable i.
Balance is 0, so i is now 0.
Set the value of balance to the result of i + 1.
Now balance is 1.
Return the key (it completed the increment() method).
Re-enter the increment() method and **get the key**.
Put the value of balance into variable i.
Balance is 1, so i is now 1.

[now thread A is sent back to runnable, but since it has not completed the synchronized method, Thread A keeps the key]

② Thread B is selected to run

Attempt to enter the increment() method. The method is synchronized, so we need to get the key.

The key is not available.

[now thread B is sent into a 'object lock not available lounge]

③ Thread A runs again, picking up where it left off (remember, it still has the key)

Set the value of balance to the result of i + 1.
Now balance is 2.
Return the key.

[now thread A is sent back to runnable, but since it has completed the increment() method, the thread does NOT hold on to the key]

④ Thread B is selected to run

Attempt to enter the increment() method. The method is synchronized, so we need to get the key.

This time, the key IS available, get the key.

Put the value of balance into variable i.

[continues to run...]

The deadly side of synchronization

Be careful when you use synchronized code, because nothing will bring your program to its knees like thread deadlock. Thread deadlock happens when you have two threads, both of which are holding a key the other thread wants. There's no way out of this scenario, so the two threads will simply sit and wait. And wait. And wait.

If you're familiar with databases or other application servers, you might recognize the problem; databases often have a locking mechanism somewhat like synchronization. But a real transaction management system can sometimes deal with deadlock. It might assume, for example, that deadlock might have occurred when two transactions are taking too long to complete. But unlike Java, the application server can do a "transaction rollback" that returns the state of the rolled-back transaction to where it was before the transaction (the atomic part) began.

Java has no mechanism to handle deadlock. It won't even *know* deadlock occurred. So it's up to you to design carefully. If you find yourself writing much multithreaded code, you might want to study "Java Threads" by Scott Oaks and Henry Wong for design tips on avoiding deadlock. One of the most common tips is to pay attention to the order in which your threads are started.

All it takes for deadlock are two objects and two threads.

A simple deadlock scenario:

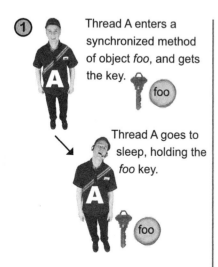

① Thread A enters a synchronized method of object *foo*, and gets the key.

Thread A goes to sleep, holding the *foo* key.

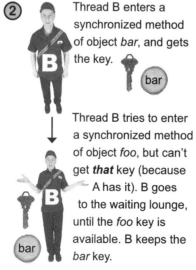

② Thread B enters a synchronized method of object *bar*, and gets the key.

Thread B tries to enter a synchronized method of object *foo*, but can't get *that* key (because A has it). B goes to the waiting lounge, until the *foo* key is available. B keeps the *bar* key.

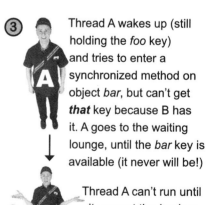

③ Thread A wakes up (still holding the *foo* key) and tries to enter a synchronized method on object *bar*, but can't get *that* key because B has it. A goes to the waiting lounge, until the *bar* key is available (it never will be!)

Thread A can't run until it can get the *bar* key, but B is holding the *bar* key and B can't run until it gets the *foo* key that A is holding and...

BULLET POINTS

- The static Thread.sleep() method forces a thread to leave the running state for at least the duration passed to the sleep method. Thread.sleep(200) puts a thread to sleep for 200 milliseconds.

- The sleep() method throws a checked exception (InterruptedException), so all calls to sleep() must be wrapped in a try/catch, or declared.

- You can use sleep() to help make sure all threads get a chance to run, although there's no guarantee that when a thread wakes up it'll go to the end of the runnable line. It might, for example, go right back to the front. In most cases, appropriately-timed sleep() calls are all you need to keep your threads switching nicely.

- You can name a thread using the (yet another surprise) setName() method. All threads get a default name, but giving them an explicit name can help you keep track of threads, especially if you're debugging with print statements.

- You can have serious problems with threads if two or more threads have access to the same object on the heap.

- Two or more threads accessing the same object can lead to data corruption if one thread, for example, leaves the running state while still in the middle of manipulating an object's critical state.

- To make your objects thread-safe, decide which statements should be treated as one atomic process. In other words, decide which methods must run to completion before another thread enters the same method on the same object.

- Use the keyword **synchronized** to modify a method declaration, when you want to prevent two threads from entering that method.

- Every object has a single lock, with a single key for that lock. Most of the time we don't care about that lock; locks come into play only when an object has synchronized methods.

- When a thread attempts to enter a synchronized method, the thread must get the key for the object (the object whose method the thread is trying to run). If the key is not available (because another thread already has it), the thread goes into a kind of waiting lounge, until the key becomes available.

- Even if an object has more than one synchronized method, there is still only one key. Once any thread has entered a synchronized method on that object, no thread can enter any other synchronized method on the same object. This restriction lets you protect your data by synchronizing any method that manipulates the data.

New and improved SimpleChatClient

Way back near the beginning of this chapter, we built the SimpleChatClient that could *send* outgoing messages to the server but couldn't receive anything. Remember? That's how we got onto this whole thread topic in the first place, because we needed a way to do two things at once: send messages *to* the server (interacting with the GUI) while simultaneously reading incoming messages *from* the server, displaying them in the scrolling text area.

Yes, there really IS an end to this chapter. But not yet...

```java
import java.io.*;
import java.net.*;
import java.util.*;
import javax.swing.*;
import java.awt.*;
import java.awt.event.*;

public class SimpleChatClient {

    JTextArea incoming;
    JTextField outgoing;
    BufferedReader reader;
    PrintWriter writer;
    Socket sock;

    public static void main(String[] args) {
        SimpleChatClient client = new SimpleChatClient();
        client.go();
    }

    public void go() {

        JFrame frame = new JFrame("Ludicrously Simple Chat Client");
        JPanel mainPanel = new JPanel();
        incoming = new JTextArea(15,50);
        incoming.setLineWrap(true);
        incoming.setWrapStyleWord(true);
        incoming.setEditable(false);
        JScrollPane qScroller = new JScrollPane(incoming);
        qScroller.setVerticalScrollBarPolicy(ScrollPaneConstants.VERTICAL_SCROLLBAR_ALWAYS);
        qScroller.setHorizontalScrollBarPolicy(ScrollPaneConstants.HORIZONTAL_SCROLLBAR_NEVER);
        outgoing = new JTextField(20);
        JButton sendButton = new JButton("Send");
        sendButton.addActionListener(new SendButtonListener());
        mainPanel.add(qScroller);
        mainPanel.add(outgoing);
        mainPanel.add(sendButton);
        setUpNetworking();

        Thread readerThread = new Thread(new IncomingReader());
        readerThread.start();

        frame.getContentPane().add(BorderLayout.CENTER, mainPanel);
        frame.setSize(400,500);
        frame.setVisible(true);

    } // close go
```

This is mostly GUI code you've seen before. Nothing special except the highlighted part where we start the new 'reader' thread.

We're starting a new thread, using a new inner class as the Runnable (job) for the thread. The thread's job is to read from the server's socket stream, displaying any incoming messages in the scrolling text area.

```
private void setUpNetworking() {

    try {
        sock = new Socket("127.0.0.1", 5000);
        InputStreamReader streamReader = new InputStreamReader(sock.getInputStream());
        reader = new BufferedReader(streamReader);
        writer = new PrintWriter(sock.getOutputStream());
        System.out.println("networking established");
    } catch(IOException ex) {
        ex.printStackTrace();
    }
} // close setUpNetworking
```

We're using the socket to get the input and output streams. We were already using the output stream to send to the server, but now we're using the input stream so that the new 'reader' thread can get messages from the server.

```
public class SendButtonListener implements ActionListener {
    public void actionPerformed(ActionEvent ev) {
        try {
            writer.println(outgoing.getText());
            writer.flush();

        } catch(Exception ex) {
            ex.printStackTrace();
        }
        outgoing.setText("");
        outgoing.requestFocus();
    }
}  // close inner class
```

Nothing new here. When the user clicks the send button, this method sends the contents of the text field to the server.

```
public class IncomingReader implements Runnable {
    public void run() {
        String message;
        try {

            while ((message = reader.readLine()) != null) {
                System.out.println("read " + message);
                incoming.append(message + "\n");

            } // close while
        } catch(Exception ex) {ex.printStackTrace();}
    } // close run
} // close inner class
```

This is what the thread does!!

In the run() method, it stays in a loop (as long as what it gets from the server is not null), reading a line at a time and adding each line to the scrolling text area (along with a new line character).

```
} // close outer class
```

Ready-bake Code

The really really simple Chat Server

You can use this server code for both versions of the Chat Client. Every possible disclaimer ever disclaimed is in effect here. To keep the code stripped down to the bare essentials, we took out a lot of parts that you'd need to make this a real server. In other words, it works, but there are at least a hundred ways to break it. If you want a Really Good Sharpen Your Pencil for after you've finished this book, come back and make this server code more robust.

Another possible Sharpen Your Pencil, that you could do right now, is to annotate this code yourself. You'll understand it much better if you work out what's happening than if we explained it to you. Then again, this is Ready-bake code, so you really don't have to understand it at all. It's here just to support the two versions of the Chat Client.

> **To run the chat client, you need two terminals. First, launch this server from one terminal, then launch the client from another terminal**

```java
import java.io.*;
import java.net.*;
import java.util.*;

public class VerySimpleChatServer {

    ArrayList clientOutputStreams;

    public class ClientHandler implements Runnable {
        BufferedReader reader;
        Socket sock;

        public ClientHandler(Socket clientSocket) {
            try {
                sock = clientSocket;
                InputStreamReader isReader = new InputStreamReader(sock.getInputStream());
                reader = new BufferedReader(isReader);

            } catch(Exception ex) {ex.printStackTrace();}
        } // close constructor

        public void run() {
            String message;
            try {
                while ((message = reader.readLine()) != null) {
                    System.out.println("read " + message);
                    tellEveryone(message);

                } // close while
            } catch(Exception ex) {ex.printStackTrace();}
        } // close run
    } // close inner class
```

```
public static void main (String[] args) {
    new VerySimpleChatServer().go();
}

public void go() {
    clientOutputStreams = new ArrayList();
    try {
      ServerSocket serverSock = new ServerSocket(5000);

      while(true) {
          Socket clientSocket = serverSock.accept();
          PrintWriter writer = new PrintWriter(clientSocket.getOutputStream());
          clientOutputStreams.add(writer);

          Thread t = new Thread(new ClientHandler(clientSocket));
          t.start();
          System.out.println("got a connection");
      }

    } catch(Exception ex) {
      ex.printStackTrace();
    }
} // close go

public void tellEveryone(String message) {

    Iterator it = clientOutputStreams.iterator();
    while(it.hasNext()) {
       try {
          PrintWriter writer = (PrintWriter) it.next();
          writer.println(message);
          writer.flush();
       } catch(Exception ex) {
           ex.printStackTrace();
       }

    } // end while

} // close tellEveryone
} // close class
```

there are no
Dumb Questions

Q: What about protecting static variable state? If you have static methods that change the static variable state, can you still use synchronization?

A: Yes! Remember that static methods run against the class and not against an individual instance of the class. So you might wonder whose object's lock would be used on a static method? After all, there might not even *be* any instances of that class. Fortunately, just as each *object* has its own lock, each loaded *class* has a lock. That means that if you have three Dog objects on your heap, you have a total of four Dog-related locks. Three belonging to the three Dog instances, and one belonging to the Dog class itself. When you synchronize a static method, Java uses the lock of the class itself. So if you synchronize two static methods in a single class, a thread will need the class lock to enter *either* of the methods.

Q: What are thread priorities? I've heard that's a way you can control scheduling.

A: Thread priorities *might* help you influence the scheduler, but they still don't offer any guarantee. Thread priorities are numerical values that tell the scheduler (if it cares) how important a thread is to you. In general, the scheduler will kick a lower priority thread out of the running state if a higher priority thread suddenly becomes runnable. But... one more time, say it with me now, "there is no guarantee." We recommend that you use priorities only if you want to influence *performance*, but never, ever rely on them for program correctness.

Q: Why don't you just synchronize all the getters and setters from the class with the data you're trying to protect? Like, why couldn't we have synchronized just the checkBalance() and withdraw() methods from class BankAccount, instead of synchronizing the makeWithdrawal() method from the Runnable's class?

A: Actually, we *should* have synchronized those methods, to prevent other threads from accessing those methods in other ways. We didn't bother, because our example didn't have any other code accessing the account.

But synchronizing the getters and setters (or in this case the checkBalance() and withdraw()) isn't enough. Remember, the point of synchronization is to make a specific section of code work ATOMICALLY. In other words, it's not just the individual methods we care about, it's methods that require **more than one step to complete**! Think about it. If we had not synchronized the makeWithdrawal() method, Ryan would have checked the balance (by calling the synchronized checkBalance()), and then immediately exited the method and returned the key!

Of course he would grab the key again, after he wakes up, so that he can call the synchronized withdraw() method, but this still leaves us with the same problem we had before synchronization! Ryan can check the balance, go to sleep, and Monica can come in and also check the balance before Ryan has a chance to wakes up and completes his withdrawal.

So synchronizing all the access methods is probably a good idea, to prevent other threads from getting in, but you still need to synchronize the methods that have statements that must execute as one atomic unit.

Code Kitchen

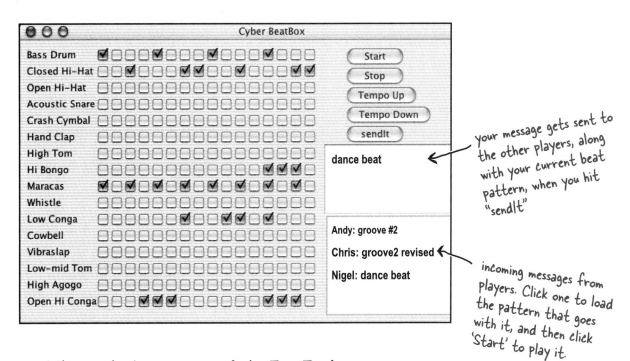

Bass Drum
Closed Hi-Hat
Open Hi-Hat
Acoustic Snare
Crash Cymbal
Hand Clap
High Tom
Hi Bongo
Maracas
Whistle
Low Conga
Cowbell
Vibraslap
Low-mid Tom
High Agogo
Open Hi Conga

Cyber BeatBox

Start
Stop
Tempo Up
Tempo Down
sendIt

dance beat

your message gets sent to the other players, along with your current beat pattern, when you hit "sendIt"

Andy: groove #2
Chris: groove2 revised
Nigel: dance beat

incoming messages from players. Click one to load the pattern that goes with it, and then click 'Start' to play it.

This is the last version of the BeatBox!

It connects to a simple MusicServer so that you can
send and receive beat patterns with other clients.

The code is really long, so the complete listing is
actually in Appendix A.

Exercise

Code Magnets

A working Java program is scrambled up on the fridge. Can you add the code snippets on the next page to the empty classes below, to make a working Java program that produces the output listed? Some of the curly braces fell on the floor and they were too small to pick up, so feel free to add as many of those as you need!

```
public class TestThreads {
```

```
class ThreadOne
```

```
class Accum {
```

```
class ThreadTwo
```

```
File Edit Window Help Sewing
% java TestThreads
one 98098
two 98099
```

Bonus Question: Why do you think we used the modifiers we did in the Accum class?

Code Magnets, continued..

```
Accum a = Accum.getAccum();
```

```
Thread one = new Thread(t1);
```

```
System.out.println("two "+a.getCount());
```

```
} catch(InterruptedException ex) { }
```

```
ThreadTwo t2 = new ThreadTwo();
```

```
try {
```

```
return counter;
```

```
counter += add;
```

```
Thread two = new Thread(t2);
```

```
implements Runnable {
```

```
one.start();
```

```
Accum a = Accum.getAccum();
```

```
Thread.sleep(50);
```

```
public static Accum getAccum() {
```

```
} catch(InterruptedException ex) { }
```

```
private static Accum a = new Accum();
```

```
private int counter = 0;
```

```
public void run() {
```

```
a.updateCounter(1);
```

```
Thread.sleep(50);
```

```
for(int x=0; x < 99; x++) {
```

```
implements Runnable {
```

```
a.updateCounter(1000);
```

```
return a;
```

```
public int getCount() {
```

```
System.out.println("one "+a.getCount());
```

```
public void updateCounter(int add) {
```

```
for(int x=0; x < 98; x++) {
```

```
two.start();
```

```
public static void main(String [] args) {
```

```
try {
```

```
public void run() {
```

```
private Accum() { }
```

```
ThreadOne t1 = new ThreadOne();
```

```
public class TestThreads {
  public static void main(String [] args) {
    ThreadOne t1 = new ThreadOne();
    ThreadTwo t2 = new ThreadTwo();
    Thread one = new Thread(t1);
    Thread two = new Thread(t2);
    one.start();
    two.start();
  }
}
```

create a static instance of class Accum

```
class Accum {
  private static Accum a = new Accum();  ←
  private int counter = 0;

  private Accum() { }  ←  A private constructor

  public static Accum getAccum() {
    return a;
  }

  public void updateCounter(int add) {
    counter += add;
  }

  public int getCount() {
    return counter;
  }
}
```

Threads from two different classes are updating the same object in a third class, because both threads are accessing a single instance of Accum. The line of code:

private static Accum a = new Accum( ); creates a static instance of Accum (remember static means one per class), and the private constructor in Accum means that no one else can make an Accum object. These two techniques (private constructor and static getter method) used together, create what's known as a 'Singleton' - an OO pattern to restrict the number of instances of an object that can exist in an application. (Usually, there's just a single instance of a Singleton—hence the name), but you can use the pattern to restrict the instance creation in whatever way you choose.)

```
class ThreadOne implements Runnable {
  Accum a = Accum.getAccum();
  public void run() {
    for(int x=0; x < 98; x++) {
      a.updateCounter(1000);
      try {
        Thread.sleep(50);
      } catch(InterruptedException ex) { }
    }
    System.out.println("one "+a.getCount());
  }
}
```

```
class ThreadTwo implements Runnable {
  Accum a = Accum.getAccum();
  public void run() {
    for(int x=0; x < 99; x++) {
      a.updateCounter(1);
      try {
        Thread.sleep(50);
      } catch(InterruptedException ex) { }
    }
    System.out.println("two "+a.getCount());
  }
}
```

Near-miss at the Airlock

As Sarah joined the on-board development team's design review meeting , she gazed out the portal at sunrise over the Indian Ocean. Even though the ship's conference room was incredibly claustrophobic, the sight of the growing blue and white crescent overtaking night on the planet below filled Sarah with awe and appreciation.

Five-Minute Mystery

This morning's meeting was focused on the control systems for the orbiter's airlocks. As the final construction phases were nearing their end, the number of spacewalks was scheduled to increase dramatically, and traffic was high both in and out of the ship's airlocks. "Good morning Sarah", said Tom, "Your timing is perfect, we're just starting the detailed design review."

"As you all know", said Tom, "Each airlock is outfitted with space-hardened GUI terminals, both inside and out. Whenever spacewalkers are entering or exiting the orbiter they will use these terminals to initiate the airlock sequences." Sarah nodded, "Tom can you tell us what the method sequences are for entry and exit?" Tom rose, and floated to the whiteboard, "First, here's the exit sequence method's pseudocode", Tom quickly wrote on the board.

```
orbiterAirlockExitSequence()

    verifyPortalStatus();

    pressurizeAirlock();

    openInnerHatch();

    confirmAirlockOccupied();

    closeInnerHatch();

    decompressAirlock();

    openOuterHatch();

    confirmAirlockVacated();

    closeOuterHatch();
```

"To ensure that the sequence is not interrupted, we have synchronized all of the methods called by the orbiterAirlockExitSequence() method", Tom explained. "We'd hate to see a returning spacewalker inadvertently catch a buddy with his space pants down!"

Everyone chuckled as Tom erased the whiteboard, but something didn't feel right to Sarah and it finally clicked as Tom began to write the entry sequence pseudocode on the whiteboard. "Wait a minute Tom!", cried Sarah, "I think we've got a big flaw in the exit sequence design, let's go back and revisit it, it could be critical!"

Why did Sarah stop the meeting? What did she suspect?

What did Sarah know?

Sarah realized that in order to ensure that the entire exit sequence would run without interruption the

`orbiterAirlockExitSequence( )` method needed to be synchronized. As the design stood, it would be possible for a returning spacewalker to interrupt the Exit Sequence! The Exit Sequence thread couldn't be interrupted in the middle of any of the lower level method calls, but it *could* be interrupted in *between* those calls. Sarah knew that the entire sequence should be run as one atomic unit, and if the `orbit erAirlockExitSequence ( )` method was synchronized, it could not be interrupted at any point.

Data structures

Sheesh... and all this time I could have just let *Java* put things in alphabetical order? Third grade really sucks. We never learn anything useful...

Sorting is a snap in Java. You have all the tools for collecting and manipulating your data without having to write your own sort algorithms (unless you're reading this right now sitting in your Computer Science 101 class, in which case, trust us—you are SO going to be writing sort code while the rest of us just call a method in the Java API). The Java Collections Framework has a data structure that should work for virtually anything you'll ever need to do. Want to keep a list that you can easily keep adding to? Want to find something by name? Want to create a list that automatically takes out all the duplicates? Sort your co-workers by the number of times they've stabbed you in the back? Sort your pets by number of tricks learned? It's all here...

Tracking song popularity on your jukebox

Congratulations on your new job—managing the automated jukebox system at Lou's Diner. There's no Java inside the jukebox itself, but each time someone plays a song, the song data is appended to a simple text file.

Your job is to manage the data to track song popularity, generate reports, and manipulate the playlists. You're not writing the entire app—some of the other software developer/ waiters are involved as well, but you're responsible for managing and sorting the data inside the Java app. And since Lou has a thing against databases, this is strictly an in-memory data collection. All you get is the file the jukebox keeps adding to. Your job is to take it from there.

You've already figured out how to read and parse the file, and so far you've been storing the data in an ArrayList.

SongList.txt

```
Pink Moon/Nick Drake
Somersault/Zero 7
Shiva Moon/Prem Joshua
Circles/BT
Deep Channel/Afro Celts
Passenger/Headmix
Listen/Tahiti 80
```

This is the file the jukebox device writes. Your code must read the file, then manipulate the song data.

Challenge #1
Sort the songs in alphabetical order

You have a list of songs in a file, where each line represents one song, and the title and artist are separated with a forward slash. So it should be simple to parse the line, and put all the songs in an ArrayList.

Your boss cares only about the song titles, so for now you can simply make a list that just has the song titles.

But you can see that the list is not in alphabetical order... what can you do?

You know that with an ArrayList, the elements are kept in the order in which they were inserted into the list, so putting them in an ArrayList won't take care of alphabetizing them, unless... maybe there's a sort() method in the ArrayList class?

Here's what you have so far, without the sort:

```java
import java.util.*;
import java.io.*;

public class Jukebox1 {

    ArrayList<String> songList = new ArrayList<String>();

    public static void main(String[] args) {
        new Jukebox1().go();
    }

    public void go() {
        getSongs();
        System.out.println(songList);
    }

    void getSongs() {
        try {
            File file = new File("SongList.txt");
            BufferedReader reader = new BufferedReader(new FileReader(file));
            String line =  null;
            while ((line= reader.readLine()) != null) {
                addSong(line);
            }

        } catch(Exception ex) {
            ex.printStackTrace();
        }
    }

    void addSong(String lineToParse) {
        String[] tokens = lineToParse.split("/");
        songList.add(tokens[0]);
    }
}
```

We'll store the song titles in an ArrayList of Strings.

The method that starts loading the file and then prints the contents of the songList ArrayList.

Nothing special here... just read the file and call the addSong() method for each line.

The addSong method works just like the Quiz-Card in the I/O chapter—you break the line (that has both the title and artist) into two pieces (tokens) using the split() method.

We only want the song title, so add only the first token to the SongList (the ArrayList).

```
File Edit Window Help Dance
%java Jukebox1
[Pink Moon, Somersault,
Shiva Moon, Circles,
Deep Channel, Passenger,
Listen]
```

The songList prints out with the songs in the order in which they were added to the ArrayList (which is the same order the songs are in within the original text file).

This is definitely NOT alphabetical!

But the ArrayList class does NOT have a sort() method!

When you look in ArrayList, there doesn't seem to be any method related to sorting. Walking up the inheritance hierarchy didn't help either—it's clear that *you can't call a sort method on the ArrayList.*

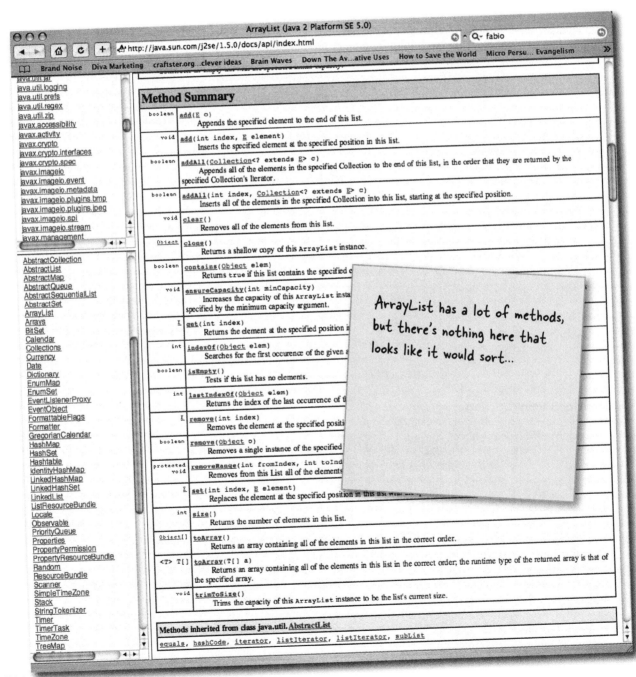

Method Summary

boolean	**add**(E o) Appends the specified element to the end of this list.
void	**add**(int index, E element) Inserts the specified element at the specified position in this list.
boolean	**addAll**(Collection<? extends E> c) Appends all of the elements in the specified Collection to the end of this list, in the order that they are returned by the specified Collection's Iterator.
boolean	**addAll**(int index, Collection<? extends E> c) Inserts all of the elements in the specified Collection into this list, starting at the specified position.
void	**clear**() Removes all of the elements from this list.
Object	**clone**() Returns a shallow copy of this ArrayList instance.
boolean	**contains**(Object elem) Returns true if this list contains the specified e
void	**ensureCapacity**(int minCapacity) Increases the capacity of this ArrayList insta specified by the minimum capacity argument.
E	**get**(int index) Returns the element at the specified position i
int	**indexOf**(Object elem) Searches for the first occurence of the given a
boolean	**isEmpty**() Tests if this list has no elements.
int	**lastIndexOf**(Object elem) Returns the index of the last occurrence of t
E	**remove**(int index) Removes the element at the specified positi
boolean	**remove**(Object o) Removes a single instance of the specified
protected void	**removeRange**(int fromIndex, int toInd Removes from this List all of the elements
E	**set**(int index, E element) Replaces the element at the specified position in this list with
int	**size**() Returns the number of elements in this list.
Object[]	**toArray**() Returns an array containing all of the elements in this list in the correct order.
<T> T[]	**toArray**(T[] a) Returns an array containing all of the elements in this list in the correct order; the runtime type of the returned array is that of the specified array.
void	**trimToSize**() Trims the capacity of this ArrayList instance to be the list's current size.

Methods inherited from class java.util.AbstractList

equals, hashCode, iterator, listIterator, listIterator, subList

ArrayList has a lot of methods, but there's nothing here that looks like it would sort...

I do see a collection class called TreeSet... and the docs say that it keeps your data sorted. I wonder if I should be using a TreeSet instead of an ArrayList...

ArrayList is <u>not</u> the only collection

Although ArrayList is the one you'll use most often, there are others for special occasions. Some of the key collection classes include:

Don't worry about trying to learn these other ones right now. We'll go into more details a little later.

➤ **TreeSet**
Keeps the elements sorted and prevents duplicates.

➤ **HashMap**
Let's you store and access elements as name/value pairs.

➤ **LinkedList**
Designed to give better performance when you insert or delete elements from the middle of the collection. (In practice, an ArrayList is still usually what you want.)

➤ **HashSet**
Prevents duplicates in the collection, and given an element, can find that element in the collection quickly.

➤ **LinkedHashMap**
Like a regular HashMap, except it can remember the order in which elements (name/value pairs) were inserted, or it can be configured to remember the order in which elements were last accessed.

You *could* use a TreeSet...
Or you could use the Collections.sort() method

If you put all the Strings (the song titles) into a **TreeSet** instead of an ArrayList, the Strings would automatically land in the right place, alphabetically sorted. Whenever you printed the list, the elements would always come out in alphabetical order.

And that's great when you need a *set* (we'll talk about sets in a few minutes) or when you know that the list must *always* stay sorted alphabetically.

On the other hand, if you don't need the list to stay sorted, TreeSet might be more expensive than you need—*every time you insert into a TreeSet, the TreeSet has to take the time to figure out where in the tree the new element must go.* With ArrayList, inserts can be blindingly fast because the new element just goes in at the end.

---

java.util.Collections

public static void **copy**(List destination, List source)

public static List **emptyList**()

public static void **fill**(List listToFill, Object objToFillItWith)

public static int **frequency**(Collection c, Object o)

public static void **reverse**(List list)

public static void **rotate**(List list, int distance)

public static void **shuffle**(List list)

public static void **sort**(List list)

public static boolea~~ All~~(List list, Object oldVal, Object newVal)

// many more met~~

Q: But you CAN add something to an ArrayList at a specific index instead of just at the end—there's an overloaded add() method that takes an int along with the element to add. So wouldn't it be slower than inserting at the end?

A: Yes, it's slower to insert something in an ArrayList somewhere *other* than at the end. So using the overloaded add(index, element) method doesn't work as quickly as calling the add(element)—which puts the added element at the end. But most of the time you use ArrayLists, you won't need to put something at a specific index.

Q: I see there's a LinkedList class, so wouldn't *that* be better for doing inserts somewhere in the middle? At least if I remember my Data Structures class from college...

A: Yes, good spot. The LinkedList *can* be quicker when you insert or remove something from the middle, but for most applications, the difference between middle inserts into a LinkedList and ArrayList is usually not enough to care about unless you're dealing with a *huge* number of elements. We'll look more at LinkedList in a few minutes.

> Hmmm... there IS a sort() method in the Collections class. It takes a List, and since ArrayList implements the List interface, ArrayList IS-A List. Thanks to polymorphism, you can pass an ArrayList to a method declared to take List.

> Note: this is NOT the real Collections class API; we simplified it here by leaving out the generic type information (which you'll see in a few pages).

Adding <u>Collections.sort()</u> to the Jukebox code

```
import java.util.*;
import java.io.*;

public class Jukebox1 {

    ArrayList<String> songList = new ArrayList<String>();

    public static void main(String[] args) {
        new Jukebox1().go();
    }

    public void go() {
        getSongs();
        System.out.println(songList);
        Collections.sort(songList);
        System.out.println(songList);
    }

    void getSongs() {
        try {
            File file = new File("SongList.txt");
            BufferedReader reader = new BufferedReader(new FileReader(file));
            String line =  null;
            while ((line= reader.readLine()) != null) {
                addSong(line);
            }

        } catch(Exception ex) {
            ex.printStackTrace();
        }
    }

    void addSong(String lineToParse) {
        String[] tokens = lineToParse.split("/");
        songList.add(tokens[0]);
    }
}
```

> The Collections.sort()
> method sorts a list of
> Strings alphabetically.

Call the static Collections
sort() method, then print the
list again. The second print out
is in alphabetical order!

```
File Edit Window Help Chill

%java Jukebox1

[Pink Moon, Somersault, Shiva Moon, Circles, Deep
Channel, Passenger, Listen]

[Circles, Deep Channel, Listen, Passenger, Pink
Moon, Shiva Moon, Somersault]
```

Before calling sort().

After calling sort().

But now you need Song objects, not just simple Strings.

Now your boss wants actual Song class instances in the list, not just Strings, so that each Song can have more data. The new jukebox device outputs more information, so this time the file will have *four* pieces (tokens) instead of just two.

The Song class is really simple, with only one interesting feature—the overridden toString() method. Remember, the toString() method is defined in class Object, so every class in Java inherits the method. And since the toString() method is called on an object when it's printed (System.out.println(anObject)), you should override it to print something more readable than the default unique identifier code. When you print a list, the toString() method will be called on each object.

SongListMore.txt

```
Pink Moon/Nick Drake/5/80
Somersault/Zero 7/4/84
Shiva Moon/Prem Joshua/6/120
Circles/BT/5/110
Deep Channel/Afro Celts/4/120
Passenger/Headmix/4/100
Listen/Tahiti 80/5/90
```

The new song file holds four attributes instead of just two. And we want ALL of them in our list, so we need to make a Song class with instance variables for all four song attributes.

```java
class Song {
    String title;
    String artist;
    String rating;
    String bpm;

    Song(String t, String a, String r, String b) {
        title = t;
        artist = a;
        rating = r;
        bpm = b;
    }

    public String getTitle() {
        return title;
    }

    public String getArtist() {
        return artist;
    }

    public String getRating() {
        return rating;
    }

    public String getBpm() {
        return bpm;
    }

    public String toString() {
        return title;
    }
}
```

Four instance variables for the four song attributes in the file.

The variables are all set in the constructor when the new Song is created.

The getter methods for the four attributes.

We override toString(), because when you do a System.out.println(aSongObject), we want to see the title. When you do a System.out.println(aListOfSongs), it calls the toString() method of EACH element in the list.

Changing the Jukebox code to use Songs instead of Strings

Your code changes only a little—the file I/O code is the same, and the parsing is the same (String.split()), except this time there will be *four* tokens for each song/line, and all four will be used to create a new Song object. And of course the ArrayList will be of type <Song> instead of <String>.

```
import java.util.*;
import java.io.*;
```

Change to an ArrayList of Song objects instead of String.

```
public class Jukebox3 {

    ArrayList<Song> songList = new ArrayList<Song>();
    public static void main(String[] args) {
        new Jukebox3().go();
    }
    public void go() {
        getSongs();
        System.out.println(songList);
        Collections.sort(songList);
        System.out.println(songList);
    }
    void getSongs() {
        try {
            File file = new File("SongList.txt");
            BufferedReader reader = new BufferedReader(new FileReader(file));
            String line = null;
            while ((line= reader.readLine()) != null) {
                addSong(line);
            }
        } catch(Exception ex) {
            ex.printStackTrace();
        }
    }

    void addSong(String lineToParse) {
        String[] tokens = lineToParse.split("/");

        Song nextSong = new Song(tokens[0], tokens[1], tokens[2], tokens[3]);
        songList.add(nextSong);
    }
}
```

Create a new Song object using the four tokens (which means the four pieces of info in the song file for this line), then add the Song to the list.

It won't compile!

Something's wrong... the Collections class clearly shows there's a sort() method, that takes a List.

ArrayList is-a List, because ArrayList implements the List interface, so... it *should* work.

But it doesn't!

The compiler says it can't find a sort method that takes an ArrayList<Song>, so maybe it doesn't like an ArrayList of Song objects? It didn't mind an ArrayList<String>, so what's the important difference between Song and String? What's the difference that's making the compiler fail?

```
File Edit Window Help Bummer
%javac Jukebox3.java
Jukebox3.java:15: cannot find symbol
symbol   : method sort(java.util.ArrayList<Song>)
location: class java.util.Collections
                    Collections.sort(songList);
                ^
1 error
```

And of course you probably already asked yourself, "What would it be sorting *on*?" How would the sort method even *know* what made one Song greater or less than another Song? Obviously if you want the song's *title* to be the value that determines how the songs are sorted, you'll need some way to tell the sort method that it needs to use the title and not, say, the beats per minute.

We'll get into all that a few pages from now, but first, let's find out why the compiler won't even let us pass a Song ArrayList to the sort() method.

WTF? I have no idea how to read the method declaration on this. It says that sort() takes a List<T>, but what is T? And what is that big thing before the return type?

The sort() method declaration

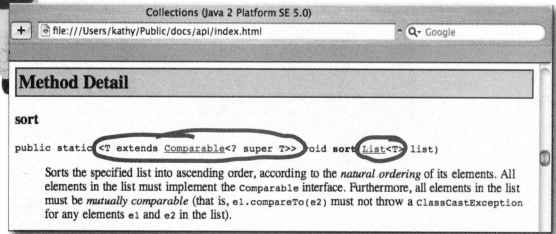

Collections (Java 2 Platform SE 5.0)

file:///Users/kathy/Public/docs/api/index.html — Q▾ Google

Method Detail

sort

`public static <T extends Comparable<? super T>> void sort(List<T> list)`

Sorts the specified list into ascending order, according to the *natural ordering* of its elements. All elements in the list must implement the `Comparable` interface. Furthermore, all elements in the list must be *mutually comparable* (that is, `e1.compareTo(e2)` must not throw a `ClassCastException` for any elements `e1` and `e2` in the list).

From the API docs (looking up the java.util.Collections class, and scrolling to the sort() method), it looks like the sort() method is declared... *strangely.* Or at least different from anything we've seen so far.

That's because the sort() method (along with other things in the whole collection framework in Java) makes heavy use of *generics.* Anytime you see something with angle brackets in Java source code or documentation, it means generics—a feature added to Java 5.0. So it looks like we'll have to learn how to interpret the documentation before we can figure out why we were able to sort String objects in an ArrayList, but not an ArrayList of Song objects.

Generics means more type-safety

We'll just say it right here—*virtually all of the code you write that deals with generics will be collection-related code.* Although generics can be used in other ways, the main point of generics is to let you write type-safe collections. In other words, code that makes the compiler stop you from putting a Dog into a list of Ducks.

Before generics (which means before Java 5.0), the compiler could not care less what you put into a collection, because all collection implementations were declared to hold type Object. You could put *anything* in any ArrayList; it was like all ArrayLists were declared as ArrayList<Object>.

WITHOUT generics

Objects go IN as a reference to SoccerBall, Fish, Guitar, and Car objects

Before generics, there was no way to declare the type of an ArrayList, so its add() method took type Object.

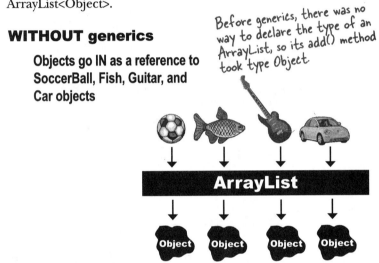

And come OUT as a reference of type Object

With generics, you can create type-safe collections where more problems are caught at compile-time instead of runtime.

Without generics, the compiler would happily let you put a Pumpkin into an ArrayList that was supposed to hold only Cat objects.

WITH generics

Objects go IN as a reference to only Fish objects

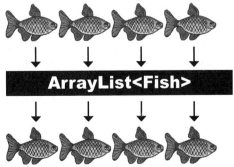

And come out as a reference of type Fish

Now with generics, you can put only Fish objects in the ArrayList<Fish>, so the objects come out as Fish references. You don't have to worry about someone sticking a Volkswagen in there, or that what you get out won't really be cast-able to a Fish reference.

Learning generics

Of the dozens of things you could learn about generics, there are really only three that matter to most programmers:

① **Creating instances of generified *classes* (like ArrayList)**

When you make an ArrayList, you have to tell it the type of objects you'll allow in the list, just as you do with plain old arrays.

```
new ArrayList<Song>()
```

② **Declaring and assigning *variables* of generic types**

How does polymorphism really work with generic types? If you have an ArrayList<Animal> reference variable, can you assign an ArrayList<Dog> to it? What about a List<Animal> reference? Can you assign an ArrayList<Animal> to it? You'll see...

```
List<Song> songList =
    new ArrayList<Song>()
```

③ **Declaring (and invoking) *methods* that take generic types**

If you have a method that takes as a parameter, say, an ArrayList of Animal objects, what does that really mean? Can you also pass it an ArrayList of Dog objects? We'll look at some subtle and tricky polymorphism issues that are very different from the way you write methods that take plain old arrays.

(This is actually the same point as #2, but that shows you how important we think it is.)

```
void foo(List<Song> list)

x.foo(songList)
```

Q: But don't I also need to learn how to create my OWN generic classes? What if I want to make a class type that lets people instantiating the class decide the type of things that class will use?

A: You probably won't do much of that. Think about it—the API designers made an entire library of collections classes covering most of the data structures you'd need, and virtually the only type of classes that really need to be generic are collection classes. In other words, classes designed to hold other elements, and you want programmers using it to specify what type those elements are when they declare and instantiate the collection class.

Yes, it is possible that you might want to *create* generic classes, but that's the exception, so we won't cover it here. (But you'll figure it out from the things we *do* cover, anyway.)

Using generic CLASSES

Since ArrayList is our most-used generified type, we'll start by looking at its documentation. They two key areas to look at in a generified class are:

1) The *class* declaration

3) The *method* declarations that let you add elements

Think of "E" as a stand-in for "the type of element you want this collection to hold and return." (E is for Element.)

Understanding ArrayList documentation
(Or, what's the true meaning of "E"?)

The "E" is a placeholder for the REAL type you use when you declare and create an ArrayList

ArrayList is a subclass of AbstractList, so whatever type you specify for the ArrayList is automatically used for the type of the AbstractList.

```
public class ArrayList<E> extends AbstractList<E> implements List<E>  ... {

        public boolean add(E o)
```

Here's the important part! Whatever "E" is determines what kind of things you're allowed to add to the ArrayList.

The type (the value of <E>) becomes the type of the List interface as well.

```
        // more code
}
```

The "E" represents the type used to create an instance of ArrayList. When you see an "E" in the ArrayList documentation, you can do a mental find/replace to exchange it for whatever <type> you use to instantiate ArrayList.

So, new ArrayList<Song> means that "E" becomes "Song", in any method or variable declaration that uses "E".

Using type parameters with ArrayList

THIS code:

```
ArrayList<String> thisList = new ArrayList<String>
```

Means ArrayList:

```
public class ArrayList<E> extends AbstractList<E> ... {


    public boolean add(E o)
    // more code
}
```

Is treated by the compiler as:

```
public class ArrayList<String> extends AbstractList<String>... {


    public boolean add(String o)
    // more code
}
```

In other words, the "E" is replaced by the *real* type (also called the *type parameter*) that you use when you create the ArrayList. And that's why the add() method for ArrayList won't let you add anything except objects of a reference type that's compatible with the type of "E". So if you make an ArrayList**<String>**, the add() method suddenly becomes **add(String o)**. If you make the ArrayList of type **Dog**, suddenly the add() method becomes **add(Dog o)**.

Q: Is "E" the only thing you can put there? Because the docs for sort used "T"...

A: You can use anything that's a legal Java identifier. That means anything that you could use for a method or variable name will work as a type parameter. But the convention is to use a single letter (so that's what you should use), and a further convention is to use "T" unless you're specifically writing a collection class, where you'd use "E" to represent the "type of the Element the collection will hold".

Using generic METHODS

A generic *class* means that the *class declaration* includes a type parameter. A generic *method* means that the method declaration uses a type parameter in its signature.

You can use type parameters in a method in several different ways:

①   Using a type parameter defined in the class declaration

```
public class ArrayList<E> extends AbstractList<E> ... {
    public boolean add(E o)
```

You can use the "E" here ONLY because it's already been defined as part of the class.

When you declare a type parameter for the class, you can simply use that type any place that you'd use a *real* class or interface type. The type declared in the method argument is essentially replaced with the type you use when you instantiate the class.

②   Using a type parameter that was NOT defined in the class declaration

```
public <T extends Animal> void takeThing(ArrayList<T> list)
```

If the class itself doesn't use a type parameter, you can still specify one for a method, by declaring it in a really unusual (but available) space—*before the return type*. This method says that T can be "any type of Animal".

Here we can use <T> because we declared "T" earlier in the method declaration.

> Wait... that can't be right. If you can take a list of Animal, why don't you just SAY that? What's wrong with just *takeThing(ArrayList<Animal> list)*?

Here's where it gets weird...

This:
```
public <T extends Animal> void takeThing(ArrayList<T> list)
```

Is NOT the same as this:
```
public void takeThing(ArrayList<Animal> list)
```

Both are legal, but they're *different!*

The first one, where **<T extends Animal>** is part of the method declaration, means that any ArrayList declared of a type that is Animal, or one of Animal's subtypes (like Dog or Cat), is legal. So you could invoke the top method using an ArrayList<Dog>, ArrayList<Cat>, or ArrayList<Animal>.

But... the one on the bottom, where the method argument is (ArrayList<Animal> list) means that *only* an ArrayList<Animal> is legal. In other words, while the first version takes an ArrayList of any type that is a type of Animal (Animal, Dog, Cat, etc.), the second version takes *only* an ArrayList of type Animal. Not ArrayList<Dog>, or ArrayList<Cat> but only ArrayList<Animal>.

And yes, it does appear to violate the point of polymorphism. but it will become clear when we revisit this in detail at the end of the chapter. For now, remember that we're only looking at this because we're still trying to figure out how to sort() that SongList, and that led us into looking at the API for the sort() method, which had this strange generic type declaration.

For now, all you need to know is that the syntax of the top version is legal, and that it means you can pass in a ArrayList object instantiated as Animal or any Animal subtype.

And now back to our sort() method...

sorting a Song

This still doesn't explain why the sort method failed on an ArrayList of Songs but worked for an ArrayList of Strings...

Remember where we were...

```
File Edit Window Help Bummer
%javac Jukebox3.java
Jukebox3.java:15: cannot find symbol
symbol   : method sort(java.util.ArrayList<Song>)
location: class java.util.Collections
                    Collections.sort(songList);
                    ^
1 error
```

```
import java.util.*;
import java.io.*;

public class Jukebox3 {
    ArrayList<Song> songList = new ArrayList<Song>();
    public static void main(String[] args) {
        new Jukebox3().go();
    }
    public void go() {
        getSongs();
        System.out.println(songList);
        Collections.sort(songList);
        System.out.println(songList);
    }
    void getSongs() {
        try {
            File file = new File("SongList.txt");
            BufferedReader reader = new BufferedReader(new FileReader(file));
            String line =  null;
            while ((line= reader.readLine()) != null) {
                addSong(line);
            }
        } catch(Exception ex) {
            ex.printStackTrace();
        }
    }
    void addSong(String lineToParse) {
        String[] tokens = lineToParse.split("/");
        Song nextSong = new Song(tokens[0], tokens[1], tokens[2], tokens[3]);
        songList.add(nextSong);
    }
}
```

This is where it breaks! It worked fine when passed in an ArrayList<String>, but as soon as we tried to sort an ArrayList<Song>, it failed.

Revisiting the sort() method

So here we are, trying to read the sort() method docs to find
out why it was OK to sort a list of Strings, but not a
list of Song objects. And it looks like the answer is...

**The sort() method can take only lists
of Comparable objects.**

**Song is NOT a subtype of
Comparable, so you cannot sort()
the list of Songs.**

At least not yet...

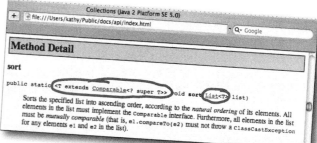

Collections (Java 2 Platform SE 5.0)

file:///Users/kathy/Public/docs/api/index.html

Q- Google

Method Detail

sort

public static <T extends Comparable<? super T>> void sort(List<T> list)

Sorts the specified list into ascending order, according to the *natural ordering* of its elements. All
elements in the list must implement the Comparable interface. Furthermore, all elements in the list
must be *mutually comparable* (that is, e1.compareTo(e2) must not throw a ClassCastException
for any elements e1 and e2 in the list).

```
public static <T extends Comparable<? super T>> void sort(List<T> list)
```

This says "Whatever 'T' is must
be of type Comparable."

(Ignore this part for now. But
if you can't, it just means
that the type parameter for
Comparable must be of type T
or one of T's supertypes.)

You can pass in only a List (or
subtype of list, like ArrayList)
that uses a parameterized type
that "extends Comparable".

> Um... I just checked the docs for
> String, and String doesn't EXTEND
> Comparable--it IMPLEMENTS it.
> **Comparable is an interface**. So it's nonsense
> to say <T *extends* Comparable>.

```
public final class String extends Object implements Serializable,
                                        Comparable<String>, CharSequence
```

In generics, "extends" means "extends or implements"

The Java engineers had to give you a way to put a constraint on a parameterized type, so that you can restrict it to, say, only subclasses of Animal. But you also need to constrain a type to allow only classes that implement a particular interface. So here's a situation where we need one kind of syntax to work for both situations—inheritance and implementation. In other words, that works for both *extends* and *implements*.

And the winning word was... *extends*. But it really means "is-a", and works regardless of whether the type on the right is an interface or a class.

In generics, the keyword "extends" really means "is-a", and works for BOTH classes and interfaces.

Comparable is an interface, so this REALLY reads, "T must be a type that implements the Comparable interface".

```
public static <T extends Comparable<? super T>> void sort(List<T> list)
```

It doesn't matter whether the thing on the right is a class or interface... you still say "extends".

Q: Why didn't they just make a new keyword, "is"?

A: Adding a new keyword to the language is a REALLY big deal because it risks breaking Java code you wrote in an earlier version. Think about it—you might be using a variable "is" (which we do use in this book to represent input streams). And since you're not allowed to use keywords as identifiers in your code, that means any earlier code that used the keyword *before* it was a reserved word, would break. So whenever there's a chance for the Sun engineers to reuse an existing keyword, as they did here with "extends", they'll usually choose that. But sometimes they don't have a choice...

A few (very few) new keywords *have* been added to the language, such as **assert** in Java 1.4 and **enum** in Java 5.0 (we look at enum in the appendix). And this does break people's code, however you sometimes have the option of compiling and running a *newer* version of Java so that it behaves as though it were an older one. You do this by passing a special flag to the compiler or JVM at the command-line, that says, "Yeah, yeah, I KNOW this is Java 1.4, but please pretend it's really 1.3, because I'm using a variable in my code named *assert* that I wrote back when you guys said it would OK!#$%".

(To see if you have a flag available, type *javac* (for the compiler) or *java* (for the JVM) at the command-line, without anything else after it, and you should see a list of available options. You'll learn more about these flags in the chapter on deployment.)

Finally we know what's wrong...
The Song class needs to implement Comparable

We can pass the ArrayList<Song> to the sort() method only if the Song class implements Comparable, since that's the way the sort() method was declared. A quick check of the API docs shows the Comparable interface is really simple, with only one method to implement:

java.lang.Comparable

```
public interface Comparable<T> {
    int compareTo(T o);
}
```

And the method documentation for compareTo() says

Returns:
a negative integer, zero, or a positive integer as this object is less than, equal to, or greater than the specified object.

It looks like the compareTo() method will be called on one Song object, passing that Song a reference to a different Song. The Song running the compareTo() method has to figure out if the Song it was passed should be sorted higher, lower, or the same in the list.

Your big job now is to decide what makes one song greater than another, and then implement the compareTo() method to reflect that. A negative number (any negative number) means the Song you were passed is greater than the Song running the method. Returning a positive number says that the Song running the method is greater than the Song passed to the compareTo() method. Returning zero means the Songs are equal (at least for the purpose of sorting... it doesn't necessarily mean they're the same object). You might, for example, have two Songs with the same title.

(Which brings up a whole different can of worms we'll look at later...)

The big question is: what makes *one* song less than, equal to, or greater than *another* song?

You can't implement the Comparable interface until you make that decision.

Sharpen your pencil

Write in your idea and pseudo code (or better, REAL code) for implementing the compareTo() method in a way that will sort() the Song objects by title.

Hint: if you're on the right track, it should take less than 3 lines of code!

The new, improved, comparable Song class

We decided we want to sort by title, so we implement the compareTo() method to compare the title of the Song passed to the method against the title of the song on which the compareTo() method was invoked. In other words, the song running the method has to decide how its title compares to the title of the method parameter.

Hmmm... we know that the String class must know about alphabetical order, because the sort() method worked on a list of Strings. We know String has a compareTo() method, so why not just call it? That way, we can simply let one title String compare itself to another, and we don't have to write the comparing/alphabetizing algorithm!

Usually these match....we're specifying the type that the implementing class can be compared against.

This means that Song objects can be compared to other Song objects, for the purpose of sorting.

```java
class Song implements Comparable<Song> {
    String title;
    String artist;
    String rating;
    String bpm;

    public int compareTo(Song s) {
        return title.compareTo(s.getTitle());
    }

    Song(String t, String a, String r, String b) {
        title = t;
        artist = a;
        rating = r;
        bpm = b;
    }

    public String getTitle() {
        return title;
    }

    public String getArtist() {
        return artist;
    }

    public String getRating() {
        return rating;
    }

    public String getBpm() {
        return bpm;
    }

    public String toString() {
        return title;
    }
}
```

The sort() method sends a Song to compareTo() to see how that Song compares to the Song on which the method was invoked.

Simple! We just pass the work on to the title String objects, since we know Strings have a compareTo() method.

This time it worked. It prints the list, then calls sort which puts the Songs in alphabetical order by title.

```
File Edit Window Help Ambient

%java Jukebox3

[Pink Moon, Somersault, Shiva Moon, Circles, Deep
Channel, Passenger, Listen]

[Circles, Deep Channel, Listen, Passenger, Pink
Moon, Shiva Moon, Somersault]
```

We can sort the list, but...

There's a new problem—Lou wants two different views of the song list, one by song title and one by artist!

But when you make a collection element comparable (by having it implement Comparable), you get only one chance to implement the compareTo() method. So what can you do?

The horrible way would be to use a flag variable in the Song class, and then do an *if* test in compareTo() and give a different result depending on whether the flag is set to use title or artist for the comparison.

But that's an awful and brittle solution, and there's something much better. Something built into the API for just this purpose—when you want to sort the same thing in more than one way.

Look at the Collections class API again. There's a second sort() method—and it takes a Comparator.

That's not good enough. Sometimes I want it to sort by artist instead of title.

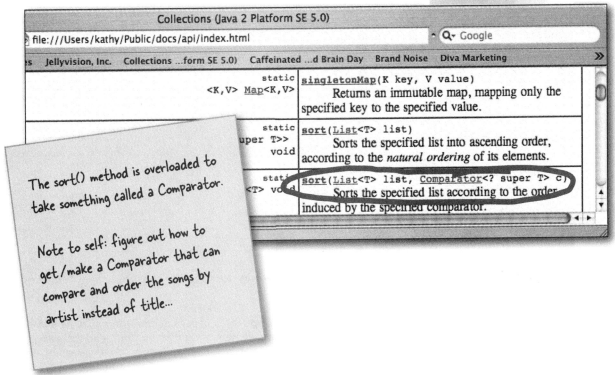

Collections (Java 2 Platform SE 5.0)

file:///Users/kathy/Public/docs/api/index.html   Q▾ Google

Jellyvision, Inc.   Collections ...form SE 5.0)   Caffeinated ...d Brain Day   Brand Noise   Diva Marketing

static <K,V> Map<K,V>	singletonMap(K key, V value) Returns an immutable map, mapping only the specified key to the specified value.
static uper T>> void	sort(List<T> list) Sorts the specified list into ascending order, according to the *natural ordering* of its elements.
stati <T> vo	sort(List<T> list, Comparator<? super T> c) Sorts the specified list according to the order induced by the specified comparator.

The sort() method is overloaded to take something called a Comparator.

Note to self: figure out how to get/make a Comparator that can compare and order the songs by artist instead of title...

Using a custom Comparator

An element in a list can compare *itself* to another of its own type in only one way, using its compareTo() method. But a Comparator is external to the element type you're comparing—it's a separate class. So you can make as many of these as you like! Want to compare songs by artist? Make an ArtistComparator. Sort by beats per minute? Make a BPMComparator.

Then all you need to do is call the overloaded sort() method that takes the List and the Comparator that will help the sort() method put things in order.

The sort() method that takes a Comparator will use the Comparator instead of the element's own compareTo() method, when it puts the elements in order. In other words, if your sort() method gets a Comparator, it won't even *call* the compareTo() method of the elements in the list. The sort() method will instead invoke the **compare()** method on the Comparator.

So, the rules are:

> ► Invoking the one-argument sort(List o) method means the list element's compareTo() method determines the order. So the elements in the list MUST implement the Comparable interface.

> ► Invoking sort(List o, Comparator c) means the list element's compareTo() method will NOT be called, and the Comparator's compare() method will be used instead. That means the elements in the list do NOT need to implement the Comparable interface.

java.util.Comparator

```
public interface Comparator<T> {
    int compare(T o1, T o2);
}
```

If you pass a Comparator to the sort() method, the sort order is determined by the Comparator rather than the element's own compareTo() method.

Q: So does this mean that if you have a class that doesn't implement Comparable, and you don't have the source code, you could still put the things in order by creating a Comparator?

A: That's right. The other option (if it's possible) would be to subclass the element and make the subclass implement Comparable.

Q: But why doesn't *every* class implement Comparable?

A: Do you really believe that *everything* can be ordered? If you have element types that just don't lend themselves to any kind of natural ordering, then you'd be misleading other programmers if you implement Comparable. And you aren't taking a huge risk by not implementing Comparable, since a programmer can compare anything in any way that he chooses using his own custom Comparator.

Updating the Jukebox to use a Comparator

We did three new things in this code:

1) Created an inner class that implements Comparator (and thus the *compare()* method that does the work previously done by *compareTo()*).

2) Made an instance of the Comparator inner class.

3) Called the overloaded sort() method, giving it both the song list and the instance of the Comparator inner class.

Note: we also updated the Song class toString() method to print both the song title and the artist. (It prints *title: artist* regardless of how the list is sorted.)

```java
import java.util.*;
import java.io.*;

public class Jukebox5 {
    ArrayList<Song> songList = new ArrayList<Song>();
    public static void main(String[] args) {
        new Jukebox5().go();
    }
```

Create a new inner class that implements Comparator (note that its type parameter matches the type we're going to compare—in this case Song objects.)

```java
    class ArtistCompare implements Comparator<Song> {
        public int compare(Song one, Song two) {
            return one.getArtist().compareTo(two.getArtist());
        }
    }
}
```

This becomes a String (the artist)

We're letting the String variables (for artist) do the actual comparison, since Strings already know how to alphabetize themselves.

```java
    public void go() {
        getSongs();
        System.out.println(songList);
        Collections.sort(songList);
        System.out.println(songList);
```

Make an instance of the Comparator inner class.

```java
        ArtistCompare artistCompare = new ArtistCompare();
        Collections.sort(songList, artistCompare);
```

Invoke sort(), passing it the list and a reference to the new custom Comparator object.

```java
        System.out.println(songList);
    }

    void getSongs() {
        // I/O code here
    }

    void addSong(String lineToParse) {
        // parse line and add to song list
    }
}
```

Note: we've made sort-by-title the default sort, by keeping the compareTo() method in Song use the titles. But another way to design this would be to implement both the title sorting and artist sorting as inner Comparator classes, and not have Song implement Comparable at all. That means we'd always use the two-arg version of Collections.sort().

```
import _____;

public class SortMountains {

  LinkedList_____ mtn = new LinkedList_____();

  class NameCompare _____ {
    public int compare(Mountain one, Mountain two) {

      return _____;
    }
  }
  class HeightCompare _____ {
    public int compare(Mountain one, Mountain two) {

      return (_____);
    }
  }
  public static void main(String [] args) {
    new SortMountain().go();
  }
  public void go() {
    mtn.add(new Mountain("Longs", 14255));
    mtn.add(new Mountain("Elbert", 14433));
    mtn.add(new Mountain("Maroon", 14156));
    mtn.add(new Mountain("Castle", 14265));

    System.out.println("as entered:\n" + mtn);
    NameCompare nc = new NameCompare();

    _____;
    System.out.println("by name:\n" + mtn);
    HeightCompare hc = new HeightCompare();

    _____;
    System.out.println("by height:\n" + mtn);
  }
}

class Mountain {

  _____;

  _____;

  _____ {

    _____;

    _____;
  }
  _____ {

    _____;
  }
}
```

Reverse Engineer

Assume this code exists in a single file. Your job is to fill in the blanks so the the program will create the output shown.

Note: answers are at the end of the chapter.

Output:

```
File  Edit  Window  Help  ThisOne'sForBob
%java SortMountains
as entered:
[Longs 14255, Elbert 14433, Maroon 14156, Castle 14265]
by name:
[Castle 14265, Elbert 14433, Longs 14255, Maroon 14156]
by height:
[Elbert 14433, Castle 14265, Longs 14255, Maroon 14156]
```

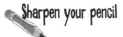 Sharpen your pencil

Fill-in-the-blanks

For each of the questions below, fill in the blank with one of the words from the "possible answers" list, to correctly answer the question. Answers are at the end of the chapter.

Possible Answers:

Comparator,

Comparable,

compareTo( ),

compare( ),

yes,

no

Given the following compilable statement:

```
Collections.sort(myArrayList);
```

1. What must the class of the objects stored in `myArrayList` implement? _____

2. What method must the class of the objects stored in `myArrayList` implement? _____

3. Can the class of the objects stored in `myArrayList` implement both Comparator AND Comparable? _____

Given the following compilable statement:

```
Collections.sort(myArrayList, myCompare);
```

4. Can the class of the objects stored in `myArrayList` implement Comparable? _____

5. Can the class of the objects stored in `myArrayList` implement Comparator? _____

6. Must the class of the objects stored in `myArrayList` implement Comparable? _____

7. Must the class of the objects stored in `myArrayList` implement Comparator? _____

8. What must the class of the `myCompare` object implement? _____

9. What method must the class of the `myCompare` object implement? _____

Uh-oh. The sorting all works, but now we have duplicates...

The sorting works great, now we know how to sort on both *title* (using the Song object's compareTo() method) and *artist* (using the Comparator's compare() method). But there's a new problem we didn't notice with a test sample of the jukebox text file—**the sorted list contains duplicates.**

It appears that the diner jukebox just keeps writing to the file regardless of whether the same song has already been played (and thus written) to the text file. The SongListMore.txt jukebox text file is a complete record of every song that was played, and might contain the same song multiple times.

```
File Edit Window Help TooManyNotes

%java Jukebox4

[Pink Moon: Nick Drake, Somersault: Zero 7, Shiva Moon: Prem
Joshua, Circles: BT, Deep Channel: Afro Celts, Passenger:
Headmix, Listen: Tahiti 80, Listen: Tahiti 80, Listen: Tahiti
80, Circles: BT]

[Circles: BT, Circles: BT, Deep Channel: Afro Celts, Listen:
Tahiti 80, Listen: Tahiti 80, Listen: Tahiti 80, Passenger:
Headmix, Pink Moon: Nick Drake, Shiva Moon: Prem Joshua,
Somersault: Zero 7]

[Deep Channel: Afro Celts, Circles: BT, Circles: BT, Passenger:
Headmix, Pink Moon: Nick Drake, Shiva Moon: Prem Joshua, Listen:
Tahiti 80, Listen: Tahiti 80, Listen: Tahiti 80, Somersault:
Zero 7]
```

— *Before sorting.*

After sorting using the Song's own compareTo() method (sort by title).

After sorting using the ArtistCompare Comparator (sort by artist name).

SongListMore.txt

```
Pink Moon/Nick Drake/5/80
Somersault/Zero 7/4/84
Shiva Moon/Prem Joshua/6/120
Circles/BT/5/110
Deep Channel/Afro Celts/4/120
Passenger/Headmix/4/100
Listen/Tahiti 80/5/90
Listen/Tahiti 80/5/90
Listen/Tahiti 80/5/90
Circles/BT/5/110
```

The SongListMore text file now has duplicates in it, because the jukebox machine is writing every song played, in order. Somebody decided to play "Listen" three times in a row, followed by "Circles", a song that had been played earlier.

We can't change the way the text file is written because sometimes we're going to need all that information. We have to change the java code.

We need a Set instead of a List

From the Collection API, we find three main interfaces, **List**, **Set**, and **Map**. ArrayList is a **List**, but it looks like *Set* is exactly what we need.

▶ **LIST** - when *sequence* matters

Collections that know about *index position.*

Lists know where something is in the list. You can have more than one element referencing the same object.

Duplicates OK.

List

▶ **SET** - when *uniqueness* matters

Collections that *do not allow duplicates.*

Sets know whether something is already in the collection. You can never have more than one element referencing the same object (or more than one element referencing two objects that are considered equal—we'll look at what object equality means in a moment).

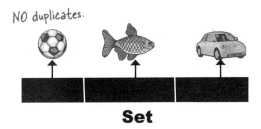

NO duplicates.

Set

▶ **MAP** - when *finding something by key* matters

Collections that use *key-value pairs.*
Maps know the value associated with a given key. You can have two keys that reference the same value, but you cannot have duplicate keys. Although keys are typically String names (so that you can make name/value property lists, for example), a key can be any object.

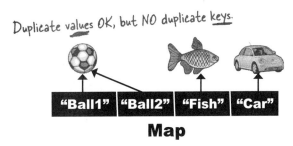

Duplicate values OK, but NO duplicate keys.

"Ball1" | "Ball2" | "Fish" | "Car"
Map

The Collection API (part of it)

Notice that the Map interface doesn't actually extend the Collection interface, but Map is still considered part of the "Collection Framework" (also known as the "Collection API"). So Maps are still collections, even though they don't include java.util.Collection in their inheritance tree.

(Note: this is not the complete collection API; there are other classes and interfaces, but these are the ones we care most about.)

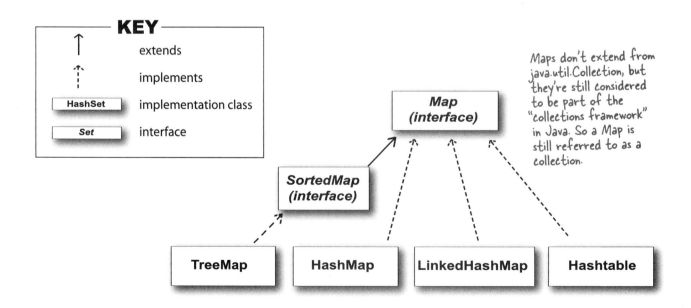

Maps don't extend from java.util.Collection, but they're still considered to be part of the "collections framework" in Java. So a Map is still referred to as a collection.

Using a HashSet instead of ArrayList

We added on to the Jukebox to put the songs in a HashSet. (Note: we left out some of the Jukebox code, but you can copy it from earlier versions. And to make it easier to read the output, we went back to the earlier version of the Song's toString() method, so that it prints only the title instead of title *and* artist.)

```java
import java.util.*;
import java.io.*;

public class Jukebox6 {
    ArrayList<Song> songList = new ArrayList<Song>();
    // main method etc.

    public void go() {
        getSongs();
        System.out.println(songList);
        Collections.sort(songList);
        System.out.println(songList);

        HashSet<Song> songSet = new HashSet<Song>();
        songSet.addAll(songList);
        System.out.println(songSet);
    }
    // getSongs() and addSong() methods
}
```

We didn't change getSongs(), so it still puts the songs in an ArrayList

Here we create a new HashSet parameterized to hold Songs.

HashSet has a simple addAll() method that can take another collection and use it to populate the HashSet. It's the same as if we added each song one at a time (except much simpler).

```
File Edit Window Help GetBetterMusic

%java Jukebox6

[Pink Moon, Somersault, Shiva Moon, Circles, Deep Channel,
Passenger, Listen, Listen, Listen, Circles]

[Circles, Circles, Deep Channel, Listen, Listen, Listen,
Passenger, Pink Moon, Shiva Moon, Somersault]

[Pink Moon, Listen, Shiva Moon, Circles, Listen, Deep Channel,
Passenger, Circles, Listen, Somersault]
```

Before sorting the ArrayList.

After sorting the ArrayList (by title).

After putting it into a HashSet, and printing the HashSet (we didn't call sort() again).

The Set didn't help!! We still have all the duplicates!

(And it lost its sort order when we put the list into a HashSet, but we'll worry about that one later...)

What makes two objects equal?

First, we have to ask—what makes two Song references duplicates? They must be considered *equal*. Is it simply two references to the very same object, or is it two separate objects that both have the same *title*?

This brings up a key issue: *reference* equality vs. *object* equality.

> If two objects *foo* and *bar* are equal, *foo.equals(bar)* must be *true*, and both *foo* and *bar* must return the same value from *hashCode()*. For a Set to treat two objects as duplicates, you must override the hashCode() and equals() methods inherited from class Object, so that you can make two different objects be viewed as equal.

▶ Reference equality
Two references, one object on the heap.

Two references that refer to the same object on the heap are equal. Period. If you call the **hashCode()** method on both references, you'll get the same result. If you don't override the hashCode() method, the default behavior (remember, you inherited this from class Object) is that each object will get a unique number (most versions of Java assign a hashcode based on the object's memory address on the heap, so no two objects will have the same hashcode).

If you want to know if two *references* are really referring to the same object, use the == operator, which (remember) compares the bits in the variables. If both references point to the same object, the bits will be identical.

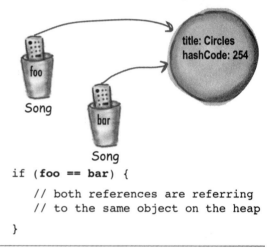

```
if (foo == bar) {
    // both references are referring
    // to the same object on the heap
}
```

▶ Object equality
Two references, two objects on the heap, but the objects are considered *meaningfully equivalent.*

If you want to treat two different Song objects as equal (for example if you decided that two Songs are the same if they have matching *title* variables), you must override *both* the **hashCode()** and **equals()** methods inherited from class Object.

As we said above, if you *don't* override hashCode(), the default behavior (from Object) is to give each object a unique hashcode value. So you must override hashCode() to be sure that two equivalent objects return the same hashcode. But you must also override equals() so that if you call it on *either* object, passing in the other object, always returns *true*.

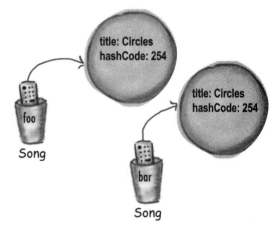

```
if (foo.equals(bar) && foo.hashCode() == bar.hashCode()) {
    // both references are referring to either a
    // a single object, or to two objects that are equal
}
```

How a HashSet checks for duplicates: hashCode() and equals()

When you put an object into a Hashset, it uses the object's hashcode value to determine where to put the object in the Set. But it also compares the object's hashcode to the hashcode of all the other objects in the HashSet, and if there's no matching hashcode, the HashSet assumes that this new object is not a duplicate.

In other words, if the hashcodes are different, the HashSet assumes there's no way the objects can be equal!

So you must override hashCode() to make sure the objects have the same value.

But two objects with the same hashCode() might *not* be equal (more on this on the next page), so if the

HashSet finds a matching hashcode for two objects—one you're inserting and one already in the set—the HashSet will then call one of the object's equals() methods to see if these hashcode-matched objects really *are* equal.

And if they're equal, the HashSet knows that the object you're attempting to add is a duplicate of something in the Set, so the add doesn't happen.

You don't get an exception, but the HashSet's add() method returns a boolean to tell you (if you care) whether the new object was added. So if the add() method returns *false*, you know the new object was a duplicate of something already in the set.

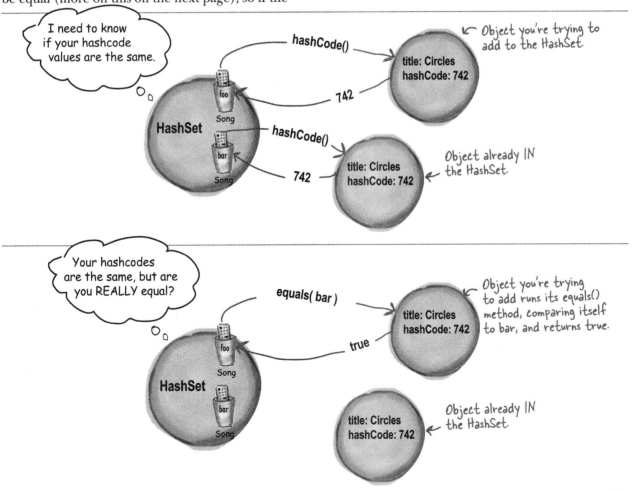

The Song class with overridden hashCode() and equals()

```
class Song implements Comparable<Song>{
    String title;
    String artist;
    String rating;
    String bpm;

    public boolean equals(Object aSong) {
        Song s = (Song) aSong;
        return getTitle().equals(s.getTitle());
    }

    public int hashCode() {
        return title.hashCode();
    }

    public int compareTo(Song s) {
        return title.compareTo(s.getTitle());
    }

    Song(String t, String a, String r, String b) {
        title = t;
        artist = a;
        rating = r;
        bpm = b;
    }

    public String getTitle() {
        return title;
    }

    public String getArtist() {
        return artist;
    }

    public String getRating() {
        return rating;
    }

    public String getBpm() {
        return bpm;
    }

    public String toString() {
        return title;
    }
}
```

The HashSet (or anyone else calling this method) sends it another Song.

The GREAT news is that title is a String, and Strings have an overridden equals() method. So all we have to do is ask one title if it's equal to the other song's title.

Same deal here... the String class has an overridden hashCode() method, so you can just return the result of calling hashCode() on the title. Notice how hashCode() and equals() are using the SAME instance variable.

Now it works! No duplicates when we print out the HashSet. But we didn't call sort() again, and when we put the ArrayList into the HashSet, the HashSet didn't preserve the sort order.

File Edit Window Help RebootWindows

```
%java Jukebox6

[Pink Moon, Somersault, Shiva Moon, Circles,
Deep Channel, Passenger, Listen, Listen,
Listen, Circles]

[Circles, Circles, Deep Channel, Listen,
Listen, Listen, Passenger, Pink Moon, Shiva
Moon, Somersault]

[Pink Moon, Listen, Shiva Moon, Circles,
Deep Channel, Passenger, Somersault]
```

Java Object Law For HashCode() and equals()

The API docs for class Object state the rules you MUST follow:

▶ If two objects are equal, they MUST have matching hashcodes.

▶ If two objects are equal, calling equals() on either object MUST return true. In other words, if (a.equals(b)) then (b.equals(a)).

▶ If two objects have the same hashcode value, they are NOT required to be equal. But if they're equal, they MUST have the same hashcode value.

▶ So, if you override equals(), you MUST override hashCode().

▶ The default behavior of hashCode() is to generate a unique integer for each object on the heap. So if you don't override hashCode() in a class, no two objects of that type can EVER be considered equal.

▶ The default behavior of equals() is to do an == comparison. In other words, to test whether the two references refer to a single object on the heap. So if you don't override equals() in a class, no two objects can EVER be considered equal since references to two different objects will always contain a different bit pattern.

a.equals(b) must also mean that *a.hashCode() == b.hashCode()*

But *a.hashCode() == b.hashCode()* does NOT have to mean *a.equals(b)*

there are no Dumb Questions

Q: How come hashcodes can be the same even if objects aren't equal?

A: HashSets use hashcodes to store the elements in a way that makes it much faster to access. If you try to find an object in an ArrayList by giving the ArrayList a copy of the object (as opposed to an index value), the ArrayList has to start searching from the beginning, looking at each element in the list to see if it matches. But a HashSet can find an object much more quickly, because it uses the hashcode as a kind of label on the "bucket" where it stored the element. So if you say, "I want you to find an object in the set that's exactly like this one..." the HashSet gets the hashcode value from the copy of the Song you give it (say, 742), and then the HashSet says, "Oh, I know exactly where the object with hashcode #742 is stored...", and it goes right to the #742 bucket.

This isn't the whole story you get in a computer science class, but it's enough for you to use HashSets effectively. In reality, developing a good hashcode algorithm is the subject of many a PhD thesis, and more than we want to cover in this book.

The point is that hashcodes can be the same without necessarily guaranteeing that the objects are equal, because the "hashing algorithm" used in the hashCode() method might happen to return the same value for multiple objects. And yes, that means that multiple objects would all land in the same bucket in the HashSet (because each bucket represents a single hashcode value), but that's not the end of the world. It might mean that the HashSet is just a little less efficient (or that it's filled with an extremely large number of elements), but if the HashSet finds more than one object in the same hashcode bucket, the HashSet will simply use the equals() method to see if there's a perfect match. In other words, hashcode values are sometimes used to narrow down the search, but to find the one exact match, the HashSet still has to take all the objects in that one bucket (the bucket for all objects with the same hashcode) and then call equals() on them to see if the object it's looking for is in that bucket.

And if we want the set to stay sorted, we've got TreeSet

TreeSet is similar to HashSet in that it prevents duplicates. But it also *keeps* the list sorted. It works just like the sort() method in that if you make a TreeSet using the set's no-arg constructor, the TreeSet uses each object's compareTo() method for the sort. But you have the option of passing a Comparator to the TreeSet constructor, to have the TreeSet use that instead. The downside to TreeSet is that if you don't *need* sorting, you're still paying for it with a small performance hit. But you'll probably find that the hit is almost impossible to notice for most apps.

```java
import java.util.*;
import java.io.*;
public class Jukebox8 {
   ArrayList<Song> songList = new ArrayList<Song>();
   int val;

   public static void main(String[] args) {
      new Jukebox8().go();
   }

   public void go() {
      getSongs();
      System.out.println(songList);
      Collections.sort(songList);
      System.out.println(songList);
      TreeSet<Song> songSet = new TreeSet<Song>();
      songSet.addAll(songList);
      System.out.println(songSet);
   }

   void getSongs() {
      try {
         File file = new File("SongListMore.txt");
         BufferedReader reader = new BufferedReader(new FileReader(file));
         String line =  null;
         while ((line= reader.readLine()) != null) {
             addSong(line);
         }

      } catch(Exception ex) {
         ex.printStackTrace();
      }
   }

   void addSong(String lineToParse) {
      String[] tokens = lineToParse.split("/");
      Song nextSong = new Song(tokens[0], tokens[1], tokens[2], tokens[3]);
      songList.add(nextSong);
   }
}
```

Instantiate a TreeSet instead of HashSet. Calling the no-arg TreeSet constructor means the set will use the Song object's compareTo() method for the sort.

(We could have passed in a Comparator.)

We can add all the songs from the HashSet using addAll(). (Or we could have added the songs individually using songSet.add() just the way we added songs to the ArrayList.)

What you MUST know about TreeSet...

TreeSet looks easy, but make sure you really understand what you need to
do to use it. We thought it was so important that we made it an exercise so
you'd *have* to think about it. Do NOT turn the page until you've done this.
We mean it.

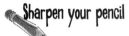 **Sharpen your pencil**

Look at this code.
Read it carefully, then
answer the questions
below. (Note: there
are no syntax errors
in this code.)

```java
import java.util.*;

public class TestTree {
    public static void main (String[] args) {
        new TestTree().go();
    }

    public void go() {
        Book b1 = new Book("How Cats Work");
        Book b2 = new Book("Remix your Body");
        Book b3 = new Book("Finding Emo");

        TreeSet<Book> tree = new TreeSet<Book>();
        tree.add(b1);
        tree.add(b2);
        tree.add(b3);
        System.out.println(tree);
    }
}

class Book {
    String title;
    public Book(String t) {
        title = t;
    }
}
```

1). What is the result when you compile this code?

_____

2). If it compiles, what is the result when you run the TestTree class?

_____

3). If there is a problem (either compile-time or runtime) with this code, how would you fix it?

_____

TreeSet elements MUST be comparable

TreeSet can't read the programmer's mind to figure out how the object's should be sorted. You have to tell the TreeSet *how*.

To use a TreeSet, one of these things must be true:

▶ **The elements in the list must be of a type that implements *Comparable***

The Book class on the previous page didn't implement Comparable, so it wouldn't work at runtime. Think about it, the poor TreeSet's sole purpose in life is to keep your elements sorted, and once again—it had no idea how to sort Book objects! It doesn't fail at compile-time, because the TreeSet add() method doesn't take a Comparable type, The TreeSet add() method takes whatever type you used when you created the TreeSet. In other words, if you say new TreeSet<Book>() the add() method is essentially add(Book). And there's no requirement that the Book class implement Comparable! But it fails at runtime when you add the second element to the set. That's the first time the set tries to call one of the object's compareTo() methods and... can't.

```java
class Book implements Comparable {
   String title;
   public Book(String t) {
      title = t;
   }
   public int compareTo(Object b) {
      Book book = (Book) b;
      return (title.compareTo(book.title));
   }
}
```

OR

▶ **You use the TreeSet's overloaded constructor that takes a *Comparator***

TreeSet works a lot like the sort() method—you have a choice of using the element's compareTo() method, assuming the element type implemented the Comparable interface, OR you can use a custom Comparator that knows how to sort the elements in the set. To use a custom Comparator, you call the TreeSet constructor that takes a Comparator.

```java
public class BookCompare implements Comparator<Book> {
   public int compare(Book one, Book two) {
      return (one.title.compareTo(two.title));
   }
}

class Test {
   public void go() {
      Book b1 = new Book("How Cats Work");
      Book b2 = new Book("Remix your Body");
      Book b3 = new Book("Finding Emo");
      BookCompare bCompare = new BookCompare();
      TreeSet<Book> tree = new TreeSet<Book>(bCompare);
      tree.add(new Book("How Cats Work"));
      tree.add(new Book("Finding Emo"));
      tree.add(new Book("Remix your Body"));
      System.out.println(tree);
   }
}
```

We've seen Lists and Sets, now we'll use a Map

Lists and Sets are great, but sometimes a Map is the best collection (not Collection with a capital "C"—remember that Maps are part of Java collections but they don't implement the Collection interface).

Imagine you want a collection that acts like a property list, where you give it a name and it gives you back the value associated with that name. Although keys will often be Strings, they can be any Java object (or, through autoboxing, a primitive).

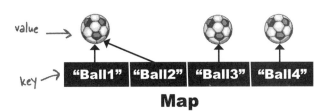

value →
key →
"Ball1" "Ball2" "Ball3" "Ball4"
Map

Each element in a Map is actually TWO objects—a _key_ and a _value_. You can have duplicate _values_, but NOT duplicate _keys_.

Map example

```
import java.util.*;

public class TestMap {

    public static void main(String[] args) {

        HashMap<String, Integer> scores = new HashMap<String, Integer>();

        scores.put("Kathy", 42);
        scores.put("Bert", 343);
        scores.put("Skyler", 420);

        System.out.println(scores);
        System.out.println(scores.get("Bert"));
    }
}
```

HashMap needs TWO type parameters—one for the key and one for the value.

Use put() instead of add(), and now of course it takes two arguments (key, value).

The get() method takes a key, and returns the value (in this case, an Integer).

```
File Edit Window Help WhereAmI
%java TestMap

{Skyler=420, Bert=343, Kathy=42}
343
```

When you print a Map, it gives you the key=value, in braces { } instead of the brackets [ ] you see when you print lists and sets.

Finally, back to generics

Remember earlier in the chapter we talked about how methods that take arguments with generic types can be... *weird*. And we mean weird in the polymorphic sense. If things start to feel strange here, just keep going—it takes a few pages to really tell the whole story.

We'll start with a reminder on how *array* arguments work, polymorphically, and then look at doing the same thing with generic lists. The code below compiles and runs without errors:

If a method argument is an *array* of Animals, it will also take an array of any Animal subtype.

In other words, if a method is declared as:

void foo(Animal[] a) { }

Assuming Dog extends Animal, you are free to call both:

foo(anAnimalArray);
foo(aDogArray);

Here's how it works with regular *arrays*:

```
import java.util.*;

public class TestGenerics1 {
    public static void main(String[] args) {
        new TestGenerics1().go();
    }

    public void go() {
        Animal[] animals = {new Dog(), new Cat(), new Dog()};
        Dog[] dogs = {new Dog(), new Dog(), new Dog()};
        takeAnimals(animals);
        takeAnimals(dogs);
    }

    public void takeAnimals(Animal[] animals) {
        for(Animal a: animals) {
            a.eat();
        }
    }
}
```

Declare and create an Animal array, that holds both dogs and cats.

Declare and create a Dog array, that holds only Dogs (the compiler won't let you put a Cat in).

← Call takeAnimals(), using both array types as arguments...

← The crucial point is that the takeAnimals() method can take an Animal[] or a Dog[], since Dog IS-A Animal. Polymorphism in action.

Remember, we can call ONLY the methods declared in type animal, since the animals parameter is of type Animal array, and we didn't do any casting. (What would we cast it to? That array might hold both Dogs and Cats.)

```
abstract class Animal {
    void eat() {
        System.out.println("animal eating");
    }
}
class Dog extends Animal {
    void bark() { }
}
class Cat extends Animal {
    void meow() { }
}
```

The simplified Animal class hierarchy.

Using polymorphic arguments and generics

So we saw how the whole thing worked with arrays, but will it work the same way when we switch from an array to an ArrayList? Sounds reasonable, doesn't it?

First, let's try it with only the Animal ArrayList. We made just a few changes to the go() method:

Passing in just ArrayList<Animal>

A simple change from Animal[] to ArrayList<Animal>.

```
public void go() {
    ArrayList<Animal> animals = new ArrayList<Animal>();
    animals.add(new Dog());
    animals.add(new Cat());       ← We have to add one at a time since there's no
    animals.add(new Dog());           shortcut syntax like there is for array creation.

    takeAnimals(animals);   ← This is the same code, except now the "animals"
}                               variable refers to an ArrayList instead of array.
```

```
public void takeAnimals(ArrayList<Animal> animals) {
    for(Animal a: animals) {
    a.eat();
    }
}
```
The method now takes an ArrayList instead of an array, but everything else is the same. Remember, that for loop syntax works for both arrays and collections.

Compiles and runs just fine

```
File Edit Window Help CatFoodIsBetter
%java TestGenerics2

animal eating
animal eating
animal eating
animal eating
animal eating
animal eating
```

But will it work with ArrayList<Dog> ?

Because of polymorphism, the compiler let us pass a Dog array to a method with an Animal array argument. No problem. And an ArrayList<Animal> can be passed to a method with an ArrayList<Animal> argument. So the big question is, will the ArrayList<Animal> argument accept an ArrayList<Dog>? If it works with arrays, shouldn't it work here too?

Passing in just ArrayList<Dog>

```
public void go() {
    ArrayList<Animal> animals = new ArrayList<Animal>();
    animals.add(new Dog());
    animals.add(new Cat());
    animals.add(new Dog());
    takeAnimals(animals);    ←── We know this line worked fine.

    ArrayList<Dog> dogs = new ArrayList<Dog>();
    dogs.add(new Dog());                    Make a Dog ArrayList and put a couple dogs in.
    dogs.add(new Dog());
    takeAnimals(dogs);   ←── Will this work now that we changed
}                              from an array to an ArrayList?


public void takeAnimals(ArrayList<Animal> animals) {
    for(Animal a: animals) {
      a.eat();
    }
}
```

When we compile it:

```
File Edit Window Help CatsAreSmarter

%java TestGenerics3

TestGenerics3.java:21: takeAnimals(java.util.
ArrayList<Animal>) in TestGenerics3 cannot be applied to
(java.util.ArrayList<Dog>)
    takeAnimals(dogs);
    ^
1 error
```

It looked so right, but went so wrong...

> And I'm supposed to be OK with this? That totally screws my animal simulation where the veterinary program takes a list of any type of animal, so that a dog kennel can send a list of dogs, and a cat kennel can send a list of cats... now you're saying I can't do that if I use collections instead of arrays?

What could happen if it *were* allowed...

Imagine the compiler let you get away with that. It let you pass an ArrayList<Dog> to a method declared as:

```
public void takeAnimals(ArrayList<Animal> animals) {
    for(Animal a: animals) {
        a.eat();
    }
}
```

There's nothing in that method that *looks* harmful, right? After all, the whole point of polymorphism is that anything an Animal can do (in this case, the eat() method), a Dog can do as well. So what's the problem with having the method call eat() on each of the Dog references?

Nothing. Nothing at all.

There's nothing wrong with *that* code. But imagine *this* code instead:

```
public void takeAnimals(ArrayList<Animal> animals) {
    animals.add(new Cat());
}
```
← Yikes!! We just stuck a Cat in what might be a Dogs-only ArrayList.

So that's the problem. There's certainly nothing wrong with adding a Cat to an ArrayList<Animal>, and that's the whole point of having an ArrayList of a supertype like Animal—so that you can put all types of animals in a single Animal ArrayList.

But if you passed a Dog ArrayList—one meant to hold ONLY Dogs— to this method that takes an Animal ArrayList, then suddenly you'd end up with a Cat in the Dog list. The compiler knows that if it lets you pass a Dog ArrayList into the method like that, someone could, at runtime, add a Cat to your Dog list. So instead, the compiler just won't let you take the risk.

If you declare a method to take ArrayList<Animal> it can take ONLY an ArrayList<Animal>, not ArrayList<Dog> or ArrayList<Cat>.

Wait a minute... if this is why they won't let you pass a Dog ArrayList into a method that takes an Animal ArrayList—to stop you from possibly putting a Cat in what was actually a Dog list, then why does it work with *arrays*? Don't you have the same problem with arrays? Can't you still add a Cat object to a Dog[]?

Array types are checked again at runtime, but collection type checks happen only when you compile

Let's say you *do* add a Cat to an array declared as Dog[] (an array that was passed into a method argument declared as Animal[], which is a perfectly legal assignment for arrays).

```
public void go() {
    Dog[] dogs = {new Dog(), new Dog(), new Dog()};
    takeAnimals(dogs);
}

public void takeAnimals(Animal[] animals) {
    animals[0] = new Cat();
}
```

We put a new Cat into a Dog array. The compiler allowed it, because it knows that you might have passed a Cat array or Animal array to the method, so to the compiler it was possible that this was OK.

It compiles, but when we run it:

Whew! At least the JVM stopped it.

```
File Edit Window Help CatsAreSmarter
%java TestGenerics1
Exception in thread "main" java.lang.ArrayStoreException:
Cat
        at TestGenerics1.takeAnimals(TestGenerics1.java:16)
        at TestGenerics1.go(TestGenerics1.java:12)
        at TestGenerics1.main(TestGenerics1.java:5)
```

Wouldn't it be dreamy if there were a way to still use polymorphic collection types as method arguments, so that my veterinary program could take Dog lists and Cat lists? That way I could loop through the lists and call their immunize() method, but it would still have to be safe so that you couldn't add a Cat in to the Dog list. But I guess that's just a fantasy...

Wildcards to the rescue

It looks unusual, but there *is* a way to create a method argument that can accept an ArrayList of any Animal subtype. The simplest way is to use a **wildcard**—added to the Java language explicitly for this reason.

```
public void takeAnimals(ArrayList<? extends Animal> animals) {
    for(Animal a: animals) {
        a.eat();
    }
}
```

Remember, the keyword "extends" here means either <u>extends</u> OR <u>implements</u> depending on the type. So if you want to take an ArrayList of types that implement the Pet interface, you'd declare it as:

ArrayList<? extends Pet>

So now you're wondering, "What's the *difference*? Don't you have the same problem as before? The method above isn't doing anything dangerous—calling a method any Animal subtype is guaranteed to have—but can't someone still change this to add a Cat to the *animals* list, even though it's really an ArrayList<Dog>? And since it's not checked again at runtime, how is this any different from declaring it without the wildcard?"

And you'd be right for wondering. The answer is NO. When you use the wildcard <?> in your declaration, the compiler won't let you do anything that adds to the list!

> **When you use a wildcard in your method argument, the compiler will STOP you from doing anything that could hurt the list referenced by the method parameter.**
>
> **You can still invoke methods on the elements in the list, but you cannot add elements to the list.**
>
> **In other words, you can do things *with* the list elements, but you can't put *new* things in the list. So you're safe at runtime, because the compiler won't let you do anything that might be horrible at runtime.**
>
> **So, this is OK inside takeAnimals():**
>
> ```
> for(Animal a: animals) {
>     a.eat();
> }
> ```
>
> **But THIS would not compile:**
>
> ```
> animals.add(new Cat());
> ```

Alternate syntax for doing the same thing

You probably remember that when we looked at the sort() method, it used a generic type, but with an unusual format where the type parameter was declared before the return type. It's just a different way of declaring the type parameter, but the results are the same:

This:

```
public <T extends Animal> void takeThing(ArrayList<T> list)
```

Does the same thing as this:

```
public void takeThing(ArrayList<? extends Animal> list)
```

there are no Dumb Questions

Q: If they both do the same thing, why would you use one over the other?

A: It all depends on whether you want to use "T" some-where else. For example, what if you want the method to have two arguments—both of which are lists of a type that extend Animal? In that case, it's more efficient to just declare the type parameter once:

```
public <T extends Animal> void takeThing(ArrayList<T> one, ArrayList<T> two)
```

Instead of typing:

```
public void takeThing(ArrayList<? extends Animal> one,
                      ArrayList<? extends Animal> two)
```

BE the compiler, advanced

Your job is to play compiler and determine which of these statements would compile. But some of this code wasn't covered in the chapter, so you need to work out the answers based on what you DID learn, applying the "rules" to these new situations. In some cases, you might have to guess, but the point is to come up with a reasonable answer based on what you know so far.

(Note: assume that this code is within a legal class and method.)

Compiles?

```
ArrayList<Dog> dogs1 = new ArrayList<Animal>();
```

```
ArrayList<Animal> animals1 = new ArrayList<Dog>();
```

```
List<Animal> list = new ArrayList<Animal>();
```

```
ArrayList<Dog> dogs = new ArrayList<Dog>();
```

```
ArrayList<Animal> animals = dogs;
```

```
List<Dog> dogList = dogs;
```

```
ArrayList<Object> objects = new ArrayList<Object>();
```

```
List<Object> objList = objects;
```

```
ArrayList<Object> objs = new ArrayList<Dog>();
```

```java
import java.util.*;

public class SortMountains {

  LinkedList<Mountain> mtn = new LinkedList<Mountain>();

  class NameCompare implements Comparator <Mountain> {
    public int compare(Mountain one, Mountain two) {

      return one.name.compareTo(two.name);

    }
  }

  class HeightCompare implements Comparator <Mountain> {
    public int compare(Mountain one, Mountain two) {

      return (two.height - one.height);

    }
  }

  public static void main(String [] args) {
    new SortMountain().go();
  }

  public void go() {
    mtn.add(new Mountain("Longs", 14255));
    mtn.add(new Mountain("Elbert", 14433));
    mtn.add(new Mountain("Maroon", 14156));
    mtn.add(new Mountain("Castle", 14265));

    System.out.println("as entered:\n" + mtn);
    NameCompare nc = new NameCompare();

    Collections.sort(mtn, nc);
    System.out.println("by name:\n" + mtn);
    HeightCompare hc = new HeightCompare();

    Collections.sort(mtn, hc);
    System.out.println("by height:\n" + mtn);
  }
}

class Mountain {
  String name;
  int height;

  Mountain(String n, int h) {
    name = n;
    height = h;
  }
  public String toString( ) {
    return name + " " + height;
  }
```

Did you notice that the height list is in DESCENDING sequence? :)

Output:

```
File  Edit  Window  Help  ThisOne'sForBob
%java SortMountains
as entered:
[Longs 14255, Elbert 14433, Maroon 14156, Castle 14265]
by name:
[Castle 14265, Elbert 14433, Longs 14255, Maroon 14156]
by height:
[Elbert 14433, Castle 14265, Longs 14255, Maroon 14156]
```

Exercise Solution

Possible Answers:

Comparator,

Comparable,

compareTo( ),

compare( ),

yes,

no

Given the following compilable statement:

```
Collections.sort(myArrayList);
```

1. What must the class of the objects stored in myArrayList implement? **Comparable**

2. What method must the class of the objects stored in myArrayList implement? **compareTo( )**

3. Can the class of the objects stored in myArrayList implement both
   Comparator AND Comparable? **yes**

Given the following compilable statement:

```
Collections.sort(myArrayList, myCompare);
```

4. Can the class of the objects stored in myArrayList implement Comparable? **yes**

5. Can the class of the objects stored in myArrayList implement Comparator? **yes**

6. Must the class of the objects stored in myArrayList implement Comparable? **no**

7. Must the class of the objects stored in myArrayList implement Comparator? **no**

8. What must the class of the myCompare object implement? **Comparator**

9. What method must the class of the myCompare object implement? **compare( )**

BE the compiler solution

Compiles?

☐ `ArrayList<Dog> dogs1 = new ArrayList<Animal>();`

☐ `ArrayList<Animal> animals1 = new ArrayList<Dog>();`

☒ `List<Animal> list = new ArrayList<Animal>();`

☐ `ArrayList<Dog> dogs = new ArrayList<Dog>();`

☐ `ArrayList<Animal> animals = dogs;`

☒ `List<Dog> dogList = dogs;`

☒ `ArrayList<Object> objects = new ArrayList<Object>();`

☒ `List<Object> objList = objects;`

☐ `ArrayList<Object> objs = new ArrayList<Dog>();`

Release Your Code

It's time to let go. You wrote your code. You tested your code. You refined your code. You told everyone you know that if you never saw a line of code again, that'd be fine. But in the end, you've created a work of art. The thing actually runs! But now what? *How* do you give it to end users? *What* exactly do you give to end users? What if you don't even know who your end users are? In these final two chapters, we'll explore how to organize, package, and deploy your Java code. We'll look at local, semi-local, and remote deployment options including executable jars, Java Web Start, RMI, and Servlets. In this chapter, we'll spend most of our time on organizing and packaging your code—things you'll need to know regardless of your ultimate deployment choice. In the final chapter, we'll finish with one of the coolest things you can do in Java. Relax. Releasing your code is not saying goodbye. There's always maintenance...

Deploying your application

What exactly *is* a Java application? In other words, once you're done with development, what is it that you deliver? Chances are, your end-users don't have a system identical to yours. More importantly, they don't have your application. So now it's time to get your program in shape for deployment into The Outside World. In this chapter, we'll look at local deployments, including Executable Jars and the part-local/part-remote technology called Java Web Start. In the next chapter, we'll look at the more remote deployment options, including RMI and Servlets.

Deployment options

100% Local   Combination   100% Remote

① **Local**
The entire application runs on the end-user's computer, as a stand-alone, probably GUI, program, deployed as an executable JAR (we'll look at JAR in a few pages.)

② **Combination of local and remote**
The application is distributed with a client portion running on the user's local system, connected to a server where other parts of the application are running.

③ **Remote**
The entire Java application runs on a server system, with the client accessing the system through some non-Java means, probably a web browser.

But before we really get into the whole deployment thing, let's take a step back and look at what happens when you've finished programming your app and you simply want to pull out the class files to give them to an end-user. What's really *in* that working directory?

A Java program is a bunch of classes. That's the output of your development.

The real question is what to do with those classes when you're done.

Brain Barbell

What are the advantages and disadvantages of delivering your Java program as a local, stand-alone application running on the end-user's computer?

What are the advantages and disadvantages of delivering your Java program as web-based system where the user interacts with a web browser, and the Java code runs as servlets on the server?

It's finally done!

Imagine this scenario...

Bob's happily at work on the final pieces of his cool new Java program. After weeks of being in the "I'm-just-one-compile-away" mode, this time he's really done. The program is a fairly sophisticated GUI app, but since the bulk of it is Swing code, he's made only nine classes of his own.

At last, it's time to deliver the program to the client. He figures all he has to do is copy the nine class files, since the client already has the Java API installed. He starts by doing an **ls** on the directory where all his files are...

What the... ?

Whoa! Something strange has happened. Instead of 18 files (nine source code files and nine compiled class files), he sees 31 files, many of which have very strange names like:

Account$FileListener.class

Chart$SaveListener.class

and on it goes. He had completely forgotten that the compiler has to generate class files for all those inner class GUI event listeners he made, and that's what all the strangely-named classes are.

Now he has to carefully extract all the class files he needs. If he leaves even one of them out, his program won't work. But it's tricky since he doesn't want to accidentally send the client one of his *source* code files, yet everything is in the same directory in one big mess.

Separate source code and class files

A single directory with a pile of source code and class files is a mess. It turns out, Bob should have been organizing his files from the beginning, keeping the source code and compiled code separate. In other words, making sure his compiled class files didn't land in the same directory as his source code.

The key is a combination of directory structure organization and the -d compiler option.

There are dozens of ways you can organize your files, and your company might have a specific way they want you to do it. We recommend an organizational scheme that's become almost standard, though.

With this scheme, you create a project directory, and inside that you create a directory called **source** and a directory called **classes**. You start by saving your source code (.java files) into the **source** directory. Then the trick is to compile your code in such a way that the output (the .class files) ends up in the *classes* directory.

And there's a nice compiler flag, **-d**, that lets you do that.

But I thought I didn't have a choice about putting the class files in with the source files. When you compile, they just *go* there, so what do I do?

Compiling with the -d (directory) flag

```
%cd MyProject/source
%javac  -d ../classes  MyApp.java
```

tells the compiler to put the compiled code (class files) into the "classes: directory that's one directory up and back down again from the current working directory.

the last thing is still the name of the java file to compile

By using the **-d** flag, *you* get to decide which *directory* the compiled code lands in, rather than accepting the default of class files landing in the same directory as the source code. To compile all the .java files in the source directory, use:

```
%javac  -d ../classes  *.java
```

*.java compiles ALL source files in the current directory

Running your code

```
%cd MyProject/classes
%java Mini
```

run your program from the 'classes' directory.

compiled code lands here

compile from THIS directory

MyProject

classes   **source**

run your main() from here

```
101101
101101
10101000010
1010 10 0
01010  1
1010101
10101010
1001010101
```
MyApp.class

```
Lorper
iure eugue
tat vero
conse
eugueroLore
do eliquis
do del dip
```
MyApp.java

(troubleshooting note: everything in this chapter assumes that the current working directory (i.e. the ".") is in your classpath. If you have explicitly set a classpath environment variable, be certain that it contains the ".")

Put your Java in a JAR

A **JAR** file is a **J**ava **AR**chive. It's based on the pkzip file format, and it lets you bundle all your classes so that instead of presenting your client with 28 class files, you hand over just a single JAR file. If you're familiar with the tar command on UNIX, you'll recognize the jar tool commands. (Note: when we say JAR in all caps, we're referring to the archive *file*. When we use lowercase, we're referring to the *jar tool* you use to create JAR files.)

The question is, what does the client *do* with the JAR? How do you get it to *run*?

You make the JAR *executable*.

An executable JAR means the end-user doesn't have to pull the class files out before running the program. The user can run the app while the class files are still in the JAR. The trick is to create a *manifest* file, that goes in the JAR and holds information about the files in the JAR. To make a JAR executable, the manifest must tell the JVM *which class has the main() method!*

Making an executable JAR

① **Make sure all of your class files are in the classes directory**

We're going to refine this in a few pages, but for now, keep all your class files sitting in the directory named 'classes'.

② **Create a manifest.txt file that states which class has the main() method**

Make a text file named manifest.txt that has a one line:

Main-Class: MyApp ← don't put the .class on the end

Press the return key after typing the Main-Class line, or your manifest may not work correctly. Put the manifest file into the "classes" directory.

③ **Run the jar tool to create a JAR file that contains everything in the classes directory, plus the manifest.**

```
%cd MiniProject/classes
%jar -cvmf manifest.txt app1.jar *.class
OR
%jar -cvmf manifest.txt app1.jar MyApp.class
```

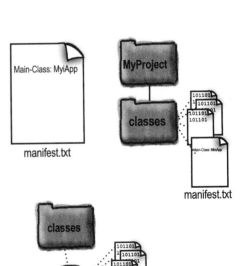

100% Local   **Combination**   **100% Remote**

Most 100% local Java apps are deployed as executable JAR files.

Running (executing) the JAR

Java (the JVM) is capable of loading a class from a JAR, and calling the main() method of that class. In fact, the entire application can *stay* in the JAR. Once the ball is rolling (i.e., the main() method starts running), the JVM doesn't care *where* your classes come from, as long as it can find them. And one of the places the JVM looks is within any JAR files in the classpath. If it can *see* a JAR, the JVM will *look* in that JAR when it needs to find and load a class.

The JVM has to 'see' the JAR, so it must be in your classpath. The easiest way to make the JAR visible is to make your working directory the place where the JAR is.

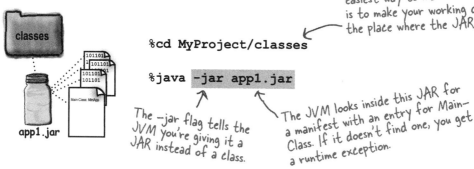

```
%cd MyProject/classes
```

```
%java -jar app1.jar
```

The -jar flag tells the JVM you're giving it a JAR instead of a class.

The JVM looks inside this JAR for a manifest with an entry for Main-Class. If it doesn't find one, you get a runtime exception.

Depending on how your operating system is configured, you might even be able to simply double-click the JAR file to launch it. This works on most flavors of Windows, and Mac OS X. You can usually make this happen by selecting the JAR and telling the OS to "Open with..." (or whatever the equivalent is on your operating system).

---

there are no Dumb Questions

Q: Why can't I just JAR up an entire directory?

A: The JVM looks inside the JAR and expects to find what it needs *right there*. It won't go digging into other directories, unless the class is part of a package, and even *then* the JVM looks only in the directories that match the package statement?

Q: What did you just say?

A: You can't put your class files into some arbitrary directory and JAR them up that way. But if your classes belong to packages, you can JAR up the entire package directory structure. In fact, you *must*. We'll explain all this on the next page, so you can relax.

Put your classes in packages!

So you've written some nicely reusable class files, and you've posted them in your internal development library for other programmers to use. While basking in the glow of having just delivered some of the (in your humble opinion) best examples of OO ever conceived, you get a phone call. A frantic one. Two of your classes have the same name as the classes Fred just delivered to the library. And all hell is breaking loose out there, as naming collisions and ambiguities bring development to its knees.

And all because you didn't use packages! Well, you did use packages, in the sense of using classes in the Java API that are, of course, in packages. But you didn't put your own classes into packages, and in the Real World, that's Really Bad.

We're going to modify the organizational structure from the previous pages, just a little, to put classes into a package, and to JAR the entire package. Pay very close attention to the subtle and picky details. Even the tiniest deviation can stop your code from compiling and/or running.

Packages prevent class name conflicts

Although packages aren't just for preventing name collisions, that's a key feature. You might write a class named Customer and a class named Account and a class named ShoppingCart. And what do you know, half of all developers working in enterprise e-commerce have probably written classes with those names. In an OO world, that's just dangerous. If part of the point of OO is to write reusable components, developers need to be able to piece together components from a variety of sources, and build something new out of them. Your components have to be able to 'play well with others', including those you didn't write or even know about.

Remember way back in chapter 6 when we discussed how a package name is like the full name of a class, technically known as the *fully-qualified name*. Class ArrayList is really **java.util.ArrayList**, JButton is really **javax.swing.JButton**, and Socket is really **java.net.Socket**. Notice that two of those classes, ArrayList and Socket, both have *java* as their "first name". In other words, the first part of their fully-qualified names is "java". Think of a hierarchy when you think of package structures, and organize your classes accordingly.

Package structure of the Java API for:

java.text.NumberFormat

java.util.ArrayList

java.awt.FlowLayout

java.awt.event.ActionEvent

java.net.Socket

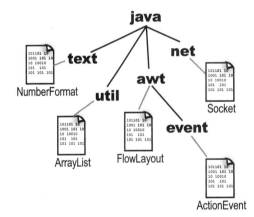

What does this picture look like to you? Doesn't it look a whole lot like a directory hierarchy?

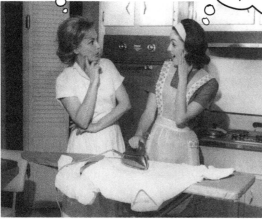

> ...so I finally settled on foo.bar.Heisenberg for my quantum baking class

> Why, that's the same name I was thinking of for my sub-atomic ironing class! Guess I'll just have to come up with something else.

Preventing package name conflicts

Putting your class in a package reduces the chances of naming conflicts with other classes, but what's to stop two programmers from coming up with identical *package* names? In other words, what's to stop two programmers, each with a class named Account, from putting the class in a package named shopping.customers? Both classes, in that case, would *still* have the same name:

shopping.customers.Account

Sun strongly suggests a package naming convention that greatly reduces that risk—prepend every class with your reverse domain name. Remember, domain names are guaranteed to be unique. Two different guys can be named Bartholomew Simpson, but two different domains cannot be named doh.com.

Packages can prevent name conflicts, but only if you choose a package name that's guaranteed to be unique. The best way to do that is to preface your packages with your reverse domain name.

com.headfirstbooks.Book
‿‿‿‿‿‿‿‿‿‿‿‿‿
    package name   class name

Reverse domain package names

→ com.headfirstjava.projects.Chart ← the class name is always capitalized

start the package with your reverse domain, separated by a dot (.), then add your own organizational structure after that

projects.Chart might be a common name, but adding com.headfirstjava means we have to worry about only our own in-house developers.

To put your class in a package:

① Choose a package name

We're using **com.headfirstjava** as our
example. The class name is PackageExercise,
so the fully-qualified name of the class is now:
com.headfirstjava.PackageExercise.

② Put a package statement in your class

It must be the first statement in the source
code file, above any import statements. There
can be only one package statement per source
code file, so **all classes in a source file must
be in the same package**. That includes inner
classes, of course.

```
package com.headfirstjava;

import javax.swing.*;

public class PackageExercise {
    // life-altering code here
}
```

③ Set up a matching directory structure

It's not enough to *say* your class is in a package,
by merely putting a package statement in
the code. Your class isn't *truly* in a package
until you put the class in a matching directory
structure. So, if the fully-qualified class name
is com.headfirstjava.PackageExercise, you
must put the PackageExercise source code in a
directory named **headfirstjava**, which *must* be in
a directory named **com**.
It is *possible* to compile without doing that, but
trust us—it's not worth the other problems
you'll have. Keep your source code in a directory
structure that matches the package structure,
and you'll avoid a ton of painful headaches down
the road.

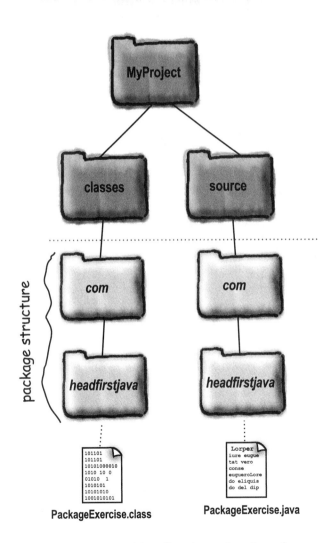

You must put a class into a directory structure that matches the package hierarchy.

Set up a matching directory structure for
both the source and classes trees.

Compiling and running with packages

When your class is in a package, it's a little trickier to compile and run. The main issue is that both the compiler and JVM have to be capable of finding your class and all of the other classes it uses. For the classes in the core API, that's never a problem. Java always knows where its own stuff is. But for your classes, the solution of compiling from the same directory where the source files are simply won't work (or at least not *reliably*). We guarantee, though, that if you follow the structure we describe on this page, you'll be successful. There are other ways to do it, but this is the one we've found the most reliable and the easiest to stick to.

Compiling with the -d (directory) flag

```
%cd MyProject/source
```
← stay in the source directory! Do NOT cd down into the directory where the .java file is!

```
%javac  -d ../classes  com/headfirstjava/PackageExercise.java
```

-d tells the compiler to put the compiled code (class files) into the classes directory, within the right package structure!! Yes, it knows.

Now you have to specify the PATH to get to the actual source file.

To compile all the .java files in the com.headfirstjava package, use:

```
%javac  -d ../classes  com/headfirstjava/*.java
```

compiles every source (.java) file in this directory

Running your code

```
%cd MyProject/classes
```
run your program from the 'classes' directory.

```
%java com.headfirstjava.PackageExercise
```

You MUST give the fully-qualified class name! The JVM will see that, and immediately look inside its current directory (classes) and expect to find a directory named com, where it expects to find a directory named headfirstjava, and in there it expects to find the class. If the class is in the "com" directory, or even in "classes", it won't work!

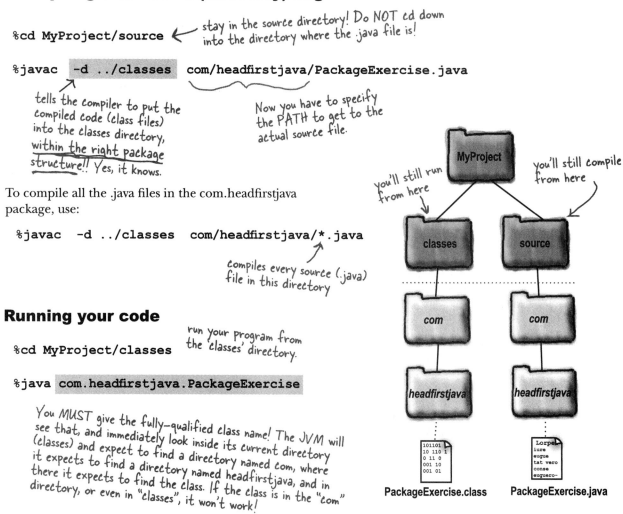

you'll still run from here

you'll still compile from here

MyProject

classes   source

com   com

headfirstjava   headfirstjava

PackageExercise.class   PackageExercise.java

The -d flag is even cooler than we said

Compiling with the **-d** flag is wonderful because not only does it let you send your compiled class files into a directory other than the one where the source file is, but it also knows to put the class into the correct directory structure for the package the class is in.

But it gets even better!

Let's say that you have a nice directory structure all set up for your source code. But you haven't set up a matching directory structure for your classes directory. Not a problem! Compiling with -d tells the compiler to not just *put* your classes into correct directory tree, but to the directories if they don't

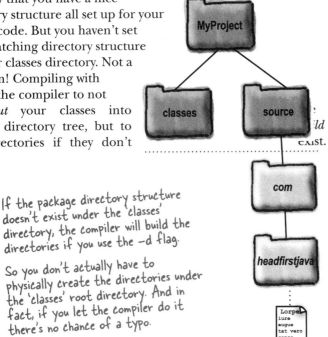

PackageExercise.java

If the package directory structure doesn't exist under the 'classes' directory, the compiler will build the directories if you use the -d flag.

So you don't actually have to physically create the directories under the 'classes' root directory. And in fact, if you let the compiler do it there's no chance of a typo.

> **The -d flag tells the compiler, "Put the class into its package directory structure, using the class specified after the -d as the root directory. But... if the directories aren't there, create them first and *then* put the class in the right place!"**

Q: I tried to cd into the directory where my main class was, but now the JVM says it can't find my class! But it's right THERE in the current directory!

A: Once your class is in a package, you can't call it by its 'short' name. You MUST specify, at the command-line, the fully-qualified name of the class whose main() method you want to run. But since the fully-qualified name includes the *package* structure, Java insists that the class be in a matching *directory* structure. So if at the command-line you say:

`%java com.foo.Book`

the JVM will look in its current directory (and the rest of its classpath), for a directory named "com". *It will not look for a class named Book, until it has found a directory named "com" with a directory inside named "foo".* Only then will the JVM accept that its found the correct Book class. If it finds a Book class anywhere else, it assumes the class isn't in the right structure, even if it is! The JVM won't for example, look back up the directory tree to say, "Oh, I can see that above us is a directory named com, so this must be the right package..."

Making an executable JAR with packages

When your class is in a package, the package directory structure must be inside the JAR! You can't just pop your classes in the JAR the way we did pre-packages. And you must be sure that you don't include any other directories above your package. The first directory of your package (usually com) must be the first directory within the JAR! If you were to accidentally include the directory *above* the package (e.g. the "classes" directory), the JAR wouldn't work correctly.

Making an executable JAR

(1) **Make sure all of your class files are within the correct package structure, under the classes directory.**

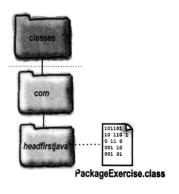

PackageExercise.class

(2) **Create a manifest.txt file that states which class has the main() method, and be sure to use the fully-qualified class name!**

Make a text file named manifest.txt that has a single line:

`Main-Class: com.headfirstjava.PackageExercise`

Put the manifest file into the classes directory

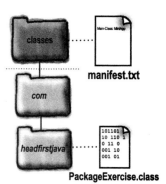

manifest.txt

PackageExercise.class

(3) **Run the jar tool to create a JAR file that contains the package directories plus the manifest**

The only thing you need to include is the 'com' directory, and the entire package (and all classes) will go into the JAR.

`%cd MyProject/classes`

All you specify is the com directory! And you'll get everything in it!

`%jar -cvmf  manifest.txt  packEx.jar  com`

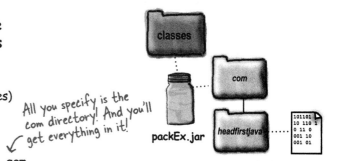

packEx.jar

PackageExercise.class

So where did the manifest file go?

Why don't we look inside the JAR and find out? From the command-line, the jar tool can do more than just create and run a JAR. You can extract the contents of a JAR (just like 'unzipping' or 'untarring').

Imagine you've put the packEx.jar into a directory named Skyler.

we put the JAR file into a directory named Skyler

jar commands for listing and extracting

① **List the contents of a JAR**

```
% jar -tf packEx.jar
```

↑ -tf stands for 'Table File' as in "show me a table of the JAR file"

```
File Edit  Window Help Pickle
% cd Skyler
% jar -tf packEx.jar
META-INF/
META-INF/MANIFEST.MF
com/
com/headfirstjava/
com/headfirstjava/
PackageExercise.class
```

the jar tool automatically builds a META-INF directory, and puts the manifest inside.

MANIFEST.MF

PackageExercise.class

② **Extract the contents of a JAR (i.e. unjar)**

```
% cd Skyler
% jar -xf packEx.jar
```

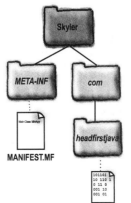

↑ -xf stands for 'Extract File' and it works just like unzipping or untarring. If you extract the packEx.jar, you'll see the META-INF directory and the com directory directory in your current directory

MANIFEST.MF

PackageExercise.class

META-INF stands for 'meta information'. The jar tool creates the META-INF directory as well as the MANIFEST.MF file. It also takes the contents of *your* manifest file, and puts it into the MANIFEST.MF file. So, *your* manifest *file* doesn't go into the JAR, but the *contents* of it are put into the 'real' manifest (MANIFEST.MF).

Sharpen your pencil

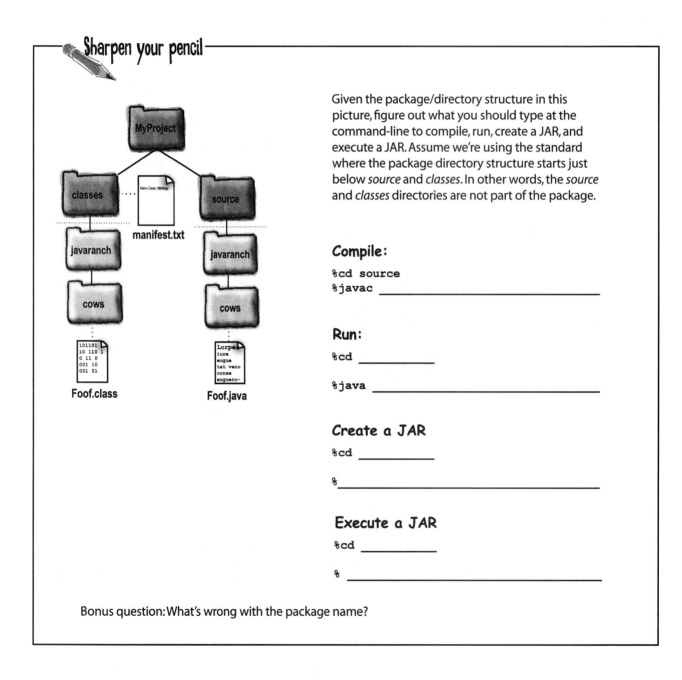

Given the package/directory structure in this picture, figure out what you should type at the command-line to compile, run, create a JAR, and execute a JAR. Assume we're using the standard where the package directory structure starts just below *source* and *classes*. In other words, the *source* and *classes* directories are not part of the package.

Compile:
```
%cd source
%javac _____
```

Run:
```
%cd _____
%java _____
```

Create a JAR
```
%cd _____
%_____
```

Execute a JAR
```
%cd _____
%_____
```

Bonus question: What's wrong with the package name?

there are no Dumb Questions

Q: What happens if you try to run an executable JAR, and the end-user doesn't have java installed?

A: Nothing will run, since without a JVM, Java code can't run. The end-user must have Java installed.

Q: How can I get Java installed on the end-user's machine?

Ideally, you can create a custom installer and distribute it along with your application. Several companies offer installer programs ranging from simple to extremely powerful. An installer program could, for example, detect whether or not the end-user has an appropriate version of Java installed, and if not, install and configure Java before installing your application. Installshield, InstallAnywhere, and DeployDirector all offer Java installer solutions.

Another cool thing about some of the installer programs is that you can even make a deployment CD-ROM that includes installers for all major Java platforms, so... one CD to rule them all. If the user's running on Solaris, for example, the Solaris version of Java is installed. On Windows, the Windows, version, etc. If you have the budget, this is by far the easiest way for your end-users to get the right version of Java installed and configured.

BULLET POINTS

- Organize your project so that your source code and class files are not in the same directory.

- A standard organization structure is to create a *project* directory, and then put a *source* directory and a *classes* directory inside the project directory.

- Organizing your classes into packages prevents naming collisions with other classes, if you prepend your reverse domain name on to the front of a class name.

- To put a class in a package, put a package statement at the top of the source code file, before any import statements:
  ```
  package com.wickedlysmart;
  ```

- To be in a package, a class must be in a *directory structure that exactly matches the package structure*. For a class, com.wickedlysmart.Foo, the Foo class must be in a directory named *wickedlysmart*, which is in a directory named *com*.

- To make your compiled class land in the correct package directory structure under the *classes* directory, use the **-d** compiler flag:
  ```
  % cd source
  % javac -d ../classes com/wickedlysmart/Foo.java
  ```

- To run your code, cd to the classes directory, and give the fully-qualified name of your class:
  ```
  % cd classes
  % java com.wickedlysmart.Foo
  ```

- You can bundle your classes into JAR (Java ARchive) files. JAR is based on the pkzip format.

- You can make an executable JAR file by putting a manifest into the JAR that states which class has the main() method. To create a manifest file, make a text file with an entry like the following (for example):
  ```
  Main-Class: com.wickedlysmart.Foo
  ```

- Be sure you hit the return key after typing the Main-Class line, or your manifest file may not work.

- To create a JAR file, type:
  ```
  jar -cvfm manifest.txt MyJar.jar com
  ```

- The entire package directory structure (and *only* the directories matching the package) must be immediately inside the JAR file.

- To run an executable JAR file, type:
  ```
  java -jar MyJar.jar
  ```

Executable JAR files are nice, but wouldn't it be dreamy if there were a way to make a rich, stand-alone client GUI that could be distributed over the Web? So that you wouldn't have to press and distribute all those CD-ROMs. And wouldn't it be just wonderful if the program could automatically update itself, replacing just the pieces that changed? The clients would always be up-to-date, and you'd never have to worry about delivering new

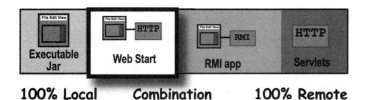

100% Local   Combination   100% Remote

Java Web Start

With Java Web Start (JWS), your application is launched for the first time from a Web browser (get it? *Web Start?*) but it runs as a stand-alone application (well, *almost*), without the constraints of the browser. And once it's downloaded to the end-user's machine (which happens the first time the user accesses the browser link that starts the download), it *stays* there.

Java Web Start is, among other things, a small Java program that lives on the client machine and works much like a browser plug-in (the way, say, Adobe Acrobat Reader opens when your browser gets a .pdf file). This Java program is called the **Java Web Start 'helper app'**, and its key purpose is to manage the downloading, updating, and launching (executing) of *your* JWS apps.

When JWS downloads your application (an executable JAR), it invokes the main() method for your app. After that, the end-user can launch your application directory from the JWS helper app *without* having to go back through the Web page link.

But that's not the best part. The amazing thing about JWS is its ability to detect when even a small part of application (say, a single class file) has changed on the server, and—without any end-user intervention—download and integrate the updated code.

There's still an issue, of course, like how does the end-user *get* Java and Java Web Start? They need both—Java to run the app, and Java Web Start (a small Java application itself) to handle retrieving and launching the app. But even *that* has been solved. You can set things up so that if your end-users don't have JWS, they can download it from Sun. And if they *do* have JWS, but their version of Java is out-of-date (because you've specified in your JWS app that you need a specific version of Java), the Java 2 Standard Edition can be downloaded to the end-user machine.

Best of all, it's simple to use. You can serve up a JWS app much like any other type of Web resource such as a plain old HTML page or a JPEG image. You set up a Web (HTML) page with a link to your JWS application, and you're in business.

In the end, your JWS application isn't much more than an executable JAR that end-users can download from the Web.

End-users launch a Java Web Start app by clicking on a link in a Web page. But once the app downloads, it runs outside the browser, just like any other stand-alone Java application. In fact, a Java Web Start app is just an executable JAR that's distributed over the Web.

How Java Web Start works

① **The client clicks on a Web page link to your JWS application (a .jnlp file).**

The Web page link

`<a href="MyApp.jnlp">Click</a>`

② **The Web server (HTTP) gets the request and sends back a .jnlp file (this is NOT the JAR).**

The .jnlp file is an XML document that states the name of the application's executable JAR file.

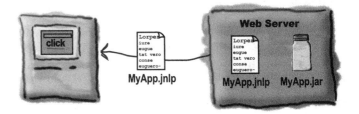

③ **Java Web Start (a small 'helper app' on the client) is started up by the browser. The JWS helper app reads the .jnlp file, and asks the server for the MyApp.jar file.**

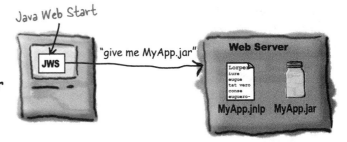

④ **The Web server 'serves' up the requested .jar file.**

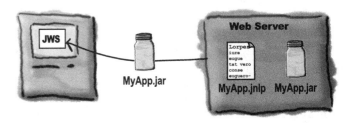

⑤ **Java Web Start gets the JAR and starts the application by calling the specified main( ) method (just like an executable JAR).**

Next time the user wants to run this app, he can open the Java Web Start application and from there launch your app, without even being online.

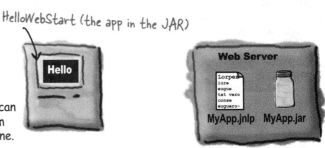

The .jnlp file

To make a Java Web Start app, you need to .jnlp (Java Network Launch Protocol) file that describes your application. This is the file the JWS app reads and uses to find your JAR and launch the app (by calling the JAR's main() method). A .jnlp file is a simple XML document that has several different things you can put in, but as a minimum, it should look like this:

```xml
<?xml version="1.0" encoding="utf-8"?>


<jnlp spec="0.2 1.0"
        codebase="http://127.0.0.1/~kathy"
        href="MyApp.jnlp">
```

The 'codebase' tag is where you specify the 'root' of where your web start stuff is on the server. We're testing this on our localhost, so we're using the local loopback address "127.0.0.1". For web start apps on our internet web server, this would say, "http://www.wickedlysmart.com"

This is the location of the .jnlp file relative to the codebase. This example shows that MyApp.jnlp is available in the root directory of the web server, not nested in some other directory.

```xml
    <information>
        <title>kathy App</title>
        <vendor>Wickedly Smart</vendor>
        <homepage href="index.html"/>
        <description>Head First WebStart demo</description>
        <icon href="kathys.gif"/>
        <offline-allowed/>
    </information>
```

Be sure to include all of these tags, or your app might not work correctly! The 'information' tags are used by the JWS helper app, mostly for displaying when the user wants to relaunch a previously-downloaded application.

This means the user can run your program without being connected to the internet. If the user is offline, it means the automatic-updating feature won't work.

```xml
    <resources>
        <j2se version="1.3+"/>
        <jar href="MyApp.jar"/>
    </resources>
```

This says that your app needs version 1.3 of Java, or greater.

The name of your executable JAR! You might have other JAR files as well, that hold other classes or even sounds and images used by your app.

```xml
    <application-desc main-class="HelloWebStart"/>
</jnlp>
```

This is like the mainfest Main-Class entry... it says which class in the JAR has the main() method.

Steps for making and deploying a Java Web Start app

① Make an executable JAR for your application.

MyApp.jar

② Write a .jnlp file.

MyApp.jnlp

③ Place your JAR and .jnlp files on your Web server.

MyApp.jnlp   MyApp.jar

④ Add a new mime type to your Web server.

`application/x-java-jnlp-file`

This causes the server to send the .jnlp file with the correct header, so that when the browser receives the .jnlp file it knows what it is and knows to start the JWS helper app.

⑤ Create a Web page with a link to your .jnlp file

MyJWSApp.html

```
<HTML>
  <BODY>
    <a href="MyApp2.jnlp">Launch My Application</a>
  </BODY>
</HTML>
```

What's First?

Look at the sequence of events below, and place them in the order in which they occur in a JWS application.

1.

2.

3.

4.

5.

6.

7.

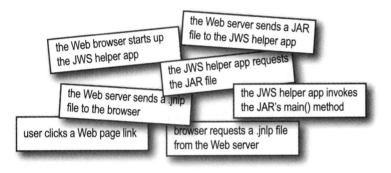

the Web browser starts up the JWS helper app

the Web server sends a JAR file to the JWS helper app

the JWS helper app requests the JAR file

the Web server sends a .jnlp file to the browser

the JWS helper app invokes the JAR's main() method

user clicks a Web page link

browser requests a .jnlp file from the Web server

---

there are no Dumb Questions

Q: How is Java Web Start different from an applet?

A: Applets can't live outside of a Web browser. An applet is downloaded from the Web as part of a Web page rather than simply from a Web page. In other words, to the browser, the applet is just like a JPEG or any other resource. The browser uses either a Java plug-in or the browser's own built-in Java (far less common today) to run the applet. Applets don't have the same level of functionality for things such as automatic updating, and they must always be launched from the browser. With JWS applications, once they're downloaded from the Web, the user doesn't even have to be using a browser to relaunch the application locally. Instead, the user can start up the JWS helper app, and use it to launch the already-downloaded application again.

Q: What are the security restrictions of JWS?

A: JWS apps have several limitations including being restricted from reading and writing to the user's hard drive. But... JWS has its own API with a special open and save dialog box so that, with the user's permission, your app can save and read its own files in a special, restricted area of the user's drive.

BULLET POINTS

- Java Web Start technology lets you deploy a stand-alone client application from the Web.

- Java Web Start includes a 'helper app' that must be installed on the client (along with Java).

- A Java Web Start (JWS) app has two pieces: an executable JAR and a .jnlp file.

- A .jnlp file is a simple XML document that describes your JWS application. It includes tags for specifying the name and location of the JAR, and the name of the class with the main() method.

- When a browser gets a .jnlp file from the server (because the user clicked on a link to the .jnlp file), the browser starts up the JWS helper app.

- The JWS helper app reads the .jnlp file and requests the executable JAR from the Web server.

- When the JWS gets the JAR, it invokes the main() method (specified in the .jnlp file).

We explored packaging, deployment, and JWS in this chapter. Your job is to decide whether each of the following statements is true or false.

☝ TRUE OR FALSE 👎

1. The Java compiler has a flag, -d, that lets you decide where your .class files should go.

2. A JAR is a standard directory where your .class files should reside.

3. When creating a Java Archive you must create a file called jar.mf.

4. The supporting file in a Java Archive declares which class has the main() method.

5. JAR files must be unzipped before the JVM can use the classes inside.

6. At the command line, Java Archives are invoked using the -arch flag.

7. Package structures are meaningfully represented using hierarchies.

8. Using your company's domain name is not recommended when naming packages.

9. Different classes within a source file can belong to different packages.

10. When compiling classes in a package, the -p flag is highly recommended.

11. When compiling classes in a package, the full name must mirror the directory tree.

12. Judicious use of the -d flag can help to assure that there are no typos in your class tree.

13. Extracting a JAR with packages will create a directory called meta-inf.

14. Extracting a JAR with packages will create a file called manifest.mf.

15. The JWS helper app always runs in conjunction with a browser.

16. JWS applications require a .nlp (Network Launch Protocol) file to work properly.

17. A JWS's main method is specified in its JAR file.

Exercise

Summary-Cross 7.0

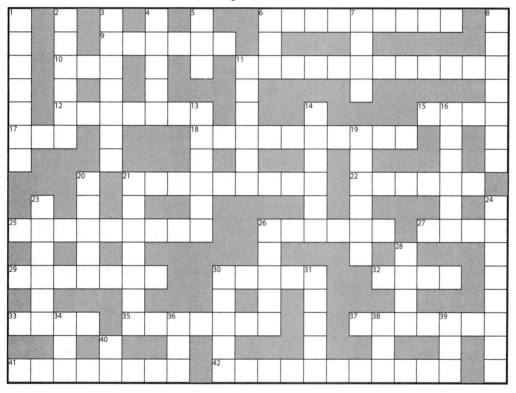

Anything in the book is fair game for this one!

Across

6. Won't travel
9. Don't split me
10. Release-able
11. Got the key
12. I/O gang
15. Flatten
17. Encapsulated returner
18. Ship this one
21. Make it so
22. I/O sieve
25. Disk leaf
26. Mine is unique
27. GUI's target
29. Java team
30. Factory
32. For a while
33. Atomic * 8
35. Good as new
37. Pairs event
41. Where do I start
42. A little firewall

Down

1. Pushy widgets
2. _____ of my desire
3. 'Abandoned' moniker
4. A chunk
5. Math not trig
6. Be brave
7. Arrange well
8. Swing slang
11. I/O canals
13. Organized release
14. Not for an instance
16. Who's allowed
19. Efficiency expert
20. Early exit
21. Common wrapper
23. Yes or no
24. Java jackets
26. Not behavior
28. Socket's suite
30. I/O cleanup
31. Milli-nap
34. Trig method
36. Encaps method
38. JNLP format
39. VB's final
40. Java branch

Exercise
Solutions

1. | user clicks a Web page link |

2. | browser requests a .jnlp file from the Web server |

3. | the Web server sends a .jnlp file to the browser |

4. | the Web browser starts up the JWS helper app |

5. | the JWS helper app requests the JAR file |

6. | the Web server sends a JAR file to the JWS helper app |

7. | the JWS helper app invokes the JAR's main() method |

True   1. The Java compiler has a flag, -d, that lets you decide where your .class files should go.

False   2. A JAR is a standard directory where your .class files should reside.

False   3. When creating a Java Archive you must create a file called jar,mf.

True   4. The supporting file in a Java Archive declares which class has the main() method.

False   5. JAR files must be unzipped before the JVM can use the classes inside.

False   6. At the command line, Java Archives are invoked using the -arch flag.

True   7. Package structures are meaningfully represented using hierarchies.

False   8. Using your company's domain name is not recommended when naming packages.

False   9. Different classes within a source file can belong to different packages.

False   10. When compiling classes in a package, the -p flag is highly recommended.

True   11. When compiling classes in a package, the full name must mirror the directory tree.

True   12. Judicious use of the -d flag can help to assure that there are no typos in your tree.

True   13. Extracting a JAR with packages will create a directory called meta-inf.

True   14. Extracting a JAR with packages will create a file called manifest.mf.

False   15. The JWS helper app always runs in conjunction with a browser.

False   16. JWS applications require a .nlp (Network Launch Protocol) file to work properly.

False   17. A JWS's main method is specified in its JAR file.

Summary-Cross 7.0

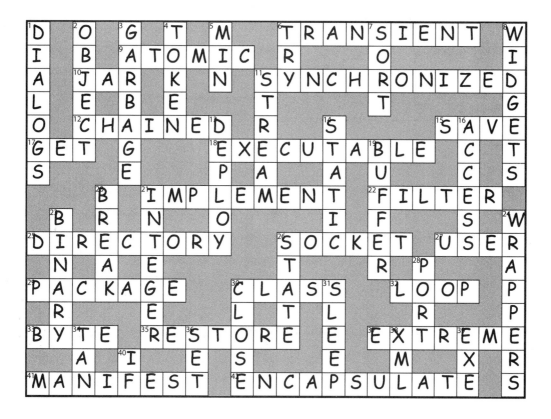

Distributed Computing

Everyone says long-distance relationships are hard, but with RMI, it's easy. No matter how far apart we *really* are, RMI makes it *seem* like we're together.

Being remote doesn't have to be a bad thing. Sure, things *are* easier when all the parts of your application are in one place, in one heap, with one JVM to rule them all. But that's not always possible. Or desirable. What if your application handles powerful computations, but the end-users are on a wimpy little Java-enabled device? What if your app needs data from a database, but for security reasons, only code on your server can access the database? Imagine a big e-commerce back-end, that has to run within a transaction-management system? Sometimes, part of your app *must* run on a server, while another part (usually a client) must run on a *different* machine. In this chapter, we'll learn to use Java's amazingly simple Remote Method Invocation (RMI) technology. We'll also take a quick peek at Servlets, Enterprise Java Beans (EJB), and Jini, and look at the ways in which EJB and Jini *depend* on RMI. We'll end the book by writing one of the coolest things you can make in Java, a *universal service browser*.

100% Local   Combination   100% Remote

Method calls are always between two objects on the <u>same</u> heap.

So far in this book, every method we've invoked has been on an object running in the same virtual machine as the caller. In other words, the calling object and the callee (the object we're invoking the method on) live on the same heap.

```java
class Foo {
    void go() {
        Bar b = new Bar();
        b.doStuff();
    }
    public static void main (String[] args) {
        Foo f = new Foo();
        f.go();
    }
}
```

In the code above, we know that the Foo instance referenced by *f* and the Bar object referenced by *b* are both on the same heap, run by the same JVM. Remember, the JVM is responsible for stuffing bits into the reference variable that represent *how to get to an object on the heap*. The JVM always knows where each object is, and how to get to it. But the JVM can know about references on only its *own* heap! You can't, for example, have a JVM running on one machine knowing about the heap space of a JVM running on a *different* machine. In fact, a JVM running on one machine can't know anything about a different JVM running on the *same* machine. It makes no difference if the JVMs are on the same or different physical machines; it matters only that the two JVMs are, well, two different invocations of the JVM.

one heap, two objects

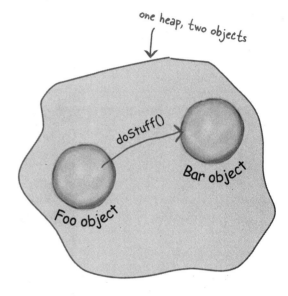

In most applications, when one object calls a method on another, both objects are on the same heap. In other words, both are running within the same JVM.

What if you want to invoke a method on an object running on another machine?

We know how to get information from one machine to another—with Sockets and I/O. We open a Socket connection to another machine, and get an OutputStream and write some data to it.

But what if we actually want to *call a method* on something running in another machine... another JVM? Of course we could always build our own protocol, and when you send data to a ServerSocket the server could parse it, figure out what you meant, do the work, and send back the result on another stream. What a pain, though. Think how much nicer it would be to just get a reference to the object on the other machine, and call a method.

powerful, fast, loves to crunch through big calculations

Imagine two computers...

tiny, wimpy, painfully slow at calculations

Little

Big

Big has something Little wants.
Compute power.

Little wants to send some data to Big, so that Big can do the heavy computing.

Little wants simply to call a method...

```
double doCalcUsingDatabase(CalcNumbers numbers)
```

and get back the result.

But how can Little get a reference to an object on Big?

Object A, running on Little, wants to call a method on Object B running on Big.

The question is, how do we get an object on one machine (which means a different heap/JVM) to call a method on another machine?

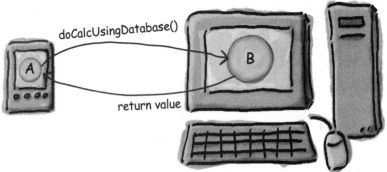

But you can't do that.

Well, not directly anyway. You can't get a reference to something on another heap. If you say:

Dog d = ???

Whatever *d* is referencing must be in the same heap space as the code running the statement.

But imagine you want to design something that will use Sockets and I/O to communicate your intention (a method invocation on an object running on another machine), yet still *feel* as though you were making a local method call.

In other words, you want to cause a method invocation on a *remote* object (i.e., an object in a heap somewhere else), but with code that lets you *pretend* that you're invoking a method on a local object. The ease of a plain old everyday method call, but the power of remote method invocation. That's our goal.

That's what RMI (Remote Method Invocation) gives you!

But let's step back and imagine how you would design RMI if you were doing it yourself. Understanding what you'd have to build yourself will help you learn how RMI works.

A design for remote method calls

Create four things: server, client, server helper, client helper

① Create client and server apps. The server app is the **remote service** that has an object with the method that the client wants to invoke.

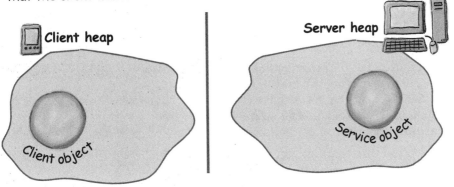

② Create client and server 'helpers'. They'll handle all the low-level networking and I/O details so your client and service can pretend like they're in the same heap.

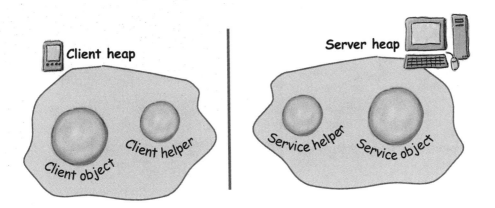

The role of the 'helpers'

The 'helpers' are the objects that actually do the communicating. They make it possible for the client to *act* as though its calling a method on a local object. In fact, it *is*. The client calls a method on the client helper, *as if the client helper were the actual service. The client helper is a proxy for the Real Thing.*

In other words, the client object *thinks* it's calling a method on the remote service, because the client helper is *pretending* to be the service object. **Pretending to be the thing with the method the client wants to call!**

But the client helper isn't really the remote service. Although the client helper *acts* like it (because it has the same method that the service is advertising), the client helper doesn't have any of the actual method logic the client is expecting. Instead, the client helper contacts the server, transfers information about the method call (e.g., name of the method, arguments, etc.), and waits for a return from the server.

On the server side, the service helper receives the request from the client helper (through a Socket connection), unpacks the information about the call, and then invokes the *real* method on the *real* service object. So to the service object, the call is local. It's coming from the service helper, not a remote client.

The service helper gets the return value from the service, packs it up, and ships it back (over a Socket's output stream) to the client helper. The client helper unpacks the information and returns the value to the client object.

> Your client object gets to act like it's making remote method calls. But what it's <u>really</u> doing is calling methods on a heap-local 'proxy' object that handles all the low-level details of Sockets and streams.

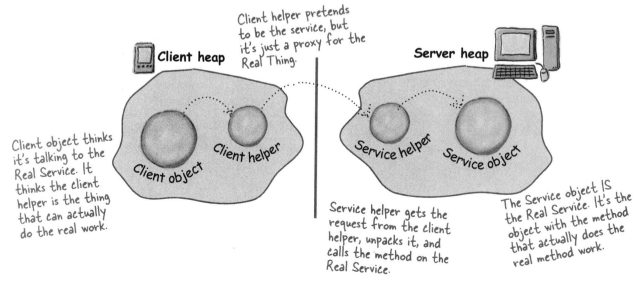

Client helper pretends to be the service, but it's just a proxy for the Real Thing.

Client object thinks it's talking to the Real Service. It thinks the client helper is the thing that can actually do the real work.

Service helper gets the request from the client helper, unpacks it, and calls the method on the Real Service.

The Service object IS the Real Service. It's the object with the method that actually does the real method work.

How the method call happens

(1) Client object calls doBigThing() on the client helper object

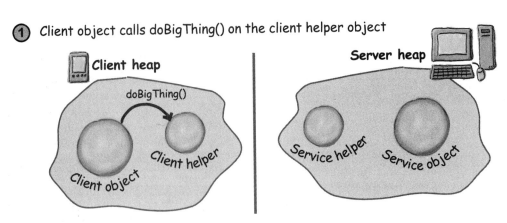

(2) Client helper packages up information about the call
(arguments, method name, etc.) and ships it over the
network to the service helper.

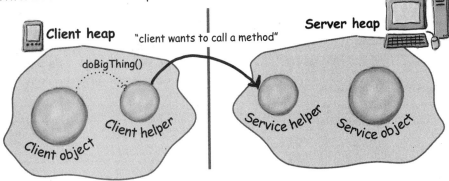

(3) Service helper unpacks the information from the client helper,
finds out which method to call (and on which object) and
invokes the _real_ method on the _real_ service object.

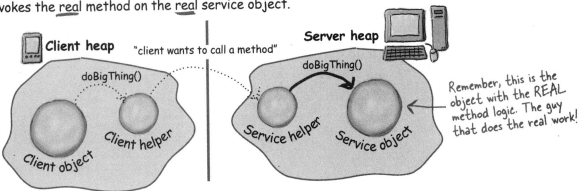

Remember, this is the object with the REAL method logic. The guy that does the real work!

Java RMI gives you the client and service helper objects!

In Java, RMI builds the client and service helper objects for you, and it even knows how to make the client helper look like the Real Service. In other words, RMI knows how to give the client helper object the same methods you want to call on the remote service.

Plus, RMI provides all the runtime infrastructure to make it work, including a lookup service so that the client can find and get the client helper (the proxy for the Real Service).

With RMI, you don't write *any* of the networking or I/O code yourself. The client gets to call remote methods (i.e. the ones the Real Service has) just like normal method calls on objects running in the client's own local JVM.

Almost.

There is one difference between RMI calls and local (normal) method calls. Remember that even though to the client it looks like the method call is local, the client helper sends the method call across the network. So there is networking and I/O. And what do we know about networking and I/O methods?

They're risky!

They throw exceptions all over the place.

So, the client does have to acknowledge the risk. The client has to acknowledge that when it calls a remote method, even though to the client it's just a local call to the proxy/helper object, the call *ultimately* involves Sockets and streams. The client's original call is *local*, but the proxy turns it into a *remote* call. A remote call just means a method that's invoked on an object on another JVM. *How* the information about that call gets transferred from one JVM to another depends on the protocol used by the helper objects.

With RMI, you have a choice of protocols: JRMP or IIOP. JRMP is RMI's 'native' protocol, the one made just for Java-to-Java remote calls. IIOP, on the other hand, is the protocol for CORBA (Common Object Request Broker Architecture), and lets you make remote calls on things which aren't necessarily Java objects. CORBA is usually *much* more painful than RMI, because if you don't have Java on both ends, there's an awful lot of translation and conversion that has to happen.

But thankfully, all we care about is Java-to-Java, so we're sticking with plain old, remarkably easy RMI.

In RMI, the client helper is a 'stub' and the server helper is a 'skeleton'.

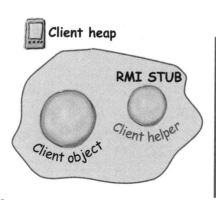

Client heap

RMI STUB

Client helper

Client object

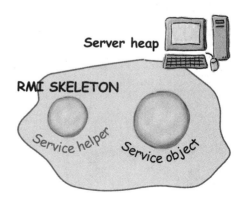

Server heap

RMI SKELETON

Service helper

Service object

Making the Remote Service

This is an **overview** of the five steps for making the remote service (that runs on the server). Don't worry, each step is explained in detail over the next few pages.

Server

Step one:

Make a Remote Interface

The remote interface defines the methods that a client can call remotely. It's what the client will use as the polymorphic class type for your service. Both the Stub and actual service will implement this!

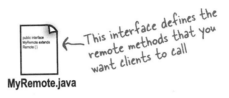
MyRemote.java

This interface defines the remote methods that you want clients to call

Step two:

Make a Remote Implementation

This is the class that does the Real Work. It has the real implementation of the remote methods defined in the remote interface. It's the object that the client wants to call methods on.

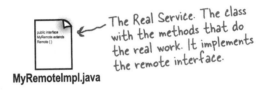
MyRemoteImpl.java

The Real Service. The class with the methods that do the real work. It implements the remote interface.

Step three:

Generate the stubs and skeletons using rmic

These are the client and server 'helpers'. You don't have to create these classes or ever look at the source code that generates them. It's all handled automatically when you run the rmic tool that ships with your Java development kit.

Running rmic against the actual service implementation class...

spits out two new classes for the helper objects

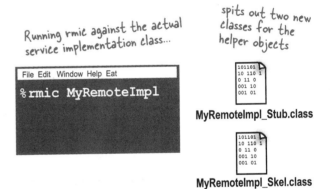

```
File Edit Window Help Eat
%rmic MyRemoteImpl
```

MyRemoteImpl_Stub.class

MyRemoteImpl_Skel.class

Step four:

Start the RMI registry (rmiregistry)

The *rmiregistry* is like the white pages of a phone book. It's where the user goes to get the proxy (the client stub/helper object).

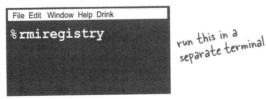

```
File Edit Window Help Drink
%rmiregistry
```

run this in a separate terminal

Step five:

Start the remote service

You have to get the service object up and running. Your service implementation class instantiates an instance of the service and registers it with the RMI registry. Registering it makes the service available for clients.

```
File Edit Window Help BeMerry
%java MyRemoteImpl
```

Step one: Make a Remote Interface

MyRemote.java

① Extend java.rmi.Remote

Remote is a 'marker' interface, which means it has no methods. It has special meaning for RMI, though, so you must follow this rule. Notice that we say 'extends' here. One interface is allowed to *extend* another interface.

```
public interface MyRemote extends Remote {
```

Your interface has to announce that it's for remote method calls. An interface can't implement anything, but it can extend other interfaces.

② Declare that all methods throw a RemoteException

The remote interface is the one the client uses as the polymorphic type for the service. In other words, the client invokes methods on something that implements the remote interface. That something is the stub, of course, and since the stub is doing networking and I/O, all kinds of Bad Things can happen. The client has to acknowledge the risks by handling or declaring the remote exceptions. If the methods in an interface declare exceptions, any code calling methods on a reference of that type (the interface type) must handle or declare the exceptions.

```
import java.rmi.*;
```
the Remote interface is in java.rmi

```
public interface MyRemote extends Remote {
    public String sayHello() throws RemoteException;
}
```

Every remote method call is considered 'risky'. Declaring RemoteException on every method forces the client to pay attention and acknowledge that things might not work.

③ Be sure arguments and return values are primitives or Serializable

Arguments and return values of a remote method must be either primitive or Serializable. Think about it. Any argument to a remote method has to be packaged up and shipped across the network, and that's done through Serialization. Same thing with return values. If you use primitives, Strings, and the majority of types in the API (including arrays and collections), you'll be fine. If you are passing around your own types, just be sure that you make your classes implement Serializable.

```
public String sayHello() throws RemoteException;
```

This return value is gonna be shipped over the wire from the server back to the client, so it must be Serializable. That's how args and return values get packaged up and sent.

Step two: Make a Remote Implementation

MyRemoteImpl.java

(1) Implement the Remote interface

Your service has to implement the remote interface—the one
with the methods your client is going to call.

```
public class MyRemoteImpl extends UnicastRemoteObject implements MyRemote {
    public String sayHello() {
        return "Server says, 'Hey'";
    }
    // more code in class
}
```

The compiler will make sure that you've implemented all the methods from the interface you implement. In this case, there's only one.

(2) Extend UnicastRemoteObject

In order to work as a remote service object, your object needs some
functionality related to 'being remote'. The simplest way is to extend
UnicastRemoteObject (from the java.rmi.server package) and let that
class (your superclass) do the work for you.

```
public class MyRemoteImpl extends UnicastRemoteObject implements MyRemote {
```

(3) Write a no-arg constructor that declares a RemoteException

Your new superclass, UnicastRemoteObject, has one little problem—its
constructor throws a RemoteException. The only way to deal with this is
to declare a constructor for your remote implementation, just so that you
have a place to declare the RemoteException. Remember, when a class is
instantiated, its superclass constructor is always called. If your superclass
constructor throws an exception, you have no choice but to declare that
your constructor also throws an exception.

```
public MyRemoteImpl() throws RemoteException { }
```

You don't have to put anything in the constructor. You just need a way to declare that your superclass constructor throws an exception.

(4) Register the service with the RMI registry

Now that you've got a remote service, you have to make it available to
remote clients. You do this by instantiating it and putting it into the RMI
registry (which must be running or this line of code fails). When you
register the implementation object, the RMI system actually puts the *stub* in
the registry, since that's what the client really needs. Register your service
using the static rebind() method of the java.rmi.Naming class.

```
try {
    MyRemote service = new MyRemoteImpl();
    Naming.rebind("Remote Hello", service);
} catch(Exception ex) {...}
```

Give your service a name (that clients can use to look it up in the registry) and register it with the RMI registry. When you bind the service object, RMI swaps the service for the stub and puts the stub in the registry.

Step three: generate stubs and skeletons

① Run rmic on the remote implementation class (not the remote interface)

The rmic tool, that comes with the Java software development kit, takes a service implementation and creates two new classes, the stub and the skeleton. It uses a naming convention that is the name of your remote implementation, with either _Stub or _Skeleton added to the end. There are other options with rmic, including not generating skeletons, seeing what the source code for these classes looked like, and even using IIOP as the protocol. The way we're doing it here is the way you'll usually do it. The classes will land in the current directory (i.e. whatever you did a cd to). Remember, *rmic* must be able to see your implementation class, so you'll probably run rmic from the directory where your remote implementation is. (We're deliberately not using packages here, to make it simpler. In the Real World, you'll need to account for package directory structures and fully-qualified names).

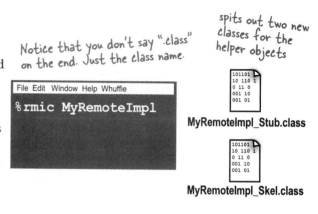

Notice that you don't say ".class" on the end. Just the class name.

spits out two new classes for the helper objects

```
File Edit Window Help Whuffie
%rmic MyRemoteImpl
```

MyRemoteImpl_Stub.class

MyRemoteImpl_Skel.class

Step four: run rmiregistry

① Bring up a terminal and start the rmiregistry.

Be sure you start it from a directory that has access to your classes. The simplest way is to start it from your 'classes' directory.

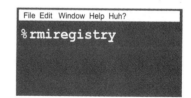

```
File Edit Window Help Huh?
%rmiregistry
```

Step five: start the service

① Bring up another terminal and start your service

This might be from a main() method in your remote implementation class, or from a separate launcher class. In this simple example, we put the starter code in the implementation class, in a main method that instantiates the object and registers it with RMI registry.

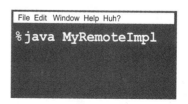

```
File Edit Window Help Huh?
%java MyRemoteImpl
```

Complete code for the server side

Server

The Remote interface:

RemoteException and Remote interface are in java.rmi package

```java
import java.rmi.*;

public interface MyRemote extends Remote {

    public String sayHello() throws RemoteException;
}
```

Your interface MUST extend java.rmi.Remote

All of your remote methods must declare a RemoteException

The Remote service (the implementation):

UnicastRemoteObject is in the java.rmi.server package

extending UnicastRemoteObject is the easiest way to make a remote object

```java
import java.rmi.*;
import java.rmi.server.*;

public class MyRemoteImpl extends UnicastRemoteObject implements MyRemote {

    public String sayHello() {
        return "Server says, 'Hey'";
    }

    public MyRemoteImpl() throws RemoteException { }

    public static void main (String[] args) {

        try {
            MyRemote service = new MyRemoteImpl();
            Naming.rebind("Remote Hello", service);
        } catch(Exception ex) {
            ex.printStackTrace();
        }
    }
}
```

You have to implement all the interface methods, of course. But notice that you do NOT have to declare the RemoteException.

you MUST implement your remote interface!!

your superclass constructor (for UnicastRemoteObject) declares an exception, so YOU must write a constructor, because it means that your constructor is calling risky code (its super constructor)

Make the remote object, then 'bind' it to the rmiregistry using the static Naming.rebind(). The name you register it under is the name clients will need to look it up in the rmi registry.

How does the client get the stub <u>object?</u>

The client has to get the stub object, since that's the thing the
client will call methods on. And that's where the RMI registry
comes in. The client does a 'lookup', like going to the white pages
of a phone book, and essentially says, "Here's a name, and I'd like
the stub that goes with that name."

This must be the name that the service was registered under

lookup() is a static method of the Naming class

```
MyRemote service = (MyRemote)    Naming.lookup("rmi://127.0.0.1/Remote Hello");
```

The client always uses the remote implementation as the type of the service. In fact, the client never needs to know the actual class name of your remote service.

You have to cast it to the interface, since the lookup method returns type Object.

your host name or IP address goes here

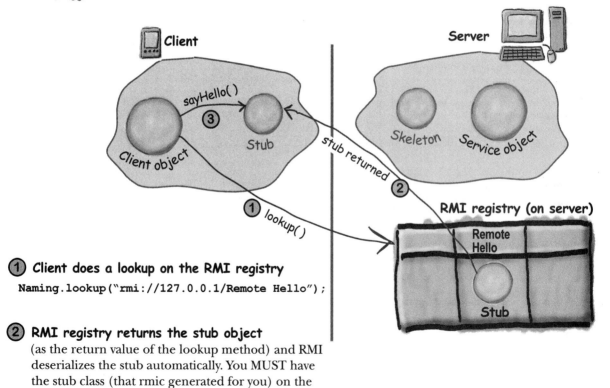

Client

sayHello( )

③

Stub

Client object

① lookup( )

stub returned ②

Server

Skeleton   Service object

RMI registry (on server)

Remote Hello

Stub

① **Client does a lookup on the RMI registry**
   `Naming.lookup("rmi://127.0.0.1/Remote Hello");`

② **RMI registry returns the stub object**
   (as the return value of the lookup method) and RMI
   deserializes the stub automatically. You MUST have
   the stub class (that rmic generated for you) on the
   client or the stub won't be deserialized.

③ **Client invokes a method on the stub, as
   though the stub IS the real service**

How does the client get the stub class?

Now we get to the interesting question. Somehow, someway, the client must have the stub class (that you generated earlier using rmic) at the time the client does the lookup, or else the stub won't be deserialized on the client and the whole thing blows up. In a simple system, you can simply hand-deliver the stub class to the client.

There's a much cooler way, though, although it's beyond the scope of this book. But just in case you're interested, the cooler way is called "dynamic class downloading". With dynamic class downloading, a stub object (or really any Serialized object) is 'stamped' with a URL that tells the RMI system on the client where to find the class file for that object. Then, in the process of deserializing an object, if RMI can't find the class locally, it uses that URL to do an HTTP Get to retrieve the class file. So you'd need a simple Web server to serve up class files, and you'd also need to change some security parameters on the client. There are a few other tricky issues with dynamic class downloading, but that's the overview.

Complete client code

```java
import java.rmi.*;

public class MyRemoteClient {
    public static void main (String[] args) {
        new MyRemoteClient().go();
    }

    public void go() {

        try {
            MyRemote service = (MyRemote) Naming.lookup("rmi://127.0.0.1/Remote Hello");

            String s = service.sayHello();

            System.out.println(s);
        } catch(Exception ex) {
            ex.printStackTrace();
        }
    }
}
```

The Naming class (for doing the rmiregistry lookup) is in the java.rmi package

It comes out of the registry as type Object, so don't forget the cast

You need the IP address or hostname

and the name used to bind/rebind the service

It looks just like a regular old method call! (Except it must acknowledge the RemoteException)

Be sure each machine has the class files it needs.

The top three things programmers do wrong with RMI are:

1) Forget to start rmiregistry before starting remote service (when you register the service using Naming.rebind(), the rmiregistry must be running!)

2) Forget to make arguments and return types serializable (you won't know until runtime; this is not something the compiler will detect.)

3) Forget to give the stub class to the client.

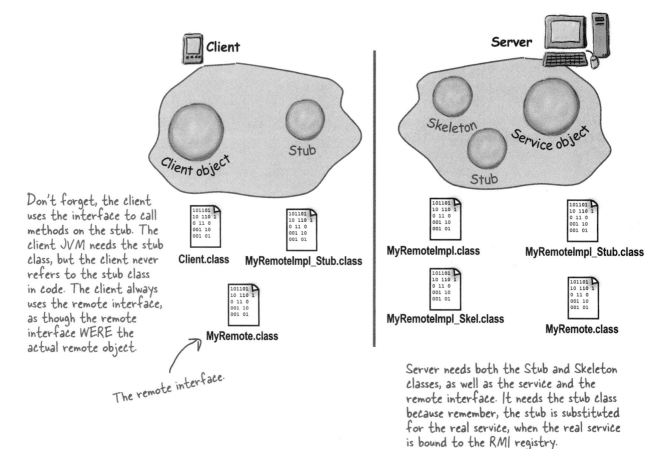

Don't forget, the client uses the interface to call methods on the stub. The client JVM needs the stub class, but the client never refers to the stub class in code. The client always uses the remote interface, as though the remote interface WERE the actual remote object.

Client object
Stub

Client.class   **MyRemoteImpl_Stub.class**

MyRemote.class

The remote interface.

Skeleton   **Service object**
Stub

MyRemoteImpl.class   **MyRemoteImpl_Stub.class**

MyRemoteImpl_Skel.class   **MyRemote.class**

Server needs both the Stub and Skeleton classes, as well as the service and the remote interface. It needs the stub class because remember, the stub is substituted for the real service, when the real service is bound to the RMI registry.

 Sharpen your pencil

What's First?

Look at the sequence of events below, and place them in the order in which they occur in a Java RMI application.

1.

2.

3.

4.

5.

6.

7.

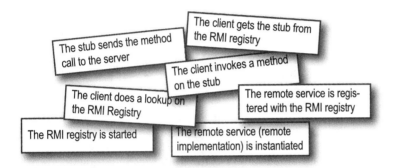

The client gets the stub from the RMI registry

The stub sends the method call to the server

The client invokes a method on the stub

The client does a lookup on the RMI Registry

The remote service is registered with the RMI registry

The RMI registry is started

The remote service (remote implementation) is instantiated

BULLET POINTS

- An object on one heap cannot get a normal Java reference to an object on a different heap (which means running on a different JVM)

- Java Remote Method Invocation (RMI) makes it *seem* like you're calling a method on a remote object (i.e. an object in a different JVM), but you aren't.

- When a client calls a method on a remote object, the client is really calling a method on a *proxy* of the remote object. The proxy is called a 'stub'.

- A stub is a client helper object that takes care of the low-level networking details (sockets, streams, serialization, etc.) by packaging and sending method calls to the server.

- To build a remote service (in other words, an object that a remote client can ultimately call methods on), you must start with a remote interface.

- A remote interface must extend the java.rmi.Remote interface, and all methods must declare RemoteException.

- Your remote service implements your remote interface.

- Your remote service should extend UnicastRemoteObject. (Technically there are other ways to create a remote object, but extending UnicastRemoteObject is the simplest).

- Your remote service class must have a constructor, and the constructor must declare a RemoteException (because the superclass constructor declares one).

- Your remote service must be instantiated, and the object registered with the RMI registry.

- To register a remote service, use the static Naming.rebind("Service Name", serviceInstance);

- The RMI registry must be running on the same machine as the remote service, before you try to register a remote object with the RMI registry.

- The client looks up your remote service using the static Naming.lookup("rmi://MyHostName/ServiceName");

- Almost everything related to RMI can throw a RemoteException (checked by the compiler). This includes registering or looking up a service in the reigstry, and *all* remote method calls from the client to the stub.

Yeah, but who really *uses* RMI?

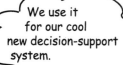

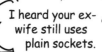

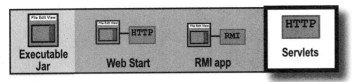

100% Local   Combination   100% Remote

What about Servlets?

Servlets are Java programs that run on (and with) an HTTP web server. When a client uses a web browser to interact with a web page, a request is sent back to the web server. If the request needs the help of a Java servlet, the web server runs (or calls, if the servlet is already running) the servlet code. Servlet code is simply code that runs on the server, to do work as a result of whatever the client requests (for example, save information to a text file or database on the server). If you're familiar with CGI scripts written in Perl, you know exactly what we're talking about. Web developers use CGI scripts or servlets to do everything from sending user-submitted info to a database, to running a web-site's discussion board.

And even servlets can use RMI!

By far, the most common use of J2EE technology is to mix servlets and EJBs together, where servlets are the client of the EJB. And in that case, *the servlet is using RMI to talk to the EJBs.* (Although the way you use RMI with EJB is a *little* different from the process we just looked at.)

(1) Client fills out a registration form and clicks 'submit'.
    The HTTP server (i.e. web server) gets the request, sees that
    it's for a servlet, and sends the request to the servlet.

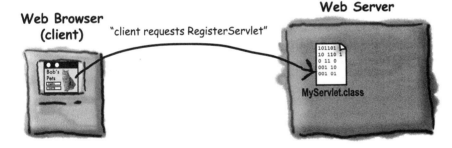

(2) Servlet (Java code) runs, adds data to the database,
    composes a web page (with custom info) and sends it back to
    the client where it displays in the browser.

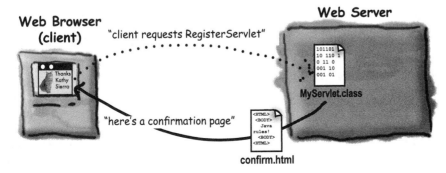

Step for making and running a servlet

Web Server

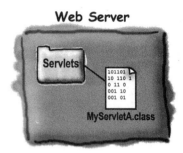

MyServletA.class

(1) Find out where your servlets need to be placed.

For these examples, we'll assume that you already have a web server up and running, and that it's already configured to support servlets. The most important thing is to find out exactly where your servlet class files have to be placed in order for your server to 'see' them. If you have a web site hosted by an ISP, the hosting service can tell you where to put your servlets, just as they'll tell you where to place your CGI scripts.

(2) Get the servlets.jar and add it to your classpath

Servlets aren't part of the standard Java libraries; you need the servlets classes packaged into the servlets.jar file. You can download the servlets classes from java.sun.com, or you can get them from your Java-enabled web server (like Apache Tomcat, at the apache.org site). Without these classes, you won't be able to compile your servlets.

servlets.jar

(3) Write a servlet class by extending HttpServlet

A servlet is just a Java class that extends HttpServlet (from the javax.servlet.http package). There are other types of servlets you can make, but most of the time we care only about HttpServlet.

```
public class MyServletA extends HttpServlet { ... }
```

MyServletA.class

(4) Write an HTML page that invokes your servlet

When the user clicks a link that references your servlet, the web server will find the servlet and invoke the appropriate method depending on the HTTP command (GET, POST, etc.)

```
<a href="servlets/MyServletA">This is the most amazing servlet.</a>
```

MyPage.html

Web Server

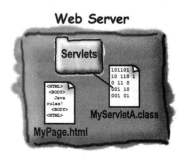

(5) Make your servlet and HTML page available to your server

This is completely dependent on your web server (and more specifically, on which *version* of Java Servlets that you're using). Your ISP may simply tell you to drop it into a "Servlets" directory on your web site. But if you're using, say, the latest version of Tomcat, you'll have a lot more work to do to get the servlet (and web page) into the right location. (We just happen to have a book on this too .)

A very simple Servlet

```
import java.io.*;
import javax.servlet.*;
import javax.servlet.http.*;
```

Besides io, we need to import two of the servlet packages. Remember, these two packages are NOT part of the Java standard libraries -- you have to download them separately

```
public class MyServletA extends HttpServlet {
```

Most 'normal' servlets will extend HttpServlet, then override one or more methods.

Override the doGet for simple HTTP GET messages.

The web server calls this method, handing you the client's request (you can get data out of it) and a 'response' object that you'll use to send back a response (a page).

```
    public void doGet (HttpServletRequest request, HttpServletResponse response)
                          throws  ServletException, IOException  {
```

```
        response.setContentType("text/html");
```

This tells the server (and browser) what kind of 'thing' is coming back from the server as a reuslt of this servlet running.

```
        PrintWriter out = response.getWriter();
```

The response object gives us an output stream to 'write' information back out to the server.

```
        String message = "If you're reading this, it worked!";
```

```
        out.println("<HTML><BODY>");
        out.println("<H1>" + message + "</H1>");
        out.println("</BODY></HTML>");
        out.close();
    }
}
```

What we 'write' is an HTML page! The page gets delivered through the server back to the browser, just like any other HTML page, even though this is a page that never existed until now. In other words, there's no .html file somewhere with this stuff in it.

What the web page looks like:

HTML page with a link to this servlet

click the link to trigger the servlet →

This an amazing servlet.

```
<HTML>
  <BODY>
     <a href="servlets/MyServletA">This is an amazing servlet.</a>
  </BODY>
</HTML>
```

BULLET POINTS

- Servlets are Java classes that run entirely on (and/or within) an HTTP (web) server.

- Servlets are useful for running code on the server as a result of client interaction with a web page. For example, if a client submits information in a web page form, the servlet can process the information, add it to a database, and send back a customized, confirmation response page.

- To compile a servlet, you need the servlet packages which are in the servlets.jar file. The servlet classes are not part of the Java standard libraries, so you need to download the servlets.jar from java.sun.com or get them from a servlet-capable web server. (Note: the Servlet library is included with the Java 2 Enterprise Edition (J2EE))

- To run a servlet, you must have a web server capable of running servlets, such as the Tomcat server from apache.org.

- Your servlet must be placed in a location that's specific to your particular web server, so you'll need to find that out before you try to run your servlets. If you have a web site hosted by an ISP that supports servlets, the ISP will tell you which directory to place your servlets in.

- A typical servlet extends HttpServlet and overrides one or more servlet methods, such as doGet() or doPost().

- The web server starts the servlet and calls the appropriate method (doGet(), etc.) based on the client's request.

- The servlet can send back a response by getting a PrintWriter output stream from the response parameter of the doGet() method.

- The servlet 'writes' out an HTML page, complete with tags).

there are no Dumb Questions

Q: What's a JSP, and how does it relate to servlets?

A: JSP stands for Java Server Pages. In the end, the web server turns a JSP into a servlet, but the difference between a servlet and a JSP is what YOU (the developer) actually create. With a servlet, you write a Java *class* that contains *HTML* in the output statements (if you're sending back an HTML page to the client). But with a JSP, it's the opposite—you write an *HTML* page that contains *Java* code!

This gives you the ability to have dynamic web pages where you write the page as a normal HTML page, except you embed Java code (and other tags that "trigger" Java code at runtime) that gets processed at runtime. In other words, part of the page is customized at runtime when the Java code runs.

The main benefit of JSP over regular servlets is that it's just a lot easier to write the HTML part of a servlet as a JSP page than to write HTML in the torturous print out statements in the servlet's response. Imagine a reasonably complex HTML page, and now imagine formatting it within println statements. Yikes!

But for many applications, it isn't necessary to use JSPs because the servlet doesn't need to send a dynamic response, or the HTML is simple enough not to be such a big pain. And, there are still many web servers out there that support servlets but do not support JSPs, so you're stuck.

Another benefit of JSPs is that you can separate the work by having the Java developers write the servlets and the web page developers write the JSPs. That's the promised benefit, anyway. In reality, there's still a Java learning curve (and a tag learning curve) for anyone writing a JSP, so to think that an HTML web page designer can bang out JSPs is not realistic. Well, not without tools. But that's the good news—authoring tools are starting to appear, that help web page designers create JSPs without writing the code from scratch.

Q: Is this all you're gonna say about servlets? After such a *huge* thing on RMI?

A: Yes. RMI is part of the Java language, and all the classes for RMI are in the standard libraries. Servlets and JSPs are *not* part of the Java language; they're considered *standard extensions*. You can run RMI on any modern JVM, but Servlets and JSPs require a properly configured web server with a servlet "container". This is our way of saying, "it's beyond the scope of this book." But you can read much more in the lovely *Head First Servlets & JSP*.

Just for fun, let's make the Phrase-O-Matic work as a servlet

Now that we told you that we won't say any more about servlets, we can't resist servletizing (yes, we *can* verbify it) the Phrase-O-Matic from chapter 1. A servlet is still just Java. And Java code can call Java code from other classes. So a servlet is free to call a method on the Phrase-O-Matic. All you have to do is drop the Phrase-O-Matic class into the same directory as your servlet, and you're in business. (The Phrase-O-Matic code is on the next page).

> Try my new web-enabled phrase-o-matic and you'll be a slick talker just like the boss or those guys in marketing.

```java
import java.io.*;

import javax.servlet.*;
import javax.servlet.http.*;

public class KathyServlet extends HttpServlet {
    public void doGet (HttpServletRequest request, HttpServletResponse response)
                                        throws ServletException, IOException  {

        String title = "PhraseOMatic has generated the following phrase.";

        response.setContentType("text/html");
        PrintWriter out = response.getWriter();

        out.println("<HTML><HEAD><TITLE>");
        out.println("PhraseOmatic");
        out.println("</TITLE></HEAD><BODY>");
        out.println("<H1>" + title + "</H1>");
        out.println("<P>" + PhraseOMatic.makePhrase());
        out.println("<P><a href=\"KathyServlet\">make another phrase</a></p>");
        out.println("</BODY></HTML>");

        out.close();
    }
}
```

See? Your servlet can call methods on another class. In this case, we're calling the static makePhrase() method of the PhraseOMatic class (on the next page)

Phrase-O-Matic code, servlet-friendly

This is a slightly different version from the code in chapter one. In the original, we ran the entire thing in a main() method, and we had to rerun the program each time to generate a new phrase at the command-line. In this version, the code simply returns a String (with the phrase) when you invoke the static makePhrase() method. That way, you can call the method from any other code and get back a String with the randomly-composed phrase.

Please note that these long String[] array assignments are a victim of word-processing here—don't type in the hyphens! Just keep on typing and let your code editor do the wrapping. And whatever you do, don't hit the return key in the middle of a String (i.e. something between double quotes).

```java
public class PhraseOMatic {
    public static String makePhrase() {

        // make three sets of words to choose from
        String[] wordListOne = {"24/7","multi-Tier","30,000 foot","B-to-B","win-win","front-
end", "web-based","pervasive", "smart", "six-sigma","critical-path", "dynamic"};

        String[] wordListTwo = {"empowered", "sticky", "valued-added", "oriented", "centric",
"distributed", "clustered", "branded","outside-the-box", "positioned", "networked", "fo-
cused", "leveraged", "aligned", "targeted", "shared", "cooperative", "accelerated"};

        String[] wordListThree = {"process", "tipping point", "solution", "architecture",
"core competency", "strategy", "mindshare", "portal", "space", "vision", "paradigm", "mis-
sion"};

        // find out how many words are in each list
        int oneLength = wordListOne.length;
        int twoLength = wordListTwo.length;
        int threeLength = wordListThree.length;

        // generate three random numbers, to pull random words from each list
        int rand1 = (int) (Math.random() * oneLength);
        int rand2 = (int) (Math.random() * twoLength);
        int rand3 = (int) (Math.random() * threeLength);

        // now build a phrase
        String phrase = wordListOne[rand1] + " " + wordListTwo[rand2] + " " +
wordListThree[rand3];

        // now return it
        return ("What we need is a " + phrase);
    }
}
```

Enterprise JavaBeans: RMI on steroids

RMI is great for writing and running remote services. But you wouldn't run something like an Amazon or eBay on RMI alone. For a large, deadly serious, enterprise application, you need something more. You need something that can handle transactions, heavy concurrency issues (like a gazillion people are hitting your server at once to buy those organic dog kibbles), security (not just anyone should hit your payroll database), and data management. For that, you need an *enterprise application server*.

In Java, that means a Java 2 Enterprise Edition (J2EE) server. A J2EE server includes both a web server and an Enterprise JavaBeans(EJB) server, so that you can deploy an application that includes both servlets and EJBs. Like servlets, EJB is way beyond the scope of this book, and there's no way to show "just a little" EJB example with code, but we *will* take a quick look at how it works. (For a much more detailed treatment of EJB, we can recommend the lively Head First EJB certification study guide.)

An EJB server adds a bunch of services that you don't get with straight RMI. Things like transactions, security, concurrency, database management, and networking.

An EJB server steps into the middle of an RMI call and layers in all of the services.

The bean object is protected from direct client access! Only the server can actually talk to the bean. This lets the server do things like say, "Whoa! This client doesn't have the security clearance to call this method..." Almost everything you pay for in an EJB server happens right HERE, where the server steps in!

Here's where the EJB server gets involved! The EJB object intercepts the calls to the bean (the bean holds the real business logic) and layers in all the services provided by the EJB server (security, transactions, etc.)

This client could be ANYTHING, but typically an EJB client is a servlet running in the same J2EE server.

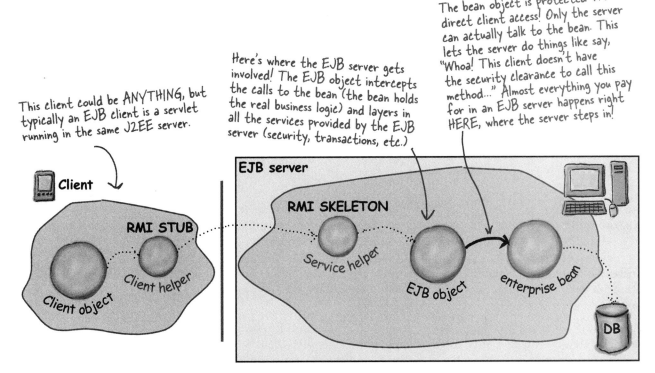

- Client
- RMI STUB
- Client helper
- Client object
- EJB server
- RMI SKELETON
- Service helper
- EJB object
- enterprise bean
- DB

This is only a small part of the EJB picture!

For our final trick... a little Jini

We love Jini. We think Jini is pretty much the best thing in Java. If EJB is RMI on steroids (with a bunch of managers), Jini is RMI with *wings*. Pure Java *bliss*. Like the EJB material, we can't get into any of the Jini details here, but if you know RMI, you're three-quarters of the way there. In terms of technology, anyway. In terms of *mindset*, it's time to make a big leap. No, it's time to *fly*.

Jini uses RMI (although other protocols can be involved), but gives you a few key features including:

Adaptive discovery

Self-healing networks

With RMI, remember, the client has to know the name and location of the remote service. The client code for the lookup includes the IP address or hostname of the remote service (because that's where the RMI registry is running) *and* the logical name the service was registered under.

But with Jini, the client has to know only one thing: *the interface implemented by the service!* That's it.

So how do you find things? The trick revolves around Jini lookup services. Jini lookup services are far more powerful and flexible than the RMI registry. For one thing, Jini lookup services announce themselves to the network, *automatically*. When a lookup service comes online, it sends a message (using IP multicast) out to the network saying, "I'm here, if anyone's interested."

But that's not all. Let's say you (a client) come online *after* the lookup service has already announced itself, *you* can send a message to the entire network saying, "Are there any lookup services out there?"

Except that you're not really interested in the lookup service *itself*—you're interested in the services that are *registered* with the lookup service. Things like RMI remote services, other serializable Java objects, and even devices such as printers, cameras, and coffee-makers.

And here's where it gets even more fun: when a service comes online, it will dynamically discover (and *register* itself with) any Jini lookup services on the network. When the service registers with the lookup service, the service sends a serialized object to be placed in the lookup service. That serialized object can be a stub to an RMI remote service, a driver for a networked device, or even the whole service itself that (once you get it from the lookup service) runs locally on your machine. And instead of registering by *name*, the service registers by the *interface* it implements.

Once you (the client) have a reference to a lookup service, you can say to that lookup service, "Hey, do you have anything that implements ScientificCalculator?" At that point, the lookup service will check its list of registered interfaces, and assuming it finds a match, says back to you, "Yes I *do* have something that implements that interface. Here's the serialized object the ScientificCalculator service registered with me."

Adaptive discovery in action

① Jini lookup service is launched somewhere on the network, and announces itself using IP multicast.

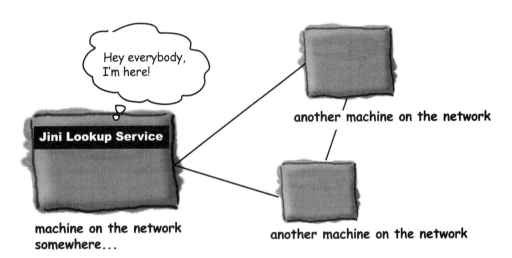

② An already-running Jini service on another machine asks to be registered with this newly-announced lookup service. It registers by capability, rather than by name. In other words, it registers as the service interface it implements. It sends a serialized object to be placed in the lookup service.

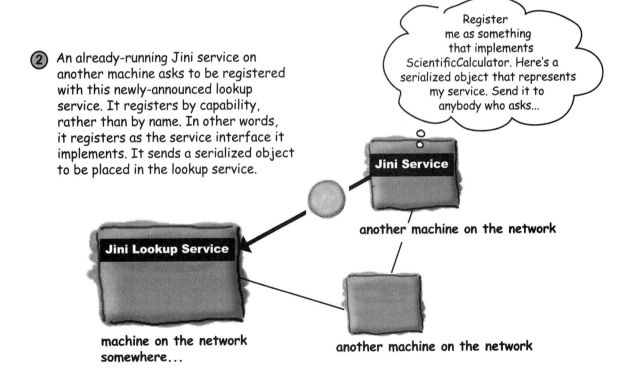

Adaptive discovery in action, continued...

(3) A client on the network wants something that implements the ScientificCalculator interface. It has no idea where (or if) that thing exists, so it asks the lookup service.

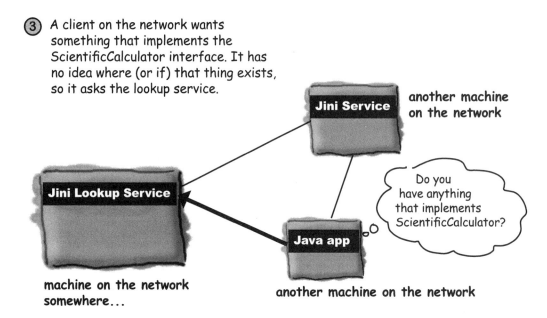

Jini Service

another machine on the network

Do you have anything that implements ScientificCalculator?

Jini Lookup Service

Java app

machine on the network somewhere...

another machine on the network

(4) The lookup service responds, since it does have something registered as a ScientificCalculator interface.

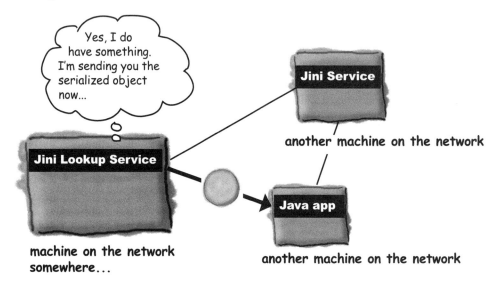

Yes, I do have something. I'm sending you the serialized object now...

Jini Service

another machine on the network

Jini Lookup Service

Java app

machine on the network somewhere...

another machine on the network

Self-healing network in action

① A Jini Service has asked to register with the lookup service. The lookup service responds with a "lease". The newly-registered service must keep renewing the lease, or the lookup service assumes the service has gone offline. The lookup service wants always to present an accurate picture to the rest of the network about which services are available.

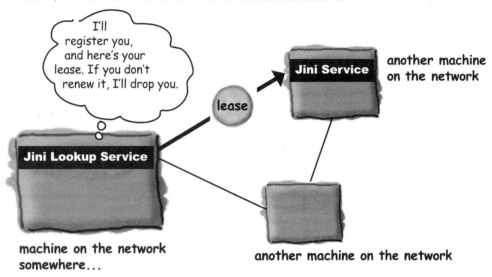

② The service goes offline (somebody shuts it down), so it fails to renew its lease with the lookup service. The lookup service drops it.

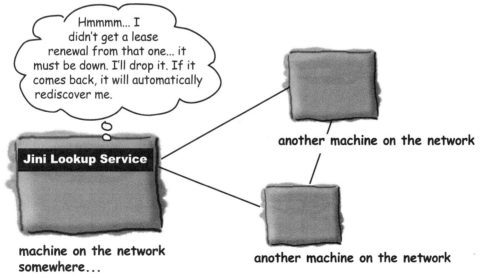

Final Project: the Universal Service browser

We're going to make something that isn't Jini-enabled, but quite easily could be. It will give you the flavor and feeling of Jini, but using straight RMI. In fact the main difference between our application and a Jini application is how the service is discovered. Instead of the Jini lookup service, which automatically announces itself and lives anywhere on the network, we're using the RMI registry which must be on the same machine as the remote service, and which does not announce itself automatically.

And instead of our service registering itself automatically with the lookup service, *we* have to register it in the RMI registry (using Naming.rebind()).

But once the client has found the service in the RMI registry, the rest of the application is almost identical to the way we'd do it in Jini. (The main thing missing is the *lease* that would let us have a self-healing network if any of the services go down.)

The universal service browser is like a specialized web browser, except instead of HTML pages, the service browser downloads and displays interactive Java GUIs that we're calling *universal services*.

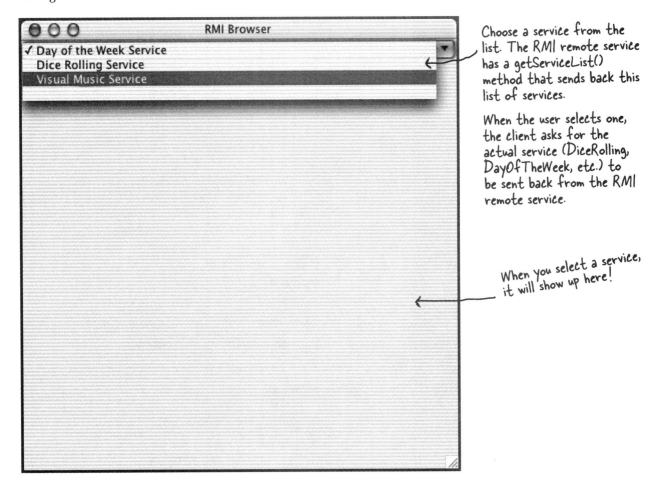

Choose a service from the list. The RMI remote service has a getServiceList() method that sends back this list of services.

When the user selects one, the client asks for the actual service (DiceRolling, DayOfTheWeek, etc.) to be sent back from the RMI remote service.

When you select a service, it will show up here!

How it works:

(1) Client starts up and does a lookup on the RMI registry for the service called "ServiceServer", and gets back the stub.

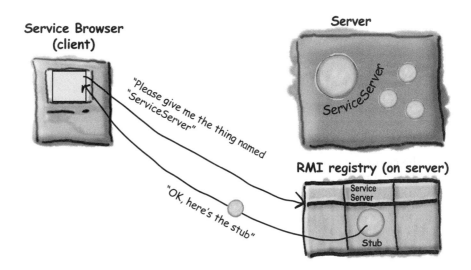

Service Browser (client)

Server

"Please give me the thing named 'ServiceServer'"

"OK, here's the stub"

RMI registry (on server)

Service Server

Stub

(2) Client calls getServiceList() on the stub. The ServiceServer returns an array of services

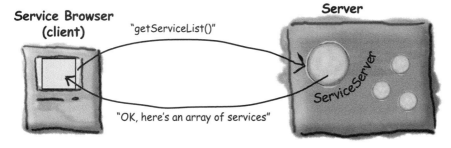

Service Browser (client)

Server

"getServiceList()"

ServiceServer

"OK, here's an array of services"

(3) Client displays the list of services in a GUI

Service Browser (client)

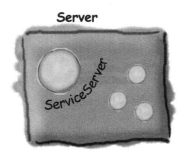

Server

ServiceServer

How it works, continued...

④ User selects from the list, so client calls the getService()
method on the remote service. The remote service returns a
serialized object that is an actual service that will run inside
the client browser.

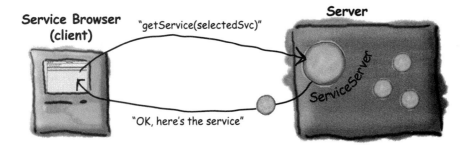

⑤ Client calls the getGuiPanel() on the serialized service object it
just got from the remote service. The GUI for that service is
displayed inside the browser, and the user can interact with it
locally. At this point, we don't need the remote service unless/until
the user decides to select another service.

Service Browser
(client)

The classes and interfaces:

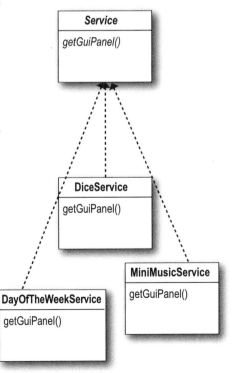

(1) interface ServiceServer implements Remote
A regular old RMI remote interface for the remote service (the remote service has the method for getting the service list and returning a selected service).

(2) class ServiceServerImpl implements ServiceServer
The actual RMI remote service (extends UnicastRemoteObject). Its job is to instantiate and store all the services (the things that will be shipped to the client), and register the server itself (ServiceServerImpl) with the RMI registry.

(3) class ServiceBrowser
The client. It builds a very simple GUI, does a lookup in the RMI registry to get the ServiceServer stub, then calls a remote method on it to get the list of services to display in the GUI list.

(4) interface Service
This is the key to everything. This very simple interface has just one method, getGuiPanel(). Every service that gets shipped over to the client must implement this interface. This is what makes the whole thing UNIVERSAL! By implementing this interface, a service can come over even though the client has no idea what the actual class (or classes) are that make up that service. All the client knows is that whatever comes over, it implements the Service interface, so it MUST have a getGuiPanel() method.
The client gets a serialized object as a result of calling getService(selectedSvc) on the ServiceServer stub, and all the client says to that object is, "I don't know who or what you are, but I DO know that you implement the Service interface, so I know I can call getGuiPanel() on you. And since getGuiPanel() returns a JPanel, I'll just slap it into the browser GUI and start interacting with it!

(5) class DiceService implements Service
Got dice? If not, but you need some, use this service to roll anywhere from 1 to 6 virtual dice for you.

(6) class MiniMusicService implements Service
Remember that fabulous little 'music video' program from the first GUI Code Kitchen? We've turned it into a service, and you can play it over and over and over until your roommates finally leave.

(7) class DayOfTheWeekService implements Service
Were you born on a Friday? Type in your birthday and find out.

interface ServiceServer (the remote interface)

```
import java.rmi.*;

public interface ServiceServer extends Remote {

    Object[] getServiceList() throws RemoteException;

    Service getService(Object serviceKey) throws RemoteException;
}
```

A normal RMI remote interface, defines the two methods the remote service will have.

interface Service (what the GUI services implement)

```
import javax.swing.*;
import java.io.*;

public interface Service extends Serializable {
    public JPanel getGuiPanel();
}
```

A plain old (i.e. non-remote) interface, that defines the one method that any universal service must have—getGuiPanel(). The interface extends Serializable, so that any class implementing the Service interface will automatically be Serializable.

That's a must, because the services get shipped over the wire from the server, as a result of the client calling getService() on the remote ServiceServer.

class ServiceServerImpl (the remote implementation)

```java
import java.rmi.*;
import java.util.*;
import java.rmi.server.*;
```

A normal RMI implementation

```java
public class ServiceServerImpl extends UnicastRemoteObject implements ServiceServer  {

    HashMap serviceList;
```
The services will be stored in a HashMap collection. Instead of putting ONE object in the collection, you put TWO -- a key object (like a String) and a value object (whatever you want). (see appendix B for more on HashMap)

```java
    public ServiceServerImpl() throws RemoteException {
        setUpServices();
    }
```
When the constructor is called, initialize the actual universal services (DiceService, MiniMusicService, etc.)

```java
    private void setUpServices() {
        serviceList = new HashMap();
        serviceList.put("Dice Rolling Service", new DiceService());
        serviceList.put("Day of the Week Service", new DayOfTheWeekService());
        serviceList.put("Visual Music Service", new MiniMusicService());
    }
```
Make the services (the actual service objects) and put them into the HashMap, with a String name (for the 'key').

```java
    public Object[] getServiceList() {
        System.out.println("in remote");
        return serviceList.keySet().toArray();
    }
```
Client calls this in order to get a list of services to display in the browser (so the user can select one). We send an array of type Object (even though it has Strings inside) by making an array of just the KEYS that are in the HashMap. We won't send an actual Service object unless the client asks for it by calling getService().

```java
    public Service getService(Object serviceKey) throws RemoteException {
        Service theService = (Service) serviceList.get(serviceKey);
        return theService;
    }
```
Client calls this method after the user selects a service from the displayed list of services (that it got from the method above). This code uses the key (the same key originally sent to the client) to get the corresponding service out of the HashMap.

```java
    public static void main (String[] args) {
        try {
            Naming.rebind("ServiceServer", new ServiceServerImpl());
        } catch(Exception ex) {
            ex.printStackTrace();
        }
        System.out.println("Remote service is running");
    }
}
```

class ServiceBrowser (the client)

```java
import java.awt.*;
import javax.swing.*;
import java.rmi.*;
import java.awt.event.*;


public class ServiceBrowser {

   JPanel mainPanel;
   JComboBox serviceList;
   ServiceServer server;


   public void buildGUI() {
      JFrame frame = new JFrame("RMI Browser");
      mainPanel = new JPanel();
      frame.getContentPane().add(BorderLayout.CENTER, mainPanel);

      Object[] services = getServicesList();

      serviceList = new JComboBox(services);

      frame.getContentPane().add(BorderLayout.NORTH, serviceList);

      serviceList.addActionListener(new MyListListener());

      frame.setSize(500,500);
      frame.setVisible(true);

   }

   void loadService(Object serviceSelection) {
       try {
          Service svc = server.getService(serviceSelection);

          mainPanel.removeAll();
          mainPanel.add(svc.getGuiPanel());
          mainPanel.validate();
          mainPanel.repaint();
       } catch(Exception ex) {
          ex.printStackTrace();
       }
   }
}
```

this method does the RMI registry lookup, gets the stub, and calls getServiceList(). (The actual method is on the next page).

Add the services (an array of Objects) to the JComboBox (the list). The JComboBox knows how to make displayable Strings out of each thing in the array.

Here's where we add the actual service to the GUI, after the user has selected one. (This method is called by the event listener on the JComboBox). We call getService() on the remote server (the stub for ServiceServer) and pass it the String that was displayed in the list (which is the SAME String we originally got from the server when we called getServiceList()). The server returns the actual service (serialized), which is automatically deserialized (thanks to RMI) and we simply call the getGuiPanel() on the service and add the result (a JPanel) to the browser's mainPanel.

```
Object[] getServicesList() {
   Object obj = null;
   Object[] services = null;

   try {

      obj = Naming.lookup("rmi://127.0.0.1/ServiceServer");

   }
   catch(Exception ex) {
    ex.printStackTrace();
   }
   server = (ServiceServer) obj;

   try {

      services = server.getServiceList();

   } catch(Exception ex) {
      ex.printStackTrace();
   }
   return services;

}

class MyListListener implements ActionListener {
   public void actionPerformed(ActionEvent ev) {

      Object selection =  serviceList.getSelectedItem();
      loadService(selection);

   }
 }

public static void main(String[] args) {
   new ServiceBrowser().buildGUI();
}

}
```

Do the RMI lookup, and get the stub

Cast the stub to the remote interface type, so that we can call getServiceList() on it

getServiceList() gives us the array of Objects, that we display in the JComboBox for the user to select from.

If we're here, it means the user made a selection from the JComboBox list. So, take the selection they made and load the appropriate service. (see the loadService method on the previous page, that asks the server for the service that corresponds with this selection)

class DiceService (a universal service, implements Service)

```java
import javax.swing.*;
import java.awt.event.*;
import java.io.*;

public class DiceService implements Service {

    JLabel label;
    JComboBox numOfDice;


    public JPanel getGuiPanel() {
        JPanel panel = new JPanel();
        JButton button = new JButton("Roll 'em!");
        String[] choices = {"1", "2", "3", "4", "5"};
        numOfDice = new JComboBox(choices);
        label = new JLabel("dice values here");
        button.addActionListener(new RollEmListener());
        panel.add(numOfDice);
        panel.add(button);
        panel.add(label);
        return panel;
    }

    public class RollEmListener implements ActionListener {
        public void actionPerformed(ActionEvent ev) {
            // roll the dice
            String diceOutput = "";
            String selection = (String)  numOfDice.getSelectedItem();
            int numOfDiceToRoll = Integer.parseInt(selection);
            for (int i = 0; i < numOfDiceToRoll; i++) {
                int r = (int) ((Math.random() * 6) + 1);
                diceOutput += (" " + r);
            }
            label.setText(diceOutput);

        }
    }
}
```

Here's the one important method! The method of the Service interface— the one the client's gonna call when this service is selected and loaded. You can do whatever you want in the getGuiPanel() method, so it builds the actual dice-rolling GUI.

Sharpen your pencil

Think about ways to improve the DiceService. One suggestion: using what you learned in the GUI chapters, make the dice graphical. Use a rectangle, and draw the appropriate number of circles on each one, corresponding to the roll for that particular die.

class MiniMusicService (a universal service, implements Service)

```java
import javax.sound.midi.*;
import java.io.*;
import javax.swing.*;
import java.awt.*;
import java.awt.event.*;

public class MiniMusicService implements Service {

    MyDrawPanel myPanel;

    public JPanel getGuiPanel() {
        JPanel mainPanel = new JPanel();
        myPanel = new MyDrawPanel();
        JButton playItButton = new JButton("Play it");
        playItButton.addActionListener(new PlayItListener());
        mainPanel.add(myPanel);
        mainPanel.add(playItButton);
        return mainPanel;
    }

    public class PlayItListener implements ActionListener {
      public void actionPerformed(ActionEvent ev) {

        try {

          Sequencer sequencer = MidiSystem.getSequencer();
          sequencer.open();

          sequencer.addControllerEventListener(myPanel, new int[] {127});
          Sequence seq = new Sequence(Sequence.PPQ, 4);
          Track track = seq.createTrack();

          for (int i = 0; i < 100; i+= 4) {

              int rNum = (int) ((Math.random() * 50) + 1);
              if (rNum < 38) {   // so now only do it if num <38 (75% of the time)
                track.add(makeEvent(144,1,rNum,100,i));
                track.add(makeEvent(176,1,127,0,i));
                track.add(makeEvent(128,1,rNum,100,i + 2));
              }
          } // end loop

          sequencer.setSequence(seq);
          sequencer.start();
          sequencer.setTempoInBPM(220);
        } catch (Exception ex) {ex.printStackTrace();}

      } // close actionperformed
    } // close inner class
```

The service method! All it does is display a button and the drawing service (where the rectangles will eventually be painted).

This is all the music stuff from the Code Kitchen in chapter 12, so we won't annotate it again here.

class MiniMusicService, continued...

```java
public MidiEvent makeEvent(int comd, int chan, int one, int two, int tick) {
    MidiEvent event = null;
        try {
           ShortMessage a = new ShortMessage();
           a.setMessage(comd, chan, one, two);
           event = new MidiEvent(a, tick);

          }catch(Exception e) { }
      return event;
      }


class MyDrawPanel extends JPanel implements ControllerEventListener {

    // only if we got an event do we want to paint
    boolean msg = false;

    public void controlChange(ShortMessage event) {
       msg = true;
       repaint();
  }

    public Dimension getPreferredSize() {
      return new Dimension(300,300);
    }

    public void paintComponent(Graphics g) {
       if (msg) {

          Graphics2D g2 = (Graphics2D) g;

          int r = (int) (Math.random() * 250);
          int gr = (int) (Math.random() * 250);
          int b = (int) (Math.random() * 250);

          g.setColor(new Color(r,gr,b));

          int ht = (int) ((Math.random() * 120) + 10);
          int width = (int) ((Math.random() * 120) + 10);

          int x = (int) ((Math.random() * 40) + 10);
          int y =  (int) ((Math.random() * 40) + 10);

          g.fillRect(x,y,ht, width);
          msg = false;

      } // close if
    } // close method
  } // close inner class
} // close class
```

Nothing new on this entire page. You've seen it all in the graphics CodeKitchen. If you want another exercise, try annotating this code yourself, then compare it with the CodeKitchen in the "A very graphic story" chapter.

class DayOfTheWeekService (a universal service, implements Service)

```java
import javax.swing.*;
import java.awt.event.*;
import java.awt.*;
import java.io.*;
import java.util.*;
import java.text.*;

public class DayOfTheWeekService implements Service {

    JLabel outputLabel;
    JComboBox month;
    JTextField day;
    JTextField year;

    public JPanel getGuiPanel() {
        JPanel panel = new JPanel();
        JButton button = new JButton("Do it!");
        button.addActionListener(new DoItListener());
        outputLabel = new JLabel("date appears here");
        DateFormatSymbols dateStuff = new DateFormatSymbols();
        month = new JComboBox(dateStuff.getMonths());
        day = new JTextField(8);
        year = new JTextField(8);
        JPanel inputPanel = new JPanel(new GridLayout(3,2));
        inputPanel.add(new JLabel("Month"));
        inputPanel.add(month);
        inputPanel.add(new JLabel("Day"));
        inputPanel.add(day);
        inputPanel.add(new JLabel("Year"));
        inputPanel.add(year);
        panel.add(inputPanel);
        panel.add(button);
        panel.add(outputLabel);
        return panel;
    }

    public class DoItListener implements ActionListener {
        public void actionPerformed(ActionEvent ev) {
            int monthNum = month.getSelectedIndex();
            int dayNum = Integer.parseInt(day.getText());
            int yearNum = Integer.parseInt(year.getText());
            Calendar c = Calendar.getInstance();
            c.set(Calendar.MONTH, monthNum);
            c.set(Calendar.DAY_OF_MONTH, dayNum);
            c.set(Calendar.YEAR, yearNum);
            Date date = c.getTime();
            String dayOfWeek = (new SimpleDateFormat("EEEE")).format(date);
            outputLabel.setText(dayOfWeek);
        }
    }
}
```

The Service interface method that builds the GUI

Refer to chapter 10 if you need a reminder of how number and date formatting works. This code is slightly different, however, because it uses the Calendar class. Also, the SimpleDateFormat lets us specify a pattern for how the date should print out.

Congratulations!
You made it to the end.

**Of course, there's still the two appendices.
And the index.
And then there's the web site...
There's no escape, really.**

Appendix A:
Final Code Kitchen

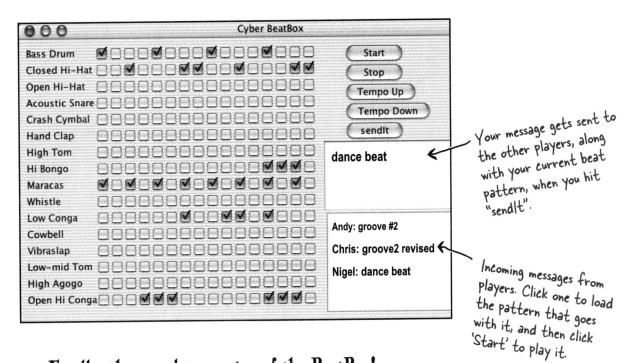

Your message gets sent to the other players, along with your current beat pattern, when you hit "sendlt".

Incoming messages from players. Click one to load the pattern that goes with it, and then click 'Start' to play it.

Finally, the complete version of the BeatBox!

It connects to a simple MusicServer so that you can send and receive beat patterns with other clients.

Final BeatBox client program

Most of this code is the same as the code from the CodeKitchens in the previous chapters, so we don't annotate the whole thing again. The new parts include:

GUI - two new components are added for the text area that displays incoming messages (actually a scrolling list) and the text field.

NETWORKING - just like the SimpleChatClient in this chapter, the BeatBox now connects to the server and gets an input and output stream.

THREADS - again, just like the SimpleChatClient, we start a 'reader' class that keeps looking for incoming messages from the server. But instead of just text, the messages coming in include TWO objects: the String message and the serialized ArrayList (the thing that holds the state of all the checkboxes.)

```java
import java.awt.*;
import javax.swing.*;
import java.io.*;
import javax.sound.midi.*;
import java.util.*;
import java.awt.event.*;
import java.net.*;
import javax.swing.event.*;

public class BeatBoxFinal {

    JFrame theFrame;
    JPanel mainPanel;
    JList incomingList;
    JTextField userMessage;
    ArrayList<JCheckBox> checkboxList;
    int nextNum;
    Vector<String> listVector = new Vector<String>();
    String userName;
    ObjectOutputStream out;
    ObjectInputStream in;
    HashMap<String, boolean[]> otherSeqsMap = new HashMap<String, boolean[]>();

    Sequencer sequencer;
    Sequence sequence;
    Sequence mySequence = null;
    Track track;


    String[] instrumentNames = {"Bass Drum", "Closed Hi-Hat", "Open Hi-Hat","Acoustic
    Snare", "Crash Cymbal", "Hand Clap", "High Tom", "Hi Bongo", "Maracas", "Whistle",
    "Low Conga", "Cowbell", "Vibraslap", "Low-mid Tom", "High Agogo", "Open Hi Conga"};

    int[] instruments = {35,42,46,38,49,39,50,60,70,72,64,56,58,47,67,63};
```

```java
public static void main (String[] args) {
   new BeatBoxFinal().startUp(args[0]);  // args[0] is your user ID/screen name
}
```

Add a command-line argument for your screen name.
Example: % java BeatBoxFinal theFlash

```java
public void startUp(String name) {
    userName = name;
    // open connection to the server
    try {
      Socket sock = new Socket("127.0.0.1", 4242);
      out = new ObjectOutputStream(sock.getOutputStream());
      in = new ObjectInputStream(sock.getInputStream());
      Thread remote = new Thread(new RemoteReader());
      remote.start();
    } catch(Exception ex) {
        System.out.println("couldn't connect - you'll have to play alone.");
    }
    setUpMidi();
    buildGUI();
} // close startUp
```

Nothing new... set up the networking, I/O, and make (and start) the reader thread.

```java
 public void buildGUI() {

    theFrame = new JFrame("Cyber BeatBox");
    BorderLayout layout = new BorderLayout();
    JPanel background = new JPanel(layout);
    background.setBorder(BorderFactory.createEmptyBorder(10,10,10,10));

    checkboxList = new ArrayList<JCheckBox>();

    Box buttonBox = new Box(BoxLayout.Y_AXIS);
    JButton start = new JButton("Start");
    start.addActionListener(new MyStartListener());
    buttonBox.add(start);

    JButton stop = new JButton("Stop");
    stop.addActionListener(new MyStopListener());
    buttonBox.add(stop);

    JButton upTempo = new JButton("Tempo Up");
    upTempo.addActionListener(new MyUpTempoListener());
    buttonBox.add(upTempo);

    JButton downTempo = new JButton("Tempo Down");
    downTempo.addActionListener(new MyDownTempoListener());
    buttonBox.add(downTempo);

    JButton sendIt = new JButton("sendIt");
    sendIt.addActionListener(new MySendListener());
    buttonBox.add(sendIt);

    userMessage = new JTextField();
```

GUI code, nothing new here

final BeatBox code

```
      buttonBox.add(userMessage);

      incomingList = new JList();
      incomingList.addListSelectionListener(new MyListSelectionListener());
      incomingList.setSelectionMode(ListSelectionModel.SINGLE_SELECTION);
      JScrollPane theList = new JScrollPane(incomingList);
      buttonBox.add(theList);
      incomingList.setListData(listVector); // no data to start with

      Box nameBox = new Box(BoxLayout.Y_AXIS);
      for (int i = 0; i < 16; i++) {
          nameBox.add(new Label(instrumentNames[i]));
      }

      background.add(BorderLayout.EAST, buttonBox);
      background.add(BorderLayout.WEST, nameBox);

      theFrame.getContentPane().add(background);
      GridLayout grid = new GridLayout(16,16);
      grid.setVgap(1);
      grid.setHgap(2);
      mainPanel = new JPanel(grid);
      background.add(BorderLayout.CENTER, mainPanel);

      for (int i = 0; i < 256; i++) {
          JCheckBox c = new JCheckBox();
          c.setSelected(false);
          checkboxList.add(c);
          mainPanel.add(c);
      } // end loop

      theFrame.setBounds(50,50,300,300);
      theFrame.pack();
      theFrame.setVisible(true);
    } // close buildGUI

    public void setUpMidi() {
        try {
        sequencer = MidiSystem.getSequencer();
        sequencer.open();
        sequence = new Sequence(Sequence.PPQ,4);
        track = sequence.createTrack();
        sequencer.setTempoInBPM(120);
    } catch(Exception e) {e.printStackTrace();}

} // close setUpMidi
```

JList is a component we haven't used before. This is where the incoming messages are displayed. Only instead of a normal chat where you just LOOK at the messages, in this app you can SELECT a message from the list to load and play the attached beat pattern.

Nothing else on this page is new

Get the Sequencer, make a Sequence, and make a Track

```
public void buildTrackAndStart() {
    ArrayList<Integer> trackList = null; // this will hold the instruments for each
    sequence.deleteTrack(track);
    track = sequence.createTrack();

    for (int i = 0; i < 16; i++) {

        trackList = new ArrayList<Integer>();

        for (int j = 0; j < 16; j++) {
            JCheckBox jc = (JCheckBox) checkboxList.get(j + (16*i));
            if (jc.isSelected()) {
                int key = instruments[i];
                trackList.add(new Integer(key));
            } else {
                trackList.add(null);  // because this slot should be empty in the track
            }
        } // close inner loop
        makeTracks(trackList);
    } // close outer loop
    track.add(makeEvent(192,9,1,0,15)); // - so we always go to full 16 beats
    try {
        sequencer.setSequence(sequence);
        sequencer.setLoopCount(sequencer.LOOP_CONTINUOUSLY);
        sequencer.start();
        sequencer.setTempoInBPM(120);
    } catch(Exception e) {e.printStackTrace();}
} // close method


public class MyStartListener implements ActionListener {
    public void actionPerformed(ActionEvent a) {
        buildTrackAndStart();
    } // close actionPerformed
} // close inner class


public class MyStopListener implements ActionListener {
    public void actionPerformed(ActionEvent a) {
        sequencer.stop();
    } // close actionPerformed
} // close inner class


public class MyUpTempoListener implements ActionListener {
    public void actionPerformed(ActionEvent a) {
        float tempoFactor = sequencer.getTempoFactor();
        sequencer.setTempoFactor((float)(tempoFactor * 1.03));
    } // close actionPerformed
} // close inner class
```

Build a track by walking through the checkboxes to get their state, and mapping that to an instrument (and making the MidiEvent for it). This is pretty complex, but it is EXACTLY as it was in the previous chapters, so refer to previous CodeKitchens to get the full explanation again.

The GUI listeners. Exactly the same as the previous chapter's version.

```
    public class MyDownTempoListener implements ActionListener {
        public void actionPerformed(ActionEvent a) {
          float tempoFactor = sequencer.getTempoFactor();
          sequencer.setTempoFactor((float)(tempoFactor * .97));
        }
    }

    public class MySendListener implements ActionListener {
        public void actionPerformed(ActionEvent a) {
           // make an arraylist of just the STATE of the checkboxes
            boolean[] checkboxState = new boolean[256];
            for (int i = 0; i < 256; i++) {
                JCheckBox check = (JCheckBox) checkboxList.get(i);
                if (check.isSelected()) {
                    checkboxState[i] = true;
                }
            } // close loop
          String messageToSend = null;
          try {
              out.writeObject(userName + nextNum++ + ": " + userMessage.getText());
              out.writeObject(checkboxState);
          } catch(Exception ex) {
              System.out.println("Sorry dude. Could not send it to the server.");
          }
          userMessage.setText("");
        } // close actionPerformed
    } // close inner class

    public class MyListSelectionListener implements ListSelectionListener {
        public void valueChanged(ListSelectionEvent le) {
          if (!le.getValueIsAdjusting()) {
              String selected = (String) incomingList.getSelectedValue();
              if (selected != null) {
                  // now go to the map, and change the sequence
                  boolean[] selectedState = (boolean[]) otherSeqsMap.get(selected);
                  changeSequence(selectedState);
                  sequencer.stop();
                  buildTrackAndStart();
              }
          }
        } // close valueChanged
    } // close inner class
```

This is new... it's a lot like the SimpleChatClient, except instead of sending a String message, we serialize two objects (the String message and the beat pattern) and write those two objects to the socket output stream (to the server).

This is also new -- a ListSelectionListener that tells us when the user made a selection on the list of messages. When the user selects a message, we IMMEDIATELY load the associated beat pattern (it's in the HashMap called otherSeqsMap) and start playing it. There's some if tests because of little quirky things about getting ListSelectionEvents.

```
public class RemoteReader implements Runnable {
    boolean[] checkboxState = null;
    String nameToShow = null;
    Object obj = null;
    public void run() {
      try {
        while((obj=in.readObject()) != null) {
          System.out.println("got an object from server");
          System.out.println(obj.getClass());
          String nameToShow = (String) obj;
          checkboxState = (boolean[]) in.readObject();
          otherSeqsMap.put(nameToShow, checkboxState);
          listVector.add(nameToShow);
          incomingList.setListData(listVector);
        } // close while
      } catch(Exception ex) {ex.printStackTrace();}
    } // close run
} // close inner class
```

This is the thread job -- read in data from the server. In this code, 'data' will always be two serialized objects: the String message and the beat pattern (an ArrayList of checkbox state values)

When a message comes in, we read (deserialize) the two objects (the message and the ArrayList of Boolean checkbox state values) and add it to the JList component. Adding to a JList is a two-step thing: you keep a Vector of the lists data (Vector is an old-fashioned ArrayList), and then tell the JList to use that Vector as it's source for what to display in the list.

```
public class MyPlayMineListener implements ActionListener {
    public void actionPerformed(ActionEvent a) {
      if (mySequence != null) {
        sequence = mySequence;   // restore to my original
      }
    } // close actionPerformed
} // close inner class
```

This method is called when the user selects something from the list. We IMMEDIATELY change the pattern to the one they selected.

```
public void changeSequence(boolean[] checkboxState) {
   for (int i = 0; i < 256; i++) {
      JCheckBox check = (JCheckBox) checkboxList.get(i);
       if (checkboxState[i]) {
          check.setSelected(true);
       } else {
          check.setSelected(false);
       }
   } // close loop
} // close changeSequence
```

All the MIDI stuff is exactly the same as it was in the previous version.

```
public void makeTracks(ArrayList list) {
   Iterator it = list.iterator();
   for (int i = 0; i < 16; i++) {
      Integer num = (Integer) it.next();
      if (num != null) {
         int numKey = num.intValue();
         track.add(makeEvent(144,9,numKey, 100, i));
         track.add(makeEvent(128,9,numKey,100, i + 1));
      }
   } // close loop
} // close makeTracks()
```

```
public  MidiEvent makeEvent(int comd, int chan, int one, int two, int tick) {
    MidiEvent event = null;
    try {
      ShortMessage a = new ShortMessage();
      a.setMessage(comd, chan, one, two);
      event = new MidiEvent(a, tick);
    }catch(Exception e) { }
    return event;
  } // close makeEvent

} // close class
```

Nothing new. Just like the last version.

Sharpen your pencil

What are some of the ways you can improve this program?

Here are a few ideas to get you started:

1) Once you select a pattern, whatever current pattern was playing is blown away. If that was a new pattern you were working on (or a modification of another one), you're out of luck. You might want to pop up a dialog box that asks the user if he'd like to save the current pattern.

2) If you fail to type in a command-line argument, you just get an exception when you run it! Put something in the main method that checks to see if you've passed in a command-line argument. If the user doesn't supply one, either pick a default or print out a message that says they need to run it again, but this time with an argument for their screen name.

3) It might be nice to have a feature where you can click a button and it will generate a random pattern for you. You might hit on one you really like. Better yet, have another feature that lets you load in existing 'foundation' patterns, like one for jazz, rock, reggae, etc. that the user can add to.

You can find existing patterns on the Head First Java web start.

Final BeatBox server program

Most of this code is identical to the SimpleChatServer we made in the Networking and Threads chapter. The only difference, in fact, is that this server receives, and then re-sends, two serialized objects instead of a plain String (although one of the serialized objects happens to *be* a String).

```java
import java.io.*;
import java.net.*;
import java.util.*;

public class MusicServer {

    ArrayList<ObjectOutputStream> clientOutputStreams;

    public static void main (String[] args) {
        new MusicServer().go();
    }

    public class ClientHandler implements Runnable {

        ObjectInputStream in;
        Socket clientSocket;

        public ClientHandler(Socket socket) {
          try {
            clientSocket = socket;
             in = new ObjectInputStream(clientSocket.getInputStream());

          } catch(Exception ex) {ex.printStackTrace();}
         } // close constructor


        public void run() {
            Object o2 = null;
            Object o1 = null;
          try {

            while ((o1 = in.readObject()) != null) {

              o2 = in.readObject();

              System.out.println("read two objects");
              tellEveryone(o1, o2);
            } // close while

          } catch(Exception ex) {ex.printStackTrace();}
        } // close run
    } // close inner class
```

```
public void go() {
   clientOutputStreams = new ArrayList<ObjectOutputStream>();

      try {
        ServerSocket serverSock = new ServerSocket(4242);

        while(true) {
           Socket clientSocket = serverSock.accept();
           ObjectOutputStream out = new ObjectOutputStream(clientSocket.getOutputStream());
           clientOutputStreams.add(out);

           Thread t = new Thread(new ClientHandler(clientSocket));
           t.start();

           System.out.println("got a connection");
        }
     }catch(Exception ex) {
       ex.printStackTrace();
     }
} // close go

public void tellEveryone(Object one, Object two) {
   Iterator it = clientOutputStreams.iterator();
   while(it.hasNext()) {
     try {
        ObjectOutputStream out = (ObjectOutputStream) it.next();
        out.writeObject(one);
        out.writeObject(two);
      }catch(Exception ex) {ex.printStackTrace();}
   }
} // close tellEveryone

} // close class
```

Appendix B

The Top Ten Topics that almost made it into the Real Book...

You mean, there's still MORE? Doesn't this book EVER end?

We covered a lot of ground, and you're almost finished with this book. We'll miss you, but before we let you go, we wouldn't feel right about sending you out into JavaLand without a little more preparation. We can't possibly fit everything you'll need to know into this relatively small appendix. Actually, we *did* originally include everything you need to know about Java (not already covered by the other chapters), by reducing the type point size to .00003. It all fit, but nobody could read it. So, we threw most of it away, but kept the best bits for this Top Ten appendix.

This really *is* the end of the book. Except for the index (a must-read!).

#10 Bit Manipulation

Why do you care?

We've talked about the fact that there are 8 bits in a byte, 16 bits in a short, and so on. You might have occasion to turn individual bits on or off. For instance you might find yourself writing code for your new Java enabled toaster, and realize that due to severe memory limitations, certain toaster settings are controlled at the bit level. For easier reading, we're showing only the last 8 bits in the comments rather than the full 32 for an int).

Bitwise NOT Operator: ~

This operator 'flips all the bits' of a primitive.

```
int x = 10;    //     bits are 00001010
x = ~x;        // bits are now 11110101
```

The next three operators compare two primitives on a bit by bit basis, and return a result based on comparing these bits. We'll use the following example for the next three operators:

```
int x = 10;    // bits are 00001010

int y =  6;    // bits are 00000110
```

Bitwise AND Operator: &

This operator returns a value whose bits are turned on only if *both* original bits are turned on:

```
int a = x & y;  // bits are 00000010
```

Bitwise OR Operator: |

This operator returns a value whose bits are turned on only if *either* of the original bits are turned on:

```
int a = x | y;  // bits are 00001110
```

Bitwise XOR (exclusive OR) Operator: ^

This operator returns a value whose bits are turned on only if *exactly one* of the original bits are turned on:

```
int a = x ^ y;  // bits are 00001100
```

The Shift Operators

These operators take a single integer primitive and shift (or slide) all of its bits in one direction or another. If you want to dust off your binary math skills, you might realize that shifting bits *left* effectively *multiplies* a number by a power of two, and shifting bits *right* effectively *divides* a number by a power of two.

We'll use the following example for the next three operators:

```
int x = -11;   //     bits are 11110101
```

Ok, ok, we've been putting it off, here is the world's shortest explanation of storing negative numbers, and *two's complement*. Remember, the leftmost bit of an integer number is called the **sign bit**. A negative integer number in Java *always* has its sign bit turned *on* (i.e. set to 1). A positive integer number always has its sign bit turned *off* (0). Java uses the *two's complement* formula to store negative numbers. To change a number's sign using two's complement, flip all the bits, then add 1 (with a byte, for example, that would mean adding 00000001 to the flipped value).

Right Shift Operator: >>

This operator shifts all of a number's bits right by a certain number, and fills all of the bits on the left side with whatever the original leftmost bit was. **The sign bit does *not* change:**

```
int y = x >> 2;  // bits are 11111101
```

Unsigned Right Shift Operator: >>>

Just like the right shift operator BUT it ALWAYS fills the leftmost bits with zeros. **The sign bit *might* change:**

```
int y = x >>> 2;  // bits are 00111101
```

Left Shift Operator: <<

Just like the unsigned right shift operator, but in the other direction; the rightmost bits are filled with zeros. **The sign bit might change.**

```
int y = x << 2;  // bits are 11010100
```

#9 Immutability

Why do you care that <u>Strings are Immutable?</u>

When your Java programs start to get big, you'll inevitably end up with lots and lots of String objects. For security purposes, and for the sake of conserving memory (remember your Java programs can run on teeny Java-enabled cell phones), Strings in Java are immutable. What this means is that when you say:

```
String s = "0";

for (int x = 1; x < 10; x++) {
  s = s + x;
}
```

What's actually happening is that you're creating ten String objects (with values "0", "01", "012", through "0123456789"). In the end *s* is referring to the String with the value "0123456789", but at this point there are *ten* Strings in existence!

Whenever you make a new String, the JVM puts it into a special part of memory called the 'String Pool' (sounds refreshing doesn't it?). If there is already a String in the String Pool with the same value, the JVM doesn't create a duplicate, it simply refers your reference variable to the existing entry. The JVM can get away with this because Strings are immutable; one reference variable can't change a String's value out from under another reference variable referring to the same String.

The other issue with the String pool is that the Garbage Collector *doesn't go there*. So in our example, unless by coincidence you later happen to make a String called "01234", for instance, the first nine Strings created in our *for* loop will just sit around wasting memory.

How does this save memory?

Well, if you're not careful, *it doesn't!* But if you understand how String immutability works, than you can sometimes take advantage of it to save memory. If you have to do a lot of String manipulations (like concatenations, etc.), however, there is another class StringBuilder, better suited for that purpose. We'll talk more about StringBuilder in a few pages.

Why do you care that <u>Wrappers are</u> Immutable?

In the Math chapter we talked about the two main uses of the wrapper classes:

- Wrapping a primitive so it can pretend to be an object.

- Using the static utility methods (for example, Integer.parseInt()).

It's important to remember that when you create a wrapper object like:

```
Integer iWrap = new Integer(42);
```

That's it for that wrapper object. Its value will *always* be 42. **There is no setter method for a wrapper object.** You can, of course, refer *iWrap* to a *different* wrapper object, but then you'll have *two* objects. Once you create a wrapper object, there's no way to change the *value* of that object!

Make it Stick

Java is
Pass
by value

threads
wait()
notify()

Wash
Cat

Roses are red, violets are blue.
Strings are immutable, wrappers are too.

Oh look! A bonus Make it Stick.
Right here in the appendix.

#8   Assertions

We haven't talked much about how to debug your Java program while you're developing it. We believe that you should learn Java at the command line, as we've been doing throughout the book. Once you're a Java pro, if you decide to use an IDE*, you might have other debugging tools to use. In the old days, when a Java programmer wanted to debug her code, she'd stick a bunch of System.out.println( ) statements throughout the program, printing current variable values, and "I got here" messages, to see if the flow control was working properly. (The ready-bake code in chapter 6 left some debugging 'print' statements in the code.) Then, once the program was working correctly, she'd go through and take all those System.out.println( ) statements back out again. It was tedious and error prone. But as of Java 1.4 (and 5.0), debugging got a whole lot easier. The answer?

Assertions

Assertions are like System.out.println( ) statements on steroids. Add them to your code as you would add println statements. The Java 5.0 compiler assumes you'll be compiling source files that are 5.0 compatible, so as of Java 5.0, compiling with assertions is enabled by default.

At runtime, if you do nothing, the assert statements you added to your code will be ignored by the JVM, and won't slow down your program. But if you tell the JVM to *enable* your assertions, they will help you do your debugging, without changing a line of code!

Some folks have complained about having to leave assert statements in their production code, but leaving them in can be really valuable when your code is already deployed in the field. If your client is having trouble, you can instruct the client to run the program with assertions enabled, and have the client send you the output. If the assertions were stripped out of your deployed code, you'd never have that option. And there is almost no downside; when assertions are not enabled, they are completely ignored by the JVM, so there's no performance hit to worry about.

How to make Assertions work

Add assertion statements to your code wherever you believe that something *must be true*. For instance:

```
assert (height > 0);

// if true, program continues normally

// if false, throw an AssertionError
```

You can add a little more information to the stack trace by saying:

```
assert (height > 0) : "height = " +
height + " weight = " + weight;
```

The expression after the colon can be any legal Java expression *that resolves to a non-null value.* But whatever you do, ***don't create assertions that change an object's state!*** If you do, enabling assertions at runtime might change how your program performs.

Compiling and running with Assertions

To *compile* with assertions:

```
javac TestDriveGame.java
```

(Notice that no command line options were necessary.)

To *run* with assertions:

```
java -ea TestDriveGame
```

* IDE stands for Integrated Development Environment and includes tools such as Eclipse, Borland's JBuilder, or the open source NetBeans (netbeans.org).

#7 Block Scope

In chapter 9, we talked about how local variables
live only as long as the method in which they're
declared stays on the stack. But some variables can
have even *shorter* lifespans. Inside of methods, we
often create *blocks* of code. We've been doing this
all along, but we haven't explicitly *talked* in terms of
blocks. Typically, blocks of code occur within methods,
and are bounded by curly braces { }. Some common
examples of code blocks that you'll recognize include
loops (*for, while*) and conditional expressions (like *if*
statements).

Let's look at an example:

```
void doStuff() {         ← start of the method block

    int x = 0;     ← local variable scoped to the entire method

    for(int y = 0; y < 5; y++) {    ← beginning of a for loop block, and y is
                                       scoped to only the for loop!


        x = x + y;    ← No problem, x and y are both in scope

    }   ← end of the for loop block


    x = x * y;  ← Aack! Won't compile! y is out of scope here! (this is not
                   the way it works in some other languages, so beware!)
}
   ← end of the method block, now x is also out of scope
```

In the previous example, *y* was a block variable,
declared inside a block, and *y* went out of scope as
soon as the for loop ended. Your Java programs will
be more debuggable and expandable if you use local
variables instead of instance variables, and block
variables instead of local variables, whenever possible.
The compiler will make sure that you don't try to use
a variable that's gone out of scope, so you don't have
to worry about runtime meltdowns.

#6   Linked Invocations

While you did see a little of this in this book, we tried to keep our syntax as clean and readable as possible. There are, however, many legal shortcuts in Java, that you'll no doubt be exposed to, especially if you have to read a lot code you didn't write. One of the more common constructs you will encounter is known as *linked invocations*. For example:

```
StringBuffer sb = new StringBuffer("spring");

sb = sb.delete(3,6).insert(2,"umme").deleteCharAt(1);

System.out.println("sb = " + sb);
// result is sb = summer
```

What in the world is happening in the second line of code? Admittedly, this is a contrived example, but you need to learn how to decipher these.

1 - Work from left to right.

2 - Find the result of the leftmost method call, in this case `sb.delete(3,6)`. If you look up StringBuffer in the API docs, you'll see that the `delete()` method returns a StringBuffer object. The result of running the `delete()` method is a StringBuffer object with the value "spr".

3 - The next leftmost method (`insert()`) is called on the newly created StringBuffer object "spr". The result of that method call (the `insert()` method), is *also* a StringBuffer object (although it doesn't have to be the same type as the previous method return), and so it goes, the returned object is used to call the next method to the right. In theory, you can link as many methods as you want in a single statement (although it's rare to see more than three linked methods in a single statement). Without linking, the second line of code from above would be more readable, and look something like this:

```
sb = sb.delete(3,6);
sb = sb.insert(2,"umme");
sb = sb.deleteCharAt(1);
```

But here's a more common, and useful example, that you saw us using, but we thought we'd point it out again here. This is for when your main() method needs to invoke an instance method of the main class, but you don't need to keep a *reference* to the instance of the class. In other words, the main() needs to create the instance *only* so that main() can invoke one of the instance's *methods*.

```
class Foo {
    public static void main(String [] args) [
       new Foo().go();   ⟵   we want to call go(), but we don't care about
    }                          the Foo instance, so we don't bother assigning
    void go() {                the new Foo object to a reference.
      // here's what we REALLY want...
    }

}
```

#5 Anonymous and Static Nested Classes

Nested classes come in many flavors

In the GUI event-handling section of the book, we started using inner (nested) classes as a solution for implementing listener interfaces. That's the most common, practical, and readable form of an inner class—where the class is simply nested within the curly braces of another enclosing class. And remember, it means you need an instance of the outer class in order to get an instance of the inner class, because the inner class is a *member* of the outer/enclosing class.

But there are other kinds of inner classes including *static* and *anonymous*. We're not going into the details here, but we don't want you to be thrown by strange syntax when you see it in someone's code. Because out of virtually anything you can do with the Java language, perhaps nothing produces more bizarre-looking code than anonymous inner classes. But we'll start with something simpler—static nested classes.

Static nested classes

You already know what static means—something tied to the class, not a particular instance. A static nested class looks just like the non-static classes we used for event listeners, except they're marked with the keyword `static`.

```
public class FooOuter {
    static class BarInner {
        void sayIt() {
            System.out.println("method of a static inner class");
        }
    }
}

class Test {
    public static void main (String[] args) {
        FooOuter.BarInner foo = new FooOuter.BarInner();
        foo.sayIt();
    }
}
```

A static nested class is just that—a class enclosed within another, and marked with the static modifier.

Because a static nested class is...static, you don't use an instance of the outer class. You just use the name of the class, the same way you invoke static methods or access static variables.

Static nested classes are more like regular non-nested classes in that they don't enjoy a special relationship with an enclosing outer object. But because static nested classes are still considered a *member* of the enclosing/outer class, they still get access to any private members of the outer class... but *only the ones that are also static*. Since the static nested class isn't connected to an instance of the outer class, it doesn't have any special way to access the non-static (instance) variables and methods.

#5   Anonymous and Static Nested Classes, continued

The difference between *nested* and *inner*

Any Java class that's defined within the scope of another class is known as a ***nested*** class. It doesn't matter if it's anonymous, static, normal, whatever. If it's inside another class, it's technically considered a *nested* class. But *non-static* nested classes are often referred to as *inner* classes, which is what we called them earlier in the book. The bottom line: all inner classes are nested classes, but not all nested classes are inner classes.

Anonymous inner classes

Imagine you're writing some GUI code, and suddenly realize that you need an instance of a class that implements ActionListener. But you realize you don't *have* an instance of an ActionListener. Then you realize that you also never wrote a *class* for that listener. You have two choices at that point:

1) Write an inner class in your code, the way we did in our GUI code, and then instantiate it and pass that instance into the button's event registration (addActionListener()) method.

OR

2) Create an *anonymous* inner class and instantiate it, right there, just-in-time. **Literally right where you are at the point you need the listener object.** That's right, you create the class and the instance in the place where you'd normally be supplying just the instance. Think about that for a moment—it means you pass the entire *class* where you'd normally pass only an *instance* into a method argument!

```
import java.awt.event.*;
import javax.swing.*;
public class TestAnon {
    public static void main (String[] args) {

        JFrame frame = new JFrame();
        JButton button = new JButton("click");
        frame.getContentPane().add(button);
        // button.addActionListener(quitListener);
```

We made a frame and added a button, and now we need to register an action listener with the button. Except we never made a class that implements the ActionListener interface...

Normally we'd do something like this—passing in a reference to an instance of an inner class... an inner class that implements ActionListener (and the actionPerformed() method).

This statement:

```
        button.addActionListener (new ActionListener() {
            public void actionPerformed(ActionEvent ev) {
                System.exit(0);
            }
        });
```

ends down here!

But now instead of passing in an object reference, we pass in... the whole new class definition!! In other words, we write the class that implements ActionListener RIGHT HERE WHERE WE NEED IT. The syntax also creates an instance of the class automatically.

Notice that we say "new ActionListener()" even though ActionListener is an interface and so you can't MAKE an instance of it! But this syntax really means, "create a new class (with no name) that implements the ActionListener interface, and by the way, here's the implementation of the interface methods .actionPerformed().

```
    }
}
```

#4   Access Levels and Access Modifiers (Who Sees What)

Java has *four* access *levels* and *three* access *modifiers*. There are only *three* modifiers because the *default* (what you get when you don't use any access modifier) *is* one of the four access levels.

Access Levels (in order of how restrictive they are, from least to most restrictive)

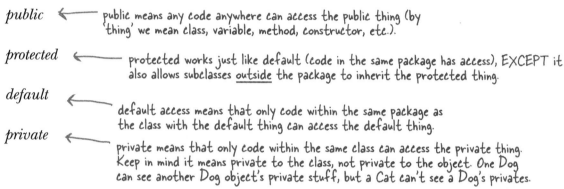

public ← public means any code anywhere can access the public thing (by 'thing' we mean class, variable, method, constructor, etc.).

protected ← protected works just like default (code in the same package has access), EXCEPT it also allows subclasses <u>outside</u> the package to inherit the protected thing.

default ← default access means that only code within the same package as the class with the default thing can access the default thing.

private ← private means that only code within the same class can access the private thing. Keep in mind it means private to the class, not private to the object. One Dog can see another Dog object's private stuff, but a Cat can't see a Dog's privates.

Access modifiers

```
public
protected
private
```

Most of the time you'll use only public and private access levels.

public

Use public for classes, constants (static final variables), and methods that you're exposing to other code (for example getters and setters) and most constructors.

private

Use private for virtually all instance variables, and for methods that you don't want outside code to call (in other words, methods *used* by the public methods of your class).

But although you might not use the other two (protected and default), you still need to know what they do because you'll see them in other code.

#4 Access Levels and Access Modifiers, cont.

default and protected

default

Both protected and default access levels are tied to packages. Default access is simple—it means that only code *within the same package* can access code with default access. So a default class, for example (which means a class that isn't explicitly declared as *public*) can be accessed by only classes within the same package as the default class.

But what does it really mean to *access* a class? Code that does not have access to a class is not allowed to even *think* about the class. And by think, we mean *use* the class in code. For example, if you don't have access to a class, because of access restriction, you aren't allowed to instantiate the class or even declare it as a type for a variable, argument, or return value. You simply can't type it into your code at all! If you do, the compiler will complain.

Think about the implications—a default class with public methods means the public methods aren't really public at all. You can't access a method if you can't *see* the class.

Why would anyone want to restrict access to code within the same package? Typically, packages are designed as a group of classes that work together as a related set. So it might make sense that classes within the same package need to access one another's code, while as a package, only a small number of classes and methods are exposed to the outside world (i.e. code outside that package).

OK, that's default. It's simple—if something has default access (which, remember, means no explicit access modifier!), only code within the same package as the default *thing* (class, variable, method, inner class) can access that *thing*.

Then what's *protected* for?

protected

Protected access is almost identical to default access, with one exception: it allows sub-classes to *inherit* the protected thing, *even if those subclasses are outside the package of the super-class they extend.* That's it. That's *all* protected buys you—the ability to let your subclasses be outside your superclass package, yet still *inherit* pieces of the class, including methods and constructors.

Many developers find very little reason to use protected, but it is used in some designs, and some day you might find it to be exactly what you need. One of the interesting things about protected is that—unlike the other access levels—protected access applies only to inheritance. If a subclass-outside-the-package has a *reference* to an instance of the superclass (the superclass that has, say, a protected method), the subclass can't access the pro-tected method using that superclass reference! The only way the subclass can access that method is by *inheriting* it. In other words, the subclass-outside-the-package doesn't have *access* to the protected method, it just *has* the method, through inheritance.

#3   String and StringBuffer/StringBuilder Methods

Two of the most commonly used classes in the Java API are String and StringBuffer (remember from #9 a few pages back, Strings are immutable, so a StringBuffer/StringBuilder can be a lot mor efficient if you're manipulating a String). As of Java 5.0 you should use the String*Builder* class instead of String*Buffer*, unless your String manipulations need to be thread-safe, which is not common. Here's a brief overview of the **key** methods in these classes:

Both String and StringBuffer/StringBuilder classes have:

    char charAt(int index);   // what char is at a certain position

    int length();   // how long is this

    String substring(int start, int end);   // get a part of this

    String toString();   // what's the String value of this

To concatenate Strings:

    String concat(string);   // for the String class

    String append(String);   // for StringBuffer & StringBuilder

The String class has:

    String replace(char old, char new);   // replace all occurences of a char
    String substring(int begin, int end);   // get a portion of a String
    char [] toCharArray();   // convert to an array of chars
    String toLowerCase();   // convert all characters to lower case
    String toUpperCase();   // convert all characters to upper case
    String trim();   // remove whitespace from the ends
    String valueOf(char [])   // make a String out of a char array
    String valueOf(int i)   // make a String out of a primitive
                                             // other primitives are supported as well

The StringBuffer & StringBuilder classes have:

    StringBxxxx delete(int start, int end);   // delete a portion

    StringBxxxx insert(int offset, any primitive or a char []); // insert something

    StringBxxxx replace(int start, int end, String s);   // replace this part with this String

    StringBxxxx reverse();   // reverse the SB from front to back

    void setCharAt(int index, char ch);   // replace a given character

Note: StringBxxxx refers to either String*Buffer* or String*Builder,* as appropriate.

#2 Multidimensional Arrays

In most languages, if you create, say, a 4 x 2 two-dimensional array, you would visualize a rectangle, 4 elements by 2 elements, with a total of 8 elements. But in Java, such an array would actually be *5* arrays linked together! In Java, a two dimensional array is simply *an array of arrays*. (A three dimensional array is an array of arrays of arrays, but we'll leave that for you to play with.) Here's how it works

```
int[][] a2d  = new int [4][2];
```

The JVM creates an array with 4 elements. *Each* of these four elements is actually a reference variable referring to a (newly created), int array with 2 elements.

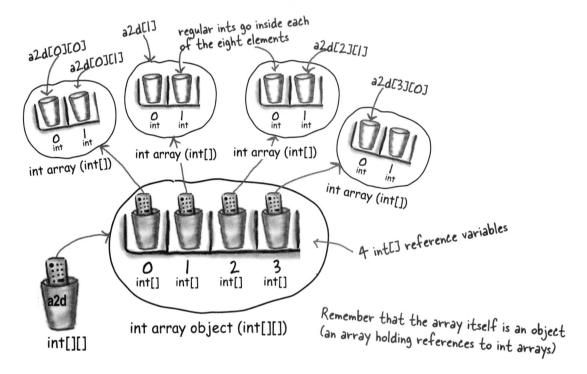

int array object (int[][])

Remember that the array itself is an object (an array holding references to int arrays)

Working with multidimensional arrays

- To access the second element in the third array: `int x = a2d[2][1];`   `// remember, 0 based!`
- To make a one-dimensional reference to one of the sub-arrays: `int[] copy = a2d[1];`
- Short-cut initialization of a 2 x 3 array: `int[][] x = { { 2,3,4 }, { 7,8,9 } };`
- To make a 2d array with irregular dimensions:

```
int[][] y = new int [2][];     //  makes only the first array, with a length of 2
y[0] = new int [3];    // makes the first sub-array 3 elements in length
y[1] = new int [5];    // makes the second sub-array 5 elements in length
```

And the number one topic that didn't quite make it in...

#1 Enumerations (also called Enumerated Types or Enums)

We've talked about constants that are defined in the API, for instance, **JFrame.EXIT_ON_CLOSE**. You can also create your own constants by marking a variable **static final**. But sometimes you'll want to create a set of constant values to represent the *only* valid values for a variable. This set of valid values is commonly referred to as an *enumeration*. Before Java 5.0 you could only do a half-baked job of creating an enumeration in Java. As of Java 5.0 you can create full fledged enumerations that will be the envy of all your pre-Java 5.0-using friends.

Who's in the band?

Let's say that you're creating a website for your favorite band, and you want to make sure that all of the comments are directed to a particular band member.

The old way to fake an "enum":

```
public static final int JERRY = 1;
public static final int BOBBY = 2;
public static final int PHIL = 3;

// later in the code


if (selectedBandMember == JERRY) {
  // do JERRY related stuff
}
```

We're hoping that by the time we got here "selectedBandMember" has a valid value!

The good news about this technique is that it DOES make the code easier to read. The other good news is that you can't ever change the value of the fake enums you've created; JERRY will always be 1. The bad news is that there's no easy or good way to make sure that the value of selectedBandMember will always be 1, 2, or 3. If some hard to find piece of code sets selectedBandMember equal to 812, it's pretty likely your code will break...

#1 Enumerations, cont.

The same situation using a genuine Java 5.0 enum. While this is a very basic enumeration, most enumerations usually *are* this simple.

A new, official "enum":

```
public enum Members { JERRY, BOBBY, PHIL };
public Members selectedBandMember;

// later in the code

if (selectedBandMember == Members.JERRY) {
  // do JERRY related stuff
}
```

This kind of looks like a simple class definition doesn't it? It turns out that enums ARE a special kind of class. Here we've created a new enumerated type called "Members".

The "selectedBandMember" variable is of type "Members", and can ONLY have a value of "JERRY", "BOBBY", or "PHIL".

No need to worry about this variable's value!

The syntax to refer to an enum "instance".

Your enum extends java.lang.Enum

When you create an enum, you're creating a new class, and *you're implicitly extending* `java.lang.Enum`. You can declare an enum as its own standalone class, in its own source file, or as a member of another class.

Using "if" and "switch" with Enums

Using the enum we just created, we can perform branches in our code using either the `if` or `switch` statement. Also notice that we can compare enum instances using either `==` or the `.equals()` method. Usually `==` is considered better style.

Assigning an enum value to a variable.

```
Members n = Members.BOBBY;
if (n.equals(Members.JERRY)) System.out.println("Jerrrry!");
if (n == Members.BOBBY) System.out.println("Rat Dog");

Members ifName = Members.PHIL;
switch (ifName) {
  case JERRY: System.out.print("make it sing ");
  case PHIL: System.out.print("go deep ");
  case BOBBY: System.out.println("Cassidy! ");
}
```

Both of these work fine! "Rat Dog" is printed.

Pop Quiz! What's the output?

Answer: go deep Cassidy!

#1   Enumerations, completed

A really tricked-out version of a similar enum

You can add a bunch of things to your enum like a constructor, methods, variables, and something called a constant-specific class body. They're not common, but you might run into them:

```java
public class HfjEnum {

  enum Names {
    JERRY("lead guitar") { public String sings() {
                  return "plaintively"; }
                },
    BOBBY("rhythm guitar") { public String sings() {
                    return "hoarsely"; }
                },
    PHIL("bass");

    private String instrument;

    Names(String instrument) {
      this.instrument = instrument;
    }
    public String getInstrument() {
      return this.instrument;
    }
    public String sings() {
      return "occasionally";
    }
  }

  public static void main(String [] args) {
    for (Names n : Names.values()) {
      System.out.print(n);
      System.out.print(", instrument: "+ n.getInstrument());
      System.out.println(", sings: " + n.sings());
    }
  }
}
```

This is an argument passed in to the constructor declared below.

These are the so-called "constant-specific class bodies". Think of them as overriding the basic enum method (in this case the "sing()" method), if sing() is called on a variable with an enum value of JERRY or BOBBY.

This is the enum's constructor. It runs once for each declared enum value (in this case it runs three times).

You'll see these methods being called from "main()".

Every enum comes with a built-in "values()" method which is typically used in a "for" loop as shown.

```
File  Edit  Window  Help  Bootleg
%java HfjEnum

JERRY, instrument: lead guitar, sings: plaintively
BOBBY, instrument: rhythm guitar, sings: hoarsely
PHIL, instrument: bass, sings: occasionally
%
```

Notice that the basic "sing()" method is only called when the enum value has no constant-specific class body.

Five-Minute Mystery

A Long Trip Home

Captain Byte of the Flatland starship "Traverser" had received an urgent, Top Secret transmission from headquarters. The message contained 30 heavily encrypted navigational codes that the Traverser would need to successfully plot a course home through enemy sectors. The enemy Hackarians, from a neighboring galaxy, had devised a devilish code-scrambling ray that was capable of creating bogus objects on the heap of the Traverser's only navigational computer. In addition, the alien ray could alter valid reference variables so that they referred to these bogus objects. The only defense the Traverser crew had against this evil Hackarian ray was to run an inline virus checker which could be imbedded into the Traverser's state of the art Java 1.4 code.

Captain Byte gave Ensign Smith the following programming instructions to process the critical navigational codes:

"Put the first five codes in an array of type ParsecKey. Put the last 25 codes in a five by five, two dimensional array of type QuadrantKey. Pass these two arrays into the plotCourse() method of the public final class ShipNavigation. Once the course object is returned run the inline virus checker against all the programs reference variables and then run the NavSim program and bring me the results."

A few minutes later Ensign Smith returned with the NavSim output. "NavSim output ready for review, sir", declared Ensign Smith. "Fine", replied the Captain, "Please review your work". "Yes sir!", responded the Ensign, "First I declared and constructed an array of type ParsecKey with the following code; ParsecKey [] p = new ParsecKey[5]; , next I declared and constructed an array of type QuadrantKey with the following code: QuadrantKey [] [] q = new QuadrantKey [5] [5]; . Next, I loaded the first 5 codes into the ParsecKey array using a 'for' loop, and then I loaded the last 25 codes into the QuadrantKey array using nested 'for' loops. Next, I ran the virus checker against all 32 reference variables, 1 for the ParsecKey array, and 5 for its elements, 1 for the QuadrantKey array, and 25 for its elements. Once the virus check returned with no viruses detected, I ran the NavSim program and re-ran the virus checker, just to be safe... Sir ! "

Captain Byte gave the Ensign a cool, long stare and said calmly, "Ensign, you are confined to quarters for endangering the safety of this ship, I don't want to see your face on this bridge again until you have properly learned your Java! Lieutenant Boolean, take over for the Ensign and do this job correctly!"

Why did the captain confine the Ensign to his quarters?

Five-Minute Mystery Solution

A Long Trip Home

Captain Byte knew that in Java, multidimensional arrays are actually arrays of arrays. The five by five QuadrantKey array 'q', would actually need a total of 31 reference variables to be able to access all of its components:

1 - reference variable for 'q'

5 - reference variables for q[0] - q[4]

25 - reference variables for q[0][0] - q[4][4]

The ensign had forgotten the reference variables for the five one dimensional arrays embedded in the 'q' array. Any of those five reference variables could have been corrupted by the Hackarian ray, and the ensign's test would never reveal the problem.

Index

T

talking head 203

TCP ports 475

Telluride 30

testing
   extreme programming 101

text
   parsing with String.split() 458 458
   read from a file. *See also* I/O
   write to a file 447

text area (JTextArea) 414

text field (JTextField) 413

Thread.sleep() 501–503

threads
   about 489–515
   deadlock 516
   locks 509
   lost update problem 512–514
   run() 493, 494
   Runnable 492, 493, 494
   Ryan and Monica problem 505–507
   scheduling 496, 496–498
   sleep() 501–503
   stack 490–491
   start() 492
   starting 492
   states 495, 496
   summary 500, 517
   synchronized 510–512
   unpredictability 498–499

throw
   exceptions 323–326
   throws 323–326

transient 439

TreeMap 558

TreeSet 533, 558, 564–566, 566

try
   blocks 321, 326

type 50
   parameter 137, 542, 544

type-safety 540
   and generics 540

U

universal service browser 636–648

V

variables
   assigning 52, 262
   declaring 50, 54, 84, 236–238
   local 85, 236–238
   nulling 262
   primitive 51, 52
   references 54, 55, 56, 185–186
   scope 236–238
   static. *See* static

variable declarations 50
   instance 84
   primitive 51
   reference 54

virtual method invocation 175

W

web start. *See* Java Web Start

while loops 11, 115

wildcard 574

wine 202

wrapper 287
   autoboxing 288–289
   conversion utilities 292
   Integer.parseInt() 104, 106, 117

writing. *See* I/O

This isn't goodbye

Bring your brain over to
wickedlysmart.com

Don't you know about the web site? We've got answers to some of the Sharpens, examples, the Code Kitchens, Ready-bake Code, and daily updates from the Head First author blogs!